Alleged Assasination Plots Involving Foreign Leaders

Alleged Assasination Plots Involving Foreign Leaders

AN INTERIM REPORT
OF THE
SELECT COMMITTEE
TO STUDY GOVERNMENTAL OPERATIONS
WITH RESPECT TO
INTELLIGENCE ACTIVITIES
UNITED STATES SENATE
TOGETHER WITH
ADDITIONAL SUPPLEMENTAL , AND SEPARATE
VIEWS

GOVERNMENT REPRINTS PRESS
Washington, D.C.

© Ross & Perry, Inc. 2001 All rights reserved.

No claim to U.S. government work contained throughout this book.

Protected under the Berne Convention. Published 2001

Printed in The United States of America
Ross & Perry, Inc. Publishers
717 Second St., N.E., Suite 200
Washington, D.C. 20002
Telephone (202) 675-8300
Facsimile (202) 675-8400
info@RossPerry.com

SAN 253-8555

Government Reprints Press Edition 2001

Government Reprints Press is an Imprint of Ross & Perry, Inc.

Library of Congress Control Number: 2001093414

http://www.GPOreprints.com

ISBN 1-931641-59-5

♾ The paper used in this publication meets the requirements for permanence established by the American National Standard for Information Sciences "Permanence of Paper for Printed Library Materials" (ANSI Z39.48-1984).

All rights reserved. No copyrighted part of this publication may be reproduced, stored in a retrieval system, or transmitted, in any form or by any means, electronic, photocopying, recording, or otherwise, without the prior written permission of the publisher.

CONTENTS

	Page
Prologue	XIII
I. Introduction and Summary	1
A. Committee's Mandate	1
B. Committee Decision To Make Report Public	2
C. Scope of Committee's Investigation	2
D. Summary of Findings and Conclusions	4
1. The Questions Presented	4
2. Summary of Findings and Conclusions on the Plots	4
3. Summary of Findings and Conclusions on The Issues of Authority and Control	6
II. Covert Action as a Vehicle for Foreign Policy Implementation	9
A. Policy Development and Approval Mechanism	9
B. The Concept of "Plausible Denial"	11
III. Assassination Planning and Plots	13
A. Congo	13
1. Introduction	13
2. Dulles Cable to Leopoldville: August 26, 1960	14
3. CIA Encouragement of Congolese Efforts to "Eliminate" Lumumba	16
4. The Plot to Assassinate Lumumba	19
(a) Bissell/Tweedy Meetings on Feasibility of Assassinating Lumumba	19
(b) Bissell/Scheider Meetings on Preparations for Assassinating "An African Leader"	20
(c) Scheider Mission to the Congo on an Assassination Operation	21
(d) Congo Station Officer Told to Expect Scheider: Dulles Cables About "Elimination" of Lumumba	22
(e) Assassination Instructions Issued to Station Officer and Lethal Substances Delivered: September 26, 1960	24
(f) Hedgman's Impression That President Eisenhower Ordered Lumumba's Assassination	25
(g) Steps in Furtherance of the Assassination Operation	26
(i) Hedgman's Testimony About Confirmation from Headquarters of the Assassination Plan	26
(ii) "Exploratory Steps"	27
(iii) The Assassination Operation Moves Forward After Scheider's Return to Headquarters: October 5-7, 1960	29
(iv) Headquarters Continues to Place "Highest Priority" on the Assassination Operation	30
(h) Tweedy/Bissell Testimony: Extent of Implementation; Extent of Authorization	33
(i) Tweedy's Testimony About the Scope of the Assassination Operation	33
(ii) Bissell's Testimony About Moving the Assassination Operation From Planning to Implementation	36

III. Assassination Planning and Plots—Continued
  A. Congo—Continued
    5. The Question of a Connection Between the Assassination Plot and Other Actions of CIA Officers and Their Agents in the Congo_____ 37
      (a) Mulroney's Assignment in the Congo_____ 37
        (i) Mulroney's Testimony That He Went to the Congo After Refusing an Assassination Assignment From Bissell_____ 37
        (ii) Bissell's Testimony About the Assignment to Mulroney_____ 40
        (iii) Mulroney Informed of Virus in Station Safe Upon Arriving in Congo: November 3, 1960_____ 41
        (iv) Mulroney's Plan to "Neutralize" Lumumba_____ 42
      (b) QJ/WIN's Mission in the Congo: November–December 1960_____ 43
      (c) WI/ROGUE Asks QJ/WIN to Join "Execution Squad": December 1960_____ 45
    6. The Question of Whether the CIA Was Involved in Bringing About Lumumba's Death in Katanga Province_____ 48
      (a) Lumumba's Imprisonment After Leaving U.N. Custody: November 27–December 3, 1960_____ 48
      (b) Lumumba's Death_____ 49
    7. The Question of the Level at Which the Assassination Plot Was Authorized_____ 51
      (a) High-Level Meetings at Which "Getting Rid of Lumumba" Was Discussed_____ 53
        (i) Dillon's Testimony About Pentagon Meeting: Summer 1960_____ 53
        (ii) Robert Johnson's Testimony That He Understood the President to Order Lumumba's Assassination at an NSC Meeting_____ 55
        (iii) Special Group Agrees to Consider Anything That Might Get Rid of Lumumba: August 25, 1960_____ 60
        (iv) Dulles Reminded by Gray of "Top-Level Feeling" That "Vigorous Action" was Necessary in the Congo: September 7–8, 1960_____ 62
        (v) Dulles Tells NSC That Lumumba Remains a Grave Danger Until "Disposed Of": September 21, 1960_____ 62
      (b) Testimony of Eisenhower White House Officials_____ 64
      (c) Bissell's Assumptions About Authorization by President Eisenhower and Allen Dulles_____ 65
      (d) The Impression of Scheider and Hedgman That the Assassination Operation Had Presidential Authorization_____ 67
  B. Cuba_____ 71
    1. The Assassination Plots_____ 71
      (a) Plots: Early 1960_____ 72
        (i) Plots to Destroy Castro's Public Image_____ 72
        (ii) Accident Plot_____ 72
        (iii) Poison Cigars_____ 73
      (b) Use of Underworld Figures—Phase I (Pre-Bay of Pigs)_____ 74
        (i) The Initial Plan_____ 74
        (ii) Contact with the Syndicate_____ 75
        (iii) Las Vegas Wiretap_____ 77
          (1) CIA Involvement in the Wiretap_____ 77
          (2) Consequences of the Wiretap_____ 79
        (iv) Poison is Prepared and Delivered to Cuba_____ 79
      (c) Use of Underworld Figures: Phase II (Post-Bay of Pigs)_____ 82
        (i) Change in Leadership_____ 82
        (ii) The Operation is Reactivated_____ 83
      (d) Plans in Early 1963_____ 85
      (e) AM/LASH_____ 86
        (i) Origin of the Project_____ 86
        (ii) The Poison Pen Device_____ 88
        (iii) Providing AM/LASH with Arms_____ 89

III. Assassination Planning and Plots—Continued
B. Cuba—Continued

		Page
2. At What Level Were the Castro Plots Known About or Authorized Within the Central Intelligence Agency?		91
(a) The Question Presented		91
(i) Dulles		92
(ii) McCone		92
(b) Did Allen Dulles Know of or Authorize the Initial Plots Against Castro?		92
(i) Dulles' Approval of J.C. King's December 1959 Memorandum		92
(ii) Dulles' January 1960 Statement to the Special Group		93
(iii) Meetings in March 1960		93
(iv) Recision of Accident Plot in July 1960		94
(v) Briefing of Dulles on Use of Underworld Figures in September 1960		94
(1) Evidence Concerning What Dulles Was Told		94
(2) Evidence Concerning When the Briefing Occurred		97
(vi) Edwards' Communications to the Justice Department in 1961 and 1962		97
(vii) General Cabell's Remarks to the Special Group in November 1960		98
(c) Did John McCone Know of or Authorize Assassination Plots During His Tenure as DCI?		99
(i) McCone's Testimony		99
(ii) Testimony of Helms, Bissell and Other Subordinate Agency Employees		100
(iii) Helms and Harvey Did Not Brief McCone About the Assassination Plots		102
(iv) The Question of Whether General Carter, McCone's Deputy Director, Learned About the Underworld Plot and Informed McCone		106
(v) The August 1963 Briefing of McCone		107
3. At What Level Were the Castro Plots Known About or Authorized Outside of the Central Intelligence Agency?		108
(a) The Question of Knowledge and Authorization Outside the Central Intelligence Agency in the Eisenhower Administration		109
(i) Summary		109
(ii) Richard Bissell's Testimony		110
(1) Lack of Personal Knowledge		110
(2) Assumptions Concerning Dulles		111
(iii) Testimony of White House Officials		111
(1) Gordon Gray		111
(2) Andrew Goodpaster		112
(3) Thomas Parrott		113
(4) John Eisenhower		113
(iv) Documentary Evidence		114
(1) Inspector General's Report		114
(2) Contemporaneous Documents		114
(b) The Question of Knowledge and Authorization Outside the Central Intelligence Agency During the Kennedy Administration		116
(i) Pre-Bay of Pigs Assassination Plot		117
(1) Bissell's Testimony Concerning His Assumption That Dulles Told the President		117
(2) Bissell's Testimony Regarding His Own Actions		118
(3) Kennedy Administration Officials' Testimony		119
(4) The Question of Whether Assassination Efforts Were Disclosed in Various Briefings of Administration Officials		120
a. Briefing of the President-Elect		120
b. Discussion with Bundy on "Executive Action Capability"		121
c. Taylor/Kennedy Bay of Pigs Inquiry		121
(5) Conversation Between President Kennedy and Senator George Smathers		123

III. Assassination Planning and Plots—Continued
  B. Cuba—Continued
    3. At What Level Were the Castro Plots Known About or Authorized Outside of the Central Intelligence Agency?—Con.
      (b) The Question of Knowledge and Authorization Outside of the Central Intelligence Agency During the Kennedy Administration—Continued
        (i) Pre-Bay of Pigs Assassination Plot—Continued

	Page
(6) The Question of Whether the President or the Attorney General Might Have Learned of the Assassination Effort from the Cuban Participants	124
(7) The Question of Whether the Assassination Operation Involving Underworld Figures Was Known About by Attorney General Kennedy or President Kennedy as Revealed by Investigations of Giancana and Rosselli	125
a. 1960	125
b. 1961	126
c. 1962	129
(1) Did President Kennedy Learn Anything About Assassination Plots as a Result of the FBI Investigation of Giancana and Rosselli?	129
(2) The Formal Decision to Forego Prosecution	131
(a) Events Leading Up to a Formal Briefing of the Attorney General	131
(b) Briefing of the Attorney General on May 7, 1962	131
(aa) The Attorney General Was Told That the Operation Had Involved an Assassination Attempt	132
(bb) Evidence Concerning Whether The Attorney General Was Told That the Operation Had Been Terminated	132
(ii) Post-Bay of Pigs Underworld Plot—MONGOOSE Period	134
(1) Events Preceding the Establishment of MONGOOSE	135
a. The Taylor/Kennedy Board of Inquiry	135
b. National Security Action Memorandum 100 of October 5, 1961, and the CIA Intelligence Estimate	136
c. President Kennedy's November 9, 1961 Conversation with Tad Szulc	138
d. President Kennedy's Speech of November 16, 1961	139
(2) Operation MONGOOSE	139
a. The Creation of Operation MONGOOSE	139
(1) The Special Group (Augmented) (SGA)	140
(2) General Lansdale Named Chief-of-Operations of MONGOOSE	140
(3) CIA Organization for MONGOOSE	140
b. Lansdale's Theory and Objective for MONGOOSE	140
c. Bissell's Testimony Concerning Presidential Instructions to Act More Vigorously	141
d. The January 19, 1962 Special Group Meeting	141
e. General Lansdale's MONGOOSE Planning Tasks	142
f. Lansdale's Rejection of a Suggestion that a Propaganda Campaign, Including Rewards for Assassination, Be Explored	144
g. The control System MONGOOSE Operations	144
h. The Pattern of MONGOOSE Action	146

III. Assassination Planning and Plots—Continued
  B. Cuba—Continued
    3. At What Level Were the Castro Plots Known About or Authorized Outside of the Central Intelligence Agency?—Con.
      (b) The Question of Knowledge and Authorization Outside of the Central Intelligence Agency During the Kennedy Administration—Continued
        (ii) Post-Bay of Pigs Underworld Plot—MONGOOSE Period—Continued

	Page
(3) Evidence Bearing on Knowledge of and Authorization for the Assassination Plot, Phase II	148
a. Helms' Testimony Concerning Authority	148
(1) Helms' Perception of Authority	148
(2) Helms' Testimony Concerning the Absence of a Direct Order and Why He Did Not Inform Administration Officials	150
(3) Helms' Perception of Robert Kennedy's Position on Assassination	150
(4) Helms' Testimony as to Why He Did Not Obtain a Direct Order	151
(5) Helms' Perception of the Relation of Special Group Controls to Assassination Activity	152
b. Harvey's Testimony Concerning Authority	153
(1) Harvey's Perception of Authority	153
(2) Harvey and the Special Group (Augmented)	153
c. Testimony of Kennedy Administration Officials	154
(4) The August 10, 1962 Special Group (Augmented) Meeting	161
a. The Contemporaneous Documents	161
(1) Lansdale's August 13, 1962 Memorandum	161
(2) Harvey's August 14, 1962 Memorandum	162
(3) The Minutes of the August 10, 1962 Meeting	162
(4) The August 10 Meeting	163
b. The Testimony	164
(1) Testimony About the August 10 Meeting	164
(a) McCone	164
(b) Harvey	164
(c) Goodwin	164
(d) McNamara	165
(2) Testimony About Events After the August 10, 1962 Meeting	165
(a) McCone	165
(b) Harvey	165
(c) Elder	165
(d) Lansdale	165
(3) Testimony of Reporters About Lansdale's Comments on the August 10 Meeting	167
(a) The Martin Report	168
(b) The O'Leary Report	169
(iii) The Question of Whether the AM/LASH Plot (1963–1965) Was Known About or Authorized by Administration Officials Outside the CIA	170
(1) Kennedy Administration's Policy Toward Cuba in 1963	170
a. Organizational Changes	170
b. Discussion of the Contingency of Castro's Death	170
c. The Standing Group's Discussion of United States Policy Toward Cuba	172
d. The Special Group's Authorization of a Sabotage Program Against Cuba	173
e. The Diplomatic Effort to Explore an Accommodation with Castro	173

III. Assassination Planning and Plots—Continued
  B. Cuba—Continued
    3. At What Level Were the Castro Plots Known About or Authorized Outside of the Central Intelligence Agency?—Con.
      (b) The Question of Knowledge and Authorization Outside of the Central Intelligence Agency During the Kennedy Administration—Continued
        (iii) The Question of Whether the AM/LASH Plot (1963–1965) Was Known About or Authorized by Administration Officials Outside the CIA—Continued

	Page
(2) Testimony on the Question of Authorization for the AM/LASH Poison Pen Device	174
a. The October Meeting with AM/LASH and the Use of Robert Kennedy's Name Without Obtaining His Approval	174
b. The Delivery of the Poison Pen on November 22, 1963	175
(3) The Question of Authorization in the Johnson Administration	176
a. Summary of the Assassination Activity	176
b. The Issue of Authorization	176
c. The Covert Action Program Against Cuba in 1964–1965	177
d. The Special Group Investigation of Reported Castro Assassination Plots by Cuban Exiles	177
e. Helms' Report to Rusk	178
f. Helms' Briefing of President Johnson on the 1967 Inspector General's Report	179
(4) Helms' Testimony on Authorization in the Johnson Administration	179
C. Institutionalizing Assassination: The "Executive Action" Capability	181
1. Introduction	181
2. The Question of White House Initiation, Authorization, or Knowledge of the Executive Action Project	182
3. The Question of Authorization or Knowledge of the Executive Action Project by the DCI	187
4. The Question of Whether Project ZR/RIFLE Was Connected to Any Actual Assassination Plots	187
(a) Conversation Between Bissell and Bundy	188
(b) Bissell's Instruction to Harvey to Take Over Responsibility for Underworld Contact: November 1961	188
(c) Use of QJ/WIN in Africa	189
D. Trujillo	191
1. Summary	191
2. Background	191
3. Initial Contact With Dissidents and Request for Arms	192
(a) Dissident Contacts	192
(b) The Request for Sniper Rifles	193
4. Summer and Fall of 1960	194
(a) Diplomatic Development—Withdrawal of United States Personnel	194
(b) Dearborn Reports Assassination May Be Only Way To Overthrow Trujillo Regime	195
(c) Efforts to Convince Trujillo to Abdicate	196
(d) CIA Plans of October 1960	196
(e) December 1960 Special Group Plan of Covert Actions	196
5. January 12, 1961 Special Group Approval of "Limited Supplies of Small Arms and Other Material"	196
(a) Memorandum Underlying the Special Group Action	197
6. January 20, 1961–April 17, 1961 (the Kennedy Administration through the Bay of Pigs)	197
(a) Specific Events Indirectly Linking United States to Dissidents' Assassination Plans	198
(i) Assassination Discussions and Requests for Explosives	198

III. Assassination Planning and Plots—Continued
  D. Trujillo—Continued
    6. January 20, 1961–April 17, 1961 (the Kennedy Administration through the Bay of Pigs—Continued
      (a) Specific Events Indirectly Linking United States to Dissident's Assassination Plans—Continued

	Page
(ii) The Passage of Pistols	199
(1) Pouching to the Dominican Republic	199
(2) Reason for the CIA Instruction Not To Tell Dearborn	199
(3) Were the Pistols Related to Assassination?	200
(iii) Passing of the Carbines	200
(1) Request by the Station and by Dearborn and Approval by CIA	200
(2) Were the Carbines Related to Assassination?	200
(3) Failure to Disclose to State Department Officials in Washington	201
(iv) Requests for and Pouching of the Machine Guns	201
(1) Requests for Machine Guns	201
(2) Pouching of Machine Guns Approved by Bissell	202

      (b) Knowledge of Senior American Officials (Pre-Bay of Pigs) ... 202
    7. April 17, 1961–May 31, 1961 (Bay of Pigs Through Trujillo Assassination) ... 205
      (a) Decision Not to Pass the Machine Guns and Unsuccessful United States Attempt to Stop Assassination Effort ... 205
      (b) Further Consideration of Passing Machine Guns ... 207
      (c) Special Group Meetings of May 4 and May 18, 1961 ... 208
      (d) Final Requests by Dissidents for Machine Guns ... 208
      (e) Dearborn in Washington for Consultation—Drafting of Contingency Plans ... 209
      (f) Cable of May 29, 1961 ... 212
    8. May 30, 1961 and Immediately Thereafter ... 213
      (a) Trujillo Assassinated ... 213
      (b) Cables to Washington ... 213
      (c) Immediate Post-Assassination Period ... 214
  E. Diem ... 217
    1. Summary ... 217
    2. The Abortive Coup of August 1963 ... 217
    3. The November 1963 Coup ... 220
  F. Schneider ... 225
    1. Summary ... 225
    2. The President's Initial Instruction and Background ... 227
      (a) September 15 White House Meeting ... 227
      (b) Background: Tracks I and II ... 229
      (c) CIA Views of Difficulty of Project ... 232
    3. CIA's Implementation of Track II ... 233
      (a) Evolution of CIA Strategy ... 233
        (i) The "Constitutional Coup" Approach ... 233
        (ii) Military Solution ... 234
      (b) The Chile Task Force ... 235
      (c) Use of the U.S. Military Attache and Interagency Relations ... 235
      (d) Agents Who Posed as Third Country Nationals ... 238
      (e) Chief of Station ... 239
    4. CIA Efforts to Promote a Coup ... 239
      (a) The Chilean Conspirators ... 239
      (b) Contacts Prior to October 15 ... 240
      (c) October 15 Decision ... 242
      (d) Coup Planning and Attempts After October 15 ... 243
      (e) The Shooting of General Schneider ... 245
      (f) Post October 22 Events ... 246
    5. CIA/White House Communication During Track II ... 246
      (a) September ... 247
      (b) October ... 248
      (c) December ... 253
      (d) Did Track II End? ... 253

	Page
IV. Findings and Conclusions	255
A. Findings Concerning the Plots Themselves	255
1. Officials of the United States Government Initiated Plots to Assassinate Fidel Castro and Patrice Lumumba	255
2. No Foreign Leaders Were Killed as a Result of Assassination Plots Initiated by Officials of the United States	256
3. American Officials Encouraged or Were Privy to Coup Plots Which Resulted in the Deaths of Trujillo, Diem, and Schneider	256
4. The Plots Occurred in a Cold War Atmosphere Perceived to be of Crisis Proportions	256
5. American Officials Had Exaggerated Notions About Their Ability to Control the Actions of Coup Leaders	256
6. CIA Officials Made Use of Known Underworld Figures in Assassination Efforts	257
B. Conclusions Concerning the Plots Themselves	257
1. The United States Should Not Engage in Assassination	257
(a) Distinction Between Targeted Assassinations Instigated by the United States and Support for Dissidents Seeking to Overthrow Local Governments	257
(b) The Setting In Which the Assassination Plots Occurred Explains, But Does Not Justify Them	258
2. The United States Should Not Make Use of Underworld Figures for Their Criminal Talents	259
C. Findings and Conclusions Relating to Authorization and Control	260
1. The Apparent Lack of Accountability in the Command and Control System Was Such That the Assassination Plots Could Have Been Undertaken Without Express Authorization	261
2. Findings Relating to the Level at Which the Plots Were Authorized	261
(a) Diem	261
(b) Schneider	262
(c) Trujillo	262
(d) Lumumba	263
(e) Castro	263
3. CIA Officials Involved in the Assassination Operations Perceived Assassination to Have Been a Permissible Course of Action	264
4. The Failure in Communication Between Agency Officials in Charge of the Assassination Operations and their Superiors in the Agency and in the Administration was Due to: (a) The Failure of Subordinates to Disclose Their Plans and Operations to Their Superiors; and (b) The Failure of Superiors in the Climate of Violence and Aggressive Covert Actions Sanctioned by the Administrations to Rule Out Assassination as a Tool of Foreign Policy; To Make Clear to Their Subordinates That Assassination Was Impermissible; Or To Inquire Further After Receiving Indications That It Was Being Considered	267
(a) Agency Officials Failed on Several Occasions to Reveal the Plots to Their Superiors, Or To Do So With Sufficient Detail and Clarity	267
(i) Castro	267
(ii) Trujillo	270
(iii) Schneider	272
(b) Administration Officials Failed to Rule Out Assassination As a Tool of Foreign Policy, To Make Clear to Their Subordinates That Assassination Was Impermissible or To Inquire Further After Receiving Indications That Assassination Was Being Considered	273
(i) Trujillo	273
(ii) Schneider	273
(iii) Lumumba	273
(iv) Castro	274

IV. Findings and Conclusions—Continued
  C. Findings and Conclusions Relating to Authorization and Control—Continued
    5. Practices Current at the Time in Which the Assassination Plots Occurred Were Revealed by the Record To Create the Risk of Confusion, Rashness and Irresponsibility in the Very Areas Where Clarity and Sober Judgment Were Most Necessary... 277
      (a) The Danger Inherent in Overextending the Doctrine of Plausible Denial... 277
      (b) The Danger of Using "Circumlocution" and "Euphemism". 278
      (c) The Danger of Generalized Instructions................... 278
      (d) The Danger of "Floating Authorization"................... 278
      (e) The Problems Connected With Creating New Covert Capabilities... 279
V. Recommendations.. 281
  A. General Agreement That the United States Must Not Engage in Assassination... 281
  B. CIA Directives Banning Assassination............................. 282
  C. The Need for a Statute... 282
Epilogue.. 285
Statement of Joinder.. 286
Appendix A... 289
Appendix B... 291
Separate Views of Senator Philip A. Hart................................ 297
Additional Views of Senator Robert Morgan............................... 299
Additional Views of Senator Howard H. Baker, Jr......................... 303
Additional Views of Senator Barry Goldwater............................. 341
Supplemental Views of Senator Charles McC. Mathias, Jr.................. 345
Abbreviations of Citations.. 347

PROLOGUE

The events discussed in this Interim Report must be viewed in the context of United States policy and actions designed to counter the threat of spreading Communism. Following the end of World War II, many nations in Eastern Europe and elsewhere fell under Communist influence or control. The defeat of the Axis powers was accompanied by rapid disintegration of the Western colonial empires. The Second World War had no sooner ended than a new struggle began. The Communist threat, emanating from what came to be called the "Sino-Soviet bloc," led to a policy of containment intended to prevent further encroachment into the "Free World."

United States strategy for conducting the Cold War called for the establishment of interlocking treaty arrangements and military bases throughout the world. Concern over the expansion of an aggressive Communist monolith led the United States to fight two major wars in Asia. In addition, it was considered necessary to wage a relentless cold war against Communist expansion wherever it appeared in the "back alleys of the world." This called for a full range of covert activities in response to the operations of Communist clandestine services.

The fear of Communist expansion was particularly acute in the United States when Fidel Castro emerged as Cuba's leader in the late 1950's. His takeover was seen as the first significant penetration by the Communists into the Western Hemisphere. United States leaders, including most Members of Congress, called for vigorous action to stem the Communist infection in this hemisphere. These policies rested on widespread popular support and encouragement.

Throughout this period, the United States felt impelled to respond to threats which were, or seemed to be, skirmishes in a global Cold War against Communism. Castro's Cuba raised the spectre of a Soviet outpost at America's doorstep. Events in the Dominican Republic appeared to offer an additional opportunity for the Russians and their allies. The Congo, freed from Belgian rule, occupied the strategic center of the African continent, and the prospect of Communist penetration there was viewed as a threat to American interests in emerging African nations. There was great concern that a Communist takeover in Indochina would have a "domino effect" throughout Asia. Even the election in 1970 of a Marxist president in Chile was seen by some as a threat similar to that of Castro's takeover in Cuba.

The Committee regards the unfortunate events dealt with in this Interim Report as an aberration, explainable at least in part, but not justified, by the pressures of the time. The Committee believes that it is still in the national interest of the United States to help nations achieve self-determination and resist Communist domination. However, it is clear that this interest cannot justify resorting to the kind of abuses covered in this report. Indeed, the Committee has resolved that steps must be taken to prevent those abuses from happening again.

I. INTRODUCTION AND SUMMARY

This interim report covers allegations of United States involvement in assassination plots against foreign political leaders. The report also examines certain other instances in which foreign political leaders in fact were killed and the United States was in some manner involved in activity leading up to the killing, but in which it would be incorrect to say that the purpose of United States involvement had been to encourage assassination.

The evidence establishes that the United States was implicated in several assassination plots. The Committee believes that, short of war, assassination is incompatible with American principles, international order, and morality. It should be rejected as a tool of foreign policy.

Our inquiry also reveals serious problems with respect to United States involvement in coups directed against foreign governments. Some of these problems are addressed here on the basis of our investigation to date; others we raise as questions to be answered after our investigation into covert action has been completed.

We stress the interim nature of this report. In the course of the Committee's continuing work, other alleged assassination plots may surface, and new evidence concerning the cases covered herein may come to light. However, it is the Committee's view that these cases have been developed in sufficient detail to clarify the issues which are at the heart of the Committee's mandate to recommend legislative and other reforms.

Thorough treatment of the assassination question has lengthened the Committee's schedule, but has greatly increased the Committee's awareness of the hard issues it must face in the months ahead. These issues include problems of domestic and foreign intelligence collection, counterintelligence, foreign covert operations, mechanisms of command and control, and assessment of the effectiveness of the total United States intelligence effort. The Committee intends, nevertheless, to complete, by February 1976, its main job of undertaking the first comprehensive review of the intelligence community.

A. COMMITTEE'S MANDATE

Senate Resolution 21 instructs the Committee to investigate the full range of governmental intelligence activities and the extent, if any, to which such activities were "illegal, improper or unethical." In addition to that broad general mandate, the Committee is required to investigate, study and make recommendations concerning various specific matters, several of which relate to the assassination issue.[1]

---

[1] For example, S. Res. 21 requires the Committee to study and investigate the following:
The extent and necessity of * * * covert intelligence activities * * * abroad;
[The] nature and extent of executive branch oversight of all United States intelligence activities;
The need for improved, strengthened, or consolidated oversight of United States intelligence activities by the Congress * * * and the need for new legislation.

Although the Rockefeller Commission initiated an inquiry into reported assassination plots, the Commission declared it was unable, for a variety of reasons, to complete its inquiry. At the direction of the President, the Executive Branch turned over to the Select Committee the work the Commission had done, along with certain other documents relating to assassination.

B. Committee Decision to Make Report Public

This report raises important questions of national policy. We believe that the public is entitled to know what instrumentalities of their Government have done.[1] Further, our recommendations can only be judged in light of the factual record. Therefore, this interim report should be made public.

The Committee believes the truth about the assassination allegations should be told because democracy depends upon a well-informed electorate. We reject any contention that the facts disclosed in this report should be kept secret because they are embarrassing to the United States. Despite the temporary injury to our national reputation, the Committee believes that foreign peoples will, upon sober reflection, respect the United States more for keeping faith with its democratic ideal than they will condemn us for the misconduct revealed. We doubt that any other country would have the courage to make such disclosures.

The fact that portions of the story have already been made public only accentuates the need for full disclosure. Innuendo and misleading partial disclosures are not fair to the individuals involved. Nor are they a responsible way to lay the groundwork for informed public policy judgments.

C. Scope of Committee's Investigation

Investigating the assassination issue has been an unpleasant duty, but one that the Committee had to meet. The Committee has compiled a massive record in the months that the inquiry has been underway. The record comprises over 8,000 pages of sworn testimony taken from over 75 witnesses during 60 hearing days and numerous staff interviews. The documents which the Committee has obtained include raw files from agencies and departments, the White House, and the Presidential libraries of the Administrations of former Presidents Dwight Eisenhower, John Kennedy and Lyndon Johnson.[2]

We have obtained two types of evidence: *first*, evidence relating to the general setting in which the events occurred, the national policy of the time, and the normal operating procedures, including channels of command and control; and *second*, evidence relating to the specific events.

A Senate Committee is not a court. It looks to the past, not to determine guilt or innocence, but in order to make recommendations for the future. When we found the evidence to be ambiguous—as we did on

---

[1] When the name of a participant in the plot did not add to the presentation and its inclusion may have placed in jeopardy his life or livelihood, the Committee, on occasion, resorted, on balance, to the use of an alias or a general description of the individual or his position.

[2] The Committee has served both general and specific document requests upon the Executive Branch. The Administration represented to the Committee that it has produced all the relevant documents.

some issues—we have set out both sides, in order that the evidence may speak for itself.

Despite the number of witnesses and documents examined by the Committee, the available evidence has certain shortcomings.

Many of the events considered occurred as long as fifteen years ago. With one exception, they occurred during the administrations of Presidents now dead. Other high officials whose testimony might have shed additional light on the thorny issues of authorization and control are also dead. Moreover, with the passage of time, the memories of those still alive have dimmed.

The Committee has often faced the difficult task of distinguishing refreshed recollection from speculation. In many instances, witnesses were unable to testify from independent recollection and had to rely on documents contemporaneous with the events to refresh their recollections. While informed speculation is of some assistance, it can only be assigned limited weight in judging specific events.

Although assassination is not a subject on which one would expect many records or documents to be made or retained, there were, in fact, more relevant contemporaneous documents than expected. In addition, in 1967 the Central Intelligence Agency had made an internal study of the Castro, Trujillo and Diem assassination allegations.[1] That study was quite useful, particularly in suggesting leads for uncovering the story of the actual assassination activity. Unfortunately, the working papers relating to that investigation were destroyed upon the completion of the Report, pursuant to instructions from CIA Director Richard Helms. (Memorandum for the Record, 5/23/67) These notes were destroyed because of their sensitivity and because the information they contained had already been incorporated into the Report. In fairness to Director Helms, it should be added, however, that he was responsible for requesting the preparation of the Inspector General's Report and for preserving the Report.

Some ambiguities in the evidence result from the practice of concealing CIA covert operations from the world and performing them in such a way that if discovered, the role of the United States could be plausibly denied. An extension of the doctrine of "plausible deniability" had the result that communications between the Agency and high Administration officials were often convoluted and imprecise.[2]

The evidence contains sharp conflicts, some of which relate to basic facts. But the most important conflicts relate not so much to basic facts as to differing perceptions and opinions based upon relatively undisputed facts. With respect to both kinds of conflicts, the Committee has attempted to set forth the evidence extensively so that it may speak for itself, and in our section on findings and conclusions, we suggest resolutions for some of the conflicts. However, because

---

[1] Those studies were made at the direction of CIA Director Richard Helms to provide him with information to answer questions from President Johnson. The President's questions concerning Castro were provoked by a Drew Pearson newspaper column in March 1967. The column alleged that the CIA had attempted to kill Castro using the Mafia. The President also asked Helms for information concerning possible United States involvement in the assassinations of Trujillo and Diem.

[2] For a full discussion of this doctrine, see pages 11–12.

the Committee's main task is to find lessons for the future, resolving conflicts in the evidence may be less important than making certain that the system which produced the ambiguities is corrected.

D. SUMMARY OF FINDINGS AND CONCLUSIONS

1. THE QUESTIONS PRESENTED

The Committee sought to answer four broad questions:

Assassination plots.—Did United States officials instigate, attempt, aid and abet, or acquiesce in plots to assassinate foreign leaders?

Involvement in other killings.—Did United States officials assist foreign dissidents in a way which significantly contributed to the killing of foreign leaders?

Authorization.—Where there was involvement by United States officials in assassination plots or other killings, were such activities authorized and if so, at what levels of our Government?

Communication and control.—Even if not authorized in fact, were the assassination activities perceived by those involved to be within the scope of their lawful authority? If they were so perceived, was there inadequate control exercised by higher authorities over the agencies to prevent such misinterpretation?

2. SUMMARY OF FINDINGS AND CONCLUSIONS ON THE PLOTS

The Committee investigated alleged United States involvement in assassination plots in five foreign countries:[1]

Country	Individual involved[2]
Cuba	Fidel Castro.
Congo (Zaire)	Patrice Lumumba.
Dominican Republic	Rafael Trujillo.
Chile	General Rene Schneider.
South Vietnam	Ngo Dinh Diem.

The evidence concerning each alleged assassination can be summarized as follows:[3]

Patrice Lumumba (Congo/Zaire).—In the Fall of 1960, two CIA officials were asked by superiors to assassinate Lumumba. Poisons were sent to the Congo and some exploratory steps were taken toward gaining access to Lumumba. Subsequently, in early 1961, Lumumba was killed by Congolese rivals. It does not appear from the evidence that the United States was in any way involved in the killing.

Fidel Castro (Cuba).—United States Government personnel plotted to kill Castro from 1960 to 1965. American underworld figures and

---

[1] In addition to the plots discussed in the body of this report, the Committee received some evidence of CIA involvement in plans to assassinate President Sukarno of Indonesia and "Papa Doc" Duvalier of Haiti. Former Deputy Director for Plans Richard Bissell testified that the assassination of Sukarno had been "contemplated" by the CIA, but that planning had proceeded no farther than identifying an "asset" whom it was believed might be recruited to kill Sukarno. Arms were supplied to dissident groups in Indonesia, but, according to Bissell, those arms were not intended for assassination. (Bissell, 6/11/75, p. 89)
Walter Elder, Executive Assistant to CIA Director John McCone, testified that the Director authorized the CIA to furnish arms to dissidents planning the overthrow of Haiti's dictator, Duvalier. Elder told the Committee that while the assassination of Duvalier was not contemplated by the CIA, the arms were furnished "to help [the dissidents] take what measures were deemed necessary to replace the government," and it was realized that Duvalier might be killed in the course of the overthrow. (Elder, 8/13/75, p. 79)

[2] Assassination plots against the Cuban leadership sometimes contemplated action against Raul Castro and Che Guevarra. In South Vietnam Diem's brother Ngo Dinh Nhu was killed at the same time as Diem.

[3] Section III contains a detailed treatment of the evidence on each country.

Cubans hostile to Castro were used in these plots, and were provided encouragement and material support by the United States.

Rafael Trujillo (Dominican Republic).—Trujillo was shot by Dominican dissidents on May 31, 1961. From early in 1960 and continuing to the time of the assassination, the United States Government generally supported these dissidents. Some Government personnel were aware that the dissidents intended to kill Trujillo. Three pistols and three carbines were furnished by American officials, although a request for machine guns was later refused. There is conflicting evidence concerning whether the weapons were knowingly supplied for use in the assassination and whether any of them were present at the scene.

Ngo Dinh Diem (South Vietnam).—Diem and his brother, Nhu, were killed on November 2, 1963, in the course of a South Vietnamese Generals' coup. Although the United States Government supported the coup, there is no evidence that American officials favored the assassination. Indeed, it appears that the assassination of Diem was not part of the Generals' pre-coup planning but was instead a spontaneous act which occurred during the coup and was carried out without United States involvement or support.

General Rene Schneider (Chile).—On October 25, 1970, General Schneider died of gunshot wounds inflicted three days earlier while resisting a kidnap attempt. Schneider, as Commander-in-Chief of the Army and a constitutionalist opposed to military coups, was considered an obstacle in efforts to prevent Salvador Allende from assuming the office of President of Chile. The United States Government supported, and sought to instigate a military coup to block Allende. U.S. officials supplied financial aid, machine guns and other equipment to various military figures who opposed Allende. Although the CIA continued to support coup plotters up to Schneider's shooting, the record indicates that the CIA had withdrawn active support of the group which carried out the actual kidnap attempt on October 22, which resulted in Schneider's death. Further, it does not appear that any of the equipment supplied by the CIA to coup plotters in Chile was used in the kidnapping. There is no evidence of a plan to kill Schneider or that United States officials specifically anticipated that Schneider would be shot during the abduction.

Assassination capability (Executive action).—In addition to these five cases, the Committee has received evidence that ranking Government officials discussed, and may have authorized, the establishment within the CIA of a generalized assassination capability. During these discussions, the concept of assassination was not affirmatively disavowed.

Similarities and differences among the plots.—The assassination plots all involved Third World countries, most of which were relatively small and none of which possessed great political or military strength. Apart from that similarity, there were significant differences among the plots:

    (1) Whether United States officials initiated the plot, or were responding to requests of local dissidents for aid.

    (2) Whether the plot was specifically intended to kill a foreign leader, or whether the leader's death was a reasonably foreseeable consequence of an attempt to overthrow the government.

The Castro and Lumumba cases are examples of plots conceived by United States officials to kill foreign leaders.

In the Trujillo case, although the United States Government certainly opposed his regime, it did not initiate the plot. Rather, United States officials responded to requests for aid from local dissidents whose aim clearly was to assassinate Trujillo. By aiding them, this country was implicated in the assassination, regardless of whether the weapons actually supplied were meant to kill Trujillo or were only intended as symbols of support for the dissidents.

The Schneider case differs from the Castro and Trujillo cases. The United States Government, with full knowledge that Chilean dissidents considered General Schneider an obstacle to their plans, sought a coup and provided support to the dissidents. However, even though the support included weapons, it appears that the intention of both the dissidents and the United States officials was to abduct General Schneider, not to kill him. Similarly, in the Diem case, some United States officials wanted Diem removed and supported a coup to accomplish his removal, but there is no evidence that any of those officials sought the death of Diem himself.

3. SUMMARY OF FINDINGS AND CONCLUSIONS ON THE ISSUES OF AUTHORITY AND CONTROL

To put the inquiry into assassination allegations in context, two points must be made clear. First, there is no doubt that the United States Government opposed the various leaders in question. Officials at the highest levels objected to the Castro and Trujillo regimes, believed the accession of Allende to power in Chile would be harmful to American interests, and thought of Lumumba as a dangerous force in the heart of Africa. Second, the evidence on assassinations has to be viewed in the context of other, more massive activities against the regimes in question. For example, the plots against Fidel Castro personally cannot be understood without considering the fully authorized, comprehensive assaults upon his regime, such as the Bay of Pigs invasion in 1961 and Operation MONGOOSE in 1962.

Once methods of coercion and violence are chosen, the probability of loss of life is always present. There is, however, a significant difference between a coldblooded, targeted, intentional killing of an individual foreign leader and other forms of intervening in the affairs of foreign nations. Therefore, the Committee has endeavored to explore as fully as possible the questions of how and why the plots happened, whether they were authorized, and if so, at what level.

The picture that emerges from the evidence is not a clear one. This may be due to the system of deniability and the consequent state of the evidence which, even after our long investigation, remains conflicting and inconclusive. Or it may be that there were in fact serious shortcomings in the system of authorization so that an activity such as assassination could have been undertaken by an agency of the United States Government without express authority.

The Committee finds that the system of executive command and control was so ambiguous that it is difficult to be certain at what levels assassination activity was known and authorized. This situation creates the disturbing prospect that Government officials might have undertaken the assassination plots without it having been uncontrovertibly clear that there was explicit authorization from the Presidents. It is also possible that there might have been a successful "plausible denial" in which Presidential authorization was issued but is now obscured. Whether or not the respective Presidents knew of or authorized the plots, as chief executive officer of the United States, each must bear the ultimate responsibility for the activities of his subordinates.

The Committee makes four other major findings.[1] The first relates to the Committee's inability to make a finding that the assassination plots were authorized by the Presidents or other persons above the governmental agency or agencies involved. The second explains why certain officials may have perceived that, according to their judgment and experience, assassination was an acceptable course of action. The third criticizes agency officials for failing on several occasions to disclose their plans and activities to superior authorities, or for failing to do so with sufficient detail and clarity. The fourth criticizes Administration officials for not ruling out assassination, particularly after certain Administration officials had become aware of prior assassination plans and the establishment of a general assassination capability.

There is admittedly a tension among the findings. This tension reflects a basic conflict in the evidence. While there are some conflicts over facts, it may be more important that there appeared to have been two differing perceptions of the same facts. This distinction may be the result of the differing backgrounds of those persons experienced in covert operations as distinguished from those who were not. Words of urgency which may have meant killing to the former, may have meant nothing of the sort to the latter.

While we are critical of certain individual actions, the Committee is also mindful of the inherent problems in a system which relies on secrecy, compartmentation, circumlocution, and the avoidance of clear responsibility. This system creates the risk of confusion and rashness in the very areas where clarity and sober judgment are most necessary. Hence, before reviewing the evidence relating to the cases, we briefly deal with the general subject of covert action.

---

[1] The Committee's findings are elaborated in Section IV, *infra*.

II. COVERT ACTION AS A VEHICLE FOR FOREIGN POLICY IMPLEMENTATION

Covert action is activity which is meant to further the sponsoring nation's foreign policy objectives, and to be concealed in order to permit that nation to plausibly deny responsibility.

The National Security Act of 1947 [1] which established the Central Intelligence Agency did not include specific authority for covert operations. However, it created the National Security Council, and gave that body authority to direct the CIA to "perform such other functions and duties related to intelligence affecting the national security as the National Security Council may from time to time direct." At its first meeting in December 1947, the NSC issued a top secret directive granting the CIA authority to conduct covert operations. From 1955 to 1970, the basic authority for covert operations was a directive of the National Security Council, NSC 5412/2.[2]

This directive instructed the CIA to counter, reduce and discredit "International Communism" throughout the world in a manner consistent with United States foreign and military policies. It also directed the CIA to undertake covert operations to achieve this end and defined covert operations as any covert activities related to propaganda, economic warfare, political action (including sabotage, demolition and assistance to resistance movements) and all activities compatible with the directive.[3] In 1962, the CIA's General Counsel rendered the opinion that the Agency's activities were "not inhibited by any limitations other than those broadly set forth in NSC 5412/2." (CIA General Counsel Memorandum 4/6/62)

A. POLICY DEVELOPMENT AND APPROVAL MECHANISM

In his 1962 memorandum, CIA's General Counsel made it clear that the CIA considered itself responsible for developing proposals and plans to implement the objectives of NSC 5412/2.[4] The memorandum also stated that even in developing ideas or plans it was incumbent on the Agency not only to coordinate with other executive departments and agencies, but also to "obtain necessary policy approval." The Committee has been faced with determining whether CIA officials thought

---

[1] (P.L. 80-253).
[2] Today the basic authority for CIA covert action operations is National Security Decision Memorandum 40, which superseded NSC 5412/2 on February 17, 1970.
[3] By contrast NSDM 40 of 1970 described covert actions as those secret activities designed to further official United States programs and policies abroad. It made no reference to communism.
[4] The memorandum stated:
"CIA must necessarily be responsible for planning. Occasionally suggestions for action will come from outside sources but, to depend entirely on such requirements would be an evasion of the Agency's responsibilities. Also, the average person, both in government and outside, is thinking along normal lines and to develop clandestine cold war activities properly, persons knowing both the capabilities and limitations of clandestine action must be studying and devising how such actions can be undertaken effectively."
With respect to policy approval, the General Counsel said:
"Both in developing ideas or plans for action it is incumbent upon the Agency to obtain necessary policy approval, and for this purpose these matters should be explored with proper officials in other departments and agencies, particularly in the Departments of State and Defense, so the determination can be made as to whether any one proposal should go to the Special Group or higher for policy determination."

it was "necessary" to obtain express approval for assassination plans and, if so, whether such approval was in fact either sought or granted.

Beginning in 1955, the responsibility for authorizing CIA covert action operations lay with the Special Group, a subcommittee of the National Security Council composed of the President's Assistant for National Security Affairs, the Director of Central Intelligence, the Deputy Secretary of Defense and the Under Secretary of State for Political Affairs. Today this group is known as the 40 Committee, and its membership has been expanded to include the Chairman of the Joint Chiefs of Staff. During 1962 another NSC subcommittee was established to oversee covert operations in Cuba. This subcommittee was the Special Group (Augmented); its membership included the Special Group, the Attorney General, and certain other high officials.

In exercising control over covert operations, the Special Group was charged with considering the objectives of proposed activities, determining whether the activities would accomplish the objectives, assessing the likelihood of success, and deciding whether the activities would be "proper" and in the national interest. The Chairman of the Special Group was usually responsible for determining which projects required Presidential consideration and for keeping him abreast of developments.

Authorization procedures, however, have not always been clear and tidy, nor have they always been followed. Prior to 1955, there were few formal procedures. Procedures from 1955 through 1963 were characterized in an internal CIA memorandum as "somewhat cloudy and * * * based on value judgments by the DCI." (Memorandum for the Record, C/CA/PEG, "Policy Coordination of CIA's Covert Action Operations", 2/21/67)

The existence of formal procedures for planning and implementing covert actions does not necessarily rule out the possibility that other, more informal procedures might be used. The granting of authority to an executive agency to plan covert action does not preempt Presidential authority to develop and mandate foreign policy. Formal procedures may be disregarded by either high Administration officials or officers in the CIA. In the Schneider incident, for example, President Nixon instructed CIA officials not to consult with the 40 Committee or other policy-making bodies.[1] In the plot to assassinate Castro using underworld figures, CIA officials decided not to inform the Special Group of their activities. One CIA operation, an aspect of which was to develop an assassination capability, was assigned to a senior case officer as a special task. His responsibility to develop this capability did not fall within the Special Group's review of covert operations, even though this same officer was responsible to the Special Group (Augmented) on other matters.

The Central Intelligence Agency also has a formal chain of command. At the top of the structure of the CIA is the Director of Central Intelligence (DCI) and his immediate subordinate, the Deputy Director of Central Intelligence (DDCI). Together they are responsible for the administration and supervision of the Agency. Beneath the DCI, and directly responsible to him, are the four operational components of the Agency. During the period covered by this report, the

---

[1] The Special Group was renamed the 303 Committee in 1964. In 1970 its name was changed again—this time to the 40 Committee.

component responsible for clandestine operations was the Directorate of Plans, headed by the Deputy Director for Plans (DDP).[1] The Directorate of Plans was organized around regional geographic divisions. These divisions worked with their respective overseas stations (headed by a Chief of Station (COS)) in planning and implementing the Directorate's operations. The divisions which played a part in the events considered in this report were the Western Hemisphere Division (WH) which was responsible for Latin America, the African Division (AF), and the Far Eastern Division (FE).

In addition to the regional divisions, the Directorate of Plans also included three staff-level units which provided some oversight and coordination of division projects. The staff units had no approval authority over the divisions. However, they could criticize and suggest modifications of projects sponsored by divisions. The three staffs were: Foreign Intelligence, Counterintelligence, and Covert Action.

When functioning in accordance with stated organizational procedures, the Directorate of Plans operated under a graduated approval process. Individual project proposals generally originated either from the field stations or from the divisions and were approved at varying levels within the Directorate, depending on the estimated cost and risk of the operation. Low-cost, low-risk projects could be approved at the Deputy Director for Plans level; extremely high-cost, high-risk projects required the approval of the DCI. Covert action proposals also required approval of the Special Group.

Also within the Directorate of Plans was a Technical Services Division (TSD) which developed and provided technical and support material required in the execution of operations. A separate Directorate, the Directorate of Support, handled financial and administrative matters. The Office of Security, a component of the Directorate of Support, was largely responsible for providing protection for clandestine installations and, as discussed at length in the Castro study, was occasionally called on for operational assistance.

B. The Concept of "Plausible Denial"

Non-attribution to the United States for covert operations was the original and principal purpose of the so-called doctrine of "plausible denial."

Evidence before the Committee clearly demonstrates that this concept, designed to protect the United States and its operatives from the consequences of disclosures, has been expanded to mask decisions of the President and his senior staff members. A further consequence of the expansion of this doctrine is that subordinates, in an effort to permit their superiors to "plausibly deny" operations, fail to fully inform them about those operations.

"Plausible denial" has shaped the processes for approving and evaluating covert actions. For example, the 40 Committee and its predecessor, the Special Group, have served as "circuit breakers" for Presidents, thus avoiding consideration of covert action by the Oval office.

"Plausible denial" can also lead to the use of euphemism and circumlocution, which are designed to allow the President and other

---

[1] The Directorate of Plans is presently called the Directorate of Operations, and is headed by the Deputy Director for Operations (DDO).

senior officials to deny knowledge of an operation should it be disclosed. The converse may also occur; a President could communicate his desire for a sensitive operation in an indirect, circumlocutious manner. An additional possibility is that the President may, in fact, not be fully and accurately informed about a sensitive operation because he failed to receive the "circumlocutious" message. The evidence discussed below reveals that serious problems of assessing intent and ensuring both control and accountability may result from the use of "plausible denial."

III. ASSASSINATION PLANNING AND THE PLOTS

A. CONGO

1. INTRODUCTION

The Committee has received solid evidence of a plot to assassinate Patrice Lumumba. Strong hostility to Lumumba, voiced at the very highest levels of government may have been intended to initiate an assassination operation; at the least it engendered such an operation. The evidence indicates that it is likely that President Eisenhower's expression of strong concern about Lumumba at a meeting of the National Security Council on August 18, 1960, was taken by Allen Dulles as authority to assassinate Lumumba.[1] There is, however, testimony by Eisenhower Administration officials, and ambiguity and lack of clarity in the records of high-level policy meetings, which tends to contradict the evidence that the President intended an assassination effort against Lumumba.

The week after the August 18 NSC meeting, a presidential advisor reminded the Special Group of the "necessity for very straightforward action" against Lumumba and prompted a decision not to rule out consideration of "any particular kind of activity which might contribute to getting rid of Lumumba." The following day, Dulles cabled a CIA Station Officer in Leopoldville, Republic of the Congo,[2] that "in high quarters" the "removal" of Lumumba was "an urgent and prime objective." Shorty thereafter the CIA's clandestine service formulated a plot to assassinate Lumumba. The plot proceeded to the point that lethal substances and instruments specifically intended for use in an assassination were delivered by the CIA to the Congo Station. There is no evidence that these instruments of assassination were actually used against Lumumba.

A thread of historical background is necessary to weave these broad questions together with the documents and testimony received by the Committee.

In the summer of 1960, there was great concern at the highest levels in the United States government about the role of Patrice Lumumba in the Congo. Lumumba, who served briefly as Premier of the newly independent nation, was viewed with alarm by United States policymakers because of what they perceived as his magnetic public appeal and his leanings toward the Soviet Union.

Under the leadership of Lumumba and the new President, Joseph Kasavubu, the Congo declared its independence from Belgium on June 30, 1960.[3] In the turbulent month that followed, Lumumba

---

[1] Indeed, one NSC staff member present at the August 18 meeting, believed that he witnessed a presidential order to assassinate Lumumba.
[2] Since the period in which the events under examination occurred, the names of many geographical units and governmental institutions have changed. For instance, the nation formerly known as the Republic of the Congo is now the Republic of Zaire and the present capital city, Kinshasa, was known then as Leopoldville. For the sake of clarity in dealing with many of the documents involved in this section, the names used in this report are those which applied in the early 1960's.
[3] For detailed reporting of the events in the Congo during this period, see the *New York Times*, especially July 7, 1960, 7:3; July 14, 1960, 1:1; July 16, 1960, 1:1 and 3:2; July 28, 1960, 3:7; September 3, 1960, 3:2; September 6, 1960, 1:8; December 3, 1960, 1:8; January 18, 1961, 3:1; February 14, 1961, 1:1.

(13)

threatened to invite Soviet troops to hasten the withdrawal of Belgian armed forces. The United Nations Security Council requested Belgium's withdrawal and dispatched a neutral force to the Congo to preserve order. In late July, Lumumba visited Washington and received pledges of economic aid from Secretary of State Christian Herter. By the beginning of September, Soviet airplanes, trucks, and technicians were arriving in the province where Lumumba's support was strongest.

In mid-September, after losing a struggle for the leadership of the government to Kasavubu and Joseph Mobutu, Chief of Staff of the Congolese armed forces, Lumumba sought protection from the United Nations forces in Leopoldville. Early in December, Mobutu's troops captured Lumumba while he was traveling toward his stronghold at Stanleyville and imprisoned him. On January 17, 1961, the central government of the Congo transferred Lumumba to the custody of authorities in Katanga province, which was then asserting its own independence from the Congo. Several weeks later, Katanga authorities announced Lumumba's death.

Accounts of the circumstances and timing of Lumumba's death vary. The United Nations investigation concluded that Lumumba was killed on January 17, 1961.[1]

2. DULLES CABLE TO LEOPOLDVILLE: AUGUST 26, 1960

The Congo declared its independence from Belgium on June 30, 1960. Shortly thereafter, the CIA assigned a new officer to its Leopoldville Station. The "Station Officer"[2] said that assassinating Lumumba was not discussed during his CIA briefings prior to departing for the Congo, nor during his brief return to Headquarters in connection with Lumumba's visit to Washington in late July. (Hedgman, 8/21/75, pp. 8–9)

During August, there was increasing concern about Lumumba's political strength in the Congo among the national security policymakers of the Eisenhower Administration.[3] This concern was nurtured by intelligence reports such as that cabled to CIA Headquarters by the Station Officer:

> EMBASSY AND STATION BELIEVE CONGO EXPERIENCING CLASSIC COMMUNIST EFFORT TAKEOVER GOVERNMENT. MANY FORCES AT WORK HERE: SOVIETS * * * COMMUNIST PARTY, ETC. ALTHOUGH DIFFICULT DETERMINE MAJOR INFLUENCING FACTORS TO PREDICT OUTCOME STRUGGLE FOR POWER, DECISIVE PERIOD NOT FAR OFF. WHETHER OR NOT LUMUMBA ACTUALLY COMMIE OR JUST PLAYING COMMIE GAME TO ASSIST HIS SOLIDIFYING POWER, ANTI-WEST FORCES RAPIDLY INCREASING POWER CONGO AND THERE MAY BE LITTLE TIME LEFT IN WHICH TAKE ACTION TO AVOID ANOTHER CUBA. (CIA Cable, Leopoldville to Director, 8/18/60)

---

[1] Report of the Commission of Investigation. U.N. Security Council, Official Records. Supplement for October, November, and December, 11/11/61, p. 117. (Cited hereinafter as "U.N. Report, 11/11/61.")

[2] Victor Hedgman was one of the CIA officers in Leopoldville attached to the Congo Station and will be referred to hereinafter as "Station Officer."

[3] See Section 7, infra, for a full discussion of the prevailing anti-Lumumba attitude in the United States government as shown by minutes of the National Security Council and Special Group and the testimony of high Administration officials.

This cable stated the Station's operational "objective [of] replacing Lumumba with pro Western Group." Bronson Tweedy, who was Chief of the Africa Division of CIA's clandestine services, replied that he was seeking State Department approval for the proposed operation based upon "your and our belief Lumumba must be removed if possible." (CIA Cable, Tweedy to Leopoldville, 8/18/60) On August 19, DDP Richard Bissell, Director of CIA's covert operations branch, signed a follow-up cable to Leopoldville, saying: "You are authorized proceed with operation." (CIA Cable, Director to Leopoldville, 8/19/60)

Several days later, the Station Officer reported:

ANTI-LUMUMBA LEADERS APPROACHED KASAVUBU WITH PLAN ASSASSINATE LUMUMBA * * * KASAVUBU REFUSED AGREE SAYING HE RELUCTANT RESORT VIOLENCE AND NO OTHER LEADER SUFFICIENT STATURE REPLACE LUMUMBA. (CIA Cable, Leopoldville to Director, 8/24/60)

On August 25, Director of Central Intelligence, Allen Dulles attended a meeting of the Special Group—the National Security Council subcommittee responsible for the planning of covert operations.[1] In response to the outline of some CIA plans for political actions against Lumumba, such as arranging a vote of no confidence by the Congolese Parliament, Gordon Gray, the Special Assistant to the President for National Security Affairs reported that the President "had expressed extremely strong feelings on the necessity for very straightforward action in this situation, and he wondered whether the plans as outlined were sufficient to accomplish this." (Special Group Minutes, 8/25/60) The Special Group "finally agreed that planning for the Congo would not necessarily rule out 'consideration' of any particular kind of activity which might contribute to getting rid of Lumumba." (Special Group Minutes, 8/25/60)

The next day, Allen Dulles signed a cable [2] to the Leopoldville Station Officer stating:

IN HIGH QUARTERS HERE IT IS THE CLEAR-CUT CONCLUSION THAT IF [LUMUMBA] CONTINUES TO HOLD HIGH OFFICE, THE INEVITABLE RESULT WILL AT BEST BE CHAOS AND AT WORST PAVE THE WAY TO COMMUNIST TAKEOVER OF THE CONGO WITH DISASTROUS CONSEQUENCES FOR THE PRESTIGE OF THE UN AND FOR THE INTERESTS OF THE FREE WORLD GENERALLY. CONSEQUENTLY WE CONCLUDE THAT HIS REMOVAL MUST BE AN URGENT AND PRIME OBJECTIVE AND THAT UNDER EXISTING CONDITIONS THIS SHOULD BE A HIGH PRIORITY OF OUR COVERT ACTION. (CIA Cable, Dulles to Station Officer, 8/26/60) [3]

---

[1] The August 25th Special Group meeting and the testimony about its significance for the issue of authorization is discussed in detail in Section 7(a)(iii), *infra*.
That meeting was preceded by an NSC meeting on August 18, at which an NSC staff executive heard the President make a statement that impressed him as an order for the assassination of Lumumba. (Johnson, 6/18/75, pp. 6–7) The testimony about this NSC meeting is set forth in detail at Section 7(a)(ii), *infra*.
[2] Cables issued under the personal signature of the DCI are a relative rarity in CIA communications and call attention to the importance and sensitivity of the matter discussed. By contrast, cable traffic to and from CIA field stations routinely refers to the sender or recipient as "Director" which simply denotes "CIA Headquarters."
[3] The bracketed words in cables throughout this section signify that a cryptonym, pseudonym, or other coded reference has been translated in order to maintain the security of CIA communications and to render the cable traffic comprehensible. The translations were provided to the Committee by the CIA Review Staff and by various witnesses.

The cable said that the Station Officer was to be given "wider authority"—along the lines of the previously authorized operation to replace Lumumba with a pro-Western group—"including even more aggressive action if it can remain covert . . . we realize that targets of opportunity may present themselves to you." Dulles' cable also authorized the expenditure of up to $100,000 "to carry out any crash programs on which you do not have the opportunity to consult HQS," and assured the Station Officer that the message had been "seen and approved at competent level" in the State Department. (CIA Cable, 8/26/60) The cable continued:

> TO THE EXTENT THAT AMBASSADOR MAY DESIRE TO BE CONSULTED, YOU SHOULD SEEK HIS CONCURRENCE. IF IN ANY PARTICULAR CASE, HE DOES NOT WISH TO BE CONSULTED YOU CAN ACT ON YOUR OWN AUTHORITY WHERE TIME DOES NOT PERMIT REFERRAL HERE.

This cable raises the question of whether the DCI was contemplating action against Lumumba for which the United States would want to be in a position to "plausibly deny" responsibility. On its face, the cable could have been read as authorizing only the "removal" of Lumumba from office. DDP Richard Bissell was "almost certain" that he was informed about the Dulles cable shortly after its transmission. He testified that it was his "belief" that the cable was a circumlocutious means of indicating that the President wanted Lumumba killed.[1] (Bissell, 9/10/75, pp. 12, 33, 64–65)

Bronson Tweedy testified that he may have seen Dulles' cable of August 26, before it was transmitted and that he "might even have drafted it." Tweedy called this cable the "most authoritative statement" on the "policy consensus in Washington about the need for the removal of Lumumba" by any means, including assassination. He said that he "never knew" specifically who was involved in formulating this policy. But he believed that the cable indicated that Dulles had received authorization at the "policy level" which "certainly * * * would have involved the National Security Council." Tweedy testified that the $100,000 was probably intended for "political operations against Lumumba * * * not assassination-type programs." (Tweedy, 10/9/75 I, p. 5, II, pp. 5–7, 24, 26)

3. CIA ENCOURAGEMENT OF CONGOLESE EFFORTS TO "ELIMINATE" LUMUMBA

On September 5, 1960, President Kasavubu dismissed Premier Lumumba from the government despite the strong support for Lumumba in the Congolese Parliament. After losing the ensuing power struggle with Kasavubu and Mobutu, who seized power by a military coup on September 14, Lumumba asked the United Nations peace-keeping force for protection.

The evidence indicates that the ouster of Lumumba did not alleviate the concern about him in the United States government. Rather, CIA and high Administration officials[2] continued to view him as a threat.

---

[1] See Section 7(c), *infra* for additional testimony by Bissell on the question of authorization for the assassination effort against Lumumba. Bissell testified, *inter alia*, that Dulles would have used the phrase "highest quarters" to refer to the President.

[2] A detailed treatment of the expressions of continued concern over Lumumba at the National Security Council level is set forth in Section 7, *infra*.

During this period, CIA officers in the Congo advised and aided Congolese contacts known to have an intent to assassinate Lumumba. The officers also urged the "permanent disposal" of Lumumba by some of these Congolese contacts. Moreover, the CIA opposed reopening Parliament after the coup because of the likelihood that Parliament would return Lumumba to power.

The day after Kasavubu deposed Lumumba, two CIA officers met with a high-level Congolese politician who was in close contact with the Leopoldville Station. The Station reported to CIA Headquarters:

> TO [STATION OFFICER] COMMENT THAT LUMUMBA IN OPPOSITION IS ALMOST AS DANGEROUS AS IN OFFICE, [THE CONGOLESE, POLITICIAN] INDICATED UNDERSTOOD AND IMPLIED MIGHT PHYSICALLY ELIMINATE LUMUMBA. (CIA Cable, Leopoldville to Director, 9/7/60)

The cable also stated that the Station Officer had offered to assist this politician "in preparation new government program" and assured him that the United States would supply technicians. (CIA Cable, 9/7/60)

As the struggle for power raged, Bronson Tweedy summarized the prevalent apprehension of the United States about Lumumba's ability to influence events in the Congo by virtue of his personality, irrespective of his official position:

> LUMUMBA TALENTS AND DYNAMISM APPEAR OVERRIDING FACTOR IN REESTABLISHING HIS POSITION EACH TIME IT SEEMS HALF LOST. IN OTHER WORDS EACH TIME LUMUMBA HAS OPPORTUNITY HAVE LAST WORD HE CAN SWAY EVENTS TO HIS ADVANTAGE. (CIA Cable, Director to Leopoldville, 9/13/60)

The day after Mobutu's coup, the Station Officer reported that he was serving as an advisor to a Congolese effort to "eliminate" Lumumba due to his "fear" that Lumumba might, in fact, have been strengthened by placing himself in U.N. custody, which afforded a safe base of operations. Hedgman concluded: "Only solution is remove him from scene soonest." (CIA Cable, Leopoldville to Director, 9/15/60)

On September 17, another CIA operative in the Congo met with a leading Congolese senator. The cable to CIA Headquarters concerning the meeting reported:

> [CONGOLESE SENATOR] REQUESTED CLANDESTINE SUPPLY SMALL ARMS TO EQUIP * * * TROOPS RECENTLY ARRIVED [LEOPOLDVILLE] AREA * * * [THE SENATOR] SAYS THIS WOULD PROVIDE CORE ARMED MEN WILLING AND ABLE TAKE DIRECT ACTION * * * [SENATOR] RELUCTANTLY AGREES LUMUMBA MUST GO PERMANENTLY. DISTRUSTS [ANOTHER CONGOLESE LEADER] BUT WILLING MAKE PEACE WITH HIM FOR PURPOSES ELIMINATION LUMUMBA. (CIA Cable, Leopoldville to Director, 9/17/60)

The CIA operative told the Congolese senator that "he would explore possibility obtaining arms" and he recommended to CIA headquarters that they should:

> HAVE [ARMS] SUPPLIES READY TO GO AT NEAREST BASE PEND-

ING [UNITED STATES] DECISION THAT SUPPLY WARRANTED AND NECESSARY. (CIA Cable, 9/17/60)[1]

Several days later, the Station Officer warned a key Congolese leader about coup plots led by Lumumba and two of his supporters, and: "Urged arrest or other more permanent disposal of Lumumba, Gizenga, and Mulele." (CIA Cable, Leopoldville to Director, 9/20/61) Gizenga and Mulele were Lumumba's lieutenants who led his supporters while Lumumba was in U.N. custody.

Throughout the fall of 1960, while Lumumba remained in U.N. protective custody,[2] the CIA continued to view him as a serious political threat. One concern was that if Parliament were re-opened and the moderates failed to obtain a majority vote, the "pressures for [Lumumba's] return will be almost irresistible." (CIA Cable, Leopoldville to Director, 10/26/60).[3] Another concern at CIA Headquarters was that foreign powers would intervene in the Congo and bring Lumumba to power. (CIA Cable, Director to Leopoldville, 10/17/60) Lumumba was also viewed by the CIA and the Administration as a stalking horse for "what appeared to be a Soviet effort to take over the Congo." (Hedgman, 8/21/75, pp. 10, 45)[4]

After Lumumba was in U.N. custody, the Leopoldville Station continued to maintain close contact with Congolese who expressed a desire to assassinate Lumumba.[5] CIA officers encouraged and offered to aid these Congolese in their efforts against Lumumba, although there is

---

[1] This recommendation proved to be in line with large scale planning at CIA Headquarters for clandestine paramilitary support to anti-Lumumba elements. On October 6, 1960, Richard Bissell and Bronson Tweedy signed a cable concerning plans which the Station Officer was instructed not to discuss with State Department representatives or operational contacts:

[IN] VIEW UNCERTAIN OUTCOME CURRENT DEVELOPMENTS [CIA] CONDUCTING CONTINGENCY PLANNING FOR CONGO AT REQUEST POLICY ECHELONS. THIS PLANNING DESIGNED TO PREPARE FOR SITUATION IN WAY [UNITED STATES] WOULD PROVIDE CLANDESTINE SUPPORT TO ELEMENTS IN ARMED OPPOSITION TO LUMUMBA. CONTEMPLATED ACTION INCLUDES PROVISION ARMS, SUPPLIES AND PERHAPS SOME TRAINING TO ANTI-LUMUMBA RESISTANCE GROUPS. (CIA Cable, Director in Leopoldville, 10/6/60)

[2] Both Richard Bissell and Bronson Tweedy confirmed that the CIA continued to view Lumumba as a threat even after he placed himself in U.N. custody. (Bissell, 9/10/75, pp. 68–69, 79; Tweedy, 9/9/75, pp. 48–50) Two factors were mentioned consistently in testimony by government officials to substantiate this view: first, Lumumba was a spellbinding orator with the ability to stir masses of people to action; and second, the U.N. forces did not restrain Lumumba's freedom of movement and the Congolese army surrounding them were often lax in maintaining their vigil. (Mulroney, 9/11/75, pp. 22–24; Dillon, 9/2/75. p. 49) As CIA officer Michael J. Mulroney put it, the fact that Lumumba was in United Nations custody "did not result in a cessation of his political activity." (Mulroney, 9/11/75, p. 23)

[3] A CIA Cable from Leopoldville to the Director on November 3, 1960 returned to this theme: the opening of the Congolese Parliament by the United Nations is opposed because it "WOULD PROBABLY RETURN LUMUMBA TO POWER."

[4] See Section 7, *infra*, for a treatment of the expression of this viewpoint at high-level policy meetings.

Tweedy expressed an even broader "domino theory" about the impact of Lumumba's leadership in the Congo upon events in the rest of Africa:

"The concern with Lumumba was not really the concern with Lumumba as a person. It was concern at this very pregnant point in the new African development [with] the effect on the balance of the Continent of a disintegration of the Congo. [I]t was the general feeling that Lumumba had it within his power to bring about this dissolution, and this was the fear that it would merely be the start—the Congo, after all, was the largest geographical expression. Contained in it were enormously important mineral resources * * *. The Congo itself, is adjacent to Nigeria, which at that point was considered to be one of the main hopes of the future stability of Africa. [I]f the Congo had fallen, then the chances were Nigeria would be seized with the same infection.

"This was why Washington * * * was so concerned about Lumumba, not because there was something unique about Lumumba, but it was the Congo." (Tweedy, 10/9/75 II, p. 42)

[5] A Congolese in contact with the CIA "IMPLIED HE TRYING HAVE [LUMUMBA] KILLED BUT ADDED THIS MOST DIFFICULT AS JOB WOULD HAVE BE DONE BY AFRICAN WITH NO APPARENT INVOLVEMENT WHITE MAN." (CIA Cable, Leopoldville to Director, 10/28/60)

no evidence that aid was ever provided for the specific purpose of assassination.

4. THE PLOT TO ASSASSINATE LUMUMBA

Summary

In the Summer of 1960, DDP Richard Bissell asked the Chief of the Africa Division, Bronson Tweedy, to explore the feasibility of assassinating Patrice Lumumba. Bissell also asked a CIA scientist, Joseph Scheider, to make preparations to assassinate or incapacitate an unspecified "African leader." According to Scheider, Bissell said that the assignment had the "highest authority." Scheider procured toxic biological materials in response to Bissell's request, and was then ordered by Tweedy to take these materials to the Station Officer in Leopoldville. According to Scheider, there was no explicit requirement that the Station check back with Headquarters for final approval before proceeding to assassinate Lumumba. Tweedy maintained, however, that whether or not he had explicitly levied such a requirement, the Station Officer was not authorized to move from exploring means of assassination to actually attempting to kill Lumumba without referring the matter to Headquarters for a policy decision.

In late September, Scheider delivered the lethal substances to the Station Officer in Leopoldville and instructed him to assassinate Patrice Lumumba. The Station Officer testified that after requesting and receiving confirmation from CIA Headquarters that he was to carry out Scheider's instructions, he proceeded to take "exploratory steps" in furtherance of the assassination plot. The Station Officer also testified that he was told by Scheider that President Eisenhower had ordered the assassination of Lumumba. Scheider's testimony generally substantiated this account, although he acknowledged that his meetings with Bissell and Tweedy were the only bases for his impression about Presidential authorization. Scheider's mission to the Congo was preceded and followed by cables from Headquarters urging the "elimination" of Lumumba transmitted through an extraordinarily restricted "Eyes Only" channel—including two messages bearing the personal signature of Allen Dulles.

The toxic substances were never used. But there is no evidence that the assassination operation was terminated before Lumumba's death. There is, however, no suggestion of a connection between the assassination plot and the events which actually led to Lumumba's death.[1]

(a) *Bissell/Tweedy Meetings on Feasibility of Assassinating Lumumba*

Bronson Tweedy testified that Richard Bissell initiated a discussion with him in the summer of 1960 about the feasibility of assassinating Patrice Lumumba, and that they discussed the subject "more than once" during the following fall. Tweedy said the first such conversation probably took place shortly before Dulles' cable of August 26, instructing the Station Officer that Lumumba's "removal" was a "high priority of our covert action."[2] Whether his talk with Bissell was

---
[1] See Section 6, *infra*, for a discussion of the evidence about the circumstances surrounding Lumumba's death in Katanga.
[2] See Section 2, *supra*.

"shortly before or shortly after" the Dulles cable, it was clear to Tweedy that the two events "were totally in tandem." (Tweedy, 9/9/75, pp. 14–15; 10/9/75 II, p. 6)

Tweedy testified that he did not recall the exact exchange but the point of the conversation was clear:

> What Mr. Bissell was saying to me was that there was agreement, policy agreement, in Washington that Lumumba must be removed from the position of control and influence in the Congo * * * and that among the possibilities of that elimination was indeed assassination.
>
> * * * The purpose of his conversation with me was to initiate correspondence with the Station for them to explore with Headquarters the possibility of * * * assassination, or indeed any other means of removing Lumumba from power * * * to have the Station start reviewing possibilities, assets, and discussing them with Headquarters in detail in the same way we would with any operation. (Tweedy, 10/9/75 II, pp. 6, 8)

Tweedy was "sure" that in his discussions with Bissell poisoning "must have" been mentioned as one means of assassination that was being considered and which the Station Officer should explore. (Tweedy, 9/9/75, pp. 26–27)

Tweedy testified that Bissell assigned him the task of working out the "operational details," such as assessing possible agents and the security of the operation, and of finding "some solution that looked as if it made sense, and had a promise of success." Tweedy stated that Bissell "never said * * * go ahead and do it in your own good time without any further reference to me." Rather, Tweedy operated under the impression that if a feasible means of assassinating Lumumba were developed, the decision on proceeding with an assassination attempt was to be referred to Bissell. (Tweedy, 10/9/75 I, pp. 7, 17–18)

Tweedy stated that he did not know whether Bissell had consulted with any "higher authority" about exploring the possibilities for assassinating Lumumba. Tweedy said, that generally, when he received an instruction from Bissell:

> I would proceed with it on the basis that he was authorized to give me instructions and it was up to him to bloody well know what he was empowered to tell me to do. (Tweedy, 9/9/75, p. 13)[1]

(b) *Bissell/Scheider Meetings on Preparations for Assassinating "An African Leader"*

Joseph Scheider[2] testified that he had "two or three conversations" with Richard Bissell in 1960 about the Agency's technical capability to assassinate foreign leaders. In the late spring or early summer, Bissell asked Scheider generally about technical means of assassination or incapacitation that could be developed or procured by the CIA.

---

[1] When asked whether he considered declining Bissell's assignment to move toward the assassination of Lumumba, Tweedy responded:
TWEEDY: I certainly did not attempt to decline it, and I felt, in view of the position of the government on the thing, that at least the exploration of this, or possibility of removing Lumumba from power in the Congo was an objective worth pursuing.
Q: Including killing him?
TWEEDY: Yes. I suspect I was ready to consider this * * * Getting rid of him was an objective worth pursuing, and if the government and my betters wished to pursue it, professionally, I was perfectly willing to play my role in it, yes * * *. Having to do it all over again, it would be my strong recommendation that we not get into it. (Tweedy, 10/9/75, II, pp. 39–41)

[2] During the events discussed in the Lumumba case, Joseph Scheider served as Special Assistant to the DDP (Bissell) for Scientific Matters. Scheider holds a degree in bio-organic chemistry. (Scheider, 10/7/75, pp. 13, 25–29)

Scheider informed Bissell that the CIA had access to lethal or potentially lethal biological materials that could be used in this manner. Following their intial "general discussion," Scheider said he discussed assassination capabilities with Bissell in the context of "one or two meetings about Africa." (Scheider, 10/7/75, pp. 6–7, 41)

Scheider testified that in the late summer or early fall, Bissell asked him to make all preparations necessary for having biological materials ready on short notice for use in the assassination of an unspecified African leader, "in case the decision was to go ahead." [1] Scheider testified that Bissell told him that "he had direction from the highest authority * * * for getting into that kind of operation." Scheider stated that the reference to "highest authority" by Bissell "signified to me that he meant the President." [2] (Scheider, 10/7/75, pp. 51–55, 58; 10/9/75, p. 8)

Scheider said that he "must have" outlined to Bissell the steps he planned to take to execute Bissell's orders. (Scheider, 10/7/75, p. 58) After the meeting, Scheider reviewed a list of biological materials available at the Army Chemical Corps installation at Fort Detrick, Maryland which would produce diseases that would "either kill the individual or incapacitate him so severely that he would be out of action." (Scheider, 10/7/75, pp. 63–64; 10/9/75, pp. 8–9, 12) [3] Scheider selected one material from the list which "was supposed to produce a disease that was * * * indigenous to that area [of Africa] and that could be fatal." (Scheider, 10/7/75, p. 63) Scheider testified that he obtained this material and made preparation for its use:

> We had to get it bottled and packaged in a way that it could pass for something else and I needed to have a second material that could absolutely inactivate it in case that is what I desired to do for some contingency. (Scheider, 10/7/75, p. 64)

Scheider also "prepared a packet of * * * accessory materials," such as hypodermic needles, rubber gloves, and gauze masks, "that would be used in the handling of this pretty dangerous material." (Scheider, 10/7/75, p. 59)

(c) *Scheider Mission to the Congo on an Assassination Operation*

Scheider testified that he remembered "very clearly" a conversation with Tweedy and the Deputy Chief of the Africa Division in September 1960 which "triggered" his trip to the Congo after he had prepared toxic biological materials and accessories for use in an assassination operation. (Scheider, 10/7/75, pp. 41, 65) According to Scheider, Tweedy and his Deputy asked him to take the toxic materials to the Congo and deliver instructions from Headquarters to the Station Officer: "to mount an operation, if he could do it securely * * * to either seriously incapacitate or eliminate Lumumba." (Scheider, 10/7/75, p. 66)

---

[1] Scheider said it was possible that Bissell subsequently gave him the "go signal" for his trip to the Congo and specified Lumumba as the target of the assassination operation. (Scheider, 10/7/75, pp. 65, 113–114; 10/7/75, p. 8) Scheider had a clearer memory, however, of another meeting, where the top officers of CIA's Africa Division, acting under Bissell's authority, actually dispatched to the Congo. (See Section 4(c), *infra*)

[2] See Section 7(d), *infra* for additional testimony by Scheider about the question of Presidential authorization for the assassination of Lumumba.

[3] Scheider said that there were "seven or eight materials" on the list, including tularemia ("rabbit fever"), brucellosis (undulant fever), tuberculosis, anthrax, smallpox, and Venezuelan equine encephalitis ('sleeping sickness"). (Scheider, 10/7/75, p. 64; 10/9/75. p. 9)

Scheider said that he was directed to provide technical support to the Station Officer's attempt to find a feasible means of carrying out the assassination operation:

They urged me to be sure that * * * if these technical materials were used * * * I was to make the technical judgments if there were any reasons the things shouldn't go, that was my responsibility. (Scheider, 10/7/75, p. 68)[1]

According to Scheider, the Station Officer was to be responsible for "the operations aspects, what assets to use and other non-technical considerations." Scheider said that in the course of directing him to carry instructions to the Station Officer in the Congo, Tweedy and his Deputy "referred to the previous conversation I had with Bissell," and left Scheider with, "the impression that Bissell's statements to me in our previous meeting held and that they were carrying this message from Bissell to me." (Scheider, 10/9/75, pp. 13, 15, 69)

Although he did not have a specific recollection, Scheider stated that it was "probable" that he would have "checked with Bissell" to validate the extraordinary assignment he received from Tweedy and his Deputy, if indeed he had not actually received the initial assignment itself from Bissell. (Scheider, 10/7/75, pp. 113–114)

After being informed of Scheider's testimony about their meeting, and reviewing the contemporaneous cable traffic, Tweedy stated that it was "perfectly clear" that he had met with Scheider. He assumed that he had ordered Scheider to deliver lethal materials to the Leopoldville Station Officer and to serve as a technical adviser to the Station Officer's attempts to find a feasible means of assassinating Lumumba. (Tweedy, 10/9/75 I, pp. 18–21; 10/9/75 II, p. 9)

Tweedy said that his Deputy Chief was the only other person in the Africa Division who would have known that the assassination of Lumumba was being considered. (Tweedy, 9/9/75. p. 64) Tweedy assumed Scheider had "already been given his marching orders to go to the Congo by Mr. Bissell, not by me." (Tweedy, 10/9/75 II, p. 11)

Scheider testified that he departed for the Congo within a week of his meeting with Tweedy and his Deputy (Scheider, 10/9/75, p. 15)

(d) Congo Station Officer Told To Expect Scheider: Dulles Cables About "Elimination" of Lumumba

On September 19, 1960, several days after Lumumba placed himself in the protective custody of the United Nations peacekeeping force in Leopoldville, Richard Bissell and Bronson Tweedy sent a cryptic cable to Leopoldville to arrange a clandestine meeting between the Station Officer and "Joseph Braun," who was traveling to the Congo

---

[1] When asked if he had considered declining to undertake the assignment to provide technical support to an assassination operation, Scheider stated:

"I think that my view of the job at the time and the responsibilities I had was in the context of a silent war that was being waged, although I realize that one of my stances could have been * * * as a conscientious objector to this war. That was not my view. I felt that a decision had been made * * * at the highest level that this be done and that as unpleasant a responsibility as it was, it was my responsibility to carry out my part of that." (Scheider, 10/9/75, p. 63)

on an unspecified assignment. Joseph Scheider testified that "Joseph Braun" was his alias and was used because this was "an extremely sensitive operation." (Scheider, 10/7/75, pp. 78, 80) The cable informed the Station Officer:

> ["JOE"] SHOULD ARRIVE APPROX 27 SEPT * * * WILL ANNOUNCE HIMSELF AS "JOE FROM PARIS" * * * IT URGENT YOU SHOULD SEE ["JOE"] SOONEST POSSIBLE AFTER HE PHONES YOU. HE WILL FULLY IDENTIFY HIMSELF AND EXPLAIN HIS ASSIGNMENT TO YOU. (CIA Cable, Bissell, Tweedy to the Station Officer, 9/19/60)

The cable bore the codeword "PROP," which indicated extraordinary sensitivity and restricted circulation at CIA headquarters to Dulles, Bissell, Tweedy, and Tweedy's Deputy. The PROP designator restricted circulation in the Congo to the Station Officer. (Tweedy, 10/9/75 I, pp. 14–15; II, pp. 9, 37)

Tweedy testified that the PROP channel was established and used exclusively for the assassination operation. (Tweedy, 10/9/75 II, p. 37; 10/9/75 I, pp. 48–49) The Bissell/Tweedy cable informed the Station Officer that the PROP channel was to be used for:

> ALL [CABLE] TRAFFIC THIS OP, WHICH YOU INSTRUCTED HOLD ENTIRELY TO YOURSELF. (CIA Cable, 9/19/60)

Tweedy testified that the fact that he and Bissell both signed the cable indicated that authorization for Scheider's trip to the Congo had come from Bissell. Tweedy stated that Bissell "signed off" on cables originated by a Division Chief "on matters of particular sensitivity or so important that the DDP wished to be constantly informed about correspondence." Tweedy said that Bissell read much of the cable traffic on this operation and was "generally briefed on the progress of the planning." (Tweedy, 10/9/75 I, pp. 14, 54)

The Station Officer, Victor Hedgman testified to a clear, independent recollection of receiving the Tweedy/Bissell cable. He stated that in September of 1960 he received a "most unusual" cable from CIA Headquarters which advised that:

> someone who I would have recognized would arrive with instructions for me * * * I believe the message was also marked for my eyes only * * *and contained instructions that I was not to discuss the message with anyone.

He said that the cable did not specify the kind of instructions he was to receive, and it "did not refer to Lumumba in any way." (Hedgman, 8/21/75, pp. 11–13, 43)

Three days after the Bissell/Tweedy cable, Tweedy sent another cable through the PROP channel which stated that if it was decided that "support for prop objectives [was] essential" a third country national should be used as an agent in the assassination operation to completely conceal the American role.[1] (CIA Cable, 9/22/60) Tweedy testified that "PROP objectives" referred to an assassination attempt. (Tweedy, 10/9/75 I, p. 30) Tweedy also indicated to the Station Officer and his "colleague" Scheider:

---

[1] Tweedy also expressed reservations about two agents that the Station Officer was considering for this operation and said "WE ARE CONSIDERING A THIRD NATIONAL CUTOUT CONTACT CANDIDATE AVAILABLE HERE WHO MIGHT FILL BILL." (CIA Cable, 9/22/60) This is probably a reference to agent OJ/WIN, who was later dispatched to the Congo. His mission is discussed in Sections 5(b)–5(c), *infra*.

> YOU AND COLLEAGUE[1] UNDERSTAND WE CANNOT READ OVER YOUR SHOULDER AS YOU PLAN AND ASSESS OPPORTUNITIES. OUR PRIMARY CONCERN MUST BE CONCEALMENT [AMERICAN] ROLE, UNLESS OUTSTANDING OPPORTUNITY EMERGES WHICH MAKES CALCULATED RISK FIRST CLASS BET. READY ENTERTAIN ANY SERIOUS PROPOSALS YOU MAKE BASED OUR HIGH REGARD BOTH YOUR PROFESSIONAL JUDGMENTS. (CIA Cable, 9/22/60)

On September 24, the DCI personally sent a cable to Leopoldville stating:

> WE WISH GIVE EVERY POSSIBLE SUPPORT IN ELIMINATING LUMUMBA FROM ANY POSSIBILITY RESUMING GOVERNMENTAL POSITION OR IF HE FAILS IN LEOPOLDVILLE, SETTING HIMSELF IN STANLEYVILLE OR ELSEWHERE. (CIA Cable, Dulles to Leopoldville, 9/24/60)

Dulles had expressed a similar view three days before in President Eisenhower's presence at an NSC meeting.[2]

Scheider recalled that Tweedy and his Deputy had told him that the Station Officer would receive a communication assuring him that there was support at CIA Headquarters for the assignment Scheider was to give him. (Scheider, 10/7/75, pp. 88–90)

(e) Assassination Instructions Issued to Station Officer and Lethal Substances Delivered: September 26, 1960

Station Officer Hedgman reported through the PROP channel that he had contacted Scheider on September 26. (CIA Cable, Leopoldville to Tweedy, 9/27/60)

According to Hedgman:

> HEDGMAN: It is my recollection that he advised me, or my instructions were, to eliminate Lumumba.
> Q: By eliminate, do you mean assassinate?
> HEDGMAN: Yes, I would say that was * * * my understanding of the primary means. I don't think it was probably limited to that, if there was some other way of * * * removing him from a position of political threat. (Hedgman, 8/21/75, pp. 17–18)

Hedgman said that he and Scheider also may have discussed non-lethal means of removing Lumumba as a "political threat", but he could not "recall with certainty on that." (Hedgman, 8/21/75, p. 28)

Scheider testified:

> I explained to him [Station Officer] what Tweedy and his Deputy had told me, that Headquarters wanted him to see if he could use this [biological] capability I brought against Lumumba [and] to caution him that it had to be done * * * without attribution to the USA. (Scheider, 10/9/75, p. 16)

The Station Officer testified that he received "rubber gloves, a mask, and a syringe" along with lethal biological material from Scheider, who also instructed him in their use.[3] Hedgman indicated that this

---

[1] Tweedy identified Scheider as the "colleague" referred to in this cable. (Tweedy, 10/9/75 I, p. 32) Scheider was en route to the Congo at this point.
[2] Dulles' statement at the NSC meeting of September 21, 1960 is discussed in detail at Section 7(a)(v), *infra*.
[3] Scheider testified that he sent the medical paraphernalia via diplomatic pouch. (Scheider, 10/7/75, pp. 59, 99)

paraphernalia was for administering the poison to Lumumba for the purpose of assassination. (Hedgman, 8/21/75, pp. 18–21, 24) Scheider explained that the toxic material was to be injected into some substance that Lumumba would ingest: "it had to do with anything he could get to his mouth, whether it was food or a toothbrush, * * * [so] that some of the material could get to his mouth." (Scheider, 10/7/75, p. 100)

Hedgman said that the means of assassination was not restricted to use of the toxic material provided by Scheider. (Hedgman, 8/21/75, p. 19)

He testified that he may have "suggested" shooting Lumumba to Scheider as an alternative to poisoning. (Hedgman, 8/21/75, pp. 19, 27–29) Scheider said it was his "impression" that Tweedy and his Deputy empowered him to tell the Station Officer that he could pursue other means of assassination. (Scheider, 10/7/75, pp. 100–101) Station Officer Hedgman testified that, although the selection of a mode of assassination was left to his judgment, there was a firm requirement that:

[I]f I implemented these instructions * * * it had to be a way which could not be traced back * * * either to an American or the United States government. (Hedgman, 8/21/75, p. 19)

Hedgman said Scheider assured him that the poisons were produced to: [leave] normal traces found in people that die of certain diseases." (Hedgman, 8/21/75, p. 23.)

Hedgman said that he had an "emotional reaction of great surprise" when it first became clear that Scheider had come to discuss an assassination plan. (Hedgman, 8/21/75, p. 30) He told Scheider he "would explore this." (Hedgman, 8/21/75, p. 46) and left Scheider with the impression "that I was going to look into it and try and figure if there was a way * * * I believe I stressed the difficulty of trying to carry out such an operation." (Hedgman, 8/21/75, p. 47) Scheider said that the Station Officer was "sober [and] grim" but willing to proceed with the operation. (Scheider, 10/7/75, pp. 98, 121)

The Station Officer's report of his initial contact with Scheider was clearly an affirmative response to the assignment, and said that he and Scheider were "on same wavelength." (CIA Cable, Leopoldville to Tweedy, 9/27/60) Hedgman was "afraid" that the central government was "weakening under" foreign pressure to effect a reconciliation with Lumumba, and said:

HENCE BELIEVE MOST RAPID ACTION CONSISTENT WITH SECURITY INDICATED. (CIA Cable, 9/27/60)[1]

(f) Hedgman's Impression That President Eisenhower Ordered Lumumba's Assassination

Station Officer Hedgman testified that Scheider indicated to him that President Eisenhower had authorized the assassination of Lumumba.[2]

---

[1] Scheider interpreted this cable to mean that Hedgman was informing Headquarters: "that he has talked to me and that he is going to go ahead and see if he could mount the operation * * * [H]e believes we ought to do it, if it is going to be done, as quickly as we can." (Scheider, 10/7/75, p. 121)

[2] See Section 7(d), *infra*, for a more detailed treatment of the testimony of the Station Officer and Scheider on the question of Presidential authorization for the assassination of Lumumba.

Hedgman had a "quite strong recollection" of asking about the source of authority for the assignment:

> HEDGMAN: I must have * * * pointed out that this was not a common or usual Agency tactic * * * never in my training or previous work in the Agency had I ever heard any references to such methods. And it is my recollection I asked on whose authority these instructions were issued.
> Q: And what did Mr. Scheider reply?
> HEDGMAN: It is my recollection that he identified the President * * * and I cannot recall whether he said "the President," or whether he identified him by name. (Hedgman, 8/21/75, pp. 30–31)

Hedgman explained that Scheider told him "something to the effect that the President had instructed the Director" to assassinate Lumumba. (Hedgman, 8/21/75, pp. 32, 34)

Scheider stated that he had an "independent recollection" of telling the Station Officer about his meetings with Bissell, Tweedy, and Tweedy's Deputy, including Bissell's reference to "the highest authority." (Scheider, 10/7/75, p. 102) Scheider believed that he left the Station Officer with the impression that there was presidential authorization for an assassination attempt against Lumumba. (Scheider, 10/7/75, pp. 90, 102–103)

(g) Steps in Furtherance of the Assassination Operation

(i) Hedgman's Testimony About Confirmation From Headquarters of the Assassination Plan.

Hedgman's testimony, taken fifteen years after the events in question and without the benefit of reviewing the cables discussed above, was compatible with the picture presented by the cables of a fully authorized and tightly restricted assassination operation. The only variance is that the cables portray Hedgman as taking an affirmative, aggressive attitude toward the assignment, while he testified that his pursuit of the operation was less vigorous.

The Station Officer testified that soon after cabling his request for confirmation that he was to carry out the assassination assignment, he received a reply from Headquarters, which he characterized as follows:

> I believe I received a reply which I interpreted to mean yes, that he was the messenger and his instructions were * * * duly authorized. (Hedgman, 8/21/75, pp. 37–38)

Despite the cryptic nature of the cables, Hedgman said "I was convinced that yes, it was right," but he had no "desire to carry out these instructions." (Hedgman, 8/21/75, pp. 44, 50, 106) Hedgman stated:

> "I think probably that I would have gone back and advised that I intended to carry out and sought final approval before carrying it out had I been going to do it, had there been a way to do it. I did not see it as * * * a matter which could be accomplished practically, certainly. (Hedgman, 8/21/75, pp. 51–52)

Hedgman said that his reason for seeking a final approval would have been to receive assurances about the practicality of the specific mode of assassination that he planned to use. (Hedgman, 8/21/75, p. 53)

All CIA officers involved in the plot to kill Lumumba testified that, by virtue of the standard operating procedure of the clandestine services, there was an implicit requirement that a field officer check back with Headquarters for approval of any major operational plan.[1] Moreover, Hedgman's cable communications with Headquarters indicate that he consistently informed Tweedy of each significant step in the formulation of assassination plans, thus allowing Headquarters the opportunity to amend or disapprove the plans. The personal cable from Dulles to the Station Officer on August 26, made it clear, however, that if Lumumba appeared as a "target of opportunity" in a situation where time did not permit referral to headquarters, Hedgman was authorized to proceed with the assassination.

The Station Officer testified that for several months after receiving Scheider's instructions he took "exploratory steps in furtherance of the assassination plot." He sent several cables to CIA Headquarters which "probably reflected further steps I had taken," and stated that his cables to Headquarters were essentially "progress reports" on his attempts to find access to Lumumba. (Hedgman, 8/21/75, pp. 50, 59–60)

The cable traffic conforms to the Station Officer's recollection. For two months after Scheider's arrival in the Congo, a regular stream of messages assessing prospects for the assassination operation flowed through the PROP channel between Headquarters and Leopoldville.

(ii) "Exploratory Steps"

On the basis of his talks with Scheider, Station Officer Hedgman listed a number of "possibilities" for covert action against Lumumba. At the top of the list was the suggestion that a particular agent be used in the following manner:

HAVE HIM TAKE REFUGE WITH BIG BROTHER. WOULD THUS ACT AS INSIDE MAN TO BRUSH UP DETAILS TO RAZOR EDGE. (CIA Cable, 9/27/60)

Tweedy testified that "Big Brother" referred to Lumumba. (Tweedy, 10/9/75 II, p. 13) Tweedy and Scheider both said that this cable indicated that Hedgman's top priority plan was to instruct his agent to infiltrate Lumumba's entourage to explore means of poisoning Lumumba. (Tweedy, 10/9/75 I, p. 38, II, pp. 13–14; Scheider, 10/7/75, pp. 124–125) The Station Officer reported that he would begin to follow this course by recalling the agent to Leopoldville, and informed Headquarters:

BELIEVE MOST RAPID ACTION CONSISTENT WITH SECURITY INDICATED * * * PLAN PROCEED ON BASIS PRIORITIES AS LISTED ABOVE, UNLESS INSTRUCTED TO CONTRARY. (CIA Cable, 9/27/60)

Scheider testified that at this point the Station Officer was reporting to Headquarters that he was proceeding to "go ahead" to carry out Scheider's instructions as quickly as possible. (Scheider, 10/7/75, pp. 121–123) Tweedy's Deputy stated that the form of the Station Officer's request would have satisfied the standard requirement for confirmation of an operational plan:

* * * it is my professional opinion that, under normal operational procedure at that time, the Station Officer would have been expected to advise Headquarters that he was preparing to implement the plan unless advised to the contrary. (Deputy Chief, Africa Division, affidavit, 10/17/75, p. 5)

---

[1] See Tweedy, 10/9/75, I, pp. 10, 24–27; Hedgman, 8/21/75, pp. 39, 51–53; Scheider, 10/7/75, p. 92; Deputy Chief, Africa Division, affidavit, 10/17/75, p. 5.

On September 30, the Station Officer specifically urged Headquarters to authorize "exploratory conversations" to launch his top priority plan:

> NO REALLY AIRTIGHT OP POSSIBLE WITH ASSETS NOW AVAILABLE. MUST CHOOSE BETWEEN CANCELLING OP OR ACCEPTING CALCULATED RISKS OF VARYING DEGREES.
>
> * * * [IN] VIEW NECESSITY ACT IMMEDIATELY, IF AT ALL, URGE HQS AUTHORIZE EXPLORATORY CONVERSATIONS TO DETERMINE IF [AGENT] WILLING TAKE ROLE AS ACTIVE AGENT OR CUT-OUT THIS OP. (WOULD APPROACH ON HYPOTHETICAL BASIS AND NOT REVEAL PLANS.) IF HE APPEARS WILLING ACCEPT ROLE, WE BELIEVE IT NECESSARY REVEAL OBJECTIVE OP TO HIM.
>
> * * * REQUEST HQS REPLY [IMMEDIATELY]. (CIA Cable, Leopoldville to Tweedy, 9/30/60)

Headquarters replied:

> YOU ARE AUTHORIZED HAVE EXPLORATORY TALKS WITH [AGENT] TO ASSESS HIS ATTITUDE TOWARD POSSIBLE ACTIVE AGENT OR CUTOUT ROLE * * *. IT DOES APPEAR FROM HERE THAT OF POSSIBILITIES AVAILABLE [THIS AGENT] IS BEST * * * WE WILL WEIGH VERY CAREFULLY YOUR INITIAL ASSESSMENT HIS ATTITUDE AS WELL AS ANY SPECIFIC APPROACHES THAT MAY EMERGE * * * APPRECIATE MANNER YOUR APPROACH TO PROBLEM. "HOPE * * * FOR MODERATE HASTE" (CIA Cable, Deputy Chief, Africa Division to Leopoldville, 9/30/60)

Tweedy and his Deputy made it clear that the agent was being viewed as a potential assassin. (Tweedy, 10/9/75 I, p. 41; Deputy Chief, Africa Division, affidavit, 10/17/75, p. 4) Tweedy stated that it would have been proper for his Deputy to issue this cable authorizing the Station Officer to take the assassination operation "one step further" and it was "quite possible" that Richard Bissell was informed of this directive. (Tweedy, 10/9/75 I, pp. 42–43)

On October 7, the Station Officer reported to Headquarters on his meeting with the agent who was his best candidate for gaining access to Lumumba:

> CONDUCTED EXPLORATORY CONVERSATION WITH [AGENT] * * * AFTER EXPLORING ALL POSSIBILITIES [AGENT] SUGGESTED SOLUTION RECOMMENDED BY HQS. ALTHOUGH DID NOT PICK UP BALL, BELIEVE HE PREPARED TAKE ANY ROLE NECESSARY WITHIN LIMITS SECURITY ACCOMPLISH OBJECTIVE. (CIA Cable, Station Officer to Tweedy, 10/7/60)

The Station Officer testified that the subject "explored" was the agent's ability to find a means to inject the toxic material into Lumumba's food or toothpaste:

> I believe that I queried the agent who had access to Lumumba, and his entourage, in detail about just what access he actually had, as opposed to speaking to people. In other words, did he have access to the bathroom, did he have access to the kitchen, things of that sort.
>
> I have a recollection of having queried him on that without specifying why I wanted to know this. (Hedgman, 8/21/75, pp. 48, 60)

The Station Officer said that he was left with doubts about the wisdom or practicality of the assassination plot:

> [C]ertainly I looked on it as a pretty wild scheme professionally. I did not think that it * * * was practical professionally, certainly, in a short time, if you

were going to keep the U.S. out of it * * * I explored it, but I doubt that I ever really expected to carry it out. (Hedgman, 8/21/75, p. 11)

(iii) The Assassination Operation Moves Forward After Scheider's Return to Headquarters: October 5-7, 1960

Despite the Station Officer's testimony about the dubious practicality of the assassination operation, the cables indicate that he planned to continue his efforts to implement the operation and sought the resources to do so successfully. For example, he urged Headquarters to send an alternate agent:

> IF HQS BELIEVE [AGENT'S CIRCUMSTANCES] BAR HIS PARTICIPATION, WISH STRESS NECESSITY PROVIDE STATION WITH QUALIFIED THIRD COUNTRY NATIONAL. (CIA Cable, Leopoldville to Tweedy, 10/7/60)

Tweedy cabled the Station Officer that he "had good discussion your colleague 7 Oct"—referring to a debriefing of Scheider upon his return to the United States. Tweedy indicated that he continued to support the assassination operation and advised (Tweedy, 10/9/75 II, pp. 48-49):

> BE ASSURED DID NOT EXPECT PROP OBJECTIVES BE REACHED IN SHORT PERIOD * * * CONSIDERING DISPATCHING THIRD COUNTRY NATIONAL OPERATIVE WHO, WHEN HE ARRIVES, SHOULD BE ASSESSED BY YOU OVER PERIOD TO SEE WHETHER HE MIGHT PLAY ACTIVE OR CUTOUT ROLE ON FULL TIME BASIS. IF YOU CONCLUDE HE SUITABLE AND BEARING IN MIND HEAVY EXTRA LOAD THIS PLACES ON YOU, WOULD EXPECT DISPATCH [TEMPORARY DUTY] SENIOR CASE OFFICER RUN THIS OP * * * UNDER YOUR DIRECTION. (CIA Cable, Tweedy to Station Officer, 10/7/60) [1]

According to the report of the Station Officer, Joseph Scheider left the Congo to return to Headquarters on October 5 in view of the "expiration date his material" (CIA Cable, Leopoldville to Tweedy, 10/7/60)—a reference to the date beyond which the substances would no longer have lethal strength. (Scheider, 10/7/75, pp. 132-133) The cable from the Station Officer further stated that:

> [JOE] LEFT CERTAIN ITEMS OF CONTINUING USEFULNESS. [STATION OFFICER] PLANS CONTINUE TRY IMPLEMENT OP. (CIA Cable, Leopoldville to Tweedy, 10/7/60)

Notwithstanding the influence of the Station Officer's October 7 cable that some toxic substances were left with Hedgman, Scheider specifically recalled that he had "destroyed the viability" of the biological material and disposed of it in the Congo River before he departed for the United States on October 5, 1960. (Scheider, 10/7/75, pp. 133, 117, 135-136; 10/9/75, p. 20) In the only real conflict between his testimony and Scheider's, Hedgman testified that the toxic material was

---

[1] See Sections 5(b)-5(c), *infra*, for a detailed account of the activities in the Congo of two "third country national" agents: QJ/WIN and WI/ROGUE. See Section 5(a), *infra*, for discussion of the temporary duty assignment in the Congo of senior case officer" Michael Mulroney.

not disposed of until after Lumumba was imprisoned by the Congolese in early December. (Hedgman, 8/21/75, pp. 85–86) [1]

The central point remains that the Station Officer planned to continue the assassination effort, by whatever means, even after Scheider's departure. (Scheider, 10/7/75, p. 143) Scheider was under the impression that the Station Officer was still authorized to move ahead with an assassination attempt against Lumumba at that point, although he would have continued to submit his plans to Headquarters. (Scheider, 10/7/75, p. 135; 10/9/75, pp. 20–21) [2]

(iv) Headquarters Continues to Place "Highest Priority" on the Assassination Operation

SUMMARY

The cable traffic during this period demonstrates that there was a clear intent at Headquarters to authorize and support rapid progress of the assassination operation. Even after Lumumba placed himself in the protective custody of the United Nations, CIA Headquarters continued to regard his assassination as the "highest priority" of covert action in the Congo. The cables also show an intent at Headquarters to severely restrict knowledge of the assassination operation among officers in CIA's Africa Division and among United States diplomatic personnel in the Congo, excluding even those who were aware of, and involved in, other covert activities.

The Station Officer, despite the burden of his other operational responsibilities, was actively exploring, evaluating, and reporting on the means and agents that might be used in an attempt to assassinate Lumumba. When his implementation of the assassination operation was thwarted by the failure of his prime candidate to gain access to Lumumba, Hedgman requested additional operational and supervisory personnel to help him carry out the assignment, which he apparently pursued until Lumumba was imprisoned by Congolese authorities.

---

[1] Scheider said he destroyed and disposed of the toxic materials: "for the reason that it didn't look like on this trip he could mount the operational * * * assets to do the job and * * * the material was not refrigerated and unstable." He said that he and the Station Offices "both felt that we shouldn't go ahead with this until there were no doubts." (Scheider, 10/7/75, p. 116) The Station Officer had been unable "to find a secure enough agent with the right access" to Lumumba before the potency of the biological material was "no longer reliable." (Scheider, 10/9/75, p. 28: 10/7/75, pp. 132–133) Scheider speculated that the Station Officer's reference to retaining "items of continuing usefulness" may have meant the gloves, mask, and hypodermic syringe left with Hedgman. Scheider said: "perhaps he is talking about leaving these accessory materials in case there will be a round two of this, and someone brings more material." (Scheider, 10/7/75, p. 135)

In support of his position the Station Officer speculated that it was "possible" that he had preserved the poisons in his safe until after Lumumba's death. (Hedgman, 8/21/75, p. 85) He said that after Scheider's visit, he locked the toxic material in the bottom drawer of his safe, "probably" sealed in an envelope marked "Eyes Only" with his name on it. (Hedgman, 8/21/75, pp. 48–49) He did not recall taking the materials out of his safe except when he disposed of them months later. (Hedgman, 8/21/75, p. 84)

Both Scheider and the Station Officer specifically recalled disposing of the toxic material in the Congo River and each recalled performing the act alone. (Scheider, 10/7/75, pp. 117–118; Hedgman, 8/21/75, p. 84)

The Station Officer's testimony is bolstered by Michael Malroney's account that when he arrived in the Congo nearly a month after Scheider had returned to Headquarters. Hedgman informed him that there was a lethal virus in the station safe. (See Section 5(a)(iii), *infra*.) Moreover, the Station Officer distinctly remembered disposing of the medical paraphernalia. (Hedgman, 8/21/75, p. 84) This would indicate that, at the least, the operation had not been "stood down" to the point of disposing of all traces of the plot until long after Scheider's departure from the Congo.

[2] For Tweedy's testimony about the operational authority possessed by the Station Officer on October 7, see Section 4(h), *infra*.

On October 15, 1960, shortly after Tweedy offered additional manpower for the assassination operation, a significant pair of cables were sent from CIA Headquarters to Leopoldville.

One cable was issued by a desk officer in CIA's Africa Division, released under Bronson Tweedy's signature, and transmitted through standard CIA channels, thus permitting distribution of the message to appropriate personnel in the CIA Station and the United States Embassy. (Tweedy, 10/9/75 I, pp. 60–62) The cable discussed the possibility of covertly supplying certain Congolese leaders with funds and military aid and advised:

> ONLY DIRECT ACTION WE CAN NOW STAND BEHIND IS TO SUPPORT IMMOBILIZING OR ARRESTING [LUMUMBA], DESIRABLE AS MORE DEFINITIVE ACTION MIGHT BE. ANY ACTION TAKEN WOULD HAVE TO BE ENTIRELY CONGOLESE. (CIA Cable, Director to Leopoldville, 10/15/60)

On the same day Tweedy dispatched, a second cable, via the PROP channel for Hedgman's "Eyes Only," which prevented the message from being distributed to anyone else, including the Ambassador.[1] Tweedy's Deputy stated that "the cable which carried the PROP indicator would have controlling authority as between the two cables." (Deputy Chief, Africa Division affidavit, 10/17/75, p. 4) The second cable stated:

> YOU WILL NOTE FROM CABLE THROUGH NORMAL CHANNEL CURRENTLY BEING TRANSMITTED A PARA[GRAPH] ON PROP TYPE SUGGESTIONS. YOU WILL PROBABLY RECEIVE MORE ALONG THESE LINES AS STUMBLING BLOC [LUMUMBA] REPRESENTS INCREASINGLY APPARENT ALL STUDYING CONGO SITUATION CLOSELY AND HIS DISPOSITION SPONTANEOUSLY BECOMES NUMBER ONE CONSIDERATION.
>
> RAISE ABOVE SO YOU NOT CONFUSED BY ANY APPARENT DUPLICATION. THIS CHANNEL REMAINS FOR SPECIFIC PURPOSE YOU DISCUSSED WITH COLLEAGUE AND ALSO REMAINS HIGHEST PRIORITY. (CIA Cable, Tweedy to Station Officer, 10/15/60)

Tweedy testified that the "specific purpose discussed with colleague" referred to the Station Officer's discussion of "assassination with Scheider." He stated that the premise of his message was that "there is no solution to the Congo as long as Lumumba stays in a position of power or influence there." (Tweedy, 10/9/75 I, pp. 59, 60)[2]

Tweedy went on to request the Station Officer's reaction to the prospect of sending a senior CIA case officer to the Congo on a "direct assignment * * * to concentrate entirely this aspect" (CIA Cable, Tweedy to Station Officer, 10/15/60).[3]

---

[1] Hedgman testified that he did not discuss the assassination operation with anyone at the United States embassy in Leopoldville. Moreover, he testified that he never discussed the prospect of assassinating Lumumba with Clare H. T. Timberlake, who was the Ambassador to the Congo at that time. (Hedgman, 8/21/75, p. 91)

[2] See Section 4(h), *infra*, for Tweedy's testimony on the conditions under which he believed the operation was authorized to proceed.

This referred to CIA officer Michael Mulroney (Tweedy, 10/9/75 I, p. 56), who testified that in late October he was asked by Richard Bissell to undertake the mission of assassinating Lumumba.

[3] For a full account of the meeting between Bissell and Mulroney and Mulroney's subsequent activities in the Congo, see Section 5(a), *infra*.

The cable also provided an insight into why the assassination operation had not progressed more rapidly under the Station Officer:

> SEEMS TO US YOUR OTHER COMMITMENTS TOO HEAVY GIVE NECESSARY CONCENTRATION PROP.

In contradiction of the limitations on anti-Lumumba activity outlined in the cable sent through normal channels, Tweedy's cable suggested:

> POSSIBILITY USE COMMANDO TYPE GROUP FOR ABDUCTION [LUMUMBA], EITHER VIA ASSAULT ON HOUSE UP CLIFF FROM RIVER OR, MORE PROBABLY, IF [LUMUMBA] ATTEMPTS ANOTHER BREAKOUT INTO TOWN * * * REQUEST YOUR VIEWS. (CIA Cable, Tweedy to Station Officer, 10/15/60)

Two days later the Station Officer made a number of points in a reply to Tweedy. First, the agent he had picked for the assassination operation had difficulty infiltrating Lumumba's inner circle:[1]

> HAS NOT BEEN ABLE PENETRATE ENTOURAGE. THUS HE HAS NOT BEEN ABLE PROVIDE OPS INTEL NEEDED THIS JOB. * * * ALTHOUGH MAINTAINING PRIORITY INTEREST THIS OP, ABLE DEVOTE ONLY LIMITED AMOUNT TIME, VIEW MULTIPLE OPS COMMITMENTS. * * * BELIEVE EARLY ASSIGNMENT SENIOR CASE OFFICER HANDLE PROP OPS EXCELLENT IDEA * * * IF CASE OFFICER AVAILABLE [STATION OFFICER] WOULD DEVOTE AS MUCH TIME AS POSSIBLE TO ASSISTING AND DIRECTING HIS EFFORTS, (CIA Cable, 10/17/60)

The Station Officer concluded this cable with the following cryptic recommendation, reminiscent of his testimony that he may have "suggested" shooting Lumumba to Scheider as an alternative to poisoning (Hedgman, 8/21/75, pp. 27-29):

> IF CASE OFFICER SENT, RECOMMEND HQS POUCH SOONEST HIGH POWERED FOREIGN MAKE RIFLE WITH TELESCOPIC SCOPE AND SILENCER. HUNTING GOOD HERE WHEN LIGHTS RIGHT. HOWEVER AS HUNTING RIFLES NOW FORBIDDEN, WOULD KEEP RIFLE IN OFFICE PENDING OPENING OF HUNTING SEASON. (CIA Cable, 10/17/60)

Tweedy testified that the Station Officer's recommendation clearly referred to sending to the Congo via diplomatic pouch a weapon suited for assassinating Lumumba. (Tweedy, 10/9/75 I, p. 64) Senior case officer Mulroney stated that he never heard discussion at Headquarters of sending a sniper-type weapon to the Congo, nor did he have any knowledge that such a weapon had been "pouched" to the Congo. (Mulroney affidavit, 11/7/75)

The oblique suggestion of shooting Lumumba at the "opening of hunting season" could be interpreted as a plan to assassinate Lumumba as soon as he was seen outside the residence where he remained in U.N. protective custody. Tweedy interpreted the cable to mean that "an operational plan involving a rifle" had not yet been formulated by the Station Officer and that the "opening of hunting season" would depend upon approval of such a plan by CIA headquarters. (Tweedy, 10/9/75 I, pp. 64-65)

---

[1] This agent left Leopoldville "sometime in October" and their discussions terminated. (Hedgman, 8/21/75, p. 61)

A report sent the next month by the Station Officer through the PROP channel for Tweedy's "Eyes Alone" indicated that, whatever the intention about moving forward with a plan for assassination by rifle fire, Lumumba was being viewed as a "target" and his movements were under close surveillance. Hedgman's cable described the stalemate which prevailed from mid-September until Lumumba's departure for Stanleyville on November 27; Lumumba was virtually a prisoner in U.N. custody, and inaccessible to CIA agents and the Congolese:

> TARGET HAS NOT LEFT BUILDING IN SEVERAL WEEKS. HOUSE GUARDED DAY AND NIGHT BY CONGOLESE AND UN TROOPS * * *. CONGOLESE TROOPS ARE THERE TO PREVENT TARGET'S ESCAPE AND TO ARREST HIM IF HE ATTEMPTS. UN TROOPS THERE TO PREVENT STORMING OF PALACE BY CONGOLESE. CONCENTRIC RINGS OF DEFENSE MAKE ESTABLISHMENT OF OBSERVATION POST IMPOSSIBLE. ATTEMPTING GET COVERAGE OF ANY MOVEMENT INTO OR OUT OF HOUSE BY CONGOLESE * * *. TARGET HAS DISMISSED MOST OF SERVANTS SO ENTRY THIS MEANS SEEMS REMOTE. (CIA Cable, Station Officer to Tweedy, 11/14/60)

(*h*) *Tweedy/Bissell Testimony: Extent of Implementation; Extent of Authorization*

SUMMARY

The testimony of Richard Bissell and Bronson Tweedy is at some variance from the picture of the assassination plot presented by the Station Officer and by the cable traffic from the period.

The cables demonstrate that CIA Headquarters placed the "highest priority" on the effort to assassinate Lumumba. They also show that the assassination operation involving Scheider and the Station Officer was initiated by a cable signed personally by Bissell and Tweedy and transmitted in a specially restricted cable channel established solely for communications about this operation. Bissell and Tweedy both testified to an absence of independent recollection of Scheider's assignment in the Congo and of any specific operation to poison Lumumba.

The cables appear to indicate that the Station Officer was authorized to proceed with an assassination attempt if he determined it to be a feasible, secure operation and if time did not permit referral to Headquarters for approval. Tweedy alone testified that the Station Officer was empowered only to explore and assess the means of assassinating Lumumba and not to proceed with an assassination attempt even when "time did not permit" referral to Headquarters.

(*i*) *Tweedy's Testimony About the Scope of the Assassination Operation*

As Chief of the Africa Division, Bronson Tweedy had the principal supervisory responsibility at CIA Headquarters for the operations of the Station Officer Hedgman in Leopoldville. Most of the reports and recommendations cabled by Hedgman on the assassination operation were marked for Tweedy's "Eyes Only." Through Tweedy, instructions were issued, plans were approved, and progress reports were assessed concerning the effort to assassinate Lumumba.[1]

Before reviewing all of the cables, Tweedy testified that he had no knowledge of the plot to poison Lumumba. (Tweedy, 9/9/75, pp. 30–31) He stated that if Scheider went to the Congo as a courier carrying lethal biological material, "I will bet I knew it, but I don't recall it." (Tweedy, 9/9/75, p. 35)

Tweedy commented that rather than questioning the truth of the Station Officer's testimony,[2] the discrepancies between their testimony could be attributed to his own lack of recall.[3]

Even after he reviewed the cables on the PROP operation, Tweedy said that he did not recall talking to Scheider about an assignment to the Congo, although he assumed he had done so. Tweedy's review enabled him to "recall the circumstances in which these things occurred; and there's no question that Mr. Scheider went to the Congo." (Tweedy, 10/9/75 I, p. 13; II, pp. 5–6)[4]

Despite Tweedy's lack of recollection about the actual plot to poison Lumumba, he recalled discussing the feasibility of an assassination attempt against Lumumba with Bissell and communicating with the Station Officer about gaining access to Lumumba for this purpose. (Tweedy, 9/9/75, pp. 14–15, 19–21)

Tweedy characterized his discussions with Bissell about assassinating Lumumba as "contingency planning" (Tweedy, 9/9/75, p. 28):

TWEEDY. * * * I think it came up in the sense that Dick would have said we probably better be thinking about whether it might ever be necessary or desirable to get rid of Lumumba, in which case we presumably should be in position to assess whether we could do it or not successfully.
Q. Do it, meaning carry off an assassination?
TWEEDY. Yes, but it was never discussed with him in any other sense but a planning exercise. * * * never were we instructed to do anything of this kind. We were instructed to ask whether such a thing would be feasible and to have the Station Officer thinking along those lines as well. (Tweedy, 9/9/75, pp. 15, 28)

Tweedy testified that Bissell never authorized him to proceed beyond the planning stage to move forward with an assassination attempt. (Tweedy, 10/9/75 I, p. 17)

---

[1] Tweedy personally signed both the cable which initially informed the Station Officer that "JOE" would arrive in Leopoldville with an assignment (CIA Cable, Bissell, Tweedy to Station Officer, 9/19/60) and the cable of October 7 indicating that he had debriefed Scheider upon his return from the Congo. (CIA Cable, Tweedy to Station Officer, 10/7/60) Tweedy was also the "Eyes Only" recipient of Hedgman's reports on Scheider's arrival in the Congo (CIA Cable, Station Officer to Tweedy, 9/27/60) and of subsequent communications about the top priority plan that emerged from the discussions between Scheider and Hedgman: i.e., infiltrating an agent into Lumumba's entourage to administer a lethal poison to the Congolese leader. (CIA Cable, Station Officer to Tweedy, 9/30/60; CIA Cable, Station Officer to Tweedy, 10/7/60; CIA Cable, Station Officer to Tweedy, 10/17/60) See Sections 4(a)–4(e) *supra* for a full treatment of the cables sent in the PROP channel between Tweedy and the Station Officer in Leopoldville.
[2] Tweedy expressed a high regard for the credibility of the Station Officer. Tweedy said that he never had occasion to doubt Hedgman's veracity or integrity, adding, "I would trust his memory and I certainly trust his integrity." (Tweedy, 9/9/75, p. 36)
[3] Tweedy explained his difficulty in recalling the assassination operation:
"[T]he things that I recall the most vividly about all my African experiences were * * * the things I was basically concerned with all the time, which was putting this Division together and the rest of it. When it comes to operational detail I start getting fuzzy and you would have thought with something like thinking about Mr. Lumumba in these terms that I would have gone to bed and got up thinking about Lumumba, I can assure you this wasn't the case." (Tweedy, 9/9/75, p. 34)
[4] For a detailed treatment of Tweedy's testimony on Scheider's assignment to the Congo and the assassination operation against Lumumba, see Sections 4(a)–(g), *supra*.

Tweedy characterized the entire assassination operation as "exploratory":

> This involved the launching of the idea with the field so they could make the proper operational explorations into the feasibility of this, reporting back to Headquarters for guidance. At no point was the field given carte blanche if they thought they had found a way to do the job, just to carry it out with no further reference. (Tweedy, 10/9/75 II, p. 22)

He testified that the period of exploration of access to Lumumba remained "a planning interval and at no point can I recall that I ever felt it was imminent that somebody would say 'go'." (Tweedy, 9/9/75, pp. 18–19)

Tweedy stated that, despite his inability to specifically recall his directive to Scheider, he would not have given the Station Officer an instruction "to use this [toxic] material and go ahead and assassinate Lumumba, as if * * * that is all the authority that was necessary." He said that:

> Under no circumstances would that instruction have been given by me without reference to higher authority up through the chain of command * * * my higher authority, in the first instance, would be Mr. Bissell * * * and I know Mr. Bissell would have talked to Mr Dulles. (Tweedy, 10/9/75 I, pp. 17–18; 10/9/75 II, pp. 25, 33)

It is difficult to reconcile some of the cables and the testimony of Scheider and Hedgman with Tweedy's testimony that there was "no misunderstanding" that the PROP operation was purely exploratory "contingency planning" and that no authorization was granted for attempting an assassination without checking back with headquarters.

For example, Dulles' August 26 directive appeared to indicate wide latitude for making operational decisions in the field "where time does not permit referral" to Headquarters.

Tweedy testified that sending a potentially lethal biological material with a short period of toxicity to the Congo did not mean that the Station Officer was empowered to take action without seeking final approval from Headquarters.

> TWEEDY: If, as a result of the Station focusing on the problem for the first time, as a result of Headquarters' request, they had come up with a plan that they thought was exceedingly solid and which Headquarters approved, it is not surprising, perhaps, that we wanted the materials there to take advantage of such * * * an unlikely event.
>
> Q: Because Scheider took lethal materials to the Congo with him that had such a short period of lethality, were you not contemplating at that time that the operation might well move from the exploration phase to the implementation phase just as soon as Scheider and Hedgman determined that it was feasible?
>
> TWEEDY: I think I would put it quite differently. I think that I would say that we would have been remiss in not being in a position to exploit, if we reached the point where we all agreed that the thing was possible. (Tweedy, 10/9/75 I, pp. 49–50)

The dispatch of toxic material and medical paraphernalia to the Congo certainly demonstrates that the "exploration" of the feasibility of assassinating Lumumba had progressed beyond mere "assessment" and "contingency planning."

Tweedy further disagreed that the Station Officer's October 7 message that he would "continue try implement op[eration]" signified that the Officer was prepared to proceed to "implement" an assassination attempt:

> He would continue to explore the possibilities of this operation and continue to report to Headquarters. That is all this means. It does not mean that * * * he would try to pull off the operation without further reference to Headquarters * * * [H]e was to continue to explore it to determine whether or not there was a feasible means. (Tweedy, 10/9/75 II, pp. 14–15)

Finally, Tweedy's recollection that a "go ahead" on the assassination operation was never imminent is brought into question by the cable he sent for Hedgman's "Eyes Only" on October 15 to assure him that there was a policy-level consensus that Lumumba's "disposition spontaneously becomes number one consideration" and that the PROP operation "remains highest priority." (CIA Cable, Tweedy to Station, 10/15/60)

(ii) *Bissell's Testimony About Moving the Assassination Operation From Planning to Implementation*

Richard Bissell testified that he did not remember discussing the feasibility of assassinating Lumumba with Bronson Tweedy, but it seemed "entirely probable" to him that such discussions took place. Bissell, who did not review the cable traffic, said he "may have" given Tweedy specific instructions about steps to further an assassination plan, but he did not remember doing so. He said that seeking information from the Station Officer about access for poisoning or assassinating Lumumba by other means would "almost certainly" have been a "major part" of his "planning and preparatory activity" but he had no specific recollection of cable communications on this subject. He did recall that the Station Officer had an agent who supposedly had direct access to Lumumba. (Bissell, 9/10/75, pp. 3, 4, 6–8, 80)

Bissell testified that he "most certainly" approved any cables that Tweedy sent to the Station Officer seeking information about gaining access to Lumumba because in "a matter of this sensitivity," Tweedy probably would have referred cables to him for final dispatch. But Bissell added:

> I think Mr. Tweedy, on the basis of an oral authorization from me, would have had the authority to send such a cable without my signing off on it. (Bissell, 9/10/75, p. 8)

Bissell's failure to recall discussing his assignment to Michael Mulroney [1] with Tweedy provided a basis for his speculation that Tweedy might also have been unaware of the true purpose of Scheider's visit. (Bissell, 9/10/75, pp. 20–22)

Bissell did not recall cables concerning Scheider's mission, and confirming that Scheider's instructions were to be followed; but he said "this sounds highly likely * * * I would expect, given the background, that the confirmation would have been forthcoming." (Bissell, 9/10/75, p. 43)

Bissell said that it was "very probable" that he discussed the assassination of Lumumba with Scheider, who was then his science advisor. On a number of occasions he and Scheider had discussed "the availability of means of incapacitation, including assassination." Although he had no "specific recollection," Bissell assumed that, if

---

[1] Bissell's assignment to Mulroney is discussed in Sections 5(a)(i) and 5(a)(ii), *infra*.

Scheider went to the Congo, Bissell would have approved the mission, which "might very well" have dealt with the assassination of Lumumba. (Bissell, 9/10/75, pp. 14, 60, 18, 20, 44)

Bissell testified that it would not have been against CIA policy in the fall of 1960 to send poisons to the Congo. He characterized "the act of taking the kit to the Congo * * * as still in the planning stage." (Bissell, 9/10/75, pp. 35, 49). He acknowledged, however, that:

> It would indeed have been rather unusual to send such materials—a specific kit * * * of this sort—out to a relatively small Station, unless planning for their use was quite far along. (Bissell, 9/10/7, p. 37)

Nonetheless, Bissell said that he "probably believed" that he had sufficient authority at that point to direct CIA officers to move from the stage of planning to implementation. (Bissell, 9/10/75, pp. 60–61) Although he did not have a specific recollection, Bissell assumed that if Scheider had instructed Hedgman to assassinate Lumumba, Scheider would not have been acting beyond the mandate given to him by Bissell and the assassination plot would then have "passed into an implementation phase." (Bissell, 9/10/75, pp. 39, 41, 49)

5. THE QUESTION OF A CONNECTION BETWEEN THE ASSASSINATION PLOT AND OTHER ACTIONS OF CIA OFFICERS AND THEIR AGENTS IN THE CONGO

SUMMARY

Michael Mulroney, a senior CIA officer in the Directorate for Plans, testified that in October 1960 he had been asked by Richard Bissell to go to the Congo to carry out the assassination of Lumumba. Mulroney said that he refused to participate in an assassination operation, but proceeded to the Congo to attempt to draw Lumumba away from the protective custody of the U.N. guard and place him in the hands of Congolese authorities. (Mulroney, 6/9/75, pp. 11–14)

Shortly after Mulroney's arrival in the Congo, he was joined by QJ/WIN, a CIA agent with a criminal background.[1] Late in 1960, WI/ROGUE, one of Hedgman's operatives approached QJ/WIN with a proposition to join an "execution squad." (CIA Cable, Leopoldville to Director, 12/7/60)

It is unlikely that Mulroney was actually involved in implementing the assassination assignment. Whether there was any connection between the assassination plot and either of the two operatives—QJ/WIN and WI/ROGUE—is less clear.

(a) Mulroney's Assignment in the Congo

(i) Mulroney's Testimony That He Went to the Congo After Refusing an Assassination Assignment From Bissell

In early October, 1960, several PROP cables discussed a plan to send a "senior case officer" to the Congo to aid the overburdened Station Officer with the assassination operation.[2] Shortly after the Sta-

---
[1] See Part III, Section c, of this Report for a discussion of the CIA's use of QJ/WIN in developing a stand-by assassination capability in the Executive Action project.
[2] See Section 4(g), *supra*, for full treatment of these cables.

tion Officer's request on October 17, for a senior case officer to concentrate on the assassination operation. Bissell broached the subject with Mulroney. At the time, Mulroney was the Deputy Chief of an extraordinarily secret unit within the Directorate of Plans. (Mulroney, 6/9/75, p. 8)

Mulroney testified that in October of 1960, Bissell asked him to undertake the mission of assassinating Patrice Lumumba:

MULRONEY: He called me in and told me he wanted to go down to the Belgian Congo, the former Belgian Congo, and to eliminate Lumumba * * *.
Q: What did you understand him to mean by eliminate?
MULRONEY: To kill him and thereby eliminate his influence.
Q: What was the basis for your interpreting his remarks, whatever his precise language, as meaning that he was talking about assassination rather than merely neutralizing him through some other means?
MULRONEY: It was not neutralization * * * clearly the context of our talk was to kill him. (Mulroney, 6/9/75, pp. 11–12, 19, 43)

Mulroney testified:

I told him that I would absolutely not have any part of killing Lumumba. He said, I want you to go over and talk to Joseph Scheider. (Mulroney, 6/9/75, p. 12)

Mulroney said that it was "inconceivable that Bissell would direct such a mission without the personal permission of Allen Dulles":

I assumed that he had authority from Mr. Dulles in such an important issue, but it was not discussed [with me], nor did he purport to have higher authority to do it. (Mulroney, 9/9/75, pp. 15, 44)

Mulroney then met promptly with Scheider and testified that he was "sure that Mr. Bissell had called Scheider and told him I was coming over" to his office. Scheider told Mulroney "that there were four or five * * * lethal means of disposing of Lumumba * * *. One of the methods was a virus and the others included poison." Mulroney said that Scheider "didn't even hint * * * that he had been in the Congo and that he had transported any lethal agent to the Congo." (Mulroney, 6/9/75, pp. 12–13; 9/11/75, pp. 7–7A)

Mulroney testified that after speaking with Scheider:

I then left his office, and I went back to Mr. Bissell's office, and I told him in no way would I have any part in the assassination of Lumumba * * * and reasserted in absolute terms that I would not be involved in a murder attempt. (Mulroney, 9/11/75, p. 43) [1]

Mulroney said that in one of his two conversations with Bissell about Lumumba, he raised the prospect "that conspiracy to commit murder being done in the District of Columbia might be in violation

---

[1] When asked at the conclusion of his testimony to add anything to the record that he felt was necessary to present a full picture of the operation against Lumumba, Mulroney volunteered a statement about the moral climate in which it took place:
"All the people that I knew acted in good faith. I think they acted in the light of * * * maybe not their consciences, but in the light of their concept of patriotism. [T]hey felt that this was in the best interests of the U.S. I think that we have to much of the 'good German' in us, in that we do something because the boss says it is okay. And they are not essentially evil people. But you can do an awful lot of wrong in this.
"* * * This is such a dishonest business that only honest people can be in it. That is the only thing that will save the Agency and make you trust the integrity of what they report * * *. An intelligence officer * * * must be scrupulous and he must be moral * * * he must have personal integrity * * *. They must be particularly conscious of the moral element in intelligence operations." (Mulroney, 9/11/75, pp. 57, 61)
Earlier in his testimony, Mulroney succinctly summarized his philosophical opposition to assassinating Lumumba: "murder corrupts." (Mulroney, 9/11/75, p. 9)

of federal law." He said that Bissell "airily dismissed" this prospect. (Mulroney, 6/9/75, p. 14)

Although he refused to participate in assassination, Mulroney agreed to go to the Congo on a general mission to "neutralize" Lumumba "as a political factor" (Mulroney, 9/11/75, pp. 43–44):

> I said I would go down and I would have no compunction about operating to draw Lumumba out [of UN custody], to run an operation to neutralize his operations which were against Western interests, against, I thought, American interests. (Mulroney, 6/9/75, p. 13)[1]

Although Mulroney did not formulate a precise plan until he reached the Congo, he discussed a general strategy with Bissell:

> MULRONEY: I told Mr. Bissell that I would be willing to go down to neutralize his activities and operations and try to bring him out [of UN custody] and turn him over to the Congolese authorities.
> Senator MONDALE: Was it discussed then that his life might be taken by the Congolese authorities?
> MULRONEY: It was, I think, considered * * * not to have him killed, but then it would have been a Congolese being judged by Congolese for Congolese crimes. Yes, I think it was discussed. (Mulroney, 6/9/75, p. 38)

According to Mulroney there was a "very, very high probability" that Lumumba would receive capital punishment at the hands of the Congolese authorities. But he "had no compunction about bringing him out and then having him tried by a jury of his peers." (Mulroney, 6/9/75, pp. 24, 14)

Despite Mulroney's expressed aversion to assassination and his agreement to undertake a more general mission to "neutralize" Lumumba's influence, Bissell continued pressing him to consider an assassination operation:

> In leaving at the conclusion of our second discussion * * * he said, well, I wouldn't rule out that possibility—meaning the possibility of the elimination or the killing of Lumumba * * *. In other words, even though you have said this, don't rule it out * * *. There is no question about it, he said, I wouldn't rule this other out, meaning the elimination or the assassination. (Mulroney, 9/11/75, p. 45)

Mulroney distinctly recalled that after his second discussion with Bissell, he met with Richard Helms, who was then Deputy to the DDP and Chief of Operations in the clandestine services division, in order to make his opposition to assassinating Lumumba a matter of record (Mulroney, 9/11/75, pp. 44–45):

> [I]n the Agency, since you don't have documents, you have to be awfully canny and you have to get things on record, and I went into Mr. Helms' office, and I said, Dick, here is what Mr. Bissell proposed to me, and I told him that I would under no conditions do it, and Helms said, 'you're absolutely right.' (Mulroney 6/9/75, pp. 15–16)

Helms testified that it was "likely" that he had such a conversation with Mulroney and he assumed that Mulroney's version of their conversation was correct. (Helms, 9/16/75, pp. 22–23)[2]

---

[1] Bissell also recalled that, after discussing assassination with Mulroney, Mulroney went to the Congo "with the assignment * * * of looking at other ways of neutralizing Lumumba." (Bissell, 9/10/75, p. 53)
[2] Helms testified that he did not inquire further into the subject of this conversation in any way. He did not recall why Mulroney had gone to the Congo or what his mission was. (Helms, 9/16/75, pp. 32–33)

William Harvey was Mulroney's immediate superior at that time [1] He testified:

> Mr. Mulroney came to me and said that he had been approached by Richard Bissell * * * to undertake an operation in the Congo, one of the objectives of which was the elimination of Patrice Lumumba. He also told me that he had declined to undertake this assignment. (Harvey, 6/25/75, p. 9)

Harvey said that in a later conversation with Bissell, Bissell told him that he had asked Mulroney to undertake such an operation. (Harvey, 6/25/75, p. 9)

Tweedy's Deputy, who aided in making preparations for Mulroney's trip to the Congo, recalled that Mulroney had "reacted negatively" to Bissell's request to undertake an assassination operation. (Deputy Chief, Africa Division affidavit, 10/17/75, p. 2) He stated:

> Despite the fact that Mulroney had expressed a negative reaction to this assignment, it was clear to me that when Mulroney went to the Congo, exploration of the feasibility of assassinating Lumumba was part of his assignment from Bissell. As far as I know, Mulroney was not under assignment to attempt to assassinate Lumumba, but rather merely to make plans for such an operation. (Deputy Chief, Africa Division affidavit, 10/17/75, p. 2)

In Tweedy's mind, Mulroney's eventual mission to the Congo was also linked to assessing the possibility for assassinating Lumumba rather than to a general plan to draw Lumumba out of U.N. custody. (Tweedy, 9/9/75, pp. 24, 26)

Mulroney testified, however, that because he was "morally opposed to assassination" he would "absolutely not" have explored the means by which such access could be gained, nor would he have undertaken a mission to the Congo to assess an assassination operation even if it were directed by someone else. (Mulroney, 9/11/75, p. 26)

Mulroney said that he departed for the Congo within forty-eight hours of his second discussion with Bissell. (Mulroney, 9/11/75, pp. 45–46)

(ii) Bissell's Testimony About the Assignment to Mulroney

Bissell remembered "very clearly" that he and Mulroney discussed the assassination of Lumumba in the fall of 1960 (Bissell, 6/9/75, pp. 74–75) and that Mulroney reacted negatively. (Bissell, 9/11/75, p. 18) Accordingly to Bissell, Mulroney said that assassination "was an inappropriate action and that the desired object could be accomplished better in other ways." (Bissell, 6/11/75, p. 54)

Bissell's testimony differs from Mulroney's account on only one important point—the degree to which Bissell's initial assignment to Mulroney contemplated the mounting of an operation as opposed to contingency planning. Mulroney flatly testified that Bissell requested him to attempt to kill Lumumba. In his first testimony on the subject, Bissell said that he asked Mulroney "to investigate the possibility of killing Lumumba." (Bissell, 6/11/75, p. 54; *see also* pp. 55, 75) In a later appearance, however, Bissell stated that Mulroney "had been asked to plan and prepare for" the assassination of Lumumba. (Bissell, 9/10/75, p. 24)

---

[1] Harvey was later centrally involved in the Castro case and the Executive Action project. See Parts III(B) and Part III(C), *infra*.

Bissell said that after his conversations with Mulroney, he considered "postponing" the assassination operation:

> I seem to recollect that after this conversation with him, I wanted this put very much on the back burner and inactivated for quite some time. Now that doesn't rule out the possibility that some action through completely different channels might have gone forward. But the best of my recollection is, I viewed this not only as terminating the assignment for him, but also as reason for at least postponing anything further along that line. (Bissell, 9/10/75, pp. 25–26)

(iii) Mulroney Informed of Virus in Station Safe Upon Arriving in Congo: November 3, 1960

On October 29, the Station Officer was informed that Michael Mulroney would soon arrive in Leopoldville "in furtherance this project." (CIA Cable, Deputy Chief, Africa Division, to Station Officer 10/29/60) On November 3, Mulroney arrived in Leopoldville. (CIA Cable, Leopoldville to Director, 11/4/60) Hedgman said it was "very possible" that he regarded the dispatch to the Congo of a senior officer as a signal that CIA Headquarters was "dissatisfied with my handling" of Scheider's instructions. (Hedgman, 8/21/75, p. 42)

Hedgman had only a general picture of Mulroney's assignment:

> I understood it to be that—similar to mine, that is, the removal or neutralization of Lumumba * * * I have no clear recollection of his discussing the assassination. (Hedgman, 8/21/75, p. 54)

Station Officer Hedgman said that he did not recall if Mulroney indicated whether he was considering assassination as a means of "neutralizing" Lumumba. Hedgman said, "in view of my instructions, I may have assumed that he was" considering assassination. Generally, however, the Station Officer perceived Mulroney as unenthusiastic about his assignment. (Hedgman, 8/21/75, pp. 55, 56, 88–89)

When Mulroney arrived in the Congo, he met with the Station Officer, who informed him that there was "a virus in the safe." (Mulroney, 9/11/75, p. 7–A; 6/9/75, p. 16) Mulroney said he assumed it was a "lethal agent," although the Station Officer was not explicit:

> I knew it wasn't for somebody to get his polio shot up to date. (Mulroney, 6/9/75, pp. 16, 37)[1]

Mulroney said that he did not recall the Station Officer's mentioning the source of the virus, but:

> It would have had to have come from Washington, in my estimation, and I would think, since it had been discussed with Scheider that it probably would have emanated from his office. (Mulroney, 6/9/75, p. 28)[2]

Hedgman did not recall discussing Scheider's trip to the Congo with Mulroney, but "assumed" that he did so. (Hedgman, 8/21/75, pp. 60–61)

---

[1] Mulroney added that if the virus was to be used for medical purposes, "It would have been in the custody of the State Department" personnel, not the CIA Station. (Mulroney, 6/9/75, p. 36)

[2] When Mulroney was informed about Hedgman's testimony concerning Scheider's trip to the Congo and the plot to poison Lumumba, he said, "I believe absolutely in its credibility. Mulroney found nothing in the facts as he knew them, nor in Hedgman's character, to raise a question about that testimony. He regarded Hedgman as "an honest and a decent man—a totally truthful man." (Mulroney, 9/11/75, pp. 19, 53, 56)

Mulroney was "certain" that the virus had arrived before he did. (Mulroney, 6/9/75, p. 24) He was surprised to learn that such a virus was at the Leopoldville Station because he had refused an assassination mission before departing for the Congo. (Mulroney, 6/9/75, p. 17)

Mulroney stated that he knew of no other instance where a CIA Station had possessed lethal biological substances. He assumed that its purpose was assassination, probably targeted against Lumumba (Mulroney, 9/11/75, p. 50):

> My feeling definitely is that it was for a specific purpose, and was just not an all-purpose capability there, being held for targets of opportunity, unspecified targets. (Mulroney. 9/11/75. p. 49)

Mulroney said that the Station Officer never indicated that Mulroney was to employ the virus, that he "never discussed his assassination effort, he never even indicated that this was one." (Mulroney, 9/11/75, pp. 52, 54)

While Station Officer Hedgman had no direct recollection of discussing the assassination operation with Mulroney, he "assumed" that he had at least mentioned the problem of gaining access to Lumumba for the purpose of assassinating him. (Hedgman, 8/21/75, pp. 55, 60)

Mulroney was "sure" that he "related everything" to Hedgman about his conversations with Bissell concerning the assassination of Lumumba. (Mulroney, 9/11/75, p. 46) Hedgman, however, did not recall learning this from Mulroney. (Hedgman, 8/21/75, p. 56)

Mulroney said that his discussions of assassination with Hedgman were general and philosophical, dealing with "the morality of assassinations." (Mulroney, 9/11/75, pp. 46, 54):

> From my point of view I told him I had moral objections to it, not just qualms, but objections. I didn't think it was the right thing to do. (Mulroney, 9/11/75, p. 9)

When asked to characterize Hedgman's attitude toward assassination based on those discussions, Mulroney said:

> He would not have been opposed in principle to assassination in the interests of national security * * *. I know that he is a man of great moral perception and decency and honor * * *. And that it would disturb him to be engaged in something like that. But I think I would have to say that in our conversations, my memory of those, at no time would he rule it out as being a possibility. (Mulroney, 9/11/75, p. 18)

(iv) Mulroney's Plan to "Neutralize" Lumumba

After Mulroney arrived in the Congo, he formulated a plan for "neutralizing" Lumumba by drawing him away from the custody of the U.N. force which was guarding his residence:

> Mulroney: [W]hat I wanted to do was to get him out, to trick him out, if I could, and then turn him over * * * to the legal authorities and let him stand trial. Because he had atrocity attributed to him for which he could very well stand trial.
> Q: And for which he could very well have received capital punishment?
> Mulroney: Yes. And I am not opposed to capital punishment. (Mulroney, 9/11/75, pp. 20–21)[1]

---

[1] When Mulroney's mission to draw Lumumba out of the hands of the U.N. was described to C. Douglas Dillon, who was Undersecretary of State at that time, Dillon testified that it conformed to United States policy toward Lumumba. (Dillon, 9/21/75, p. 50)

According to an earlier report from the Station Officer, it was the view of the Special Representative of the Secretary General of the United Nations that arrest by Congolese authorities was "JUST A TRICK TO ASSASSINATE LUMUMBA." (CIA Cable, Station Officer to Director, 10/11/60) The Station Officer proceeded to recommend Lumumba's arrest in the same cable:

> STATION HAS CONSISTENTLY URGED [CONGOLESE] LEADERS ARREST LUMUMBA IN BELIEF LUMUMBA WILL CONTINUE BE THREAT TO STABILITY CONGO UNTIL REMOVED FROM SCENE.

To implement his plan, Mulroney made arrangements to rent "an observation post over the palace in which Lumumba was safely ensconced." He also made the acquaintance of a U.N. guard to recruit him for an attempt to lure Lumumba outside U.N. protective custody. (Mulroney, 6/9/75, p. 20; 9/11/75, p. 21) Mulroney said that he cabled progress reports to CIA Headquarters, and kept the Station Officer informed about his activities. (Mulroney, 9/11/75, pp. 26–27, 56)

Mulroney arranged for CIA agent QJ/WIN, to come to the Congo to work with him:

> What I wanted to use him for was * * * counter-espionage. * * * I had to screen the U.S. participation in this * * * by using a foreign national whom we knew, trusted, and had worked with * * * the idea was for me to use him as an alter ego. (Mulroney, 6/9/75, pp. 19–20)

In mid-November, two cables from Leopoldville urged CIA Headquarters to send QJ/WIN:

> LOCAL OPERATIONAL CIRCUMSTANCES REQUIRE IMMEDIATE EXPEDITION OF QJ/WIN TRAVEL TO LEOPOLDVILLE. (CIA Cable, Leopoldville to Director, 11/13/60; see also 11/11/60)

The cables did not explain the "operational circumstances."

(b) *QJ/WIN's Mission in the Congo: November–December 1960*

QJ/WIN was a foreign citizen with a criminal background, recruited in Europe. (Memo to CIA Finance Division, Re: Payments to QJ/WIN, 1/31/61) In November 1960, agent QJ/WIN was dispatched to the Congo to undertake a mission that "might involve a large element of personal risk." (CIA Cable, 11/2/60)[1]

A cable from Headquarters to Leopoldville stated:

> In view of the extreme sensitivity of the objective for which we want [QJ/WIN] to perform his task, he was not told precisely what we want him to do * * *. Instead, he was told * * * that we would like to have him spot, assess, and recommend some dependable, quick-witted persons for our use * * *. It was thought best to withhold our true, specific requirements pending the final decision to use [him]. (CIA Cable, 11/2/60)

This message itself was deemed too sensitive to be retained at the station: "this dispatch should be reduced to cryptic necessary notes and destroyed after the first reading." (CIA Cable, 11/2/60)

QJ/WIN arrived in Leopoldville on November 21, 1960, and returned to Europe in late December 1960. (CIA Cable, 11/29/60; CIA Cable, Director to Leopoldville, 12/9/60)

Mulroney described QJ/WIN as follows:

> MULRONEY: * * * I would say that he would not be a man of many scruples.
> Q: So he was a man capable of doing anything?
> MULRONEY: I would think so, yes.
> Q: And that would include assassination?
> MULRONEY: I would think so. (Mulroney, 9/11/75, pp. 35–36)

But Mulroney had no knowledge that QJ/WIN was ever used for an assassination operation. (Mulroney, 9/11/75, pp. 36, 42)

---

[1] An additional purpose in dispatching QJ/WIN was to send him from the Congo to another African country for an unspecified mission. QJ/WIN's mission to this country is not explained in the cable traffic between CIA Headquarters and the various stations that dealt with him.
There is no indication in CIA files as to whether QJ/WIN completed this operation. Mulroney said he had no knowledge of any assignment that would have taken QJ/WIN to this other country. (Mulroney, 9/11/75, pp. 32–33) William Harvey stated that he recalled that QJ/WIN might have been sent to an African country other than the Congo, but Harvey was "almost certain that this was not connected in any way to an assassination mission." (Harvey affidavit, 9/14/75, p. 5)

Mulroney said that, as far as he knew, he was the only CIA officer with supervisory responsibility for QJ/WIN, and QJ/WIN did not report independently to anyone else. When asked if it was possible that QJ/WIN had an assignment independent of his operations for Mulroney, he said:

> Yes, that is possible—or it could have been that somebody contacted him after he got down there, that they wanted him to do something along the lines of assassination. I don't know. (Mulroney, 9/11/75, pp. 28, 29)

Mulroney discounted this possibility as "highly unlikely" because it would be a departure from standard CIA practice by placing an agent in a position of knowledge superior to that of his supervising officer. (Mulroney, 9/11/75, p. 29)

Despite Mulroney's doubt that QJ/WIN had an independent line of responsibility to Station Officer Hedgman, Hedgman's November 29 cable to Tweedy reported that QJ/WIN had begun implementing a plan to "pierce both Congolese and U.N. guards" to enter Lumumba's residence and "provide escort out of residence." (CIA Cable, Station Officer to Tweedy, 11/29/60) Mulroney said that he had directed QJ/WIN to make the acquaintance of the member of U.N. force. (Mulroney, 9/11/75, p. 21) By this point, Lumumba had already left U.N. custody to travel toward his stronghold at Stanleyville. This did not deter QJ/WIN:

> VIEW CHANGE IN LOCATION TARGET, QJ/WIN ANXIOUS GO STANLEYVILLE AND EXPRESSED DESIRE EXECUTE PLAN BY HIMSELF WITHOUT USING ANY APPARAT. (CIA Cable, 11/29/60)

It is unclear whether this latter "plan" contemplated assassination as well as abduction. Headquarters replied affirmatively the next day in language which could have been interpreted as an assassination order:

> CONCUR QJ/WIN GO STANLEYVILLE * * *. WE ARE PREPARED CONSIDER DIRECT ACTION BY QJ/WIN BUT WOULD LIKE YOUR READING ON SECURITY FACTORS. HOW CLOSE WOULD THIS PLACE [UNITED STATES] TO THE ACTION? (CIA Cable, Chief of Africa Division to Station Officer, 11/30/60)

Mulroney said that QJ/WIN's stay in the Congo was "coextensive with my own, allowing for the fact that he came after I did." (Mulroney, 6/9/75, p. 19)

In a memorandum to arrange the accounting for QJ/WIN's activities in the Congo, William Harvey, Mulroney's immediate superior in the Directorate of Plans, noted: "QJ/WIN was sent on this trip for a specific, highly sensitive operational purpose which has been completed." (Memo for Finance Division from Harvey, 1/11/61) Mulroney explained Harvey's reference by saying that once Lumumba was in the hands of the Congolese authorities "the reason for the mounting of the project * * * had become moot." When asked if he and QJ/WIN were responsible for Lumumba's departure from U.N. custody and subsequent capture, Mulroney replied: "Absolutely not." (Mulroney, 9/11/75, p. 35)[1]

---

[1] Harvey did not recall the meaning of the memorandum, but he assumed that the mere fact that Mulroney had returned from the Congo would have constituted the "completion" of QJ/WIN's mission. (Harvey affidavit, 9/14/75, p. 2)

Despite the suggestive language of the cables at the end of November about the prospect of "direct action" by QJ/WIN and an indication in the Inspector General's Report that QJ/WIN may have been recruited initially for an assassination mission [1] there is no clear evidence that QJ/WIN was actually involved in any assassination plan or attempt. The Inspector General's Report may have accurately reported a plan for the use of QJ/WIN which predated Mulroney's refusal to accept the assassination assignment from Bissell. But there is no evidence from which to conclude that QJ/WIN was actually used for such an operation.

Station Officer Hedgman had a "vague recollection" that QJ/WIN was in the Congo working for Mulroney. But Hedgman did not recall why QJ/WIN was in the Congo and said that QJ/WIN was not one of his major operatives. (Hedgman, 8/21/75, p. 95) Bissell and Tweedy did not recall anything about QJ/WIN's activities in the Congo. (Bissell, 9/10/75, pp. 54–57; Tweedy, 9/9/75, pp. 54, 61)

Harvey, whose division "loaned" QJ/WIN to the Congo Station, testified:

I was kept informed of the arrangements for QJ/WIN's trip to the Congo and, subsequently, of his presence in the Congo. I do not know specifically what QJ/WIN did in the Congo. I do not think that I ever had such knowledge * * *. If QJ/WIN were to be used on an assassination mission, it would have been cleared with me. I was never informed that he was to be used for such a mission. (Harvey affidavit, 9/14/75, pp. 3–4) [2]

A 1962 CIA cable indicates the value the CIA accorded QJ/WIN and the inherent difficulty for an intelligence agency in employing criminals. The CIA had learned that QJ/WIN was about to go on trial in Europe on smuggling charges and Headquarters suggested:

IF * * * INFOR[MATION] TRUE WE MAY WISH ATTEMPT QUASH CHARGES OR ARRANGE SOMEHOW SALVAGE QJ/WIN FOR OUR PURPOSES. (CIA Cable, 1962)

(c) *WI/ROGUE Asks QJ/WIN to Join "Execution Squad": December 1960*

The only suggestion that QJ/WIN had any connection with assassination was a report that WI/ROGUE, another asset of the Congo Station, once asked QJ/WIN to join an "execution squad."

WI/ROGUE was an "essentially stateless" soldier of fortune, "a forger and former bank robber." (Inspector General Memo, 3/14/75) [3]

---

[1] The CIA Inspector General's Report said that QJ/WIN "had been recruited earlier * * * for use in a special operation in the Congo (the assassination of Patrice Lumumba) to be run by Michael Mulroney." (I.G. Report, p. 38)
As explained above, Bissell and Mulroney testified that Mulroney had refused to be associated with an assassination operation. See sections 5(a) (ii) and (iii).
[2] Harvey stated that the memoranda concerning QJ/WIN were probably written for his signature by the officer who supervised QJ/WIN's activities in Europe. (Harvey affidavit, 9/14/75, pp. 1, 4)
Harvey said that in later discussions he held with Scheider concerning the development of a general assassination capability, Scheider never mentioned QJ/WIN's activities in the Congo, nor did Scheider refer to his own trip to Leopoldville. Harvey also stated that before the formation of that project, QJ/WIN's case officer had not previously used him "as an assassination capability or even viewed him as such." (Harvey affidavit, 9/14/75, pp. 7, 8) See discussion in Part III, Section C.
[3] This information was derived from a report on WI/ROGUE's assignment to the Congo prepared by a former Africa Division officer on March 14, 1975 at the request of the CIA Office of the Inspector General.

The CIA sent him to the Congo after providing him with plastic surgery and a toupee so that Europeans traveling in the Congo would not recognize him. (I.G. Memo, 3/14/75) The CIA characterized WI/ROGUE as a man who "learns quickly and carries out any assignment without regard for danger." (CIA Cable, Africa Division to Leopoldville, 10/27/60) CIA's Africa Division recommended WI/ROGUE as an agent in the following terms:

> He is indeed aware of the precepts of right and wrong, but if he is given an assignment which may be morally wrong in the eyes of the world, but necessary because his case officer ordered him to carry it out, then it is right, and he will dutifully undertake appropriate action for its execution without pangs of conscience. In a word, he can rationalize all actions.

Station Officer Hedgman described WI/ROGUE as "a man with a rather unsavory reputation, who would try anything once, at least." Hedgman used him as "a general utility agent" because "I felt we needed surveillance capability, developing new contacts, various things." Hedgman supervised WI/ROGUE directly and did not put him in touch with Mulroney. (Hedgman, 8/21/75, pp. 96-97)

A report on agent WI/ROGUE, prepared for the CIA Inspector General's Office in 1975, described the training he received:

> On 19 September 1960 two members of Africa Division met with him to discuss "an operational assignment in Africa Division." In connection with this assignment, WI/ROGUE was to be trained in demolitions, small arms, and medical immunization. (I.G. Memo, 3/14/75)[1]

The report also outlined WI/ROGUE's assignment to the Congo and recorded no mention of the use to which WI/ROGUE's "medical immunization" training would be put:

> In October 1960 a cable to Leopoldville stated that * * * Headquarters [had] * * * intent to use him as utility agent in order to "(a) organize and conduct a surveillance team; (b) intercept packages; (c) blow up bridges; and (d) execute other assignments requiring positive action. His utilization is not to be restricted to Leopoldville." (I.G. Memo, 3/14/75)

WI/ROGUE made his initial contact with Hedgman in Leopoldville on December 2, 1960. Hedgman instructed him to "build cover during initial period;" and to "spot persons for [a] surveillance team" of intelligence agents in the province where Lumumba's support was strongest. (CIA Cable, 12/17/60)

Soon thereafter Hedgman cabled Headquarters:

> QJ/WIN WHO RESIDES SAME HOTEL AS WI/ROGUE REPORTED * * * WI/ROGUE SMELLED AS THOUGH HE IN INTEL BUSINESS. STATION DENIED ANY INFO ON WI/ROGUE. 14 DEC QJ/WIN REPORTED WI/ROGUE HAD OFFERED HIM THREE HUNDRED DOLLARS PER MONTH TO PARTICIPATE IN INTEL NET AND BE MEMBER "EXECUTION SQUAD." WHEN QJ/WIN SAID HE NOT INTERESTED, WI/ROGUE ADDED THERE WOULD BE BONUSES FOR SPECIAL JOBS. UNDER QJ/WIN QUESTIONING, WI/ROGUE LATER SAID HE WORKING FOR [AMERICAN] SERVICE.
> * * * IN DISCUSSING LOCAL CONTACTS, WI/ROGUE MENTIONED QJ/WIN BUT DID NOT ADMIT TO HAVING TRIED RECRUIT HIM. WHEN [STATION OFFICER] TRIED LEARN WHETHER WI/ROGUE

---

[1] A case officer who prepared WI/ROGUE for his mission in the Congo stated that he had no knowledge that WI/ROGUE received any training in "medical immunization." The case officer assumed that an unclear cable reference to the fact that WI/ROGUE received innoculations before his journey was misinterpreted in the memorandum prepared for the Inspector General's Office on March 14, 1975. (WI/ROGUE Case Offier affidavit, 11/14/75)

HAD MADE APPROACH LATTER CLAIMED HAD TAKEN NO STEPS. [STATION OFFICER] WAS UNABLE CONTRADICT, AS DID NOT WISH REVEAL QJ/WIN CONNECTION [WITH CIA]. (CIA Cable, Leopoldville to Director, 12/17/60)

The cable also expressed Hedgman's concern about WI/ROGUE's actions:

> * * * LEOP CONCERNED BY WI/ROGUE FREE WHEELING AND LACK SECURITY. STATION HAS ENOUGH HEADACHES WITHOUT WORRYING ABOUT AGENT WHO NOT ABLE HANDLE FINANCES AND WHO NOT WILLING FOLLOW INSTRUCTIONS. IF HQS DESIRES, WILLING KEEP HIM ON PROBATION, BUT IF CONTINUE HAVE DIFFICULTIES, BELIEVE WI/ROGUE RECALL BEST SOLUTION. (CIA Cable, Leopoldville to Director, 12/17/60)

Hedgman explained WI/ROGUE's attempt to recruit QJ/WIN for an execution squad as an unauthorized unexpected contact. He testified that he had not instructed WI/ROGUE to make this kind of proposition to QJ/WIN or anyone else:

> I would like to stress that I don't know what WI/ROGUE was talking about as an "execution squad," and I am sure he was never asked to go out and execute anyone. (Hedgman, 8/21/75, p. 100)

Hedgman suggested that WI/ROGUE had concocted the idea of an execution squad:

> His idea of what an intelligence operative should do, I think, had been gathered by reading a few novels or something of the sort. (Hedgman, 8/21/75, p. 100)

Mulroney said he knew of no attempt by anyone connected with the CIA to recruit an execution squad and he did not remember WI/ROGUE. (Mulroney 9/11/75, pp. 39–42) He stated that QJ/WIN was considered for use on "strong arm squad[s]," unrelated to assassinations:

> Surveillance teams where you have to go into crime areas * * * where you need a fellow that if he gets in a box can fight his way out of it. (Mulroney, 9/11/75, p. 36)

Richard Bissell recalled nothing about WI/ROGUE's approach to QJ/WIN. (Bissell, 9/11/75, p. 71) Bronson Tweedy remembered that WI/ROGUE was "dispatched on a general purpose mission" to the Congo. But Tweedy testified that WI/ROGUE would "absolutely not" have been used on an assassination mission against Lumumba because "he was basically dispatched, assessed and dealt with by the balance of the Division" rather than by the two people in the Africa Division, Tweedy and his Deputy, who would have known that the assassination of Lumumba was being considered. (Tweedy, 9/9/75, pp. 63–65)

The Station Officer said that if WI/ROGUE had been involved in an actual assassination plan, he would have transmitted messages concerning WI/ROGUE in the PROP channel. Instead, he limited distribution of the cable about WI/ROGUE in a routine manner—as a CIA officer would "normally do * * * when you speak in a derogatory manner of an asset." (Hedgman, 8/21/75, pp. 101–102)

Hedgman maintained that WI/ROGUE's proposition to QJ/WIN to join an "execution squad" could be attributed to WI/ROGUE's "freewheeling" nature:

> I had difficulty controlling him in that he was not a professional intelligence officer as such. He seemed to act on his own without seeking guidance or author

ity * * * I found he was rather an unguided missile * * * the kind of man that could get you in trouble before you knew you were in trouble. (Hedgman, 8/21/75, pp. 96-97)

But Hedgman did not disavow all responsibility for WI/ROGUE's actions:

[I]f you give a man an order and he carries it out and causes a problem for the Station, then you accept responsibility. (Hedgman, 8/21/75, p. 97)

In sum, the testimony of the CIA officers involved in the PROP operation and the concern about WI/ROGUE's "freewheeling" in Hedgman's cable suggests that agent WI/ROGUE's attempt to form an "execution squad" was an unauthorized, maverick action, unconnected to any CIA operation. However, the fact that WI/ROGUE was to be trained in "medical immunization" (I.G. Report Memo, 3/14/75) precludes a definitive conclusion to that effect.

6. THE QUESTION OF WHETHER THE CIA WAS INVOLVED IN BRINGING ABOUT LUMUMBA'S DEATH IN KATANGA PROVINCE

The CIA officers most closely connected with the plot to poison Lumumba testified uniformly that they knew of no CIA involvement in Lumumba's death. The Congo Station had advance knowledge of the central government's plan to transport Lumumba into the hands of his bitterest enemies, where he was likely to be killed. But there is no evidentiary basis for concluding that the CIA conspired in this plan or was connected to the events in Katanga that resulted in Lumumba's death.

(a) Lumumba's Imprisonment After Leaving U.N. Custody: November 27–December 3, 1960

The only suggestion that the CIA may have been involved in the capture of Lumumba by Mobutu's troops after Lumumba left U.N. custody on November 27, is a PROP cable from the Station Officer to Tweedy on November 14. The cable stated that a CIA agent had learned that Lumumba's

POLITICAL FOLLOWERS IN STANLEYVILLE DESIRE THAT HE BREAK OUT OF HIS CONFINEMENT AND PROCEED TO THAT CITY BY CAR TO ENGAGE IN POLITICAL ACTIVITY. * * * DECISION ON BREAKOUT WILL PROBABLY BE MADE SHORTLY. STATION EXPECTS TO BE ADVISED BY [AGENT] OF DECISION WAS MADE. * * * STATION HAS SEVERAL POSSIBLE ASSETS TO USE IN EVENT OF BREAKOUT AND STUDYING SEVERAL PLANS OF ACTION. (CIA Cable, Station Officer to Tweedy, 11/14/60)

There is no other evidence that the CIA actually learned in advance of Lumumba's plan to depart for Stanleyville. In fact, a cable from Leopoldville on the day after Lumumba's escape evidenced the Station's complete ignorance about the circumstances of Lumumba's departure. (CIA Cable, Leopoldville to Director, 11/28/60) However, the same cable raises a question concerning whether the CIA was involved in Lumumba's subsequent capture en route by Congolese troops:

[STATION] WORKING WITH [CONGOLESE GOVERNMENT] TO GET ROADS BLOCKED AND TROOPS ALERTED [BLOCK] POSSIBLE ESCAPE ROUTE. (CIA Cable, 11/28/60)

Station Officer Hedgman testified that he was "quite certain that there was no Agency involvement in any way" in Lumumba's departure from U.N. custody and that he had no advance knowledge of Lumumba's plan. He stated that he consulted with Congolese officers about the possible routes Lumumba might take to Stanleyville, but he was "not a major assistance" in tracking down Lumumba prior to his capture. (Hedgman, 8/21/75, pp. 63-65)

Mulroney, who had planned to draw Lumumba out of U.N. custody and turn him over to Congolese authorities, testified that Lumumba escaped by his own devices and was not tricked by the CIA. (Mulroney, 9/11/75, p. 22)

(b) Lumumba's Death

The contemporaneous cable traffic shows that the CIA was kept informed of Lumumba's condition and movements in January of 1961 by the Congolese and that the CIA continued to consider Lumumba a serious political threat. Despite the fact that the Station Officer knew of a plan to deliver Lumumba into the hands of his enemies at a time when the CIA was convinced that "drastic steps" were necessary to prevent Lumumba's return to power, there is no evidence of CIA involvement in this plan or in bringing about the death of Lumumba in Katanga.

There is no doubt that the CIA and the Congolese government shared a concern in January 1961 that Lumumba might return to power, particularly since the Congolese army and police were threatening to mutiny if they were not given substantial pay raises. Station Officer Hedgman reported that a mutiny "almost certainly would * * * bring about [Lumumba] return power" and said he had advised the Congolese government of his opinion that the army garrison at Leopoldville

> WILL MUTINY WITHIN TWO OR THREE DAYS UNLESS DRASTIC ACTION TAKEN SATISFY COMPLAINTS. (CIA Cable, Leopoldville to Director, 1/12/61)

Hedgman urged Headquarters to consider an immediate reaction to the crisis. (CIA Cable, 1/12/61) This cable, which was sent through the ordinary channel, made no reference, even indirectly, to assassination, and instead recommended a different course of action.

The next day, Hedgman cabled Headquarters:

> STATION AND EMBASSY BELIEVE PRESENT GOVERNMENT MAY FALL WITHIN FEW DAYS. RESULT WOULD ALMOST CERTAINLY BE CHAOS AND RETURN [LUMUMBA] TO POWER. (CIA Cable, Leopoldville to Director, 1/13/61)

Hedgman advised that reopening the Congolese Parliament under United Nations supervision was unacceptable because:

> THE COMBINATION OF [LUMUMBA'S] POWERS AS DEMAGOGUE, HIS ABLE USE OF GOON SQUADS AND PROPAGANDA AND SPIRIT OF DEFEAT WITHIN [GOVERNMENT] COALITION WHICH WOULD INCREASE RAPIDLY UNDER SUCH CONDITIONS WOULD ALMOST CERTAINLY INSURE [LUMUMBA] VICTORY IN PARLIAMENT. * * * REFUSAL TAKE DRASTIC STEPS AT THIS TIME WILL LEAD TO DEFEAT OF [UNITED STATES] POLICY IN CONGO. (CIA Cable, Leopoldville to Director, 1/13/61)

On January 14, Hedgman was advised by a Congolese government leader that Lumumba was to be transferred from the Thysville military camp, where he had been held since shortly after Mobutu's troops captured him, to a prison in Bakwanga, the capital of another Congolese province reported to be the "home territory of * * * Lumumba's sworn enemy." (CIA Cable, Leopoldville to Director, 1/17/61; CIA Information Report, 1/17/61)

On January 17, authorities in Leopoldville placed Lumumba and two of his leading supporters, Maurice Mpolo and Joseph Okito, aboard an airplane bound for Bakwanga. Apparently the aircraft was redirected in midflight to Elisabethville in Katanga Province "when it was learned that United Nations troops were at Bakwanga airport." On February 13, the government of Katanga reported that Lumumba and his two companions escaped the previous day and died at the hands of hostile villagers. (U.N. Report, 11/12/61, pp. 98–100, 109)

The United Nations Commission on Investigation was "not convinced by the version of the facts given by the provincial government of Katanga." The Commission concluded instead, that Lumumba was killed on January 17, almost immediately after his arrival in Katanga, probably with the knowledge of the central government and at the behest of the Katanga authorities. (U.N. Report, 11/11/61, pp. 100, 117):

> The Commission wishes to put on record its view that President Kasavubu and his aides, on the one hand, and the provincial government of Katanga headed by Mr. Tshombe on the other, should not escape responsibility for the death of Mr. Lumumba, Mr. Okito, and Mr. Mpolo. For Mr. Kasavubu and his aides had handed over Mr. Lumumba and his colleagues to the Katanga authorities knowing full well, in doing so, that they were throwing them into the hands of their bitterest political enemies. The government of the province of Katanga in turn not only failed to safeguard the lives of the three prisoners but also had, by its action, contributed, directly or indirectly, to the murder of the prisoners. (U.N. Report, 11/11/61, p. 118)

Cables from the Station Officer demonstrated no CIA involvement in the plan to transport Lumumba to Bakwanga. But the Station Officer clearly had prior knowledge of the plan to transfer Lumumba to a state where it was probable that he would be killed. Other supporters of Lumumba who had been sent to Bakwanga earlier by Leopoldville authorities

> Were killed there in horrible circumstances, and the place was known as the 'slaughterhouse.' It was therefore improbable that Mr. Lumumba and his companions would have met a different fate at Bakwanga if they had been taken there. (U.N. Report, 11/11/61, p. 109)

After learning that Lumumba was to be flown to Bakwanga, the Station Officer cabled:

> IT NOW MORE IMPORTANT THAN EVER SUPPORT THOSE SINGLE ELEMENTS WHICH CAN STRENGTHEN FABRIC OVERALL * * * OPPOSITION [LUMUMBA]. WISH ASSURE HQS WE TRYING SHORE UP * * * DEFENSES ONLY IN TERMS OUR OWN OBJECTIVES DENY CONGO GOVT CONTROL [LUMUMBA]. (CIA Cable, Leopoldville to Director, 1/16/61)

Despite his perception of an urgent need to prevent Lumumba's return to power at this time, the Station Officer testified that the CIA was not involved in bringing about Lumumba's death in Katanga and that he did not have any first-hand knowledge of the circumstances of Lumumba's death. (Hedgman, 8/25/75, pp. 31, 33)[1]

---

[1] Hedgman also testified that he had no discussions with the Congolese central government, after Lumumba was in its custody, about executing Lumumba or sending him to Katanga. Hedgman said:
To the best of my knowledge, neither the Station nor the Embassy had any input in the decision to send him to Katanga * * * I think there was a general assumption, once we learned he had been sent to Katanga, that his goose was cooked, because Tshombe hated him and looked on him as a danger and rival. (Hedgman, 8/21/75, p. 78)

In late November, Hedgman attended a meeting of CIA officers from African Stations with Bissell and Tweedy. Hedgman testified that he briefed Bissell and Tweedy on developments in the Congo, including Lumumba's flight from Leopoldville, but he could not recall any discussion at the meeting of the possibility of assassinating Lumumba. (Hedgman, 8/21/75, pp. 66, 68)

Two days after Lumumba was flown to Katanga, the CIA Base Chief in Elisabethville sent an unusual message to headquarters:

THANKS FOR PATRICE. IF WE HAD KNOWN HE WAS COMING WE WOULD HAVE BAKED A SNAKE.

The cable also reported that the Base's sources had provided "no advance word whatsoever" of Lumumba's flight to Katanga and that the Congolese central government "does not plan to liquidate Lumumba." (CIA Cable, Elisabethville to Director, 1/19/61)

This cable indicates that the CIA did not have knowledge of the central government's decision to transfer Lumumba from Thysville military camp to a place where he would be in the hands of his avowed enemies. This cable indicates that the CIA was not kept informed of Lumumba's treatment after he arrived in Katanga because, according to the report of the United Nations Commission, Lumumba had already been killed when the cable was sent.[1]

On February 10, several weeks after Lumumba died, but before his death was announced by the Katanga government, the Elisabethville Base cabled Headquarters that "Lumumba fate is best kept secret in Katanga." (CIA Cable, Elisabethville to Director, 2/10/61) The cable gave different versions from several sources about Lumumba's death. Hedgman testified that the cable conformed to his recollection that the CIA "did not have any hard information" as of that date about Lumumba's fate after arrival in Katanga. (Hedgman, 8/25/75, p. 34)

Hedgman acknowledged that the CIA was in close contact with some Congolese officials who "quite clearly knew" that Lumumba was to be shipped to Katanga "because they were involved." But Hedgman said that these Congolese contacts "were not acting under CIA instructions if and when they did this." (Hedgman, 8/21/75, p. 35)

Tweedy and Mulroney agreed with Hedgman's account that the CIA was not involved in the events that led to Lumumba's death.[2]

7. THE QUESTION OF THE LEVEL AT WHICH THE ASSASSINATION PLOT WAS AUTHORIZED

Summary

The chain of events revealed by the documents and testimony is strong enough to permit a reasonable inference that the plot to assassinate Lumumba was authorized by President Eisenhower. Neverthe-

---

[1] Hedgman testified that neither he nor the Elisabethville Base knew of a Congolese plan to send Lumumba to Katanga. (Hedgman, 8/25/75, pp. 25-26)
[2] When asked if there was any CIA involvement, Tweedy replied that there was "none whatsoever." Tweedy stated that "the fate of Lumumba in the end was purely an African event." (Tweedy, 9/9/75, p. 53) Mulroney testified "CIA had absolutely no connection, to my certain knowledge, with the death of Patrice Lumumba." (Mulroney, 6/9/75, p. 20)
During his tenure as DCI, several years after Lumumba's death, Richard Helms was told by CIA investigators that "it was clear that the Agency had not murdered Lumumba," and that "the Agency had no involvement" in the events that led to Lumumba's death. (Helms, 9/16/75, p. 26)

less, there is enough countervailing testimony by Eisenhower Administration officials and enough ambiguity and lack of clarity in the records of high-level policy meetings to preclude the Committee from making a finding that the President intended an assassination effort against Lumumba.

It is clear that the Director of Central Intelligence, Allen Dulles, authorized an assassination plot. There is, however, no evidence of United States involvement in bringing about the death of Lumumba at the hands of Congolese authorities in Katanga.

Strong expressions of hostility toward Lumumba from the President and his national security assistant, followed immediately by CIA steps in furtherance of an assassination operation against Lumumba, are part of a sequence of events that, at the least, make it appear that Dulles believed assassination was a permissible means of complying with pressure from the President to remove Lumumba from the political scene.

The chain of significant events in the Lumumba case begins with the testimony that President Eisenhower made a statement at a meeting of the National Security Council in the summer or early fall of 1960 that came across to one staff member in attendance as an order for the assassination of Patrice Lumumba. The next link is a memorandum of the Special Group meeting of August 25, 1960, which indicated that when the President's "extremely strong feelings on the necessity for very straightforward action" were conveyed, the Special Group

* * * agreed that planning for the Congo would not necessarily rule out "consideration" of any particular kind of activity which might contribute to getting rid of Lumumba. (Special Group Minutes, 8/25/60)

The following day, CIA Director Allen Dulles, who had attended the Special Group meeting, personally cabled to the Station Officer in Leopoldville that Lumumba's

REMOVAL MUST BE AN URGENT AND PRIME OBJECTIVE * * * A HIGH PRIORITY OF OUR COVERT ACTION. YOU CAN ACT ON YOUR OWN AUTHORITY WHERE TIME DOES NOT PERMIT REFERRAL HERE. (CIA Cable, Dulles to Station Officer, 8/26/60)

Although the Dulles cable does not explicitly mention assassination, Richard Bissell—the CIA official under whose aegis the assassination effort against Lumumba took place—testified that, in his opinion, this cable was a direct outgrowth of the Special Group meeting and signaled to him that the President had authorized assassination as one means of effecting Lumumba's "removal." (Bissell, 9/10/75, pp. 33-34,, 61-62; see Section 7(c), *infra*) Bronson Tweedy, who had direct operational responsibility at Headquarters for activities against Lumumba, testified that the Dulles cable confirmed the policy that no measure, including assassination, was to be overlooked in the attempt to remove Lumumba from a position of influence. (Tweedy, 10/9/75, pp. 4-5)

On September 19, 1960, Bissell and Tweedy cabled Station Officer Hedgman to expect a messenger from CIA Headquarters. Two days later, in the presence of the President at a meeting of the National Security Council, Allen Dulles stated that Lumumba "would remain a grave danger as long as he was not yet disposed of." (Memorandum, 460th NSC Meeting, 9/21/60) Five days after this meeting, CIA scientist, Joseph Scheider, arrived in Leopoldville and provided the Station Officer with toxic biological substances, instructed him to assassinate Lumumba, and informed him that the President had authorized this operation.

Two mitigating factors weaken this chain just enough so that it will not support an absolute finding of Presidential authorization for the assassination effort against Lumumba.

First, the two officials of the Eisenhower Administration responsible to the President for national security affairs and present at the NSC meetings in question testified that they knew of no Presidential approval for, or knowledge of, an assassination operation.

Second, the minutes of discussions at meetings of the National Security Council and its Special Group do not record an explicit Presidential order for the assassination of Lumumba. The Secretary of the Special Group maintained that his memoranda reflected the actual language used at the meetings without omission or euphemism for extremely sensitive statements. (Parrott, 7/10/75, p. 19) All other NSC staff executives stated however, that there was a strong possibility that a statement as sensitive as an assassination order would have been omitted from the record or handled by means of euphemism. Several high Government officials involved in policymaking and planning for covert operations testified that the language in these minutes clearly indicated that assassination was contemplated at the NSC as one means of eliminating Lumumba as a political threat; other officials testified to the contrary.

(a) High-Level Meetings at which "Getting Rid of Lumumba" Was Discussed

(i) Dillon's Testimony About Pentagon Meeting: Summer 1960

In late July 1960, Patrice Lumumba visited the United States and met with Secretary of State Christian Herter and Undersecretary of State C. Douglas Dillon. While Lumumba was in Washington, D.C., Secretary Herter pledged aid to the newly formed Government of the Republic of the Congo.

According to Dillon, Lumumba impressed American officials as an irrational, almost "psychotic" personality:

When he was in the State Department meeting, either with me or with the Secretary in my presence * * * he would never look you in the eye. He looked up at the sky. And a tremendous flow of words came out. He spoke in French, and he spoke it very fluently. And his words didn't ever have any relation to the particular things that we wanted to discuss * * *. You had a feeling that he was a person that was gripped by this fervor that I can only characterize as messianic * * *. [H]e was just not a rational being. (Dillon, 9/2/75, p. 24)

Dillon said that the willingness of the United States government to work with Lumumba vanished after these meetings:

[T]he impression that was left was * * * very bad, that this was an individual whom it was impossible to deal with. And the feelings of the Government as a result of this sharpened very considerably at that time * * *. We [had] hoped to see him and see what we could do to come to a better understanding with him. (Dillon, 9/2/75, pp. 23–24)

Dillon testified that shortly after Lumumba's visit in late July or August, he was present at a meeting at the Pentagon attended by representatives of the State Department, Defense Department, Joint Chiefs of Staff and the CIA. (Dillon, 9/2/75, pp. 17–20, 25–26)[1] According to Dillon, "a question regarding the possibility of an assassination attempt against Lumumba was briefly raised. Dillon did not recall anything about the language used in raising the question. Dillon assumed that when the subject of Lumumba's assassination was raised, "it was turned off by the CIA" because "the CIA people, whoever they were, were negative to any such action." This opposition "wasn't moral," according to Dillon, but rather an objection on the grounds that it was "not a possible thing." Dillon said the CIA reaction "might have been" made out of the feeling that the group was too large for such a sensitive discussion. (Dillon, 9/2/75, pp. 15–17, 25, 30, 60)

Dillon did not remember who lodged the negative reaction to the assassination question although he thought it "would have to have been either Allen Dulles, or possibly [General] Cabell * * * most likely Cabell."[2] (Dillon, 9/2/75, pp. 22, 25) Dillon thought it was "very likely" that Richard Bissell attended the meeting. (Dillon, 9/2/75, p. 21)

Dillon stated that this discussion could not have served as authorization for an actual assassination effort against Lumumba, but he believed that the CIA:

Could have decided they wanted to develop the capability * * * just by knowing the concern that everyone had about Lumumba. * * * They wouldn't have had to tell anyone about that. That is just developing their own internal capability, and then they would have to come and get permission. (Dillon, 9/2/75, pp. 30, 31)

Dillon testified that he had never heard any mention of the plot to poison Lumumba nor, even a hint that the CIA asked permission to mount such an operation. (Dillon, 9/2/75, p. 50) But after he was informed of the poison plot, Dillon made the following comment about the Pentagon meeting:

I think it is * * * likely that it might have been the beginning of this whole idea on the CIA's part that they should develop such a capacity. And maybe they didn't have it then and went to work to develop it beginning in August. (Dillon, 9/2/75, p. 61)

Dillon said that it was unlikely that formal notes were taken at the meeting or preserved because it was a small "ad hoc" group rather than an official body. Such interdepartmental meetings were "not unusual," according to Dillon. (Dillon, 9/2/75, p. 18)

The only officials Dillon named as probable participants other than the CIA representatives were Deputy Secretary of Defense James Douglas and Assistant Secretary of Defense John N. Irwin II. (Dillon, 9/2/75, pp. 19, 21) Douglas stated that it was possible that he attended such a meeting at the Pentagon, but he did not recall it. Nor did he recall the question of Lumumba's assassination ever being raised in his presence. (Douglas affidavit, 9/5/75) Irwin stated that it was

---

[1] Dillon was unable to recall the precise date of this meeting. (Dillon, 9/2/75, pp. 25–26)
[2] General Cabell was Allen Dulles' Deputy DCI at this time.

"likely" that he attended the meeting to which Dillon referred, but he did not remember whether he was present "at any meeting at the Pentagon where the question of assassinating Patrice Lumumba was raised." (Irwin affidavit, 9/22/75, p. 3)

(ii) Robert Johnson's Testimony That He Understood the President to Order Lumumba's Assassination at an NSC Meeting

Robert H. Johnson, a member of the National Security Council staff from 1951 to January 1962, offered what he termed a "clue" to the extent of Presidential involvement in the decision to assassinate Lumumba. (Johnson, 6/18/75, pp. 4–5)[1] Johnson recounted the following occurrence at an NSC meeting, in the summer of 1960, which began with a briefing on world developments by the DCI:

At some time during that discussion, President Eisenhower said something—I can no longer remember his words—that came across to me as an order for the assassination of Lumumba who was then at the center of political conflict and controversy in the Congo. There was no discussion; the meeting simply moved on. I remember my sense of that moment quite clearly because the President's statement came as a great shock to me. I cannot, however, reconstruct the moment more specifically.

Although I was convinced at the time—and remained convinced when I thought about it later—that the President's statement was intended as an order for the assassination of Lumumba, I must confess that in thinking about the incident more recently I have had some doubts. As is well known, it was quite uncharacteristic of President Eisenhower to make or announce policy decisions in NSC meetings. Certainly, it was strange if he departed from that normal pattern on a subject so sensitive as this. Moreover, it was not long after this, I believe, that Lumumba was dismissed as premier by Kasavubu in an action that was a quasi-coup. I have come to wonder whether what I really heard was only an order for some such political action. All I can tell you with any certainty at the present moment is my sense of that moment in the Cabinet Room of the White House. (Johnson, 6/18/75, pp. 6–7)

Johnson "presumed" that the President made his statement while "looking toward the Director of Central Intelligence." (Johnson, 6/18/75, p. 11) He was unable to recall with any greater specificity the words used by the President. (Johnson, 9/13/75, p. 10) Johnson was asked:

Q: * * * Would it be fair to say that although you allow for the possibility that a coup or some more general political action was being discussed, it is your clear impression that you had heard an order for the assassination of Lumumba?
JOHNSON: It was my clear impression at the time.
Q: And it remains your impression now?

---

[1] Robert Johnson introduced his testimony before the Committee with the following statement:

"* * * I would like to preface my remarks by pointing out that my decision to offer testimony to this committee has involved for me a profound personal, moral dilemma. In my role as a member of the NSC Staff for ten and one-half years, I was privy to a great deal of information that involved relationships of confidentiality with high officials of the United States government. I have always taken very seriously the responsibilities implied in such relationships.

"These responsibilities extend, in my view, far beyond questions of security classification or other legal or foreign policy concerns. They relate to the very basis of human society and government—to the relationships of trust without which no free society can long survive and no government can operate.

"I have been forced by recent developments, however to weigh against these considerable responsibilities, my broader responsibilities as a citizen on an issue that involves major questions of public morality, as well as questions of sound policy. Having done so, I have concluded, not without a great deal of reluctance, to come to your committee with information bearing upon your inquiry into government decisions relating to the assassination of foreign leaders." (Johnson, 6/18/75, pp. 4–5)

After his tenure on the staff of the National Security Council, Robert Johnson served from 1962 to 1967 on the Policy Planning Council at the Department of State.

JOHNSON: It remains my impression now. I have reflected on this other kind of possibility; but that is the sense * * * that persists. (Johnson, 9/13/75, pp. 24–25)[1]

Johnson stated that the incident provoked a strong reaction from him:

I was surprised * * * that I would ever hear a President say anything like this in my presence or the presence of a group of people. I was startled. (Johnson, 6/18/75, p. 13)

A succinct summary of Johnson's testimony was elicited by Senator Mathias in the following exchange:

Senator MATHIAS: * * * What comes across is that you do have a memory, if not of exact words, but of your own reaction really to a Presidential order which you considered to be an order for an assassination.
JOHNSON: That is correct.
Senator MATHIAS: And that although precise words have escaped you in the passage of fifteen years, that sense of shock remains?
JOHNSON: Right. Yes, sir. (Johnson, 6/18/75, p. 8)

After the meeting, Johnson, who was responsible for writing the memorandum of the discussion, consulted with a senior official on the NSC staff to determine how to handle the President's statement in the memorandum and in the debriefing of the NSC Planning Board that followed each meeting:

I suspect—but no longer have an exact recollection—that I omitted it from the debriefing. I also do not recall how I handled the subject in the memo of the meeting, though I suspect that some kind of reference to the President's statement was made. (Johnson, 6/18/75, p. 7)

In his second appearance before the Committee, Johnson stated that it was "quite likely that it [the President's statement] was handled through some kind of euphemism or may have been omitted altogether." (Johnson, 9/13/75, p. 21)[2]

---

[1] Johnson further explained that his allowance for the possibility that he had heard an order for a coup did not disturb his recollection of hearing an assassination order:
"It was a retrospective reflection on what I had heard, and since this coup did occur, it occurred to me that it was possible that that is what I heard, but that would not change my sense of the moment when I heard the President speak, which I felt then, and I continue to feel, was a statement designed to direct the disposal, assassination, of Lumumba." (Johnson, 9/13/75, p. 12)

[2] In 1960, Johnson was Director of the Planning Board Secretariat—third in command on the NSC staff. He attended NSC meetings to take notes on the discussions whenever one of the two senior NSC officials was absent.
Johnson testified that the person with whom he consulted about the manner of recording the President's statement in the minutes was one of the two top NSC staff officials at that time: NCS Executive Secretary James Lay or Deputy Executive Secretary Marion Boggs. (Johnson, 9/13/75, pp. 12–13) Johnson could not recall which of the two officials he had consulted, but he "inferred" that it must have been the "top career NSC staff person present" at the meeting where he heard the President's statement. (Johnson, 9/13/75, p. 12) At both of the NSC meetings where the President and Johnson were present for a discussion of Lumumba—August 18 and September 7—James Lay was absent and Marion Boggs served as Acting Executive Secretary.
Marion Bogg's statement about his method of handling the situation described by Johnson is in accord with Johnson's testimony:
"I have no independent recollection of being consulted by Mr. Johnson about how to handle in the memorandum of discussion any sensitive statement regarding Lumumba. I am not saying I was not consulted; merely that I do not remember such an incident. If I had been consulted, I would almost certainly have directed Mr. Johnson to omit the matter from the memorandum of discussion." (Boggs affidavit, 10/10/75, p. 2)
James Lay, who attended other NSC meetings where Lumumba was discussed (*e.g.*, September 21, 1960), also confirmed the fact that NSC minutes would not be likely to record a statement as sensitive as a Presidential order for an assassination, if such an order were given:
"If extremely sensitive matters were discussed at an NSC meeting, it was sometimes the practice that the official NSC minutes would record only the general subject discussed without identifying the specially sensitive subject of the discussion. In highly sensitive cases, no reference to the subject would be made in the NSC minutes." (Lay affidavit, 9/8/75, p. 2)

As Johnson stated, his testimony standing alone is "a clue, rather than precise evidence of Presidential involvement in decision making with respect to assassinations." (Johnson, 6/18/75, p. 5) To determine the significance of this "clue," it must be placed in the context of the records of the NSC meetings attended by Johnson, testimony about those meetings, and the series of events that preceded the dispatch of poisons to the Congo for Lumumba's assassination.

In the summer of 1960, Robert Johnson attended four NSC meetings at which developments in the Congo were discussed. The President was not in attendance on two of those occasions—July 15 and July 21. (NSC Minutes, 7/15/60; NSC Minutes, 7/21/60) The attitude toward Lumumba at these first two meetings was vehement:

> Mr. Dulles said that in Lumumba we were faced with a person who was a Castro or worse * * * Mr. Dulles went on to describe Mr. Lumumba's background which he described as "harrowing" * * * It is safe to go on the assumption that Lumumba has been bought by the Communists; this also, however, fits with his own orientation. (NSC Minutes, 7/21/60)

The President presided over the other two NSC meetings—on August 18 and September 7. After looking at the records of those meetings, Johnson was unable to determine with certainty at which meeting he heard the President's statement.[1] (Johnson, 9/13/75, p. 16)

The chronology of meetings, cables, and events in the Congo during this period makes it most likely that Johnson's testimony refers to the NSC meeting of August 18, 1960.

The meeting of August 18 took place at the beginning of the series of events that preceded the dispatch of Scheider to Leopoldville with poisons for assassinating Lumumba.[2] The September 7 meeting took place in the midst of these events.

The NSC meeting of August 18, 1960 was held three weeks before Lumumba's dismissal by Kasavubu, which Johnson remembers as taking place "not long after" he heard the President's statement. The only other meeting at which Johnson could have heard the statement by the President was held two days after this event, on September 7.[3]

Robert Johnson's memorandum of the meeting of August 18, 1960 indicates that Acting Secretary of State C. Douglas Dillon[4] intro-

---

[1] Johnson testified without benefit of review of the complete Memorandum of Discussion of the meeting of September 7 because the Committee had not received it at that point. Instead, he reviewed the Record of Action which summarized the decisions made at that meeting. As discussed at Section (7)(a)(iv), *infra*, when the complete minutes of the meetings of August 18 and September 7 are compared, it is clear that the subject of Lumumba's role in the Congo received far more attention at the meeting of August 18.
[2] Each of the major events in this series is discussed in detail in other sections of the report and summarized at the beginning of section 7, *supra*.
[3] See Section 7(a)(iv), *infra*, for an analysis of the substance of the NSC discussion on September 7, 1960.
[4] In 1960, Dillon served as Undersecretary of State, the "number two position in the State Department." The title was subsequently changed to Deputy Secretary of State. In this post, Dillon frequently served as Acting Secretary of State and either attended or was kept informed about NSC and Special Group meetings. Dillon later served as Secretary of the Treasury under President Kennedy. (Dillon, 9/2/75, pp. 2–4)

duced the discussion of United States policy toward the Congo. In the course of his remarks, Dillon maintained that the presence of United Nations troops in the Congo was necessary to prevent Soviet intervention at Lumumba's request:

> If * * * Lumumba carried out his threat to force the U.N. out, he might then offer to accept help from anyone. * * * The elimination of the U.N. would be a disaster which, Secretary Dillon stated, we should do everything we could to prevent. If the U.N. were forced out, we might be faced by a situation where the Soviets intervened by invitation of the Congo.
>
> * * * Secretary Dillon said that he [Lumumba] was working to serve the purposes of the Soviets and Mr. Dulles pointed out that Lumumba was in Soviet pay. (NSC Minutes, 8/18/60)

Dillon's remarks prompted the only statements about Lumumba attributed to the President in the Memorandum of the August 18 meeting:

> The President said that the possibility that the U.N. would be forced out was simply inconceivable. We should keep the U.N. in the Congo even if we had to ask for European troops to do it. We should do so even if such action was used by the Soviets as the basis for starting a fight. Mr. Dillon indicated that this was State's feeling but that the Secretary General and Mr. Lodge doubted whether, if the Congo put up really determined opposition to the U.N., the U.N. could stay in. In response, the President stated that Mr. Lodge was wrong to this extent— we were talking of one man forcing us out of the Congo; of Lumumba supported by the Soviets. There was no indication, the President stated, that the Congolese did not want U.N. support and the maintenance of order. Secretary Dillon reiterated that this was State's feeling about the matter. The situation that would be created by a U.N. withdrawal was altogether too ghastly to contemplate. (NSC Minutes, 8/18/60)

As reported, this statement clearly does not contain an order for the assassination of Lumumba. But the statement does indicate extreme Presidential concern focused on Lumumba: the President was so disturbed by the situation in the Congo that he was willing to risk a fight with the Soviet Union and he felt that Lumumba was the "one man" who was responsible for this situation, a man who did not represent the sentiment of the Congolese people in the President's estimation.

After reviewing NSC documents and being informed of Robert Johnson's testimony, Douglas Dillon stated his "opinion that it is most likely that the NSC meeting of August 18, 1960 is the meeting referred to by Mr. Johnson." (Dillon affidavit, 9/15/75, p. 2) However, Dillon testified that he did not "remember such a thing" as a "clearcut order" from the President for the assassination of Lumumba. (Dillon, 9/2/75, pp. 32-33) Dillon explained how he thought the President may have expressed himself about Lumumba:

> DILLON: It could have been in view of this feeling of everybody that Lumumba was [a] very difficult if not impossible person to deal with, and was dangerous to the peace and safety of the world, that the President expressed himself, we will have to do whatever is necessary to get rid of him. I don't know that I would have taken that as a clearcut order as Mr. Johnson apparently did. And I think perhaps others present may have interpreted it other ways. (Dillon, 9/2/75, pp. 32-33)
>
> Q: Did you ever hear the President make such a remark about Lumumba, let's get rid of him, or let's take action right away on this?
>
> DILLON: I don't remember that. But certainly this was the general feeling of Government at that time, and it wouldn't have been if the President hadn't agreed with it. (Dillon, 9/2/75, p. 33)

Dillon said that he would have thought that such a statement "was not a direct order to have an assassination." But he testified that it was "perfectly possible" that Allen Dulles would have translated such strong Presidential language about "getting rid of" Lumumba into authorization for an assassination effort. (Dillon, 9/2/75, pp. 33, 34–35):

> I think that Allen Dulles would have been quite responsive to what he considered implicit authorization, because he felt very strongly that we should not involve the President directly in things of this nature. And he was perfectly willing to take the responsibility personally that maybe some of his successors wouldn't have been. And so I think that this is a perfectly plausible thing, knowing Allen Dulles. (Dillon, 9/2/75, p. 34)

According to President Eisenhower's national security advisor, Gordon Gray, Dulles would have placed the CIA in a questionable position if he mounted an assassination operation on the basis of such "implicit authorization." Gray testified that the CIA would have been acting beyond its authority if it undertook an assassination operation without a specific order to do so. (Gray, 9/9/75, p. 18)

Marion Boggs, who attended the meeting of August 18, as Acting Executive Secretary of the NSC, stated after reviewing the Memorandum of Discussion at that Meeting:

> I recall the discussion at that meeting, but have no independent recollection of any statements or discussion not summarized in the memorandum. Specifically, I have no recollection of any statement, order or reference by the President (or anyone else present at the meeting) which could be interpreted as favoring action by the United States to bring about the assassination of Lumumba.[1] (Boggs affidavit, 10/10/75, pp. 1–2)

There are at least four possible explanations of the failure of NSC records to reveal whether the President ordered the assassination of Lumumba at one of the meetings where Robert Johnson was present.

First, an assassination order could have been issued but omitted from the records. Johnson testified that it was "very likely" that the Presidential statement he heard would have been handled by means of a euphemistic reference or by complete omission "rather than given as [a] * * * direct quotation" in the Memorandum of Discussion. (Johnson, 9/13/75, p. 14) NSC staff executives Marion Boggs and James Lay substantiated Johnson's testimony about the manner of handling such a statement in the records.

Second, as illustrated by Douglas Dillon's testimony, the President could have made a general statement about "getting rid of" Lumumba with the intent to convey to Allen Dulles implicit authorization for an assassination effort.

Third, despite general discussions about removing Lumumba, the President may not have intended to order the assassination of Lumumba even though Allen Dulles may have thought it had been authorized. The three White House staff members responsible to the President for national security affairs testified that there was no such order.[2]

---

[1] Boggs added:
"Based on my whole experience with the NSC, I would have considered it highly unusual if a matter of this nature had been referred to in a Council meeting where a number of persons with no 'need to know' were present." (Boggs affidavit, 10/10/75, p. 2.)
[2] See Section 7(b), *infra*, for a general treatment of the testimony of Gray, Goodpaster, and Eisenhower.

Fourth, whatever language he used, the President may have intended to authorize "contingency planning" for an assassination effort against Lumumba, while reserving decision on whether to authorize an actual assassination attempt. This interpretation can be supported by a strict construction of the decision of the Special Group on August 25, in response to the "strong feelings" of the President, not to rule out " 'consideration' of any particular kind of activity which might contribute to getting rid of Lumumba" and by the testimony of Bronson Tweedy that the assassination operation was limited to "exploratory activity." [1]

(iii) *Special Group Agrees to Consider Anything That Might Get Rid of Lumumba: August 25, 1960*

On August 25, 1960, five men [2] attended a meeting of the Special Group, the subcommittee of the National Security Council responsible for planning covert operations. Thomas Parrott, a CIA officer who served as Secretary to the Group, began the meeting by outlining the CIA operations that had been undertaken in "mounting an anti-Lumumba campaign in the Congo." (Special Group Minutes, 8/25/60) This campaign involved covert operations through certain labor groups and "the planned attempt * * * to arrange a vote of no confidence in Lumumba" in the Congolese Senate. (Special Group Minutes, 8/25/60) The outline of this campaign evoked the followed dialogue:

> The Group agreed that the action contemplated is very much in order. Mr. Gray commented, however, that his associates had expressed extremely strong feelings on the necessity for very straightforward action in this situation, and he wondered whether the plans as outlined were sufficient to accomplish this. Mr. Dulles replied that he had taken the comments referred to seriously and had every intention of proceeding as vigorously as the situation permits or requires, but added that he must necessarily put himself in a position of interpreting instructions of this kind within the bounds of necessity and capability. It was finally agreed that planning for the Congo would not necessarily rule out "consideration" of any particular kind of activity which might contribute to getting rid of Lumumba. (Special Group Minutes, 8/25/60, p. 1)

Both Gordon Gray and Thomas Parrott testified that the reference to Gray's "associates" was a euphemism for President Eisenhower which was employed to preserve "plausible deniability" by the President of discussion of covert operations memorialized in Special Group Minutes. (Gray, 7/9/75, p. 27; Parrott, 7/10/75, pp. 8-9)

The four living participants at the meeting have all stated that they do not recall any discussion of or planning for the assassination of Lumumba. Gray said that he did not consider the President's desire for "very straightforward action" to include "any thought in his mind of assassination." Parrott testified to the same effect, maintaining that he would have recorded a discussion of assassination in explicit terms in the Special Group Minutes if such a discussion had taken place. (Gray, 7/9/75, pp. 27, 32; Parrott, 7/10/75, pp. 25-26; Merchant

---

[1] This interpretation of the Special Group minutes must be posed against the testimony of other witnesses who construed the minutes as authorizing action, as well as planning an assassination operation. (Special Group Minutes, 8/25/60, p. 1; see Section 7(a)(ii) *infra*) See Section 4(h)(ii), *supra*, for a detailed discussion of Tweedy's testimony.

[2] The four standing members of the Special Group were in attendance: Allen Dulles, Director of Central Intelligence; Gordon Gray, Special Assistant to the President for National Security Affairs; Livingston Merchant, Undersecretary of State for Political Affairs; and John N. Irwin II, Assistant Secretary of Defense. Also in attendance was Thomas A. Parrott, Secretary to the Special Group.

affidavit, 9/8/75, p. 1; Irwin affidavit, 9/22/75, pp. 1-2) John N. Irwin II acknowledged, however, that while he did not have "any direct recollection of the substance of that meeting," the reference in the minutes to the planning for "getting rid of Lumumba" was "broad enough to cover a discussion of assassination." (Irwin affidavit, 9/22/75, p. 2)

Irwin's interpretation was shared by Douglas Dillon and Richard Bissell who were not participants at this Special Group meeting but were involved in the planning and policymaking for covert operations in the Congo during this period.

As a participant in NSC meetings of this period, Dillon said that he would read the Special Group minutes of August 25 to indicate that assassination was within the bounds of the kind of activity that might be used to "get rid of" Lumumba. Dillon noted that the reference in the minutes to Dulles' statement that he "had taken the comments referred to seriously" probably pointed to the President's statement at the NSC meeting on August 18. (Dillon, 9/2/75, pp. 39–42) When asked whether the CIA would have the authority to mount an assassination effort against Lumumba on the basis of the discussion at the Special Group, Dillon said:

> They would certainly have the authority to plan. It is a close question whether this would be enough to actually go ahead with it. But certainly the way this thing worked, as far as I know, they didn't do anything just on their own. I think they would have checked back at least with the senior people in the State Department or the Defense Department. (Dillon, 9/2/75, p. 43)

Dillon said that if the CIA checked with the State Department, it might have done so in a way that would not appear on any record. (Dillon, 9/2/75, p. 43) Dillon added that "to protect the President as the public representative of the U.S. from any bad publicity in connection with this," Allen Dulles "wouldn't return to the President" to seek further approval if an assassination operation were mounted. (Dillon, 9/2/75, pp. 42–43)

Bissell stated that in his opinion the language of the August 25 Special Group Minutes indicated that the assassination of Lumumba was part of a general NSC strategy and was within the CIA's mandate for removing Lumumba from the political scene. (Bissell, 9/10/75, pp. 29, 32) He added:

> The Agency had put a top priority, probably, on a range of different methods of getting rid of Lumumba in the sense of either destroying him physically, incapacitating him, or eliminating his political influence. (Bissell, 9/10/75, p. 29)

Bissell pointed to the Special Group Minutes of August 25 as a "prime example" of the circumlocutious manner in which a topic like assassination would be discussed by high government officials:

> BISSELL: When you use the language that no particular means were ruled out, that is obviously what it meant, and it meant that to everybody in the room. * * * Meant that if it had to be assassination, that that was a permissible means. You don't use language of that kind except to mean in effect, the Director is being told, get rid of the guy, and if you have to use extreme means up to and including assassination, go ahead. (Bissell, 9/10/75, pp. 32–33)

Bissell added that this message was, "in effect," being given to Dulles by the President through his representative, Gordon Gray. (Bissell, 9/10/75, p. 33)

(iv) Dulles Reminded by Gray of "Top-Level Feeling" That "Vigorous Action" Was Necessary in the Congo: September 7–8, 1960

The Memorandum of Discussion from the NSC meeting of September 7, 1960—the only other meeting at which Johnson could have heard the President's statement—records only a brief, general discussion of developments in the Congo. As part of Allen Dulles' introductory intelligence briefing on world events, the Memorandum contained his remarks on the situation in the Congo following Kasavubu's dismissal of Lumumba from the government. Neither the length nor the substance of the record of this discussion indicates that Lumumba's role in the Congo received the same intense consideration as the NSC had given it on August 18.[1] There is no record of any statement by the President during the September 7 discussion. (NSC Minutes, 9/7/60, pp. 4–5)

In the course of Dulles' briefing, he expressed his continuing concern over the amount of personnel and equipment that was being sent to the Congo by the Soviet Union, primarily to aid Lumumba. Dulles concluded this part of his briefing with an observation that demonstrated that Lumumba's dismissal from the government had not lessened the extent to which he was regarded at the NSC as a potent political threat in any power struggle in the Congo:

Mr. Dulles stated that Lumumba always seemed to come out on top in each of these struggles. (NSC Minutes, 9/7/60, p. 5)

At a Special Group Meeting the next day, Gordon Gray made a pointed reminder to Allen Dulles of the President's concern about the Congo:

Mr. Gray said that he hoped that Agency people in the field are fully aware of the top-level feeling in Washington that vigorous action would not be amiss. (Special Group Minutes, 9/8/60)

(v) Dulles Tells NSC That Lumumba Remains a Grave Danger Until "Disposed of": September 21, 1960

In the course of his intelligence briefing to the NSC on September 21, 1960, Allen Dulles stressed the danger of Soviet influence in the Congo. Despite the fact that Lumumba had been deposed as Premier and was in U.N. custody, Dulles continued to regard him as a threat, especially in light of reports of an impending reconciliation between Lumumba and the post-coup Congolese government. In the presence of the President, Dulles concluded:

Mobutu appeared to be the effective power in the Congo for the moment but Lumumba was not yet disposed of and remained a grave danger as long as he was not disposed of. (NSC Minutes, 9/21/60)

Three days after this NSC meeting, Dulles sent a personal cable to the Station Officer in Leopoldville which included the following message:

WE WISH GIVE EVERY POSSIBLE SUPPORT IN ELIMINATING LUMUMBA FROM ANY POSSIBILITY RESUMING GOVERNMENTAL POSITION OR IF HE FAILS IN LEOP[OLDVILLE], SETTING HIMSELF IN STANLEYVILLE OR ELSEWHERE (CIA Cable, Dulles, Tweedy to Leopoldville, 9/24/60)

---

[1] The NSC minutes of the meeting of September 7 deal with the discussion of the Congo in two pages. (NSC Minutes, 9/7/60, pp. 4–5). By comparison, the August 18 meeting required an extraordinarily lengthy (fifteen pages) summary of discussion on the Congo and related policy problems in Africa, indicating that this topic was the focal point of the meeting. (NSC Minutes, 8/18/60, pp. 1–15)

On September 26, Joseph Scheider, under assignment from CIA Headquarters, arrived in Leopoldville, provided the Station Officer with poisons, conveyed Headquarters' instruction to assassinate Lumumba, and assured him that there was Presidential authorization for this mission.[1]

Marion Boggs, the NSC Deputy Executive Secretary, who wrote the Memorandum of Discussion of September 21, did not interpret Dulles' remark as referring to assassination:

> I have examined the memorandum (which I prepared) summarizing the discussion of the Congo at the September 21, 1960 meeting of the NSC. I recall the discussion and believe it is accurately and adequately summarized in the memorandum. I have no recollection of any discussion of a possible assassination of Lumumba at this meeting. With specific reference to the statement of the Director of Central Intelligence * * * I believe this is almost a literal rendering of what Mr. Dulles said. My own interpretation of this statement * * * was that Mr. Dulles was speaking in the context of efforts being made within the Congolese government to force Lumumba from power. I did not interpret it as referring to assassination.[2] (Boggs affidavit, 10/10/75, pp. 2–3)

Boggs, however, was not in a position to analyze Dulles' remark in the context of the actual planning for covert operations that took place during this period because Boggs was not privy to most such discussions. (Boggs affidavit, 10/10/75, p. 2)

Dillon, who attended this NSC meeting as Acting Secretary of State, did not recall the discussion. Dillon said that the minutes "could mean that" assassination would have been one acceptable means of "disposing of" Lumumba, although he felt that "getting him out [of the Congo] or locking him up" would have been a preferable disposition of Lumumba at that point since he was already out of office. (Dillon, 9/2/75, pp. 47–48)[3] When reminded of the fact that Lumumba's movement and communications were not restricted by the U.N. force and that the Congolese army continued to seek his arrest after the September 21 meeting, Dillon acknowledged that during this period Lumumba continued to be viewed by the United States as a potential threat and a volatile force in the Congo:

> * * *. He had this tremendous ability to stir up a crowd or a group. And if he could have gotten out and started to talk to a battalion of the Congolese Army, he probably would have had them in the palm of his hand in five minutes. (Dillon, 9/20/75, p. 49)

Irwin, who attended the NSC meeting as Assistant Secretary of Defense, stated that although he had no recollection of the discussion, the language of these minutes, like that of the August 25 minutes, was "broad enough to cover a discussion of assassination." (Irwin affidavit, 9/22/75, p. 2)

Bissell testified that, based upon his understanding of the policy of the NSC toward Lumumba even after Lumumba was in U.N. custody, he would read the minutes of September 21 to indicate that assassination was contemplated "as one possible means" of "disposing of" Lumumba [4] (Bissell, 9/10/75, p. 70)

---

[1] See Sections 4(e)–4(f), *supra*.
[2] NSC Executive Secretary James Lay, who was also present at the meeting of September 21, 1960, stated: "I cannot recall whether there was any discussion of assassinating Lumumba at any NSC meetings." (Lay affidavit, 9/8/75, p. 1)
[3] See Section 3, *supra*, for discussion of CIA cable traffic indicating that Lumumba continued to be regarded as capable of taking over the government after he was deposed and that pressure to "eliminate" him did not cease until his death.
[4] Bissell was not present at the NSC meeting. (NSC Minutes, 9/21/60)

Bissell's opinion stands in opposition to Gordon Gray's testimony. Gray stated that he could not remember the NSC discussion, but he interpreted the reference to "disposing of" Lumumba as "in the same category as 'get rid of', 'eliminate'." (Gray, 7/9/75, p. 59) He said: "It was not my impression that we had in mind the assassination of Lumumba.") (Gray, 7/9/75, p. 60)[1]

(b) Testimony of Eisenhower White House Officials

Gordon Gray and Andrew Goodpaster—the two members of President Eisenhower's staff who were responsible for national security affairs—both testified that they had no knowledge of any Presidential consideration of assassination during their tenure.[2]

Gray served as Special Assistant to the President for National Security Affairs, in which capacity he coordinated the National Security Council and represented the President at Special Group meetings. Gray testified that, despite the prevalent attitude of hostility toward Lumumba in the Administration, he did not recall President Eisenhower "ever saying anything that contemplated killing Lumumba." (Gray, 7/9/75, p. 28)[3] When asked to interpret phrases such as "getting rid of" or "disposing of" Lumumba, from the minutes of particular NSC and Special Group Meetings, Gray stated:

> It is the intent of the user of the expression or the phrase that is controlling and there may well have been in the Central Intelligence Agency plans and/or discussions of assassinations, but * * * at the level of the Forty Committee [Special Group] or a higher level than that, the National Security Council, there was no active discussion in any way planning assassination.
> * * * I agree that assassination could have been on the minds of some people when they used these words 'eliminate' or 'get rid of' * * * I am just trying to say it was not seriously considered as a program of action by the President or even the Forty [Special] Group. (Gray, 7/9/75, pp. 16–17)

Goodpaster, the White House Staff Secretary to President Eisenhower, said that he and Gray were the "principal channels" between the President and the CIA, outside of NSC meetings. Goodpaster was responsible for "handling with the President all matters of day-to-day operations in the general fields of international affairs and security affairs." He regularly attended NSC meetings and was listed among the participants at the NSC meetings of August 18, 1960 and September 21, 1960. (Goodpaster, 7/17/75, pp. 3, 4)

When asked if he ever heard about any assassination effort during the Eisenhower Administration, Goodpaster replied unequivocally:

> * * * at no time and in no way did I ever know of or hear about any proposal, any mention of such an activity. * * * [I]t is my belief that had such a thing been raised with the President other than in my presence, I would have known about it, and * * * it would have been a matter of such significance and sensitivity that I am confident that * * * I would have recalled it had such a thing happened. (Goodpaster, 7/17/75, p. 5)

---

[1] John Eisenhower, the President's son, who attended the NSC meeting as Assistant White House Staff Secretary, said that he had no "direct recollection" of the discussion but he found the minutes of the meeting consonant with his "recollection of the atmosphere" at the time: "The U.S. position was very much anti-Lumumba." He said:
"I would not conjecture that the words 'disposed of' meant an assassination, if for no other reason than if I had something as nasty as this to plot, I wouldn't do it in front of 21 people * * * the number present [at] the meeting." (Eisenhower, 7/18/75, pp. 9–10)
[2] For a more detailed treatment of the testimony of Gray, Goodpaster, and other Eisenhower Administration officials on the general question of discussion of assassination by the President, see Part 3, Section B(3)(a), *infra*.
[3] At the outset of his testimony on the subject, Gordon Gray acknowledged that he did not have a clear, independent recollection of Lumumba's role in the Congo. (Gray, 7/9/75, pp. 25–26)

John Eisenhower, the President's son who served under Goodpaster as Assistant White House Staff Secretary, stated that the use of assassination was contrary to the President's philosophy that "no man is indispensable." As a participant at NSC meetings who frequently attended Oval Office discussions relating to national security affairs, John Eisenhower testified that nothing that came to his attention in his experience at the White House "can be construed in my mind in the remotest way to mean any Presidential knowledge of our concurrence in any assassination plots or plans." (Eisenhower, 7/18/75, pp. 4, 14)

Each of the other Eisenhower Administration officials who was active in the Special Group in late 1960—Assistant Secretary of Defense John N. Irwin II, Undersecretary of State for Political Affairs Livingston Merchant, and Deputy Secretary of Defense James Douglas—stated that he did not recall any discussion about assassinating Lumumba. (Irwin affidavit, 9/22/75; Merchant affidavit, 9/8/75; Douglas affidavit, 9/5/75)[1]

Even if the documentary record is read to indicate that there was consideration of assassination at high-level policy meetings, there is no evidence that any officials of the Eisenhower Administration outside the CIA were aware of the specific operational details of the plot to poison Lumumba.[2]

(c) Bissell's Assumptions About Authorization by President Eisenhower and Allen Dulles

Richard Bissell's testimony on the question of high-level authorization for the effort to assassinate Lumumba is problematic. Bissell stated that he had no direct recollection of receiving such authorization and that all of his testimony on this subject "has to be described as inference." (Bissell, 9/10/75, p. 48)

Bissell began his testimony on the subject by asserting that on his own initiative he instructed Michael Mulroney to plan the assassination of Lumumba. (Bissell, 6/11/75, pp. 54–55)[3] Nevertheless, Bissell's conclusion—based on his inferences from the totality of circumstances relating to the entire assassination effort against Lumumba—was that an assassination attempt had been authorized at the highest levels of the government. (Bissell, 9/10/75, pp. 32–33, 47–49, 60–62, 65)

---

[1] Douglas Dillon testified that the subject of assassination never arose in his "direct dealings with either President Eisenhower or President Kennedy." (Dillon, 9/2/75, p. 22) He was asked by a member of the Committee, however, to speculate upon the general philosophical approach that Presidents Eisenhower and Kennedy would have taken to decision-making on the question of using assassination as a tool of foreign policy:

"Senator HART (Colorado): I would invite your speculation at this point as a sub-Cabinet officer under President Eisenhower, and as a Cabinet Officer under President Kennedy, I think the Committee would be interested in your view as to the attitude of each of them toward this subject, that is to say, the elimination, violent elimination of foreign leaders.

"DILLON: Well, that is a difficult thing to speculate on in a totally different atmosphere. But I think probably both of them would have approached it in a very pragmatic way, most likely, simply weighed the process and consequence rather than in a way that was primarily of a moral principle. That is what would probably have been their attitude in a few cases. Certainly the idea that this was going to be a policy of the U.S., generally both of them were very much opposed to it." (Dillon, 9/2/75, pp. 22–23)

Dillon served as Undersecretary of State in the Eisenhower Administration and as Secretary of the Treasury under Kennedy.

[2] Although several CIA officers involved in the PROP operation to poison Lumumba testified that the operation was within the scope of actions authorized by the NSC and Special Group, there is no testimony that any official of the Eisenhower Administration outside the CIA had specific knowledge of the operational planning and progress.

[3] See Sections 5(a)(i) and 5(a)(ii), *supra*.

As discussed above, Bissell testified that the minutes of meetings of the Special Group on August 25, 1960 and the NSC on September 21, 1960 indicate that assassination was contemplated at the Presidential level as one acceptable means of "getting rid of Lumumba." [1]

There was "no question," according to Bissell, that the cable from Allen Dulles to the Station Officer in Leopoldville on August 26—which called for Lumumba's "removal" and authorized Hedgman to take action without consulting Headquarters if time did not permit—was a direct outgrowth of the Special Group meeting Dulles had attended the previous day. (Bissell, 9/10/75, pp. 31–32) Bissell was "almost certain" that he had been informed about the Dulles cable shortly after its transmission. (Bissell, 9/10/75, p. 12) Bissell said that he assumed that assassination was one of the means of removing Lumumba from the scene that was contemplated by Dulles' cable, despite the fact that it was not explicitly mentioned. (Bissell, 9/10/75, p. 32):

> It is my belief on the basis of the cable drafted by Allen Dulles that he regarded the action of the Special Group as authorizing implementation [of an assassination] if favorable circumstances presented themselves, if it could be done covertly. (Bissell, 9/10/75, pp. 64–65) [2]

Dulles' cable signaled to Bissell that there was Presidential authorization for him to order action to assassinate Lumumba. (Bissell, 9/10/75, pp. 61–62):

> Q: Did Mr. Dulles tell you that President Eisenhower wanted Lumumba killed?
> Mr. BISSELL: I am sure he didn't.
> Q: Did he ever tell you even circumlocutiously through this kind of cable?
> Mr. BISSELL: Yes, I think his cable says it in effect. (Bissell, 9/10/75, p. 33)

As for discussions with Dulles about the source of authorization for an assassination effort against Lumumba, Bissell stated:

> I think it is probably unlikely that Allen Dulles would have said either the President or President Eisenhower even to me. I think he would have said, this is authorized in the highest quarters, and I would have known what he meant. (Bissell, 9/10/75, p. 48)

When asked if he had sufficient authority to move beyond the consideration or planning of assassination to order implementation of a plan, Bissell said, "I probably did think I had [such] authority." (Bissell, 9/10/75, pp. 61–62)

When informed of the Station Officer's testimony about the instructions he received from Scheider, Bissell said that despite his absence of a specific recollection:

> I would strongly infer in this case that such an authorization did pass through me, as it were, if Joe Scheider gave that firm instruction to the Station Officer. (Bissell, 9/10/75, p. 40) [3]

Bissell said that the DCI would have been the source of this authorization. (Bissell, 9/10/75, p. 40)

---

[1] See Sections 7(a)(iii) and 7(a)(v).
[2] Joseph Scheider also testified that, in the context of the Dulles cable, "removal" would signify to someone familiar with "intelligence terminology" a "range of things, from just getting him out of office to killing him." (Scheider, 10/9/75, pp. 45–48)
[3] See Section 7(d), *infra*, for Scheider's testimony on his impression that Bissell had authorized his assignment to the Congo.

Bissell did not recall being informed by Scheider that Scheider had represented to the Station Officer that Lumumba's assassination had been authorized by the President. But he said that assuming he had instructed Scheider to carry poison to the Congo, "there was no possibility" that he would have issued such an instruction without authorization from Dulles. Likewise Bissell said he "probably did" tell Scheider that the mission had the approval of President Eisenhower. (Bissell, 9/10/75, pp. 46, 47) This led to Bissell's conclusion that if, in fact, the testimony of the Station Officer about Scheider's actions was accurate, then Scheider's actions were fully authorized.[1] Bissell further stated:

> Knowing Mr. Scheider, it is literally inconceivable to me that we would have acted beyond his instructions. (Bissell, 9/10/75, p. 41)

Bronson Tweedy functioned as a conduit between Bissell and Scheider for instructions relating to the PROP operation. Scheider's impression about the extent of authorization for the assassination operation stemmed ultimately from his conversation with Bissell which was referred to by Tweedy during the meeting in which Scheider was ordered to the Congo.[2]

Tweedy testified that Bissell never referred to the President as the source of authorization for the assassination operation. Tweedy said, however, that the "impression" he derived from his meetings with Bissell and from the Dulles cable of August 26 was that the Agency had authorization at the highest level of the government. But Tweedy found it "very difficult * * * to judge whether the President *per se* had been in contact with the Agency" because he was not involved in decisionmaking at "the policy level." (Tweedy, 10/9/75 I, pp. 9, 10)

Concerning the assignment of Mulroney to "plan and prepare for" the assassination of Lumumba, Bissell testified that "it was my own idea to give Mulroney this assignment." But he said that this assignment was made only after an assassination mission against Lumumba already had authorization above the level of DDP. (Bissell, 9/10/75, pp. 24, 50; see also pp. 32–33, 47–48, 60–62)

(d) *The Impression of Scheider and Hedgman That the Assassination Operation had Presidential Authorization*

The Station Officer and Scheider shared the impression that the President authorized an assassination effort against Lumumba.[3] This impression was derived solely from conversations Scheider had with Bissell and Tweedy. Thus, the testimony of Scheider and the Station Officer does not, in itself, establish Presidential authorization. Neither Scheider nor the Station Officer had first-hand knowledge of any statements by Allen Dulles about Presidential authorization—statements which Bissell assumed he had heard, although he had no specific recollection. Moreover, Scheider may have misconstrued Bissell's reference to "highest authority."

---

[1] Q: In light of the entire atmosphere at the Agency and the policy at the Agency at the time Mr. Scheider's representation to the Station Officer that the President had instructed the DCI to carry out this mission would not have been beyond the pale of Mr. Scheider's authority, at that point?
BISSELL. No, it would not. (Bissell, 9/10/75, p. 65)
[2] See Section 7(d), *infra*.
[3] See Section 4(f), *infra*, for additional testimony of the Station Officer and Scheider on this issue.

Station Officer Hedgman testified that Scheider indicated to him that President Eisenhower had authorized the assassination of Lumumba by an order to Dulles. Hedgman stated that Scheider initially conveyed this account of Presidential authorization when Hedgman asked him about the source of authority for the Lumumba assassination assignment. (Hedgman, 8/21/75, pp. 30-34)

Hedgman was under the clear impression that the President was the ultimate source of the assassination operation:

> Q: Your understanding then was that these instructions were instructions coming to you from the office of the President?
> HEDGMAN: That's correct.
> Q: Or that he had instructed the Agency, and they were passed on to you?
> HEDGMAN: That's right.
> Q: You are not the least unclear whether * * * the President's name had been invoked in some fashion?
> HEDGMAN: At the time, I certainly felt that I was under instructions from the President, yes. (Hedgman, 8/21/75, pp 32-33)

Hedgman cautioned:

> [A]fter fifteen years, I cannot be 100 percent certain, but I have always, since that date, had the impression in my mind that these orders had come from the President. (Hedgman, 8/21/75, p. 34; *accord*, p. 102)

Hedgman testified that he was under the impression that a "policy decision" had been made—that assassination had been "approved" as "one means" of eliminating Lumumba as a political threat (Hedgman 8/21/75, p. 52):

> I thought the policy decision had been made in the White House, not in the Agency, and that the Agency had been selected as the Executive agent if you will, to carry out a political decision. (Hedgman, 8/21/75, p. 52.)

Although Hedgman assumed that the President had not personally selected the means of assassination, he testified that he was under the impression that the President had authorized the CIA to proceed to take action:

> HEDGMAN: * * * I doubt that I thought the President had said, you use this system. But my understanding is the President had made a decision that an act should take place, but then put that into the hands of the Agency to carry out his decision.
> Q: Whatever that act was to be, it was clearly to be assassination or the death of the foreign political leader?
> HEDGMAN: Yes. (Hedgman, 8/21/75, p. 104)

The Station Officer's impression about Presidential authorization stemmed from his conversations with Scheider in the Congo and from his reading of the cable traffic from CIA Headquarters which, in fact, never explicitly mentioned the President although it referred to "high quarters." [1]

Joseph Scheider's testimony about these discussions is compatible with Hedgman's account. (Scheider, 10/7/75, pp. 107-108) Despite the fact that he did not recall mentioning the President by name to Hedgman, Scheider believed that he left Hedgman with the impression that there was Presidential authorization for an assassination attempt against Lumumba. (Scheider, 10/7/75, pp. 103-104, 110; 10/9/75, p. 17) However, Scheider made it clear that the basis for his own knowledge about Presidential authorization for the assassination

---

[1] See Section 7(c) for Bissell's interpretation of the reference to "high quarters" in the Dulles cable of August 26, 1960.

of Lumumba were the statements to him by Bissell, Tweedy, and Tweedy's Deputy. (Scheider, 10/9/75, pp. 10;/7/75, p. 90)

Scheider testified that in the late summer or early fall of 1960, Richard Bissell asked him to make all the preparations necessary for toxic materials to be ready on short notice for use in the assassination of an unspecified African leader, "in case the decision was to go ahead." [1] (Scheider, 10/7/75, pp. 51–55; 10/9/75, p. 8) Scheider had a specific recollection that Bissell told him that "he had direction from the highest authority" for undertaking an assassination operation. (Scheider, 10/7/75, pp. 51–52, 58):

> SCHEIDER: The memory I carry was that he indicated that he had the highest authority for getting into that kind of an operation.
> Q: Getting into an operation which would result in the death or incapacitation of a foreign leader?
> SCHEIDER: Yes, yes, yes. (Scheider, 10/7/75, p. 52)

Scheider acknowledged the possibility that he "may have been wrong" in his assumptions of Presidential authorization which he based on Bissell's words:

> The specific words, as best I can recollect them, [were] "on the highest authority." (Scheider, 10/9/75, p. 11).

Scheider testified that there was a basis of experience for his assumption that "highest authority" signified the President. He said he "had heard it before" at the CIA and had always interpreted it to denote the President. (Scheider, 10/9/75, p. 51) Likewise, Bronson Tweedy testified that " 'highest authority' was a term that we used in the Agency and it was generally recognized as meaning 'the President'." (Tweedy, 10/9/75 II, p. 20)

According to Scheider, Allen Dulles would have approved the assassination operation before Bissell broached the subject with other CIA officers:

> I would have assumed that Bissell would never have told me that it was to be undertaken under the highest authority until his line ran through Dulles and until Dulles was in on it. (Scheider, 10/7/75, p. 76)

Scheider said that he left the meeting with Bissell under the impression that the Presidential authorization extended only to making preparations to carry out an assassination mission and that the implementation of such a plan might require a separate "go ahead." (Scheider, 10/7/75, pp. 53, 56–8) As far as Scheider was concerned, the "go ahead" on the assassination operation was given to him shortly thereafter by Tweedy and his Deputy.[2] When they instructed him on his Congo trip, Scheider said Tweedy and his Deputy "referred to the previous conversation I had with Bissell" and they conveyed to Scheider the impression that Bissell "felt the operation had Presidential authority." (Scheider, 10/7/75, pp. 65, 69, 71; 10/9/75, p. 13)[3] Scheider interpreted the statements by Tweedy and his Deputy to mean that Bissell's reference to "highest authority" for the operation had carried over from planning to the implementation stage. (Scheider, 10/7/75, p. 90)

---

[1] See section 4(b), *infra*, for a full treatment of Scheider's meetings with Bissell and his preparation of toxic biological materials and medical paraphernalia pursuant to Bissell's directive.

[2] See Section 4(c), *infra*, for a detailed account of the testimony about the meeting of Tweedy, his Deputy, and Scheider.

[3] Tweedy was unable to shed much light on the discussion of authorization at his meeting with Scheider:
"I do not recall that Scheider and I ever discussed higher authority and approval. I do not say that it did not occur." (Tweedy, 10/9/75 I, p. 65)

Scheider's impression that there was Presidential authorization for the assassination operation clearly had a powerful influence on the Station Officer's attitude toward undertaking such an assignment.

Hedgman had severe doubts about the wisdom of a policy of assassination in the Congo. At the conclusion of his testimony about the assassination plot, he was asked to give a general characterization of the advisability of the plot and the tenor of the times in which it took place. His response indicated that although he was willing to carry out what he considered a duly authorized order, he was not convinced of the necessity of assassinating Lumumba:

> I looked upon the Agency as an executive arm of the Presidency * * *. Therefore, I suppose I thought that it was an order issued in due form from an authorized authority.
>
> On the other hand, I looked at it as a kind of operation that I could do without, that I thought that probably the Agency and the U.S. government could get along without. I didn't regard Lumumba as the kind of person who was going to bring on World War III.
>
> I might have had a somewhat different attitude if I thought that one man could bring on World War III and result in the deaths of millions of people or something, but I didn't see him in that light. I saw his as a danger to the political position of the United States in Africa, but nothing more than that. (Hedgman, 8/21/75, pp. 110–111)

B. CUBA

The facts with respect to Cuba are divided into three broad sections.
The first describes the plots against Fidel Castro's life without addressing the question of authorization.

The second deals with whether or not the successive Directors of Central Intelligence, Allen Dulles and John McCone, authorized or knew about the various plots. (Although we have separated the evidence relating to the DCI's from that relating to other high administration officials, it is important to remember that the Director of Central Intelligence is the principal advisor to the President on intelligence matters and a member of major administrative policy-making councils, as well as head of the Central Intelligence Agency.)

The third section covers the evidence concerning whether or not other high officials—including the various Presidents—authorized or knew about the plots. This section also considers the evidence relating to whether or not the CIA officials involved believed the plots to be consistent with the general policy objectives of the various administrations even if those officials had no personal knowledge as to whether the plots were or were not specifically authorized by higher authority.

1. THE ASSASSINATION PLOTS

We have found concrete evidence of at least eight plots involving the CIA to assassinate Fidel Castro from 1960 to 1965.[1] Although some of the assassination plots did not advance beyond the stage of planning and preparation, one plot, involving the use of underworld figures, reportedly twice progressed to the point of sending poison pills to Cuba and dispatching teams to commit the deed. Another plot involved furnishing weapons and other assassination devices to a Cuban dissident. The proposed assassination devices ran the gamut from high-powered rifles to poison pills, poison pens, deadly bacterial powders, and other devices which strain the imagination.

---

[1] In August 1975, Fidel Castro gave Senator George McGovern a list of twenty-four alleged attempts to assassinate him in which Castro claimed the CIA had been involved. The Committee forwarded this list to the CIA and requested it to respond to those allegations. The CIA's fourteen-page response concluded:
"In summary, of the * * * incidents described in Castro's report, the files reviewed indicate that CIA had no involvement in fifteen of the cases: i.e., never had any contact with the individuals mentoned or was not in contact with them at the time of the alleged incidents. In the remaining nine cases, CIA had operational relationships with some of the individuals mentioned but not for the purpose of assassination. * * * Of the cases reviewed, nothing has been found to substantiate the charges that CIA directed its agents to assassinate Castro.
The Committee has found no evidence that the CIA was involved in the attempts on Castro's life enumerated in the allegations that Castro gave to Senator McGovern. The CIA's involvement in other plots against Castro and the top figures in his Government are set forth below.

The most ironic of these plots took place on November 22, 1963—the very day that President Kennedy was shot in Dallas—when a CIA official offered a poison pen to a Cuban for use against Castro while at the same time an emissary from President Kennedy was meeting with Castro to explore the possibility of improved relations.

The following narrative sets forth the facts of assassination plots against Castro as established before the Committee by witnesses and documentary evidence. The question of the level and degree of authorization of the plots is considered in the sections that follow.

(a) *Plots: Early 1960*

(i) *Plots to Destroy Castro's Public Image*

Efforts against Castro did not begin with assassination attempts.

From March through August 1960, during the last year of the Eisenhower Administration, the CIA considered plans to undermine Castro's charismatic appeal by sabotaging his speeches. According to the 1967 Report of the CIA's Inspector General, an official in the Technical Services Division (TSD) recalled discussing a scheme to spray Castro's broadcasting studio with a chemical which produced effects similar to LSD, but the scheme was rejected because the chemical was unreliable. During this period, TSD impregnated a box of cigars with a chemical which produced temporary disorientation, hoping to induce Castro to smoke one of the cigars before delivering a speech. The Inspector General also reported a plan to destroy Castro's image as "The Beard" by dusting his shoes with thallium salts, a strong depilatory that would cause his beard to fall out. The depilatory was to be administered during a trip outside Cuba, when it was anticipated Castro would leave his shoes outside the door of his hotel room to be shined. TSD procured the chemical and tested it on animals, but apparently abandoned the scheme because Castro cancelled his trip. (I.G. Report, pp. 10–13)

(ii) *Accident Plot*

The first action against the life of a Cuban leader sponsored by the CIA of which the Committee is aware took place in 1960. A Cuban who had volunteered to assist the CIA in gathering intelligence informed his case officer in Havana that he would probably be in contact with Raul Castro. (Memo to Inspector General, 1/17/75) CIA Headquarters and field stations were requested to inform the Havana Station of any intelligence needs that the Cuban might fulfill. The case officer testified that he and the Cuban contemplated only acquiring intelligence information and that assassination was not proposed by them.[1]

The cable from the Havana Station was received at Headquarters on the night of July 20. The duty officer, who was summoned to Headquarters from his home, contacted Tracy Barnes, Deputy to Richard Bissell, CIA's Deputy Director for Plans and the man in charge of

---

[1] A cable to Headquarters requesting any intelligence needs supports this account.

CIA's covert action directorate. The duty officer also contacted J. C. King, Chief of the Western Hemisphere Division within the Directorate for Plans.[1]

Following their instructions, he sent a cable to the Havana Station early in the morning of July 21, stating: "Possible removal top three leaders is receiving serious consideration at HQS." The cable inquired whether the Cuban was sufficiently motivated to risk "arranging an accident" involving Raul Castro and advised that the station could "at discretion contact subject to determine willingness to cooperate and his suggestions on details". Ten thousand dollars was authorized as payment "after successful completion," but no advance payment was permitted because of the possibility that the Cuban was a double agent. According to the case officer, this cable represented "quite a departure from the conventional activities we'd been asked to handle." (Case Officer interview, 8/4/75, p. 2)[2]

The case officer contacted the Cuban and told him of the proposal. The case officer avoided the word "assassinate" but made it clear that the CIA contemplated an "accident to neutralize this leader's [Raul's] influence." (Case Officer interview, 8/4/75, p. 2) After being assured that his sons would be given a college education in the event of his death, the Cuban agreed to take a "calculated risk," limited to possibilities that might pass as accidental. (Cable, Havana to Director, 7/22/60)

Immediately after returning to the station the case officer was told that a cable had just arrived stating: "Do not pursue ref. Would like to drop matter." (Cable, Director to Havana, 7/22/60; Memo to I. G., 1/17/75) This cable was signed by Tracy Barnes.

It was, of course, too late to "drop the matter" since the Cuban had already left to contact Raul Castro. When the Cuban returned, he told the case officer that he had not had an opportunity to arrange an accident.

(iii) Poison Cigars

A notation in the records of the Operations Division, CIA's Office of Medical Services, indicates that on August 16, 1960, an official was given a box of Castro's favorite cigars with instructions to treat them with lethal poison. (I. G. Report, p. 21) The cigars were contaminated with a botulinum toxin so potent that a person would die after putting one in his mouth. (I. G. Report, p. 22) The official reported that the cigars were ready on October 7, 1960; TSD notes indicate that they were delivered to an unidentified person on February 13, 1961. (I. G. Report, p. 22) The record does not disclose whether an attempt was made to pass the cigars to Castro.

---

[1] The duty officer testified that he must have spoken with King because he would not otherwise have signed the cable "by direction, J. C. King." (Duty Officer, 8/11/75, p. 16) He also would "very definitely" have read the cable to Barnes before sending it, because "Barnes was the man to whom we went . . . for our authority and for work connected with the [Cuban] project." (Duty Officer, pp. 4, 25) Since King at that time was giving only "nominal attention" to Cuban affairs, the officer concluded that a proposal of the gravity of an assassination could only have "come from Mr. Barnes". (Duty Officer, 8/11/75, p. 24)
[2] The duty officer remembered the cable and some of the surrounding facts for precisely that reason: "[I]t was an unusual type of [cable], and I say this because I can remember it 15 years later." (Duty Officer, 8/11/75, p 14.) The case officer recalled that when he saw the cable, he "swallowed hard." (Case Officer interview, 8/4/75, p. 3)

(b) Use of Underworld Figures—Phase I (Pre-Bay of Pigs)

(i) The Initial Plan

In August 1960, the CIA took steps to enlist members of the criminal underworld with gambling syndicate contacts to aid in assassinating Castro. The origin of the plot is uncertain. According to the 1967 Inspector General's Report,

> Bissell recalls that the idea originated with J. C. King, then Chief of W. H. Division, although King now recalls having only had limited knowledge of such a plan and at a much later date—about mid-1962. (I. G. Report, p. 14)

Bissell testified that:

> I remember a conversation which I would have put in early autumn or late summer between myself and Colonel Edwards [Director of the Office of Security], and I have some dim recollection of some earlier conversation I had had with Colonel J. C. King, Chief of the Western Hemisphere Division, and the subject matter of both of those conversations was a capability to eliminate Castro if such action should be decided upon. (Bissell, 6/9/75, p. 19)

The earliest concrete evidence of the operation is a conversation between DDP Bissell and Colonel Sheffield Edwards, Director of the Office of Security.[1] Edwards recalled that Bissell asked him to locate someone who could assassinate Castro. (Edwards, 5/30/75, pp. 2–3) Bissell confirmed that he requested Edwards to find someone to assassinate Castro and believed that Edwards raised the idea of contacting members of a gambling syndicate operating in Cuba.[2] (Bissell, 6/9/75, pp. 71–73)

Edwards assigned the mission to the Chief of the Operational Support Division of the Office of Security. The Support Chief recalled that Edwards had said that he and Bissell were looking for someone to "eliminate" or "assassinate" Castro. (Operational Support Chief, hereinafter "O.C.", 5/30/75, pp. 6–8, 95–96)[3]

Edwards and the Support Chief decided to rely on Robert A. Maheu to recruit someone "tough enough" to handle the job. (O.C., 5/30/75, p. 8) Maheu was an ex-FBI agent who had entered into a career as a private investigator in 1954. A former FBI associate of Maheu's was employed in the CIA's Office of Security and had arranged for the CIA to use Maheu in several sensitive covert operations in which "he didn't want to have an Agency person or a government person get caught."[4] (O.C., 5/30/75, p. 158) Maheu was initially paid a monthly

---

[1] The Inspector General's Report placed the conversation between Edwards and Bissell in August 1960. Bissell testified that he would not have remembered the exact month without having been shown the Inspector General's Report, but that "I would have remembered initial conversations early in the autumn of 1960" (Bissell, 6/9/75, p. 18).

[2] Although Castro closed the gambling casinos in Cuba when he first came to power, they were reopened for use by foreign tourists in late February 1959, and remained open until late September 1961.

[3] Howard Osborn, who became Director of the Office of Security in 1964, told the Committee that the DDP often drew upon personnel of the Office of Security, which was within a different directorate, because of the contacts and expertise that Security personnel developed in the field. This is an example of operations being carried out across formal organization lines. The fact that Bissell called on Edwards might indicate that Bissell had already formulated a plan and was relying on Edwards to put it in to practice.

[4] During 1954–1955, Maheu cooperated with the CIA in attempting to undermine a contract with the Saudi Arabian government that would have given one person virtually complete control over shipping of oil from Saudi Arabia. Although he was employed by a competitor of the person who held the contract, Maheu worked closely with the CIA. Maheu testified that, after consulting with the Agency, he arranged for a listening device to be placed in the room of the contract holder; and that he provided the impetus for the termination of the contract by publicizing its terms in a Rome newspaper which he said he had purchased with CIA funds. (Maheu, 7/30/75, pp. 14–25)

The Support Chief testified that at the CIA's request Maheu had also previously arranged for the production of a film in Hollywood purporting to depict a foreign leader with a woman in the Soviet Union. The CIA planned to circulate the film, representing it to have been produced by the Soviet Union. The film was never used. (O.C. 5/30/75, pp. 159, 162–163.) Maheu testified that he had located an actor resembling the leader and had arranged for the production of the film. (Maheu, 7/30/75, pp. 39–42)

retainer by the CIA of $500, but it was terminated after his detective agency became more lucrative. (O.C., 5/30/75, pp. 13-14; I.G. Report, p. 15) The Operational Support Chief had served as Maheu's case officer since the Agency first began using Maheu's services, and by 1960 they had become close personal friends. (Maheu, 7/30/75, p. 6)

Sometime in late August or early September 1960, the Support Chief approached Maheu about the proposed operation. (O.C. 5/30/75, p. 9; Maheu, 7/29/75, p. 6) As Maheu recalls the conversation, the Support Chief asked him to contact John Rosselli, an underworld figure with possible gambling contacts in Las Vegas, to determine if he would participate in a plan to "dispose" of Castro.[1] (Maheu, 7/29/75, p. 8) The Support Chief testified, on the other hand, that it was Maheu who raised the idea of using Rosselli. (O.C., 5/30/75, pp. 15-16)

Maheu had known Rosselli since the late 1950's. (Maheu, 7/29/75, pp. 58-60) Although Maheu claims not to have been aware of the extent of Rosselli's underworld connections and activities, he recalled that "it was certainly evident to me that he was able to accomplish things in Las Vegas when nobody else seemed to get the same kind of attention." (Maheu, 7/29/75, p. 60)

The Support Chief had previously met Rosselli at Maheu's home. (Maheu, 7/29/75, p. 8) The Support Chief and Maheu each claimed that the other had raised the idea of using Rosselli, and Maheu said the Chief was aware that Rosselli had contacts with the gambling syndicate. (Maheu, 7/29/75, p. 8; O.C., 5/30/75, pp. 15-16)

At first Maheu was reluctant to become involved in the operation because it might interfere with his relationship with his new client, Howard Hughes.[2] He finally agreed to participate because he felt that he owed the Agency a committment. (O.C., 5/30/75, pp. 12-13, 103) The Inspector General's Report states that:

> Edwards and Maheu agreed that Maheu would approach Rosselli as the representative of businessmen with interests in Cuba who saw the elimination of Castro as the first essential step to the recovery of their investments. (I.G. Report, p. 16)

The Support Chief also recalled that Maheu was to use this cover story when he presented the plan to Rosselli, (O.C., 5/30/75, p. 16) but Rosselli said that the story was developed after he had been contacted, and was used as a mutual "cover" by him, the Chief, and Maheu in dealing with Cubans who were subsequently recruited for the project. (Rosselli, 6/24/75, pp. 16-17) The Support Chief testified that Maheu was told to offer money, probably $150,000, for Castro's assassination.[3] (O.C., 5/30/75, pp. 16, 111; Memo, Osborn to DCI, 6/24/66)

(ii) Contact With the Syndicate

According to Rosselli, he and Maheu met at the Brown Derby Restaurant in Beverly Hills in early September 1960. Rosselli testi-

---
[1] Maheu testified that he was told that the plan to assassinate Castro was one phase of a larger project to invade Cuba. (Maheu, 7/29/75, pp. 7, 13, 47)
[2] Maheu told the Committee that at that time, Hughes was becoming an important client, and that devoting time to the CIA's assassination plot was hindering his work for Hughes. He testified that shortly before the election in November 1960, while he was in Miami working on the assassination project, Hughes phoned and asked him to return to the West Coast. Maheu testified that since he did "not want to lose" Hughes as a client, he "definitely told him that the project was on behalf of the United States Government, that it included plans to dispose of Mr. Castro in connection with a pending invasion." (Maheu, 7/29/75, pp. 22-23)
[3] The Inspector General's Report states that "Maheu was authorized to tell Rosselli that his clients' were willing to pay $150,000 for Castro's removal." (I.G. Report, p. 16) The evidence varies, however, with respect to the amount that was offered.

fied that Maheu told him that "high government officials" needed his cooperation in getting rid of Castro, and that he asked him to help recruit Cubans to do the job. (Rosselli, 6/24/75, p. 8) Maheu's recollection of that meeting was that "I informed him that I had been asked by my Government to solicit his cooperation in this particular venture." (Maheu, 7/29/75, p. 9)

Maheu stated that Rosselli "was very hesitant about participating in the project, and he finally said that he felt that he had an obligation to his government, and he finally agreed to participate." (Maheu, 7/29/75, p. 10) Maheu and Rosselli both testified that Rosselli insisted on meeting with a representative of the Government. (Maheu, 7/29/75, p. 9; Rosselli, 6/24/75, p. 9)

A meeting was arranged for Maheu and Rosselli with the Support Chief at the Plaza Hotel in New York. The Inspector General's Report placed the meeting on September 14, 1960. (I.G. Report, p. 16) Rosselli testified that he could not recall the precise date of the meeting, but that it had occurred during Castro's visit to the United Nations, which the New York Times Index places from September 18 through September 28, 1960. (Rosselli, 6/24/75, p. 10)

The Support Chief testified that he was introduced to Rosselli as a business associate of Maheu. He said that Maheu told Rosselli that Maheu represented international business interests which were pooling money to pay for the assassination of Castro. (O.C., 5/30/75, p. 26) Rosselli claimed that Maheu told him at that time that the Support Chief was with the CIA,[1] (Rosselli, 6/24/75, pp. 11, 85)

It was arranged that Rosselli would go to Florida and recruit Cubans for the operation. (Rosselli, 6/24/75, pp. 11-12) Edwards informed Bissell that contact had been made with the gambling syndicate. (Bissell, 6/9/75, pp. 20-21; I.G. Report, p. 17)

During the week of September 24, 1960 the Support Chief, Maheu, and Rosselli met in Miami to work out the details of the operation. (O.C. 5/30/75, pp. 25-26; Rosselli, 6/24/75, p. 12; I.G. Report, p. 18) Rosselli used the cover name "John Rawlston" and represented himself to the Cuban contacts as an agent of "* * * some business interests of Wall Street that had * * * nickel interests and properties around in Cuba, and I was getting financial assistance from them." (Rosselli, 6/24/75, pp. 9, 17)

Maheu handled the details of setting up the operation and keeping the Support Chief informed of developments. After Rosselli and Maheu had been in Miami for a short time, and certainly prior to October 18.[2] Rosselli introduced Maheu to two individuals on whom

---

[1] The weight of the testimony indicates that Rosselli realized the CIA was behind the assassination attempt at an early stage. Mahue substantially confirmed his account (Mahue, 7/29/75, p. 111) The support chief recalled that about three weeks after the New York meeting, Rosselli told him, "I am not kidding, I know who you work for." (O.C., 5/30/75, p. 26.)

[2] Maheu recalls that he first met "Sam Gold" (Giancana) after November 1960, when he was staying at the Fountainebleu Hotel. (Maheu, 7/29/75, p. 17) Other evidence indicates that the meeting took place earlier. When they first went to Miami, Maheu and Rosselli stayed at the Kennilworth Hotel (Maheu, 7/29/75, pp. 15-16); FBI records reveal that Maheu and Rosselli (alias J. A. Rollins) were registered at the Kennilworth from October 11-30. (FBI summary, p. 10). Giancana must have been involved in the operation during the October period at the Kennilworth because (1) the wiretap of the apartment, discussed *infra*, was made on October 30; (2) on October 18, the FBI sent a memorandum to Bissell stating that Giancana had been telling several people that he was involved in an assassination attempt against Castro. No reference is made to the CIA in this memorandum. (See *infra*, p. 79)

Rosselli intended to rely: "Sam Gold," who would serve as a "back-up man" (Rosselli, 6/24/75, p. 15), or "key" man (Maheu, 7/29/75, p. 17), and "Joe," whom "Gold" said would serve as a courier to Cuba and make arrangements there. (I.G., Report p. 19) The Support Chief, who was using the name "Jim Olds," said he had met "Sam" and "Joe" once, and then only briefly. (O.C., 5/30/75, pp. 26–29)

The Support Chief testified that he learned the true identities of his associates one morning when Maheu called and asked him to examine the "Parade" supplement to the *Miami Times*.[1] An article on the Attorney General's ten-most-wanted criminals list revealed that "Sam Gold" was Momo Salvatore Giancana, a Chicago-based gangster,[2] and "Joe" was Santos Trafficante, the Cosa Nostra chieftain in Cuba.[3] (I.G., Report, p. 19) The Support Chief reported his discovery to Edwards, (O.C. 5/30/75, pp. 31, 33) but did not know whether Edwards reported this fact to his superiors. (O.C., 5/30/75, pp. 32, 41) The Support Chief testified that this incident occurred after "we were up to our ears in it," a month or so after Giancana had been brought into the operation, but prior to giving the poison pills to Rosselli. (O.C. 5/30/75, pp. 30, 44)

Maheu recalled that it was Giancana's job to locate someone in Castro's entourage who could accomplish the assassination. (Maheu, 7/29/75, p. 19) and that he met almost daily with Giancana over a substantial period of time. (Maheu, 7/29/75, p. 18) Although Maheu described Giancana as playing a "key role," (Maheu, 7/29/75, p. 34) Rosselli claimed that none of the Cubans eventually used in the operation were acquired through Giancana's contacts. (Rosselli, 6/24/75, p. 15)

(iii) Las Vegas Wiretap

In late October 1960, Maheu arranged for a Florida investigator, Edward DuBois, to place an electronic "bug" in a room in Las Vegas. (Maheu, 7/29/75, p. 36)[4] DuBois' employee, Arthur J. Balletti, flew to Las Vegas and installed a tap on the phone. (Maheu, 7/29/75, p. 38) The Support Chief characterized the ensuing events as a "Keystone Comedy act." (O.C., 5/30/75, p. 68). On October 31, 1960, Balletti, believing that the apartment would be vacant for the afternoon, left the wiretap equipment unattended. A maid discovered the equipment and notified the local sheriff, who arrested Balletti and brought him to the jail. Balletti called Maheu in Miami, tying "Maheu into this thing up to his ear." (O.C., 5/30/75, pp. 36–37) Balletti's bail was paid by Rosselli. (Rosselli, 6/24/75, p. 52)

(1) CIA Involvement In The Wiretap.—The Committee received conflicting evidence on whether the Agency was consulted prior to

---

[1] A search of supplements to all Miami papers during this period did not reveal the article described by the Support Chief.
[2] Sam Giancana was murdered in his home on June 20, 1975.
[3] Trafficante made regular trips between Miami and Cuba on gambling syndicate business. (I.G., Report, pp. 19–20)
[4] According to the Support Chief and Rosselli, DuBois had been requested to place what they characterized as a "legal" electronic bug against the wall from an adjacent apartment. Balletti instead installed an electronic tap on the phone. (O.C., 5/30/75, pp. 67–68; Maheu, 7/29/75, pp. 36–37)

the installation of the tap.[1] The Support Chief testified that he had called Edwards and cleared the placement of an electronic "bug" in the apartment prior to the installation of the tap. (O.C., 5/30/75, pp. 67–71) Maheu recalled that he had initially asked the Support Chief if the CIA would handle the job, and that the Chief had told him that:

> He would call Mr. Edwards and see if they would have the capability of accomplishing this * * * and that subsequently he informed me that Mr. Edwards had said that they would not do it, but approved paying for it if we hired an independent private detective to put it on. (Maheu, 7/29/75, p. 37)

On the other hand, Edwards, in a May 14, 1962 memorandum for the Attorney General (discussed at length, *infra*, p. 131), stated that "At the time of the incident neither the Agency nor the undersigned knew of the proposed technical installation."[2]

The Inspector General's Report accepted Edwards' assertion that "the Agency was first unwitting and then a reluctant accessory after the fact," but offered no further evidence to support that contention. (I.G. Report, p. 67)

The Committee also received conflicting evidence concerning whether the tap had been placed to keep Giancana in Miami or to check on security leaks. The Support Chief testified that during the early stages of negotiations with the gambling syndicate, Maheu informed him that a girl friend of Giancana was having an affair with the target of the tap. Giancana wanted Maheu to bug that person's room; otherwise, Giancana threatened to fly to Las Vegas himself. Maheu was concerned that Giancana's departure would disrupt the negotiations, and secured the Chief's permission to arrange for a bug to insure Giancana's presence and cooperation. (O.C., 5/30/75, pp. 68–69) Maheu substantially confirmed this account. (Maheu, 7/29/75, pp. 25–30)[3]

There is some evidence, however, suggesting that the CIA itself may have instituted the tap to determine whether Giancana was leaking information about his involvement in an assassination attempt

---

[1] Regardless of whether the CIA initially authorized the tap, it is apparent that the CIA paid for the tap. DuBois told FBI agents that Maheu had paid him a retainer of $1,000. (File R-505, p. 14). The Support Chief confirmed that CIA "indirectly" paid for the tap because "we paid Maheu a certain amount of money, and he just paid it out of what we were giving him."
"Q: But it was understood, or you understood, that out of the money the CIA made available to Maheu, DuBois would be paid for the tap?
"A: Yes.

* * * * * * *

"Q: And Colonel Edwards * * * knew somebody was being employed in order to accomplish a tap?
"A: That is right." (O.C., 5/30/75, p. 69)

[2] However, a memorandum by J. Edgar Hoover states that the Attorney General said he had been told by Edwards in 1962 that the "CIA admitted that they had assisted Maheu in making the installation." (Memo from Hoover, 5/10/62)

[3] An acquaintance of Giancana's, Joseph Shimon, testified that Giancana had told him that Giancana had asked Rosselli to request Maheu to arrange for surveillance of the room to determine the occupant's relationship with Giancana's girl friend. (Shimon, 9/20/75, p. 21) Shimon stated that Giancana had told him that Giancana had paid Mahen $5,000 for the tap, that the CIA had not known about the tap in advance, and that Maheu subsequently decided to use his connection with the CIA operation to avoid prosecution for his involvement in the tap. (Shimon, 9/20/75, p. 23) Maheu testified that he did not recall having been paid for the tap. (Maheu, 9/23/75, p. 7)

against Castro.¹ An October 18, 1960 memorandum from J. Edgar Hoover to Bissell, stated that "a source whose reliability has not been tested" reported:

> [D]uring recent conversations with several friends, Giancana stated that Fidel Castro was to be done away with very shortly. When doubt was expressed regarding this statement, Giancana reportedly assured those present that Castro's assassination would occur in November. Moreover, he allegedly indicated that he had already met with the assassin-to-be on three occasions. * * * Giancana claimed that everything has been perfected for the killing of Castro, and that the "assassin" had arranged with a girl, not further described, to drop a "pill" in some drink or food of Castro's. (Memo, Hoover to DCI (Att: DDP), 10/18/60)

Rosselli testified that Maheu had given him two explanations for the tap on different occasions: First, that Giancana was concerned that his girl friend was having an affair; and, second, that he had arranged the tap to determine whether Giancana had told his girl friend about the assassination plot, and whether she was spreading the story. (Rosselli, 6/24/75, pp. 47–48) Maheu gave the second explanation to the FBI when he was questioned about his involvement in the tap (Summary File by FBI), and Edwards wrote in the memorandum to the Attorney General:

> Maheu stated that Sam Giancana thought that [Giancana's girl friend] might know of the proposed operation and might pass on the information to * * * a friend of [Giancana's girl friend]. (Memo Edwards to Attorney General, 5/14/62)

(2) Consequences Of The Wiretap.—Edwards told Maheu that if he was "approached by the FBI, he could refer them to me to be briefed that he was engaged in an intelligence operation directed at Cuba". (Memo, Edwards to Attorney General, 5/14/62) FBI records indicate that on April 18, 1961, Maheu informed the FBI that the tap involved the CIA, and suggested that Edwards be contacted. (Memo 4/20/61) Edwards subsequently informed the Bureau that the CIA would object to Maheu's prosecution because it might reveal sensitive information relating to the abortive Bay of Pigs invasion.²

In a memo dated April 24, 1962, Herbert J. Miller, Assistant Attorney General, Criminal Division, advised the Attorney General that the "national interest" would preclude any prosecutions based upon the tap. Following a briefing of the Attorney General by the CIA, a decision was made not to prosecute.³

(iv) Poison Is Prepared And Delivered to Cuba

The Inspector General's Report described conversations among Bissell, Edwards, and the Chief of the Technical Services Division

---

[1] When Rosselli talked with Giancana after the wiretap had been discovered, Giancana "laughed * * * I remember his expression, smoking a cigar, he almost swallowed it laughing about it" (Rosselli, 6/24/75, p. 52). Rosselli claims that he was "perturbed" because "It was blowing everything, blowing every kind of cover that I had tried to arrange to keep quiet" (Rosselli, 6/24/75, p. 52).
Rosselli said that he told Giancana that the CIA was involved in the operation "in order to have him keep his mouth shut" (Rosselli, 6/24/75, pp. 26–27).
[2] Details of the discussions between the CIA and FBI are described fully *infra* at pp. 125–135.
[3] Mahen subsequently drew on his involvement with the CIA to avoid testifying before Senator Edward Long's Committee investigating invasions of privacy in 1966. According to the Inspector General's Report, when Maheu learned that the Committee intended to call him, "he applied pressure on the Agency in a variety of ways—suggesting that publicity might expose his past sensitive work for the CIA." (I.G. Report, pp. 73–74) Lawrence Houston, General Counsel for the CIA, met with Mahen and his attorney, Edward P. Morgan, and informed Senator Long that Maheu had been involved in CIA operations (Houston, 6/2/75, pp. 58–60). As a result, the Long Committee did not call Maheu to testify.

(TSD), concerning the most effective method of poisoning Castro. (I.G. Report, pp. 23-33) There is some evidence that Giancana or Rosselli originated the idea of depositing a poison pill in Castro's drink to give the "asset" a chance to escape. (I.G. Report, p. 25) The Support Chief recalled Rosselli's request for something "nice and clean, without getting into any kind of out and out ambushing", preferably a poison that would disappear without a trace. (O.C. 5/30/75, p. 116) The Inspector General's Report cited the Support Chief as stating that the Agency had first considered a "gangland-style killing" in which Castro would be gunned down. Giancana reportedly opposed the idea because it would be difficult to recruit someone for such a dangerous operation, and suggested instead the use of poison. (I.G. Report, p. 25)

Edwards rejected the first batch of pills prepared by TSD because they would not dissolve in water. A second batch, containing botulinum toxin, "did the job expected of them" when tested on monkeys. (I.G. Report, pp. 25-26; O.C. 5/30/75, p. 43) The Support Chief received the pills from TSD, probably in February 1961, with assurances that they were lethal,[1] and then gave them to Rosselli. (O.C., 5/30/75, p. 43)

The record clearly establishes that the pills were given to a Cuban for delivery to the island some time prior to the Bay of Pigs invasion in mid-April 1961. There are discrepancies in the record, however, concerning whether one or two attempts were made during that period, and the precise date on which the passage[s] occurred. The Inspector General's Report states that in late February or March 1961, Rosselli reported to the Support Chief that the pills had been delivered to an official close to Castro who may have received kickbacks from the gambling interests. (I.G. Report, p. 23) The Report states that the official returned the pills after a few weeks, perhaps because he had lost his position in the Cuban Government, and thus access to Castro, before he received the pills. (I.G. Report, p. 28) The Report concludes that yet another attempt was made in April 1961, with the aid of a leading figure in the Cuban exile movement.

Rosselli and the Support Chief testified that the Cuban official described by the Inspector General as having made the first attempt was indeed involved in the assassination plot, and they ascribed his failure to a case of "cold feet." (Rosselli, 6/24/75, p. 24; O.C. 5/30/75, p. 44) Rosselli was certain, however, that only one attempt to assassinate Castro had been made prior to the Bay of Pigs, (Rosselli, 6/24/75, p. 26) and the Support Chief and Maheu did not clarify the matter. It is possible then, that only one pre-Bay of Pigs attempt was made, and that the Cuban exile leader was the contact in the United States who arranged for the Cuban described in the Inspector General's Report to administer the poison.

In any event, Rosselli told the Support Chief that Trafficante believed a certain leading figure in the Cuban exile movement might be able to accomplish the assassination. (I.G. Report, p. 29)[2] The Inspec-

---

[1] Records of the TSD still extant when the I.G. Report was written in 1967 indicate that the pills were tested on February 10 and delivered to the Support Chief sometime thereafter.

[2] The Support Chief testified that he met this Cuban only once, and that after the meeting the Cuban told Rosselli:

"Look, I don't know [sic] like the CIA and you can't tell me that this guy isn't a CIA man." The Support Chief recalled, "I don't know whether I showed it or what, but he suspected that I wasn't what I was represented to be." (O.C., 5/30/75, p. 22)

tor General's Report suggests that this Cuban may have been receiving funds from Trafficante and other racketeers interested in securing "gambling, prostitution, and dope monopolies" in Cuba after the overthrow of Castro. The Report speculated that the Cuban was interested in the assassination scheme as a means of financing the purchase of arms and communications equipment. (I.G. Report, p. 31)

The Cuban claimed to have a contact inside a restaurant frequented by Castro. (Rosselli, 6/24/75, p. 21) As a prerequisite to the deal, he demanded cash and $1.000 worth of communications equipment. (I.G. Report, pp. 31, 32; O.C., 5/30/75, p. 23) The Support Chief recalled that Colonel J. C. King, head of the Western Hemisphere Division, gave him $50,000 in Bissell's office to pay the Cuban if he successfully assassinated Castro. (O.C., 5/30/75, pp. 17–21) The Support Chief stated that Bissell also authorized him to give the Cuban the requested electronics equipment. (O.C., 5/30/75, pp. 20–24)

Bissell testified that he did not doubt that some cash was given to the Support Chief, and that he was aware that the poison pills had been prepared. Bissell did not recall the meeting described above, and considered it unlikely that the Support Chief would have been given the money in his office. (Bissell, 6/11/75, p. 40) The Inspector General's Report, relying on an Office of Security memorandum to the DDCI dated June 24, 1966, as well as on an interview with the person who signed the voucher for the funds, placed the amount passed at $10,000. (I.G. Report, pp. 31–32) If the Inspector General's conclusions were correct, the funds which Bissell allegedly authorized were probably the advance payment to the Cuban, and not the $150,000 that was to be paid to him after Castro's death.

The record does clearly reflect, however, that communications equipment was delivered to the Cuban [1] and that he was paid advance money to cover his expenses, probably in the amount of $10,000. (I.G. Report, p. 32) The money and pills were delivered at a meeting between Maheu, Rosselli, Trafficante, and the Cuban at the Fountainebleau Hotel in Miami. As Rosselli recalled, Maheu:

* * * opened his briefcase and dumped a whole lot of money on his lap * * * and also came up with the capsules and he explained how they were going to be used. As far as I remember, they couldn't be used in boiling soups and things like that, but they could be used in water or otherwise, but they couldn't last forever. * * * It had to be done as quickly as possible. (Rosselli, 6/24/75, p. 21)[2]

A different version of the delivery of the pills to the Cuban was given to the Committee by Joseph Shimon, a friend of Rosselli and Giancana who testified that he was present when the passage occurred. Shimon testified that he had accompanied Maheu to Miami to see the third Patterson-Johansson World Heavyweight Championship fight, which took place on March 12, 1961. (Shimon, 9/20/75, pp. 6–8) According to Shimon, he, Giancana, Rosselli, and Maheu shared a suite in the Fountainebleau Hotel. During a conversation, Maheu stated that he had a "contract" to assassinate Castro, and had been

---

[1] The Support Chief testified that a man from the communications office delivered the communications equipment that the Cuban had requested to Miami. (O.C., 5/30/75, p. 20) Maheu recalled delivering an automobile which he had been told contained communications equipment to an empty lot. (Maheu, 7/29/75, p. 52)

[2] Maheu denied that this dramatic event ever occurred, and did not recall being present at a meeting at which the pills were passed. (Maheu, 7/29/75, pp. 40–41). Maheu did recall that the Support Chief showed him the pills in an envelope and told him that the pills would be given to a Cuban. (Maheu, 7/29/75, p. 40)

provided with a "liquid" by the CIA to accomplish the task. (Shimon, 9/20/75, p. 9) [1] Shimon testified that Maheu had said the liquid was to be put in Castro's food, that Castro would become ill and die after two or three days, and that an autopsy would not reveal what had killed him. (Shimon, 9/20/75, pp. 9–10)

Shimon testified that the Cuban was contacted outside the Boom Boom Room of the Fountainebleau Hotel. Shimon said that Rosselli left with the Cuban, and that Maheu said, "Johnny's going to handle everything, this is Johnny's contract." (Shimon, 9/20/75, p. 11) Shimon testified that Giancana subsequently told him "I am not in it, and they are asking me for the names of some guys who used to work in casinos. * * * Maheu's conning the hell out of the CIA." (Shimon, 9/20/75, p. 12)

Shimon testified that a few days later, he received a phone call from Maheu, who said: "* * * did you see the paper? Castro's ill. He's going to be sick two or three days. Wow, we got him." (Shimon, 9/20/75, p. 12) [2]

Rosselli testified that he did not recall Shimon's having been present when the pills were delivered to the Cuban. (Rosselli, 9/22/75, p. 5) Maheu recalled having seen the fight with Rosselli and Giancana, but did not recall whether Shimon had been present, and denied that the poison had been delivered in the lobby of the Fountainebleau. (Maheu 9/23/75, pp. 14–15)

The attempt met with failure. According to the Inspector General's Report, Edwards believed the scheme failed because Castro stopped visiting the restaurant where the "asset" was employed. Maheu suggested an alternative reason. He recalled being informed that after the pills had been delivered to Cuba, "the go signal still had to be received before in fact they were administered." (Maheu, 9/23/75, p. 42) He testified that he was informed by the Support Chief sometime after the operation that the Cubans had an opportunity to administer the pills to Fidel Castro and either Che Guevarra or Raul Castro, but that the "go signal" never came. (Maheu 7/29/75, pp. 43–44, 60–61) Maheu did not know who was responsible for giving the signal. (Maheu, 9/23/75, pp. 44–45) The Cuban subsequently returned the cash and the pills. (O.C., 5/30/75, pp. 19–20; Memo, Osborn to DCI, 6/24/66)

The date of the Cuban operation is unclear. The Inspector General's Report places it in March–April 1961, prior to the Bay of Pigs. (I.G. Report, p. 29) Shimon's testimony puts it around March 12, 1961. Bissell testified that the effort against Castro was called off after the Bay of Pigs, (Bissell, 6/11/75, p. 52) and Maheu testified that he had no involvement in the operation after the Bay of Pigs. (Maheu, 9/23/75, p. 50) The Support Chief however, was certain that it occured during early 1962. (O.C., 5/30/75, pp. 47–48)

(c) *Use of Underworld Figures: Phase II (Post Bay of Pigs)*

(i) *Change in Leadership*

The Inspector General's Report divides the gambling syndicate operation into Phase I, terminating with the Bay of Pigs, and Phase

---

[1] Maheu said that the poison, which he was shown on one occasion by the Support Chief, consisted of five or six gelatin capsules filled with a liquid. (Maheu, 9/23/75, pp. 35–36) Rosselli described the poison as "capsules." (Rosselli, 9/22/75, p. 4)

[2] The Committee has been unable to locate the newspaper account described by Shimon.

II, continuing with the transfer of the operation to William Harvey in late 1961.¹ The distinction between a clearly demarcated Phase I and Phase II may be an artificial one, as there is considerable evidence that the operation was continuous, perhaps lying dormant for the period immediately following the Bay of Pigs.²

In early 1961, Harvey was assigned the responsibility for establishing a general capability within the CIA for disabling foreign leaders, including assassination as a "last resort." (Bissell, 6/9/75, p. 73; Harvey, 6/25/75, pp. 34–35) The capability was called Executive Action and was later included under the cryptonym ZR/RIFLE. Executive Action and the evidence relating to its connection to the "White House" and to whether or not it involved action as well as "capability" is discussed extensively *infra* in Section (III)(c), p. 181.

Harvey's notes reflect that Bissell asked him to take over the gambling syndicate operation from Edwards and that they discussed the "application of ZR/RIFLE program to Cuba" on November 16, 1961. (I.G. Report, p. 39) Bissell confirmed that the conversation took place and accepted the November date as accurate. (Bissell, 7/17/75, pp. 12–13) He also testified that the operation "was not reactivated, in other words, no instructions went out to Rosselli or to others * * * to renew the attempt, until after I had left the Agency in February 1962." (Bissell, 6/11/75, pp. 52–53.) Harvey agreed that his conversation with Bissell was limited to exploring the feasibility of using the gambling syndicate against Castro. (Harvey, 7/11/75, p. 60)

Richard Helms replaced Bissell as DDP in February 1962. As such, he was Harvey's superior. The degree to which Helms knew about and participated in the assassination plot is discussed in the section of this Report dealing with the level to which the plots were authorized within the Agency.

(ii) The Operation Is Reactivated

In early April 1962, Harvey, who testified that he was acting on "explicit orders" from Helms, (Harvey, 7/11/75, p. 18), requested Edwards to put him in touch with Rosselli. (Edwards memo, 5/14/62) The Support Chief first introduced Harvey to Rosselli in Miami, where Harvey told Rosselli to maintain his Cuban contacts, but not to deal with Maheu or Giancana, (O.C., 5/30/75, p. 50; Rosselli, 6/24/75, pp. 27–30) whom he had decided were "untrustworthy" and "surplus." (Harvey, 6/25/75, p. 65) The Support Chief recalled that initially Rosselli did not trust Harvey although they subsequently developed a close friendship. (O.C., 5/30/75, p. 52)

---

¹ Harvey had a long background in clandestine activities. At the time the gambling syndicate operation was moved under Harvey's supervision, he was responsible for a number of important activities and soon thereafter was selected to head of Task Force W, the CIA component of the Kennedy Administration's cover effort to oust Castro.
² Harevy said that he took over a "going operation" from Edwards (I.G. Report, p. 42; Harvey, 6/25/75, p. 67) and emphasized that: "I would like to make as clear as I can that there was no Phase 1, Phase 2 in this. This is an ongoing matter which I was injected into * * *. (Harvey, 6/25/75, p. 90)
Continuity was provided by retaining the Support Chief as the case officer for the project well into May 1962. During interviews for the Inspector General's Report, the Support Chief recalled that there was "something going on" between the Bay of Pigs and Harvey's assumption of control (I.G. Report, p. 43). When testifying before the Committee, the Support Chief firmly recalled several trips to Miami in the fall of 1961, and "right up to the time I turned it over to Harvey I was in and out of Miami." (O.C. 5/30/75, pp. 89–90).

Harvey, the Support Chief and Rosselli met for a second time in New York on April 8–9, 1962. (I.G. Report, p. 43) A notation made during this time in the files of the Technical Services Division indicates that four poison pills were given to the Support Chief on April 18, 1962. (I.G. Report, pp. 46–47) The pills were passed to Harvey, who arrived in Miami on April 21, and found Rosselli already in touch with the same Cuban who had been involved in the pre-Bay of Pigs pill passage. (I.G. Report, p. 47) He gave the pills to Rosselli, explaining that "these would work anywhere and at any time with anything." (Rosselli, 6/24/75, p. 31) Rosselli testified that he told Harvey that the Cubans intended to use the pills to assassinate Che Guevara as well as Fidel and Raul Castro. According to Rosselli's testimony, Harvey approved of the targets, stating "everything is all right, what they want to do." (Rosselli, 6/24/75, p. 34)

The Cuban requested arms and equipment as a *quid pro quo* for carrying out the assassination operation. (O.C., 5/30/75, pp. 53–54) With the help of the CIA's Miami station which ran covert operations against Cuba (JM/WAVE), Harvey procured explosives, detonators, rifles, handguns, radios, and boat radar costing about $5,000. (I.G. Report, p. 49) Harvey and the chief of the JM/WAVE station rented a U-Haul truck under an assumed name and delivered the equipment to a parking lot. (Harvey, 6/25/75, p. 63) The keys were given to Rosselli, who watched the delivery with the Support Chief from across the street. (O.C., 5/30/75, pp. 92–93) The truckload of equipment was finally picked up by either the Cuban or Rosselli's agent. (I.G. Report, pp. 49–50; Rosselli, 6/24/75, p. 40) Harvey testified that the arms "could" have been for use in the assassination attempt, but that they were not given to the Cuban solely for that purpose. (Harvey, 7/11/75, p. 9)

Rosselli kept Harvey informed of the operation's progress. Sometime in May 1962, he reported that the pills and guns had arrived in Cuba. (Harvey, p. 64; Rosselli, 6/24/75, pp. 34, 42–43) On June 21, he told Harvey that the Cuban had dispatched a three-man team to Cuba. The Inspector General's report described the team's mission as "vague" and conjectured that the team would kill Castro or recruit others to do the job, using the poison pills if the opportunity arose. (I.G. Report, 6/2/75, p. 51)

Harvey met Rosselli in Miami on September 7 and 11, 1962. The Cuban was reported to be preparing to send in another three-man team to penetrate Castro's bodyguard. Harvey was told that the pills, referred to as "the medicine," were still "safe" in Cuba. (Harvey, 6/25/75, p. 103; I.G. Report p. 51)

Harvey testified that by this time he had grave doubts about whether the operation would ever take place, and told Rosselli that "there's not much likelihood that this is going anyplace, or that it should be continued." (Harvey, 6/25/75, p. 104) The second team never left for Cuba, claiming that "conditions" in Cuba were not right. (I.G. Report, pp. 51–52) During early January 1963, Harvey paid Rosselli $2,700 to defray the Cuban's expenses. (I.G. Report, p. 52). Harvey terminated the operation in mid-February 1963. At a meeting with Rosselli in Los Angeles, it was agreed that Rosselli would taper off his communications with the Cubans. (I.G. Report, pp. 52–53) Rosselli testified that he simply broke off contact with the Cubans.

However, he never informed them that the offer of $150,000 for Castro's assassination had been withdrawn.[1] (Rosselli, 6/24/75, p. 45)

The agency personnel who dealt with Rosselli attributed his motivation to patriotism [2] and testified that he was not paid for his services. According to the Support Chief, Rosselli "paid his way, he paid his own hotel fees, he paid his own travel. * * * And he never took a nickel, he said, no, as long as it is for the Government of the United States, this is the least I can do, because I owe it a lot." (O.C., 5/30/75, p. 27)

Edwards agreed that Rosselli was "never paid a cent," (Edwards, 5/30/75, p. 16) and Maheu testified that "Giancana was paid nothing at all, not even for expenses, and that Mr. Rosselli was given a pittance that did not even begin to cover his expenses." (Maheu, 7/29/75, p. 68) It is clear, however, that the CIA did pay Rosselli's hotel bill during his stay in Miami in October 1960.[3] The CIA's involvement with Rosselli caused the Agency some difficulty during Rosselli's subsequent prosecutions for fraudulent gambling activities and living in the country under an assumed name.[4]

(d) Plans in Early 1963

Two plans to assassinate Castro were explored by Task Force W, the CIA section then concerned with covert Cuban operations, in early 1963. Desmond Fitzgerald (now deceased), Chief of the Task Force, asked his assistant to determine whether an exotic seashell, rigged to explode, could be deposited in an area where Castro commonly went skin diving. (Assistant, 9/18/75, p. 28) The idea was explored by the Technical Services Division and discarded as impractical. (Helms, 6/13/75, p. 135; I.G. Report, p. 77)

A second plan involved having James Donovan (who was negotiating with Castro for the release of prisoners taken during the Bay of Pigs operation) present Castro with a contaminated diving suit.[5] (Colby, 5/21/75, pp. 38–39)

---

[1] "Q: As far as those Cubans knew, then the offer which they understood from you to come from Wall Street was still outstanding?
"A: I don't know if they still think so * * * I didn't see them after that to tell them that. (Rosselli, 6/24/75, p. 45)"

[2] Rosselli claims that he was motivated by "honor and dedication." (Rosselli, 6/24/75, p. 59)

In 1943, Rosselli had been convicted of extorting money from motion picture producers to insure studios against labor strikes, and during the period of his contacts with the CIA, Rosselli was deeply involved in hotel and gambling operations in Las Vegas. (File R-505, Summary of FBI Documents) It is possible that he believed cooperating with the government in the assassination operation might serve him well in the future.

[3] FBI reports reveal that Rosselli's expenses at the Kennilworth Hotel, where he was registered from October 11–30, 1960, under the name of J. A. Rollins, were paid by Maheu. FBI file summary p. 10) Maheu's expenses were reimbursed by the CIA.

[4] In May 1966, the FBI threatened to deport Rosselli for living in the United States under an assumed name unless he cooperated in an investigation of the Mafia. (Rosselli, whose true name is Filippo Saco, was born in Italy and was allegedly brought illegally into the United States while still a child.) Rosselli contacted Edwards, who informed the FBI that Rosselli wanted to "keep square with the Bureau," but was afraid that gangsters might kill him for "talking." (Memo, Osborn to FBI, 5/27/66) After Rosselli was arrested for fraudulent gambling activities at the Friars Club in Beverly Hills in 1967, he requested Harvey, who had left the Agency, to represent him. (Memo for Record by Osborn, 12/11/67) Harvey contacted the Agency and suggested that it prevent the prosecution. (Osborn Memo, *supra*) Rosselli was subsequently convicted of violating United States interstate gambling laws. In 1971, the CIA approached the Immigration and Naturalization Service, Department of Justice, to "forestall public disclosure of Rosselli's past operational activity with CIA" that might occur if deportation proceedings were brought. (Letter, CIA to Select Committee, 7/21/75) It was agreed that CIA would be kept informed of developments in that case. The deportation order is presently being litigated in the courts.

[5] Donovan was not aware of the plan.

The Inspector General's Report dates this operation in January 1963, when Fitzgerald replaced Harvey as Chief of Task Force W, although it is unclear whether Harvey or Fitzgerald conceived the plan. (I.G. Report, p. 75) It is likely that the activity took place earlier, since Donovan had completed his negotiations by the middle of January 1963. Helms characterized the plan as "cockeyed." (Helms, 6/13/75, p. 135)

The Technical Services Division bought a diving suit, dusted the inside with a fungus that would produce a chronic skin disease (Madura foot), and contaminated the breathing apparatus with a tubercule bacillus. The Inspector General's Report states that the plan was abandoned because Donovan gave Castro a different diving suit on his own initiative. (I.G., Report, p. 75) Helms testified that the diving suit never left the laboratory. (Helms, 6/13/75, p. 135)

(e) AM/LASH

(i) Origin of the Project

In early 1961, a CIA official met with a highly-placed Cuban official to determine if the Cuban would cooperate in efforts against the Castro regime. (I.G. Report, p. 78) The Cuban was referred to by the cryptonym AM/LASH.[1] The meeting was inconclusive, but led to subsequent meetings at which AM/LASH agreed to cooperate with the CIA.

The CIA regarded AM/LASH as an important "asset" inside Cuba. As a high-ranking leader who enjoyed the confidence of Fidel Castro, AM/LASH could keep the CIA informed of the internal workings of the regime. (Case Officer 2, 8/1/75, pp. 23, 40) It was also believed that he might play a part in fomenting a coup within Cuba. (Case Officer 2, 8/1/75, p. 43)[2]

From the first contact with AM/LASH until the latter part of 1963, it was uncertain whether he would defect or remain in Cuba. His initial requests to the CIA and FBI for aid in defecting were rebuffed. (I.G. Report, pp. 80, 82–83) When Case Officer 1 joined the operation in June 1962, his assignment was to ensure that AM/LASH would "stay in place and report to us." (Case Officer 1, 8/11/75, p. 38) At a meeting in the fall of 1963, AM/LASH 1 stated that he would remain in Cuba if he "could do something really significant for the creation of a new Cuba" and expressed a desire to plan the "execution" of Fidel Castro. (Case Officer 1 Contact Report) The subject of assassinating Castro was again discussed by AM/LASH and the case officer at another meeting a few days later. The case officer's contact report states that assassination was raised in discussing AM/LASH's role in Cuba, and that AM/LASH was visibly upset. "It was not the act that he objected to, but merely the choice of

---

[1] The Committee has taken the testimony of the two case officers involved in the AM/LASH project. Case officer 1 dealt with AM/LASH through September 1963; Case officer 2 continued until mid-1965. (Case Officer 2, 8/1/75, p. 11) The Committee has agreed not to divulge their names as they are still in active service with the Agency.

[2] AM/LASH was the major "asset" in the AM/LASH operation. During this period the CIA also sponsored a separate operation to "penetrate the Cuban military to encourage either defections or an attempt to produce information from dissidents, or perhaps even to forming a group which would be capable of replacing the then present government in Cuba. (Case Officer 1, 8/11/75, pp. 18, 22) The case officers for AM/LASH were also involved in this second related program.

the word used to describe it. 'Eliminate' was acceptable." (Case Officer 1, Contact Report)

Each case officer testified that he did not ask AM/LASH to assassinate Castro. The record clearly reveals, however, that both officers were aware of his desire to take such action. A cable to Headquarters reporting on a 1963 meeting with AM/LASH stated:

> Have no intention give AM/LASH physical elimination mission as requirement but recognize this something he could or might try to carry out on his own initiative.[1]

At a meeting late in the fall of 1963, AM/LASH again raised the possibility of defecting, but indicated that he would be willing to continue working against the Castro Regime if he received firm assurances of American support. According to Case Officer 2, AM/LASH requested military supplies, a device with which to protect himself if his plots against Castro were discovered, and a meeting with Attorney General Robert Kennedy. (Case Officer 2, 8/1/75, pp. 48–49)

Desmond Fitzgerald, Chief of the Special Affairs Staff,[2] agreed to meet AM/LASH and give him the assurances he sought. The Inspector General's Report states that Fitzgerald consulted with the DDP, Helms, who agreed that Fitzgerald should hold himself out as a personal representative of Attorney General Kennedy. (I.G. Report, p. 89)[3]

Helms testified that he did not recall the conversation with Fitzgerald. He also said that he had not consulted the Attorney General and speculated that his reason for not having done so might have been because "this was so central to the whole theme of what we had been trying to do * * * (find someone inside Cuba who might head a government and have a group to replace Castro). This is obviously what we had been pushing, what everybody had been pushing for us to try to do, and it is in that context that I would have made some remark like this." (Helms, 6/13/75, p. 117)

Helms recalled that he told Fitzgerald to "go ahead and say that from the standpoint of political support, the United States government will be behind you if you are successful. This had nothing to do with killings. This had only to do with the political action part of it." (Helms, 6/13/75, p. 131)

Fitzgerald met AM/LASH in late fall 1963 and promised him that the United States would support a coup against Castro. (Case

---

[1] Case Officer 1 testified that AM/LASH discussed "eliminating" Castro, although he attributed such remarks to AM/LASH's "mercurial" nature, and stated that no specific plans for assassinations were ever discussed. (Case Officer 1, 8/11/75, pp. 39–41, 62) The Case Officer who took over from the AM/LASH project in September 1963 recalled being briefed by Case Officer 1 on AM/LASH's belief that Castro's assassination was a necessary first step in a coup. (Case Officer 2, 8/1/75, p. 28)

The second AM/LASH Case Officer described the context in which AM/LASH generally raised the topic of assassination:

"You also must recognize that AM/LASH was a rather temperamental man whose temperament was of a mercurial nature and whereas he may have said something like this in one fit of pique, he would settle down and talk about organizing a regular military coup in the next breath." (Case Officer 2, 8/1/75, p. 29)

[2] The Special Affairs Staff (SAS) was the name given to Task Force W in early 1963 when Fitzgerald replaced Harvey as head of the covert Cuban operations. The AM/LASH Case Officers reported directly to Fitzgerald.

[3] The contact plan for the proposed meeting stated: "Fitzgerald will represent self as personal representative of Robert F. Kennedy who travelled to (foreign city) for specific purpose meeting AM/LASH and giving him assurances of full support with a change of the present government in Cuba."

Officer 2, 8/1/75, p. 60) [1] When later interviewed for the Inspector General's Report, Fitzgerald recalled that AM/LASH repeatedly requested an assassination weapon, particularly a "high-powered rifle with telescopic sights that could be used to kill Castro from a distance." Fitzgerald stated that he told AM/LASH that the United States would have "no part of an attempt on Castro's life." (I.G. Report, p. 90) Case Officer 2 recalled that AM/LASH raised the prospect of assassinating Castro, but did not propose an explicit plan. (Case Officer 2, 8/1/75, pp. 62, 85) AM/LASH was, however, "convinced that Castro had to be removed from power before a coup could be undertaken in Cuba." (Case Officer 2, 8/1/75, p. 61)

AM/LASH also requested high-powered rifles and grenades. (Case Officer 2, 8/1/75, p. 77) A memorandum by Case Officer 2 states:

C/SAS [Fitzgerald] approved telling AM/LASH he would be given a cache inside Cuba. Cache could, if he requested it, include * * * high-powered rifles with scopes * * *.

AM/LASH was told on November 22, 1963 that the cache would be dropped in Cuba. (Case Officer 2, 8/1/75, p. 92)

(ii) The Poison Pen Device

Another device offered to AM/LASH was a ball-point pen rigged with a hypodermic needle. (Case Officer 2, 8/1/75, p. 110) The needle was designed to be so fine that the victim would not notice its insertion. Case Officer 2, 8/1/75, p. 103)

According to the Inspector General's Report, when Case Officer 2 was interviewed in 1967, he stated that AM/LASH had requested the Agency to "devise some technical means of doing the job that would not automatically cause him to lose his own life in the try." (I.G. Report, p. 92)

The Report concluded that: "although none of the participants so stated, it may be inferred that they were seeking a means of assassination of a sort that AM/LASH might reasonably have been expected to have devised himself." (I.G. Report, p. 92)

Fitzgerald's assistant told the Committee that the pen was intended to show "bona fides" and "the orders were to do something to get rid of Castro * * * and we thought this other method might work whereas a rifle wouldn't." (Assistant, 9/18/75, p. 26)

Helms confirmed that the pen was manufactured "to take care of a request from him that he have some device for getting rid of Castro, for killing him, murdering him, whatever the case may be." (Helms, 6/13/75, p. 113)

"* * * [t]his was a temporizing gesture." (Helms, 6/11/75, p. 133) [2]

---

[1] Case Officer 2 was present at the meeting. He did not recall whether Robert Kennedy's name was used. (Case Officer 2, 8/1/75, p. 60)
[2] In his testimony before the Committee, Case Officer 2 offered a conflicting story. He said that the purpose of the pen was "to provide AM/LASH with a device which would serve him to protect him in case he was confronted with and charged with being involved in a military coup against Castro." (Case Officer 2, 8/1/75, p. 107) According to the case officer, AM/LASH had requested an "esoteric device" which could easily be concealed which he could use in self-defense. (Case Officer 2, 8/1/75, pp. 98–99) The device was not intended for offensive use against any person, but was rather "a kind of psychological crutch . . . to help him think that we were interested in his own protection, his own security. (Case Officer 2, 8/1/75, pp. 104–105) This version is wholly inconsistent with documents in the CIA files, some of which were written by the AM/LASH case officer, which establish that AM/LASH intended to kill Castro, and that the CIA knew his desire and endeavored to supply the means that he needed. These documents are set forth in the following text.

On November 22, 1963, Fitzgerald and the case officer met with AM/LASH and offered him the poison pen, recommending that he use Blackleaf-40, a deadly poison which is commercially available. (Case Officer 2, 8/1/75, p. 112) The Inspector General's Report noted that "it is likely that at the very moment President Kennedy was shot, a CIA officer was meeting with a Cuban agent * * * and giving him an assassination device for use against Castro." (I.G. Report, p. 94)

The case officer later recalled that AM/LASH did not "think much of the device," and complained that CIA could surely "come up with something more sophisticated than that." (I.G. Report, p. 93a).

The case officer recalled offering the pen to AM/LASH, but could not remember whether AM/LASH threw it away then or took it with him. (Case Officer 2, 8/1/75, pp. 105, 110) He did recall that AM/LASH said he would not take the pen back to Cuba, but did not know what AM/LASH in fact did with the pen. (Case Officer 2, 8/1/75, pp. 110–111)

An entry in the CIA AM/LASH files written in 1965 states:

Although Fitzgerald and the case officer assured AM/LASH on November 22, 1963 that CIA would give him everything he needed (telescopic sight, silencer, all the money he wanted) the situation changed when the case officer and Fitzgerald left the meeting to discover that President Kennedy had been assassinated. Because of this fact, plans with AM/LASH changed and it was decided that we could have no part in the assassination of a government leader (including Castro) and would not aid AM/LASH in this attempt * * *. AM/LASH was not informed of (this decision) until he was seen by the case officer in November, 1964.

In fact, however, assassination efforts involving AM/LASH continued into 1965.

(iii) Providing AM/LASH with Arms

CIA cables indicate that one cache of arms for AM/LASH was delivered in Cuba in March 1964 and another in June. An entry in the AM/LASH file for May 5, 1964 states that the case officer requested the Technical Services Division to produce, on a "crash basis," a silencer which would fit an FAL rifle. The contact report of a meeting between the case officer and a confidante of AM/LASH states that AM/LASH was subsequently informed that it was not feasible to make a silencer for an FAL rifle.

Toward the latter part of 1964, AM/LASH became more insistent that the assassination of the Cuban leadership was a necessary initial step in a successful coup. (Case Officer 2, 8/1/75, pp. 129–133) A memorandum written in the fall of 1964 stated:

AM/LASH was told and fully understands that the United States Government cannot become involved to any degree in the "first step" of his plan. If he needs support, he realizes he will have to get it elsewhere. FYI: This is where B-1 could fit in nicely in giving any support he would request.

Documents in the AM/LASH file establish that in early 1965, the CIA put AM/LASH in contact with B-1, the leader of an anti-Castro group. As the Case Officer explained to the Inspector General:

* * * What had happened was that SAS had contrived to put B-1 and AM/LASH together in such a way that neither of them knew that the contact had been engineered by CIA. The thought was that B-1 needed a man inside and

AM/LASH wanted a silenced weapon, which CIA was unwilling to furnish to him directly. By putting the two together, B-1 might get its man inside Cuba and AM/LASH might get his silenced weapon—from B-1. (I.G., Report p. 101)

A report of a meeting between a case officer and B-1 states that B-1, in his initial contacts with AM/LASH, discussed plans for assassinating Castro. AM/LASH suggested that guerrilla raids against Cuba should be stepped up one month before the "attempt on Fidel Castro" to "prepare the public and raise the morale and resistance spirit of the people." B-1 reported that:

> AM/LASH believed that the only solution to the problems in Cuba would be to get rid of Fidel Castro. He is able either to shoot him with a silencer or place a bomb in some place where Fidel will be. He might use, for example, a small bomb, that he can carry and place, or with his group attack the residence where Fidel lives * * * B-1 is going to provide AM/LASH with escape routes and places where B-1 is able to pick him up. He will memorize these points and escape routes * * * Next, B-1 is to provide AM/LASH either a silencer for a FAL or a rifle with a silencer.

A CIA document dated January 3, 1965 states that B-1, in a lengthy interview with a case officer, said that he and AM/LASH had reached firm agreement on the following points:

> 1. B-1 is to provide AM/LASH with a silencer for the FAL; if this is impossible, B-1 is to cache in a designated location a rifle with a scope and silencer plus several bombs, concealed either in a suitcase, a lamp or some other concealment device which he would be able to carry, and place next to Fidel Castro.
> 2. B-1 is to provide AM/LASH with escape routes controlled by B-1 and not by the Americans. The lack of confidence built up by the Bay of Pigs looms large.
> 3. B-1 is to prepare one of the western provinces, either Pinar del Rio or Havana, with arms caches and a clandestine underground mechanism. This would be a fall back position and a safe area where men and weapons are available to the group.
> 4. B-1 is to be in Cuba one week before the elimination of Fidel, but no one, including AM/LASH, will know B-1's location.
> 5. B-1 is to arrange for recognition by at least five Latin American countries as soon as Fidel is neutralized and a junta is formed. This junta will be established even though Raul Castro and Che Guevara may still be alive and may still be in control of part of the country. This is the reason AM/LASH requested that B-1 be able to establish some control over one of the provinces so that the junta can be formed in that location.
> 6. One month to the day before the neutralization of Fidel, B-1 will increase the number of commando attacks to a maximum in order to raise the spirit and morale of the people inside Cuba. In all communiques, in all radio messages, in all propaganda put out by B-1 he must relate that the raid was possible thanks to the information received from clandestine sources inside Cuba and from the clandestine underground apparatus directed by "P". This will be AM/LASH's war name.

A CIA cable dated in early 1965 stated that B-1 had given AM/LASH a silencer and that AM/LASH had "small, highly concentrated explosives." Shortly afterwards, a CIA station cabled that AM/LASH would soon receive "one pistol with silencer and one FAL rifle with a silencer from B-1's secretary." A subsequent cable reported that "B-1 had three packages of special items made up by his technical people and delivered to AM/LASH." (I.G., Report p. 103)

In June 1965, CIA terminated all contact with AM/LASH and his associates for reasons related to security. (I.G., Report pp. 104–105)

2. AT WHAT LEVEL WERE THE CASTRO PLOTS KNOWN ABOUT OR AUTHORIZED WITHIN THE CENTRAL INTELLIGENCE AGENCY?

(a) The Question Presented

As explained in the preceding section, Richard Bissell clearly authorized the two attempts to assassinate Cuban leaders that occurred during his tenure as Deputy Director of Plans—the incident involving a Cuban in contact with Raul Castro and the attempt involving underworld figures that took place prior to the Bay of Pigs. It is also clear that Bissell's successor, Richard Helms, authorized and was aware of the attempt on Castro's life involving underworld figures that took place the year following the Bay of Pigs, although the degree of Helms' participation in the details of the plot is not certain.[1]

Helms also authorized and was aware of the AM/LASH operation, although it is not certain that he knew that AM/LASH intended to assassinate Castro.[2] The evidence indicates that the exploding seashell and diving suit schemes were abandoned at the laboratory stage and that no authorization was sought for their development or eventual use.

This section deals with whether the Director of Central Intelligence, Allen Dulles, and his successor, John McCone, authorized or were aware of the assassination plots. Dulles served as DCI from 1953 to November 1961. McCone was DCI from November 1961 to April 1965.[3] General Charles Cabell served as Deputy Director of Central Intelligence under Dulles and continued into the early months of McCone's term. He was replaced as DDCI in April 1962 by General Marshall Carter.

In summary, the evidence relating to Dulles and McCone (and their respective Deputy DCI's) is as follows:

(i) *Dulles.*—Bissell and Edwards testified that they were certain that both Dulles and his Deputy General Cabell were aware of and authorized the initial phase of the assassination plot involving underworld figures. They acknowledged, however, that Dulles and Cabell were not told about the plot until after the underworld figures had been contacted. The words said to have been used to brief the Director and his Deputy—"an intelligence operation"—do not convey on their

---

[1] William Harvey testified that he kept Helms informed of the operation involving the underworld at all stages. (Harvey, 6/25/75, pp. 65–66) When interviewed for the Inspector General's Report, Harvey said that he briefed Helms on his first meeting with Rosselli, and "thereafter he regularly briefed Helms on the status of the Castro operation." (I.G. Report, p. 41).

Helms' recollection was less certain. Helms did recall that he was briefed by Harvey when Harvey first contacted Rosselli in April 1962. He remembered that he "reluctantly" had approved the operation, but that he had no confidence that it would succeed. (Helms, 7/17/75, p. 23)

When asked if he authorized sending the poison pills to Florida, Helms testified:

"I believe they were poison pills, and I don't recall necessarily approving them, but since Harvey alleges to have them and says that he took them to Miami, I must have authorized them in some fashion." (Helms, 6/13/75, p. 44)

Helms confirmed that Harvey was "reporting quite regularly what was going on. Whether he reported everything or not, I do not know." It was Helms' expectation that Harvey would have reported to him a matter such as the pills. (Helms, 6/13/75, p. 105) However, Helms also testified:

"You saw the I.G. Report says that I was kept currently informed. Maybe I was and maybe I wasn't, and today I don't remember it, as I have said. But I do not recall ever having been convinced that any attempt was really made on Castro's life." (Helms, 7/18/75, p. 32)

[2] Whether Helms was aware of AMLASH's intention specifically to assassinate Castro, as opposed to AM/LASH's potential for leading a coup against Castro, is discussed infra, pp. 174–175.

[3] Bissell served as DDP from January 1, 1959, to February 17, 1962. (President Kennedy decided to replace Dulles and Bissell because of the failure of the Bay of Pigs (Bissell, 6/9/75, pp. 6–8)] Helms, who had been Bissell's Deputy, succeeded Bissell in February 1962 as DDP. He was appointed DDCI in April 1965, and DCI in June 1966.

face that the plot involved assassination, although Bissell and Edwards insist that the real meaning must have been understood. Certain other evidence before the Committee suggests that Dulles and Cabell did know about the assassination plots; other evidence suggests that they did not. (See subsection (b) below.)

(ii) *McCone.*—McCone testified that he did not know about or authorize the plots. Helms, Bissell and Harvey all testified that they did not know whether McCone knew of the assassination plots. Each said, however, that he did not tell McCone of the assassination efforts either when McCone assumed the position of DCI in November 1961 or at any time thereafter until August 1963, when Helms gave McCone a memorandum from which McCone concluded that the operation with underworld figures prior to the Bay of Pigs had involved assassination. The Inspector General's Report states that Harvey received Helms' approval not to brief McCone when the assassination efforts were resumed in 1962. Harvey testified this accorded with his recollection. On other occasions when it would have been appropriate to do so, Helms and Harvey did not tell McCone about assassination activity. Helms did not recall any agreement not to brief McCone, but he did not question the position taken by Harvey or the Inspector General's Report. Helms did say that McCone never told him not to assassinate Castro. (These matters, as well as the various reasons put forward by Harvey and Helms for not briefing McCone, are set forth in Section (c) below.)

(b) *Did Allen Dulles Know of or Authorize the Initial Plots Against Castro.*[1]

Both Allen Dulles and General Cabell are deceased. The Committee's investigation of this question relied on the available documents and the testimony of those who served under Dulles and Cabell who are still living.[2]

(i) *Dulles' Approval of J. C. King's December 1959 Memorandum.*—On December 11, 1959, J. C. King, head of CIA's Western Hemisphere Division, wrote a memorandum to Dulles observing that a "far left" dictatorship now existed in Cuba which, "if" permitted to stand, will encourage similar actions against U.S. holdings in other Latin American countries.

One of King's four "Recommended Actions" was:

> Thorough consideration be given to the elimination of Fidel Castro. None of those close of Fidel, such as his brother Raul or his companion Che Guevara, have the same mesmeric appeal to the masses. Many informed people believe that the disappearance of Fidel would greatly accelerate the fall of the present Government.

A handwritten note indicates that Dulles, with Bissell's concurrence, approved the recommendations.[3]

---

[1] This evidence relates to the aborted incident in July 1960 and what the Inspector General's Report referred to as the initial phase of the assassination effort involving the underworld. With respect to the "schemes" prior to that operation, the I. G. Report concluded it could "find no evidence that any of the schemes were approved at any level higher than division, if that." (I. G. Report, p. 10)

[2] The Inspector General questioned neither Dulles nor Cabell in preparing his Report in 1967, although both were then alive.

[3] The Committee received this document on November 15, 1975, after printing of this Report had begun. As a consequence, there was no opportunity to question either King or Bissell concerning the meaning of "elimination", what consideration was in fact given to Castro's "elimination", and whether any planning resulting from this document in fact led to the actual plots. In this regard it should be noted that Bissell had a "dim recollection" of a conversation prior to early autumn or late summer 1960 with King (the author of the above memorandum) concerning a "capability to eliminate Castro if such action should be decided upon". (Bissell, 6/9/75, p. 19) See p. 74.

(ii) Dulles' January 1960 Statement to the Special Group.—On January 13, 1960, Allen Dulles, in what was apparently the first Special Group discussion of a covert program to overthrow Castro, emphasized that "a quick elimination of Castro" was not contemplated by the CIA. (Special Group Minutes, 1/13/60) According to the minutes, Dulles first "noted the possibility that over the long run the U.S. will not be able to tolerate the Castro regime in Cuba, and suggested that covert contingency planning to accomplish the fall of the Castro government might be in order." Then in response to the State Department representative's comment that "timing was very important so as to permit a solidly based opposition to take over," Dulles "* * * emphasized that we do not have in mind a quick elimination of Castro, but rather actions designed to enable responsible opposition leaders to get a foothold."

(iii) Meetings in March 1960.—According to a memorandum of a meeting on March 9, 1960, J. C. King, Chief of CIA's Western Hemisphere Division, told the Task Force which was in charge of Cuban operations:

That the DCI is presenting a special policy paper to the NSC 5412 representatives. He mentioned growing evidence that certain of the "Heads" in the Castro government have been pushing for an attack on the U.S. Navy installation at Guantanamo Bay and said that an attack on the installation is in fact, possible.
3. Col. King stated * * * *that unless Fidel and Raul Castro and Che Guevara could be eliminated in one package—which is highly unlikely—this operation can be a long, drawn-out affair and the present government will only be overthrown by the use of force.*" [Memo for the Record, March 9, 1960. (Emphasis added.)]

A lengthy meeting of the National Security Council on the following day involved a discussion of American policy to "bring another government to power in Cuba." The minutes of that meeting report that:

Admiral Burke thought we needed a Cuban leader around whom anti-Castro elements could rally. Mr. Dulles said some anti-Castro leaders existed, but they are not in Cuba at present. The President said we might have another Black Hole of Calcutta in Cuba, and he wondered what we could do about such a situation * * * *Mr. Dulles reported that a plan to effect the situation in Cuba was being worked on. Admiral Burke suggested that any plan for the removal of Cuban leaders should be a package deal, since many of the leaders around Castro were even worse than Castro.* (*Id.*, 9) (Emphasis added.)

On March 14, Dulles and J. C. King attended a Special Group meeting at the White House. The minutes state that:

There was a general discussion as to what would be the effect on the Cuban scene if *Fidel and Raul Castro and Che Guevara should disappear simultaneously.* Admiral Burke said that the only organized group within Cuba today were the Communists and there was therefore the danger that they might move into control. Mr. Dulles felt this might not be disadvantageous because it would facilitate a multilateral action by OAS. Col. King said there were few leaders capable of taking over so far identified. [Memo for the Record, March 15, 1960 (Emphasis added.)]

Participants in these National Security Council and Special Group meetings testified that assassination was neither discussed nor considered. That testimony and details concerning the context of those meetings is set forth fully in the section dealing with whether President Eisenhower was aware of the plots against Castro.

(iv) Rescission of Accident Plot in July 1960.—As discussed above (pp. 72–73), in July 1960, Bissell's assistant, Tracy Barnes, approved sending a cable to CIA's Havana station stating that "possible removal of top three leaders receiving serious consideration at Head-

quarters," and giving instructions to carry out a plan to kill Raul Castro. J. C. King was the authenticating officer on the cable. A few hours later a second cable, bearing only Barnes' signature, rescinded the first.

King told the Committee that he remembered nothing of this event, and Barnes is deceased. Bissell testified that he did not remember the incident and that he did not know whether Dulles had known about the cable. (Bissell, 9/10/75, p. 74) When asked why the cable might have been rescinded, Bissell speculated that

> It may well have embodied a judgment on Dulles' part that this effort concerning Raul Castro was altogether too risky, and technically not sufficiently likely of success (Bissell, 9/10/75, p. 76)

He speculated further that Headquarters might have been considering the elimination of all three Cuban leaders, and that the cable authorizing the assassination of Raul was rescinded because it fell short of that broader objective. (Bissell, 9/10/75, pp. 76–77)

The Executive Officer to the Chief of the Cuba covert action project sent the cables and testified that he had "heard" that Dulles had countermanded the plan and had indicated that "assassination was not to be considered." (Duty Officer, 8/11/75, p. 29)[1]

The officer added, however, that he had no personal knowledge of the reason for calling off the plan, or even if Dulles had been the one who called it off. He further testified that:

> [Dulles] indicated that assassination was not to be considered * * * This would be conforming with what I had understood the general practice was. (Duty Officer, 8/11/75, pp. 29–30)

(v) *Briefing of Dulles on Use of Underworld Figures in September 1960.*

(1) *Evidence concerning what Dulles Was Told.*—Bissell recalled that "in the latter part of September " there was "a meeting in which Col. Edwards and I briefed Mr. Dulles and General Cabell" about the plan to assassinate Castro. (Bissell, 6/9/75, p. 20) Bissell testified that "Colonel Edwards outlined in somewhat circumlocutious terms the plan that he had discussed with syndicate representatives." (Bissell, 6/9/75, p. 22) He stated that Edwards had said :

---

[1] The countermanding cable to the Havana station, which was "Operational Immediate," was sent the morning after the cable of the previous night. The officer who sent that cable testified :

"* * * I saw the cable and was told that, to the best of my knowledge, my memory is that the Director [Dulles], not the Deputy Director [Bissell] * * * had countermanded the cable and had directed that—had indicated that assassination was not to be considered." (Duty Officer, 8/11/75, p. 29)

The officer stated that he did not talk to either Dulles or Bissell about the countermanding cable, but that he did see the cable and in all likelihood heard of the reason for Dulles' reaction in discussions the same morning with his superior, the Chief of the Cuba project. (Duty Officer, 8/11/75, pp. 30–32)

That contact had been made with [the underworld], that a plan had been prepared for their use, and I think he either said in as many words or strongly inferred that the plan would be put into effect unless at that time or subsequently he was told by Mr. Dulles that it should not be." (Bissell, 6/9/75, p. 22)[1]

The CIA's 1967 Inspector General's Report, based on interviews with Edwards and Bissell, said Dulles and Cabell were briefed as follows:

> The discussion was circumspect. Edwards deliberately avoided the use of any "bad words." The descriptive term used was "an intelligence operation." Edwards is quite sure that the DCI and the DDCI clearly understood the nature of the operation he was discussing. He recalls describing the channel as being "from A to B to C." As he then envisioned it, A was Maheu, B was Rosselli, and C was the principal in Cuba. Edwards recalls that Mr. Dulles merely nodded, presumably in understanding and approval. Certainly there was no opposition. Edwards states that, while there was no formal approval as such, he felt that he clearly had tacit approval to use his own judgment. (I.G. Report, pp. 17–18)

Bissell testified that the description sounded "highly plausible." (Bissell, 6/9/75, p. 24) Edwards said it was "accurate." (Edwards, 5/30/75, p. 11)

In light of the manner in which Bissell and Edwards described briefing Dulles, the question arises as to whether Dulles in fact would have understood that the operation involved assassination. The Inspector General, in attempting to "conjecture as to just what the Director did approve," decided:

> It is safe to conclude, given the men participating and the general subject of the meeting, that there was little likelihood of misunderstanding—even though the details were deliberately blurred and the specific intended result was never stated to unmistakable language. It is also reasonable to conclude that the pointed avoidance of "bad words" emphasized to the participants the extreme sensitivity of the operation. (I.G. Report, p. 18)

Bissell testified that:

> I can only say that I am quite sure I came away from that meeting—and there was, I think subsequent occasions when this came up between Mr. Dulles and myself, and I am quite convinced that he knew the nature of the operation.
> Q. What were the subsequent conversations you had with Mr. Dulles in which you concluded that he knew that this was an assassination effort?
> BISSELL. * * * it's really a guess on my part that such conversations occurred * * * I do believe they did occur in that during the entire autumn I suppose I must have spoken to Mr. Dulles practically daily about some aspect of the whole Cuban operation and I am virtually certain that he would in one or another of those conversations and probably more than once have asked if there was anything to report about the Sheffield Edwards' operation. He also may have been in direct contact with Edwards at that time. (Bissell, 6/9/75, pp. 24–25)

When asked by the Chairman why, in this context, persons within the Agency talked "in riddles to one another," Bissell replied that:

> * * * I think there was a reluctance to spread even on an oral record some aspects of this operation.
> CHAIRMAN. Did the reluctance spring from the fact that it simply grated against your conscience to have to speak more explicitly?
> BISSELL. I don't think it grated against my conscience. I think it may have been a feeling that the Director preferred the use of the sort of language that is described in the Inspector General's Report. (Bissell, 6/9/75, p. 25)

---

[1] Bissell testified that he was relying on the dating provided in the Inspector General's Report, but that his statements concerning what was said at the meeting were based on his unaided recollection. (Bissell, 6/9/75, pp. 20–22)

Bissell, in a subsequent appearance before the Committee, again addressed the issue of whether he and Edwards had made it clear to Dulles that what was involved was an assassination operation:

I thought I made clear that it was my impression—and I believe the impression incidentally that I thought was confirmed in the [I.G. Report]—that in discussing this with Dulles and Cabell * * * the objective of the operation was made unmistakably clear to them. The terms "an intelligence operation," I think someone said, was that not a cover designation? But we would not under any circumstances have told Allen Dulles that this was an intelligence collection operation. If I said that on Monday, I must have given a wrong impression. (Bissell, 6/11/75, p. 24)

On the other hand, the only author of the Inspector General's Report still with the CIA testified that in his opinion a "pointed avoidance of 'bad words'" would have made it less likely that an "intelligence operation" would have been understood as an assassination attempt, and that "it was open to question how clearly this was stated to Mr. Dulles and whether or not Mr. Dulles understood." (Colby/I.G., 5/23/75, p. 10)

Sheffield Edwards was quite infirm when examined by the Committee and has since died.[1] Edwards testified before the Committee as follows:

* * * [T]his possible project was approved by Allen Dulles, Director of CIA, and by General Cabell, the Deputy Director. They are both dead.

The CHAIRMAN. How do you know, Colonel, that the project had been approved by these two gentlemen?

Edwards. I personally briefed Allen Dulles * * * and Cabell (Edwards, 5/30/75, pp. 5-6)

In his interview with the Rockefeller Commission, Edwards testified:

Q. Now, who inside the Agency besides Bissell did you have any contact with on the top echelon?
A. Very important. The plan was approved by Allen Dulles and General Cabell. (Edwards, Rockefeller Comm., 4/9/75, p. 5.)

The Support Chief who had been the case officer for the operation involving underworld figures testified that when he and Edwards discussed the matter in 1975, prior to giving evidence to the Rockefeller Commission, he was sure that Edwards had told him Dulles had approved the plot. (O.C., 5/30/75, pp. 58-59) He added that he was "reasonably sure" or "knew" in the "back of my mind" that either Edwards or Bissell had also told him of Dulles' knowledge when the plot was underway in 1960-62. (O.C., 5/30/75, pp. 33-34; 36; 60)[2]

A review of Dulles' calendar for August through December 1960 showed no meeting involving Dulles, Cabell, Bissell and Edwards.[3] Of course, such a meeting could have occurred without having been noted on Dulles' calendar.

---

[1] As its investigation proceeded, the Committee sought to reexamine Edwards but he died before this could be accomplished. The Committee was unable to examine Edwards concerning either the claimed briefing of Dulles and Cabell, or his conflicting statements about Dulles in two memoranda. Those conflicting memoranda are set forth, *infra*, at p. 97-98.

[2] In June 1966, Howard J. Osborn, Edwards' successor as Director of Security, wrote a memorandum for Helms on the Las Vegas tap stating that "the DCI was briefed and gave his approval." When questioned about this memorandum, Osborn stated that he had no firsthand knowledge of the briefing, and that he had most likely obtained this statement from Edwards or the Support Chief.

[3] The calendar also reflects no meetings during the period between Dulles, Edwards and Bissell, or between Dulles and Edwards.

(2) Evidence Concerning When the Briefing Occurred.—Bissell and the Inspector General's Report (which relied on Edwards) placed the briefing of Dulles in "the latter part of September 1960."

Bissell did not have a clear independent recollection of the dates involved, but recalled that discussions concerning the possible use of syndicate members against Castro began "in the autumn of 1960." [1] He recalled initial discussions among himself, Edwards, and Colonel J. C. King, Chief of the Western Hemisphere Division, which he said occurred before Dulles and Cabell were approached about assassinating Castro. According to Bissell,

> those conversations, the subject matter was a capability to eliminate Castro if such action should be decided upon.
> It is, therefore, accurate to say that my best recollection of those conversations (with Edwards and King) is that they addressed themselves to the existence or non-existence of the capability. They were not conclusive or decisive conversations * * * nor would they have revealed a prior decision to implement such a plan by anybody. (Bissell, 6/9/75, p. 19)

The testimony regarding the dates during which assassination planning was undertaken was inexact, and the Committee cannot place those events precisely. According to the Inspector General's Report, the Support Chief contacted Rosselli in early September 1960, and during the week of September 25, the Chief, Maheu, and Rosselli met with Giancana and Trafficante in Miami. (I.G. Report, pp. 18–19) Bissell testified about the sequence of events:

> Q. Well, before we came to the meeting [with Dulles], you had been informed prior to that, had you not, that contact had been made with the Mafia?
> Mr. BISSELL. I had.
> Q. Now were you informed that the Mafia had been given the go ahead to proceed with actual efforts to assassinate Castro?
> BISSELL. Not that early, to my best recollection. I cannot date that at all well. I would suppose that it was within the next two or three weeks. (Bissell, 6/9/75, pp. 20–21.)

On the other hand, Rosselli's testimony suggests that prior to the "latter part of September" 1960, Maheu had indicated that a large sum of money would be paid for Castro's death. (Rosselli, 6/28/75 p. 17) And in a memorandum dated May 14, 1962, Edwards indicated that the briefing of "senior officials" took place after the money had been offered.

It is clear, then, that even if Dulles was informed about the use of underworld figures to assassinate Castro, subordinate agency officials had previously decided to take steps toward arranging for the killing of Castro, including discussing it with organized crime leaders.

(vi) Edwards' Communications to the Justice Department in 1961 and 1962.—As fully described *supra*, pp. 77–79, the FBI discovered in late 1960 that Maheu had been involved in an illegal wiretap in Las Vegas. In April 1961, Maheu told the FBI that the tap had been placed in connection with a CIA operation, and suggested that the FBI contact Edwards to verify this fact.

---

[1] Q. When did you first become aware of any plan or effort to assassinate Mr. Castro—
BISSELL. Well, I became aware of planning a contingency basis for such an operation. My recollection is August * * *
Q. August of 1960?
BISSELL. '60, correct * * * but without reading [the I.G. Report], I would have remembered initial conversations early in the autumn of 1960. (Bissell, 6/9/75, pp. 17–18)

An FBI report of a May 3, 1961 interview with Edwards (in which Edwards vaguely described the use of Giancana as relating to "clandestine efforts against the Castro Government" with no mention of assassination, and a copy of which was given to the Attorney General) stated:

> Col. Edwards advised that only Mr. Bissell (Director of Plans, CIA) and two others in CIA were aware of the Giancana-Maheu activity in behalf of CIA's program *and Allen Dulles was completely unaware of Edwards contact with Maheu in this connection.* He added that Mr. Bissell, in his recent briefings of Gen. Taylor and the Attorney General in connection with their inquiries into CIA relating to the Cuban situation, told the Attorney General that some of the associated planning included the use of Giancana and the underworld against Castro. (FBI memorandum entitled, "Arthur James Balletti, et al.," May 22, 1961) (Emphasis added.)

Bissell said he was certain, however, that the statement regarding Dulles' knowledge about the operation was wrong, and testified:

> Now it (the FBI memorandum) is just flatly contrary to my recollection that Allen Dulles was unaware of these contacts, as I have testified several times. Also, I submit it is quite implausible that I would have briefed General Taylor and the Attorney General—and incidentally, I have no recollection of briefing those two gentlemen except as members of the Board of Inquiry that I have described, of which Allen Dulles himself was a member—it is quite implausible that I would have briefed them on a matter which had been going on for some months, and about which the Director, Mr. Dulles himself, had never been informed. (Bissell, 6/11/75, p. 27)

When asked to speculate on why Edwards would have told the FBI that Dulles was unaware of Edwards' contact with Maheu, Bissell replied:

> I can only surmise that he believed he could secure the cooperation of the Justice Department that he required without in any way involving his superior, Mr. Dulles, and simply did this in a protective fashion. (Bissell, 7/17/75, p. 20)

A year later, on May 7, 1962, Edwards and CIA's General Counsel met with Attorney General Robert Kennedy. (That meeting is discussed extensively below at p. 131 et seq.) Edwards' memorandum of the meeting indicated that he had said that after Rosselli and Giancana had been offered $150,000, Edwards had "then briefed the proper senior officials of [the] Agency" (without specifying whom) and they had "duly orally approved."[1] It further states that "knowledge" of the project had been "kept to a total of six persons."[2]

Dulles had left the Agency before the time of Edwards' second statement.

(*vii*) *General Cabell's Remarks to the Special Group in November 1960.*—Bissell and Edwards testified that Cabell was aware of the Castro plots (Bissell, 6/9/75, p. 22; Edwards, 5/30/75, pp. 5–6)[3]

---

[1] On the same day he wrote the memorandum for the Attorney General, Edwards wrote another memorandum for his own files indicating that after putting Harvey in contact with Rosselli in early April, he had "cautioned him [Harvey] that I felt that any future projects of this nature should have the tacit approval of the Director of Central Intelligence." (5/14/62. Memorandum for the Record) This memorandum, which contained other information which Harvey and Edwards had agreed to include to "falsify" the record, is discussed *infra*, p. 134.
[2] The 1967 Inspector General's Report surmised that thirteen people knew of the plot, including Dulles, based upon Bissell's and Edwards' account of the Dulles briefing.
[3] The Inspector General's Report stated, "With Bissell present, Edwards briefed the Director (Dulles) and the DDCI (Cabell) on the existence of a plan involving members of the syndicate. * * * Edwards is quite sure that the DCI and the DDCI clearly understood the nature of the operation he was discussing." (I.G. Report, p. 17)
The Support Chief testified that prior to the Support Chief's testifying before the Rockefeller Commission, Edwards told him that Cabell had been aware of and authorized the project. (O.C., 5/30/75, p. 64)

The evidence indicates that the meeting between Dulles, Bissell, Edwards, and Cabell occurred sometime "in the autumn" of 1960, probably in late September. The minutes of a meeting of the Special Group on November 3, 1960, reflect the following remarks:

> Finally, Mr. [Livingston] Merchant [Under Secretary of State for Political Affairs] asked whether any real planning had been done for taking direct positive action against Fidel, Raul and Che Guevara. He said that without these three the Cuban Government would be leaderless and probably brainless. He conceded that it would be necessary to act against all three simultaneously. General Cabell pointed out that action of this kind is uncertain of results and highly dangerous in conception and execution, because the instruments must be Cubans. He felt that, particularly because of the necessity of simultaneous action, it would have to be concluded that Mr. Merchant's suggestion is beyond our capabilities. (Special Group Minutes, 11/3/60)

Exactly what the term "direct positive action" meant to the speaker or those listening is uncertain. Merchant was ill and unable to testify; others present at the meeting could not recall what the words meant at the time they were uttered, although some have testified that they could refer to assassination.[1]

Bissell was also asked about the minutes of the November 3 meeting. After reading the reference to "direct positive action," Bissell said, "I find it difficult to understand." (Bissell, 7/17/75, p. 18) He then was asked,

> Q. Do you, in light of the November 3 minutes remain firm that Cabell was knowledgeable (of the assassination plots)?
> A. It casts some doubt on that in my mind.

When asked if it cast "some significant doubt in light of (Cabell's) character," Bissell answered, "Yes." (Bissell, 7/17/75, pp. 22–23)

(c) *Did John McCone Know of or Authorize Assassination Plots During His Tenure as DCI?*

The CIA considered several assassination plots against Castro during McCone's tenure as Director. Harvey initiated his contact with Rosselli in April 1962, and that operation continued into early 1963. In early 1963 the CIA looked into the possibility of assassinating Castro with an exploding seashell and contaminated diving suit. AM/LASH was offered a poison pen device in November 1963, and caches of arms were delivered to Cuba for his use in the following years.

(i) *McCone's testimony.*—McCone testified that he was not aware of the plots to assassinate Castro which took place during the years in which he was DCI, and that he did not authorize those plots. (McCone, 6/6/75, pp. 33, 44–45)[2] He testified that he was not briefed about the assassination plots by Dulles, Bissell, Helms, or anyone else when he succeeded Dulles as Director in November 1961 (McCone, 6/6/75, pp.

---

[1] "Q. Do you read * * * direct, positive action * * * as meaning killing (Fidel Castro. Raul Castro and Che Guevara)?
"A. I would read it that way, yes. (Lansdale, 7/8/75, p. 103)
"Q. * * * would you agree that the words 'direct positive action' appear to question whether there's been any planning in connection with assassinating (the Castros and Guevara)?
"A. I think the phrase 'positive action' could include assassinations, but * * * I'm not sure what was in Mr. Merchant's mind." (Gray, 7/9/75, p. 9.)
[2] McCone testified that he first learned of the Rosselli operation in August 1963, long after it had been terminated. See discussion *infra*, pp. 107–108.

6-7, 17), and that if he had ever been asked about the plots, he would have disapproved. McCone testified:

> I had no knowledge of any authorized plan or planning that might lead to a request for authorization. Of course, during those days it was almost common for one person or another to say, "we ought to dispose of Castro" * * * [b]ut at no time did anyone come to me, or come to other authorities to my knowledge, with a plan for the actual undertaking of an assassination. (McCone, 6/6/75, p. 3)

McCone also testified:

> Senator Hart of Colorado: Did you ever discuss the subject of assassinations with your predecessor, Mr. Dulles?
> McCone: No, I did not.[1]

(ii) *Testimony of Helms, Bissell, and other Subordinate Agency Employees.*—Bissell was DDP under McCone for three months, from November 1961 until February 1962. Helms assumed the duties of DDP from Bissell and served throughout the balance of McCone's terms as Director.

Bissell testified about McCone's knowledge as follows:

> Q. Your testimony is that you never discussed assassinations with Mr. McCone?
> A. That is correct.
> Q. * * * [D]id you tell McCone anything about that conversation with Mr. Harvey in which you at least told him to take over the relationship with the criminal syndicate?
> A. I don't remember so doing. (Bissell, 6/11/75, p. 19)

Helms testified that he did not recall ever having discussed the assassination plots with McCone while the plots were continuing.[2] When asked whether McCone was aware of the assassination plots against Castro, Helms testified:

> No, it isn't my impression that I told him, at least I don't have any impression, unfortunately * * *. Mr. McCone is an honorable man. He has done his own testifying, and all I can say is that I do not know specifically whether he was aware or not. (Helms, 6/13/75, pp. 90, 101-102)

Helms further testified:

> Senator MONDALE. I believe Mr. McCone testified that he never heard of any of these attempts when he was Director. Would you have any reason to disagree with his testimony?
> HELMS. Sir, I have always liked McCone and I don't want to get into an altercation with him. He had access to Harvey and everybody else just the way I had and he had regular access to the Attorney General.

*   *   *   *   *   *   *

> Senator MONDALE. If you were a member of this Committee wouldn't you assume that Mr. McCone was unaware of the assassination attempts while they were underway?
> HELMS. I don't know how to answer that, Senator Mondale. He was involved in this up to his scuppers just the way everybody else was that was in it, and I just don't know. I have no reason to impugn his integrity. On the other hand,

---

[1] Walt Elder, McCone's Executive Assistant, testified that Dulles gave McCone from ten to twelve informal briefings between September and November 1961. He also said that Dulles and McCone travelled together on a briefing trip to Europe to enable McCone to get "up to speed" on CIA activities. (Elder, 8/13/75, p. 13)
[2] Helms testified that he first informed McCone about the plot using underworld figures in August 1963. See discussion *supra* at p. 107.

I don't understand how it was he didn't hear about some of these things that he claims that he didn't. (Helms, 7/17/75, pp. 32–33)

* * * * * * *

HELMS. I honestly didn't recall that Mr. McCone was not informed and when I was told that there was evidence that he wasn't informed, I was trying to scratch my head as to why I didn't tell him at the time and my surmises are the best I can come up with. I am really surprised I did not discuss it with him at the time. My relations with him were good, and so my surmises are just the best I am able to do in 1975 over an episode that took place that many years ago. (Helms, 6/13/75, p. 90)

Several other Agency officials who were aware of the assassination plots testified that they had not told McCone of the plots. William Harvey testified that he never spoke with McCone about the operation involving underworld figures or assassination and that, to the best of his knowledge, McCone had not been told about the project. (Harvey, 6/25/75, p. 66)

Sheffield Edwards, when asked whether he had informed McCone about the plot, replied:

EDWARDS. No, I did not inform Mr. McCone.
Q. Was there a reason for why you did not inform Mr. McCone?
EDWARDS. Well, I did not want to drag Mr. McCone into this thing that in my opinion had petered out, and I did not want to involve him. (Edwards, 5/30/75, p. 18)

The Support Chief who had been the case officer for the operation under Edwards, testified that he recalled that Edwards had told him during a discussion about the plots in 1965 that Edwards had not briefed McCone on the operation.

As a matter of fact, I don't think he ever knew about it. From later conversations with Colonel Edwards, not recently, we talked about it, and he said that he was convinced that Mr. McCone never knew about it, it wasn't on his watch, so to speak, and he didn't want to get him involved. (O.C., 5/30/75, pp. 37, 39)

George McManus, Helms' Special Assistant for Cuba during the relevant period, testified that he had not been told about the assassination activities, and gave his opinion that if McCone had been asked to approve an assassination, he "would have reacted violently, immediately." [1]

Walter Elder, McCone's Executive Assistant, testified that he had not known of the underworld operation until August 1963, after it had been terminated, and that in his opinion McCone did not learn of the operation prior to that time. (Elder, 8/13/75, p. 15) [2]

With respect to the Cuban assassination matters, where his knowledge was only secondhand, William Colby said "Mr. McCone did not know of it." (Colby, 5/21/75, p. 101)

---

[1] McManus advanced two reasons for this opinion: (1) "McCone had a great love for the President of the United States and he sort of looked at him as an older son or a brother, a very protective sense he had about the President, President Kennedy, and McCone would have immediately said Jesus, this is a no win ball game.
(2) "Second, as an individual, he would have found it morally reprehensible." (McManus, 7/22/75, p. 33)
McManus also testified: "I always assumed that Mr. Helms would keep the Director fully informed of any activity that he thought was sensitive. * * * Under most circumstances, and indeed under all circumstances you can imagine, Helms would have told McCone, with the exception of a situation in which Helms had been told by higher authority not to tell him." (McManus, pp. 32–34)
McManus told the Committee that he had had no knowledge of the assassination plots prior to reading about them in the newspaper. However, the Inspector General's Report stated in 1967 that McManus was aware of such plots. (I.G. Report, pp. 75–76)
[2] In August 1963 Helms gave McCone a copy of Edwards' May 14, 1962 memorandum to the Attorney General. See discussion *infra* at p. 107.

(iii) *Helms and Harvey Did Not Brief McCone About the Assassination Plots.*—McCone assumed the position of DCI in November 1961. It was also in November 1961 that Bissell asked Harvey to assume operational control over the Castro plot involving underworld figures. Richard Helms replaced Bissell in February of 1962 and was subsequently briefed by Harvey on the existence of the assassination plots. Helms was Harvey's immediate superior and the person to whom he reported about the Castro plot activities.

Harvey testified that in the spring of 1962, when he was preparing to contact Rosselli:

* * * I briefed Helms generally on the takeover of Rosselli, on the doubts about the operation, on the possible * * * future of it, and to the extent it had then been possible, the assessment of Rosselli and the cutting out of various individuals. (Harvey, 6/25/75, p. 65)[1]

Harvey testified that after so informing Helms

[T]here was a fairly detailed discussion between myself and Helms as to whether or not the Director should at that time be briefed concerning this. For a variety of reasons which were tossed back and forth, we agreed that it was not necessary or advisable to brief him at that time.
I then said, as I recall, to Mr. Helms, if you decide in the future that he should be briefed, I would like to know about it in advance to which, to my best recollection, he agreed. (Harvey, 6/25/75, p. 66)

Harvey offered the following explanation for why he and Helms had decided not to discuss the matter with McCone at that time:

There were several reasons for this. One, this operation at that stage had not been assessed. It was obviously questionable on several grounds. It obviously involved knowledge by too many people. We were not even sure at that point it had any remote possibility or rather any real possibility for success. It had arisen with full authority insofar as either of us knew long before I knew anything about it, and before the then-Director became Director of the Agency.
I saw no reason at that time to charge him with knowledge of this, at least until we reached the point where it appeared it might come to fruition or had a chance to assess the individuals involved and determine exactly the problem we faced, including the possible problem—and it was a very, or it appeared to be, and in my opinion was, at that time, a very real possibility of this government being blackmailed either by Cubans for political purposes or by figures in organized crime for their own self-protection or aggrandizement, which, as it turned out, did not happen, but at that time was a very pregnant possibility. (Harvey, 6/25/75, pp. 67-68)
I am definitely not saying that there was any effort to hide or conceal any information from the Director. There was not. This was a discussion as to whether or not it was even necessary or appropriate at this point to take details of this particular operation in an unassessed form to the then-Director at that time. (Harvey, 6/25/75, p. 69)

Harvey stated that he did not have any reason to believe that the assassination activities would have been "disapproved by the Director" had McCone been advised of the project. (Harvey, 6/25/75, p. 69) Harvey said that he had thought the plots "were completely authorized at every appropriate level within and beyond the Agency." (Harvey, 7/11/75, p. 66) When asked why McCone had not been given an opportunity to consider the plot, Harvey replied:

---

[1] Harvey testified that when he took over the Rosselli operation, he had "cut out" both Maheu and Giancana because "regardless of what I may have thought of their trustworthiness * * * they were surplus to the operation." (Harvey, 6/25/75, p. 65)

One of the things that I don't know from my own * * * knowledge * * * is who was briefed in exactly what terms at the time of the so called Las Vegas flop that involved attempts to place a technical surveillance * * * in the Las Vegas hotel room. (Harvey, 7/11/75, p. 46)

Harvey was queried on whether the reasons he had given for not briefing McCone were actually "reasons why he should [have been] briefed forthwith." Harvey replied:

Well, Senator Huddleston, it will be quite easy in looking at it now to say, well I can see your argument. All I can say to you in answer is at that time I didn't feel that it was necessary or advisable. I did not make this decision except in consultation, and had I been disagreed with, that would have been it. And I am not off-loading this on Richard Helms or attempting to at all. It isn't all that easy for me to go back this many years and sort of recast all of the reasoning and be sure I am accurate. And I don't also want to evade it by saying, well, it seemed like a good idea at the time. But actually it did. In other words, this was not something that either Helms or myself felt that at that stage there was any point in attempting to brief the Director on it until, at least, we had a somewhat better handle on it * * *. (Harvey, 7/11/75, pp. 67–68)

* * * * * * *

And I might also add, if I may, * * * as far as either one of us knew at that point he [McCone] might have been or should have been briefed, if you want it that way, by either Allen Dulles or Richard Bissell. (Harvey, 7/11/75, pp. 67–71)

The 1967 report, prepared by the Inspector General for Helms, states that Harvey said: "When he briefed Helms on Rosselli, he obtained Helms' approval not to brief the Director." (I.G. Report, p. 41)

Helms testified that he did not recall this conversation, but that he had no reason to doubt the accuracy of Harvey's testimony and the Inspector General's Report. (Helms, 6/13/75, pp. 32, 106)

Helms, when asked about Harvey's testimony that he and Harvey had agreed not to brief McCone, stated "I frankly don't recall having agreed to this."

My recollection is that I had very grave doubts about the wisdom of this * * *. And as I recall it, we had so few assets inside Cuba at that time that I was willing to try almost anything. But the thing did not loom large in my mind at that time. I was enormously busy with a lot of other things, taking over a new job [as DDP]. Mr. McCone was relatively new in the Agency and I guess I must have thought to myself, well this is going to look peculiar to him and I doubt very much this is going to go anyplace, but if it does, then that is time enough to bring him into the picture. (Helms, 6/13/75, p. 33)

Helms also stated:

It was a Mafia connection and Mr. McCone was relatively new to the organization and this was, you know, not a very savory effort. (Helms, 6/13/75, p. 92)

Helms later testified that he did not "recall ever having been convinced that any attempt was really made on Castro's life."

He said:

I am having a very difficult time justifying before this Committee, because there is something in here that doesn't come together, even for me, I am sorry to say. Because if this was all that clear, as everybody seems to think it was, that there were those pills in that restaurant in Cuba and Castro was about to die, I certainly would have talked to McCone about it. And this never was that clear, I am sorry to say, but it never was, not at that time. (Helms, 7/17/75, p. 34)

On May 7, 1962, Edwards and the CIA's General Counsel, Lawrence Houston, briefed Attorney General Robert Kennedy on the operation involving underworld figures, describing it as terminated.[1]

Harvey told the Inspector General that:

> * * * on 14 May he briefed Helms on the meeting with the Attorney General, as told to him by Edwards. Harvey, too, advised against briefing Mr. McCone and General Carter and states that Helms concurred in this. (I.G. Report, p. 65)

Harvey testified that he had probably told Helms:

> Any briefing of the Director on the discussion with the Attorney General concerning this should come from Colonel Edwards and Larry Houston, the General Counsel, and not from the DDP unless we are asked. (Harvey, 6/25/75, p. 99)

Helms testified that he did not recall this conversation and remarked:

> It seems odd to me only because, if the Attorney General had been briefed on something it would seem very logical that it would be very important to brief the Director at that time on the same thing. (Helms, 6/13/75, p. 107)

Harvey supplied poison pills and weapons to Rosselli and his Cuban associates during a trip to Miami in late April 1962.[2] At a Special Group meeting on April 26, General Taylor requested that Harvey "attend the next meeting and report on agent activities." (Memo from McCone, 4/27/62) On April 26, Harvey was sent a memorandum informing him of General Taylor's request and McCone's wish to meet with Harvey and Lansdale "immediately on your return to discuss the Task Force Activities." (Memo, Elder to Harvey, 4/27/72)

Harvey testified that upon his return, he reported to the Special Group on the "status of the active and potential sources inside Cuba * * *":

> Q. Did you report on the passage of the pills to Rosselli?
> HARVEY. No, I did not.
> Q. Which you had just accomplished in Miami * * * for the purpose of assassinating Fidel Castro.
> HARVEY. No.
> Q. And did you report that to Mr. McCone when he asked you to tell him what you had done in Miami?
> HARVEY. No, I did not. (Harvey, 7/11/75, pp. 16–17)

Harvey stated that he did not tell McCone or the Special Group about the operation at that time because:

> I did not consider either, (a) that this should be in any sense in this amorphous stage, surfaced to the Special Group, nor, as I have attempted to explain before that it should be briefed to John McCone at that point in the state that it was

---

[1] The briefing is described *supra* at p. 131.
According to the Inspector General's Report, Harvey and Rosselli had a farewell dinner before Harvey went on another assignment in June 1963. The meeting was observed by the FBI, and Sam Papich, the FBI liaison with the CIA, notified Harvey that FBI Director Hoover would be informed. Harvey asked Papich to call him if he felt that Hoover would inform the Director about the incident.
"Harvey said that he then told Mr. Helms of the incident and that Helms agreed that there was no need to brief McCone unless a call from Hoover was expected." (I.G. Report, p. 54)

[2] Harvey described the trip to Miami as: "one of a number of periodic trips for the purpose of reviewing in toto * * * the actual and potential operations at the Miami base * * * and this covered the whole gamut from personnel administration, operational support in the way of small craft (and) so on * * *" (Harvey, 7/11/75, pp. 15–16)

in with as little as we knew about it, and with all of the attendant background which at that point, and I was not personally cognizant of all of this, had been going on for approximately, as I recall, two to two-and-a-half years. (Harvey, 7/11/75, p. 18)

Harvey attended an August 10, 1962 meeting of the Special Group Augmented.[1] He testified that Secretary of Defense Robert McNamara suggested at that meeting that the Special Group "consider the elimination or assassination of Fidel." (Harvey, 7/11/75, p. 30) Harvey said that on the day following this Special Group meeting.

> In connection with a morning briefing of John McCone, the question again came up and I expressed some opinion as to the inappropriateness of this having been raised in this form and at that forum [Special Group meeting], at which point Mr. McCone stated in substance that he agreed and also that he had felt so strongly that he had, I believe, the preceding afternoon or evening, personally called the gentleman who made the proposal or suggestion and had stated similar views as to the inappropriateness and that he [McCone] said in addition * * * if I got myself involved in something like this, I might end up getting myself excommunicated. (Harvey, 6/25/75, p. 71)

Harvey stated that he did not tell McCone on that occasion about the actual assassination operation involving Rosselli.

> I would like to recast the time that this took place. This was August of '62. This was at the start of the so-called Missile Crisis * * *.
> A tentative decision had been made at that point that the only sensible thing to do with [the Rosselli operation] was to terminate it as rapidly and cleanly as it could be done * * * I am sure that I had discussed with Rosselli, at least on a tentative basis, by August, the probable necessity of terminating this * * *.

According to the Inspector General's Report, the "medicine" was reported to be still in Cuba at this time. (I.G. Report, pp. 51–52) Harvey testified that the report was referring to the poison pills. (Harvey, 6/25/75, p. 105) [2]

In relation to the August 10 meeting, Helms was asked whether he believed McCone would have stopped an assassination attempt if he had known that one was underway. Helms stated:

> HELMS. The reason I say I don't know * * * is that elsewhere Mr. McCone states that he went to see Mr. McNamara in connection with this August 1962 affair and told Mr. McNamara that he wouldn't have anything to do with this, that I have no recollection, that I don't believe he ever said anything to me about his not wanting to have anything to do with it.
> Q. And you were close to Mr. McCone in that period? You are his Deputy for Plans?
> HELMS. I saw him almost daily.
> Q. And is it your belief that if he had made any such statement to Mr. McNamara that he would have come to you and told you about it at some point?
> HELMS. I just don't know why he didn't but I don't recall any such statement. As I said, and I would like to repeat it, Mr. McCone had given me my job, he had promoted me, I felt close to him, I felt loyal to him, and I would not have violated an instruction he gave me if I could have possibly helped it.
> Q. But in any event, it is your judgment that he did not indicate that he was opposed to assassinations?
> HELMS. Not to me.

---

[1] This meeting and the raising of the suggestion of assassination is discussed in depth at pages 161–169.
[2] Harvey said: "I may have deferred for a period of a few weeks giving an actual order to terminate this as soon as possible * * *" (Harvey, 6/25/75, p. 74)

Walter Elder, McCone's Executive Assistant, testified, however, that he had personally told Helms of McCone's opposition to assassination after the August 10 meeting.[1]

(iv) *The Question of Whether General Carter, McCone's Deputy Director, Learned About the Underworld Plot and Informed McCone.*—As fully described in other sections of this report, the fact that Giancana and Rosselli had been involved in a CIA operation directed against Cuba was brought to the attention of the FBI sometime in mid-1961, although the FBI was not told that the objective of the operation had been to assassinate Castro. The CIA opposed prosecution of Giancana and Rosselli for their involvement in the Las Vegas wiretap because of a concern that the Agency's association with them might be revealed. In the course of communications between the CIA and law enforcement agencies, CIA's general counsel, Lawrence Houston, wrote in a memorandum dated April 26, 1962:

> I * * * briefed the DDCI in view of the possibility that the Attorney General might call him or the Director in the case. General Carter understood the situation and said in due time we might brief the Director. (Memo, Houston to Edwards, 4/26/62)

The Attorney General was subsequently briefed by Houston and Sheffield Edwards; a memorandum of that meeting written by Edwards states that the Attorney General was told that the operation had been terminated.

The Inspector General's Report inquired into precisely what Houston had told Carter and concluded:

> Edwards states that the briefing of the Attorney General and the forwarding of a memorandum of record was carried out without briefing the Director (John McCone), the DDCI (General Carter), or the DDP (Richard Helms). He felt that, since they had not been privy to the operation when it was underway, they should be protected from involvement in it after the fact. Houston had briefed the DDCI on the fact that there was a matter involving the Department of Justice, but Houston had not given the DDCI the specifics. He feels it would have been normal for him to have briefed the DCI in view of the Attorney General's interest, but he also feels quite sure that he would have remembered doing it and does not. He suggested that Edwards' deliberate avoidance of such briefings may have led him also to avoid making any briefings. He recalls no disagreements with Edwards on this point and concludes that he must have accepted Edwards' decision not to brief. (I. G. Report, pp. 63-64)

When testifying before the Committee, Houston could not recall whether he had told Carter that the operation had involved assassination. (Houston, 6/17/75, p. 16) Houston testified that he had learned from Edwards "within a matter of days before we went to see the Attorney General," that the purpose of the operation had been to assassinate Castro. (Houston, 6/17/75, p. 6) Since Houston's discussion with Carter took place, at the earliest, nearly two weeks prior to

---

[1] Elder told the Committee:
"I told Mr. Helms that Mr. McCone had expressed his feeling * * * that assassination could not be condoned and would not be approved. Furthermore, I conveyed Mr. McCone's statement that it would be unthinkable to record in writing any consideration of assassination because it left the impression that the subject had received serious consideration by governmental policy makers, which it had not. Mr. Helms responded, 'I understand.' The point is that I made Mr. Helms aware of the strength of Mr. McCone's opposition to assassination. I know that Mr. Helms could not have been under any misapprehension about Mr. McCone's feeling after this conversation." (Elder Affidavit)

Helms, after reading Elder's affidavit, testified: "I do not have any recollection of such a conversation * * * let me say that in not recalling this conversation, I very seriously doubt that it ever took place." (Helms, 9/16/75, pp. 16, 19)

the Attorney General's briefing,[1] it is possible that he did not know at the time of that conversation that assassination was involved.

General Marshall S. Carter was appointed Deputy Director of the CIA in mid-April 1962. When shown the Houston memorandum by the Committee, Carter testified that he did not recall the meeting with Houston, that he had not been told about the assassination plot during his tenure in the Agency, and that he had never briefed McCone on either the assassination plot or the CIA's use of Giancana and Rosselli. (Carter, 9/19/75, pp. 61, 63)

After reading the sentence of Houston's memorandum stating that Carter had said "in due time we might brief the Director," Carter testified "it is surely contrary to every operational procedure that I've ever followed." (Carter, 9/19/75, p. 61)[2] When asked to explain what might have occurred, he testified:

> Memorandums for the record have very little validity in fact. When you sit down after the fact and write it down, as I say, he could have very easily have come to me and said this is the kind of problem we're faced with. We've had it before. I think you ought to know that we're asking the Department of Justice not to prosecute this character because he's been trying to do a job for us. I think under those circumstances, if it were presented in that way, then I might very well have said, well, you know what you're doing, it's your baliwick, you've done it before, go ahead and do it. (Carter, 9/19/75, p. 67)

(v) *The August 1963 Briefing of McCone.*—An August 16, 1963, *Chicago Sun Times* article claimed that the CIA had had a connection with Giancana.[3] McCone asked Helms for a report about the article. McCone testified that when Helms came to see him, he brought the following memorandum:

> 1. Attached is the only copy in the Agency of a memorandum on subject, the ribbon copy of which was sent to the Attorney General in May of 1962. I was vaguely aware of the existence of such a memorandum since I was informed that it had been written as a result of a briefing given by Colonel Edwards and Lawrence Houston to the Attorney General in May of last year.
> 2. I spoke with Colonel Edwards on the telephone last evening, and, in the absence of Mr. Bannerman on leave, I was with Colonel Edwards' assistance able to locate this copy. As far as I am aware, this is the only written information available on Agency relationships with subject. I hope that this will serve your purpose.
> 3. I assume you are aware of the nature of the operation discussed in the attachment. (Memorandum to Director of Central Intelligence, re: Sam Giancana, from Helms, 8/16/63)[4]

Attached to Helms' memorandum to the DCI was the May 14, 1962, memorandum from Sheffield Edwards to the Attorney General which

---

[1] The memorandum is dated April 26, 1962. The Attorney General was briefed on May 7.
[2] Carter further observed that, since he was new in the Agency at that time, he would have immediately brought the matter to the Director's attention if he had believed it was important and if it had been presented to him by Houston as requiring the Director's consideration. After reviewing other memoranda involved in the case, Carter testified that "this would have appeared to have been a matter that the staff, in the light of the past activities, had been well able to handle." (Carter, 9/19/75, p. 65)
[3] The 8/16/63 *Chicago Sun Times* article stated that "Justice Department sources" believed that Giancana never did any spying for the CIA, but pretended to go along with the Agency "in the hopes that the Justice Department's drive to put him behind bars might be slowed—or at least affected—by his ruse of cooperation with another government agency."
[4] When asked whether this entry in the memorandum suggested that he had previously been aware of the operation, McCone testified that Helms had orally informed him "on that day in August" that it involved assassination. (McCone, 6/6/75, p. 9)

described the operation as having been terminated *before* McCone became DCI. (See discussion, *infra.* p. 132.)

Neither McCone nor Helms was able to remember what precisely was said at the meeting. Walter Elder, who was then McCone's Executive Assistant, recalled:

> Mr. Helms came in with [the memorandum]. He handed it to [McCone] who read it and * * * handed it back without any particular comment other than to say, "Well, this did not happen during my tenure."
>
> * * * *
>
> Q. Was anything else said?
> A. No, he had very little to say about it.
> Q. Did Mr. Helms then leave?
> A. Mr. Helms left. (Elder, 8/13/75, pp. 16–17, 58)

Elder testified that he had concluded that the operation involved assassination from reading the two memoranda that were given to McCone. (Elder, 8/13/75, p. 60) Elder "further concluded that [McCone] was perfectly aware of what Mr. Helms was trying to say to him." (Elder, 8/13/75, p. 60) Elder further testified:

> Q. Other than that conversation that you just described between yourself and Mr. McCone, did he have anything else to say about that memorandum?
> Mr. ELDER. No.
> Q. I take it then he did not tell either you or Mr. Helms that we absolutely could not have this activity going on in the future?
> Mr. ELDER. No. (Elder, 8/13/75, p. 61)

McCone testified that he could not recall whether Helms had told him that the operation referred to in the memorandum had involved assassination, but he did remember that the part of the memorandum stating that $150,000 was to be paid to the principals on completion of the operation had indicated to him when he first saw the memorandum that the aim of the project had been to assassinate Castro. (McCone, 10/9/75, pp. 35–36)

The Inspector General's Report concluded that:

> This is the earliest date on which we have evidence of Mr. McCone's being aware of any aspect of the scheme to assassinate Castro using members of the gambling syndicate. (I.G. Report, p. 70)

3. AT WHAT LEVEL WERE THE CASTRO PLOTS AUTHORIZED OR KNOWN ABOUT OUTSIDE OF THE CENTRAL INTELLIGENCE AGENCY?

The ensuing section sets forth evidence bearing on whether officials outside the CIA in either the Eisenhower, Kennedy, or Johnson Administrations knew about or authorized the attempted assassination of Fidel Castro. The reader is reminded that the early phases of the assassination effort against Castro occurred during the same time as the plot to assassinate Patrice Lumumba (August 1960 through January 1961) and the CIA's involvement with dissidents bent on assassinating Raphael Trujillo (February 1960 through May 1961). The evidence discussed here must be read in conjunction with evidence relating to those other plots to fully understand the authorization and knowledge issues and the milieu within which the various plots occurred.

The first part of this section reviews evidence relating to whether officials of the Eisenhower Administration were aware of or authorized the assassination efforts against Castro undertaken by the CIA during that time—the abortive 1960 "accident" plot and the initiation of the plot involving underworld figures. The second part of this section examines evidence relating to whether officials of the Kennedy Administration were aware of or authorized the continuation of the plot involving the underworld and sending poison to Cuba prior to the Bay of Pigs. Also considered in that part is evidence bearing on events which occurred after the Bay of Pigs that sheds light on whether Kennedy Administration officials subsequently learned of that attempt. The third part of this section examines evidence relating to whether officials of the Kennedy Administration authorized or knew about the second attempt to assassinate Castro involving John Rosselli which began in April 1962. This part closely examines the Administration's effort to overthrow the Castro regime—Operation MONGOOSE—for any bearing it might have on the perception of Agency officials that assassination was within the sphere of permissible activity.

The final parts examine evidence relating to whether the assassination activity during the last year of the Kennedy Administration and in the Johnson Administration—Operation AM/LASH—was authorized or known about by top Administration officials outside the CIA and whether that plot was consistent with general efforts sanctioned by the Administrations to overthrow Castro's government.

(a) *The Question of Knowledge and Authorization Outside The Central Intelligence Agency in The Eisenhower Administration*

(i) *Summary*

The evidence as to whether Allen Dulles, CIA Director during the Eisenhower Administration, was informed of the Castro assassination operation is not clear.

Even assuming that Dulles was informed, authorization outside the CIA for a Castro assassination could, according to the testimony, only have come from President Eisenhower, from someone speaking for him, or from the Special Group. At issue, then is whether President Eisenhower, his close aides, or the Special Group authorized or had knowledge of the Castro assassination plots.

The Committee took testimony on this issue from Richard Bissell and from President Eisenhower's principal staff assistants. In summary, the evidence was:

(a) Bissell testified that he did not inform the Special Group or President Eisenhower of the Castro assassination operation, and that he had no personal knowledge that Allen Dulles had informed either President Eisenhower or the Special Group. However, Bissell expressed the belief that Allen Dulles would have advised President Eisenhower (but not the Special Group) in a "circumlocutious" or "oblique" way. Bissell based this "pure personal opinion" on his understanding of Dulles' practice regarding other particularly sensitive covert operations. But Bissell testified that Dulles never told him that he had so advised President Eisenhower about the Castro assassination operation, even though Dulles had told Bissell when he had employed this "circumlocutious" approach to the President on certain other occasions.

(b) Gordon Gray, Eisenhower's Special Assistant for National Security Affairs and the President's representative on the Special Group, testified that the Special Group never approved a Castro assassination, and that President Eisenhower had charged the Special Group with the responsibility of authorizing all important covert operations. A review of the records of Special Group meetings shows that a query concerning a plan to take "direct positive action" against Castro caused Allen Dulles' Deputy, General Cabell, to advise that such action was beyond the CIA's capability. Gray, Andrew Goodpaster (the President's staff secretary responsible for national security operational matters) and John Eisenhower (Assistant Staff Secretary) each stated that he believed that President Eisenhower would not have considered such a matter in a private meeting with Dulles, would not have approved Castro's assassination, and would not have discussed such a matter without telling him. Each concluded as a matter of opinion that President Eisenhower was never told, and each denied having heard anything about any assassination.

(c) In addition to the Inspector General's Report (which concluded that it could not say that any assassination activity carried on during this period was responsive to Administration pressure), the documentary evidence shows that Castro's removal was discussed at two meetings of the National Security Council and the Special Group in March 1960. The minutes of these meetings indicate that the discussions involved a general consideration of a proposal to train a Cuban exile force to invade Cuba and an assessment that Castro's overthrow might result in a Communist takeover. Gray and Admiral Arleigh Burke, Chief of Naval Operations from 1955 through 1961, testified that these discussions of Castro's removal did not refer to assassination, but rather to the problem of creating an anti-Castro exile force strong enough to ensure a non-Communist successor to the Castro regime. Apparently there was no assassination activity steming directly from those meetings. Another Special Group document stated that planning for "direct positive action" against Cuban leaders was raised at a meeting in the Fall of 1960, shortly after Phase I of the CIA/underworld assassination operation was initiated. The DDCI told the Special Group, however, that such action was beyond the CIA's capability.

(ii) *Richard Bissell's Testimony*

(1) *Lack of Personal Knowledge*

Bissell testified that he knew nothing of authorization outside the CIA for the Castro assassination effort. (Bissell, 6/9/75, p. 30) Bissell testified that he met frequently with the Special Group in the fall of 1960 to discuss Cuban operations, but that he never informed the Special Group or any Administration official that there was a plot underway involving the use of underworld figures to assassinate Castro. (Bissell, 6/9/75, pp. 25–29) Bissell said he did not do so because as Deputy Director of Plans, he reported to the Director, and under Agency procedures, relied on the Director to inform the appropriate persons outside the Agency.

(2) *Assumptions Concerning Dulles*

Based on his belief that Dulles had been briefed about the operation involving underworld figures and understood that it involved assassination, Bissell testified that:

> I went on the assumption that, in a matter of this sensitivity, the Director would handle higher level clearances. By clearance, I mean authorization [1] (Bissell, 6/9/75, p. 26)

Bissell stated that although he believed that Dulles "probably" talked with President Eisenhower:

> the Mafia operation was not regarded as of enormous importance and there were much more important matters to talk about with the President. (Bissell, 7/17/75, p. 25)

Bissell testified that he was only "guessing" that Dulles had informed Eisenhower, and that the President had then given his authorization, "perhaps only tacitly." (Bissell, 7/17/75, pp. 38–39; 6/11/75, p. 6) Bissell said that this guess was "not based on hard evidence," but was "pure personal opinion" (Bissell, 6/9/75, p. 61), derived from his knowledge of "command relationship, of Allen Dulles as an individual, and of his [Dulles'] mode of operations." (Bissell, 6/11/75, p. 6) Bissell emphasized, however:

> I still want to be quite clear, I do not have any recollection of the Director telling me that on this specific operation he had made such an approach and received assent, approval, tacit or otherwise. (Bissell, 6/11/75, p. 11)

In describing the manner in which Dulles might have informed the President of the assassination plot involving underworld figures, Bissell said circumlocution would have been used "to protect the President" in accord with the concept of "plausible deniability." [2]

> My guess is that indeed whoever informed him, that is Dulles directly or Dulles through a staff member, would have had the same desire ... to shield the President and to shield him in the sense of intimating or making clear that something of the sort was going forward, but giving the President as little information about it as possible, and the purpose of it would have been to give the President an opportunity, if he so elected, to cancel it, to order it cancelled, or to allow it to continue but without, in effect, extracting from him an explicit endorsement of the detailed specific plan. (Bissell, 6/9/75, p. 61)

On other occasions involving sensitive covert operations, Bissell said that Dulles had used just such a "circumlocutious approach" with President Eisenhower. (Bissell, 6/11/75, p. 10)

(*iii*) *Testimony of White House Officials*

(1) *Gordon Gray*

Gordon Gray served as President Eisenhower's Special Assistant for National Security Affairs from July 1958 to January 20, 1961. (Gray, 7/9/75, p. 4) Gray was also the President's representative on

---

[1] Bissell reiterated this view in a subsequent appearance: "* * * I felt that the responsibility for obtaining necessary authorization should remain with the Director." (Bissell, 6/11/75, p. 4)

[2] Bissell explained the "plausible deniability" practice as follows:
"Any covert operations, but especially covert operations ... that if successful, would have very visible consequences, it was of course, an objective to carry out in such a way that they could be plausibly disclaimed by the U.S. Government." (Bissell, 6/11/75, p. 5.) Bissell apparently assumed that a corollary to that doctrine required the use of "oblique," "circumlocutious" langage.

the Special Group. (Gray, 7/9/75, p. 4) President Eisenhower instructed Gray that all covert actions impinging on the sovereignty of other countries must be deliberated by the Special Group. (Gray, 7/9/75, p. 6) Gray testified that from July 1958 to January 20, 1961, the Special Group never approved an action to assassinate Castro (Gray, 7/9/75, p. 6) and that no such suggestion was made by Bissell. (Gray, 7/9/75, p. 37)

Gray testified that:

> I find it very difficult to believe, and I do not believe, that Mr. Dulles would have gone independently to him [President Eisenhower] with such a proposal without, for that matter, my knowing about it from Mr. Dulles. (Gray, 7/9/75, p. 35) [1]

Gray further testified that his relationship with President Eisenhower was such that President Eisenhower "would discuss with me anything that came to his attention independently of me." (Gray, 7/9/75, p. 7) And Gray testified that President Eisenhower never discussed with him the subject of a Castro assassination or of the use of the underworld figures and Cubans in such an effort. (Gray, 7/9/75, p. 7)

(2) *Andrew Goodpaster*

Goodpaster served as President Eisenhower's Staff Secretary and Defense Liaison Officer during the last two years of the Eisenhower Administration. (Goodpaster, 7/17/75, p. 3) In addition to responsibility for the President's schedule and supervision of the White House staff, Goodpaster was responsible for handling with the President "all matters of day to day operations" in the foreign affairs and national security field, including the activities of the CIA and the Departments of State and Defense. (Goodpaster, 7/17/75, p. 3) Goodpaster testified that he had a "very close personal relationship" with President Eisenhower and saw the President "essentially every day when [President Eisenhower] was in Washington." (Goodpaster, 7/17/75, p. 4) Gordon Gray and Goodpaster served as the channels between the CIA and the President, and Goodpaster had particular responsibility for "operations in which [President Eisenhower] might take a personal part." (Goodpaster, 7/17/75, p. 4)

Goodpaster testified that he never heard any mention of assassination efforts. (Goodpaster, 7/17/75, p. 5) He said that President Eisenhower never told him about any assassination effort and that it was his belief, under White House procedures and by virtue of his close relationship with President Eisenhower, that if an assassination plan or operation had ever been raised with the President, he (Goodpaster) would have learned of it. (Goodpaster, 7/17/75, p. 5)

> That was simply not the President's way of doing business. He had made it very clear to us how he wanted to handle matters of this kind, and we had set up procedures to see that they were then handled that way. (Goodpaster, 7/17/75, pp. 6–7)

---

[1] Gray pointed out "that I was not with President Eisenhower twenty-four hours a day. It was a few minutes every day, practically every day." (Gray, 7/9/75, p. 35)

According to the records of the Eisenhower Library, Dulles was alone with President Eisenhower on one occasion in the fall of 1960. That meeting lasted ten minutes and occurred on November 25, 1960. The record of the previous portion of the meeting attended by Gray indicates only that, in addition to discussion of operations in another country, "there was also some discussion of Cuba." (Memorandum, November 28, 1960, by Gordon Gray, of Meeting with the President, November 25, 1960, at 10:40 a.m.)

General Goodpaster testified that he found Bissell's assumption of a "circumlocutious" personal conversation between Dulles and the President "completely unlikely."

According to Goodpaster, after the collapse of the Paris Summit Conference between President Eisenhower and Premier Khrushchev as a result of the U-2 incident in the spring of 1960, the Eisenhower Administration reviewed its procedures for approval of CIA operations and tightened them. Goodpaster said that this review was carried out

> with the aim in mind of being sure we had full and explicit understanding of any proposals that came to us and we knew from [President Eisenhower] that in doing that we were responsive to a desire on his part. (Goodpaster, 7/17/75, p. 7)

Goodpaster also said John Foster Dulles was a confidant of the President while Allen Dulles was not. (Goodpaster, 7/17/75, p. 8)

(3) *Thomas Parrott*

Thomas Parrott, a CIA officer, served as Secretary of the Special Group from 1957 until October 1963. (Parrott, 7/10/75, p. 4) Parrott stated that by virtue of this assignment, he was Allen Dulles' assistant in the Special Group. He came to know Dulles well, and gained an understanding of the Director's method of expression and his practice in dealing with the President.[1] (Parrott, 7/10/75, pp. 13–14)

Parrott testified that early in 1959, President Eisenhower directed the Special Group to meet at least once a week to consider, approve, or reject all significant covert action operations. (Parrott, 7/10/75, p. 4) He said that:

> as evidenced in his * * * revitalization * * * of this Committee [the Special Group], [President Eisenhower was] highly conscious of the necessity to be protective * * * in this field, and I just cannot conceive that [President Eisenhower] would have gone off and mounted some kind of covert operation on his own. This certainly would not have been consistent with President Eisenhower's staff method of doing business * * *[2]

(4) *John Eisenhower*

John Eisenhower was Goodpaster's Assistant Staff Secretary from mid-1958 to the end of his father's Administration. (Eisenhower, 7/18/75, pp. 5, 9) Eisenhower testified that his father had confided in him about secret matters "to a very large extent." (Eisenhower, 7/18/75, p. 3) For example, he said that after the Potsdam Conference in July 1945, his father had told him that the United States had developed the atomic bomb (Eisenhower, 7/18/75, p. 3) and that as early as 1956, President Eisenhower had told him of the secret U-2 flights. (Eisenhower, 7/18/75, p. 4)

John Eisenhower said that President Eisenhower never told him of any CIA activity involving an assassination plan or attempt concerning Castro and it was his opinion that President Eisenhower would have told him if the President had known about such activity.

---

[1] Parrott testified:
"I saw him [Allen Dulles] several times a week for hours at a time. I had known him somewhat before . . . but I got to know him very well indeed during these four years." (Parrott, 7/10/75, p. 13)

[2] Parrott further testified that Allen Dulles followed a practice of insisting upon specific orders rather than "tacit approval" and he also found Bissell's assumptions regarding a circumlocutious conversation between President Eisenhower and Allen Dulles "hard to believe." (Parrott, 7/10/75, p. 14)

(Eisenhower, 7/18/75, p. 5) He also said that President Eisenhower did not discuss important subjects circumlocutiously. (Eisenhower, 7/18/75, p. 8) He told the Committee that President Eisenhower believed that no leader was indispensable, and thus assassination was not an alternative in the conduct of foreign policy. (Eisenhower, 7/18/75, p. 14)

(iv) Documentary Evidence

(1) The Inspector General's Report.—The concluding section of the Inspector General's Report advanced several possible responses to Drew Pearson's public charges about CIA links with the underworld.[1] One question posed in the Inspector General's Report was: "Can CIA state or imply that it was merely an instrument of policy?" The answer given was:

> Not in this case. While it is true that Phase Two (the attempt commencing in April 1962) was carried out in an atmosphere of intense Kennedy Administration pressure to do something about Castro, such is not true of the earlier phase. (I.G. Report, p. 132)

(2) The Contemporaneous Documents.—The Committee also examined records of the National Security Council, the Special Group, and other relevant White House files bearing on the question of authorization for the period from Castro's rise to power to the end of the Eisenhower Administration. Three documents were found which contained references arguably related to the subject of assassination.

In March 1960, the National Security Council and the Special Group focused on America's Cuban policy. President Eisenhower had just returned from a foreign trip in which:

> Latin American Presidents had counseled further forbearance by the U.S. in the hope that the members of the Organization of American States would finally see the potential danger in Cuba and take concerted action. (Memorandum of March 10, 1960 NSC Meeting)

Castro was characterized as hostile, but his Communist ties were apparently then unclear.[2] The minutes of the March 10, 1960, NSC meeting stated:

> There is no apparent alternative to the present government in the event Castro disappears. Indeed the result of Castro's disappearance might be a Communist takeover.

The general covert action plan against Cuba came out of these March 1960 meetings of the NSC and Special Group.[3]

The record of the NSC meeting of March 10, 1960 (at which President Eisenhower was present), states that Admiral Arleigh Burke, in commenting on Allen Dulles' statement that the Cuba covert action plan was in preparation, "suggested that any plan for the removal of Cuban leaders should be a package deal, since many of the Cuban leaders around Castro were even worse than Castro." According to the minutes of the Special Group meeting on March 14, 1960 (which

---

[1] On March 3, 1967, Drew Pearson stated in his newspaper column that there was a United States "plot" to assassinate Castro, and that "one version claims that underworld figures actually were recruited to carry out the plot." (Pearson, Washington *Merry Go-Round*, March 3, 1967)

[2] Castro apparently first announced publicly that he was a "Marxist-Lenist" on December 2, 1961. (David Larson, *Cuba Crisis of 1962*, p. 304)

[3] As Gray testified, this plan covered four areas; sabotage, economic sanctions, propaganda, and training of a Cuban exile force for a possible invasion. Gray stated that this plan had nothing to do with assassination. (Gray, 7/9/75, p. 17)

President Eisenhower did not attend), "there was a general discussion as to what would be the effect on the Cuban scene if Fidel and Raul Castro and Che Guevara should disappear simultaneously."

Admiral Burke stated in an affidavit [1] that although he did not recall the March 10, 1960, NSC meeting, he did have a clear recollection of discussions of Cuba policy in the spring of 1960. (Burke affidavit)

Burke stated that the reference to his suggestion at the March 10 meeting "clearly refers to the general covert action plan reported by Allen Dulles at that meeting and to the general consideration given at that time in the U.S. Government to identify Cuban groups with which the U.S. might work to overthrow the Castro regime." (Burke affidavit) Burke continued:

> In this connection, it was my view that the U.S. must support those Cuban groups who would have a sufficient power base among the Cuban people, not merely to overthrow Castro, but to be able to cope with and dismantle his organization as well. It was my firm belief at the time that many people in Castro's organization were Communist and that Castro was probably a Communist. I therefore advocated that any effort to support groups so as to achieve Castro's overthrow must focus, not merely on the leaders at the top of the Castro regime, but on the very strong organization that had been the key to Castro's rise to power, and was the basis for his power.

* * * * * * *

> The question of a Castro assassination never arose at the March 10, 1960 NSC meeting or at any other meeting or discussion that I attended or in which I participated. It is my firm conviction based on five years of close association with President Eisenhower during my service as Chief of Naval Operations, that President Eisenhower would never have tolerated such a discussion, or have permitted anyone to propose assassination, nor would he have ever authorized, condoned, or permitted an assassination attempt. (Burke affidavit)

Gordon Gray testified that the March 10 and March 14, 1960 meetings dealt with plans to overthrow the Castro government, rather than with assassinating Castro. He said that Admiral Burke's comment at the March 10 NSC meeting was part of a lengthy and general discussion about Cuba. Burke's reference to a "package deal" for the removal of Cuban leaders was in direct response to a comment by Allen Dulles that "a plan to affect the situation in Cuba was being worked on." (Gray, 7/9/75, pp. 13–14) Gray said he believed that Dulles "was certainly referring to" the Eisenhower Administration's plan to train Cuban exiles for an invasion, rather than to a targeted attempt on Castro's life.[2] (Gray, 7/9/75, pp. 14, 45) Gray testified that viewing Burke's remarks in context, he believed it was clear that "Admiral Burke * * * was expressing his opinion that if you have any plan [for the overthrow of Castro] it ought to take these factors into

---

[1] Admiral Burke was unable to testify in person because he was hospitalized.

[2] The memorandum of an internal CIA meeting shows that the first meeting of the CIA task force established to plan the training of a Cuban exile force was held on March 9, 1960, the day before the March 10, NSA meeting. The CIA task force discussed "an operation directed at the overthrow of the Castro regime" and described that operation as one in which a Cuban exile force would be trained for "6–7 months." In the discussion of this operation, it was noted that a principal problem was the weakness of the Cuban exile groups which "had no real leader and are divided into many parts," but it was hoped that during the long training period the "opposition groups will have been merged and will have formed a government-in-exile to which all trained elements could be attached." (Memorandum March 9, 1960)

According to the memorandum of the meeting, J. C. King, Chief of the CIA's Western Hemisphere Division, had stated, "unless Fidel and Raul Castro and Che Guevara could be eliminated in one package—which is highly unlikely—this operation can be a long, drawn-out affair and the present government will only be overthrown by the use of force." (*Id.*, p. 1)

consideration, that you might end up with a Communist government."
(Gray, 7/9/75, p. 45)

Admiral Burke stated that the "general discussion" at the March 14 Special Group meeting "clearly did not involve a discussion of assassination of Cuban leaders, but to the possible effects should only those leaders be overthrown by a group not powerful enough to also master the organization those leaders had established in Cuba." [1] (Burke affidavit) Burke added:

> Thus, it was consistent with my views then that I should have been recorded in the record of the March 14 meeting as warning in this discussion that the Communists might move into control even if these three top leaders should be overthrown. As stated above, I strongly believed that a strong, organized group must be in the forefront of any effort to overthrow the Castro government. (Burke affidavit)

When the question of "whether any real planning had been done for taking direct positive action against Fidel, Raul and Che Guevara" was subsequently raised at a Special Group meeting on November 3, 1960, General Cabell reportedly said:

> that action of this kind is uncertain of results and highly dangerous in conception and execution, because the instruments must be Cubans. He felt that, particularly because of the necessity for simultaneous action, it would have to be concluded that (such action) is beyond our capabilities. (Minutes Special Group Meeting, November 3, 1960)

The reference to "direct positive action" is ambiguous and subject to different interpretations, including a suggestion that assassination be explored.[2]

However, it is clear that at most a question was being asked. Moreover, assuming that "direct positive action" meant killing, it is significant that shortly after assassination plots were begun, the CIA Deputy Director told the Special Group that such action was "beyond our capabilities."

(b) The Question of Knowledge and Authorization Outside The Central Intelligence Agency during the Kennedy Administration

We have divided the evidence on whether or not assassination plots were authorized during the Kennedy Administration into three sections. The first primarily relates to the assassination operation involving underworld figures prior to the Bay of Pigs invasion in April 1961. The second deals with the post-Bay of Pigs period, and

---

[1] The record of the March 14 meeting states: "Admiral Burke said that the organized group within Cuba today was the Communists and there was therefore the danger they might move into control."

[2] Testimony varied as to the meaning of the phrase "direct positive action" and of General Cabell's response in the November 3, 1960 memorandum.

Gray testified that it could be taken to include assassination, but he did not know whether Mr. Merchant intended to refer to assassination or not. (Gray, 7/9/75, p. 9)

Parrott, the author of the memorandum, testified that, although he had no recollection of the November 3, 1960 meeting, it was his opinion, based on the context of weekly Special Group meetings and discussion in the fall of 1960, that this discussion centered on the possibility of a palace coup, as opposed to a paramilitary operation mounted from outside Cuba; General Cabell was indicating that "we simply do not have agents inside of Cuba to carry out this kind" of a coup. (Parrott, 7/10/75, pp. 19–21) Parrott also testified that the phrase "direct positive action" was not a euphemism, and that he did not employ euphemisms in Special Group records, except for references to the President. (Parrott, 7/10/75, pp. 19–21)

Bissell testified that he found it "difficult to understand" that General Cabell would have told the Special Group that it was beyond the CIA's capabilities to take "direct positive action" (if that referred to assassination) in light of Bissell's assumption that General Cabell was informed of the CIA/underworld assassination effort. (Bissell, 7/17/75, pp. 15–18)

Mr. Merchant was unable to testify because of ill health and orders of his physician.

the Rosselli operation in the spring of 1962. That section also discusses Operation Mongoose. A third section discusses the 1963 laboratory schemes and the AM/LASH plot.

(*i*) *Pre-Bay Of Pigs Assassination Plot*

The testimony was essentially the same as for the Eisenhower Administration. Bissell again said he assumed and believed that Dulles had met with President Kennedy and informed him, in a circumlocutious fashion, that the operation had been planned and was being attempted. Bissell also testified that he (Bissell) informed neither the President nor any other officials outside the CIA about the assassination efforts. Each Kennedy Administration official who testified said that he had not known about or authorized the plots, and did not believe the President would have authorized an assassination.

(1) *Bissell's Testimony Concerning His Assumption That Dulles Told The President.*—Richard Bissell continued as DDP, the principal agency official responsible for efforts against the Castro regime, including both the Bay of Pigs operation and the assassination plots, when Kennedy became President in January, 1961. Bissell is the only surviving CIA policy maker with first hand knowledge of high-level decisions in the pre-Bay of Pigs phase of the Castro assassination plot involving underworld figures. Although Bissell testified that Allen Dulles never told him that Dulles had informed President Kennedy about the underworld plot, Bissell told the Committee that he believed Dulles had so informed President Kennedy and that the plot had accordingly been approved by the highest authority.[1]

Senator BAKER. * * * you have no reason to think that he [Dulles] didn't or he did [brief the President]. But the question I put was whether or not in the ordinary course of the operations of the CIA as you know them under their traditions, their rules and regulations, and their policies in your opinion—was the President, President-elect briefed or was he not?

BISSELL. I believe at some stage the President and the President-elect both were advised that such an operation had been planned and was being attempted.

Senator BAKER. By whom?

BISSELL. I would guess through some channel by Allen Dulles.

The CHAIRMAN. But you're guessing, aren't you?

Mr. BISSELL. I am, Mr. Chairman, and I have said that I cannot recollect the giving of such briefing at the meeting with the President-elect in November or in any meeting with President Eisenhower. (Bissell, 6/9/75, pp. 38–39)

Bissell characterized his belief that the President had been informed as "a pure personal opinion" (Bissell, 6/9/75, pp. 60–61); on another occasion the following exchange occurred:

Senator MORGAN. Mr. Bissell, it's a serious matter to attribute knowledge of this sort to the President of the United States, especially one who cannot speak for himself. Is it fair to assume that out of an abundance of caution you are simply telling us that you have no knowledge unless you are absolutely certain? * * * I gather that you think * * * it [assassination plot information] came out but because of the seriousness of the accusation you are just being extremely cautious * * * is that a fair assumption to make?

BISSELL. That is very close to a fair assumption, sir. It's just that I have no direct knowledge, first-hand knowledge of his [President Kennedy's] being advised, but my belief is that he knew of it [assassination plans]. (Bissell, 6/9/75, pp. 55–56)

---

[1] Bissell never asked Dulles whether Dulles had informed President Kennedy's National Security Adviser, McGeorge Bundy about the plot. (Bissell, 6/9/75, p. 34.)

Bissell said that he had not personally informed White House officials or the President of the assassination plot because he "left the question of advising senior officials of the government and obtaining clearances in Allen Dulles' hands." (Bissell, 6/9/75, pp. 29, 33) As with President Eisenhower, Bissell once again "assumed" that Dulles "had at least intimated [to President Kennedy] that some such thing was underway." (Bissell, 6/9/75, p. 33) [1]

Bissell speculated that Dulles would have engaged in a "circumlocutious" conversation using "rather general terms," although Dulles did not mention such a briefing to Bissell, as he had on some past occasions when he had circumlocutiously briefed President Eisenhower on sensitive matters. (Bissell, 6/11/75, pp. 6, 10–14)

Bissell repeatedly coupled Eisenhower and Kennedy when he speculated that the Presidents would have been advised in a manner calculated to maintain "plausible deniability." (Bissell, 6/9/75, pp. 38, 57; 6/11/75, pp. 5–6):

> In the case of an operation of high sensitivity of the sort that we are discussing, there was a further objective that would have been pursued at various levels, and that was specifically with respect to the President, to protect the President. And, therefore, the way in which I believe that Allen Dulles would have attempted to do that was to have indicated to the two successive Presidents the general objective of the operation that was contemplated, to make that sufficiently clear so that the President—either President Eisenhower or President Kennedy—could have ordered the termination of the operation, but to give the President just as little information about it as possible beyond an understanding of its general purpose. Such an approach to the President would have had as its purpose to leave him in the position to deny knowledge of the operation if it should surface.
>
> My belief—a belief based, as I have said, only to my knowledge of command relationship of Allen Dulles as an individual, and of his mode of operations—is that authorization was obtained by him in the manner that I have indicated. I used the word on Monday "circumlocutious," and it was to this approach that I referred.
>
> Assuming for the moment that I am correct, since the effort would have been to minimize the possibility of embarrassment to the President, it is, I think, understandable that neither I nor anyone else in the Agency would have discussed this operation on our own initiative with, for instance, members of the White House staff.
>
> The effort would have been to hold to the absolute minimum the number of people who knew that the President had been consulted, had been notified and had given, perhaps only tacitly, his authorization. (Bissell, 6/11/75, pp. 5–6)

(2) *Bissell's Testimony Regarding His Own Actions.*—When Bissell was asked if he had informed anyone outside the CIA that Bissell was asked if he had informed anyone outside the CIA that an effort to assassinate Castro was underway, he replied, "not to my recollection." He added that he was never told that any official outside the Agency had been made aware of such an effort. (Bissell, 6/9/75, pp. 28–30)

Bissell had ample opportunity to inform appropriate officials outside the CIA of the plot. He worked closely with McGeorge Bundy, the White House liaison for Cuban affairs and formerly one of Bissell's

---

[1] Prior to the Bay of Pigs, there were many meetings at which both the President and Dulles were present. The Presidential logs from the Kennedy Administration indicate only one meeting before the Bay of Pigs invasion at which the President and Allen Dulles may have met privately. This meeting took place on March 25, 1961. (There is no record of the meeting. We feel compelled to state that the fact of this meeting, on the evidence available, is of little, if any significance or relevance.)

students at Yale University. Bissell and Bundy were also personal friends, but Bissell testified that he never told Bundy about the plot, a fact Bundy confirmed. (Bissell, 6/9/75, pp. 16, 28–29; 7/22/75, p. 31) (Bundy, 7/11/75, p. 41) Bissell testified that:

* * * almost from the beginning of the Kennedy Administration, the President himself and a number of Cabinet members and other senior officials took a very active interest in the operation(s) concerning Cuba. (Bissell, 6/9/75, p. 16)

Bissell was "almost invariably" present at meetings on Cuba in which the President and other senior officials took an "active interest." (Bissell, 6/9/75, p. 17) Bissell testified that he did not then inform any of them of the assassination plot. (Bissell, 6/9/75, p. 39)

(3) *Kennedy Administration Officials Testimony.*—The Committee has taken testimony from all living officials high in the Kennedy Administration who dealt with Cuban affairs.[1] The theme of their testimoney was that they had no knowledge of any assassination plan or attempt by the United States government before or after the Bay of Pigs invasion, and that they did not believe President Kennedy's character or style of operating would be consistent with approving assassination.

Secretary of Senate Dean Rusk testified, "I never had any reason to believe that anyone that I ever talked to knew about had any active planning of assassination underway." (Rusk, 7/10/75, p. 65)

Secretary of Defense Robert McNamara stated that he had "no knowledge or information about * * * plans or preparations for a possible assassination attempt against Premier Castro." (McNamara, 7/11/75, p. 7)

Roswell Gilpatric, Deputy Secretary of Defense under McNamara, said that killing Castro was not within the mandate of the Special Group, which he construed as having been only to weaken and undermine "the Cuban economy." (Gilpatric, 7/8/75, p. 28)

General Maxwell Taylor, who later chaired Special Group meetings on Operation MONGOOSE, stated that he had "never heard" of an assassination effort against Castro, and that he never raised the question of assassination with anyone. (Taylor, 7/9/75, pp. 7–8, 72, 19)

McGeorge Bundy stated that it was his "conviction" that "no one in the Kennedy Administration, in the White House, or in the cabinet, ever gave any authorization, approval, or instruction of any kind for any effort to assassinate anyone by the CIA." (Bundy, 7/11/75, p. 54) Bundy said that he was never told that assassination efforts were being conducted against Castro. (Bundy, 7/11/75, p. 63)

Walt W. Rostow, who shared national security duties with Bundy before moving to the Department of State, testified that during his entire tenure in government, he "never heard a reference" to an intention to undertake an assassination effort. (Rostow, 7/9/75, pp. 10, 12–13, 38)

---

[1] Most of the testimony from officials high in the Kennedy Administration covered the period after the Bay of Pigs Invasion, involving Operation MONGOOSE and related activities. (See following Section) It was during this period that high officials in the White House State Department, Defense Department, and the CIA were drawn into the detailed planning of Cuban operations. Their testimony concerning the question of authorization for the assassination plots is extensively discussed *infra*, pp. 148–161.

Asked if he had ever been told anything about CIA efforts to assassinate Castro, Richard Goodwin, Assistant Special Counsel to the President, replied, "No, I never heard of such a thing." (Goodwin, 7/18/75, p. 13)[1]

Theodore Sorensen, who said that his "first-hand knowledge" of Cuban affairs was limited to the post-Bay of Pigs period, stated that his general opinion, based on his close contact with President Kennedy, was that

* * * such an act [as assassination] was totally foreign to his character and conscience, foreign to his fundamental reverence for human life and his respect for his adversaries, foreign to his insistence upon a moral dimension in U.S. foreign policy and his concern for this country's reputation abroad and foreign to his pragmatic recognition that so horrendous but inevitably counterproductive a precedent committed by a country whose own chief of state was inevitably vulnerable could only provoke reprisals and inflame hostility. * * * (Sorensen, 7/21/75, p. 5)

Sorensen stated that President Kennedy "would not make major foreign policy decisions alone without the knowledge or participation of one or more of those senior foreign policy officials in whose judgment and discretion he had confidence." (Sorensen, 7/21/75, p. 6)

Sorensen concluded his testimony with the following exchange:

Q. Would you think it would be possible that * * * the Agency, the CIA could somehow have been under the impression that they had a tacit authorization for assassination due to a circumspect discussion that might have taken place in any of these meetings?
SORENSEN. It is possible, indeed, I think the President on more than one occasion felt that Mr. Dulles, by making rather vague and sweeping references to particular countries was seeking tacit approval without ever asking for it, and the President was rather concerned that he was not being asked for explicit directives and was not being given explicit information, so it is possible. But on something of this kind, assassination, I would doubt it very much. Either you are for it or you are not for it, and he was not for it. (Sorensen 7/21/75, pp. 32–33)

(4) *The Question of Whether Assassination Efforts Were Disclosed in Various Briefings of Administration Officials.*

a. Briefing of the President-Elect

In the latter part of November 1960, after the Presidential election, Dulles and Bissell jointly briefed President-elect Kennedy on "the most important details with respect to the operation which became the Bay of Pigs." (Bissell, 6/9/75, p. 34) Bissell testified that he did not believe the ongoing assassination efforts were mentioned to the President-elect at that meeting. (Bissell, 6/9/75, pp. 27, 35–36) Bissell surmised that the reasons he and Dulles did not tell Kennedy at that initial meeting were that they had "apparently" thought it was not an important matter,[2] and that they "would have thought that that was a matter of which he should be advised upon assuming office

---

[1] Goodwin did hear about assassination on two occasions. One involved a meeting between the President and reporter Tad Szulc in November 1961 (see discussion pp. 138–139) and the other involved the Special Group (Augmented) meeting of August 10, 1962. (See pp. 164–165.)

[2] This reason was also given by Bissell in response to the Committee's questioning of his assumption that Dulles probably told President Eisenhower about the assassination operation: "* * * the Mafia operation was not regarded as of enormous importance and there were much more important matters to talk about with the President." (Bissell, 7/17/75, p. 25)

rather than in advance." (Bissell, 6/9/75, p. 35) Bissell's latter comment led to the following exchange:

> The CHAIRMAN. Isn't it a strange distinction that you draw that on the one hand (as) a Presidential designate, as President-elect, he should have all of the details concerning a planned invasion of Cuba, but that he should not be told about an ongoing attempt to assassinate Fidel Castro?
> Mr. BISSELL. I think that in hindsight it could be regarded as peculiar, yes.
> The CHAIRMAN. * * * (I)t just seems too strange that if you were charged with briefing the man who was to become President of the U.S. on matters so important as a planned invasion of a neighboring country, and that if you knew at the time in addition to the planned invasion there was an ongoing attempt to assassinate the leader of that country, that you would tell Mr. Kennedy about one matter and not the other.
> Mr. BISSELL. Well, Mr. Chairman, it is quite possible that Mr. Dulles did say something about an attempt to or the possibility of making use of syndicate characters for this purpose. I do not remember his doing so at that briefing. My belief is that had he done so, he probably would have done so in rather general terms and that neither of us was in a position to go into detail on the matter. (Bissell, 6/9/75, p. 35)

However, Bissell also testified generally that pursuant to the doctrine of "plausible denial," efforts were made to keep matters that might be "embarrassing" away from Presidents. (Bissell, 6/11/75, pp. 5–6)

b. Discussion with Bundy on "Executive Action Capability"

Sometime early in the Kennedy Administration, Bissell discussed with Bundy a "capability" for "executive action"—a term Bissell said included various means of "eliminating the effectiveness" of foreign leaders, including assassination.[1] (Bissell, 7/22/75, p. 32) Bissell did not tell Bundy about the plot against Castro during their discussion of Executive Action capability. (Bissell, 7/22/75, p. 31; Bundy, 7/11/75, p. 41) However, Bissell did say that Castro, Trujillo, and Lumumba might have been mentioned in connection with a discussion of "research" into the capability. (Bissell, 6/11/75, pp. 50–51)

c. Taylor/Kennedy Bay of Pigs Inquiry

Following the failure of the Bay of Pigs invasion, President Kennedy convened a "court of inquiry" which reviewed "the causes of * * * [the] failure" of the operation. (Bissell, 6/9/75, pp. 42, 45) Robert Kennedy, General Maxwell Taylor, Allen Dulles, and Admiral Arleigh Burke comprised the Board. The "Taylor Report," issued on June 13, 1961 after the panel had examined the matter for several weeks, makes no mention of the assassination plot.

Bissell was questioned extensively by the Taylor/Kennedy Board. General Taylor considered Bissell to have been the principal government official in the Bay of Pigs operation. He thought Bissell much more knowledgeable than Dulles, who had deliberately removed himself from the planning and had delegated responsibility to Bissell. (Taylor, 7/9/75, p. 73)

Bissel said he had not disclosed the assassination plot to the Taylor/Kennedy Board and advanced several reasons for not having done so. First, "the question was never asked;" second, Dulles already knew about the operation; third, "by that time the assassination attempt had

---
[1] The evidence concerning who initiated the conversation, when it occurred, and what was said, is discussed extensively in section III–C.

been called off;" fourth, the assassination effort was "not germane" because it did not contribute to the failure of the Bay of Pigs. (Bissell, 6/9/75, pp. 44–46; 6/11/75, p. 39) Bissell added that he had "no reason to believe" that Allen Dulles did not discuss the plot with one or more of the other Board members. (Bissell, 6/9/75, p. 46) However, both General Taylor and Admiral Burke, the only other members of the Board still living, stated that neither Bissell nor Dulles had informed them of the assassination plot. (Taylor, 7/9/75, pp. 72–73; Burke affidavit, 8/25/75)[1]

Bissell's testimony that he had not disclosed the assassination plot to the Kennedy/Taylor Board is consistent with his statement that "I have no knowledge that Robert Kennedy was advised of this [the plot to kill Mr. Castro]." (Bissell, 6/9/75, p. 41)

The Committee tested this statement against other parts of Bissell's testimony. FBI Director Hoover sent the Attorney General a memorandum about the Las Vegas wiretap on May 22, 1961.[2] An attachment to that memorandum quoted Sheffield Edwards as saying that Bissell, in his "recent briefings" of Taylor and Kennedy "told the Attorney General that some of the associated planning included the use of Giancana and the underworld against Castro."

When Bissell was first shown this document by the Committee, he said: "I have no recollection of briefing those two gentlemen except as members of the Board of Inquiry that I have described, of which Allen Dulles himself was a member." (Bissell, 6/11/75, p. 27)

In a subsequent appearance before the Committee, Bissell again said that he had no recollection of the conversation referenced in the May 22 memorandum. (Bissell, 7/22/75, p. 56) He was sure that if such a conversation had occurred it was not before the Kennedy/Taylor Board. (Bissell, 7/22/75, p. 64)

Bissell speculated, however, that the memorandum quoted language which "I might very well have used, that is, the use of the underworld against Castro." (Bissell, 6/11/75, p. 21)

The examination of Bissell on whether he had discussed a pre-Bay of Pigs plot with the Attorney General or General Taylor and, if so, why he used such obscure and indirect language, elicited the following testimony:

Q. Did you, sometime in May of 1961 communicate the state of your awareness to the Attorney General in your briefing to him?

BISSELL. Well, there is a report which I was shown, I think it was last week, I believe it also came from the FBI, but I could be wrong about that, or indicating that I did, at that time in May, brief the Attorney General, and I think General Taylor to the effect that the Agency had been using—I don't know whether Giancana was mentioned by name, but in effect, the Underworld against the Castro regime.

Q. Did you tell them—them being the Attorney General and General Taylor—that this use included actual attempts to assassinate Mr. Castro?

BISSELL. I have no idea whether I did [.] I have no idea of the wording. I think it might quite possibly have been left in the more general terms of using the underworld against the Castro regime, or the leadership of the Castro regime.

---

[1] When asked if Bissell had ever informed him that underworld figures had been offered a large sum to assassinate Castro, General Taylor responded: "No, I never heard that, and it amazes me" (Taylor, 7/9/75, p. 72) Taylor said that during his review of the Bay of Pigs operation no mention was made of an assassination effort against Castro. (Taylor, 7/9/75, p. 72) Taylor noted that Dulles met with the Board of Inquiry some thirty or forty times. (Tayor, 7/9/75, p. 73)

[2] A handwritten note from the Attorney General to his assistant on the face of the memorandum indicates that the Attorney General had seen the document. This memorandum is discussed in detail at Section (7) (b), *infra*.

Q. Mr. Bissell, given the state of your knowledge at that time, wouldn't that have been deliberately misleading information?

BISSELL. I don't think it would have been. We were indeed doing precisely that. We were trying to use elements of the underworld against Castro and the Cuban leadership.

Q. But you had information, didn't you, that you were, in fact, trying to kill him?

BISSELL. I think that is a way of using these people against him.

Q. That's incredible. You're saying that in briefing the Attorney General you are telling him you are using the underworld against Castro, and you intended that to mean, Mr. Attorney General, we are trying to kill him?

BISSELL. I thought it signaled just exactly that to the Attorney General, I'm sure.

Q. Then it's your belief that you communicated to the Attorney General that you were, in fact, trying to kill Castro?

BISSELL. I think it is best to rest on that report we do have, which is from a source over which I had no influence and it does use the phrase I have quoted here. Now you can surmise and I can surmise as to just what the Attorney General would have read into that phrase. (Bissell, 7/22/75, pp. 53–54)

Q. Was it your intent to circumlocutiously, or otherwise, to advise the Attorney General that you were in the process of trying to kill Castro?

Mr. BISSELL. [U]nless I remembered the conversation at the time, which I don't, I don't have any recollection as to whether that was my intent or not. (Bissell, 7/22/75, p. 56)

Bissell speculated further that a "proper" briefing might have omitted any reference to the assassination plot. (Bissell, 7/22/75, p. 59) As bases for his speculation, Bissell suggested first that even if he had "thoroughly briefed" the Attorney General he would have chosen "circumlocutious" language to tell him about the activity involving Giancana. (Bissell, 7/22/75, pp. 53–56); and second that the assassination effort had been "stood down by them." (Bissell, 7/22/75, p. 59) Bissell concluded by reiterating that he had "no knowledge" that the Attorney General was "specifically advised" of the assassination plot against Castro. (Bissell, 7/22/75, p. 62)[1]

(5) *Conversation Between President Kennedy and Senator George Smathers*

George Smathers, former Senator from Florida, testified that the subject of a possible assassination of Castro arose in a conversation Smathers had with President Kennedy on the White House lawn in 1961.[2] Smathers said he had discussed the general Cuban situation with the President many times. (Smathers, 7/23/75, p. 6) Smathers had many Cuban constituents and was familiar with Latin American affairs. He was also a long-time friend of the President. (Smathers, 7/23/75, p. 6)

It was Smathers' "impression" that President Kennedy raised the subject of assassination with Smathers because someone else "had ap-

---

[1] If the FBI quotation of Edwards is to be accorded significant weight, then it is important to note that another section of it contradicts Bissell's assumption that Presidents Eisenhower and Kennedy had been circumlocutiously advised by Dulles of the assassination plot. Edwards told the FBI that "Allen Dulles was completely unaware of Edwards' contact with Meheu" in connection with Cuban operation.

Bissell's explanation for Edwards' statement was that Edwards was being "protective" of the DCI. (Bissell, 7/17/75, p. 20) But this testimony must be reconciled with Bissell's previous testimony that Dulles knew of the operation and probably would have told the President about it.

[2] Smathers' testimony about this conversation referred to the transcript of an Oral History interview he gave on March 31, 1964. That interview indicates that the conversation probably took place in 1961, before the Bay of Pigs invasion in mid-April.

White House logs of Presidential meetings indicate only two occasions in 1961 when Senator Smathers met alone with the President. Both of those meetings took place in March.

parently discussed this and other possibilities with respect to Cuba" with the President. (Smathers, 7/23/75, pp. 16, 25) Smathers had no direct knowledge of any such discussion, or who might have been involved. (Smathers, 7/23/75, pp. 18–19, 25) The President did not indicate directly that assassination had been proposed to him. (Smathers, 7/23/75, p. 18)

According to Smathers:

* * * [President Kennedy] asked me what reaction I thought there would be throughout South America were Fidel Castro to be assasketed * * * I told the President that even as much as I disliked Fidel Castro that I did not think it would be a good idea for there to be even considered an assassination of Fidel Castro, and the President of the United States completely agreed with me, that it would be a very unwise thing to do, the reason obviously being that no matter who did it and no matter how it was done and no matter what, that the United States would receive full credit for it, and the President receive full credit for it, and it would work to his great disadvantage with all of the other countries in Central and South America * * * I disapproved of it, and he completely disapproved of the idea. (Smathers, 7/23/75, pp. 6–7)

Smathers said that on a later occasion he had tried to discuss Cuba with President Kennedy and the President had made it clear to Smathers that he should not raise the subject with him again.[1]

Senator Smathers concluded his testimony by indicating that on Cuban affairs in general, he felt he was "taking a tougher stance than was the President." (Smathers, 7/23/75, p. 24) Smathers said he was "positive" that Kennedy opposed assassination. (Smathers, 7/23/75, p. 16)

(6) *The Question of Whether the President or the Attorney General Might Have Learned of the Assassination Effort from the Cuban Participants*

A memorandum for the record in CIA files dated April 24, 1961, reflects that on April 19–20, in the aftermath of the Bay of Pigs, President Kennedy and other Administration officials, including Secretary of Defense McNamara and General Lyman L. Lemnitzer, Chairman of the Joint Chiefs of Staff, met with a translator and several members of Cuban groups involved in the Bay of Pigs. One of those Cuban exile leaders had been involved in the passage of poison pills to Cuba in March or April of that year;[2] there is no evidence that any of the other Cubans at the meeting were involved in or aware of the assassination plot, and it is unclear whether that particular Cuban realized that the plot in which he was involved was sponsored by the CIA.[3] The April 24 memorandum states that the atmosphere of the meeting reflected depression over the failure of the Bay of Pigs.

---

[1] One night at dinner with Senator Smathers, the President emphasized his point by cracking his plate at the mention of Cuba. (Smathers, 7/23/75, p. 22)

[2] According to FBI memoranda dated December 21, 1960, and January 18, 1961, the Cuban was associated with anti-Castro activities financed by United States racketeers, including Santos Trafficante, who hoped to secure illegal monopolies in the event of Castro's overthrow. This same Cuban was subsequently used by Rosselli in the second passage of pills to Cuba in April 1962.

[3] Rosselli testified that he represented himself to the Cubans as an agent of American business interests that desired the removal of Castro. (Rosselli, 6/24/75, pp. 17, 89) Maheu testified that he and Rosselli held themselves out to the Cubans as representatives of American industrialists who had been financially hurt by Castro's regime, and that "at no time had we identified to them that the U.S. government in fact was behind the project." (Maheu, 7/29/75, p. 34) The Support Chief testified that he had met the Cuban exile leader with whom Rosselli had dealt only once, and that he had then been "put out as being somebody that had a client, commercial type." The Support Chief was not certain that the Cuban had not suspected his true identity, however, because the Chief testified that after that meeting, Rosselli had told him that the Cuban had remarked, "You can't tell me this guy is not a CIA man." (O.C., 5/30/75, p. 22)

On May 18, 1961, the Taylor/Kennedy Board interviewed several Cuban exile leaders who had been involved in the Bay of Pigs, including the leaders who had cooperated in the assassination plot. The summary of that session states that the subject of the inquiry was the Bay of Pigs operation. Attorney General Robert Kennedy was present.

The Cuban exile leader involved in the assassination plot may have seen the Attorney General on one further occasion shortly after the Cuban Missile Crisis in October, 1962. Rosselli testified that this Cuban then was being used by the United States Government to aid in intelligence gathering and covert operations directed at Cuba. Rosselli said that he met that Cuban and other Cuban leaders in Washington, D.C., and that the Cubans told him they "were here meeting with the Attorney General and that they were waiting for an appointment from the White House." (Rosselli, 9/22/75, p. 6) They did not tell Rosselli their reasons for seeing the Attorney General, indicating only that the meeting involved the Cuban situation generally. Rosselli said that he did not discuss the assassination operation with the Cuban leaders "because I did not want [the second leader] to hear of it, because he was not part of it." (Rosselli, 9/22/75, p. 10)

(7) *The Question of Whether or not the Assassination Operation Involving Underworld Figures was Known about by Attorney General Kennedy or President Kennedy as Revealed by Investigations of Giancana and Rosselli.*

Beginning in the fall of 1960 and continuing throughout the Bay of Pigs and MONGOOSE periods (through 1962), the CIA undertook an assassination operation against Castro involving underworld figures. Following the discovery of the wiretap in a Las Vegas hotel room on October 31, 1960,[1] the CIA began disclosing aspects of its involvement with underworld figures to the FBI, to certain Justice Department officials, and after the advent of the Kennedy Administration, to Attorney General Robert F. Kennedy.[2] This section sets forth evidence bearing on what Attorney General Robert Kennedy did or did not know about the use of underworld figures by the CIA as revealed by FBI and Justice Department investigations surrounding the discovery of the Las Vegas wiretap.

This section also discusses evidence bearing on whether or not President Kennedy knew prior to April 1962, or at any time thereafter about the pre-Bay of Pigs plot involving underworld figures. There are two issues. The first is whether the President was made aware, through either the FBI or the Attorney General, of the CIA's use of Rosselli and Giancana. The second is whether the President learned that the CIA had used Rosselli and Giancana in an attempt to assassinate Fidel Castro.

a. 1960.—On October 18, 1960, FBI Director Hoover sent a memorandum[3] to DDP Bissell with copies to some other members of the

---

[1] The wiretap was placed on the telephone by Arthur J. Balletti. Arrangements for the tap were made by Maheu through his acquaintance, Edward DuBois. (FBI memo 3/23/62) See discussion, *supra*, pp. 77–79.
[2] Robert Kennedy was Attorney General from January 1961 until September 1964. During his tenure as Attorney General he had close ties not only to law enforcement agencies (FBI and Justice), but also to the CIA. He served on the Special Group (Augmented) which supervised Operation MONGOOSE from December 1961 through October 1962.
[3] This memorandum is set forth in full, *supra*, p. 79.

intelligence community [1] stating that an informant had reported that "* * * during [a] recent conversation with several friends. Giancana stated that Fidel Castro was to be done away with very shortly. When doubt was expressed regarding this statement, Giancana reportedly assured those present that Castro's assassination would occur in November." [2] (Memo, Hoover to Bissell, 10/18/69) According to the memorandum Giancana claimed to have met with the assassin-to-be on three occasions and said that the assassination could be accomplished by dropping a pill in Castro's food. The memorandum did not specifically reveal CIA involvement.

After discovering the Las Vegas wiretap on October 31, 1960, the FBI commenced an investigation which quickly developed that Maheu and Giancana were involved in the case. In April 1961, Rosselli's involvement was discovered.

b. 1961.—The first documentary evidence indicating alleged CIA involvement with the wiretap case is an FBI report dated April 20, 1961. The report stated that on April 18, 1961, Maheu informed the FBI that the tap had played a part in a project "on behalf of the CIA relative to anti-Castro activities," a fact which could be verified by Sheffield Edwards, CIA's Director of Security.[3]

Bissell testified that he knew during the spring of 1961 that Edwards was seeking to persuade the Justice Department, via communications to the FBI, not to prosecute the parties—including Maheu, Rosselli, and Giancana—who were involved in the Las Vegas tap. Although Bissell believed that Edwards had told the Bureau the truth, he did not expect that Edwards would have revealed that the CIA operation involved assassination. (Bissell, 6/9/75, pp. 63–65)[4]

According to a May 22, 1961, FBI memorandum, on May 3, 1961, Edwards told the FBI [5] that the CIA had relied on Giancana because of Giancana's contacts with gambling figures who might have sources for use "in connection with CIA's clandestine efforts against the Castro government". Edwards reportedly said that "none of Giancana's efforts have materialized to date and that several of the plans still are working and may eventually 'pay off'". Edwards also stated that he had never been furnished details of the methods used by Giancana and Maheu because this was "dirty business" and he could not afford to

---

[1] The October 18 memo was also distributed to Assistant Attorney General J. Walter Yeagley and to Army, Air Force, Navy and State Department intelligence offices. Bissell testified that he did not recall this memorandum. (Bissell, 7/22/75, p. 40) He speculated that the CIA's copy ordinarily would have been delivered to him and he would have passed it on to Sheffield Edwards. The action copy was directed to Bissell but he surmised that a copy would also have gone to the Director. (Bissell, 7/22/75, pp. 40, 41)

[2] The FBI copy of the memorandum contained a postscript stating:
"By separate airtel (night cable), we have instructed the field to be most alert for any additional information concerning alleged plots against Castro and to submit recommendations for close surveillance of Giancana in the event he makes trip to the Miami area or other trips which may be for the purpose of contacting people implicated in this plot."

[3] Sam Papich, the FBI liaison with the CIA during this period, stated that the FBI was furious when it learned of the CIA's use of Maheu, Rosselli and Giancana in the tap because it might inhibit possible prosecutions against them in the wiretap case and in others.

An arrangement (which was informal with Edwards, but was formalized with William Harvey) was subsequently made between the CIA and the FBI. The arrangement was that Papich would be informed by Agency personnel of any CIA contacts with underworld figures, of their movements, and any intelligence which directly or indirectly related to organized crime activities in the United States. The CIA would not report to the FBI any information concerning the objectives of Agency operations.

[4] Bissell also testified that the "cover story" for the operation may have been intelligence gathering (*i.d.*, p. 66).

[5] Edwards apparently gave this information to Sam Papich.

know the specific actions of Maheu and Giancana in pursuit of any mission for the CIA.

Although Edwards did not reveal the specific objective of the Giancana operation to the FBI, he was referring to the Agency's recent assassination attempt involving the passage of poison involving a Cuban exile leader sometime between mid-March and mid-April 1961.[1]

The summary of Edwards' statements to the FBI that was sent by Hoover to Attorney General Kennedy on May 22, 1961, stated, in part that:

> Colonel Edwards advised that in connection with CIA's operation against Castro he personally contacted Robert Maheu during the fall of 1960 for the purpose of using Maheu as a "cut-out" in contacts with Sam Giancana, a known hoodlum in the Chicago area. Colonel Edwards said that since the underworld controlled gambling activities in Cuba under the Batista government, it was assumed that this element would still continue to have sources and contacts in Cuba which perhaps could be utilized successfully in connection with CIA's clandestine efforts against the Castro government. As a result, Maheu's services were solicited as a "cut-out" because of his possible entree into underworld circles. Maheu obtained Sam Giancana's assistance in this regard and according to Edwards, Giancana gave every indication of cooperating through Maheu in attempting to accomplish several clandestine efforts in Cuba. Edwards added that none of Giancana's efforts have materialized to date and that several of the plans still are working and may eventually "pay off."
>
> Colonel Edwards related that he had no direct contact with Giancana; that Giancana's activities were completely "back stopped" by Maheu and that Maheu would frequently report Giancana's action and information to Edwards. No details or methods used by Maheu or Giancana in accomplishing their missions were ever reported to Edwards. Colonel Edwards said that since this is "dirty business", he could not afford to have knowledge of the actions of Maheu and Giancana in pursuit of any mission for CIA. Colonel Edwards added that he has neither given Maheu any instruction to use technical installations of any type nor has the subject of technical installations ever come up between Edwards and Maheu in connection with Giancana's activity.
>
> Mr. Bissell, in his recent briefings of General Taylor and the Attorney General and in connection with their inquiries into CIA relating to the Cuban situation [the Taylor Board of Inquiry] told the Attorney General that some of the associated planning included the use of Giancana and the underworld against Castro.[2]

The summary of Edwards' conversation with the FBI was accompanied by a cover memorandum from Hoover stating that Edwards had acknowledged the "attempted" use of Maheu and "hoodlum elements" by the CIA in "anti-Castro activities" but that the "purpose for placing the wiretap * * * has not been determined * * *." (FBI memo to Attorney General, 5/22/61) The memorandum also explained that Maheu had contacted Giancana in connection with the CIA program and CIA had requested that the information be handled on a "need-to-know" basis.[3]

---

[1] See the preceding section for a discussion of this Cuban exile leader.
[2] For a discussion of this part of the memorandum and Bissell's testimony on it, see pp. 121–123 *supra*.
[3] At the time Hoover sent the May 22, 1961, memorandum to the Attorney General, indicating that there was a CIA/Giancana link, Bureau files already contained another memorandum revealing that Giancana had earlier talked about an assassination attempt against Castro. This earlier memorandum dated October 18, 1960, did not reveal any Giancana/CIA connections, but anyone seeing the October 18 memorandum and knowing of the CIA's association with Giancana in a project "against Castro" should have realized the connection.

Courtney Evans, the FBI's liaison with the Attorney General, however, testified that pursuant to Bureau procedure, Hoover would have received an intra-bureau memorandum giving him a detailed summary of the information that was in the files. (Evans, 8/28/75, pp. 70, 72) (footnote continued on p. 128)

Hoover's memorandum to Attorney General Kennedy was stamped "received" and a marginal notation in Kennedy's handwriting said: "Courtney I hope this will be followed up vigorously." [1] Carbon copies were sent to Deputy Attorney General Byron R. White and Assistant Attorney General Herbert J. Miller, Jr,

A memorandum from Evans to Allen Belmont, Assistant to the Director (FBI) dated June 6, 1961, stated:

> We checked with CIA and ascertained that CIA had used Maheu as an intermediary in contacting Sam Giancana, the notorious Chicago hoodlum. This was in connection with anti-Castro activities. CIA, however, did not give any instructions to Maheu to use any technical installations. In connection with this information received from CIA concerning their attempted utilization of the hoodlum element, CIA requested this information be handled on a "need-to-know" basis.
>
> We are conducting a full investigation in this wiretap case requested by the Department and the field has been instructed to press this investigation vigorously. Accordingly, the Attorney General will be orally assured that we are following up vigorously and the results of our investigation will be furnished to the Department promptly.

Entries in the FBI files indicate that the FBI vigorously pursued its investigation of the wiretap case. However, on August 16, 1961, the Assistant United States Attorney in Las Vegas reported his reluctance to proceed with the case because of deficiencies in the evidence and his concern that CIA's alleged involvement might become known. The Department of Justice files indicate no activity between September 1961, when the FBI's investigation was concluded, and January 1962, when the question of prosecution in the case was brought up for reconsideration.

An entry in the Justice Department files dated October 6, 1961, stated:

> Yesterday P.M. told me that A.G. had inquired as to status of this case and think Harold [Shapiro] got it taken care of OK.

Evans also testified that he did not recall ever having seen the October 18 memorandum, that he had never heard from any source of an assassination plot involving the Central Intelligence Agency and members of the underworld during his tenure with the Bureau, and that he never discussed assassination with the Attorney General. (Evans, 8/28/75, pp. 55-57) However, he did have discussions with the Attorney General following the May 22 memorandum. Evans testified that if the October 18 memorandum had been sent to him, it would have been sent to him by Thomas McAndrews, who was Chief of the Organized Crime Section of the Special Investigative Division of the Bureau. McAndrews, who was responsible for distributing information from the FBI to the entire intelligence community, could not recall ever having given the October 18 memorandum to Evans. When asked if he believed the information contained in that memorandum had ever been brought to the attention of Attorney General Kennedy, McAndrews testified: "I think he was briefed specifically on it, either in writing or orally * * * I think it was done. But I can't say for sure." (McAndrews, 9/17/75, p. 27)

Ralph Hill was the Special Agent in charge of the investigation of Giancana. He testified that he recalled the information in the October 18 memorandum, but that he did not recall the memorandum itself. He stated that because of the Attorney General's interest in organized crime figures, it was the practice for field reports concerning Giancana to be given to Courtney Evans, who would then forward them to the Attorney General.

The only documents the Committee has seen indicating that the FBI realized the October 18 memorandum related to the CIA/underworld figures operation, were two memoranda, both dated March 6, 1967, and both entitled "Central Intelligence Agency's Intentions to Send Hoodlums to Cuba to Assassinate Castro." The first memorandum to Attorney General Ramsey Clark stated that "it appears that data which came to our attention in October 1960 possibly pertains to the above-captioned matter." The second, an internal FBI memorandum used in the preparation of the memorandum for the Attorney General, stated that there were two other references in the files to the overall information mentioned above, one of which was the statement made by Giancana that in October 1960 he met with an individual who was to assassinate Castro in November 1960.

[1] Courtney Evans was the FBI's liaison with the Attorney General and the President. Courtney Evans had worked closely with the then Senator John Kennedy and Robert Kennedy on the McClellan Committee, which had investigated the relationship between organized labor and organized crime. During the McClellan Investigation Sam Giancana was one of the major crime figures examined. After becoming Attorney General, Robert Kennedy had singled out Giancana as one of the underworld leaders to be most intensely investigated.

With the exception of this briefing, the FBI and Justice files indicate no other activity in the Balletti wiretap case from September 1961 through January 1962. There was no activity in the assassination effort involving underworld figures from April 1961 until mid-April 1962.

c. 1962.—A note of January 29, 1962, from the head of the Administrative Regulations Division to the first and second assistants in the Criminal Division stated:

> Our primary interest was in Giancana * * * apparently detective (Maheu) has some connection with Giancana but he claims was because of CIA assignment in connection with Cuba—CIA has objected, may have to drop.

Assistant Attorney General Herbert Miller then asked the FBI to again speak with Edwards about the prosecution of Maheu. (Memo from Miller, 1/31/62)

An FBI memorandum dated February 24, 1962, set forth Miller's request that Edwards be reinterviewed about possible prosecutions in the Balletti case. A reply memorandum from the FBI to Miller on February 7, 1962, stated that Edwards had been contacted and that he objected to the prosecution.

(1) Did President Kennedy Learn Anything About Assassination Plots as a Result of the FBI Investigation of Giancana and Rosselli?

As elaborated in the previous sections of this report, all living CIA officials who were involved in the underworld assassination attempt or who were in a position to have known of the attempt have testified that they never discussed the assassination plot with the President. By May 1961, however, the Attorney General and Hoover were aware that the CIA had earlier used Giancana in an operation against Cuba and FBI files contained two memoranda which, if simultaneously reviewed, would have led one to conclude that the CIA operation had involved assassination.[1] There is no evidence that any one within the FBI concluded that the CIA had used Giancana in an assassination attempt. The Committee has uncovered a chain of events, however, which would have given Hoover an opportunity to have assembled the entire picture and to have reported the information to the President.

Evidence before the Committee indicates that a close friend of President Kennedy had frequent contact with the President from the end of 1960 through mid-1962. FBI reports and testimony indicate that the President's friend was also a close friend of John Rosselli and Sam Giancana and saw them often during this same period.[2]

On February 27, 1962, Hoover sent identical copies of a memorandum to the Attorney General and Kenneth O'Donnell, Special Assistant to the President. The memorandum stated that information developed in connection with a concentrated FBI investigation of John Rosselli revealed that Rosselli had been in contact with the President's

---

[1] The two memoranda, which are discussed in considerable detail *supra*, were the October 18, 1960, memorandum linking Giancana to an assassination plot (but not mentioning CIA) and the May 22, 1961, memorandum linking Giancana to a CIA operation against Cuba involving "dirty business" (but not mentioning assassination).

[2] White House telephone logs show 70 instances of phone contact between the White House and the President's friend whose testimony confirms frequent phone contact with the President himself.
Both the President's friend and Rosselli testified that the friend did not know about either the assassination operation or the wiretap case. Giancana was killed before he was available for questioning.

friend. The memorandum also reported that the individual was maintaining an association with Sam Giancana, described as "a prominent Chicago underworld figure." Hoover's memorandum also stated that a review of the telephone toll calls from the President's friend's residence revealed calls to the White House. The President's secretary ultimately received a copy of the memorandum and said she believed she would have shown it to the President.

The association of the President's friend with the "hoodlums" and that person's connection with the President was again brought to Hoover's attention in a memorandum preparing him for a meeting with the President planned for March 22, 1962. Courtney Evans testified that Hoover generally required a detailed summary of information in the FBI files for drafting important memoranda or preparing for significant meetings. (Evans, 8/28/75, pp. 70, 72) The FBI files on Giancana then contained information disclosing Giancana's connection with the CIA as well as his involvement in assassination plotting. (Memoranda of 10/18/60 and 5/22/61)

On March 22, Hoover had a private luncheon with President Kennedy. There is no record of what transpired at that luncheon. According to the White House logs, the last telephone contact between the White House and the President's friend occurred a few hours after the luncheon.

The fact that the President and Hoover had a luncheon at which one topic was presumably that the President's friend was also a friend of Giancana and Rosselli raises several possibilities. The first is, assuming that Hoover did in fact receive a summary of FBI information relating to Giancana prior to his luncheon with the President, whether that summary reminded the Director that Giancana had been involved in a CIA operation against Cuba that included "dirty business" and further indicated that Giancana had talked about an assassination attempt against Castro. A second is whether Hoover would then have taken the luncheon as an opportunity to fulfill his duty to bring this information to the President's attention.[1] What actually transpired at that luncheon may never be known, as both participants are dead and the FBI files contain no records relating to it.

On March 23, 1962, the day immediately following his luncheon with the President, at which Rosselli and Giancana were presumably discussed, Hoover sent a memorandum to Edwards stating:

> At the request of the Criminal Division of the Department of Justice, this matter was discussed with the CIA Director of Security on February 7, 1962, and we were advised that your agency would object to any prosecution which would necessitate the use of CIA personnel or CIA information. We were also informed that introduction of evidence concerning the CIA operation would be embarrassing to the Government.
>
> The Criminal Division has now requested that CIA specifically advise whether it would or would not object to the initiation of criminal prosecution against the subjects, Balletti, Maheu, and the individual known as J. W. Harrison for conspiracy to violate the "Wire Tapping Statute."

---

[1] The President, thus nottified, might then have inquired further of the CIA. The Presidential calendar indicates that the President had meetings at which most CIA officials witting of the assassination plot were present during the period from February 27 through April 2, 1962. All of those persons, however, have testified that the President never asked them about the assassination plot.

An early reply will be appreciated in order that we may promptly inform the Criminal Division of CIA's position in this matter.[1]

As a result of this request, the CIA did object to the prosecution of those involved in the wiretap case, thereby avoiding exposure of Giancana's and Rosselli's involvement with the Agency in an assassination plot. We now turn to events which occurred during April and May 1962 which culminated in the formal decision to forego prosecution in the wiretap case.

(2) *The Formal Decision to Forego Prosecution.*

(*a*) Events Leading up to a Formal Briefing of the Attorney General.

A memorandum for the record of April 4, 1962, reflects that Edwards met with Sam Papich, the FBI liaison to the CIA, on March 28 or 29 and told Papich that:

> Any prosecution in the matter would endanger sensitive sources and methods used in a duly authorized intelligence project and would not be in the national interest. (Edwards' memorandum, 4/4/62)

A memorandum for Assistant Attorney General Miller from Hoover dated April 10, 1962, stated that Edwards:

> Has now advised that he has no desire to impose any restriction which might hinder efforts to prosecute any individual, but he is firmly convinced that prosecution of Maheu undoubtedly would lead to exposure of most sensitive information relating to the abortive Cuban invasion in April 1961, and would result in most damaging embarrassment to the U.S. Government. He added that in view of this, his agency objects to the prosecution of Maheu. (Memo, Hoover to Miller, 4/10/62)

On April 16, 1962, Lawrence Houston, CIA General Counsel, met with Miller.[2] Houston reported to Edwards that Miller envisioned "no major difficulty in stopping action for prosecution." Houston offered to brief the Attorney General, but said that he "doubted if we would want to give the full story to anyone else in the Department," and Miller did not desire to know the "operational details." On April 20 Houston told Miller's first assistant that he was requesting Justice not to prosecute "on grounds of security," and asked to be informed if it was necessary to brief the Attorney General. (Memo, Houston to Edwards, 4/26/62)

In the latter half of April 1962 William Harvey, head of the CIA's anti-Castro effort, gave poison pills to Rosselli for use in the post-Bay of Pigs assassination effort against Fidel Castro using underworld figures.

(*b*) Briefing of the Attorney General on May 7, 1962.

An entry in Attorney General Kennedy's calendar for May 7, 1962, states "1:00—Richard Helms."[3] At 4:00 the Attorney General met

---
[1] This memorandum is peculiar in two respects. First, the CIA had already orally objected to prosecution on two occasions. Second, Hoover was quizzing the CIA on behalf of the Department of Justice, a task that would normally be performed by the Department's Criminal Division.

[2] Houston testified that he did not remember these meetings. (Houston, 6/2/75, p. 3) Miller recalled only that Houston had spoken to him about a wiretap and possible CIA embarrassment. (Miller, 8/11/75, p. 16)

[3] Helms testified that he did not recall meeting with the Attorney General on May 7 and his desk book does not reflect any such meeting. When asked if he had ever met with the Attorney General to set up a knowingly inaccurate briefing, Helms testified that he had not and that if he had, he would certainly remember it because "I would have been conniving or colluding, and I have no recollection of ever having done anything like that." (Helms, 9/16/75, p. 8)

with Houston and Edwards to be briefed on the CIA operation involving Maheu, Rosselli, and Giancana. The briefing was at the Attorney General's request. (I.G. Report, p. 62a)

On May 9, 1962, the Attorney General met with Director Hoover. Hoover prepared a memorandum for the record dated May 10, 1962, recounting what was said at that meeting. On May 11 the Attorney General requested Edwards to prepare a memorandum of the May 7 briefing. Edwards, with Houston's assistance, prepared a memorandum dated May 14, 1962, relating what had transpired at the May 7 briefing. Also, on the same day, Edwards had a telephone conversation with William Harvey. As a result of that conversation, Edwards prepared an internal memorandum for the record dated May 14, 1962, which falsely stated that the operation involving Rosselli was then being terminated.

(aa) *The Attorney General Was Told That the Operation Had Involved an Assassination Attempt*

Houston testified that the operation was described to the Attorney General as an assassination attempt. (Houston, 6/2/75, p. 14) When interviewed for the Inspector General's Report in 1967, Edwards said he briefed Kennedy "all the way." (I.G. Report, p. 62a) A memorandum by Hoover of a conference with Kennedy on May 9, two days after the briefing states:

> The Attorney General told me he wanted to advise me of a situation in the Giancana case which had considerably disturbed him. He stated a few days ago he had been advised by CIA that in connection with Giancana, CIA had hired Robert A. Maheu, a private detective in Washington, D.C., to approach Giancana with a proposition of paying $150,000 to hire some gunmen to go into Cuba and to kill Castro. (Memorandum from Hoover, 4/10/62)

(bb) *Evidence Concerning Whether the Attorney General Was Told That the Operation Had Been Terminated*

Houston, who said that he was told about the use of underworld figures for the first time by Edwards a few weeks before the briefing of the Attorney General, testified that it was his "understanding that the assassination plan aimed at Castro had been terminated completely," and that Kennedy was told "the activity had been terminated as of that time." (Houston, 6/2/75, pp. 13, 15) Edwards testified that he had also believed at the time of the briefing that the operation had been concluded and that he had so informed Kennedy. (Edwards, 5/30/75, p. 16) [1] The memorandum of the briefing prepared by Edwards describes the operation as having been "conducted during the period approximately August 1960 to May 1961." It further states:

> After the failure of the invasion of Cuba word was sent through Maheu to Rosselli to call off the operation and Rosselli was told to tell his principal that the proposal to pay one hundred fifty thousand dollars for completion of the operation had been definitely withdrawn. (Memo from Edwards, 4/14/62)

---

[1] Harvey, who was informed of the briefing by Edwards, could not recall whether Edwards told him that the Attorney General had been briefed that the operation had been terminated. (Harvey, 6/25/75, p. 99)

Based upon interviews with Houston and Edwards, the Inspector General's Report concluded that:

> The Attorney General was not told that the gambling syndicate operation had already been reactivated, nor, as far as we know, was he ever told that CIA had a continuing involvement with U.S. gangster elements. (I.G. Report, p. 65) [1]

Houston and Edwards recalled that Kennedy was upset that the CIA had used Giancana. Houston testified:

> If you have seen Mr. Kennedy's eyes get steely and his jaw set and his voice get low and precise, you get a definite feeling of unhappiness. (Houston, 6/2/75, p. 14)

In his memorandum of the meeting with the Attorney General two days after the briefing, Hoover recalled:

> I expressed great astonishment at this in view of the bad reputation of Maheu and the horrible judgment in using a man of Giancana's background for such a project. The Attorney General shared the same views. (Memo from Hoover, 5/10/62) [2]

Hoover's May 10 memorandum further states that the Attorney General said that "CIA admitted that they had assisted Maheu in making this installation and for these reasons CIA was in a position where it could not afford to have any action taken against Giancana and Maheu." [3]

According to Edwards, at the end of the briefing, Kennedy said: "I want you to let me know about these things," or words to that effect. (Edwards, 5/30/75, p. 17) Houston recalled that Kennedy said:

> In very specific terms that if we were going to get involved with Mafia personnel again he wanted to be informed first * * *. I do not remember his commenting about the operation itself. (Houston, 6/2/75, p. 14) [4]

Hoover recorded that two days after the briefing, the Attorney General told him that:

> He had asked CIA whether they had ever cleared their actions in hiring Maheu and Giancana with the Department of Justice before they did so and he was advised by CIA they had not cleared these matters with the Department of Justice. He stated he then issued orders to CIA to never again in the future take such steps without first checking with the Department of Justice. (Memo from Hoover, 5/10/62)

Edwards testified that at the time of the Kennedy briefing, he did not know that the CIA was still utilizing its underworld contacts,

---

[1] In a section entitled "The Facts As We Know Them," the I.G. Report stated that Attorney General Kennedy "was briefed on Gambling Syndicate—Phase One after it was over. He was not briefed on Phase Two." (I.G. Report, p. 118)

[2] The Hoover memorandum indicates two reasons for Attorney General Kennedy's displeasure. First, the CIA had put itself into a position where "it could not afford to have any action taken against Giancana or Maheu." Second, Hoover: "Stated as he [Kennedy] well knew the 'gutter gossip' was that the reason nothing had been done against Giancana was because of Giancana's close relationship with Frank Sinatra who, in turn, claimed to be a close friend of the Kennedy family. The Attorney General stated he realized this and it was for that reason that he was quite concerned when he received this information from CIA about Giancana and Maheu." (Sinatra is not the President's friend discussed in the preceding subsection.)

Despite the Attorney General's concern that prosecutions of parties involved in the tap might be foreclosed in the future, both Giancana and Rosselli were in fact prosecuted later for crimes unrelated to the tap.

[3] In the CIA memorandum of the briefing prepared by Edwards, Edwards wrote that "at the time of the incident, neither this Agency nor the undersigned knew of the proposed technical installation."

[4] Houston testified that Kennedy insisted "There was not to be any contact of the Mafia * * * without prior consultation with him." (Houston, 6/2/75, p. 37) When interviewed in 1967 for the Inspector General's Report, Houston had recalled Kennedy as saying: "I trust that if you ever try to do business with organized crime again—with gangsters—you will let the Attorney General know." (I.G. Report, p. 62a)

(Edwards, 5/30/75, p. 16) even though the operation had been reactivated under the Directorate of Plans, and in early April 1962, poison pills had been given to Rosselli.

As concluded by the CIA itself in the Inspector General's Report, Edwards' statement that he was not aware of these developments is implausible. In the memorandum of May 14, 1962, prepared for the Attorney General, Edwards stated that Harvey had asked him to arrange a contact with Rosselli, and that a meeting had been set for April 9. The Inspector General's Report observed:

> When the Attorney General was briefed on 7 May, Edwards knew that Harvey had been introduced to Rosselli. He must also have known that his subordinate, the Support Chief, was in Miami and roughly for what purpose (although Edwards does not now recall this). (I.G. Report, p. 65)[1]

Harvey testified that Edwards knew the operation was still in effect and that Edwards told Harvey about the briefing of the Attorney General shortly afterwards. (Harvey, 6/25/75, pp. 98–100)

In the internal memorandum for the record dated May 14, 1962, written the same day as the memorandum of the Attorney General's briefing, Edwards stated:

> On this date Mr. Harvey called me and indicated that he was dropping any plans for the use of Subject (Rosselli) for the future.

Harvey testified that the memorandum "was not true, and Colonel Edwards knew it was not true." (Harvey, 6/25/75, p. 97) Edwards confirmed that he was aware at that time that Harvey was "trying" to assume control of the operation. (Edwards, 5/30/75, p. 19)

Harvey testified that Edwards' entry would cause the record to show incorrectly that the operation had been terminated, when in fact it had not been. (Harvey, 6/25/75, p. 102) Harvey's reasons explaining the decision to "falsify" the record were:

> * * * if this ever came up in the future, the file would show that on such and such a date he was advised so and so, and he was no longer chargeable with this. * * * (Harvey, 6/25/75, p. 100)
>
> This was purely an internal document for use in closing out this operation as far as the Office of Security and its Director, that is its Chief, personally, was concerned. (Harvey, 6/25/75, p. 102)
>
> To bring this operation under some sort of sensible control, determine what it was, and attempt to insulate against what I consider a very definite potential for damage to the agency and to the government. (Harvey, 6/25/75, p. 101)

When questioned about the fact that the Attorney General had been told that the operation had been terminated when in fact it was continuing, Helms testified:

> * * * I am not able to tell you whether this operation was ongoing, whether it had really been stopped, whether it had been fairly stopped, whether there was fun and games going on between the officers involved as to, we will create a fiction that it stopped or go ahead with it. I just don't recall any of those things at all * * *. (Helms, 6/13/75, p. 109)

(ii) *Post-Bay Of Pigs Underworld Plot—MONGOOSE Period*

This section discusses evidence bearing on whether the post-Bay of Pigs operation to assassinate Castro involving underworld figures—which began in April 1962, and continued at least through the Cuban

---

[1] Papich presumably continued to receive reports from the CIA on Harvey's subsequent meetings with Rosselli.

missile crisis in October of that year—was authorized or known about by Administration officials outside of the CIA.

This issue must be considered in light of the differing perceptions of Helms and his subordinates, on the one hand, and of other members of the Kennedy Administration, including the Director of the CIA, on the other. While Helms testified that he never received a direct order to assassinate Castro, he fully believed that the CIA was at all times acting within the scope of its authority and that Castro's assassination came within the bounds of the Kennedy Administration's effort to overthrow Castro and his regime. Helms said that he inherited the Rosselli program from Bissell, and, due to its sensitive and unsavory character, it was not the type of program one would discuss in front of high officials. He stated that he never informed McCone or any other officials of the Kennedy Administration of the assassination plot. However, McCone and the surviving members of the Kennedy Administration testified that they believed a Castro assassination was impermissible without a direct order, that assassination was outside the parameters of the Administration's anti-Castro program, and each testified that to his knowledge no such order was given to Helms.

An understanding of the Kennedy Administration's 1962 covert action program for Cuba is essential to an evaluation of the testimony on the issue of authorization. That program, which was designed to overthrow the Castro regime, and the events in 1961 leading up to it are discussed below. A detailed exposition of the testimony then follows.

(1) Events Preceding the Establishment of MONGOOSE

A. THE TAYLOR/KENNEDY BOARD OF INQUIRY

On April 22, 1961, following the Bay of Pigs failure, the President requested General Maxwell Taylor to conduct a reevaluation of "our practices and programs in the areas of military and paramilitary, guerilla and anti-guerilla activity which fall short of outright war." Taylor was to give special attention to Cuba (Letter to Maxwell Taylor, 4/22/61) and Robert Kennedy was to be his principal colleague in the effort.

The resulting review concluded:

> We have been struck with the general feeling that there can be no long-term living with Castro as a neighbor. His continued presence within the hemispheric community as a dangerously effective exponent of Communism and anti-Americanism constitutes a real menace capable of eventually overthrowing the elected governments in any one or more of weak Latin American republics. * * *
> It is recommended that the Cuban situation be reappraised in the light of all presently known factors and new guidance be provided for political, military, economic and propaganda action against Castro. (Report to the President, 6/13/61, Memo No. 4, p. 8)

It is clear from the record, moreover, that the defeat at the Bay of Pigs had been regarded as a humiliation for the President personally and for the CIA institutionally.

By July 1961, the Special Group had agreed that "the basic objective toward Cuba was to provide support to a U.S. program to develop opposition to Castro and to help bring about a regime acceptable to the

U.S." (Memo for the Record, 7/21/61) Occasional harassment operations were mounted during the summer but there was no overall strategy and little activity.

B. NATIONAL SECURITY ACTION MEMORANDUM 100 OF OCTOBER 5, 1961, AND THE CIA INTELLIGENCE ESTIMATE

In the fall of 1961 the Kennedy Administration considered the consequences of Castro's removal from power and the prospects for United States military intervention if that occurred. Two studies were prepared. National Security Action Memorandum 100 (NSAM 100) directed the State Department to assess the potential courses of action open to the United States should Castro be removed from the Cuban scene, and to prepare a contingency plan with the Department of Defense for military intervention in that event. The CIA prepared an "Intelligence Estimate" on the "situation and prospects" in Cuba. The focus of these studies was on the possible courses of action open to the United States in a post-Castro Cuba, rather than on the means that might bring about Castro's removal. It does not appear, however, that assassination was excluded from the potential means by which Castro might be removed.

On October 5, 1961, McGeorge Bundy issued NSAM 100 entitled "Contingency Planning for Cuba." It was addressed to the Secretary of State and stated in full:

In confirmation of oral instructions conveyed to Assistant Secretary of State Woodward, a plan is desired for the indicated contingency.

The Special Group Minutes of October 6, 1961, state that the Group was told that in addition to an overall plan for Cuban covert operations, "a contingency plan in connection with the possible removal of Castro from the Cuban scene" was in preparation. (Memorandum for the Record of Special Group meeting, 10/6/61) An October 5, 1961 Memorandum for the Record by Thomas Parrott, Secretary to the Special Group, states that Parrott informed the Deputy Assistant Secretary for Latin American Affairs that "what was wanted was a plan against the contingency that Castro would in some way or other be removed from the Cuban scene." Parrott's memorandum stated that in preparing the plan, "the presence and positions of Raul (Castro) and Che Guevara must be taken into account," and that General Taylor had told Parrott he preferred "the President's interest in the matter not be mentioned" to the Assistant Secretary. This memorandum also said that "on the covert side, I talked to Tracy Barnes in CIA and asked that an up-to-date report be furnished as soon as possible on what is going on and what is being planned."

The CIA's Board of National Estimates (which was not part of the Directorate of Plans) prepared a study entitled "The Situation and Prospects in Cuba."[1] The CIA estimate was pessimistic about the

---

[1] The Inspector General apparently had access to an earlier draft of this intelligence estimate. (I.G. Report, p. 4) In reporting that many CIA officers interviewed in the I.G. investigation stressed that "elimination of the dominant figures in a government * * * will not necessarily cause the downfall of the government," the Report stated: "This point was stressed with respect to Castro and Cuba in an internal CIA draft paper of October 1961, which was initiated in response to General Maxwell Taylor's desire for a contingency plan. The paper took the position that the demise of Fidel Castro, from whatever cause, would offer little opportunity for the liberation of Cuba from Communist and Soviet Bloc control." (I.G. Report, p. 4)

The CIA has been unable to locate the draft paper referred to in the Inspector General's Report.

success of a Cuban internal revolt, and found that Castro's assassination would probably strengthen the Communist position in Cuba.

After reviewing the economic, military, and political situation in Cuba, the CIA estimate concluded that the Castro regime had sufficient popular support and repressive capabilities to cope with any internal threat. The concluding paragraph of the estimate, entitled "If Castro Were to Die," noted that:

> His [Castro's] loss now, by assassination or by natural causes, would have an unsettling effect, but would almost certainly not prove fatal to the regime * * * [I]ts principal surviving leaders would probably rally together in the face of a common danger. (Estimate, p. 9)

The CIA study predicted that if Castro died, "some sort of power struggle would almost certainly develop eventually," and, regardless of the outcome of such a struggle, the Communist Party's influence would be "significantly" increased.[1] (Estimate, p. 9)

Bundy testified that the contingency referred to in NSAM 100 and the related documents was "what would we do if Castro were no longer there," and that "clearly one of the possibilities would be assassination." (Bundy, 7/11/75, p. 77) However, Bundy emphasized that NSAM 100 represented an effort to assess the effect should Castro be removed from power by any means (including assassination) but "without going further with the notion [of assassination] itself."[2] (Bundy, 7/11/75, p. 77) Bundy contended that the President was not considering an assassination, but rather "what are things going to be like after Castro?" (Bundy, 7/11/75, p. 81)[3]

Taylor testified that he had no recollection of NSAM 100 or of the events described in the related documents. (Taylor, 7/9/75, p. 18) Based on his review of the documents, Taylor testified that "it sounds like purely a political consideration of the sequence of power in Cuba"[4] and he emphasized that "never at any time" did he raise the question of assassination with Parrott, or with anybody else. (Taylor, 7/9/75, p. 19)

Special Group Secretary Parrott testified that the request for a plan reflected in his memorandum of October 5, 1961, and the reference in that memorandum to the "contingency that Castro would in some way or another be removed from the Cuban scene", reflected interest in a contingency study for Castro's removal, but by means "short of being killed." (Parrott, 7/10/75, p. 83)

---

[1] A cover memorandum by Lansdale transmitting the CIA estimate to Robert Kennedy criticized the estimate's assessment that "it is highly improbable that an extensive popular uprising could be fomented" against Castro as a "conclusion of fact quite outside the area of intelligence." Lansdale stated that the estimate "seems to be the major evidence to be used to oppose your program" (referring to the proposed overall MONGOOSE operation). (Memo, Lansdale to Robert Kennedy, 11/62, p. 1) As discussed in detail at p. 140, Lansdale's basic concept for the MONGOOSE program was to overthrow Castro through an internal revolt of the Cuban people.
[2] "If people were suggesting this to you and you were curious about whether it was worth exploring, one way of getting more light on it without going any further with that notion itself would be to ask political people, not intelligence people, what they thought would happen if Castro were not there any longer." (Bundy, 7/11/75, p. 79)
[3] Bundy explained: "* * * it was precisely to insulate the President from any false inference that what he was asking about was assassination. It is easy to confuse the question, what are things going to be like after Castro, with the other question, and we were trying to focus attention on the information he obviously wanted, which is, what would happen if we did do this sort of thing, and not get one into the frame of mind of thinking that he was considering doing it." (Bundy, 7/11/75, p. 81)
[4] Taylor said he was puzzled by the wording of NSAM 100 and the related documents and stated, "I just cannot tie in the language here with a plausible explanation." (Taylor, 7/9/75, p. 18)

C. PRESIDENT KENNEDY'S NOVEMBER 9, 1961 CONVERSATION WITH TAD SZULC

In early November 1961 Tad Szulc [1] was asked by Richard Goodwin, a Special Assistant to President Kennedy, to meet with Attorney General Robert Kennedy on November 8 to discuss the situation in Cuba. The meeting was "off-the-record." Szulc attended as a friend of Goodwin's, and not as a reporter. (Szulc, 6/10/75, p. 24) During the meeting with Robert Kennedy, the discussion centered on "the situation in Cuba following the [Bay of Pigs] invasion [and] the pros and cons of some different possible actions by the United States Government in that context." (Szulc, 6/10/75, p. 25) According to Szulc the subject of assassination was not mentioned during this meeting. (Szulc, 6/10/75, p. 31)

At the close of the meeting, Robert Kennedy asked Szulc to meet with the President. (Szulc, 6/10/75, p. 25) The next day Szulc, accompanied by Goodwin, met with President Kennedy for over an hour in the Oval Office.[2] (Szulc, 6/10/75, p. 25) Szulc recalled that the President discussed "a number of his views on Cuba in the wake of the Bay of Pigs, asked me a number of questions concerning my conversations with Premier Castro, and * * * what the United States could [or] might do in * * * either a hostile way or in establishing some kind of a dialogue * * *" (Szulc, 6/10/75, pp. 25-26)

Szulc testified that after this general discussion, the President asked "what would you think if I ordered Castro to be assassinated?"[3] (Szulc, 6/10/75, pp. 26, 27; Szulc Notes of conversation with President Kennedy, 11/9/61) Szulc testified that he replied that an assassination would not necessarily cause a change in the Cuban system, and that it was Szulc's personal view that the United States should not be party to murders and political assassinations. (Szulc, 6/10/75, p. 26) Szulc said that the President responded, "I agree with you completely." Szulc stated:

> He [President Kennedy] then went on for a few minutes to make the point how strongly he and his brother felt that the United States for moral reasons should never be in a situation of having recourse to assassination. (Szulc, 6/10/75, p. 27)

Szulc's notes of the meeting with the President state:

> JFK then said he was testing me, that he felt the same way—he added "I'm glad you feel the same way"—because indeed U.S. morally must not be part [sic] to assassinations.
>
> JFK said he raised question because he was under terrific pressure from advisers (think he said intelligence people, but not positive) to okay a Castro murder. sed [sic] he was resisting pressures. (Szulc note of conversation with President Kennedy, 11/9/61)

---

[1] Tad Szulc was a reporter in the Washington Bureau of the *New York Times*. Szulc had visited Cuba in May–June 1961, following the Bay of Pigs invasion. During the course of that trip, Szulc had a "series of very long conversations" with Castro. (Szulc, 6/10/75, p. 24)

[2] Goodwin testified that President Kennedy met frequently with members of the press and others who were experts in various fields, but that it was "possible" that the meeting with Szulc may have been an occasion for the President to consider Szulc for a position in the Administration. (Goodwin, 7/18/75, pp. 29–30)

On November 2, 1961, Goodwin had addressed an "eyes only" memorandum to the President and the Attorney General outlining a suggested organization for what became the MONGOOSE operation. Goodwin proposed five "staff components," including "intelligence collection," "guerrilla and underground," and "propaganda." The memorandum stated: "As for propaganda, I thought we might ask Tad Szulc to take a leave of absence from the Times and work on this one—although we should check with [USIA Director] Ed Murrow and Dick Bissell." (Memo, Goodwin to the President and the Attorney General, 11/2/61, p. 2)

[3] Szulc made notes of the conversation with President Kennedy as soon as he returned to his office. President Kennedy's question regarding a Castro assassination appears in quotation marks in Szulc's notes, which were made the same day from "reasonably fresh" memory. (Szulc, 6/10/75, p. 30)

Szulc stated that it is "possible" and he "believed" that President Kennedy used such words as "someone in the intelligence business," to describe the source of the pressure for a Castro assassination. (Szulc, 6/10/75, p. 29) The President did not specifically identify the source of the pressure. (Szulc, 6/10/75, p. 27)

There is no evidence other than Szulc's testimony that the President was being pressured. This lack of evidence was particularly troublesome since everyone else questioned by the Committee denied ever having discussed assassination with the President, let alone having pressed him to consider it.

Goodwin recalled that, after President Kennedy asked Szulc for his reaction to the suggestion that Castro be assassinated, President Kennedy said, "well, that's the kind of thing I'm never going to do." (Goodwin, 7/18/75, p. 3) Goodwin said that several days after the meeting he referred to the previous discussion of assassination and President Kennedy said "we can't get into that kind of thing, or we would all be targets." (Goodwin, 7/18/75, pp. 4, 11)

D. PRESIDENT KENNEDY'S SPEECH OF NOVEMBER 16, 1961

A few days after the meeting with Szulc and Goodwin, and some six weeks after the issuance of NSAM 100, President Kennedy delivered a speech at the University of Washington, in which he stated:

We cannot, as a free nation, compete with our adversaries in tactics of terror, assassination, false promises, counterfeit mobs and crises. (Public Papers of the Presidents, John F. Kennedy, 1961, p. 724)

(2) Operation MONGOOSE

A. THE CREATION OF OPERATION MONGOOSE

In November 1962 the proposal for a major new covert action program to overthrow Castro was developed. The President's Assistant, Richard Goodwin, and General Edward Lansdale, who was experienced in counter-insurgency operations, played major staff roles in creating this program, which was named Operation MONGOOSE. Goodwin and Lansdale worked closely with Robert Kennedy, who took an active interest in this preparatory stage, and Goodwin advised the President that Robert Kennedy "would be the most effective commander" of the proposed operation. (Memo, Goodwin to the President, 11/1/61, p. 1) In a memorandum to Robert Kennedy outlining the MONGOOSE proposal, Lansdale stated that a "picture of the situation has emerged clearly enough to indicate what needs to be done and to support your sense of urgency concerning Cuba." (Memo, 11/15/61)

At the end of the month, President Kennedy issued a memorandum recording his decision to begin the MONGOOSE project to "use our available assets * * * to help Cuba overthrow the Communist regime." (Memo from the President to the Secretary of State, et al., 11/30/61)

The establishment of Operation MONGOOSE resulted in important organizational changes.

(1) The Special Group (Augmented) (SGA)

A new control group, the Special Group (Augmented) (SGA) was created to oversee Operation MONGOOSE. The SGA comprised the regular Special Group members (*i.e.*, McGeorge Bundy, Alexis Johnson of the Department of State, Roswell Gilpatric of the Department of Defense, John McCone, and General Lyman Lemnitzer of the Joint Chiefs) augmented by Attorney General Robert Kennedy and General Maxwell Taylor. Although Secretary of State Rusk and Secretary of Defense McNamara were not formal members of the Special Group or the Special Group (Augmented), they sometimes attended meetings.

(2) General Lansdale named Chief-of-Operations of MONGOOSE

As a result of the Bay of Pigs failure, President Kennedy distrusted the CIA and believed that someone from outside the Agency was required to oversee major covert action programs. Rather than appoint his brother, Robert Kennedy, to head MONGOOSE, as proposed by Goodwin, President Kennedy gave General Edward Lansdale the task of coordinating the CIA's MONGOOSE operations with those of the Departments of State and Defense. Lansdale had developed a reputation in the Philippines and Vietnam for having an ability to deal with revolutionary insurgencies in less developed countries. Kennedy appointed General Taylor Chairman of the Special Group Augmented. Robert Kennedy played an active role in the MONGOOSE Operation, a role unrelated to his position as Attorney General.

(3) CIA Organization for MONGOOSE

In late 1961 or early 1962, William Harvey was put in charge of the CIA's Task Force W, the CIA unit for MONGOOSE Operations. Task Force W operated under guidance from the Special Group (Augmented) and employed a total of approximately 400 people at CIA headquarters and its Miami Station. McCone and Harvey were the principal CIA participants in Operation MONGOOSE. Although Helms attended only 7 of the 40 MONGOOSE meetings, he was significantly involved, and he testified that he "was as interested" in MONGOOSE as were Harvey and McCone. (Helms, 7/18/75, p. 10)

B. LANSDALE'S THEORY AND OBJECTIVE FOR MONGOOSE

In the fall of 1961, Lansdale was asked by President Kennedy to examine the Administration's Cuba policy and to make recommendations. Lansdale testified that he reported to President Kennedy that "Castro * * * had aroused considerable affection for himself personally with the Cuban population * * *" (Lansdale, 7/8/75, p. 4), and that the United States "should take a very different course" from the "harassment" operations that had been directed against Castro up to that time. (Lansdale, 7/8/75, p. 3) Lansdale informed the President that these prior United States operations were conceived and led by Americans. (Lansdale, 7/8/75, p. 5) In contrast, Lansdale proposed in Operation MONGOOSE that the United States work with exiles, particularly professionals, who had opposed Batista and then became disillusioned with Castro. (Lansdale, 7/8/75, pp. 4, 10-11) Lansdale's ultimate objective was to have "the people themselves overthrow the Castro regime rather than U.S. engineered efforts from outside Cuba." (Lansdale, 7/8/75, p. 41)

Lansdale's concept for Operation MONGOOSE envisioned a first step involving the development of leadership elements and "a very necessary political basis" among the Cubans opposed to Castro. (Lansdale, 7/8/75, p. 11) At the same time, he sought to develop "means to infiltrate Cuba successfully" and to organize "cells and activities inside Cuba * * * who could work secretly and safely." (Lansdale, 7/8/75, p. 11) Lansdale's plan was designed so as not to "arouse premature actions, not to bring great reprisals on the people there and abort any eventual success." (Lansdale, 7/8/75, p. 11)

C. BISSELL'S TESTIMONY CONCERNING PRESIDENTIAL INSTRUCTIONS TO ACT MORE VIGOROUSLY

According to the Assistant to the head of Task Force W, sometime early in the fall of 1961, Bissell was "chewed out in the Cabinet Room of the White House by both the President and the Attorney General for, as he put it, sitting on his ass and not doing anything about getting rid of Castro and the Castro regime." (Assistant, 6/18/75, p. 8)

The Assistant said Bissell told him about the meeting and directed him to come up with some plans. (Assistant, 6/18/75, pp. 8, 36–37) Bissell did not recall the White House meeting described by the Assistant, but agreed that he had been, in essence, told to "get off your ass about Cuba." (Bissell, 7/25/75, pp. 37–38)

Bissell was asked whether he considered that instruction authority for proceeding to assassinate Castro. He said, no, and that "formal and explicit approval" would be required for assassination activity (*id.*, 38–39). Bissell also said that there was in fact no assassination activity between the pre-Bay of Pigs/Rosselli operation and his departure from the Agency in February 1962.

D. THE JANUARY 19, 1962 SPECIAL GROUP MEETING

On January 19, 1962, a meeting of principal MONGOOSE participants was held in Attorney General Kennedy's office.[1] (McManus, 7/22/75, p. 6) Notes taken at the meeting by George McManus, Helms' Executive Assistant, contain the following passages:

Conclusion Overthrow of Castro is Possible.
"* * * a solution to the Cuban problem today carried top priority in U.S. Gov[ernmen]t. No time, money, effort—or manpower is to be spared."
"Yesterday * * * the President had indicated to him that the final chapter had not been written—it's got to be done and will be done." (McManus memo 1/19/62, p. 2)

McManus attributed the words "the top priority in the U.S. Gov[ernmen]t—no time, money, effort or manpower is to be spared" to the Attorney General. (McManus, 7/22/75, pp. 8–9)

Helms stated that those words reflected the "kind of atmosphere" in which he had perceived that assassination was implicitly authorized. (Helms, 7/17/75, pp. 60–61) McManus agreed that Robert Kennedy "was very vehement in his speech" and "really wanted action," but

---
[1] Those attending included the Attorney General, Lansdale, McManus, General Craig, representing the Joint Chiefs of Staff, Don Wilson of USIA, Major Patchell of the Secretary of Defense's office, and Frank Hand of CIA. It is probable that DDP Helms was also present.

McManus disagreed with Helms' perception, stating that "it never occurred to me" that Kennedy's exhortation included permission to assassinate Castro. Nor did the spirit of the meeting as a whole leave McManus with the impression that assassination was either contemplated or authorized. (McManus, 7/22/75, pp. 9-10) [1]

E. GENERAL LANSDALE'S MONGOOSE PLANNING TASKS

On January 18, 1962, Lansdale assigned 32 planning tasks to the agencies participating in MONGOOSE. In a memorandum to the working group members, Lansdale emphasized that "it is our job to put the American genius to work on this project, quickly and effectively. This demands a change from the business as usual and a hard facing of the fact that we are in a combat situation—where we have been given full command." (Lansdale memorandum, 1/20/62)

The 32 tasks comprised a variety of activities, ranging from intelligence collection to planning for "use of U.S. military force to support the Cuban popular movement" and developing an "operational schedule for sabotage actions inside Cuba." [2] In focusing on intelligence collection, propaganda, and various sabotage actions, Lansdale's tasks were consistent with the underlying strategy of MONGOOSE to build gradually towards an internal revolt of the Cuban people.

Lansdale transmitted a copy of the tasks to Attorney General Kennedy on January 18, 1962, with a handwritten note stating: "my review does not include the sensitive work I have reported to you; I felt you preferred informing the President privately." Lansdale testified that this sensitive work did not refer to assassinations and that he "never took up assassination with either the Attorney General or the President." He said that he could not precisely recall the nature of this "sensitive work" but that it might have involved a special trip he made under cover to meet Cuban leaders in Florida to assess their political strengths. (Lansdale, 7/8/75, p. 30)

In a memorandum to the Attorney General on January 27, 1962, Lansdale referred to the possibility that "we might uncork the touchdown play independently of the institutional program we are spurring." (Memo, Lansdale to Attorney General, 1/27/62) Lansdale

---

[1] There was a great deal of evidence showing that Cuba had a high priority in the Kennedy Administration, and the very existence of a high-level group like the Special Group (Augmented) further demonstrated Cuba's importance. McNamara stated that "we were hysterical about Castro at the time of the Bay of Pigs and thereafter." (In the same context, McNamara stated, "I don't believe we contemplated assassination.") (McNamara, 7/22/75, p. 93) Similarly, General Lansdale informed the members of his interagency committee that MONGOOSE "demands a change from business-as-usual and a hard facing of the fact that you're in a combat situation where we have been given full command." (Lansdale Memo, 1/20/62)

On the other hand, Theodore Sorensen testified that "there were lots of top priorities, and it was the job of some of [us] to continually tell various agencies their particular subject was the top priority" and although Cuba was "important" it was "fairly well down on the list of the President's agenda." (Sorensen, 7/21/75, p. 12) For example, when President Kennedy told Sorensen that his first letter to Khruschev in the secret correspondence which lasted two or three years would be "the single most important document you will write during your Presidency." President Kennedy said, "Yes, we get these every day over here." (Sorensen, 7/21/75, p. 12)

[2] Parrott sarcastically characterized Lansdale's plans as follows:

"I'll give you one example of Lansdale's perspicacity. He had a wonderful plan for getting rid of Castro. This plan consisted of spreading the word that the Second Coming of Christ was imminent and that Christ was against Castro (who) was anti-Christ. And you would spread this word around Cuba, and then on whatever date it was, that there would be a manifestation of this thing. And at that time—this is absolutely true—and at that time just over the horizon there would be an American submarine which would surface off of Cuba and send up some starshells. And this would be the manifestation of the Second Coming and Castro would be overthrown * * *

Well, some wag called this operation—and somebody dubbed this—Elimination by Illumination." (Parrott, 7/10/75, pp. 49, 50)

testified that the phrase "touchdown play" was a "breezy way of referring to a Cuban revolt to overthrow the regime" rather than to Castro's assassination. (Lansdale, 7/8/75, p. 45) [1] The examples of such plays cited in the memorandum (e.g., "stir up workers in Latin America and Cuba," work through "ethnic language groups," "youth elements," or "families through the Church") do not contain any indication of assassination.[2] (Memo, Lansdale to Attorney General, 1/27/62, p. 1)

On January 19, 1962, Lansdale added an additional task to those assigned on January 18. "Task 33" involved a plan to "incapacitate" Cuban sugar workers during the harvest by the use of chemical warfare means. Lansdale testified that the plan involved using nonlethal chemicals to sicken Cubans temporarily and keep them away from the fields for a 24–48 hour period "without ill effects." The task was initially approved for planning purposes with the notation that it would require "policy determination" before final approval. After a study showed the plan to be unfeasible, it was cancelled without ever being submitted to the SGA for debate. (Lansdale, 7/8/75 p. 29; SGA Minutes, 1/30/62, p. 1)

The SGA approved Lansdale's 33 tasks for planning purposes on January 30, 1962. (SGA Minutes, 1/30/62, p. 1) On February 20, Lansdale detailed a six-phase schedule for MONGOOSE, designed to culminate in October, 1962, with an "open revolt and overthrow of the Communist regime." (Lansdale Memorandum, 2/20/62, p. 2) As one of the operations for this "Resistance" phase, Lansdale, listed "attacks on the cadre of the regime, including key leaders." (Landsdale, 7/8/75, p. 151) Lansdale's plan stated:

> This should be a "Special Target" operation * * * Gangster elements might provide the best recruitment potential for actions against police—G2 [intelligence] officials. (*Id.*, p. 151) [3]

---

[1] The testimony was as follows:
The CHAIRMAN. What precisely did you mean by "uncork the touchdown play independently of the institutional programs we are spurring?"
General LANSDALE. Well, I was holding almost daily meetings with my working group, and—in tasking, and finding how they were developing plans I was becoming more and more concerned that they kept going back to doing what I felt were *pro forma* American types of actions rather than actively exploring how to get the Cubans into this, and to have them undertake actions.
To me, the touchdown play was a Cuban revolt to overthrow the regime. I did not feel that we had gotten into the real internal part of getting Cubans into the action, and I was concerned about that.
Senator BAKER. In the same context, it is fair to say that the name of the game was to get rid of Castro or his regime and that touchdown play was one of several methods that might have been used for that purpose?
General LANSDALE. Yes.
Senator BAKER. All right, now what was the touchdown play that you had in mind here?
General LANSDALE. Well, it was a revolt by the Cubans themselves * * * a revolution that would break down the police controls of the state and to drive the top people out of power and to do that, there needed to be political actions cells, psychological propaganda action cells, and eventually when possible, guerrilla forces developed in the country in a safe place for a new government to set up and direct the revolution that would eventually move into Havana and take over. (Lansdale, 7/8/75, pp. 45–56)

[2] Lansdale's memorandum described the "touchdown play" as follows:
"It may be a special effort which professional labor operators can launch to stir up workers in Latin America and Cuba. It may be through ethnic-language groups; Spain has an untapped action potential. It could be a warming-up of the always lively youth element in Latin America and Cuba, through some contacts specially used. It could be with the families through the Church, with families resisting the disciplined destruction of social justice by the Communists. It could be an imaginative defection project which cracks the top echelon of the Communist gang now running Cuba." (Memorandum, Lansdale to Attorney General, 1/27/62)

[3] An earlier reference to use of gangster-type elements had appeared in a CIA memorandum for the SGA on January 24, 1962. Commenting on Task 5 of Lansdale's original 32 tasks (which called for planning for "defection of top Cuban government officials"), the CIA memorandum noted that planning for the task will "necessarily be based upon an appeal made inside the island by intermediaries" and listed "crime syndicates" along with other groups as possible intermediaries. (CIA Memorandum, 1/24/62)

Lansdale testified that early in the MONGOOSE operation he had suggested that working level representatives of the MONGOOSE agencies get in touch with "criminal elements" to obtain intelligence and for "possible actions against the police structure" in Cuba. (Lansdale, 7/8/75, p. 104) Lansdale conceded that his proposal to recruit gangster elements for attacks on "key leaders" contemplated the targeted killing of individuals, in addition to the casualties that might occur in the course of the revolt itself. (Lansdale, 7/8/75, p. 107)

Lansdale's 33 plans were never approved for implementation by the SGA. As discussed below, the SGA tabled Lansdale's six phase plan altogether in February 1962, and directed him to plan for and conduct an intelligence collection plan only. (SGA Minutes, 3/5/62)

F. LANSDALE'S REJECTION OF A SUGGESTION THAT A PROPAGANDA CAMPAIGN, INCLUDING REWARDS FOR ASSASSINATION, BE EXPLORED

On January 30, 1962, the representative of the Defense Department and the Joint Chiefs on the MONGOOSE Working Group forwarded for Lansdale's consideration "a concept for creating distrust and apprehension in the Cuban Communist Hierarchy." (Memo, Craig to Lansdale, 1/30/62) The concept titled Operation Bounty, was described as a "system of financial rewards, commensurate with position and stature, for killing or delivering alive known Communists." Under the concept, leaflets would be dropped in Cuba listing rewards, which ranged from $5,000 for an "informer" to $100,000 for "government officials." A reward of "2¢" was listed for Castro. Lansdale testified that the 2¢ bounty was designed "to denigrate * * * Castro in the eyes of the Cuban population." (Lansdale, 7/8/75, p. 26) Lansdale said that he "tabled" this concept when he received it because "I did not think that it was something that should be seriously undertaken or supported further." (Lansdale, 7/8/75, p. 26) He never brought Operation Bounty before the SGA.

G. THE CONTROL SYSTEM FOR MONGOOSE OPERATIONS

In establishing the MONGOOSE Operation on November 30, 1961, President Kennedy had emphasized that the SGA should be "kept closely informed" of its activities. (Memorandum by the President, 11/30/61)

In practice, as Harvey's Executive Assistant on the CIA MONGOOSE Task Force W testified, this resulted in the submission of "specific detailed plans for every activity carried out by the task force." (Assistant, 6/18/75, p. 16) The Assistant testified that those plans were submitted "in nauseating detail:"

> It went down to such things as the gradients on the beach, and the composition of the sand on the beach in many cases. Every single solitary thing was in those plans, full details, times, events, weaponry, how it was going to happen, who was going to do what * * * the full details of every single thing we did. (Assistant, 6/18/75, p. 17)

Harvey also characterized the control process as requiring the submission of "excruciating detail." It was understood that the SGA was to be given an opportunity to debate proposals and to decide after weighing their strengths and weaknesses. (Harvey, 6/25/75, pp. 114, 123–124)

The documentary evidence further illustrates the SGA's tight control procedures for MONGOOSE. For example, after Lansdale submitted his 33 tasks and his overall concept for MONGOOSE for SGA consideration in January, he was ordered to cut back his plan and limit it to an intelligence collection program for the March–May 1962 period, rather than the five-stage plan culminating in an October "popular revolution," as originally conceived by Lansdale. (Memo 3/2/62, by Lansdale) In approving the modified intelligence collection plan, the SGA pointed out that:

* * * any actions which are not specifically spelled out in the plan but seem to be desirable as the project progresses, will be brought to the Special Group for resolution. (SGA Minutes, 1962)

In addition, the Guidelines for the MONGOOSE program emphasized the SGA's responsibility for control and prior approval of important operations:

The SGA is responsible for providing policy guidance to the [MONGOOSE] project, for approving important operations and for monitoring progress. (Guidelines for Operation MONGOOSE, March 14, 1962)

The SGA request for Helms to estimate "for each week as far into the next twelve months as possible * * * the numbers and type of agents you will establish inside Cuba * * * [and] brief descriptions * * * of actions contemplated," is another example of the close control the SGA exercised over Operation MONGOOSE. (Memo, Lansdale to Helms, 3/5/62) Any proposal to supply arms and equipment to particular resistance groups inside Cuba was also required to "be submitted to the Special Group (Augmented) for decision *ad hoc*." (Lansdale Memo to the Special Group, 4/11/62, p. 1) These procedural requirements were operative at the time of Harvey's meeting with Rosselli in Miami.

The Guidelines for Operation MONGOOSE stated:

During this period, General Lansdale will continue as Chief of Operations, calling directly on the participating departments and agencies for support and implementation of agreed tasks. The heads of these departments and agencies are responsible for performance through normal command channels to higher authority.[1] (Guideline for Operation MONGOOSE, 3/14/62)

Harvey complained to McCone about the SGA control requirement for advance approval of "major operations going beyond the collection of intelligence." He stated that:

To permit requisite flexibility and professionalism for a maximum operational effort against Cuba, the tight controls exercised by the Special Group and the present time-consuming coordination and briefing procedures should, if at all possible, be made less restrictive and less stultifying. (Memo, Harvey to McCone, 4/10/62)

---

[1] The initial draft of these Guidelines had referred to the President, but was later amended to read "higher authority." (Draft Guidelines, 3/5/62, p. 2) The minutes of the consideration of these Guidelines were also amended with respect to the manner in which the Guidelines were approved. A Memorandum for Record, entitled "Discussion of Operation MONGOOSE with the President," stated:

"In the presence of the Special Group (Augmented) the President was given a progress report on Operation MONGOOSE. The Guidelines dated March 14, 1962 were circulated and were used as the basis of the discussion. After a prolonged consideration of the visibility, noise level and risks entailed, General Lansdale and the Special Group (Augmented) were given tacit authorization to proceed in accordance with the Guidelines." (SGA Memo for the Record, 3/16/62)

A note, dated March 22, 1962, appeared on the bottom of this memorandum and stated:

"This minute was read to the Special Group (Augmented) today. The Group was unanimous in feeling that no authorization, either tacit or otherwise, was given by higher authority. The members of the Group asked that the minute be amended to indicate that the Group itself had decided to proceed in accordance with the Guidelines."

Even as the Cuban Missile Crisis approached, and the increasing pressure to act against the Castro regime led to a "stepped-up" MONGOOSE plan, the SGA continued to require that all sensitive operations be submitted to it for advance approval. For example, when the SGA approved in principle a proposed set of operations on September 14, 1962, Bundy

> * * * made it clear that this did not constitute a blanket approval of every item in the paper and that sensitive ones such as sabotage, for example, will have to be presented in more detail on a case by case basis. (Memo of SGA Meeting, 9/14/62, p. 1)

Helms and the members of the SGA differed on whether or not these control requirements were consistent with Helms' perception that assassination was permissible without a direct order. That testimony is discussed in subsection (3), *infra*.

H. THE PATTERN OF MONGOOSE ACTION

The Kennedy Administration pressed the MONGOOSE operation with vigorous language. Although the collection of intelligence information was the central objective of MONGOOSE until August 1962, sabotage and paramilitary actions were also conducted,[1] including a major sabotage operation aimed at a large Cuban copper mine. Lansdale described the sabotage acts as involving "blowing up bridges to stop communications and blowing up certain production plants." (Lansdale, 7/8/75, p. 36) During the Missile Crisis in the fall of 1962, sabotage was increasingly urged.

Despite the Administration's urgings, the SGA shied away from sabotage and other violent action throughout 1962, including the period of the Missile Crisis. Helms noted in a memorandum of a meeting on October 16, 1962, that Robert Kennedy, in expressing the "general dissatisfaction of the President" with MONGOOSE, "pointed out that [MONGOOSE] had been underway for a year * * * that there had been no acts of sabotage and that even the one which had been attempted had failed twice." (Memo by Helms, 10/16/62) A memorandum to Helms from his Executive Assistant (who spent full time on Cuba matters) reviewed the MONGOOSE program in the aftermath of the Missile Crisis, and stated:

> During the past year, while one of the options of the project was to create internal dissension and resistance leading to eventual U.S. intervention, a review shows that policymakers not only shied away from the military intervention aspect but were generally apprehensive of sabotage proposals. (Memo to Helms, 10/16/62)

Harvey concurred in this SGA assessment. MONGOOSE documents bear out the operation's emphasis on intelligence gathering. The only phase of Lansdale's six-phase plan approved for January through August 1962 was described by Lansdale as "essentially an intelligence

---

[1] In early March 1962, the SGA recognized the need to begin "preliminary actions * * * involving such things as spotting, assessing and training action-type agents" but the SGA agreed that it must "keep its hand tightly" on these actions. The SGA saw, however, that such control might not be completely effective and recognized 'that many of the agents infiltrated into Cuba would be of an all-purpose type; that is, they would be trained in paramilitary skills, as well as those of exclusively intelligence concern.' It was noted that once the agents are within the country, they cannot be effectively controlled from the U.S., although every effort will be made to attempt such control." (SGA Minutes, 3/5/62)

collection" effort. (Lansdale Memo 4/11/62) The MONGOOSE Guidelines approved on March 5, 1962, stated that the acquisition of intelligence was the "immediate priority objective of U.S. efforts in the coming months." (Guidelines for Operation MONGOOSE, 3/14/62) While the Guidelines did state that covert actions would be undertaken concurrently with intelligence collection, these were to be on a scale "short of those reasonably calculated to inspire a revolt" in Cuba. The SGA stipulated that MONGOOSE action beyond the acquisition of intelligence "must be inconspicuous." (Lansdale Memo, 3/2/62)

After the intelligence collection phase ended in August 1962, the SGA considered whether to adopt a "stepped-up Course B plus," which, in contrast to Phase I, was designed to inspire a revolt against the Castro regime. (Memo for the SGA from Lansdale, 8/8/62) The SGA initially decided against this course and in favor of a "CIA variant" on August 10, 1962. (Minutes of SGA Meeting, 8/10/62) The "CIA variant," which was proposed by McCone, posted limited actions to avoid inciting a revolt and sought a split between Castro and "old-line Communists" rather than Castro's overthrow.

On August 20, Taylor told the President that the SGA saw no likelihood that Castro's Government would be overturned by internal means without direct United States military intervention, and that the SGA favored a more aggressive MONGOOSE program.[1] (Memo, Taylor to the President, 8/20/62) On August 23, McGeorge Bundy issued NSC Memorandum No. 181, which stated that, at the President's directive, "the line of activity projected for Operation MONGOOSE Plan B plus should be developed with all possible speed." On August 30, the SGA instructed the CIA to submit a list of possible sabotage targets and noted that: "The Group, by reacting to this list, could define the limits within which the Agency could operate on its own initiative." (Minutes of 8/30/62)

The onset of the Cuban Missile Crisis intially caused a reversion to the stepped-up Course B plan. At an SGA meeting on October 4, 1962, Robert Kennedy stated that the President "is concerned about progress on the MONGOOSE program and feels that more priority should be given to trying to mount sabotage operations." The Attorney General urged that "massive activity" be undertaken within the MONGOOSE framework. In response to this proposal, the SGA decided that "considerably more sabotage" should be undertaken, and that "all efforts should be made to develop new and imaginative approaches with the possibility of getting rid of the Castro regime." (Minutes of SGA Meeting, 10/14/62, p. 3) [2] However, on October 30,

---

[1] There are references in the SGA records to attacks on Soviet personnel in Cuba. The record of the SGA meeting on September 9, 1962, states: "It was suggested that the matter of attacking and harassing of Soviet personnel within Cuba should be considered." (SGA Minutes, 9/9/62)
Earlier, on August 31, 1962, Lansdale had included a task "to provoke incidents between Cubans and Bloc personnel to exacerbate tensions" in a proposed projection of actions for Phase II of MONGOOSE. (Memo to SGA, Action No. 47, 8/31/62) The Special Group thereafter decided, as a means of "emphasizing such activity," to replace that tas' with one to "cause actions by Cubans against Bloc personnel," and to note that "consideration will be given to provoking and conducting physical attacks on Bloc personnel.' (Memo to Taylor, Rusk, and McNamara, from Lansdale, 9/12/62, pp. 1–2)
[2] The SGA also decided on October 4, 1962, that Robert Kennedy would chair the Group' meetings "for the time being." (Id., p. 3.) Subsequently, at a meeting on October 16, 1962 Robert Kennedy stated that he was going to give MONGOOSE "more personal attention' in view of the lack of progress and would hold daily meetings with the working grou. representatives, i.e., Lansdale, Harvey, and the other Agency members. (Memo of Meeting by Helms, 10/16/62. p. 1) Helms testified that he did not recall any such daily meeting with the Attorney General. He had the impression there may have been several at firs but that then they ceased. (Helms, 7/17/75, pp. 54–55)

1962, the Special Group (Augmented) ordered a halt to all sabotage operations. (Lansdale Memo for the record, 10/30/62)[1]

Theodore Sorensen, a member of the Executive Committee established to deal with the Missile Crisis, testified that Cuba was the "No. 1 priority" during the Crisis. He said that although "all alternatives, plans, possibilities were exhaustively surveyed" during that time, the subject of assassination was never raised in the National Security Council or the Executive Committee. (Sorensen, 7/21/75, p. 11)

(3) EVIDENCE BEARING ON KNOWLEDGE OF AND AUTHORIZATION FOR THE ASSASSINATION PLOT, PHASE II

As discussed below, both Helms and the high Kennedy Administration officials who testified agreed that no direct order was ever given for Castro's assassination and that no senior Administration officials, including McCone, were informed about the assassination activity. Helms testified, however, that he believed the assassination activity was permissible and that it was within the scope of authority given to the Agency. McCone and other Kennedy Administration officials disagreed, testifying that assassination was impermissible without a direct order and that Castro's assassination was not within the bounds of the MONGOOSE operation.

As DDP, Helms was in charge of covert operations when the poison pills were given to Rosselli in Miami in April 1962. Helms had succeeded to this post following Bissell's retirement in February 1962. He testified that after the Bay of Pigs:

> Those of us who were still [in the Agency] were enormously anxious to try and be successful at what we were being asked to do by what was then a relatively new Administration. We wanted to earn our spurs with the President and with other officers of the Kennedy Administration. (Helms, 7/17/75, p. 4)

A. HELMS' TESTIMONY CONCERNING AUTHORITY

Helms testified that he doubted that he was informed when Harvey gave poison pills to Rosselli and that he did not recall having authorized Castro's assassination by that means. He said, however, that he had authorized that assassination plot because "we felt that we were operating as we were supposed to operate, that these things if not specifically authorized, at least were authorized in general terms." (Helms, 6/13/75, p. 61)

(1) Helms' Perception of Authority

Helms testified that the "intense" pressure exerted by the Kennedy Administration to overthrow Castro had led him to perceive that the CIA was acting within the scope of its authority in attempting

---

[1] Harvey testified that he had a "confrontation" with Robert Kennedy at the height of the Missile Crisis concerning Harvey's order that agent teams be sent into Cuba to support any conventional U.S. military operation that might occur. Harvey stated that Robert Kennedy "took a great deal of exception" to this order and, as a result, McCone ordered Harvey to stop the agent operations (Harvey, 7/11/75, pp. 80-81). Elder, McCone's assistant at the time, similarly described this incident and stated that, although Harvey had attempted to get guidance from top officials during the Missile Crisis, Harvey "earned another black mark as not being fully under control." (Elder, 8/13/75, pp. 34-35)

Castro's assassination, even though assassination was never directly ordered.[1] He said:

> I believe it was the policy at the time to get rid of Castro and if killing him was one of the things that was to be done in this connection, that was within what was expected. (Helms, 6/13/75, p. 137)
> I remember vividly [the pressure to overthrow Castro] was very intense. (Helms, 6/13/75, p. 26)

Helms stated that this pressure intensified during the period of Operation MONGOOSE and continued through much of 1963. (Helms, 6/13/75, p. 27) As the pressure increased, "obviously the extent of the means that one thought were available * * * increased too." (Helms, 6/13/75, p. 26)

Helms recalled that during the MONGOOSE period, "it was made abundantly clear * * * to everybody involved in the operation that the desire was to get rid of the Castro regime and to get rid of Castro * * * the point was that no limitations were put on this injunction." (Helms, 7/17/75, pp. 16–17)

> Senator MATHIAS. Let me draw an example from history. When Thomas Beckett was proving to be an annoyance, as Castro, the King said who will rid me of this man. He didn't say to somebody, go out and murder him. He said who will rid me of this man, and let it go at that.
> Mr. HELMS. That is a warming reference to the problem.
> Senator MATHIAS. You feel that spans the generations and the centuries?
> Mr. HELMS. I think it does, sir.
> Senator MATHIAS. And that is typical of the kind of thing which might be said, which might be taken by the Director or by anybody else as Presidential authorization to go forward?
> Mr. HELMS. That is right. But in answer to that, I realize that one sort of grows up in [the] tradition of the time and I think that any of us would have found it very difficult to discuss assassinations with a President of the U.S. I just think we all had the feeling that we're hired out to keep those things out of the Oval Office.
> Senator MATHIAS. Yet at the same time you felt that some spark had been transmitted, that that was within the permissible limits?
> Mr. HELMS. Yes, and if he had disappeared from the scene they would not have been unhappy. (Helms, 6/13/75, pp. 72–73)

Helms said that he was never told by his superiors to kill Castro, (Helms, 7/17/75, p. 15) but that:

> No member of the Kennedy Administration * * * ever told me that [assassination] was proscribed, [or] ever referred to it in that fashion * * *. Nobody ever said that [assassination] was ruled out * * * (Helms, 7/17/75, pp. 18, 43) [2]

Helms said that the delivery of poison pills for assassinating Castro:

> "with all the other things that were going on at that time * * * seemed to be within the permissible part of this effort * * *. In the perceptions of the time and the things we were trying to do this was one human life against many other human lives that were being lost." (Helms, 6/13/75, pp. 64, 99) [3]

---

[1] The extent to which pressure in fact existed "to do something about Castro" is discussed in detail in the section immediately above dealing with Operation MONGOOSE, its strategy of causing an internal revolt of the Cuban people against Castro, the strict control system established by the Special Group Augmented, and the pattern of intelligence collection and sabotage activity actually authorized and undertaken.
[2] Helms testified: "In my 25 years in the Central Intelligence Agency, I always thought I was working within authorization, that I was doing what I had been asked to do by proper authority and when I was operating on my own I was doing what I believed to be the legitimate business of the Agency as it would have been expected of me." (Helms, 6/13/75, pp. 30–31)
[3] Helms elaborated: "* * * people were losing their lives in raids, a lot of people had lost their life at the Bay of Pigs, agents were being arrested left and right and put before the wall and shot." (Helms, 6/13/75, p. 64)

(2) Helms' Testimony Concerning the Absence of a Direct Order and Why He Did Not Inform Administration Officials

Helms testified that there was no direct order to assassinate Castro. He said that his perceptions of authority did not reach the point where he could testify that he had specific instructions to kill Castro. Helms told the Committee:

> I have testified as best I could about the atmosphere of the time, what I understood was desired, and I don't want to take refuge in saying that I was instructed to specifically murder Castro * * *. (Helms, 6/13/75, p. 88)

When asked if President Kennedy had been informed of any assassination plots, Helms pointed out that "nobody wants to embarrass a President of the United States by discussing the assassination of foreign leaders in his presence." (Helms, 6/13/75, p. 29) He added that the Special Group was "the mechanism that was set up * * * to use as a circuit breaker so that these things did not explode in the President's face and that he was not held responsible for them." (Helms, 6/13/75, p. 29) He said that he had "no knowledge that a Castro assassination was ever authorized" by the SGA. (Helms, 6/13/75, pp. 28–29)

Helms testified that he never informed the SGA or any of its members that Harvey had given the pills to Rosselli in Miami "because to this day I do not recall Harvey ever having told me they were passed." (Helms, 7/18/75, p. 22)

(3) Helms' Perception of Robert Kennedy's Position on Assassination

Helms emphasized that Robert Kennedy continually pressed for tangible results in the MONGOOSE effort.[1] He testified:

> I can say absolutely fairly we were constantly in touch with each other in these matters. The Attorney General was on the phone to me, he was on the phone to Mr. Harvey, to Mr. Fitzgerald, his successor. He was on the phone even to people on Harvey's staff, as I recall it. (Helms, 7/17/75, p.13)[2]

---

[1] Q. So it was your impression that he was sort of setting the tone for the group's action or activity.
"A. Oh, yes * * * there wasn't any doubt about that. He was very much interested in this and spent a great deal of time on it." (Helms, 6/13/75, p. 22)

[2] The telephone records of the Attorney General's office indicate frequent contact between the Attorney General and Helms. Helms stated that his conversations with Robert Kennedy were "candid" and that "he and I used to deal in facts most of the time." (Helms, 6/13/75, p. 63) Helms testified about the detail of his talks with Robert Kennedy:
"For example, we had projects to land sabotage teams. Well, (the Attorney General would ask) have you got the team organized, did the team go? Well, no, we've been delayed a week because the weather is bad or the boats don't run, or something of this kind. It even got down to that degree of specificity." (Helms, 7/17/75, p. 40)
An official in the Western Hemisphere Division of the Directorate of Plans who was responsible for evaluating potential Cuban assets testified that in June or July 1962, he was told by his superior [either Harvey or Harvey's assistant] "go see the Attorney General, he has something to talk about" (Official, 9/18/75, p. 28). The official said that he went to the Justice Department and was told by the Attorney General that: "He wanted to see a man who had contact with a small group of Cubans who had a plan for creating an insurrection, or something like that * * *" (Official, 9/18/75, p. 30)
The contact recommended by the Attorney General, referred the official to five or six Cubans who claimed to have connections within Cuba and who requested weapons, money, and supplies to start an insurrection. The official said he reported to the Attorney General that the Cubans did not have a concrete plan; the Attorney General rejected the official's evaluation and ordered him to go to Guantanamo Naval Base in Cuba "using whatever assets we could get to make contact with people inside Cuba, and start working and developing this particular group." (Official, 9/18/75, p. 34) When the official protested that the CIA had agreed not to work out of Guantanamo, the Attorney General responded, "we will see about that." The official said that he then reported his conversation with the Attorney General to Harvey, who replied: "There was a meeting about that this morning. I forgot to tell you about it. I will take care of it * * *" (Official, 9/18/75, p. 35) The official said that he had no further contact with the Attorney General or the Cubans.

During one appearance before the Committee, Helms was asked by the Chairman:

> The CHAIRMAN. Since he [Kennedy] was on the phone to you repeatedly did he ever tell you to kill Castro?
> Mr. HELMS. No.
> The CHAIRMAN. He did not?
> Mr. HELMS. Not in those words, no. (Helms, 7/17/75, p. 13)[1]

Helms testified that he had never told Attorney General Kennedy about any assassination activity. He assumed that "he wasn't informed by anyone," and added that "Harvey kept phase 2 [the Rosselli plot] pretty much in his back pocket" (Helms, 6/13/75, pp. 57–58). Helms also said that the Attorney General had never told him that assasination was ruled out. (Helms, 7/17/75, p. 13) He added that he did not know if Castro's assassination would have been morally unacceptable to the Attorney General, but he believed that Robert Kennedy "would not have been unhappy if [Castro] had disappeared off the scene by whatever means." (Helms, 7/17/75, pp. 17–18)

(4) Helms' Testimony as to Why he Did Not Obtain a Direct Order

Helms testified that assassination "was not part of the CIA's policy" and was not part of its "armory." (Helms, 6/13/75, pp. 87–88) Helms said that he "never liked assassination," and banned its use five years after he became Director of Central Intelligence. (Helms, 6/13/75, p. 166) Helms also testified to his "very grave doubts about the wisdom" of dealing with underworld figures when Harvey proposed contacting Rosselli to see if gangster links to Cuba could be developed. (Helms, 6/13/75, p. 33; 7/18/75, p. 31)

Despite these reservations, Helms did not seek approval for the assassination activity. He said this was because assassination was not a subject which should be aired with higher authority. (Helms, 7/18/75, pp. 31–32) Specifically, he said he did not seek SGA approval because:

> I didn't see how one would have expected that a thing like killing or murdering or assassination would become a part of a large group of people sitting around a table in the United States Government. (Helms, 7/17/75, p. 14)

His unwillingness "to embarrass a President of the United States [by] discussing the assassination of foreign leaders in his presence" has already been noted. (Helms, 6/13/75, p. 29)

Helms gave additional testimony in response to questions concerning his failure to seek explicit authorization for assassination activity.

> Senator HUDDLESTON. * * * it did not occur to you to inquire of the Attorney General or of the Special Group or of anyone that when they kept pushing and asking for action * * * to clarify that question of whether you should actually be trying to assassinate?
> Mr. HELMS. I don't know whether it was in training, experience, tradition or exactly what one points to, but I think to go up to a Cabinet officer and say, am

---

[1] Helms immediately reiterated that his perception of authority for Castro's assassination derived from the pressure exerted by the Administration against Castro. The exchange between the Chairman and Helms continued as follows:
"The CHAIRMAN. Well, did he ever tell you in other words that clearly conveyed to you the message that he wanted to kill Castro?
"HELMS. Sir, the last time I was here [before the Committee], I did the best I could about what I believed to be the parameters under which we were working, and that was to get rid of Castro. I can't imagine any Cabinet officer wanting to sign off on something like that. I can't imagine anybody wanting something in writing saying I have just charged Mr. Jones to go out and shoot Mr. Smith." (Helms, 7/17/75, pp. 13–14)

I right in assuming that you want me to assassinate Castro or to try to assassinate Castro, is a question it wouldn't have occurred to me to ask.

* * * * * * *

Senator HUDDLESTON. * * * [because assassination has such serious consequences] it seems to fortify the thought that I would want to be dead certain, I would want to hear it from the horse's mouth in plain, simple English language before I would want to undertake that kind of activity." (Helms, 7/17/75, pp. 51–52)

* * * * * * *

"Senator MORGAN. In light of your previous statement that this is a Christian country and that this Committee has to face up to the prime moral issue of whether or not killing is * * * acceptable * * * don't you think it would have taken affirmative permission or authority to kill, rather than just saying it was not eliminated from the authority or you were not restricted * * *?
"Mr. HELMS. * * * killing was not part of the CIA's policy. It was not part of the CIA's armory * * * but in this Castro operation * * * I have testified as best I could about the atmosphere of the time, what I understood was desired [and] that this was getting rid of Castro, if he had been gotten rid of by this means that this would have been acceptable to certain individuals * * * I was just doing my best to do what I thought I was supposed to do." (Helms, 6/13/75, pp. 87–88)

When asked why he had not sought clarification from the Special Group, its members, or Robert Kennedy as to whether it was "in fact, the policy of the Government to actually kill Fidel Castro," Helms answered,

I don't know * * * There is something about the whole chain of episodes in connection with this Rosselli business that I am simply not able to bring back in a coherent fashion. And there was something about the ineffectuality of all this, or the lack of conviction that anything ever happened, that I believe in the end made this thing simply collapse, disappear. And I don't recall what I was briefed on at the time. Maybe I was kept currently informed and maybe I wasn't, and today I don't remember it * * * But I do not recall ever having been convinced that any attempt was really made on Castro's life. And since I didn't believe any attempt had been made on Castro's life, I saw no reason to pursue the matter further. (Helms, 7/18/75, pp. 31–32)

(5) *Helms' Perception of the Relation of Special Group Controls to Assassination Activity*

Helms stated that the SGA's control system for MONGOOSE was not intended to apply to assassination activity. (Helms, 7/18/75, p. 21) Helms stated that the SGA's decision on March 5, 1962, that major operations going beyond the collection of intelligence must receive advance approval referred to "rather specific items that the Special Group had on its agenda" from the outset of MONGOOSE (Helms, 7/18/75, p. 21) Helms said that since assassination was not among those items, the SGA would not have expected assassination activity to come within its purview. (Helms, 7/18/75, p. 21) As to the SGA's stated desire to "keep its hands tightly on preliminary actions" leading towards sabotage and other covert activity, Helms characterized it as the kind of injunction "that appears in all kinds of governmental minutes of meetings." (Helms, 7/18/75, pp. 16–17)

Helms stated that although there were "no limitations" on actions to remove Castro during MONGOOSE, there were restraints on sabotage operations. He did not understand the absence of specific limitations to authorize more drastic actions, such as committing the United States military to an invasion of Cuba. (Helms, 7/18/75, p. 9)[1]

---

[1] Helms testified that, although loss of life was implicit in the MONGOOSE operations, "I think there was an effort made not to take tacks that would recklessly kill a lot of people and not achieve very much. I think there was an effort, if you had a sabotage operation, not to throw a lot of hand grenades into a city, but rather take out the power plant which would actually damage the economy of the country. There was an effort made to find devices that would seem to have a useful end." (Helms, 7/17/75, pp. 63–64)

B. HARVEY'S TESTIMONY CONCERNING AUTHORITY

(1) Harvey's Perception of Authority

Harvey stressed that he was a line officer reporting to the DDP, his immediate superior within the Agency. (Harvey, 6/25/75, p. 83) He pointed out that his information about authorization from outside the agency came from the DDP:

> [A]t no time during this entire period * * * did I ever personally believe or have any feeling that I was either free-wheeling or end-running or engaging in any activity that was not in response to a considered, decided U.S. policy, properly approved, admittedly, perhaps, through channels and at levels I personally had no involvement in, or first-hand acquaintance with, and did not consider it at that point my province to, if you will, cross-examine either the Deputy Director or the Director concerning it. (Harvey, 6/25/75, p. 83)

Harvey stated that he believed that authorization for the 1962 assassination activity carried over from the period when Allen Dulles was DCI. He based his belief on statements made to him by Bissell. On the question of McCone's knowledge or authorization, the following exchange occurred between Harvey and the Chairman:

> The CHAIRMAN. That doesn't necessarily mean that because the previous director had knowledge that Mr. McCone had knowledge. It is not like a covenant that runs in the land.
> Mr. HARVEY. No, of course not, and they don't always brief their successors. (Harvey, 6/25/75, p. 85)

(2) Harvey and the Special Group (Augmented)

During the MONGOOSE period, Harvey attended many SGA meetings as the CIA's representative. He testified that he never informed the SGA or any of its members of the ongoing assassination plots and that at no time was assassination discussed at any meetings, except the one on August 10, 1962.[1]

Early in 1962, Harvey was appointed chief of Task Force W, CIA's action arm for MONGOOSE activities. In the latter part of April 1962, Harvey went to Miami where the CIA had its JM/WAVE station. Harvey testified that in addition to meeting with Rosselli and delivering the poison pills, his trip had other purposes totally unrelated to assassination:

> " * * * this was one of a number of periodic trips for the purpose of reviewing in toto * * * the actual and potential operations at the Miami base * * * and this covered the whole gamut from personnel administration, operational support in the way of small craft [and] so on * * *." (Harvey, 7/11/75, pp. 15-16)

The SGA expected to receive a report from Harvey on his April trip to Miami. While Harvey was still in Miami, Lansdale told the SGA that:

> "Upon the return of Mr. Harvey from his current field visit, more specific information on the status of agent training and operations should be made available." (Memorandum for the SGA, 4/19/62, p. 2)

On April 26, 1962, Lansdale told the SGA that Harvey was in Florida "initiating a new series of agent infiltrations" and would return to Washington on April 30. (Memo for the SGA, 4/26/62, from Lansdale) At an SGA meeting on April 26, General Taylor requested that Harvey "attend the next meeting and report on agent activities."

---

[1] This meeting and the testimony concerning it is treated in depth in the section, *infra*, pp. 161-169.

(Memo for the Record, April 26, 1962, by McCone) The next day, McCone's assistant sent Harvey a memorandum informing him of General Taylor's request and notifying him that McCone wanted to meet with Harvey and Lansdale "immediately on your return to discuss the Task Force activities." (Memo for Action, Elder to Harvey, 4/27/62)

Harvey reported to the SGA as requested. He testified that he did not inform the SGA, or any individual outside the Agency, that he had given the poison pills to Rosselli. (Harvey, 7/11/75, p. 16) Harvey said he did not tell McCone about the poison pills when he briefed the Director because he did not believe it was necessary. (Harvey, 7/11/75, p. 17)[1]

Harvey gave a progress report to the SGA on "agent teams" and the "general field of intelligence" when he reported to them following his trip to Miami. (Memo of SGA Meeting, 5/3/62) According to the minutes, Harvey reported that three agent teams had been infiltrated and that 72 actual or potential reporting sources were also in the place. The minutes of the May 3, 1962, SGA meeting make no mention of Harvey's assassination activities.

Shortly after the May 3 meeting, General Taylor gave the President what Taylor called a "routine briefing." (Taylor, 7/9/75, p. 27) General Taylor's memorandum of that briefing makes no reference to Harvey's contacts with Rosselli or the delivery of pills and guns. (Memo for Record, May 7, 1962, by General Taylor) Taylor testified that he had never heard of Harvey's delivering pills to poison Castro, or of any assassination attempts. (Taylor, 7/9/75, p. 42)

C. TESTIMONY OF KENNEDY ADMINISTRATION OFFICIALS

The Committee took testimony from the Kennedy Administration officials principally involved in the MONGOOSE operation, all of whom testified that the assassination plots were not authorized. Their testimony focused on whether any authority for a Castro assassination existed, whether they had knowledge of any Castro assassination activity, and whether it was probable that Robert Kennedy might have given Helms an assassination order through a "back channel."[2]

McCone, who testified that he had never been informed of the assassination plots, said that neither President Kennedy, Attorney General Kennedy, nor any of the Cabinet or White House staff ever discussed with him any plans or operations to assassinate Castro. (McCone, 6/6/75, p. 44)

McCone said that although the Cuban problem was discussed in terms of "dispose of Castro," or "knock off Castro," those terms were meant to refer to "the overthrow of the Communist Government in Cuba," and not to assassination. (McCone, 6/6/75, p. 44; Memo to Helms, April 14, 1967)

---

[1] Harvey explained his failure to brief the SGA in the following exchange:
"Q. * * * Did you believe that the White House did not want the Special Group to know?
"HARVEY. Well, I would have had no basis for that belief, but I would have felt that if the White House [tasked] this [operation to the CIA] and wanted the Special Group to know about it, it was up to the White House to brief the Special Group and not up to me to brief them, and I would have considered that I would have been very far out of line and would have been subject to severe censure." (Harvey, 7/11/75, p. 77)

[2] In one of Helms' subsequent appearances before the Committee he testified that Robert Kennedy never gave him such an order.

McCone told the Committee that "it is very hard for me to believe" that Robert Kennedy would have initiated an assassination effort against Castro without consulting the SGA. (McCone, 1975 p. 52)

Taylor served as Chairman of the SGA during the MONGOOSE Operation (Taylor, 7/9/75, p. 12), and as President Kennedy's Military Representative and Intelligence Advisor after the Bay of Pigs until his appointment as Chairman of the Joint Chiefs of Staff in November 1962. (Taylor, 7/9/75, p. 11; Bundy, 7/11/75, p. 25) He testified that a plan to assassinate Castro was "never" submitted to the SGA, either orally or in writing. (Taylor, 7/9/75, p. 41) He said the SGA was never told of the poison pills given to Rosselli in April 1962, and that the passage of those pills without the knowledge of the SGA was "entirely, completely out of [the] context and character of the way the [SGA] operated or the way it would accept" that an operation was properly authorized. (Taylor, 7/9/75, p. 43) Taylor testified that although the SGA was "certainly anxious for the downfall of Castro," an "assassinaton never came up" at its meetings. (Taylor, 7/9/75, p. 62)

Taylor stated "the President and the Attorney General would never have gone around" the SGA to deal with Helms or other CIA officials in planning an assassination. (Taylor, 7/9/75, p. 49) To have done so would have been "entirely contradictory to every method of operation I ever saw on the part of the President and his brother." (Taylor, 7/9/75, p. 45) Taylor acknowledged that Robert Kennedy frequently pushed for more direct action during MONGOOSE, but said that "there was no suggestion [of] assassination." (Taylor, 7/9/75, p. 67) He testified that Robert Kennedy dealt directly with Lansdale outside SGA channels "only for the purpose of imparting his own sense of urgency," but "never" would have done so on substantive issues.[1]

In General Lansdale's appearance before the Committee, the following exchange occurred:

The CHAIRMAN. You do not recall ever having discussed with the Attorney General a plan or a proposal to assassinate Fidel Castro?
General LANSDALE. No. And I am very certain Senator, that such a discussion never came up * * * neither with the Attorney General nor the President." (Lansdale, 7/8/75, p. 18)[2]

Lansdale said that he had not discussed assassination with the President or the President's brother because he "had doubts" that assassination was a "useful action, and one which I had never employed in the past, during work in coping with revolutions, and I had con-

---

[1] The evidence showed, however, that there were occasions when the Attorney General dealt with officials involved in MONGOOSE without consulting General Taylor. For example (as discussed in detail in the section on MONGOOSE operations), on January 18, 1962, General Lansdale sent a copy of his MONGOOSE program review to Robert Kennedy with a cover memorandum indicating that other "sensitive work" not in the review was to be dealt with by the President, the Attorney General, and Lansdale only. The nature of that work, which Lansdale testified involved political contacts in the Cuba exile community, is discussed at p. 142.

[2] Lansdale was questioned about the term "touchdown plays" which appeared in one set of SGA minutes:

"Senator BAKER: Now do you completely rule out the possibility that the touchdown play had to do with the possible assassination efforts against Fidel Castro?

"General LANSDALE: Yes * * * I never discussed, nor conceived, nor received orders about an assassination of Castro with my dealings with either the Attorney General or the President." (Lansdale, 7/8/75, p. 56)

siderable doubts as to its utility and I was trying to be very pragmatic."[1] (Lansdale (7/8/75, p. 31)

When asked if he thought the President was aware of efforts to depose Castro and his government, Lansdale answered:

> I am certain he was aware of efforts to dispose of the Castro regime. I am really not one to guess what he knew of assassinations, because I don't know. (*Id.*, p. 32.)

With regard to the Castro assassination attempts, Lansdale testified that Harvey "never" told him that Harvey was attempting to assassinate Castro. (Lansdale, 7/8/75, p. 24) Lansdale stated:

> I had no knowledge of such a thing. I know of no order or permission for such a thing and I was given no information at all that such a thing was going on by people who I have now learned were involved with it. (Lansdale, 7/8/75, p. 58)

When asked if Robert Kennedy might have by-passed the SGA and Lansdale to deal directly with Agency officials on a Castro assassination, Lansdale testified:

> I never knew of a direct line of communication between the President or the Attorney General and Harvey apart from me on this * * *.[2]

Bundy served as President Kennedy's Special Assistant for National Security Affairs throughout the Kennedy Administration (Bundy, 7/11/75, p. 2) and participated in the planning that led to the creation of Operation MONGOOSE. He was also a member of the SGA. (Bundy, 7/11/75, pp. 34, 87) Bundy worked on an intimate basis with the President and the Attorney General during the entire Kennedy Administration.

Bundy testified that it was his conviction that "no one in the Kennedy Administration, in the White House * * * ever gave any authorization, approval, or instruction of any kind for any effort to assassinate anyone by the CIA." (Bundy, 7/11/75, p. 54) He said that Castro's assassination was "mentioned from time to time," but "never that I can recall by the President." (Bundy, 7/11/75, p. 73) Bundy emphasized that the question came up "as something to talk about rather than to consider." (Bundy, 7/11/75, p. 73)

> The CHAIRMAN. Based upon that acquaintanceship, do you believe, under any of the circumstances that occurred during that whole period, either one of them would have authorized the assassination of Fidel Castro?
> Mr. BUNDY. I most emphatically do not * * *. If you have heard testimony that there was pressure to do something about Cuba, there was. There was an effort, both from the President in his style and from the Attorney General in his style to keep the government active in looking for ways to weaken the Cuban regime. There was. But if you, as I understand it, and not even those who pressed the matter most closely as having essentially been inspired by the

---

[1] "Senator BAKER: Is that the reason you didn't, because of the principle of deniability?
"General LANSDALE: No, it wasn't. The subject never came up, and I had no reason to bring it up with him."

[2] "Senator HUDDLESTON: You never had any reason to believe that the Attorney General had dealt directly with Mr. Harvey?
"General LANSDALE: I hadn't known about that at all, no * * *.
"Senator HUDDLESTON: * * * You have no reason to believe that he might have broached [a Castro assassination] with the Attorney General?
"General LANSDALE: I wouldn't know about that—I certainly didn't know it.
"Senator HUDDLESTON: You had no reason to believe that there was any kind of activity going on in relation to Cuba outside of what you were proposing or what was coming before the Special Group?
"General LANSDALE: No, I was supposed to know it all, and I had no indication that I did not know it all [except for one operation by Harvey unrelated to assassinations]." (Lansdale, 7/8/75, p. 48)

White House can tell you that anyone ever said to them, go and kill anyone.
Let me say one other thing about these two men, and that is that there was something that they really wanted done, they did not leave people in doubt, so that on the one hand, I would say about their character, their purposes, and their nature and the way they confronted international affairs that I find it incredible that they would have ordered or authorized explicitly or implicitly an assassination of Castro. I also feel that if, contrary to everything that I know about their character, they had had such a decision and such a purpose, people would not have been in any doubt about it. (Bundy, 7/11/75, pp. 98-99)

Bundy said that he could not explain Helms' testimony that Helms had believed the CIA had been authorized to develop and engage in assassination activity. (Bundy, 7/11/75, pp. 99-100) He said that despite the extreme sense of urgency that arose during the Cuban Missile Crisis, Castro's assassination was never discussed, and it would have been "totally inconsistent" with the policies and actions of the President and the Attorney General during that crisis. (Bundy, 7/11/75, pp. 95, 97-98)[1]

Bundy testified that he was never told that assassination efforts against Castro had been undertaken or that the CIA had used underworld figures for that purpose. (Bundy, 7/11/75, p. 63) He said that he had heard about "Executive Action * * * some time in the early months of 1961" (Bundy, 7/11/75, p. 4), but that since it had been presented to him as an untargeted capability, he did not "discourage or dissuade" the person who briefed him.[2] (Bundy, 7/11/75, pp. 4, 7, 10)

When asked if he recalled any specific covert plans against Cuba involving poisons, Bundy stated:

I have no recollection of any specific plan. I do have a very vague, essentially refreshed recollection that I heard the word poison at some point in connection with a possibility of action in Cuba. But that is as far as I have been able to take it in my own memory. (Bundy, 7/11/75, p. 42)

Bundy recalled that the proposal had seemed "impractical" because it was going to kill "a large group of people in a headquarters mess, or something of that sort." (Bundy, 7/11/75, pp. 42-43)

Bundy stated that although Robert Kennedy did spur people to greater effort during MONGOOSE, "he never took away from the existing channel of authority its authority or responsibility." (Bundy, 7/11/75, pp. 47-48) He said that Robert Kennedy and Maxwell Taylor (SGA Chairman) had "a relation of real trust and confidence." It was Bundy's opinion that Robert Kennedy would not have by-passed Taylor to develop a "back-channel" with someone else to assassinate Castro. (Bundy, 7/11/75, p. 87)

McNamara served as Secretary of Defense throughout the Kennedy Administration. He represented the Department on the Special Group and the SGA during the MONGOOSE operations.

McNamara stated that he had never heard either the President or the Attorney General propose Castro's assassination. (McNamara, 7/11/75, p. 4) He noted that: "We were hysterical about Castro at

---

[1] Bundy stated: "* * * the most important point I want to make * * * is that I find the notion that they separately, privately encouraged, ordered, or arranged efforts at assassination totally inconsistent with what I knew of both of them. And, as an example, I would cite—and one among very many—the role played by the Attorney General in the Missile Crisis, because it was he who, most emphatically, argued against a so-called surgical air strike or any other action that would bring death upon many, in favor of the more careful approach which was eventually adopted by the President in the form of a quarantine or a blockade." (Bundy, 7/11/75, p. 98)
[2] Executive Action is fully discussed in Section (III)(c).

the time of the Bay of Pigs and thereafter, and that there was pressure from [President Kennedy and the Attorney General] to do something about Castro. But I don't believe we contemplated assassination. We did, however, contemplate overthrow." (McNamara, 7/11/75, p. 93)

An exchange that occurred during McNamara's testimony captures the dilemma posed by the evidence:

The CHAIRMAN. We also have received evidence from your senior associates that they never participated in the authorization of an assassination attempt against Castro nor ever directed the CIA to undertake such attempts.

We have much testimony establishing the chain of command where covert action was concerned, and all of it has been to the effect that the Special Group or the Special Group (Augmented) had full charge of covert operations, and that in that chain of command any proposal of this character or any other proposal having to do with covert operations being directed against the Castro regime, or against Castro personally, were to be laid before the Special Group (Augmented) and were not to be undertaken except with the authority of that group and at the direction of that group.

Now, at the same time we know from the evidence that the CIA was in fact engaged during the period in a series of attempts to assassinate Castro.

Now, you see what we are faced with is this dilemma. Either the CIA was a rogue elephant rampaging out of control, over which no effective direction was being given in this matter of assassination, or there was some secret channel circumventing the whole structure of command by which the CIA and certain officials in the CIA were authorized to proceed with assassination plots and assassination attempts against Castro. Or the third and final point that I can think of is that somehow these officials of the CIA who were so engaged misunderstood or misinterpreted their scope of authority.

Now it is terribly important, if there is any way that we can find out which of these three points represented what actually happened. That is the nature, that is the quandry.

Now, is there anything that you can tell us that would assist us in finding an answer to this central question?

Mr. McNAMARA: I can only tell you what will further your uneasiness. Because I have stated before and I believe today that the CIA was a highly disciplined organization, fully under the control of senior officials of the government, so much so that I feel as a senior official of the government I must assume responsibility for the actions of the two, putting assassination aside just for the moment. But I know of no major action taken by CIA during the time I was in the government that was not properly authorized by senior officials. And when I say that I want to emphasize also that I believe with hindsight we authorized actions that were contrary to the interest of the Republic but I don't want it on the record that the CIA was uncontrolled, was operating with its own authority and we can be absolved of responsibility for what CIA did, again with exception of assassination, again which I say I never heard of.

The second point you say that you have, you know that CIA was engaged in a series of attempts of assassination. I think to use your words. I don't know that. I accept the fact that you do and that you have information I was not aware of. I find that impossible to reconcile. I just can't understand how it could have happened and I don't accept the third point, that they operated on the basis of misunderstanding, because it seems to me that the McCone position that he was opposed to it, his clear recollection and his written memo of 1967 that I was strongly opposed to it, his statement that Murrow opposed, all should eliminate any point of misunderstanding. So I frankly can't reconcile. (McNamara, 7/11/75, pp. 38–41)

McNamara concluded:

I find it almost inconceivable that the assassination attempts were carried on during the Kennedy Administration days without the senior members knowing it, and I understand the contradiction that this carries with respect to the facts. (McNamara, 7/11/75, p. 90)

He emphasized that approval of an assassination by the President or his brother would have been "totally inconsistent with everything I know about the two men." (McNamara, 7/11/75, p. 4)

Roswell Gilpatric served as Deputy Secretary of Defense throughout the Kennedy Administration and represented the Department on the Special Group and the SGA during the MONGOOSE operation. (Gilpatric, 7/8/75, p. 5)

Gilpatric testified that he understood the mandate of the Special Group during MONGOOSE was not to kill Castro, but to "so undermine, so disrupt the Cuban system under Castro that it could not be effective.[1] (Gilpatric, 7/8/75, p. 28) Gilpatric emphasized that "it was the system we had to deal with," and that words such as "get rid of Castro" were said "in the context of the system, of the * * * government he had installed and was presiding over, but of which [Castro] was only one part." (Gilpatric, 7/8/75, p. 29)

Gilpatric said he knew of no express restriction barring assassination, but that it was understood that "there were limits on the use of power," and that those limits precluded assassination. (Gilpatric, 7/8/75, p. 31) While he believed that it was "perfectly possible" that someone might reasonably have inferred that assassination was authorized, the limits imposed by the SGA would have required anyone receiving general instructions to make specific efforts to determine whether those instructions authorized assassination.[2]

Gilpatric testified that "within our charter, so to speak, the one thing that was off limits was military invasion." (Gilpatric, 7/8/75, p. 45) When asked whether the "killing of Castro by a paramilitary group [would] have been within bounds," Gilpatric responded, "I know of no restriction that would have barred it." (*Id.*) When asked if there was any concern that the raids and infiltration efforts were too limited, Gilpatric said:

> No, to the contrary. The complaint that the Attorney General had, if we assume he was reflecting the President's views on it, [was that] the steps taken by the CIA up to that point, [and] their plans were too petty, were too minor, they weren't massive enough, they weren't going to be effective enough. (Gilpatric, 7/8/75, p. 47)

---

[1] When Gilpatric was first interviewed by the Committee staff on July 7, 1975, he did not recall the Operation MONGOOSE designation and what it referenced. Nor did he recall that General Lansdale was Chief of Operations for the project, even though Gilpatric had previously recommended Lansdale for promotion to Brigadier General and had worked closely with him earlier on a Viet Nam operation. Gilpatric did generally recall the covert activities in Cuba. Gilpatric attributed his failed recollections to the lapse of time (approximately fifteen years) since the events.

Robert McNamara testified before the Committee on July 11, 1975, that he had spoken with Gilpatric on May 30, 1975. McNamara said: "* * * on May 30 in connection with my inquiries to determine exactly who General Lansdale was working for at the time of August 1962, I called * * * Ros Gilpatric * * *, and during my conversation with Mr. Gilpatric I asked him specifically what Lansdale was working for in August '62 and Mr. Gilpatric stated that he was not working for either himself, that is Gilpatric, or me in August '62, but rather for the committee that was dealing with the MONGOOSE operation." (McNamara, 7/11/75, p. 78)

[2] "Senator HUDDLESTON: * * * It's on the basis of these words that everybody admits were used, like replace or get rid of, on the basis of these kinds of conversation alone that [Helms] was firmly convinced and that apparently went right down through the whole rank of command, firmly convinced that he had that authority to move against the life of a head of state. Now this disturbs me, and I don't know whether our councils of government operate that way in all areas or not, but if they do then it seems to me it would raise a very serious question as to whether or not the troops are getting the right orders.

Mr. GILPATRIC: * * * I thought there were limits on the use of power, and that was one of them.

Senator HUDDLESTON: And going beyond that would require that somebody make a specific effort to make sure he understood precisely what they were talking about, would that be your interpretation?

Mr. GILPATRIC: It would." (Gilpatric, 7/8/75, p. 31)

Contrary to the opinion expressed by other witnesses, Gilpatric testified that "it was not unusual" for the President and the Attorney General to deal directly with people at various levels in the Executive Branch. (Gilpatric, 7/8/75, p. 58) He described Robert Kennedy as the "moving spirit" of MONGOOSE (Gilpatric, 7/8/75, p. 11) whose role was "principally to spur us on, to get going, get cracking." (Gilpatric, 7/8/75, p. 47.) Although Robert Kennedy frequently complained that the plans of the CIA and MONGOOSE were not "massive enough," and that "we should get in there and do more," Gilpatric said that the Attorney General was not urging specific proposals, and that he had desired only "to limit the Castro regime's effectiveness." (Gilpatric, 7/8/75, p. 47)

Dean Rusk served as Secretary of State throughout the Kennedy Administration and participated in a number of SGA meetings during the MONGOOSE operation. (Rusk, 7/10/75, p. 7)

Rusk testified that he had never been informed of any Castro assassination plans or undertakings and had no knowledge of any such activity. (Rusk, 7/10/75, p. 52) He found it "very hard to believe" that in the course of urging action against Castro, President Kennedy or Robert Kennedy would have sanctioned any measure against Castro personally.[1] He believed that while it was "possible" that someone might have thought that specific courses of action were authorized by the emphasis in SGA meetings, permission to commit an assassination could not have been reasonably inferred.

> It would have been an abuse of the President and the Attorney General if somebody had thought they were getting that without confirming that this was, in fact, an official, firm policy decision. (Rusk, 7/10/75, pp. 97-98)

Rusk testified that he could not imagine the President or the Attorney General having circumvented the SGA by going directly to Helms or Harvey about assassinating Castro.[2]

Theodore Sorensen served as a Special Assistant to President Kennedy during the entire Kennedy Administration. He was a member of the National Security Council Executive Committee that dealt with the Missile Crisis, but was not involved with MONGOOSE.

Sorensen testified that in all his daily personal meetings with the President and at NSC meetings he attended, there was "not at any

---

[1] "Senator HUDDLESTON: * * * [Do] your contacts with Robert Kennedy or President Kennedy, indicate to you that they were agitated to such an extent about Cuba and MONGOOSE progress that in a conversation with someone urging them to get off their rear-end and get something done that they might convey the message that they meant anything, go to any length to do something about the Castro regime?
Mr. RUSK. I find it very hard to believe that Robert Kennedy standing alone, or particularly Robert Kennedy alleging to speak for President Kennedy, would have gone down that trail * * *." (Rusk, 7/10/75, p. 96.)

[2] "Senator MONDALE: * * * We asked General Taylor yesterday whether he thought something of informal, subterranean, whatever kinds of communications from the highest level to Helms would have been possible without his knowledge, and he said he felt that was incredible, he didn't think it was possible.
Do you think that it would be likely that an informal order around channels, say to Helms or to Harvey——
The CHAIRMAN: Over a three-year period.
Senator MONDALE: Over a three-year period would have been possible without your being informed?
Mr. RUSK: Theoretically, Senator, one would have to say it is possible.
Senator MONDALE: But based on your experience?
Mr. RUSK: In terms of practicality, probability and so forth, I don't see how it could have happened.
You know those things, in these circles we were moving in could not be limited in that way. You know the echoes would come back." (Rusk, 7/10/75, p. 99)

time any mention—much less approval by [the President]—of any U.S.-sponsored plan to assassinate any foreign leaders." (Sorensen, 7/21/75, p. 4.)

(4) THE AUGUST 10, 1962 SPECIAL GROUP (AUGMENTED) MEETING

The question of liquidating Cuban leaders was raised at a meeting of the SGA on August 10, 1962. On August 13, 1962, Lansdale directed Harvey to include in a proposed plan for Phase II of MONGOOSE, an option for the "liquidation of leaders."

At the outset, it should be noted that the documents and testimony about the meeting indicate that the discussion of assassination on August 10 was unrelated to the assassination activity undertaken by Harvey and Rosselli, or to any other plans or efforts to assassinate Castro. The Inspector General's Report states:

> The subject (of a Castro assassination) was raised at a meeting at State on 10 August 1962, but is unrelated to any actual attempts at assassination. It did result in a MONGOOSE action memorandum by Lansdale assigning to CIA action for planning liquidation of leaders. (I.G. Report, p. 118)

This finding of the Inspector General is supported by both the chronology of the Castro assassination efforts and the testimony of Harvey. Harvey gave Rosselli the poison pills for use against Castro (and shortly thereafter was informed that the pills were inside Cuba) three months before the August 10 meeting. There was no Castro assassination activity during the remainder of 1962.

Harvey attended the August 10 meeting and recalled that the question of a Castro assassination was raised. He testified that the assassination discussion was not related to his activities with Rosselli. (Harvey, 7/11/75, pp. 48–50) He said that he did not regard the SGA discussion as authorization for his Rosselli operation because "the authority, as I understood it, for this particular operation went back long before the formation of the SGA." (Harvey, 7/11/75, p. 49)

A. THE CONTEMPORANEOUS DOCUMENTS

(1) Lansdale's August 13, 1962 Memorandum

Lansdale's August 13 memorandum was sent to Harvey and to the other members of Lansdale's interagency working group.[1] The Memorandum stated:

> In compliance with the desires and guidance expressed in the August 10 policy meeting on Operation MONGOOSE, we will produce an outline of an alternate Course B for submission.
> I believe the paper need contain only a statement of objectives and a list of implementing activities. The list of activities will be under the heading of: Intelligence, Political, Economic, Psychological, Paramilitary, and Military.

---

[1] Lansdale sent copies of his memorandum to Robert Hurwitch (State Department), General Benjamin Harris (Defense Department) and Donald Wilson (United States Information Agency).
When General Harris testified, he identified a document drafted by the MONGOOSE Working Group in the Defense Department shortly before the August 10 meeting. The document listed a number of steps that could be taken in the event of an intensified MONGOOSE program that might involve United States military intervention. One such step was "assassinate Castro and his handful of top men." General Harris stated that this was "not out of the ordinary in terms of contingency planning * * * it's one of the things you look at." (Harris. 8/18/75, p. 37) There was no evidence that this document was distributed outside the Defense Department's MONGOOSE Working Group.

Lansdale's memorandum then assigned to Harvey preparation of papers on the following subjects:

> Mr. HARVEY. Intelligence, Political, [words deleted], Economic, (sabotage, limited deception), and Paramilitary." (*Id.*)

According to a memorandum from Harvey to Helms on the following day, the words deleted from the quoted passage were "including liquidation of leaders." (Memo, Harvey to Helms, 8/14/62)

(2) Harvey's August 14, 1962 Memorandum

After receiving Lansdale's August 13 memorandum, Harvey wrote a memorandum to Helms. He attached a copy of the Lansdale memorandum, and noted that he had excised the words "including liquidation of leaders." Harvey's memorandum explained that:

> The question of assassination, particularly of Fidel Castro, was brought up by Secretary McNamara at the meeting of the Special Group (Augmented) in Secretary Rusk's office on 10 August. It was the obvious consensus at that meeting, in answer to a comment by Mr. Ed Murrow, that this is not a subject which has been made a matter of official record. I took careful notes on the comments at this meeting on this point, and the Special Group (Augmented) is not expecting any written comments or study on this point." (*Id.*)

Harvey's memorandum further stated that he had called Lansdale's office and pointed out "the inadmissability and stupidity of putting this type of comment in writing in such a document." (*Id.*) He also told Lansdale's office that the CIA "would write no document pertaining to this and would participate in no open meeting discussing it." (*Id.*)

(3) The Minutes of the August 10, 1962 Meeting

The minutes of the August 10 meeting contain no reference to assassination. (Memo for Record, Special Group Augmented Meeting, August 10, 1962, hereafter "August 10 Minutes") Thomas Parrott, who authored the August 10 Minutes, testified that he did not recall a discussion of assassination at that meeting, but that the fact that the minutes reflect no such discussion does not necessarily indicate that the matter had not come up. (Parrott, 7/10/75, p. 34) Parrott pointed out that his minutes "were not intended to be a verbatim transcript of everything that was said," since their purpose was "to interpret what the decisions were and to record those and to use them as a useful action document." [Parrott, 7/10/75, pp. 34–35.] Parrott testified: "we had 15 or 16 people [at the August 10, 1962 meeting] * * * all of them well informed, all of them highly articulate. This meeting, as I recall, went on for several hours. * * * Now I'm sure that particularly in a group like this that there were a great many proposals made that were just shot down immediately." (Parrott, 7/10/75, pp. 34–35)

Parrott testified that he did not record proposals that were quickly rejected. (Parrott, 7/10/75, p. 35) He said that, although he had no recollection of a discussion of Castro's assassination at the meeting, he would infer from the related documents [the Lansdale and Harvey Memoranda of August 13 and 14, respectively] that the subject was raised but "it never got off the ground * * *. Therefore, I did not record it." (Parrott, 7/10/75, p. 35)

(4) The August 10 Meeting

The purpose of the August 10 Meeting was to decide on a course of action to succeed the intelligence collection phase of MONGOOSE, scheduled to conclude in August. (McCone, 6/6/75, p. 34) Because it was a policy meeting, a larger number of officials than usual attended. The Meeting was chaired by Secretary of State Rusk and those attending included the principals of the other agencies taking part in MONGOOSE, *i.e.*, Secretary of Defense McNamara, CIA Director McCone, and USIA Director Murrow.

General Lansdale submitted a MONGOOSE proposal for a "stepped-up Course B" that would involve operations to "exert all possible diplomatic, economic, psychological, and other overt pressures to overthrow the Castro-Communist regime, without overt employment of U.S. military." (Lansdale Memo for Special Group Augmented, 8/8/62)

The SGA decided against the "stepped-up Course B." In discussing Lansdale's proposal, Rusk "emphasized the desirability of attempting to create a split between Castro and old-line Communists." McNamara questioned whether the practice of building up agents in Cuba would not lead to actions that "would hurt the U.S. in the eyes of world opinion."[1] The minutes state that McNamara's concern "led to the suggestion by General Taylor that we should consider changing the overall objective [of MONGOOSE] from one of overthrowing the Castro regime" to one of causing its failure. (SGA Minutes, 8/10/62, p. 2)

Instead of Lansdale's "stepped-up Course B," the SGA chose a plan advanced by McCone which assumed Castro's continuance in power and had the more limited objective of splitting off Castro from "old-line Communists."[2] (SGA Minutes, 8/10/62, p. 2) The decision and "action" were described as follows:

The principal members of the Special Group felt, after some discussion, that the CIA variant should be developed further for consideration at next Thursday's meeting of the Special Group. McCone was asked to stress economic sabotage, and to emphasize measures to foment a Castro-oldline Communist split.

* * * * * * *

Action to be taken: CIA to prepare a new version of its variant plan, in accordance with the above-summarized discussion. This should be ready by Wednesday, August 15. (SGA Minutes Memo, 8/10/62, pp. 2–3)

The discussion which follows treats testimony bearing on whether Lansdale's request to Harvey for an assassination plan reflected the wishes of the SGA or was contemplated by the SGA's decision to proceed with a plan of "reduced effort" that posited Castro's continuance in power.

---

[1] That remark by McNamara seems to be inconsistent with his raising the question of assassination in any sense of advocacy at the same meeting.

[2] The August 10 Minutes show that McCone pointed out that the stepped-up Course B "will risk inviting an uprising, which might result in a Hungary-type blood bath if unsupported." McCone "emphasized that the stepped-up plan should not be undertaken unless the U.S. is prepared to accept attributability for the necessary actions, including the eventual use of military force." The August 10 Minutes further stated that, in McCone's view, the CIA variant "would avoid all of these dangers because it would not invite an uprising." (SGA Minutes, 8/10/62, p. 2)

B. THE TESTIMONY

Harvey, McCone, and Goodwin recalled that the question of assassinating Castro was raised at the August 10 meeting.[1] Their testimony is discussed first with regard to the meeting itself, and second, with regard to the action that followed.

(1) Testimony About the August 10 Meeting

(a) McCone

McCone testified that "liquidation" or removal of Castro and other Cuban leaders arose at the August 10 meeting in the context of "exploring the alternatives that were available" for the next phase of MONGOOSE. (McCone, 6/6/75, p. 34) He did not recall who made this suggestion, but remembered that he and Edward Murrow took "strong exception" to it. A memorandum written by McCone in 1967 states:[2]

> I took immediate exception to this suggestion, stating that the subject was completely out of bounds as far as the USG [U.S. Government] and CIA were concerned and the idea should not be discussed nor should it appear in any papers, as the USG could not consider such actions on moral or ethical grounds.

McCone testified that there was no decision at the meeting not to include assassination in the program, and that "the subject was just dropped" after his objection. (McCone, 6/6/75, p. 37) McCone's 1967 memorandum stated that: "At no time did the suggestion receive serious consideration by the Special Group (Augmented) nor by any individual responsible for policy."

(b) Harvey

It was Harvey's recollection that the question of assassination was raised by Secretary McNamara as one of "shouldn't we consider the elimination or assassination" of Castro. (Harvey, 7/11/75, p. 30) Harvey testified:

> I think the consensus of the Group was to sweep that particular proposal or suggestion or question or consideration off the record and under the rug as rapidly as possible. There was no extensive discussion of it, no discussion, no back and forth as the whys and wherefores and possibilities and so on. (Harvey, 7/11/75, p. 30)

(c) Goodwin

Goodwin testified that he had a recollection of "limited certainty" that the subject of a Castro assassination was raised at the August 10

---

[1] Other participants (Rusk, McNamara, Bundy, and Gilpatric) did not recall the August 10 discussion.
[2] On April 14, 1967, after McCone left the CIA, he dictated a memorandum stating his recollection of the August 10, 1962 meeting. The memorandum was prompted by a telephone call from the newspaper columnist, Jack Anderson, who at that time was preparing a column on Castro assassination attempts, implicating President Kennedy and Robert Kennedy. After talking with Anderson on the telephone at Robert Kennedy's request, McCone dictated the April 14, 1967 memorandum, which stated, in part, several MONGOOSE meetings on August 8, 9, or 10, 1962, "I recall a suggestion being made to liquidate top people in the Castro regime, including Castro."

meeting,[1] but he was unable to say "with any certainty" who raised the subject. (Goodwin, 7/18/75, p. 8) [2]

(d) *McNamara*

McNamara testified that although he did not recall assassination being discussed at the SGA meeting, he did remember having expressed opposition to any assassination attempt or plan when he spoke with McCone several days later. (McNamara, 7/11/75, pp. 7, 8)

(2) *Testimony about Events After the August 10, 1962 meeting*

(a) *McCone*

McCone testified that he called McNamara after receiving Lansdale's August 13 Memorandum and:

> * * * insisted that that Memorandum be withdrawn because no decision was made on this subject, and since no decision was made, then Lansdale was quite out of order in tasking the Central Intelligence Agency to consider the matter.[3]

McCone said that McNamara agreed that Lansdale's Memorandum should be withdrawn [4] for the same reason. (McCone, 6/6/75, p. 39)

(b) *Harvey*

Harvey's demand that the words "liquidation of leaders" be excised from Lansdale's memorandum and his further statement that "the Special Group (Augmented) is not expecting any written comments or study on this point," raise an important question. Did Harvey mean that the SGA was not considering assassination or merely that the subject should not be put in writing? When Harvey was asked "was it

---

[1] In a staff interview prior to his testimony, Goodwin recalled the date of the meeting at which a Castro assassination was raised as falling in early 1961, after the Bay of Pigs. (Memorandum of Staff Interview with Goodwin, 5/27/75, p. 2) After reviewing the Minutes of the August 10, 1962 meeting and the Lansdale and Harvey memoranda of August 13 and 14, respectively, Goodwin testified that he had "misplaced the date of the meeting in my own memory." (Goodwin, 7/18/75, p. 7). In placing the incident on August 10, 1962, Goodwin stated "Now, of course, you know, it may not be. That's the best recollection I now have. It's a little better than the earlier one, but it's not certain." (Goodwin, 7/18/75, p. 8)

[2] In a magazine article in June 1975, Goodwin was quoted as stating that at one of the meetings of a White House task force on Cuba it was McNamara who said that "Castro's assassination was the only productive way of dealing with Cuba." (Branch and Crile, "The Kennedy Vendetta," *Harpers*, July, 1975, p. 61). In his testimony on July 18, 1975, Goodwin said: "that's not an exact quote" in the article, and explained: "I didn't tell [the author of the magazine article] that it was definitely McNamara, that very possibly it was McNamara. He asked me about McNamara's role, and I said it very well could have been McNamara." (Goodwin, 7/18/75, p. 33)

Goodwin told the Committee: "It's not a light matter to perhaps destroy a man's career on the basis of a fifteen year old memory of a single sentence that he might have said at a meeting without substantial certainty in your own mind, and I do not have that" (Goodwin, 7/18/75, pp. 34–35). It is difficult to reconcile this testimony with Goodwin's testimony that he told the author of the article that McNamara might very well have made the statement about assassination at the August meeting.

[3] McCone's 1967 Memorandum stated: "Immediately after the meeting, I called on Secretary McNamara personally and reemphasized my position, in which he heartily agreed. I did this because Operation MONGOOSE—an interdepartmental affair—was under the operational control of [the Defense Department] * * *."

[4] McNamara confirmed this testimony: "I agreed with Mr. McCone that no such planning should be undertaken." (McNamara, 7/11/75, p. 8.) He added: "I have no knowledge or information about any other plans or preparations for a Castro assassination." (McNamara, 7/11/75, p. 7)

understood in an unwritten way that [assassination] was to proceed," he replied:

> Not to my knowledge, no * * *. If there was any unwritten understanding on the part of the members of the Special Group concerning this, other than what was said at the meeting, I do not know of it * * *. (Harvey, 7/11/75, pp. 30–31)

Harvey said that shortly after the meeting, McCone informed him that he had told McNamara that assassination should not be discussed. McCone also told McNamara that involvement in such matters might result in his own excommunication. (Harvey, 7/11/75, p. 25)

(c) Elder

Walter Elder, McCone's Executive Assistant, was present when McCone telephoned McNamara after the August 10 meeting. Elder testified that McCone told McNamara "the subject you just brought up, I think it is highly improper. I do not think it should be discussed. It is not an action that should ever be condoned. It is not proper for us to discuss, and I intend to have it expunged from the record." (Elder, 8/13/75, p. 23)

Elder testified that this was the essence of the conversation but that he distinctly remembered "several exact phrases, like 'would not be condoned' and 'improper'." (Elder, 8/13/75, pp. 23, 24) [1]

McCone spoke with Harvey in Elder's presence after receiving Lansdale's August 13 memorandum. According to Elder, "McCone made his views quite clear in the same language and tone * * * that he used with Mr. McNamara." (Elder, 8/13/75, p. 25) Elder testified that Harvey did not then tell McCone that Harvey was engaged in a Castro assassination effort. (Elder, 8/13/75, p. 25)

Elder also described a meeting held in his office with Helms shortly after the McCone/Harvey/Elder meeting. Elder stated:

> I told Mr. Helms that Mr. McCone had expressed his feeling to Mr. McNamara and Mr. Harvey that assassination could not be condoned and would not be approved. Furthermore, I conveyed Mr. McCone's statement that it would be unthinkable to record in writing any consideration of assassination because it left the impression that the subject had received serious consideration by governmental policymakers, which it had not. Mr. Helms responded, "I understand." The point is that I made Mr. Helms aware of the strength of Mr. McCone's opposition to assassination. I know that Mr. Helms could not have been under any misapprehension about Mr. McCone's feelings after this conversation. (Elder Affidavit, 8/26/75, p. 2)

Helms, after reading Elder's affidavit, told the Committee that he had no recollection of the meeting. (Helms, 9/16/75, p. 16)

(d) Lansdale

Lansdale recalled that the subject of Castro's assassination had surfaced at the August 10 meeting. He testified that the "consensus was * * * hell no on this and there was a very violent reaction." (Lansdale,

---

[1] Elder said he heard the entire telephone conversation via a speaker phone. He said that McNamara "just more or less accepted what Mr. McCone said without comment or rejoinder." (Elder, 8/13/75, p. 24)

7/8/75, p. 20) Lansdale was questioned as to why he subsequently asked Harvey for a Castro assassination plan:

> Senator BAKER. Why did you, three days later if they all said, hell no, [go] ahead with it?
> General LANSDALE. * * * the meeting at which they said that was still on a development of my original task, which was a revolt and an overthrow of a regime. At the same time, we were getting intelligence accumulating very quickly of something very different taking place in Cuba than we had expected, which was the Soviet technicians starting to come in and the possibilities of Soviet missiles being placed there * * * At that time, I thought it would be a possibility someplace down the road in which there would be some possible need to take action such as that [assassination][1] (Lansdale, 7/8/75, p. 21)

Lansdale stated that he had one brief conversation with Harvey after the August 13 memorandum in which Harvey stated "he would look into it * * * see about developing some plans." Lansdale said that was the last he ever heard of the matter. (Lansdale, 7/8/75, p. 124) Lansdale stated that as the Cuban Missile Crisis developed, MONGOOSE "was being rapidly shifted out of consideration" and thus "I wasn't pressing for answers * * * it was very obvious that another situation was developing that would be handled quite differently in Cuba." (Lansdale, 7/8/75, p. 124)

Lansdale testified that he was "very certain" that he never discussed a Castro assassination plan or proposal with Robert Kennedy or with President Kennedy. He said that he had asked Harvey for a plan without having discussed the matter with anyone:

> Senator BAKER: * * * did you originate this idea of laying on the CIA a requirement to report on the feasibility of the assassination of Castro or did someone else suggest that?
> General LANSDALE: I did, as far as I recall.
> Senator BAKER: Who did you discuss it with before you laid on that requirement?
> General LANSDALE: I don't believe I discussed it with anyone.
> Senator BAKER: Only with Harvey?
> General LANSDALE: Only with Harvey.
> Senator BAKER: Did you ever discuss it with Helms?
> General LANSDALE: I might have, and I don't believe that I did. I think it was just with Harvey.
> Senator BAKER: Did you ever discuss it with Robert Kennedy?
> General LANSDALE: No, not that I recall.
> Senator BAKER: With the President?
> General LANSDALE: No. (Lansdale, 7/8/75, pp. 19–20)

(3) Testimony of Reporters About Lansdale's Comments on the August 10 Meeting

During the Committee's investigation, reports concerning the August 10 meeting and Lansdale's request for a Castro assassination plan appeared in the press. One report was based on statements made by Lansdale to David Martin of the Associated Press and another on Lansdale's statements to Jeremiah O'Leary of the *Washington Star-News*. Because there was conflict between Lansdale's testimony

---

[1] "Q. * * * Why, if it is true that assassination idea was turned down on August 10, did you send out your memo on August 13?
General LANSDALE. * * * I don't recall that thoroughly, I don't remember the reasons why I would.
Q. Is it your testimony that the August 10 meeting turned down assassinations as a subject to look into, and that you nevertheless asked Mr. Harvey to look into it?
General LANSDALE. I guess it is, yes. The way you put it to me now has me baffled about why I did it. I don't know." (Lansdale, 7/8/75, pp. 123–124)

to the Committee and what he was reported to have told Martin and O'Leary, the Committee invited both reporters to testify. Martin testified under subpoena. O'Leary appeared voluntarily but stated that the policy of his newspaper against disclosing news sources precluded him from elaborating on the contents of a prepared statement, which he read under oath. O'Leary stated that his news report "represents accurately my understanding of the relevant information I obtained from news sources." (O'Leary, 9/26/75, p. 5)

(a) *The Martin Report*

The lead paragraph of Martin's report stated:

Retired Maj. Gen. Edward G. Lansdale said Friday that acting on orders from President John F. Kennedy delivered through an intermediary, he developed plans for removing Cuban Premier Fidel Castro by any means including assassination.

Martin testified that this paragraph was an accurate reflection of his conclusion based on the totality of his interview with Lansdale on May 30, 1975. (Martin, 7/24/75, pp. 19–20) Lansdale testified that, after reading Martin's story, he told the reporter that "your first sentence is not only completely untrue, but there is not a single thing in your story that says it is true." (Lansdale, 7/8/75, p. 65)

In view of Martin's testimony that the report's lead paragraph was a conclusion based on his total interview with Lansdale, it should be noted that the remainder of Martin's story does not state that Lansdale was ordered by President Kennedy or the Attorney General to develop plans for Castro's assassination. The report quotes Lansdale as stating "I was working for the highest authority in the land * * * the President," and then states that Lansdale said he did not deal directly with the President, but "worked through" an intermediary who was more intimate with the President than Bundy.[1] The Committee notes that the phrases "working for" and "working through" do not carry the same meaning as the lead paragraph's conclusion that Lansdale was "acting on orders" to develop a Castro assassination plan. Subsequent paragraphs in the Martin report indicate that Lansdale told the reporter that the decision to undertake assassination planning was his own; Lansdale so testified before the Committee. According to the Martin article, Lansdale said that assassination was "one of the means he considered," that he believed assassination would not have been "incompatible" with his assignment, and that he "* * * just wanted to see if the U.S. had any such capabilities." Martin said he did not ask Lansdale specifically if Lansdale had acted on orders regarding an assassination plan, nor did Lansdale volunteer that information. Rather, Martin asked Lansdale "Who were you working for?"[2]

---

[1] Lansdale refused to provide Martin the intermediary's name for the record. The Committee did not ask Martin about Lansdale's off-the-record statements out of respect for the confidentiality of news sources (Martin, 7/24/75, p. 18)

[2] Martin testified that his interview with Lansdale involved two questions: (1) "What were you [Lansdale] doing in August 1962?" (Martin, 7/24/75, p. 16), and (2) "Who were you working for?" (Martin 7/24/75, p. 17) Martin stated that in discussing Lansdale's activities in August 1962, Lansdale stated, "I just wanted to see if the U.S. had any such capabilities" and that this included "assassination" as well as other means of disposing of Castro. As to the second question "Who were you working for?" Lansdale replied "on that project I was working for the highest authority in the land." (Martin, 7/24/75, p. 18)

In a subsequent conversation on June 4, 1975, Martin said he asked Lansdale specifically, "Were you ever ordered by President Kennedy or any other Kennedy to draw up plans to assassinate Castro?" (Martin, 7/24/75, p. 21) Martin testified that Lansdale replied "no" and that his orders were "very broad." (Martin, 7/24/75, p. 21) Martin further testified that in the June 4 conversation he asked Lansdale whether "any assassination planning you did was done on your own initiative," and that Lansdale replied "yes." (Martin 7/24/75, p. 21) Martin stated his belief that Lansdale's statements on June 4 were at variance with his prior statements on May 30. (Martin 7/24/75, p. 21) It is, of course, possible that since Martin posed different questions in the two conversations, he and Lansdale may have misunderstood each other.

(b) *The O'Leary Report*

O'Leary's report began:

Retired Maj. Gen. Edward G. Lansdale has named Robert F. Kennedy as the administration official who ordered him in 1962 to launch a CIA project to work out all feasible plans for "getting rid of" Cuban Prime Minister Fidel Castro.

Lansdale, in an interview with the Washington Star, never used the word "assassination" and said it was not used by Kennedy, then the attorney general.

But he said there could be no doubt that "that project for disposing of Castro envisioned the whole spectrum of plans from overthrowing the Cuban leader to assassinating him."

O'Leary's report contained the statement that "Lansdale said he was contacted by Robert Kennedy in mid-summer of 1962 * * *." O'Leary told the Committee that this reference modified the reference in the lead paragraph of his report. (O'Leary, 9/26/75, p. 13)

Lansdale testified that he had submitted a statement to the *Washington Star News* stating that O'Leary's report was "a distortion of my remarks." (Lansdale, 7/8/75, p. 61) Lansdale said he told the newspaper that: "perhaps someplace in the planning there is something about what to do with a leader who would threaten the lives of millions of Americans [with Soviet Missiles] * * * but I can say I never did receive any order from President Kennedy or from Robert Kennedy about taking action against Castro personally." (Lansdale, 7/18/75, pp. 61–62)

Lansdale testified that he told O'Leary that he did take orders from Robert Kennedy, but made clear that "Kennedy's orders to him were on a very wide-ranging type of thing." (Lansdale, 7/8/75, p. 62)

After the story appeared, the * * * *Washington Star* asked me what wide-ranging things were you talking about?

I said there were economic matters and military matters and military things and they were very wide-ranging things. I said perhaps all O'Leary was thinking of was assassination. I was thinking of far wider than that. (Lansdale, 7/8/75, pp. 62–63)

The O'Leary report states:

Lansdale said he is certain Robert Kennedy's instructions to him did not include the word "assassination." He said the attorney general, as best he could recall, spoke in more general terms of exploring all feasible means and practicalities of doing something "to get rid of" Castro.

(*iii*) THE QUESTION OF WHETHER THE AM/LASH PLOT (1963–1965) WAS KNOWN ABOUT OR AUTHORIZED BY ADMINISTRATION OFFICIALS OUTSIDE THE CIA

This section examines evidence relating to whether officials in the Kennedy or Johnson Administrations were aware of or authorized the CIA's use of AM/LASH as a potential assassin. The question is examined in light of the policies of those Administrations toward Cuba as well as the evidence bearing more directly on the authorization issues.

The evidence falls into a pattern similar to that described in the discussion of post-Bay of Pigs activity in the Kennedy Administration. Administration officials testified that they had never been informed about the plot and that they never intended to authorize assassination. Richard Helms, on the other hand, testified that he had believed that assassination was permissible in view of the continuing pressure to overthrow the Castro regime exerted by the respective Administrations and the failure of either Administration to place limits on the means that could be used to achieve that end.

(1) KENNEDY ADMINISTRATION'S POLICY TOWARD CUBA IN 1963

a. Organizational Changes

The MONGOOSE Operation was disbanded following the Cuban Missile Crisis, and an interagency "Cuban Coordinating Committee" was established within the State Department with responsibility for developing covert action proposals. (Bundy, 7/11/75, p. 148) The SGA was abolished, and the Special Group, chaired by McGeorge Bundy, reassumed responsibility for reviewing and approving covert actions in Cuba. (Bundy, 7/11/75, p. 148)

United States policy toward Cuba in 1963 was also formulated in the National Security Council's Standing Group, the successor to the Executive Committee which had been established for the Missile Crisis. Members of the Standing Group included Robert Kennedy, Robert McNamara, John McCone, McGeorge Bundy and Theodore Sorensen.

Four aspects of the Kennedy Administration's 1963 Cuba policy are discussed below: (1) the Standing Group's discussion of possible developments in the event of Castro's death; (2) the Standing Group's discussion of policy options; (3) the covert action program approved by the Special Group; and (4) the diplomatic effort to explore the possibility of reestablishing relations with Castro. The first three took place in the spring or early summer of 1963; the fourth—the effort to communicate with Castro—occurred at the same time the CIA offered AM/LASH the poison pen device for Castro's assassination.

b. Discussion of the Contingency of Castro's Death

In the spring of 1963, Bundy submitted to the Standing Group a memorandum entitled "Cuba Alternatives" which discussed "possible new directions" for American policy toward Cuba. (Bundy Memorandum, 4/21/63) The memorandum distinguished between events which might occur independently of actions taken by the United

States, and those which the United States might "initiate." Listed under the first category was the possibility of Castro's death. In May 1963, the Group discussed this contingency and found that the possibilities for developments favorable to the United States if Castro should die were "singularly unpromising." (Summary Record of Standing Group Meeting, 5/28/63)

When Bundy's memorandum was first discussed by the Group in April, Robert Kennedy proposed a study of the "measures we would take following contingencies such as the death of Castro or the shooting down of a U-2." (Summary Record of Standing Group Meeting, 4/23/63) Bundy's follow-up memorandum, an agenda for a future Standing Group discussion of Cuban policy, listed contingency planning for Castro's death under a category comprising events not initiated by the United States, *e.g.*, "occurrence of revolt or repression in the manner of Hungary," "attributable interference by Castro in other countries," and "the reintroduction of offensive weapons." (Bundy Memorandum, 4/29/63)

After the Standing Group's meeting on April 23, 1963, the CIA's Office of National Estimates was assigned the task of assessing possible developments if Castro should die. (Memorandum for Members of the Standing Group, 5/2/63) The resulting paper analyzed the forces likely to come into play in Cuba after Castro's death, including the roles of his top aides, Raul Castro and Che Guevara, and possible Soviet reactions. (Draft Memorandum by Office of National Estimates titled "Developments in Cuba and Possible U.S. Actions in the Event of Castro's Death," pp. 2-5) The paper concluded that "the odds are that upon Castro's death, his brother Raul or some other figure in the regime would, with Soviet backing and help, take over control"[1] The paper warned: "If Castro were to die by other than natural causes the U.S. would be widely charged with complicity, even though it is widely known that Castro has many enemies."

The paper also identified several courses of action open to the United States in the event of Castro's death, ranging from no United States initiatives, action to support a government in exile, quarantine and blockade, and outright invasion.

On May 28, 1963, the Standing Group discussed this paper. The Group decided that "all of the courses of action were singularly unpromising". (Summary Record of NSC Standing Group Meeting No. 7/63, May 28, 1963)

Bundy testified that the Standing Group "certainly posed the question" in the Spring of 1963 of what would happen if Castro died or were killed. (Bundy, 7/11/75, p. 130) However, he said that he had no recollection of Castro's assassination being considered by the Standing Group when that contingency was discussed. (Bundy, 7/11/75, p. 14)[2]

Bundy said that one reason for having requested the estimate was to make a record establishing that the United States should not be

---

[1] The paper also saw little chance that a government favorably disposed toward the United States would be able to come to power without extensive United States military support: "Anti-Moscow Cuban nationalists would require extensive U.S. help in order to win, and probably U.S. military intervention."
[2] Bundy did recall that over the period 1961 to 1963 "the subject of a Castro assassination was mentioned from time to time by different individuals," but he said that he was not aware of "much discussion in the Spring of 1963 on that subject." (Bundy, 7/11/75, p. 140)

"fussing" with assassination, and that assassination was not a sound policy. (Bundy, 7/11/75, p. 142)

Bundy said that it was not unusual to assess the implications of a foreign leader's death, and named Stalin and De Gaulle as examples. In the case of Castro, Bundy said he felt it was only prudent to attempt to assess a post-Castro Cuba since Castro was such a "dominant figure." (Bundy, 7/11/75, p. 145)

c. The Standing Group's Discussion of United States Policy Toward Cuba

The Standing Group's documents indicate it continued to assume the desirability of harassing Cuba, but recognized that there were few practical measures the United States could take to achieve Castro's overthrow.

In his April 21 memorandum on "Cuban Alternatives" Bundy identified three possible alternatives: (1) forcing "a non-Communist solution in Cuba by all necessary means," (2) insisting on "major but limited ends," or (3) moving "in the direction of a gradual development of some form of accommodation with Castro." (Bundy Memorandum, 4/21/63, p. 3) These alternatives were discussed at the Standing Group meetings on April 23 and May 28, 1963.

Sorensen participated in these meetings. He testified that the "widest possible range of alternatives" was discussed, but that "assassination was not even on the list." (Sorensen, 7/21/75, p. 4) He said that options such as forcing "a non-Communist solution in Cuba by all necessary means"

* * * could not have included or implied assassination. Instead, it expressly referred to the development of pressures and gradual escalation of the confrontation in Cuba to produce an overthrow of the regime, including a willingness to use military force to invade Cuba. Such a course was obviously not adopted by the President, and in any event expressed an approach far different from assassination. (Sorensen affidavit, 7/25/75)[1]

The record of the first Standing Group discussion of Bundy's memorandum shows that a number of alternatives (none of which involved assassination) were considered but no conclusions were reached.

The Standing Group again met on May 28, 1963. McCone argued for steps to "increase economic hardship" in Cuba, supplemented by sabotage to "create a situation in Cuba in which it would be possible to subvert military leaders to the point of their acting to overthrow Castro." (Summary Record of NSC Standing Group Meeting, 5/28/63) McNamara said that sabotage would not be "conclusive" and suggested that "economic pressures which would upset Castro" be studied. Robert Kennedy said "the U.S. must do something against Castro, even though we do not believe our actions would bring him down." (*id.*) Bundy summarized by stating that the task was "to decide now what actions we would take against Castro, acknowl-

---

[1] The Bundy memorandum also used the phrase "all necessary measures" to describe the steps the American Government was willing to take to "prevent" a direct military threat to the United States or to the Western Hemisphere from Cuba. Sorensen explained the meaning of this phrase in the context of the April 23 discussion of Kennedy Administration policy. "[this phrase] could not by any stretch of semantics or logic have included assassination or any other initiative. It reflected the purely defensive posture implemented six months earlier when long-range missiles and other offensive weapons were placed in Cuba." (Sorensen affidavit, 7/25/75)

edging that the measures practical for us to take will not result in his overthrow." (*id.*)

d. The Special Group's Authorization of a Sabotage Program Against Cuba

During the first six months of 1963, little, if any, sabotage activity against Cuba was undertaken.¹ However, on June 19, 1963, following the Standing Group's discussion of Cuba policy in the spring, President Kennedy approved a sabotage program.² (Memorandum for the Special Group, 6/19/63) In contrast to the MONGOOSE program, which sought to build toward an eventual internal revolt, the 1963 covert action program had a more limited objective, *i.e.*, "to nourish a spirit of resistance and disaffection which could lead to significant defections and other byproducts of unrest." (*id*)

After initial approval, specific intelligence and sabotage operations were submitted to the Special Group for prior authorization. On October 3, 1963, the Special Group approved nine operations in Cuba, several of which involved sabotage. On October 24, 1963, thirteen major sabotage operations, including the sabotage of an electric power plant, an oil refinery, and a sugar mill, were approved for the period from November 1963 through January 1964. (Memorandum, 7/11/75, CIA Review Staff to Select Committee, on "Approved CIA Covert Operations into Cuba")

e. The Diplomatic Effort to Explore an Accommodation with Castro

As early as January 4, 1963, Bundy proposed to President Kennedy that the possibility of communicating with Castro be explored. (Memorandum, Bundy to the President, 1/4/63) Bundy's memorandum on "Cuba Alternatives" of April 23, 1963, also listed the "gradual development of some form of accommodation with Castro" among policy alternatives. (Bundy memorandum, 4/21/63) At a meeting on June 3, 1963, the Special Group agreed it would be a "useful endeavor" to explore "various possibilities of establishing channels of communication to Castro." (Memorandum of Special Group meeting, 6/6/63)

In the fall of 1963, William Atwood was a Special Advisor to the United States Delegation to the United Nations with the rank of Ambassador. (Atwood, 7/10/75, p. 3) Atwood testified that from September until November 1963, he held a series of talks with the Cuban Ambassador to the United Nations to discuss opening negotiations on an accommodation between Castro and the United States.

Atwood said that at the outset he informed Robert Kennedy of these talks and was told that the effort "was worth pursuing." (Atwood, 7/10/75, pp. 5-9) Atwood said he regularly reported on the talks to the White House and to Adlai Stevenson, his superior at the United Nations. (Atwood, 7/10/75, pp. 6-7) Atwood stated that he was told

---

¹ At an April 3, 1963 meeting on Cuba, Bundy stated that no sabotage operations were then underway because the Special Group "had decided * * * that such activity is not worth the effort expended on it." (Memorandum of Meeting on Cuba, 4/3/63)
² The sabotage program was directed at "four major segments of the Cuban economy," (1) electric power; (2) petroleum refineries and storage facilities; (3) railroad and highway transportation and (4) production and manufacturing. (Memorandum for the Special Group, June 19, 1963, p. 1.) Operations under this program were to be conducted by CIA-controlled Cuban agents from a United States island off Florida and were to complement a similar effort designed to "develop internal resistance elements which could carry out sabotage." (*id*)

by Bundy that President Kennedy was in favor of "pushing towards an opening toward Cuba" to take Castro "out of the Soviet fold and perhaps wiping out the Bay of Pigs and maybe getting back to normal." (Atwood, 7/10/75, pp. 5-9)

Atwood said he believed that the only people who knew about his contacts with the Cubans were the President, Ambassador Averell Harriman, Ambassador Stevenson, Attorney General Kennedy, McGeorge Bundy, Bundy's assistant, and journalist Lisa Howard.[1] Atwood also testified that he arranged for a French journalist, Jean Daniel, to visit the White House prior to Daniel's scheduled trip to see Castro. (Atwood, 7/10/75, p. 19) (According to an article by Daniel in December 1963, Daniel met with President Kennedy on October 24, 1963. They discussed the prospects for reestablishing United States–Cuba relations and President Kennedy asked Daniel to report to him after seeing Castro.)[2]

On November 18, 1963, Atwood spoke by telephone with a member of Castro's staff in Cuba. (Atwood, 7/10/75, p. 8) Pursuant to White House instructions, Atwood informed Castro's staff member that the United States favored preliminary negotiations at the United Nations (rather than in Cuba as proposed by the Cubans), and that the United States desired to work out an agenda for these talks. (Atwood, 7/10/75, pp. 8-9) Atwood reported this conversation to Bundy who told him that after the Cuban agenda was received, President Kennedy wanted to see Atwood to "decide what to say and whether to go or what we should do next." (id., p. 9) Jean Daniel, the French journalist, met with Castro four days later on November 22, 1963, the same day AM/LASH was given the poison pen. On that same day, President Kennedy was assassinated.[3] With the change of Administrations, Atwood's talks with the Cubans became less frequent, and eventually ceased early in 1964. (Atwood, 7/10/75, p. 10)

(2) TESTIMONY ON THE QUESTION OF AUTHORIZATION FOR THE AM/LASH POISON PEN DEVICE

a. The October Meeting with AM/LASH and the Use of Robert Kennedy's Name Without Obtaining His Approval

Desmond Fitzgerald met AM/LASH in October 1963, and represented to AM/LASH that he was the personal representative of Robert Kennedy. He gave AM/LASH assurances of full support should AM/LASH succeed in overthrowing Castro.

The 1967 Inspector General's Report states that, according to Fitzgerald, Helms and Fitzgerald discussed the planned meeting with AM/LASH, and Helms decided "it was not necessary to seek approval from Robert Kennedy for Fitzgerald to speak in his name." (I.G. Report, pp. 88–89) When he testified before the Committee, Helms said he did not recall such a discussion with Fitzgerald. He stated

---

[1] Howard had initially placed Atwood in contact with the Cuban Ambassador after reporting to Atwood that during a trip to Cuba, she had learned Castro was anxious to establish communications with the United States. Thereafter Howard served as an intermediary in arranging Atwood's meetings with the Cubans. (Atwood, 7/10/75 pp. 4, 18.)
[2] Daniel, *"Unofficial Envoy: A Historic Report from Two Capitals,"* (*New Republic*, December 14, 1963).
[3] Daniel was with Castro when Castro received the report of President Kennedy's assassination. Daniel, *"When Castro Heard the News,"* (*New Republic*, December 7, 1963)

however, that he believed he had pre-existing authority to deal with AM/LASH regarding "a change in government" (as opposed to assassination) and that authority would have obviated the need to obtain Robert Kennedy's approval.[1] Helms testified: "I felt so sure that if I went to see Mr. Kennedy that he would have said yes, that I don't think there was any need to." (Helms, 6/13/75, p. 132)

Helms said he had considered AM/LASH to be a political action agent, not a potential assassin, and that Fitzgerald's meeting with AM/LASH and Helms' decision not to contact Robert Kennedy should be viewed in that light.

> * * * given this Cuban of his standing and all the history * * * of trying to find someone inside Cuba who might head a government and have a group to replace Castro * * * this was so central to the whole theme of everything we had been trying to do, that I [found] it totally unnecessary to ask Robert Kennedy at that point [whether] we should go ahead with this. This is obviously what he had been pushing, what everybody had been pushing for us to try to do * * * let's get on with doing it." (Helms, 6/13/75, pp. 117–118) [2]

b. The Delivery of the Poison Pen on November 22, 1963.

Helms testified that while the delivery of a poison pen to AM/LASH was not part of an assassination plot, he believed Castro's assassination was within the scope of the CIA's authority. As in the case of the 1962 plots, Helms based his belief on the vigor of the Administration's policy toward Cuba and his perception that there were no limits on the means that could be used in the effort against Castro. (Helms, 9/11/75, pp. 11–12) When asked whether it was his opinion that the offer of the poison pen to AM/LASH was authorized because it came within the scope of the 1963 program against Castro, Helms responded:

> I think the only way I know how to answer that is that I do not recall when things got cranked up in 1963 any dramatic changes or limitations being put on this operation. There was still an effort being made by whatever device, and perhaps slightly differently oriented at this time, to try to get rid of Castro * * * But I do not recall specific things being said now, [we are not] going to do this, we're not going to do that, and we're not going to do the other things, and we will do just these things. (Helms, 9/11/75, 11–12)

Each Kennedy Administration official who testified on AM/LASH agreed that he had never been informed about any assassination plot and that he knew of no order to assassinate Castro. Their statements

---

[1] The following exchange occurred in Helms' testimony.
Sen. HART of Michigan. Dealing with respect to what? A change in government, or assassination?
Mr. HELMS. A change in government, Senator Hart. This is what we were trying to do." (Helms, 6/13/75, p. 132.)

[2] As discussed above (see pp. 88), there was conflicting testimony from CIA officers concerning whether or not they viewed AM/LASH as an assassin and the purpose for giving him the poison pen. The documentary evidence, however, indicates that in 1963 AM/LASH was intent on assassinating Castro, that the CIA officers knew this, and that in addition to offering him a poison pen, the officers told AM/LASH they would supply him with high powered rifles with telescopic sights.
Helms testified that because AM/LASH "was the asset we were looking for, [w]e didn't want him to blow himself or blow anything else by getting involved in something like this [assassination] and have it fail. We wanted him to stay in place." (Helms, 6/13/75, p. 131.) Helms stated that "at no time was it the idea of [the AM/LASH] case officers, or those people in the chain behind, to use [AM/LASH] to assassinate Castro." (Helms, 6/13/75, p. 135.)
Helms further stated: "* * * there was an enormous amount of temporizing with this fellow to keep him on the team, to keep him working away at this job, but to try and persuade him that this was not the way to go about it." (Helms, 6/13/75, p. 133.) Helms testified that AM/LASH was given the poison pen "because he was insisting on something and this was a temporizing gesture rather than giving him some kind of a gun he had asked for * * *." (Helms, 6/13/75, p. 133.)

are consistent with Helms' testimony that he did not know that the AM/LASH operation involved assassination, but they again disagreed with Helms' view that an assassination plot could be undertaken without express authority. Running against the possibility that Administration officials intended an assassination of Castro was testimony that it was inconceivable that the President would have approved an assassination at the same time that he had authorized talks to explore the possibility of improved relations with Castro.[1]

(3) THE QUESTION OF AUTHORIZATION IN THE JOHNSON ADMINISTRATION

a. Summary of the Assassination Activity

The CIA delivered arms to AM/LASH in Cuba in March and June of 1964. Early in 1965, after AM/LASH had become more insistent that Castro's assassination was necessary and had asked for a silenced weapon, the Agency put AM/LASH in contact with the leader of an anti-Castro group, "B-1," with the intention that AM/LASH obtain his desired weapon from that group. The Agency subsequently learned that AM/LASH had received a silencer and other special equipment from B-1 and was preparing to assassinate Castro.

b. The Issue of Authorization

The issue of authority in the Johnson Administration is similar to that in the Kennedy Administration. The principal officials of the Kennedy Administration [2] (and DDP Helms) continued in their positions during the relevant period of the Johnson Administration (Robert Kennedy left the Administration in September 1964). Helms testified that he believed Castro's assassination was within the scope of the CIA's authority in view of Administration policy toward Cuba reflected in the AM/LASH operation in both 1963 and 1964–65. (Helms, 6/13/75, pp. 137–138) Again, there was no direct evidence that McCone or anyone outside the Agency authorized or knew about the AM/LASH plot.

The Committee examined four events that may shed light on the perceptions of the Administration and CIA officials about assassination during the early years of the Johnson Administration: (1) the covert action program against Cuba in 1964–1965; (2) the Special Group's action in investigating reports of Cuban exiles/underworld plots to assassinate Castro; (3) Helms' report to Rusk that CIA was not involved with AM/LASH in a Castro assassination plot; and (4) Helms' briefing of President Johnson on the 1967 Inspector General's Report on alleged CIA assassination plots.

---

[1] Rusk testified that "I find it extraordinarily difficult to believe" and that "I just can't conceive" President Kennedy would have authorized the passage of an asassination device for use against Castro while Atwood was exploring the possibility of normalizing relations with Castro. (Rusk, 7/10/75, pp. 85–86) Similarly, Bundy testified he "absolutely" did not believe President Kennedy would have authorized or permitted an assassination device to have been passed at the same time a possible rapprochment with Castro was being pursued. (Bundy, 7/11/75, pp. 150–151.)
On the other hand, when the possibility of exploring better relations with Castro was initially raised (but before any talks were begun) Bundy indicated that accommodation could be explored on a "separate track" while other proposed actions, such as sabotage, were going on. (Agenda for Special Group meeting of 4/29/63, p. 2)

[2] Rusk (Secretary of State), McNamara (Secretary of Defense), McCone (Director of Central Intelligence), and Bundy (Special Assistant for National Security and Chairman of the Special Group).

c. *The Covert Action Program Against Cuba in 1964–1965*

According to the minutes of a Special Group meeting on April 7, 1964, President Johnson decided to discontinue the use of CIA-controlled sabotage raids against Cuba.[1] (Memorandum of Special Group Meeting, 4/7/64) A McCone memorandum indicated that in reaching that decision, President Johnson had abandoned the objective of Castro's overthrow.

At the April 7 meeting, Rusk opposed sabotage raids because they were unproductive and had a "high noise level" that called attention to them. Rusk added he suspected the "Cuban exiles who actually conduct the raids of possibly wishing to leave fingerprints pointing to U.S. involvement in order to increase that involvement." (*Id*, p. 2) McCone disagreed noting that the covert action program relied on a "well-planned series of sabotage efforts. Bundy said that since the June 1963 approval of the current sabotage program "policy makers * * * had turned sabotage operations on and off to such an extent that [the sabotage program] simply does not, in the nature of things, appear feasible." (*Id*, p. 2) [2]

d. *The Special Group Investigation of Reported Castro Assassination Plots by Cuban Exiles*

On June 10, 1964, Helms sent McCone a memorandum stating that Agency officials had learned of several plots by Cuban exiles to assassinate Castro and other Cuban leaders. (Memorandum, Helms to McCone, 6/10/64) According to the memorandum, several of the plots involved "people apparently associated with the Mafia" who had been offered $150,000 by Cuban exiles to accomplish the deed. Helms' memorandum stated that the sources of the reports were parties to the plots who had presumably given this information to CIA officials with the expectation that they would receive legal immunity if the plots succeeded. (*Id.*)

Helms' memorandum, however, did not mention any of the CIA assassination plots against Castro.[3] To the contrary, it stated that "Agency officers made clear to each of the sources that the United

---

[1] A memorandum by Bundy on April 7, 1964, listed seven aspects of the covert action program which had been in effect. These were: (1) collection of intelligence; (2) covert propaganda to encourage low risk forms of active and passive resistance; (3) cooperation with other agencies in economic denial (4) attempts to identify and establish contact with potential dissident elements inside Cuba; (5) indirect economic sabotage; (6) CIA-controlled sabotage raiding; and (7) autonomous operations. (Memorandum for the Record of the Special Group, 4/7/64)

[2] In a memorandum the day after President Johnson's decision to stop CIA-controlled sabotage operations, McCone stated: "the real issue to be considered at the meeting and by the President was a question of whether we wished to implement the policy (outlined in certain memoranda) or abandon the basic objective of bringing about the liquidation of the Castro Communist entourage and the elimination of Communist presence in Cuba and thus rely on future events of an undisclosed nature which might accomplish this objective". (Memorandum by McCone, 4/8/64)

In the context of the Special Group's discussion, McCone's use of the words "liquidation" and "elimination" appears to be another example of inartful language. A literal interpretation of these words leaves one with the impression that assassination was contemplated. But the context of the discussion does not bear out such an interpretation. Thus in specifying what he meant by "future events of an undisclosed nature" McCone pointed to "extreme economic distress caused by a sharp drop in sugar prices." and "other external factors." (*Id.*, p. 8) McCone testified that such references as the "elimination" or "liquidation" of the Castro regime may not refer to assassination. (McCone, 6/6/75, p. 32)

[3] Moreover, according to Bundy, no one informed him at the meetings that "in earlier years there had been a relationship with * * * persons allegedly involved with the criminal syndicate—in order to accomplish the assassination of Fidel Castro." (Bundy, 7/11/75, p. 71)

States Government would not, under any circumstances, condone the planned actions." (*Id.*, p. 1)

McCone said in a Special Group Meeting on June 18, 1964, that he was "somewhat skeptical" and opposed additional investigation, but "others, including Mr. Bundy, felt that the United States was being put on notice and should do everything in its power to ascertain promptly the veracity of the reports and then undertake prevention." (Memorandum of Special Group Meeting, 6/18/64) McCone made a Memorandum of the June 18 meeting which indicated that he had dissented from the Special Group's decision. He had expressed his belief that the Special Group was "overly exercised," and that he was inclined to dismiss the matter as "Miami cocktail party talk." McCone noted, however, that the Special Group "was more concerned than I and therefore planning to discuss the subject with the Attorney General and possibly Mr. Hoover." (Memorandum, 6/18/64, p. 1)

The Special Group decided to transmit the reports to the Attorney General "as a matter of law enforcement," and when Robert Kennedy was so informed a few days later, he stated that the Justice Department would investigate. (Memorandum of Meeting, 6/22/64) The FBI then conducted an investigation and its results were submitted by McCone to the Special Group on August 19, 1964.[1] (McCone to Bundy Memorandum, 8/19/64)

e. *Helms' Report to Rusk*

In 1966 Helms sent a memorandum to Rusk reporting the CIA's relations with AM/LASH. The memorandum stated that the CIA's contact with AM/LASH was for "the express purpose" of intelligence collection. (*Id.*) Noting allegations that had come to his attention that AM/LASH had been involved with the CIA in a Castro assassination plot, Helms stated:

The Agency was not involved with [AM/LASH] in a plot to assassinate Fidel Castro. * * * nor did it ever encourage him to attempt such an act.

Helms' memorandum made no mention of the fact that CIA officers, with Helms' knowledge, had offered a poison pen to AM/LASH on November 22 1963, that the CIA had supplied arms to AM/LASH in 1964, or that the CIA had put AM/LASH in touch with B–1 to obtain a silenced weapon to assassinate Castro.

Helms told the Committee that this memorandum to Rusk was "inaccurate" and not factual. (Helms, 6/13/75, p. 115)

The CIA's copy of the memorandum contains a typed notation recommending that Helms sign the document. That notation was by Thomas Karamessines, who had become DDP. (Rusk, 7/10/75, p. 2) Helms testified that the day before his June 13, 1975, testimony to the Committee he had asked Karamessines why the memorandum to Rusk had been written in the way that it was. Helms stated he and Karamessines had concluded that they did not know the reason but Helms speculated that "it may be until we conducted the Inspector General's Investigation somewhat later we didn't have the facts straight, or

---

[1] McCone's memorandum summarized seven FBI reports on its investigation. The FBI said that several of the persons interviewed stated they had knowledge of the exiles' plot and had reported the information to the CIA. Others interviewed denied knowledge of the plans.

maybe we had the facts straight then but we did not have them straight later." (Helms, 6/13/75, p. 115)

f. Helms' Briefing of President Johnson on the 1967 Inspector General's Report

Drew Pearson's newspaper article in the spring of 1967 alleging United States involvement in plots to assassinate Fidel Castro prompted President Johnson to direct Helms, who was then DCI, to conduct an investigation. The result was the Inspector General's Report of May 23, 1967. (Helms, 6/13/75, pp. 35-36) After receiving the Report, Helms briefed the President "orally about the contents." (*Id.*, p. 36.) During his testimony, Helms was shown his handwritten notes which appeared to have been made in preparation for his briefing of the President. Those notes carried the story of CIA's involvement in assassination through mid-1963. When asked if he had told President Johnson that the Inspector General had concluded that efforts to assassinate Fidel Castro had continued into Johnson's presidency, Helms replied, "I just can't answer that, I just don't know. I can't recall having done so." (*Id.*, p. 38.) He did note that it would not have occurred to him to brief President Johnson on the 1964 AM/LASH gun deliveries because "I don't think one would have approached the AM/LASH thing as an assassination plot against Castro." (*Id.*, p. 39)[1]

(4) Helms' Testimony on Authorization in the Johnson Administration.

Helms was asked if the Agency regarded "whatever marching orders they had obtained prior to the death of President Kennedy as still being valid and operative" when President Johnson succeeded to the office. Helms replied:

> This is not very clear to me at this stage. A lot of the same officers were serving President Johnson as they served President Kennedy, and * * * I can't recall anymore whether there was any specific issue about whether this was taken up with President Johnson at any meeting or any session. If it had been, I would have thought there would have been records someplace. (Helms, 6/13/75, p. 139.)

Helms testified that with respect to the AM/LASH operation in the period 1964–1965, he had no knowledge or recollection that assassination was involved in the CIA's relationship with him. (Helms, 9/11/75, pp. 20–21) Helms said: "[t]he policy making and policy approval mechanism in President Johnson's Administration has to have gone through some changes in shifts I don't remember exactly what they were." (*Id.*, p. 22)

> So if these things [placing AM/LASH in contact with a Cuban exile leader who would supply him with an assassination device] were happening after President Kennedy was assassinated, I don't know what authorization they're working on or what their thought processes were, whether these were simply low level fellows scheming and so forth, on something that didn't have high level approval. I honestly cannot help you. I don't recall these things going on at the time. (*Id.*)

When asked whether President Johnson had been informed of or had authorized continuing efforts to assassinate Castro, Helms replied:

---

[1] Helms earlier testified that AMLASH was an intelligence and political action agent. The Inspector General Report, however, treated the AMLASH operation as an assassination plot.

The Special Group would have continued to consider these matters, and I would have assumed that whoever was chairing the Special Group would have in turn reported to the President, which was the usual practice. (*Id.*)[1]

The records of the Special Group do not show any consideration of Castro's assassination or of the AM/LASH plot during the Johnson Administration (or earlier) and there was no other evidence that McCone or anyone above the Agency was informed of or specifically authorized the AM/LASH plots.

---

[1] In an interview with Leo Janis in 1971, former President Johnson was reported to have said that when he had taken office, he had discovered that "we had been operating a damned Murder, Inc., in the Caribbean." (L. Janis. *"The Last Days of the President," Atlantic*, July 1973, pp. 35, 39, Janis was interviewed by the Committee staff and affirmed the accuracy of this remark.) The Committee has not ascertained who related this statement to Johnson. It should be noted that Johnson attended post-Trujillo assassination meetings which assessed United States involvement in that killing. His reference to Murder, Inc., may have derived from his knowledge of that episode or from general knowledge he had of other violent covert activities conducted during the Kennedy Administration.

C. INSTITUTIONALIZING ASSASSINATION: THE "EXECUTIVE ACTION" CAPABILITY

In addition to investigating actual assassination plots, the Committee has examined a project known as Executive Action which included, as one element, the development of a general, standby assassination capability. As with the plots, this examination focused on two broad questions: What happened? What was the extent and nature of authorization for the project?

1. INTRODUCTION

Sometime in early 1961, Bissell instructed Harvey, who was then Chief of a CIA Foreign Intelligence staff, to establish an "executive action capability," which would include research into a capability to assassinate foreign leaders.[1] (Bissell, 6/9/75, p. 51; Harvey, 6/25/75, pp. 36–37) At some point in early 1961 Bissell discussed the Executive Action capability with Bundy. The timing of that conversation and whether "the White House" urged that a capability be created were matters on which the evidence varied widely, as is discussed in section (2) below.

Bissell, Harvey and Helms all agreed that the "generalized" capability was never used. (Bissell 6/9/75, p. 87; Harvey 6/25/75; p. 45; Helms 6/13/75, p. 52)

---

[1] During the late spring or early summer of 1960, Richard Bissell had requested his Science Advisor, Mr. Joseph Scheider, to review the general "capability of the clandestine service in the field of incapacitation and elimination." Scheider testified that assassination was one of the "capabilities" he was asked by Bissell to research. (Scheider, 10/9/75, pp. 5–6, 24–25)

Scheider indicated that Bissell turned to him because he was knowledgeable about "substances that might be available in CIA laboratories" and because Bissell would have considered it part of my job as his technical aide." (id., 6).

Also prior to this time, there had been an internal CIA committee which passed on proposals involving the operational use of drugs, chemicals and biological agents. The purpose of this Committee is suggested by the following incident:

In February 1960, CIA's Near East Division sought the endorsement of what the Division Chief called the "Health Alteration Committee" for its proposal for a "special operation" to "incapacitate" an Iraqi Colonel believed to be "promoting Soviet bloc political interests in Iraq." The Division sought the Committee's advice on a technique, "which while not likely to result in total disablement would be certain to prevent the target from pursuing his usual activities for a minimum of three months," adding:

"We do not consciously seek subject's permanent removal from the scene; we also do not object should this complication develop." (Memo, Acting Chief N.E. Division to DC/CI, 2/25/60.)

In April, the Committee unanimously recommended to the DDP that a "disabling operation" be undertaken, noting that Chief of Operations advised that it would be "highly desirable." Bissell's deputy, Tracy Barnes, approved on behalf of Bissell. (Memo, Deputy Chief CI to DDP, 4/1/62)

The approved operation was to mail a monogrammed handkerchief containing an incapacitating agent to the colonel from an Asian country. Scheider testified that, while he did not now recall the name of the recipient, he did remember mailing from the Asian country, during the period in question, a handkerchief "treated with some kind of material for the purpose of harassing that person who received it." (Scheider Affidavit, 10/20/75; Scheider, 10/9/75, pp. 52–55; 10/18/75, pp. 55–56.)

During the course of this Committee's investigation, the CIA stated that the handkerchief was "in fact never received (if, indeed, sent)." It added that the colonel:

"Suffered a terminal illness before a firing squad in Baghdad (an event we had nothing to do with) not very long after our handkerchief proposal was considered." (Memo, Chief of Operations, N.E. Division to Assistant to the SA/DDO, 9/26/75.)

"Executive Action" was a CIA euphemism, defined as a project for research into developing means for overthrowing foreign political leaders, including a "capability to perform assassinations." (Harvey, 6/25/75, p. 34) Bissell indicated that Executive Action covered a "wide spectrum of actions" to "eliminate the effectiveness" of foreign leaders, with assassination as the "most extreme" action in the spectrum. (Bissell, 7/22/75, p. 32) The Inspector General's Report described executive action as a "general standby capability" to carry out assassination when required. (I.G. Report, p. 37) The project was given the code name ZR/RIFLE by the CIA.[1]

A single agent ("asset") was given the cryptonym QJ/WIN, and placed under Harvey's supervision for the ZR/RIFLE project. He was never used in connection with any actual assassination efforts. Helms described QJ/WIN's "capability":

If you needed somebody to carry out murder, I guess you had a man who might be prepared to carry it out. (Helms, 6/13/75, p. 50)

Harvey used QJ/WIN, to spot "individuals with criminal and underworld connections in Europe for possible multi-purpose use." (Harvey, 6/25/75, p. 50) For example, QJ/WIN reported that a potential asset in the Middle East was "the leader of a gambling syndicate" with "an available pool of assassins." (CIA file, ZR/RIFLE/Personality Sketches) However, Harvey testified that:

During the entire existence of the entire ZR/RIFLE project * * * no agent was recruited for the purpose of assassination, and no even tentative targeting or target list was ever drawn. (Harvey, 6/25/75, p. 45)

In general, project ZR/RIFLE involved assessing the problems and requirements of assassination and developing a stand-by assassination capability; more specifically, it involved "spotting" potential agents and "researching" assassination techniques that might be used. (Bissell, 7/17/75, p. 11 and 6/9/75, p. 73; Harvey, 6/25/75, pp. 37-A, 45) Bissell characterized ZR/RIFLE as "internal and purely preparatory." (Bissell, 7/22/75, p. 32) The 1967 Inspector General's Report found "no indication in the file that the Executive Action capability of ZR/RIFLE-QJ/WIN was ever used," but said that "after Harvey took over the Castro operation, he ran it as one aspect of ZR/RIFLE." (I.G. Report, pp. 40-41)

2. THE QUESTION OF WHITE HOUSE INITIATION, AUTHORIZATION, OR KNOWLEDGE OF THE EXECUTIVE ACTION PROJECT

Harvey testified that Bissell had told him that "the White House" had twice urged the creation of such a capability and the Inspector General's Report quoted notes of Harvey's (no longer in existence) to that effect. Bissell did not recall any specific conversation with the "White House," but in his initial testimony before the Committee he assumed the correctness of Harvey's notes and stated that, while he could have created the capability on his own, any urgings would have come from Bundy or Walt Rostow. In a later appearance, however, Bissell said he merely informed Bundy of the capability and that

---

[1] ZR/RIFLE was a cryptonym relating to two areas. One was the Executive Action assassination capability. The other ZR/RIFLE area is not part of the subject matter of this report. This second program was genuine, but it was also meant to provide a cover for any Executive Action operation. William Harvey had been in charge of the CIA section with general responsibility for such programs. (Harvey, 6/25/75, p. 49)

the context was a briefing by him and not urging by Bundy. Bundy said he received a briefing and gave no urging, though he raised no objections. Rostow said he never heard of the project.

William Harvey testified that he was "almost certain" that on January 25 and 26, 1961, he met with two CIA officials: Joseph Scheider, who by then had become Chief of the Technical Services Division, and a CIA recruiting officer, to discuss the feasibility of creating a capability within the Agency for "Executive Action." (Harvey, 6/25/75, p. 52) After reviewing his notes of those meetings,[1] Harvey testified that the meetings occurred after his initial discussion of Executive Action with Bissell, which, he said, might have transpired in "early January." (Harvey, 6/25/75, p. 52) When Bissell was shown these notes, he agreed with Harvey about the timing of their initial discussion. (Bissell, 7/17/75, p. 10)

Harvey testified that the Executive Action capability was intended to include assassination. (Harvey, 6/25/75, p. 35) His cryptic handwritten notes of the January 25/26 meetings, preserved at the CIA, contain phrases which suggest a discussion of assassination: "last resort beyond last resort and a confession of weakness," "the magic button," and "never mention word assassination". Harvey confirmed this interpretation. (Harvey, Ex. 1, 6/25/75)[2]

The Inspector General's Report did not mention Harvey's notes, or their dates. However, in describing Bissell's initial assignment of the Executive Action project to Harvey, the Report referred to Harvey's notes, now missing, and which quoted Bissell as saying to Harvey, "the White House had twice urged me to create such a capability." (I.G. Report, p. 37) Harvey also testified that this "urging" was men-

---

[1] Harvey was asked whether his notations "25/1-Joes" and "26/1" indicate that he spoke to Joseph Scheider and the recruiting officer in 1961.
"Q: And is it your judgment that that is January 26, 1961 and is about the subject of Executive Action?
"HARVEY. Yes, it is.
"Q: And it followed your conversation with Mr. Bissell that you have recounted?
"HARVEY. * * * [W]ell, when I first looked at this, I thought this, well, this has got to be 1962, but I am almost certain now that it is not. If this is true, this might place the first discussion that I had with Dick Bissell in early January and this is difficult to pinpoint because there were several such discussions in varying degrees of detail during the period in the Spring, and very early in 1961 to the fall of 1961 period, but I did find out fairly early on that [the recruiting officer] had—or that Bissell had discussed the question of assassination with [the recruiting officer] and this discussion, at the very least, had to take place after I know Bissell already had discussed the matter with [him]." (Harvey, 6/25/75, p. 52)
Harvey had also testified that, after receiving Bissell's initial instructions to establish an Executive Action capability:
"The first thing I did * * * was discuss in theoretical terms with a few officers whom I trusted quite implicitly the whole subject of assassination, our possible assets, our posture, going back, if you will, even to the fundamental questions of (a), is assassination a proper weapon of an American intelligence service, and (b), even if you assume that it is, is it within our capability within the framework of this government to do it effectively and properly, securely and discreetly." (Harvey, 6/25/75, pp. 37-A, 38)
The Inspector General's Report connected [the recruiting officer] and Scheider to the early stages of the Executive Action project as follows:
"Harvey says that Bissell had already discussed certain aspects of the problem with [the recruiting officer] and with Joseph Scheider. Since [the recruiting officer] was already cut in, Harvey used him in developing the Executive Action Capability * * *. Harvey's mention of him [Scheider] in this connection may explain a notation by [a CIA doctor] that Harvey instructed [the doctor] to discuss techniques with Scheider without associating the discussion with the Castro operation." (I.G. Report, pp. 37-38)
It is evident from the testimony of Harvey and Bissell that the turnover to Harvey of the Rosselli contact in November, 1961 was discussed as part of ZR/RIFLE (see Section (d), infra). Thus, their initial discussion of Executive Action can, at the least, be dated before November, 1961 and the "25/1" and "26/1" notations would have to refer to January, 1961.
[2] Harvey's notes also contained a phrase which suggests his concern that any U.S. assassination attempts might breed retaliation from other governments: "Dangers of RIS (Russian Intelligence Service) counter-action and monitor if they are blamed." (Harvey, Ex. 1, 6/25/75; Bissell, Ex. 1, 7/17/75)

tioned in his initial discussion of Executive Action with Bissell. (Harvey, 6/25/75, p. 37) However, the testimony from Bissell and from the White House aides is in conflict with Harvey's testimony as to whether such "urging" had in fact been given to Bissell.

The testimony regarding the relationship between "the White House" and the Executive Action capability is summarized as follows:

Harvey.—Harvey testified that his missing notes which had been destroyed had indicated that Bissell mentioned White House urgings to develop an Executive Action capability. (Harvey, 6/25/75, p. 37) Harvey said that he "particularly remember[ed]" that Bissell said that he received "more than one" urging from the White House. (Harvey, 6/25/75, pp. 36–37; 7/11/75, p. 59) As he testified:

> "On two occasions or on more than one occasion, and I particularly remember the more than one because I recall at the time this was clear this was not just a one-shot thing tossed out * * * the White House—I quote this much; this is exact—had urged him (Bissell)—him in this case not personally, but the Agency—to develop an Executive Action capability." (Harvey, 6/25/75, pp. 36–37)

But Harvey had no direct evidence that Bissell actually had any such discussion with "the White House." No specific individual in the White House was named to Harvey by Bissell. (Harvey, 6/25/75, p. 31) Harvey said that it would have been "improper" for him to have asked Bissell whom he had talked to and "grossly improper" for Bissell to have volunteered that name. (Harvey, 6/25/75, p. 37)

Bissell.—Bissell specifically recalled assigning Harvey to investigate the capability. (Bissell, 6/9/75, p. 51) However, Bissell did not recall "a specific conversation with anybody in the White House as the origin" of his instruction to Harvey. (Bissell, 6/9/75, p. 51)

During the course of several appearances before the Committee, Bissell's testimony varied as to whether or not he had been urged by the White House to develop an Executive Action capability.

In his initial appearances before the Committee on June 9 and 11, 1975, Bissell made statements that tended to indicate that White House authorization had been given. In response to the "twice urged" quotation of Harvey's notes in the Inspector General's Report, Bissell said, "I have no reason to believe that Harvey's quote is wrong." (Bissell, 6/9/75, p. 51) Bissell also said that as far as he knew, it was true that he was asked by the White House to create a general stand-by assassination capability. (Bissell, 6/9/75, pp. 49, 51)

Based again on Harvey's missing notes ("White House urging"), and his statement that he had no reason to challenge their accuracy, Bissell initially gave his opinion that McGeorge Bundy and Walt Rostow were the two people from whom such a request was most likely to have come because they were "the two members of the White House staff who were closest to CIA operations." (Bissell, 6/9/75, pp. 49–54)

At another point in his initial testimony, Bissell said that the creation of the capability "may have been initiated within the Agency" (*Id.*, p. 81). Two days later he said: "There is little doubt in my mind that Project RIFLE was discussed with Rostow and possibly Bundy." (Bissell, 6/11/75, p. 46)

When Bissell appeared before the Committee on July 17 and 22, his testimony, given in light of information obtained since his earlier appearances, was that there was no White House urging for the creation of the Executive Action project, although tacit approval for the "research" project was probably given by Bundy after it was established.

First, Bissell was shown the Harvey notes which had been preserved and which, without any mention of the White House, indicated Harvey had received his assignment prior to January 25/26, 1961. Those dates—just 5 days after the change in administration—made Bissell conclude that it was "very unlikely that that assignment to [Harvey] was taken as a result of White House urging or consultation." (Bissell, 7/17/75, p. 10) Bissell said that Bundy did not have any influence at the Agency before the Presidential inauguration. Bissell added that he did not remember meeting with anyone in the new administration on matters prior to the inauguration. (Bissell, 7/22/75, p. 23)

Second, when he returned in July, Bissell also said he had been convinced by telephone conversations with Rostow and Bundy after his first appearances that since Rostow's duties in 1961 had nothing to do with covert action, he had "never discussed" Executive Action with Rostow. (Bissell, 7/17/75, p. 10; 7/27/75, p. 22)

Bissell's final testimony about Bundy (given after his telephone contact with Bundy) was that he believed that he had informed Bundy about the capability after it had been created. (Bissell, 7/17/75, pp. 10–11; 7/22/75, pp. 21–22) But Bissell confirmed his original testimony that he had not briefed Bundy on the actual assassination plots against Castro already undertaken by the CIA. (Bissell, 6/11/75, p. 47; 7/22/75, p. 31) Bissell was "quite certain" that he would not have expected Bundy to mention the Executive Action capability to the President. (Bissell, 7/22/75, p. 35) He testified:

Q. Would you think the development of a capability to kill foreign leaders was a matter of sufficient importance to bring to the attention of the President?

BISSELL. In that context and at that time and given the limited scope of activities within that project, I would not." (Bissell, 7/22/75, p. 35)

Bissell said that he and Bundy had discussed an untargeted "capability" rather than the plan or approval for an assassination operation. (Bissell, 7/17/75, p. 11) Bissell said that although he does not have a specific recollection, he "might have" mentioned Castro, Lumumba, and Trujillo in the course of a discussion of Executive Action "because these were the sorts of individuals at that moment in history against whom such a capability might possibly have been employed." (Bissell, 6/11/75, p. 51)

Bissell said his impression was that in addition to expressing no unfavorable reaction to the project, Bundy actually might have given a more affirmative response. (Bissell, 7/22/75, pp. 25, 28) Bissell testified that he might have interpreted Bundy's reaction as approval (or at least no objection) for the Executive Action concept. (Bissell, 7/22/75, p. 30)

Q: * * * I think the testimony of this witness is going further in saying what you received from [Bundy] was, in your view, tantamount to approval?

BISSELL: I, at least, interpreted it as you can call it approval, or you could say no objection. He [Bundy] was briefed on something that was being done, as I now believe, on the initiative of the Agency. His [Bundy's] comment is that he made no objection to it. I suspect that his reaction was somewhat more favorable than that, but this is a matter that probably someone listening to the conversation on which such a person could have had differing interpretations. (Bissell, 7/22/75, p. 33)

All of the Bissell testimony on his Executive Action conversation with Bundy was speculative reconstruction. From his first appearance to his last, Bissell had no "clear recollection" of the events. (Bissell, 7/22/75, pp. 29, 36) But Bissell maintained that more "formal and specific and explicit approval would have been required" before any "actual overt steps in use of the capability." (Bissell, 7/22/75, p. 31)

Bissell said that Harvey's notation about White House urgings to develop an Executive Action capability may have been a slightly confused account of a Bissell/Harvey conversation subsequent to the initiation of the project in which Bissell relayed Bundy's reaction to Harvey. (Bissell, 7/22/75, p. 25)

Bissell ultimately testified that the development of an Executive Action capability was "undoubtedly," or "very much more likely" initiated within the Agency. (Bissell, 7/22/75, pp. 22, 27) He had acknowledged on his first day of testimony that this would not have been unusual:

> It was the normal practice in the Agency and an important part of its mission to create various kinds of capability long before there was any reason to be certain whether those would be used or where or how or for what purpose. The whole ongoing job of * * * a secret intelligence service of recruiting agents is of that character * * *. So it would not be particularly surprising to me if the decision to create * * * this capability had been taken without an outside request. (Bissell, 6/9/75, pp. 67–68)

Bundy.—McGeorge Bundy also testified to a conversation with Bissell, during which the Executive Action capability was discussed. Bundy's testimony comports with Bissell's on the fact that they discussed an untargeted capability, rather than an assassination operation. But Bundy said that the capability included "killing the individual." (Bundy, 7/11/75, p. 5)[1] Bundy's impression was that the CIA was "testing my reaction," not "seeking authority." (Bundy, 7/11/75, p. 15) Bundy said:

> I am sure I gave no instruction. But it is only fair to add that I do not recall that I offered any impediment either. (Bundy, 7/11/75, p. 10)

Bundy said that he did not take steps to halt the development of the Executive Action capability or "pursue the matter at all" (Bundy, 7/11/75, p. 19) because he was satisfied.

> That this was not an operational activity, and would not become such without two conditions: first, that there be a desire or a request or a guidance that there should be planning against some specific individual; and second, that there should be a decision to move against the individual. (Bundy, 7/11/75, p. 7).

Bundy believed that neither of these conditions had been fulfilled. (Bundy, 7/11/75, p. 7)

Bundy recalled the conversation with Bissell as taking place "sometime in the early months of 1961." (Bundy, 7/11/75, p. 4) When questioned about the dates in Harvey's notes, Bundy rated the chance that his conversation about Executive Action took place before January

---

[1] See p. 157, *supra*, for Bundy's testimony about having a vague recollection of hearing about poisons in relation possibly to use against a large group of people in Cuba. But he did not connect this to the conversation about executive action.

25—when Harvey was already discussing the project at the CIA pursuant to Bissell's directive—as "near zero" because the new Administration had been in office less than a week and he had been preoccupied with other problems, including the Berlin crisis and reorganizing the National Security Staff. (Bundy, 7/11/75, p. 9)

Bundy testified that he did not brief the President on the Executive Action project:

CHAIRMAN. And you have testified that you did not take the matter to the President?
BUNDY. As far as I can recall, Mr. Chairman. (Bundy, 7/11/75, p. 16)

Bundy explained that the division of responsibility for national security affairs excluded Rostow from jurisdiction over covert operations, making it unlikely that Rostow would have been briefed on a project like ZR/RIFLE. (Bundy, 7/11/75, p. 11)

Rostow.—Rostow testified that he was "morally certain" that during his entire tenure in government, he never heard a reference to executive action or "such a capability for such an intention to act by the U.S." (Rostow, 7/9/75, pp. 10, 13)[1]

3. THE QUESTION OF AUTHORIZATION OR KNOWLEDGE OF THE EXECUTIVE ACTION PROJECT BY THE DCI

Richard Bissell said he was "quite certain" that Allen Dulles had full knowledge of the Executive Action project for two reasons: first, it "would have come to the DCI's attention" when Harvey was transferred between components of the Agency and assigned to work on Cuban operations;[2] and second, Bissell "would imagine" it was mentioned to Dulles at the initiation of the project. (Bissell, 7/22/75, p. 35) Bissell and Harvey briefed Richard Helms on Project ZR/RIFLE when he became DDP. (Bissell, 6/11/75, p. 53; Harvey, 7/11/75, p. 63) But Bissell did not recall briefing John McCone about the project when McCone took over as DCI. (Bissell, 7/17/75, p. 11) McCone testified that he had no knowledge of such a project. (McCone, 6/6/75, p. 43)

William Harvey said it was assumed that the project was within the parameters permitted by the DCI. But Harvey testified that officially advising the DCI of the existence of the project was "a bridge we did not cross" and would not have crossed until "there was either specific targeting or a specific operation or a specific recruitment." (Harvey, 6/25/75, p. 59)

4. THE QUESTION OF WHETHER PROJECT ZR/RIFLE WAS CONNECTED TO ANY ACTUAL ASSASSINATION PLOTS

The Committee has sought to determine whether the CIA development of an Executive Action capability was related in any way to the actual assassination efforts. One question raised by this inquiry is whether the participants in the assassination operations might have

---

[1] *Goodpaster and Gray.*—Andrew Goodpaster and Gordon Gray were the White House officials with responsibility for national security affairs during the latter part of the Eisenhower Administration. However, there was no evidence which raised the name of either man in connection with the development of an Executive Action capability. Goodpaster and Gray testified to having no knowledge of it. (Goodpaster, 7/17/75, p. 11; Gray, 7/9/75, p. 56)

[2] Harvey's transfer to Cuban operations was not completed until late in 1961.

perceived the Executive Action capability as in some way lending legitimacy to the actual assassination efforts.

(a) *Conversation between Bissell and Bundy*

In his early testimony, Bissell said he did not have a recollection of whether he discussed the names of Castro, Lumumba, and Trujillo with anyone in the White House in the course of discussing the project to develop an executive action capability. However, Bissell testified that it was "perfectly plausible that I would have used examples." (Bissell, 6/11/75, p. 51) He continued:

> In such a discussion of a capability, I might well have used the three names that I just gave, because these were the sorts of individuals at that moment in history against whom such a capability might possibly have been employed. (Bissell, 6/11/75, p. 51)

Bissell and Bundy both testified, however, that their discussion on the development of the capability for assassination did not involve any mention of actual assassination plans or attempts (see detailed treatment at Section (b), *supra*). There is no testimony to the contrary. The account of this conversation raises a question as to whether Bissell acted properly in withholding from Bundy the fact that assassination efforts against Castro had already been mounted and were moving forward. Bundy was responsible to a new President for national security affairs and Bissell was his principal source of information about covert operations at the CIA.

(b) *Bissell's instruction to Harvey to take over responsibility for underworld contact: November 1961*

Both Bissell and Harvey recall a meeting in November 1961, in which Harvey was instructed to take over the contact with John Rosselli as part of Project ZR/RIFLE. (Bissell, 6/11/75, pp. 19, 47; Harvey, 6/25/75, p. 86; and 6/11/75, p. 19) Harvey's notes placed the meeting on November 15, 1961, (I.G. Report, p. 39), during the period in which Harvey was freed from his duties on another Agency staff and assumed direction of Task Force W which ran CIA activity against the Castro regime.

According to Bissell and Harvey, their November meeting involved only the planning and research of a capability rather than a targeted operation against Castro. (Bissell, 7/17/75, p. 13; Harvey, 7/11/75, p. 60) But Bissell acknowledged that the purpose of the Rosselli contact had been to assassinate Castro, and that "it is a fair inference that there would have been no reason to maintain it [the contact] unless there was some possibility of reactivating that operation." (Bissell, 6/11/75, p. 19) Bissell stated that because the assassination plot against Castro involving the underworld figures

> Had been stood down after the Bay of Pigs * * * and there was no authorization to pursue it actively * * * the responsibility that was given to him [Harvey] was that of taking over an inactive contact. (Bissell, 7/17/75, p. 14)

Bissell said that in effect he had asked Harvey to stand watch over the contact in case any action should be required and further testified that it was never required. However, as noted above, the Rosselli operation was reactivated by Harvey in April 1962 after Bissell had left the Agency.

The Inspector General's Report stated: "After Harvey took over the Castro operation, he ran it as one aspect of ZR/RIFLE." (I.G. Report, p. 40) Harvey recalled that during a discussion with Bissell of the creation of an Executive Action capability, Bissell advised him of "a then going operation" involving the names of Maheu and possibly Rosselli and Giancana, "which was a part of the Agency's effort to develop * * * a capability for executive action." Harvey said that at the time of this discussion, the operation had been "in train" for "approximately two years or perhaps 18 months." (Harvey, 7/11/75, pp. 54, 55, 61)

Although his "net impression" was that both the "exploratory project" and the "specific operation" were "fully authorized and approved," Harvey said he could not testify that "specific White House authority for this given operation was implied or stated." (Harvey, 7/11/75, p. 54) Bissell does not recall telling anyone in the White House that something had been done to bring a CIA officer together with the criminal syndicate. (Bissell, 6/11/75, pp. 19-20) Harvey did not recall any mention of the White House or any authority higher than the DDP in his November 1961 meeting with Bissell. (Harvey, 7/11/75, pp. 60-61)

Although Richard Helms was briefed and given administrative responsibility (as DDP) for Project ZR/RIFLE three months later, he did not recall that ZR/RIFLE was ever considered as part of the plot to assassinate Castro. (Helms, 6/13/75, p. 55) Asked whether the actual assassination efforts against Castro were related to ZR/RIFLE (Executive Action), Helms testified: "In my mind those lines never crossed." (Helms, 6/13/75, p. 52)

Bissell's testimony, however, leaves more ambiguity: "the contact with the syndicate which had Castro as its target * * * folded into the ZR/RIFLE project * * * and they became one." (Bissell, 6/11/75, p. 47) When asked whether the Executive Action capability "* * * for assassination" was "used against Castro," Bissell replied that it was "in the later phase." (Bissell, 6/11/75, p. 47) The instruction from Bissell to Harvey on November 15, 1961, however, preceded by approximately five months the reactivation of the CIA/underworld assassination operation against Castro.

(c) *Use of QJ/WIN in Africa*

QJ/WIN was a foreign citizen with a criminal background who had been recruited by the CIA for certain sensitive programs prior to Project ZR/RIFLE. As noted above, QJ/WIN's function during ZR/RIFLE was restricted to the "spotting" of potential assets for "multi-purpose" covert use. The Lumumba section of this report treats fully QJ/WIN's role.

Two factors may raise a question as to whether QJ/WIN was already being used in an *ad hoc* capacity to develop an assassination capability before ZR/RIFLE was formally initiated. First, there is a similarity in the cast of characters: Harvey, QJ/WIN, the recruiting officer, and Scheider were connected with the Lumumba matter and reappear in connection with the subsequent development of ZR/RIFLE. Second, Bissell informed Harvey that the development of an assassination capability had already been discussed with the recruiting officer and Scheider before Harvey's assignment to ZR/RIFLE. (Harvey, 6/25/75, p. 52; I.G. Report, pp. 37–38)

Nevertheless, there does not appear to be any firm evidence connecting QJ/WIN and the plot to assassinate Lumumba. (see pp. 43 to 48), supra)

D. TRUJILLO

1. SUMMARY

Rafael Trujillo was assassinated by a group of Dominican dissidents on May 30, 1961.

Trujillo was a brutal dictator, and both the Eisenhower and Kennedy Administrations encouraged the overthrow of his regime by Dominican dissidents. Toward that end the highest policy levels of both Administrations approved or condoned supplying arms to the dissidents. Although there is no evidence that the United States instigated any assassination activity, certain evidence tends to link United States officials to the assassination plans.

Material support, consisting of three pistols and three carbines, was supplied to various dissidents. While United States' officials knew that the dissidents intended to overthrow Trujillo, probably by assassination, there is no direct evidence that the weapons which were passed were used in the assassination. The evidence is inconclusive as to how high in the two Administrations information about the dissidents' assassination plots had been passed prior to the spring of 1961.

Beginning in March of 1961, the dissidents began asking United States officials for machine guns. By the time four M-3 machine guns were shipped to the CIA Station in the Dominican capital in April, it was well known that the dissidents wanted them for use in connection with the assassination. Thereafter, however, permission to deliver the machine guns to the dissidents was denied, and the guns were never passed. The day before the assassination a cable, personally authorized by President Kennedy, was sent to the United States' Consul General in the Dominican Republic stating that the United States Government, as a matter of general policy, could not condone political assassination, but at the same time indicating the United States continued to support the dissidents and stood ready to recognize them in the event they were successful in their endeavor to overthrow Trujillo.

2. BACKGROUND

Rafael Trujillo came to power in the Dominican Republic in 1930. For most of his tenure, the United States Government supported him and he was regarded throughout much of the Caribbean and Latin America as a protege of the United States. Trujillo's rule, always harsh and dictatorial, became more arbitrary during the 1950's. As a result, the United States' image was increasingly tarnished in the eyes of many Latin Americans.

Increasing American awareness of Trujillo's brutality and fear that it would lead to a Castro-type revolution caused United States' officials to consider various plans to hasten his abdication or downfall.

As early as February 1960, the Eisenhower Administration gave high level consideration to a program of covert aid to Dominican dissidents. (Special Group Minutes, 2/10/60) In April 1960 President Eisenhower approved a contingency plan for the Dominican Republic which provided, in part, that if the situation deteriorated still further:

> * * * the United States would immediately take political action to remove Trujillo from the Dominican Republic as soon as a suitable successor regime can be induced to take over with the assurance of U.S. political, economic, and—if necessary—military support. (Memo from Secretary of State Herter to the President, 4/14/60; Presidential approval indicated in Herter letter to Secretary of Defense Gates, 4/21/60)

Simultaneously, the United States was trying to organize hemispheric opposition to the Castro regime in Cuba. Latin American leaders, such as President Betancourt of Venezuela, pressed the United States to take affirmative action against Trujillo to dispel criticism that the U.S. opposed dictatorships of the left only. A belief that Castro's road to power was paved by the excesses of Batista led to concern that the Dominican Republic might also eventually fall victim to a Castro-style Communist regime. (Rusk, 7/10/75, pp. 8, 9)

3. INITIAL CONTACT WITH DISSIDENTS AND REQUEST FOR ARMS

During the spring of 1960, the U.S. Ambassador to the Dominican Republic, Joseph Farland, made initial contact with dissidents who sought to free their country from Trujillo's grasp. They asked for sniper rifles. Although documentary evidence indicates that a recommendation to provide these rifles was approved both within the State Department and the CIA, the rifles were never provided.

(a) *Dissident contacts*

Ambassador Farland established contact with a group of dissidents regarded as moderate, pro-United States and desirous of establishing a democratic form of government.[1] (Farland affidavit, 9/7/75, p. 1) Prior to his final departure from the Dominican Republic in May 1960, the Ambassador introduced his Deputy-Chief-of-Mission, Henry Dearborn, to the dissident leaders, indicating that Dearborn could be trusted. Then on June 16, 1960, CIA Headquarters[2] cabled a request that Dearborn become the "communications link" between the dissidents and CIA. The cable stated that Dearborn's role had the "*unofficial*" approval of [Assistant Secretary of State for Inter-American Affairs, Roy R.] Rubottom." (Emphasis in original.) (Cable, HQ to Station, 6/16/60)

Dearborn agreed. He requested, however, that the CIA confirm the arrangement with the dissidents as being that the United States would "clandestinely" assist the opposition to "develop effective force to ac-

---

[1] This loosely-organized group, with which contact was established, was referred to in cables, correspondence, and memoranda as "the dissidents" and is so referenced herein.
[2] As used herein "Headquarters" refers to Headquarters of the Central Intelligence Agency; "Department" indicates the Department of State.

complish Trujillo overthrow," but would not "undertake any overt action itself against Trujillo government while it is in full control of Dominican Republic." (Cable, Station to HQ, 6/17/60) CIA Headquarters confirmed Dearborn's understanding of the arrangement. (Cable, HQ to Station, 6/16/60)

(b) *The request for sniper rifles*

During the course of a cocktail party in the Dominican Republic, a leading dissident made a specific request to Ambassador Farland for a limited number of rifles with telescopic sights. The Ambassador promised to pass on the request. (Farland affidavit, 9/7/75, p. 1) He apparently did so after returning to Washington in May 1960. (CIA Memo for the Record, 6/7/61)

Documents indicate that consideration was given within the CIA to airdropping rifles into the Dominican Republic. At a June 21, 1960, meeting with an officer of the CIA's Western Hemisphere Division, Ambassador Farland reportedly suggested possible sites for the drops. (CIA memo, 6/21/60)

Documents also indicate that a meeting was held around the end of June 1960 between Assistant Secretary of State for Inter-American Affairs Roy R. Rubottom and Col. J. C. King, Chief of CIA's Western Hemisphere Division. Apparently King sought to learn the Assistant Secretary's view regarding "[to] what extent will the U.S. government participate in the overthrow of Trujillo." A number of questions were raised by King, among them:

> Would it provide a small number of sniper rifles or other devices for the removal of key Trujillo people from the scene?

King's handwritten notes indicates that Rubottom's response to that question was "yes." (CIA memo, 6/28/60; King affidavit, 7/29/75, pp. 1-2) [1]

On July 1, 1960, a memorandum directed to General Cabell, the Acting Director of Central Intelligence, was prepared for Colonel King's signature and, in his absence, signed by his principal deputy. (I.G. Report, p. 26) The memorandum stated that a principal leader of the anti-Trujillo opposition had asked Ambassador Farland for a limited number of arms to precipitate Trujillo's overthrow, and recognized that such arms presumably "would be used against key members of the Trujillo regime." The memorandum recommended that the arms be provided, since the fall of the Trujillo regime appeared inevitable, and therefore United States relations with the opposition should be as close as possible. "Providing the arms as requested would contribute significantly toward this end." (CIA memo, 7/1/60)

Specifically, the recommendation was to deliver to dissidents in the Dominican Republic 12 sterile [2] rifles with telescopic sights, together with 500 rounds of ammunition.

Paragraph 4 of the memorandum stated:

> Approval for delivery of these arms has been given by Assistant Secretary of State Roy Rubottom, who requests that the arms be placed in hands of the opposition at the earliest possible moment. (CIA Memo, 7/1/60)

---

[1] Neither King nor Rubottom recalls such a meeting, nor does either recall any proposal for supplying sniper rifles. (Rubottom affidavit, King affidavit, 7/29/75)
[2] "Sterile" rifles are regarded as "untraceable." (Bissell, 7/22/75, p. 69)

The Acting Chief of the Western Hemisphere Division's recommendation was concurred in by Richard Helms, as Acting DDP, and approved by General Cabell. (I.G. Report, p. 26)

The kind of arms approved, sterile rifles with telescopic sights, together with the statement that they presumably would be used against key members of the Trujillo regime clearly indicated the "targeted use" for which the weapons were intended. (Bissell, 7/22/75, p. 77)

On July 1, 1960, a cable was sent to Dearborn by CIA Headquarters informing him of the plan to airdrop 12 telescopically-sighted rifles into the Dominican Republic. The cable inquired whether the dissidents had the capability to realign the sights if thrown off by the drop. On July 14, 1960, Dearborn replied that the dissident leaders were against any further action in the Dominican Republic until after resolution by the OAS of a Venezuelan complaint then pending against Trujillo. The dissidents reportedly believed that sufficiently strong action by the OAS could bring Trujillo's downfall without further effort on their part. (Cable, Station to HQ, 7/14/60) The 12 sniper rifles were never furnished to the dissidents.

On August 26, 1960, Dearborn cabled Deputy Assistant Secretary of State Lester Mallory reporting on a meeting between a dissident leader and a Consulate political officer. The dissident leader was reported to have lost enthusiasm for an assassination attempt and was then speaking of an invasion from Venezuela. However, by September 1, 1960, dissidents were again speaking about the possible provision to them of arms. This time the request was for 200 rifles. For the next several months, consideration centered on providing 200 to 300 guns.

4. SUMMER AND FALL OF 1960

In August 1960, the United States interrupted diplomatic relations with the Dominican Republic and recalled most of its personnel. Dearborn was left as Consul General and *de facto* CIA Chief of Station.[1] Consideration was given both to providing arms and explosive devices and to the use of high level emissaries to persuade Trujillo to abdicate. By the end of the year, a broad plan of general support to anti-Trujillo forces, both within and without the country, was approved.

(a) Diplomatic development—withdrawal of United States personnel

Events occurring during the Summer of 1960 further intensified hemispheric opposition to the Trujillo regime. In June, agents of Trujillo tried to assassinate Venezuelan President Betancourt. As a result, the OAS censured the Trujillo government. At the same time, in August 1960, the United States interrupted diplomatic relations with the Dominican Republic and imposed economic sanctions.

With the interruption of diplomatic relations, the United States closed its Embassy. Most American personnel, including the CIA Chief

---

[1] Dearborn's role as communication's link and *de facto* Station Chief was, according to the evidence before the Committee, quite unusual. This open involvement, by the senior State Department representative, in clandestine activities was a subsequent concern within both the State Department and the CIA.

of Station, left the Dominican Republic. With the departure of the CIA Chief of Station, Dearborn became *de facto* CIA Chief of Station and was recognized as such by both CIA and the State Department. Although in January 1961, a new CIA Chief of Station came to the Dominican Republic, Dearborn continued to serve as a link to the dissidents.

(b) *Dearborn reports assassination may be only way to overthrow Trujillo regime*

Dearborn came to believe that no effort to overthrow the Trujillo government could be successful unless it involved Trujillo's assassination. He communicated this opinion to both the State Department and the CIA. In July 1960, he advised Assistant Secretary Rubottom that the dissidents were

> * * * in no way ready to carry on any type of revolutionary activity in the foreseeable future except the assassination of their principal enemy. (Letter, Dearborn to Rubottom, 7/14/60)

It is uncertain what portion of the information provided by Dearborn to State was passed above the Assistant Secretary level. Through August of 1960, only Assistant Secretary Rubottom, his Deputy, Lester Mallory, and his Staff Assistant, were, within the Latin American Division of the Department, aware of Dearborn's "current projects." (Letter, Staff Assistant to Dearborn, 8/15/60) [1]

By September 1960, Thomas Mann had replaced Roy Rubottom as Assistant Secretary for Inter-American Affairs, and the Staff Assistant had become a Special Assistant to Mr. Mann. While serving as Special Assistant to the Assistant Secretary, the Special Assistant reportedly spent ninety percent of his time coordinating State Department-CIA activities in Latin America. It was in this capacity that the Special Assistant maintained almost daily communication with officials of the CIA's Western Hemisphere Division. (Special Assistant, 7/9/75, p. 7) [2]

Mann solicited Dearborn's comments concerning plans under discussion for forcing Trujillo from power. Dearborn replied in a detailed letter which concluded:

> One further point which I should probably not even make. From a purely practical standpoint, it will be best for us, for the OAS, and for the Dominican Republic if the Dominicans put an end to Trujillo before he leaves this island. If he has his millions and is a free agent, he will devote his life from exile to preventing stable government in the D.R., to overturning democratic governments and establishing dictatorships in the Caribbean, and to assassinating his enemies. If I were a Dominican, which thank heaven I am not, I would favor destroying Trujillo as being the first necessary step in the salvation of my country and I would regard this, in fact, as my Christian duty. If you recall Dracula, you will remember it was necessary to drive a stake through his heart to prevent a continuation of his crimes. I believe sudden death would be more humane than the solution of the Nuncio who once told me he thought he should pray that Trujillo would have a long and lingering illness. (Letter, Dearborn to Mann, 10/27/60)

---

[1] Dearborn's candid reporting to State during the summer of 1960 raised concern within the Department and he was advised that certain specific information should more appropriately come through "the other channel." (presumably, CIA communications) Dearborn was advised that his cables to State were distributed to at least 19 different recipient offices. (Id.)

[2] The Special Assistant to the Assistant for Inter-American Affairs is currently serving, in another capacity, in the State Department. He is referred to hereinafter as the "Special Assistant."

(c) *Efforts to convince Trujillo to abdicate*

Throughout the fall of 1960, efforts were made on both the diplomatic and economic fronts aimed at pressuring Trujillo into relinquishing control, and ideally, leaving the Dominican Republic. The use of high level emissaries, both from within and without the ranks of government, was considered. (Special Group Minutes, 9/8/60; letter, Mann to Dearborn, 10/10/60) None of the efforts proved successful, and at the end of 1960, Trujillo was still in absolute control.

(d) *CIA plans of October 1960*

A CIA internal memorandum dated October 3, 1960 entitled "Plans of the Dominican Internal Opposition and Dominican Desk for Overthrow of the Trujillo Government" set forth plans which "have been developed on a tentative basis which appear feasible and which might be carried out * * * covertly by CIA with a minimal risk of exposure." These plans provided, in part, for the following:

> a. Delivery of approximately 300 rifles and pistols, together with ammunition and a supply of grenades, to secure cache on the South shore of the island, about 14 miles East of Ciudad Trujillo.
>
> b. Delivery to the same cache described above, of an electronic detonating device with remote control features, which could be planted by the dissidents in such manner as to *eliminate certain key Trujillo henchmen.* This might necessitate training and introducing into the country by illegal entry, a trained technican to set the bomb and detonator. (Emphasis added.) (CIA Memo, 10/3/60)

(e) *December 1960 Special Group plan of covert actions*

On December 29, 1960, the Special Group considered and approved a broad plan of covert support to anti-Trujillo forces. The plan, presented by Bissell, envisioned support to both Dominican exile groups and internal dissidents. The exile groups were to be furnished money to organize and undertake anti-Trujillo propaganda efforts and to refurbish a yacht for use in paramilitary activities. Bissell emphasized to the Special Group that "the proposed actions would not, of themselves, bring about the desired result in the near future, lacking some decisive stroke against Trujillo himself." (Special Group Minutes, 12/29/60)

5. JANUARY 12, 1961 SPECIAL GROUP APPROVAL OF "LIMITED SUPPLIES OF SMALL ARMS AND OTHER MATERIAL"

On January 12, 1961, with all members present,[1] the Special Group met and, according to its Minutes, took the following action with respect to the Dominican Republic:

> Mr. Merchant explained the feeling of the Department of State that limited supplies of small arms and other material should be made available for dissidents inside the Dominican Republic. Mr. Parrott said that we believe this can be managed securely by CIA, and that the plan would call for final transportation into the country being provided by the dissidents themselves. The Group approved the project. (Special Group Minutes, 1/12/61)

---

[1] The members of the Special Group were at the time: Livingston Merchant, Under Secretary of State for Political Affairs; Gordon Gray, Advisor to the President for National Security Affairs; John N. Irwin, Deputy Secretary of Defense; and Allen Dulles, Director of the Central Intelligence Agency.

(a) *Memorandum underlying the Special Group action*

On January 12, 1961, Thomas Mann sent a memorandum to Under Secretary Livingston Merchant. The memorandum, sent through Joseph Scott, Merchant's Special Assistant, reported the disillusionment of Dominican dissidents with the United States for its failure to furnish them with any tangible or concrete assistance. Further, it reported:

> Opposition elements have consistently asked us to supply them with "hardware" of various types. This has included quantities of conventional arms and also, rather persistently, they have asked for some of the more exotic items and devices which they associate with revolutionary effort. (Memo, Mann to Merchant, 1/12/61)

Mann suggested for Merchant's consideration and, if he approved, for discussion by the Special Group, the provision of token quantities of selected items desired by the dissidents. Mann specifically mentioned small explosive devices which would place some "sabotage potential" in the hands of dissident elements, but stated that there "would be no thought of toppling the GODR [Government of Dominican Republic] by any such minor measure." (Memo, Mann to Merchant, 1/12/61) This memorandum was drafted on January 11 by Mann's Special Assistant for CIA liaison.

A covering memorandum from Scott to Merchant, forwarding Mann's memo, was apparently taken by Merchant to the Special Group meeting. Merchant's handwritten notations indicate that the Special Group "agreed in terms of Tom Mann's memo" and that the Secretary of State was informed of that decision by late afternoon on January 12, 1961. (Memo, Scott to Merchant, 1/12/61)

There is no evidence that any member of the Special Group, other than Allen Dulles, knew that the dissidents had clearly and repeatedly expressed a desire for arms and explosives to be used by them in assassination efforts.[1] While it is, of course, possible that such information was passed orally to some or all of the members of the Special Group, and perhaps even discussed by them on January 12, 1961, there is no documentary evidence of which the Committee is aware which would establish this to be the case.

On January 19, 1961, the last day of the Eisenhower Administration, Consul General Dearborn was advised that approval had been given for supplying arms and other material to the Dominican dissidents. (Cable, HQ. to Station, 1/19/61) Shortly thereafter, Dearborn informed the Special Assistant that the dissidents were "delighted" about the decision to deliver "exotic equipment." (Cable, Dearborn to Special Assistant, 1/31/61)

6. JANUARY 20, 1961–APRIL 17, 1961 (THE KENNEDY ADMINISTRATION THROUGH THE BAY OF PIGS)

On January 20, 1961, the Kennedy Administration took office. Three of the four members of the Special Group (all except Allen Dulles) retired.

---

[1] Various CIA cables, including those dealing with the sniper rifles, indicate that copies were sent to the DCI, Allen Dulles.

Prior to the failure of the Bay of Pigs invasion on April 17, 1961, a number of significant events occurred. These events included meetings with Dominican dissidents in which specific assassination plans were discussed, requests by dissidents for explosive devices, the passage by United States officials of pistols and carbines to dissidents inside the Dominican Republic and the pouching to the Dominican Republic of machine guns which had been requested by the dissidents for use in connection with an assassination attempt.[1] These events are discussed below under subheading (a).

Evidence reflecting the degree of knowledge of these events possessed by senior American officials is treated thereafter. As used herein, "senior American officials" means individuals in the White House or serving as members of the Special Group.

(a) *Specific events indirectly linking United States to dissidents' assassination plans*

(i) *Assassination Discussions and Requests for Explosives*

At meetings held with dissident leaders in New York City on February 10 and 15, 1961, CIA officials were told repeatedly by dissident leaders that "the key to the success of the plot [to overthrow the Trujillo regime] would be the assassination of Trujillo." (CIA Memo for the Record, 2/13/61) Among the requests made of the CIA by dissident leaders were the following:

  (a) Ex-FBI agents who would plan and execute the death of Trujillo.
  (b) Cameras and other items that could be used to fire projectiles.
  (c) A slow-working chemical that could be rubbed on the palm of one's hand and transferred to Trujillo in a handshake, causing delayed lethal results.
  (d) Silencers for rifles that could kill from a distance of several miles. (*Id.*)

Other methods of assassinating Trujillo proposed by dissidents at the February 10 or February 15 meetings included poisoning Trujillo's food or medicines, ambushing his automobile, and attacking him with firearms and grenades. (CIA Memos for the Record, 2/13/61, 2/16/61)[2]

The dissidents' "latest plot," as described in the February CIA memoranda, was said to involve the planting of a powerful bomb, which could be detonated from a nearby electric device, along the route of Trujillo's evening walk. (*Id.*)

On March 13, 1961, a dissident in the Dominican Republic asked for fragmentation grenades "for use during the next week or so." This request was communicated to CIA Headquarters on March 14, 1961, and was followed the next day by an additional request for 50 fragmentation grenades, 5 rapid-fire weapons, and 10 64-mm. anti-

---

[1] As indicated in the post-Bay of Pigs section, *infra*, permission to pass these machine guns was denied and the guns were never passed.
[2] There is no record that the CIA responded affirmatively to any of these requests and the CIA officer who drafted the February 13 memorandum stated the view that some of the questions raised by the dissidents did not require an answer.

tank rockets. This further request was also passed on to CIA Headquarters. (Cable, Station to HQ, 3/15/61) There is no evidence that any of these arms were supplied to the dissidents.

The documentary record makes clear that the Special Assistant at the State Department was also advised of related developments in a March 16, 1961, "picnic" letter from Dearborn who complained that his spirits were in the doldrums because:

> * * * the members of our club are now prepared in their minds to have a picnic but do not have the ingredients for the salad. Lately they have developed a plan for the picnic, which just might work if they could find the proper food. They have asked us for a few sandwiches, hardly more, and we are not prepared to make them available. Last week we were asked to furnish three or four pineapples for a party in the near future, but I could remember nothing in my instructions that would have allowed me to contribute this ingredient. Don't think I wasn't tempted. I have rather specific guidelines to the effect that salad ingredients will be delivered outside the picnic grounds and will be brought to the area by another club. (Letter, Dearborn to Special Assistant, 3/16/16)

After reviewing his "picnic" letter, together with the requests in the March 14 and 15 cables discussed above, Dearborn concluded during his testimony before the Committee that the "pineapples" were probably the requested fragmentation grenades and the restriction on delivering salad ingredients outside of the picnic grounds was, almost certainly, meant to refer to the requirement of the January 12 Special Group decision that arms be delivered outside the Dominican Republic. (Dearborn, 7/29/75, pp. 25–27)

(ii) The Passage of Pistols

(1) *Pouching to the Dominican Republic*

In a March 15, 1961 cable, a Station officer reported that Dearborn had asked for three .38 caliber pistols for issue to several dissidents. In reply, Headquarters cabled: "Regret no authorization exists to suspend pouch regulations against shipment of arms," and indicated that their reply had been coordinated with State. (Cable, HQ to Station, 3/17/61) The Station officer then asked Headquarters to seek the necessary authorization and noted that at his last two posts he had received pistols via the pouch for "worthy purposes" and, therefore, he knew it could be done. (Cable, Station to HQ, 3/21/61) Two days later, Headquarters cabled that the pistols and ammunition were being pouched. However, the Station was instructed *not* to advise Dearborn. (Cable, HQ to Station, 3/24/61).[1]

(2) *Reason for the CIA instruction not to tell Dearborn*

A Station officer testified that he believed the "don't tell Dearborn the pistol is being pouched" language simply meant that the sending of firearms through the diplomatic pouch was not something to be unnecessarily discussed. (Didier, 7/8/75, pp. 78, 79) Dearborn said he never doubted the pouch was used, since he knew the Station had no other means of receiving weapons. (Dearborn, 7/20/75, p. 33)

---

[1] The Inspector General's Report, issued in connection with a review of these events, concludes that:

"There is no indication in the EM/DEED operational files that the pistols were actually pouched. The request for pistols appears to have been overtaken by a subsequent request for submachine guns." (I.G. Report, p. 60)

This conclusion is difficult to understand in light of the March 24, 1961, Headquarters to Station cable, which provides:

"Pouching revolvers and ammo requested TRUJ 0462 (in 20040) on 28 March. Do not advise (name Dearborn deleted) this material being pouched. Explanation follows."

(3) *Were the pistols related to assassination?*

Dearborn testified that he had asked for a single pistol for purposes completely unrelated to any assassination activity. (Dearborn, 7/29/75, pp. 29–31) He said he had been approached by a Dominican contact who lived in a remote area and who was concerned for the safety of his family in the event of political reprisals. Dearborn testified that he had believed the man's fears were well-founded and had promised to seek a pistol.[1]

Although there is no direct evidence linking any of these pistols to the assassination of Trujillo, a June 7, 1961, CIA memorandum, unsigned and with no attribution as to source, states that two of the three pistols were passed by a Station officer to a United States citizen who was in direct contact with the action element of the dissident group. It should also be noted that the assassination was apparently conducted with almost complete reliance upon hand weapons. Whether one or more of these .38 caliber Smith & Wesson pistols eventually came into the hands of the assassins and, if so, whether they were used in connection with the assassination, remain open questions.

Both Dearborn and the Station officer testified that they regarded the pistols as weapons for self-defense purposes and that they never considered them to be connected, in any way, with the then-current assassination plans. (Dearborn 7/29/75, p. 70; Didier, 7/8/75, pp. 38, 73) However, none of the Headquarters cables inquired as to the purpose for which the handguns were sought and the Station's cable stated only that Dearborn wanted them for passage to dissidents. (Cable, Station to HQ, 3/15/61) Indeed, the March 24, 1961, cable advising that the pistols were being pouched was sent in response to a request by the dissidents for machine guns to be used in an assassination effort. As with the carbines discussed below, it appears that little, if any, concern was expressed within the Agency over passing these weapons to would-be assassins.

(iii) *Passing of the Carbines*

(1) *Request by the Station and by Dearborn and approval by CIA*

In a March 26, 1961, cable to CIA Headquarters, the Station asked for permission to pass to the dissidents three 30 caliber M1 carbines. The guns had been left behind in the Consulate by Navy personnel after the United States interrupted formal diplomatic relations in August 1960. Dearborn testified that he knew of and concurred in the proposal to supply the carbines to the dissidents. (Dearborn, 7/29/75. pp. 42, 43) On March 31, 1961, CIA Headquarters cabled approval of the request to pass the carbines. (Cable, HQ to Station, 3/31/61)

(2) *Were the carbines related to assassination?*

The carbines were passed to the action group contact on April 7, 1961. (Cable, HQ to Station. 4/8/61) Eventually, they found their way into the hands of one of the assassins. Antonio de la Maza. (Cable, Station to HQ, 4/26/61; I.G. Reports, pp. 46, 49) Both Dearborn

---

[1] Dearborn is clear in his recollection that he asked the station officer to request only one pistol. (Dearborn, 7/29/75, pp. 30, 31) The station officer on the other hand, testified that if his cables requested three pistols for Dearborn then Dearborn must have asked for three pistols. (Didier 7/8/75, p. 72)

The pistols were, however, apparently sent in one package. (Cables, HQ to Station, 3/21/61, 3/24/61) and Dearborn testified that, what he believed to be the one gun, came "wrapped up" and that he passed it. (Dearborn, 7/29/75, p. 30)

and a Station officer testified that the carbines were at all times viewed as strictly a token show of support, indicating United States support of the dissidents' efforts to overthrow Trujillo. (Dearborn, 7/29/75, pp. 46–48; Didier, 7/8/75, p. 39)

(3) *Failure to Disclose to State Department Officials in Washington*

There is no indication that the request or the passage of the carbines was disclosed to State Department officials in Washington until several weeks after the passage. In fact, on April 5, Headquarters requested its Station to ask Dearborn not to comment in correspondence with State that the carbines and ammunition were being passed to the dissidents. This cable was sent while a Station officer was in Washington, and it indicated that upon his return to the Dominican Republic, he would explain the request. The Station replied that Dearborn had not commented on the carbines and ammunition in his correspondence with State and he realized the necessity not to do so. (Cable, Station to HQ, 4/6/61)

Dearborn testified, however, that he believed, at the time of his April 6 cable, that someone in the State Department had been consulted in advance and had approved the passage of the carbines. (Dearborn, 7/29/75, p. 44)

(*iv*) *Requests for and Pouching of the Machine Guns*

(1) *Requests for Machine Guns*

The Station suggested that Headquarters consider pouching an M3 machine gun on February 10, 1961. (Didier, 7/8/75, pp. 63, 64; cable, Station to HQ, 3/15/61) The request was raised again in March but no action was taken. On March 20, 1961, the Station cabled a dissident request for five M3 or comparable machine guns specifying their wish that the arms be sent via the diplomatic pouch or similar means. The dissidents were said to feel that delivery by air drop or transfer at sea would overly-tax their resources. (Cable, Station to HQ, 3/20/61)

The machine guns sought by the dissidents were clearly identified, in the Station cable, as being sought for use in connection with an attempt to assassinate Trujillo. This plan was to kill Trujillo in the apartment of his mistress and, according to the Station cable:

> To do they need five M3 or comparable machine guns, and 1500 rounds ammo for personal defense in event fire fight. Will use quiet weapons for basic job. (*Id.*)

In essence, CIA's response was that the timing for an assassination was wrong. The Station was told that precipitous or uncoordinated action could lead to the emergence of a leftist, Castro-type regime and the "mere disposal of Trujillo may create more problems than solutions." It was Headquarters' position that:

> * * * we should attempt to avoid precipitous action by the internal dissidents until opposition group and HQS are better prepared to support [assassination][1] effect a change in the regime, and cope with the aftermath. (Cable, HQ, to Station, 3/24/61)

The cable also stated that Headquarters was prepared to deliver machine guns and ammunition to the dissidents when they developed

---
[1] Word supplied by CIA previously sanitized cable.

a capability to receive them, but that security considerations precluded use of United States facilities as a carrier.[1] Soon thereafter, on April 6, 1961, while a station officer was in Washington for consultation with Headquarters, he reported on events in the Dominican Republic and:

> * * * especially on the insistence of the EMOTH [dissident] leaders that they be provided with a limited number of small arms for their own protection (specifically, five M3 .45 SMG's) (CIA Memo for the Record, 4/11/61)

(2) *Pouching of Machine Guns Approved by Bissell*

On April 7, 1961 a Pouch Restriction Waiver Request and Certification was submitted seeking permission to pouch "four M3 machine guns and 240 rounds of ammunition on a priority basis for issuance to a small action group to be used for self protection." (Pouch Restriction Waiver Request, 4/7/61)

The request, submitted on behalf of the Chief, Western Hemisphere Division, further provided:

> A determination has been made that the issuance of this equipment to the action group is desirable if for no other reason than to assure this important group's continued cooperation with and confidence in this Agency's determination to live up to its earlier commitments to the group. These commitments took the form of advising the group in January 1961 that we would provide limited arms and assistance to them provided they develop the capability to receive it. Operational circumstances have prevented this group from developing the assets capable of receiving the above equipment through normal clandestine channels such as air drops or sea infiltration. (*Id.*)

The Waiver Request was approved by Richard Bissell, as DDP, on April 10, 1961. (*Id.*)

Walter Elder, Assistant to the Director, issued a memorandum, also on April 10, which stated:

> Mr. Dulles wants no action on drops of leaflets or arms in the Dominican Republic taken without his approval. (Elder Memo, 4/10/61 [2])

The Elder memorandum suggests that Dulles did not then know that an air drop of arms was regarded as unfeasible and that consequently pouching of the arms had been approved.

The machine guns were pouched to the Dominican Republic and were received by the Station on April 19, 1961.[3] (I.G. Report, p. 42; Cable, Station to HQ, 4/19/61)

(b) *Knowledge of senior American officials (pre-Bay of Pigs)*

On February 14, 1961, prior to the passage of weapons, but a month after the generalized approval of the passage of arms by the prior Administration, a meeting of the Special Group was held with Messrs. McNamara, Gilpatric, Bowles, Bundy, Dulles, Bissell and General Cabell in attendance.

The minutes state that:

---

[1] This same cable of March 24, 1961, is the one which advised that the revolvers and ammunition were being pouched.
[2] Elder testified that this note, sent the weekend before the Bay of Pigs invasion of Cuba, was intended to make sure that there were "no unusual planes shot down or any unnecessary noise in the Dominican Republic" prior to the Cuba invasion. (Elder, 8/13/75, p. 51)
[3] Permission to pass the machine guns was never obtained and the guns never passed into the hands of the dissidents.

Mr. Dulles, assisted by Mr. Bissell, then summarized for the benefit of the new members of the Special Group the specific actions taken by the predecessor group during the past year, and also a list of significant projects which antedate the beginning of 1960 and which it is planned to continue. (Special Group Minutes, 2/14/61)

In the course of the discussion, the following point, among others, was made:

Dominican Republic—Mr. Bundy asked that a memorandum be prepared for higher authority on the subject of what plans can be made for a successor government to Trujillo. (*Id.*)

The request attributed to Bundy suggests that the Dominican Republic had been one of the matters on which Dulles and Bissell briefed the new members.

What is unclear from the February 14 minutes (just as it is unclear from the January 12 minutes) is the degree to which the Special Group was informed concerning the means by which the dissidents planned to accomplish the overthrow of the Trujillo regime. Specifically, it is not known if the new members of the Special Group were told that the dissident group had expressed the desire to assassinate Trujillo. Nor is it known if the Special Group was advised that the State Department representative in the Dominican Republic had made the assessment that the Dominican government could not be overthrown without the assassination of Trujillo.

Bissell testified that he had no clear recollection of the details of the February 14 briefing and he was unable to say whether or not the method of overthrow to be attempted by the dissidents was discussed. (Bissell, 7/22/75, pp. 101, 102) Robert McNamara, one of the new members of the Special Group in attendance for the briefing, had no recollection as to the specificity in which the Dominican Republic was discussed at the February 14 meeting. He did not recall any mention by either Dulles or Bissell of dissident plans to assassinate Trujillo. (McNamara affidavit, 7/11/75)

February memoranda

The Secretary of State sent the President a memorandum on February 15, 1961, in response to a request concerning progress to assure an orderly takeover "should Trujillo fall." The memorandum advised that:

Our representatives in the Dominican Republic have, at considerable risk to those involved, established contacts with numerous leaders of the underground opposition * * * [and] * * * the CIA has recently been authorized to arrange for delivery to them outside the Dominican Republic of small arms and sabotage equipment. (Memo, Rusk to President Kennedy, 5/15/61)

This reference to recent authorization for delivery of arms indicates that Secretary Rusk had received some briefing concerning events in the Dominican Republic and the January 1961 Special Group decision to provide arms to anti-Trujillo elements. Assistant Secretary for Inter-American Affairs, Thomas Mann; Deputy Assistant Secretary William Coerr; and the Special Assistant continued in their respective positions throughout the transition period. The Committee has been furnished no documents indicating that Secretary Rusk or Under Secretary Bowles were specifically advised as to the intentions of the Dominican dissidents to kill Trujillo; intentions of which the Bureau of Inter-American Affairs certainly had knowledge. Indeed, Secretary Rusk testified that he was not personally so advised. (Rusk, 7/10/75, pp. 41, 42)

On February 17, 1961, Richard Bissell sent a briefing paper on the Dominican Republic to McGeorge Bundy, President Kennedy's National Security Advisor. The paper, requested by Bundy for "higher authority," made note of the outstanding Special Group approval for the provision of arms and equipment to Dominican dissidents and stated that the dissidents had been informed that the United States was prepared to provide such arms and equipment as soon as they developed the capability to receive them.

The briefing paper also indicated that dissident leaders had informed CIA of "their plan of action which they felt could be implemented if they were provided with arms for 300 men, explosives, and remote control detonation devices." Various witnesses have testified, however, that supplying arms for 300 men would, standing alone, indicate a "non-targeted" use for the arms (i.e., a paramilitary or revolutionary implementation as opposed to a specifically targeted assassination use). (Bissell, 7/29/75, p. 80)

Concerning the briefing paper, Bissell testified that:

* * * it is perfectly clear that I was aware at the time of the memorandum to Mr. Bundy that these dissident groups were, and had for a long time, been hoping they could accomplish the assassination of Trujillo. As a matter of fact, the request, since some seven or eight months earlier, was a perfectly clear indication of that, so that fact was not new knowledge. (Bissell, 7/22/75, p. 102)

When asked why the memorandum did not include the fact that the dissidents intended the assassination of Trujillo, Bissell replied:

I cannot tell you, Mr. Chairman. I do not remember what considerations moved me. I don't know whether it was because this was common knowledge and it seemed to me unnecessary to include it, or as you are implying, there was an element of concealment here. I would be very surprised if it were the latter, in this case. (Bissell, 7/22/75, p. 101)

In response to questions concerning the lack of information in the February 17, 1961 briefing paper concerning the uses to which the requested arms might likely be put by the dissidents, Bissell stated:

* * * I would say that the Agency's failure, if there be a failure here was [not] to state in writing that the plans of the dissidents would include assassination attempts. (Bissell, 7/22/75, p. 99)

Bissell's briefing paper for Bundy concluded with the assessment that a violent clash might soon occur between Trujillo and the internal opposition, "which will end either with the liquidation of Trujillo and his cohorts or with a complete roll up of the internal opposition." In this regard, the fear was expressed that existing schedules for the delivery of weapons to the internal opposition might not be sufficiently timely, and it was therefore recommended that consideration be given to caching the requested arms and other materials. (Memo, Bissell to Bundy, 2/17/61)

Thus, by the middle of February 1961, the senior members of the new Administration (and in view of the "for higher authority" nature of Bundy's request, presumably President Kennedy himself) were aware of the outstanding Special Group approval for the passage of arms and other materials to opposition elements within the Dominican Republic. There was no modification or recision of the "inherited" Special Group approval and it would seem fair, therefore, to regard the approval as having been at least acquiesced in by the new Administration.

During March and early April 1961, operational levels within both the CIA and the State Department learned of increasingly detailed plans by the dissidents to assassinate Trujillo. There is no evidence that this information was passed to the White House or to any member of the Special Group, except Allen Dulles.[1] Similarly, there is no evidence that the passage of the pistols or the carbines or the pouching of the machine guns to the Dominican Republic was disclosed to anyone outside of the CIA during this period.[2]

7. APRIL 17, 1961–MAY 31, 1961 (BAY OF PIGS THROUGH TRUJILLO ASSASSINATION)

Following the failure of the Bay of Pigs invasion, attempts were made by State and CIA representatives in the Dominican Republic to dissuade the dissidents from a precipitous assassination attempt. These efforts to halt the assassination of Trujillo were the result of instructions from CIA Headquarters and were prompted by concern over filling the power vacuum which would result from Trujillo's death.

The machine guns arrived in the Dominican Republic but permission to pass them to the dissidents was never given and the guns never left the Consulate.

Dearborn returned to Washington for consultation and a contingency plan for the Dominican Republic was drafted.

The day before Trujillo's assassination, Dearborn received a cable of instructions and guidance from President Kennedy. The cable advised that the United States must not run the risk of association with political assassination, since the United States, as a matter of general policy, could not condone assassination. The cable further advised Dearborn to continue to hold open offers of material assistance to the dissidents and to advise them of United States support for them if they were successful in overthrowing the Trujillo government. The cable also reconfirmed the decision not to pass the machine guns.

(a) Decision not to pass the machine guns and unsuccessful United States attempt to stop assassination effort

By April 17, 1961, the Bay of Pigs invasion had failed. As a result, there developed a general realization that precipitous action should be avoided in the Dominican Republic until Washington was able to give further consideration to the consequences of a Trujillo overthrow and the power vacuum which would be created. (Bissell, 6/11/75, p. 113) A cable from Headquarters to the Station, on April 17, 1961, advised that it was most important that the machine guns not be passed without additional Headquarters approval.

---

[1] Copies of CIA cables, including the March 20, 1961 cable describing the plan to assassinate Trujillo in the apartment of his mistress, were apparently sent to the office of the Director of Central Intelligence.

[2] Although a copy of the CIA cable advising that the pistols were being pouched was sent to the Director's office, Dulles apparently did not receive copies of the cables approving passage of the carbines or pouching of the machine guns.

The machine guns arrived in the Dominican Republic on April 19, 1961, and Headquarters was so advised. The earlier admonition that the machine guns should be held in Station custody until further notice was repeated in a second cable from Headquarters, sent April 20, 1961. This decision was said to have been "based on judgment that filling a vacuum created by assassination now bigger question than ever view unsettled conditions in Caribbean area." (Cable, HQ to Station, 4/20/61)

The dissidents continued to press for the release of the machine guns and their requests were passed on to Headquarters in cables from Dearborn and from the Station. (Cables, Station to HQ, 4/25/61) On April 25, 1961, the Station advised Headquarters that an American living in the Dominican Republic and acting as a cut-out to the dissidents had informed the Station that Antonio de la Maza was going to attempt the assassination between April 29 and May 2. The Station also reported that this attempt would use the three carbines passed from the American Consulate, together with whatever else was available. (*Id.*)

In response to the April 25 cable, Headquarters restated that there was no approval to pass any additional arms to the dissidents and requested the Station to advise the dissidents that the United States was simply not prepared at that time to cope with the aftermath of the assassination. (See C/S comments. Cable, Station to HQ, 4/27/61) The following day, April 27, 1961, the Station replied that, based upon further discussions with the dissidents, "We doubt statement U.S. government not now prepared to cope with aftermath will dissuade them from attempt." (Cable, Station to HQ, 4/27/61)

Dearborn recalls receiving instructions that an effort be made to turn off the assassination attempt and testified that efforts to carry out the instructions were unsuccessful. In effect, the dissidents informed him that this was their affair and it could not be turned off to suit the convenience of the United States government. (Dearborn, 7/29/75, p. 52)

On April 30, 1961, Dearborn advised Headquarters that the dissidents had reported to him the assassination attempt was going to take place during the first week of May. The action group was reported to have in its possession three carbines, four to six 12-guage shotguns and other small arms. Although they reportedly still wanted the machine guns, Dearborn advised Headquarters that the group was going to go ahead with what they had, whether the United States wanted them to or not. (Cable, Station to HQ, 4/30/61)

Dearborn's cable set forth the argument of the action group that, since the United States had already assisted the group to some extent and was therefore implicated, the additional assistance of releasing the machine guns would not change the basic relationship. The cable concluded:

Owing to far-reaching political implications involved in release or non-release of requested items, Headquarters may wish discuss foregoing with State Department. (*Id.*)

Beginning with Dearborn's April 30 cable, there was a fairly constant stream of cables and reports predicting Trujillo's imminent assassination. Certain of these reports predicted the specific date or dates on which the assassination would be attempted, while others spoke of the attempt being made at the first propitious opportunity. In addition to cables sent directly to CIA Headquarters, the substance of these assassination forecasts was circulated throughout the intelligence community and the higher echelons of the government in the form of intelligence bulletins. These bulletins did not, however, contain references to any United States involvement in the assassination planning.

As a result of these reports, Robert Kennedy had a discussion with Allen Dulles, apparently sometime in the early part of May, and thereafter "looked into the matter." (June 1, 1961, dictated notes of Robert F. Kennedy.)[1] Robert Kennedy reportedly called the President and it was "decided at that time that we'd put a task force on the problem and try to work out some kind of alternative course of action in case this event did occur." Robert Kennedy's notes state that at the time he called the President, "He [the President] had known nothing about it [the reports of Trujillo's imminent assassination]." (*Id.*)

There is no record as to the specificity with which Allen Dulles discussed the matter of Trujillo's predicted assassination with Robert Kennedy. Dulles was, of course, fully informed at this time both as to the relationship between State Department and CIA representatives in the Dominican Republic and the dissidents planning Trujillo's removal, and, also, of the weapons which had been furnished to the dissidents and those which they were then requesting for use in connection with the assassination effort.

(b) *Further consideration of passing machine guns*

In response to Dearborn's cable, a cable was drafted at CIA Headquarters authorizing passage of the machine guns. The cable which was sent to Allen Dulles, with Bissell's recommendation for its dispatch, provided:

> Since it appears that opposition group has committed itself to action with or without additional support, coupled with fact ref. C items [the carbines] already made available to them for personal defense; station authorized pass ref. A items [the machine guns] to opposition member for their additional protection on their proposed endeavor." (Draft Cable, HQ to Station, 5/2/61)

The cable was never sent.

In his testimony before the Committee, Bissell characterized his reasoning for recommending release of the machine guns as

> * * * having made already a considerable investment in this dissident group and its plans that we might as well make the additional investment. (Bissell, 7/22/75, p. 127)

The following day, May 3, 1961, the Deputy Chief of the Western Hemisphere Division of CIA, who frequently acted as liaison with the State Department in matters concerning covert operations in the Dominican Republic, met with Adolph Berle, Chairman of the Interagency Task Force on Latin America.

A Berle memorandum of the meeting states that the CIA officer informed Berle that a local group in the Dominican Republic wished

---

[1] These notes were dictated by Robert Kennedy on June 1, 1961, after he learned of Trujillo's assassination.

to overthrow Trujillo and sought arms for that purpose. The memorandum continued:

> On cross examination it developed that the real plan was to assassinate Trujillo and they wanted guns for that purpose. [The CIA officer] wanted to know what the policy should be.
> I told him I could not care less for Trujillo and that this was the general sentiment. But we did not wish to have anything to do with any assassination plots anywhere, any time. [The CIA officer] said he felt the same way. (Berle, Memo of Conversation, 5/3/61)

Copies of Berle's memorandum were sent to Wymberly Coerr, the Acting Assistant Secretary for Inter-American Affairs, and to the Special Assistant.

Both the CIA officer and the Special Assistant, who had been in almost daily contact with each other since August of 1960, had been advised of the assassination plans of the dissident group. In fact, the CIA officer, along with Bissell, had signed off on the proposed cable of May 2, releasing the machine guns for passage.

(c) Special group meetings of May 4 and May 18, 1961

On the day following the Berle-CIA officer meeting, the Special Group met and, according to the Minutes:

> The DCI referred to recent reports of a new anti-Trujillo plot. He said we never know if one of these is going to work or not, and asked what is the status of contingency planning should the plot come off. Mr. Bundy said that this point is covered in the Cuba paper which will be discussed at a high level in the very near future. (Special Group Minutes, 5/4/61)

Once again, the cryptic reporting of Special Group Minutes makes subsequent analysis as to the scope of matters discussed speculative. It is not known to what extent and in what detail Allen Dulles referred to "recent reports" of a new anti-Trujillo plot. Certainly, the most recent report of such a plot was Dearborn's April 30 cable—disclosing an imminent assassination attempt potentially utilizing United States-supplied weapons.

On May 18, 1961, the Special Group again considered the situation in the Dominican Republic and, according to the Minutes:

> Cabell [Deputy DCI] noted that the internal dissidents were pressing for the release to them of certain small arms now in U.S. hands in the Dominican Republic. He inquired whether the feeling of the Group remained that these arms should not be passed. The members showed no inclination to take a contrary position at this time. (Special Group Minutes, 5/18/61)[1]

(d) Final requests by dissidents for machine guns

On May 16, 1961, Dearborn cabled the State Department (attention Acting Assistant Secretary Coerr) with an urgent request from the dissidents for the machine guns. The cable advised that the assassination attempt was scheduled for the night of May 16 and that, while the chances of success were 80 percent, provision of the machine guns would reduce the possibility of failure. The dissidents reportedly

---

[1] There was no meeting of the Special Group at which the Dominican Republic was discussed between May 4 and May 18. The language attributed to General Cabell as to whether the feeling of the Group remained not to pass the arms, tends to suggest that the question of passing these arms must have been raised prior to the May 18 Group meeting, perhaps at the May 4, 1961 meeting.

stressed to Dearborn that if the effort failed, due to United States refusal to supply the machine guns, the United States would be held responsible and would never be forgiven. Dearborn reported that he had informed the dissidents that, based on his recent conversations in Washington, he was reasonably certain that authorization could not be obtained for handing over machine gun. (Cable, Dearborn to Department, 5/16/61)

A return cable from the State Department to Dearborn, sent the same day, confirmed Dearborn's judgment. It instructed him to continue to take the same line until he received contrary instructions which clearly indicated they had been cleared in advance by the State Department itself. This cable from State was approved by Under Secretary Bowles. (Cable, Department to Dearborn, 5/16/61)

An officer in the CIA's Western Hemisphere Division referred to Dearborn's May 16 request in a memorandum he sent to the Special Assistant on the same date and asked to be advised as to the Department's policy concerning passage of the machine guns. The CIA officer noted that when this request was last taken to the Department, Berle made the decision that the weapons not be passed. (Memo to ARA from CIA, 5/16/61)

Devine responded to the CIA officer's memorandum on the same day, advising him that the Department's policy continued to be negative on the matter of passing the machine guns.[1] The CIA officer's attention was directed to the January 12, 1961 Special Group limitation concerning the passage of arms outside of the Dominican Republic. A copy of the Special Assistant's memorandum to the CIA officer was forwarded to the Office of the Under Secretary of State, to the attention of his personal assistant, Joseph Scott. (Memo, Special Assistant to [CIA officer], 5/16/61)

(e) Dearborn in Washington for consultation—drafting of contingency plans

At a meeting of the National Security Council on May 5, 1961, the question of United States policy toward the Dominican Republic was considered and it was:

Agreed that the Task Force on Cuba would prepare promptly both emergency and long-range plans for anti-communist intervention in the event of crises in Haiti or the Dominican Republican. Noted the President's view that the United States should not initiate the overthrow of Trujillo before we knew what government would succeed him, and that any action against Trujillo should be multilateral. (Record of Actions by National Security Council, 5/5/61) (Approved by the President, 5/16/61)[2]

Although the precise dates are uncertain, Dearborn was recalled to Washington to participate in drafting of these contingency plans and recommendations. Dearborn was in Washington at least from May 10 through May 13, 1961.

---

[1] By May 27, 1961, Dearborn was advising the State Department that the group was no longer requesting the arms and had accepted the fact that it must make do with what it had. (Cable, Dearborn to State, 5/27/61)

[2] As noted *supra*, p. 207, the President, prior to his May 16 approval of the NSC Record of Actions, had been informed by Robert Kennedy of the reports that Trujillo might be assassinated. Richard Goodwin of the White House staff had also received, prior to May 16, a CIA memorandum which disclosed that Dominican dissidents, intending to "neutralize" Trujillo, had been supplied by the U.S. with certain weapons and had sought further weapons.

While in Washington, Dearborn met with State Department personnel and with Richard Goodwin and Arthur Schlesinger of the White House staff. When testifying before the Committee, he was unable to recall the substance of his discussions with Goodwin and Schlesinger, aside from his general assumption that the current situation in the Dominican Republic was discussed. He did not recall any discussion with Goodwin or Schlesinger concerning arms, either those which had been passed to the dissidents or those which were being sought. (Dearborn, 7/29/75, pp. 58–61) Dearborn left the meeting at the White House, however, with the firm impression that Goodwin had been reviewing cable traffic between Washington and the Dominican Republic and was very familiar with events as they then stood. (Dearborn, 7/29/75, p. 62)

On May 11, 1961, Dearborn prepared a two-page draft document which set forth ways in which the U.S. could overtly aid and encourage the opposition to Trujillo. The draft noted that means of stepping up the covert program were considered in separate papers. (Dearborn draft document of May 11, 1961) This Dearborn draft of May 11, 1961, was apparently used as a basis for portions of the "Dominican Republic—Contingency Paper" discussed below.

Two documents entitled, "Program of Covert Action for the Dominican Republic" were provided to the Committee staff from State Department files. Each appears to be a draft of the covert activities paper described in Dearborn's May 11, 1961 memorandum. One draft recommended an expanded U.S. offer to deliver small explosive devices and arms. (Document indicating it was attached to "Dominican Republic—Contingency," dated 5/12/61 and bearing Nos. 306–308) The other draft is very similar except that it concludes that delivery of arms within the Dominican Republic to members of the underground is not recommended. (Document from State Department files bearing No. 310)

Attached to the second draft was a one-page document which the Special Assistant believes he wrote. It listed eight numbered points including the following:

1. The USG should not lend itself to direct political assassination.
2. U.S. moral posture can ill afford further tarnishing in the eyes of the world.
3. We would be encouraging the action, supplying the weapons, effecting the delivery, and then turning over only the final execution to (unskilled) local triggermen.
4. So far we have seen no real evidence of action capability. Should we entrust ourselves and our reputation to this extent in the absence thereof?
7. Can we afford a precedent which may convince the world that our diplomatic pounches are used to deliver assassination weapon? (Document from the State Department files bearing No. 313)

The other points raised in document No. 313 related to the likelihood that any such involvement by the United States would ultimately be revealed.

On May 15, 1961, Acting Assistant Secretary Coerr sent to Under Secretary Bowles a document entitled "Covert Action Programs Authorized With Respect to the Dominican Republic." That document outlined the existing Special Group approvals for covert assistance to Dominican dissidents and, while making no recommendation as to further policy, suggested that the Special Group review the outstanding approvals and communicate to interested agencies the status of such authorizations. (State Dept. document from Coerr to Bowles, 5/15/61)

During this period a document dated May 13, 1961, was prepared at the request of Richard Goodwin and was thereafter circulated within the State Department.[1] This document, entitled "Program of Covert Action for the Dominican Republic" reported:

> CIA has had in the direct custody of its Station in Ciudad Trujillo, a very limited supply of weapons and grenades. In response to the urgent requests from the internal opposition leaders for personal defense weapons attendant to their projected efforts to neutralize TRUJILLO, three (3) 38 Cal revolvers and three (3) carbines with accompanying ammunition have been passed by secure means to the opposition. The recipients have repeatedly requested additional armed support.

This memorandum is the first direct evidence of disclosure to anyone on the White House staff of the fact that arms had been passed to dissidents in the Dominican Republic.

The original ribbon copy of the memorandum has the above quoted material circled in pencil and the word "neutralize" is underscored. Goodwin testified before the Committee that he circled the above paragraph when first reading the memorandum because the information concerning passage of the arms was new to him and struck him as significant. (Goodwin, 7/18/75, pp. 48, 49)

Under the heading of "Possible Covert Actions Which Require Additional Authorization," the memorandum to Goodwin indicated that the CIA had a supply of four .45 caliber machine guns and a small number of grenades currently in the direct custody of the Station in Ciudad Trujillo and that a secure means of passing these weapons to the internal opposition "for their use in personal defense attendant to their projected efforts to remove Trujillo" could be developed by the Station. The memorandum made no recommendation to approve or disapprove passage of these weapons. (*Id.*)

On May 15, 1961, Bundy forwarded to Goodwin another memorandum. This one, entitled "The Current Situation in and Contingency Plans for the Dominican Republic," had been received by Bundy from the State Department. Attached was an underlying document which began:

> Recent reports indicate that the internal Dominican dissidents are becoming increasingly determined to oust Trujillo by any means, and their plans in this regard are well advanced.

The May 15 memorandum stressed that it was highly desirable for the United States to be identified with and to support the elements seeking to overthrow Trujillo. The attachment recommended that Consul General Dearborn inform the dissidents that if they succeed "at their own initiative and on their own responsibility in forming an acceptable provisional government they can be assured that any reasonable request for assistance from the U.S. will be promptly and favorably answered." (Documents from State Dept. files bearing Nos. 279–286)

---

[1] See Scott to Bowles memorandum of May 19, 1961, enclosing copy of Goodwin memorandum.

(f) Cable of May 29, 1961

A copy of Dearborn's cable of May 16, 1961, requesting urgent State Department guidance, was forwarded to Richard Goodwin. At the specific request of Goodwin, the State Department replied to Dearborn on May 17, and advised him to keep in mind the President's view, as expressed at the May 5 National Security Council Meeting, that the United States should not initiate the overthrow of Trujillo before knowing what government would succeed him. (Cable, Department to Dearborn, 5/17/61)

Dearborn responded on May 21, 1961, pointing out that for over a year State Department representatives in the Dominican Republic had been nurturing the effort to overthrow Trujillo and had assisted the dissidents in numerous ways, all of which were known to the Department. It was, Dearborn stated, "too late to consider whether United States will initiate overthrow of Trujillo." Dearborn invited further guidance from State.

In response to Dearborn's request for guidance, the State Department drafted a reply on May 24. The draft discussed a conflict between two objectives:

(1) To be so associated with removal Trujillo regime as to derive credit among DR dissidents and liberal elements throughout Latin America;
(2) To disassociate US from any obvious intervention in Dominican Republic and even more so from any political assassination which might occur.

It was said to be the Department's considered opinion that "former objective cannot, repeat not, easily override latter." (Draft Cable, Department to Dearborn, 5/24/61—not sent)

This State Department draft was forwarded to Under Secretary Bowles with the comment that Goodwin considered it "too negative" and that he would try his hand on a draft "for Bundy to present tomorrow morning." (Memo from Achilles to Bowles, 5/24/61)

A May 26, 1961, memorandum from Bowles to Bundy begins:

Following up on our discussion of the Dominican Republic at yesterday's meeting of the Special Group, I am forwarding you a draft telegram which we would like to send to Henry Dearborn, our Consul General in Ciudad Trujillo, supplementing the guidance he will be receiving on the recently approved contingency plans.

The minutes of the Special Group meeting on May 25, 1961, do not, however, reflect any discussion of the Dominican Republic. If, as Bowles' memorandum suggests, a discussion concerning the Dominican Republic did occur at the May 25 meeting, it is not known what the discussion involved or what decisions, if any, were made.

Richard Goodwin personally prepared alternate drafts to the proposed State Department cable to Dearborn. Goodwin testified that it was his intent in revising the cable to communicate to Dearborn, President Kennedy's personal belief that the United States "* * * didn't want to do anything that would involve us further, the United States further, in any effort to assassinate Trujillo." (Goodwin, 7/10/75, p. 32)

At the same time, Goodwin's draft raised the issue of further covert action and transfer of arms to the dissidents and advised Dearborn to hold out the arms as being available to the dissidents pending their ability to receive them.

It was the twofold intent of the cable as revised by Goodwin, (1) to express the desire to remain in the good graces of the dissidents who, it was believed, would constitute the new government following Trujillo's assassination, and (2) to avoid any action which might further involve the United States in the anticipated assassination. This dual purpose is clearly evident in the cable which advised:

* * * we must not run risk of U.S. association with political assassination, since U.S. *as matter of general policy cannot condone assassination.* This last principal is overriding and must prevail in doubtful situation. (Emphasis added)

*   *   *   *   *   *   *

Continue to inform dissident elements of U.S. support for their position.

According to Goodwin, the italicized material was inserted in the cable at the specific direction of President Kennedy. (Goodwin, 7/10/75, pp. 22, 23)

With respect to the four machine guns which were in the Consulate and which had been repeatedly requested by the dissidents, the cable advised Dearborn that the United States was unable to transfer these arms to the dissidents. Dearborn was instructed

Tell them that this is because of our suspicion that method of transfer may be unsafe. In actual fact, we feel that the transfer of arms would serve very little purpose and expose the United States to great danger of association with assassination attempt.

The cable, as revised by Goodwin and approved by President Kennedy, was sent to Dearborn on May 29, 1961. (Cable, Department to Dearborn, 5/29/61)

8. MAY 30, 1961 AND IMMEDIATELY THEREAFTER

(a) *Trujillo assassinated*

Late in the evening of May 30, 1961, Trujillo was ambushed and assassinated near San Cristobal, Dominican Republic. The assassination closely paralleled the plan disclosed by the action group to American representatives in the Dominican Republic and passed on to officials in Washington at both the CIA and the State Department. (Cable, Dearborn to Department, 4/30/61) The assassination was conducted by members of the action group, to whom the American carbines had been passed, and such sketchy information as is available indicates that one or more of the carbines was in the possession of the assassination group when Trujillo was killed. (I.G. Report, pp. 60–61) This evidence indicates, however, that the actual assassination was accomplished by handguns and shotguns. (I.G. Report, p. 61)

(b) *Cables to Washington*

After receiving the May 29 cable from Washington, both Consul General Dearborn and the CIA Station sent replies. According to Dearborn's testimony, he did not regard the May 29 cable as a change in U.S. policy concerning support for assassinations. (Dearborn, 7/29/75, p. 74)

He interpreted the May 29 cable as saying:

* * * we don't care if the Dominicans assassinate Trujillo, that is all right. But we don't want anything to pin this on us, because we aren't doing it, it is the Dominicans who are doing it. (Dearborn, 7/29/75, p. 104)

Dearborn testified that this accorded with what he said had always been his personal belief: that the U.S. should not be involved in an assassination and that if an assassination occurred it would be strictly a Dominican affair. (Dearborn, 7/29/75, pp. 100–101)

In contrast, the CIA Station officer did regard the cable as manifesting a change in U.S. policy, particularly on the question of supplying arms. (Didier, 7/8/75, p. 120) He believed the May 29 cable was the final word in United States policy on this matter and consequently felt that the government had retreated from its prior position, of offering material support to the dissidents, and had adopted a new position of withholding such support. His responsive cable to Headquarters stated:

> HQ aware extent to which U.S. government already associated with assassination. If we are to at least cover up tracks, CIA personnel directly involved in assassination preparation must be withdrawn. (Cable, Station to HQ, 5/30/61)

Immediately following the assassination, all CIA personnel in the Dominican Republic were removed from the country and within a few days Consul General Dearborn was back in Washington. The State Department cabled the CIA station in the Dominican Republic to destroy all records concerning contacts with dissidents and any related matters, except not to destroy the contingency plans or the May 29, 1961 cable to Dearborn. (Cable, HQ to Station, 5/31/61)

(c) Immediate post-assassination period

The United States Consulate in the Dominican Republic was quick to dispatch its early reports that Trujillo had been assassinated, and the United States communications network transmitted the report to President Kennedy in Paris. The President's Press Secretary, Pierre Salinger, made the first public announcement of the assassination, preceeding by several hours release of the news in the Dominican Republic. Secretary of State Rusk testified that when he learned of Salinger's announcement he was most concerned. Rusk said that Trujillo's son Ramfis was also in Paris and he was afraid that Ramfis, upon first learning of his father's death from the press secretary to the President of the United States, might reason that the United States had been in some way involved and he might therefore try to retaliate against President Kennedy. (Rusk, 7/10/75, pp. 32–33)

Following the assassination, there were several high-level meetings in Washington attended by President Kennedy, Vice President Johnson, Secretary of State Rusk, Secretary of Defense McNamara, Attorney General Kennedy, and many lower-level officials who had been involved in the Dominican Republic operation. The meetings considered the crisis in the Dominican Republic, caused by Trujillo's assassination, and attempted to ascertain the facts concerning the degree of United States involvement in the assassination. The passage of carbines to the dissidents was discussed at one such meeting. (State Department Memorandum for the files, 6/1/61)

On June 1, 1961, Robert Kennedy dictated four pages of personal notes reflecting his contemparaneous thoughts on the situation in the Dominican Republic. A review of these notes evidences considerable concern regarding the lack of information available in Washington as to events in the Dominican Republic.¹ The notes end with the following statement:

> The great problem now is that we don't know what to do because we don't (sic) what the situation is and this shouldn't be true, particularly when we have known that this situation was pending for some period of time.

There is no indication or suggestion contained in the record of those post-assassination meetings, or in the Robert Kennedy notes, of concern as to the propriety of the known United States involvement in the assassination. Nor is there any record that anyone took steps following Trujillo's assassination to reprimand or censure any of the American officials involved either on the scene or in Washington, or to otherwise make known any objections or displeasure as to the degree of United States involvement in the events which had transpired. Whether this was due to the press of other matters, including concern over Trujillo's successor and the future government of the Dominican Republic, or whether it represented a condonation or ratification of the known United States involvement, is uncertain.

In any event, when, some years later, the project covering American involvement in changing the government of the Dominican Republic was terminated by the Agency, the project was described in Agency documents as a "success" in that it assisted in moving the Dominican Republic from a totalitarian dictatorship to a Western-style democracy.

---

[1] Robert Kennedy's concern, immediately following the assassination, with the Agency's inability to provide first-hand information from the Dominican Republic as to popular support for the anti-Trujillo group, the extent of fighting, if any, in the country, and the likelihood of the dissidents seizing control of the country, was also discussed in a 1962 CIA report.

E. DIEM

1. SUMMARY

South Vietnamese President Ngo Dinh Diem and his brother, Ngo Dinh Nhu, were assassinated during a coup by Vietnamese generals on November 2, 1963. Evidence before the Committee indicates that the United States government offered encouragement for the coup, but neither desired nor was involved in the assassinations. Rather, Diem's assassination appears to have been a spontaneous act by Vietnamese generals, engendered by anger at Diem for refusing to resign or put himself in the custody of the leaders of the coup.

On one occasion, General Duong Van Minh ("Big Minh") outlined to a CIA officer the possible assassination of Nhu and another brother, Ngo Dinh Can, as one of three methods being considered for changing the government in the near future. Ambassador Henry Cabot Lodge and Deputy Chief of Mission William Trueheart [1] were informed of this possibility by the Saigon Chief of Station, who recommended that "we do not set ourselves irrevocably against the assassination plot, since the other two alternatives mean either a bloodbath in Saigon or a protracted struggle which would rip the Army and the country assunder." (CIA cable, Saigon Station to DCI, 10/5/63) Upon being informed, Director McCone sent two cables. The first stated "[w]e cannot be in the position of stimulating, approving, or supporting assassination," and the second directed that the recommendation be withdrawn because "we cannot be in position actively condoning such course of action and thereby engaging our responsibility therefor." (CIA cable, DCI to Saigon, 10/5/63; CIA cable, DCI to Saigon, 10/6/63)

2. THE ABORTIVE COUP OF AUGUST 1963

On May 8, 1963, South Vietnamese troops in the City of Hue fired on Buddhists celebrating Buddha's birthday (and carrying the Buddhist flag contrary to edicts proscribing the flying of religious flags) killing nine and wounding fourteen. This incident triggered a nationwide Buddhist protest and a sharp loss of popular confidence in the Diem regime.[2]

On May 18, United States Ambassador Frederick E. Nolting met with Diem and outlined steps which the United States desired him to take to redress the Buddhist grievances and recapture public confi-

---

[1] Trueheart is currently a consultant to the Select Committee.
[2] Senator Gravel Edition. *The Pentagon Papers*, The Defense Department History of United States Decision-making on Vietnam. pp. 207–208. Volume II, Beacon Press, Boston (hereinafter cited as Pentagon Papers). Former Public Affairs Officer of the U.S. Embassy in Saigon, John Mecklin, in his book, *Mission in Torment*, An Intimate Account of the U.S. Role in Vietnam. Doubleday and Company, 1965 (hereinafter cited as Mecklin), at pages 158–60 described the vulnerability of the Buddhists to Communist infiltration during this period noting that it "offered a classic opportunity for a Communist sleeper play."

dence. These steps included admitting responsibility for the Hue incident, compensating the victims, and reaffirming religious equality in the country. On June 8, Madame Nhu, the wife of Diem's brother, Nhu, publicly accused the Buddhists of being infiltrated with Communist agents. Trueheart, in the absence of Ambassador Nolting protested her remarks to Diem and threatened to disassociate the United States from any repressive measures against the Buddhists in the future. (Pentagon Papers, p. 308) Shortly thereafter, Madame Nhu commented on the self-immolation of Quang Duc and other Buddhist monks by stating that she would like to furnish mustard for the monks' barbecue. On June 12, Trueheart told Diem that Quang Duc's suicide had shocked the world and again warned that the United States would break with his government if he did not solve the Buddhist problem. (Pentagon Papers, p. 208)

Lucien Conein, a CIA officer in Saigon,[1] testified that the Buddhist uprisings were the catalyst that ultimately brought down the Diem regime. (Conein, 6/20/75, pp. 42–44) These events led the United States to apply "direct, relentless, and tablehammering pressure on Diem such as the United States has seldom before attempted with a sovereign friendly government." (Mecklin, p. 169)

By July 4, 1963, Generals Minh, Don, Kim, and Khiem had agreed on the necessity for a coup.[2]

In his final meeting on August 14 with Ambassador Nolting, Diem agreed to make a public statement offering concessions to the Buddhists. This statement took the form of an interview with the columnist, Marguerite Higgins, in which Diem asserted that his policy toward the Buddhists had always been conciliatory and asked for harmony and support of the government.

Shortly after midnight on August 21, 1963, Nhu ordered forces loyal to him to attack pagodas throughout Vietnam, arresting monks and sacking the sacred buildings. Over thirty monks were injured and 1,400 arrested. The American Embassy was taken by surprise and viewed the attacks as a shattering repudiation of Diem's promises to Nolting. (Pentagon Papers, p. 210)[3]

On August 24, 1963, the State Department sent a cable (Deptel 243) to the new Ambassador in Vietnam, Henry Cabot Lodge. The telegram was prepared by Roger Hilsman, Assistant Secretary of State for Far Eastern Affairs, and Under Secretary of State Averell Harriman, and was approved by President Kennedy. (Pentagon Papers, p. 235) Deptel 243 told Lodge to press Diem to take "prompt dramatic actions" to redress the grievances of the Buddhists:

We must at same time also tell key military leaders that US would find it impossible to continue support GVN [South Vietnamese Government] militarily and economically unless above steps are taken immediately which we recognize re-

---

[1] Conein testified that he had known the generals involved in the coup "for many years. Some of them I had known back even in World War II. Some of them were in powerful positions, and I was able to talk to them on a person to person basis, not as a government official." (Conein, 6/20/75, p. 17.)

[2] Conein's After-Action Report stated that: "The majority of the officers, including General Minh, desired President Diem to have honorable retirement from the political scene in South Vietnam and exile. As to Ngo Dinh Nhu and Ngo Dinh Can, there was never dissention. The attitude was that their deaths, along with Madame Ngo Dinh Nhu, would be welcomed." (Conein After-Action Report, 11/1/63, p. 10.)

[3] Conein testified that the raids might have been timed to occur when no American Ambassador was in Vietnam (Nolting had left a few days before and his replacement, Henry Cabot Lodge, had not yet arrived) (Conein, 6/20/75, p. 21).

quires removal of the Nhus from the scene. We wish give Diem reasonable opportunity to remove Nhus but if he remains obdurate, then we are prepared to accept the obvious implication that we can no longer support Diem. You may also tell appropriate military commanders we will give them direct support in any interim period of breakdown central government mechanism * * *. Concurrently with above, Ambassador and country teams should urgently examine all possible alternative leadership and make detailed plans as to how we might bring about Diem's replacement if this should become necessary.

A cable on August 25 reported the result of a conference among a station representative, Lodge, Trueheart, General Harkins [Commander, Military Assistance Command, Vietnam (MACV)] and General Weede (Chief of Staff, MACV). They accepted Deptel 243 "as a basic decision from Washington and would proceed to do their best to carry out instructions," (I.G. Report, C, pp. 7–8) but believed that Diem would refuse to remove his brother from his position in the government.

Early in the morning of August 26, 1963, the Voice of America in South Vietnam placed the blame on Nhu for the August 21 raids and absolved the army. The broadcast also reported speculation that the United States contemplated suspending aid to the South Vietnamese Government.[1] (Pentagon Papers, p. 212) Later on that same day, Lodge presented his credentials to Diem. CIA officer Conein and another CIA officer were told to see Generals Khiem and Khanh, respectively, and to convey to them the substance of Deptel 243, but to remind them that "We cannot be of any help during initial action of assuming power of state. Entirely their own action, win or lose." (DCI to Saigon, 8/26/63)

A message from the White House on August 29 authorized Harkins to confirm to the Vietnamese generals that the United States would support a coup if it had a good chance of succeeding, but did not involve United States armed forces. Lodge was authorized to suspend United States aid at his discretion. (Deptel 272, 8/29/63) A cable from the President to Lodge on the same day stated:

I have approved all the messages you are receiving from others today, and I emphasize that everything in these messages has my full support. We will do all that we can to help you conclude this operation successfully. Until the very moment of the go signal for the operation by the Generals, I must reserve a contingent right to change course and reverse previous instructions. While fully aware of your assessment of the consequences of such a reversal, I know from experience that failure is more destructive than an appearance of indecision. I would, of course, accept full responsibility for any such change as I must also bear the full responsibility for this operation and its consequences. (Cable, President Kennedy to Lodge 8/29/63)

In a reply cable, Lodge stated:

1. I fully understand that you have the right and responsibility to change course at any time. Of course I will always respect that right.

2. To be successful, this operation must be essentially a Vietnamese affair with a momentum of its own. Should this happen you may not be able to control it, i.e., the "go signal" may be given by the generals. (Cable, Lodge to President Kennedy, 8/30/63)

---

[1] In a cable to Harriman, Lodge complained that the VOA broadcast had "complicated our already difficult problem" by eliminating "the possibility of the generals' effort achieving surprise." Lodge further warned that "the US must not appear publicly in the matter, thus giving the 'kiss of death' to its friends" (Cable, Lodge to Harriman, 8/26/63).

A cable from Saigon dated August 31, 1963, stated:

> This particular coup is finished. Generals did not feel ready and did not have sufficient balance of forces. There is little doubt that GVN [South Vietnamese Government] aware US role and may have considerable detail. (CIA Cable, Sta. to Hq. 8/31/63)

Deptel 243 and the VOA broadcast set the tone for later relations between the United States representatives and the generals. Big Minh, who had initial doubts about the strength of American support, grew in confidence.

3. THE NOVEMBER 1963 COUP

American dissatisfaction with the Diem regime became increasingly apparent. On September 8, AID Director David Bell, in a television interview, stated that Congress might cut aid to South Vietnam if the Diem government did not change its course. (Pentagon Papers, p. 214) Lodge suggested a study to determine the most effective methods of cutting aid to topple the regime. (Pentagon Papers, p. 214) On September 12, with White House approval, Senator Church introduced a resolution in the Senate condemning the South Vietnamese Government for its repressive handling of the Buddhist problem and calling for an end to United States aid unless the oppressive measures were curtailed. (Pentagon Papers, pp. 214–215)

In mid-September 1963, two proposals for dealing with Diem were considered by the Administration. The first contemplated increasingly severe pressure to bring Diem in line with American policy; the second involved acquiescing in Diem's actions, recognizing that Diem and Nhu were inseparable, and attempting to salvage as much as possible. It was decided to adopt the first proposal, and to send Secretary of Defense McNamara and General Taylor on a fact-finding mission to Vietnam. (Pentagon Papers, p. 215)

On October 2, McNamara and Taylor returned to Washington and presented their findings to the National Security Council. Their report confirmed that the military effort was progressing favorably, but warned of the dangers inherent in the political turmoil and recommended bringing pressure against Diem. This pressure would include announcing the withdrawal of 1,000 American troops by the end of the year, ending support for the forces responsible for the pagoda raids, and continuing Lodge's policy of remaining aloof from the regime. The report recommended against a coup, but suggested that alternative leadership should be identified and cultivated. The recommendations were promptly approved by the President. (Pentagon Papers, pp. 215–216)

On October 3, Conein contacted Minh. Minh explained that a coup was being planned, and requested assurances of American support if it were successful. Minh outlined three courses of action [1] one of which was the assassination of Diem's brothers, Nhu and Can. (Conein, 6/20/75, p. 25; cable, Saigon to Director, 10/5/63) The Station cabled on October 5 that it had recommended to Lodge that "we do not set ourselves irrevocably against the assassination plot, since the other two alternatives mean either a blood bath in Saigon or a protracted struggle." (Cable, Saigon to Director, 10/5/63)

---

[1] The other courses of action were the encirclement of Saigon by various military units and direct confrontation between military units involved in the coup and loyalist units.

A cable from the CIA Director to Saigon responded that:

(W)e certainly cannot be in the position of stimulating, approving, or supporting assassination, but on the other hand, we are in no way responsible for stopping every such threat of which we might receive even partial knowledge. We certainly would not favor assassination of Diem. We believe engaging ourselves by taking position on this matter opens door too easily for probes of our position re others, re support of regime, et cetera. Consequently believe best approach is hands off. "However, we naturally interested in intelligence on any such plan." [1]

McCone testified that he met privately with the President and the Attorney General, taking the position that "our role was to assemble all information on intelligence as to what was going on and to report it to the appropriate authorities, but to not attempt to direct it." (McCone, 6/6/75, p. 62) He believed the United States should maintain a "hands off attitude." (McCone, 6/6/75, p. 62) McCone testified:

I felt that the President agreed with my position, despite the fact that he had great reservations concerning Diem and his conduct. I urged him to try to bring all the pressure we could on Diem to change his ways, to encourage more support throughout the country. My precise words to the President, and I remember them very clearly, was that "Mr. President, if I was manager of a baseball team, I had one pitcher, I'd keep him in the box whether he was a good pitcher or not." By that I was saying that, if Diem was removed we would have not one coup but we would have a succession of coups and political disorder in Vietnam and it might last several years and indeed it did. (McCone, 6/6/75, pp. 62–63)

McCone stated that he did not discuss assassination with the President, but rather "whether we should let the coup go or use our influences not to." He left the meeting believing that the President agreed with his "hands-off" recommendation. (McCone, 6/6/75, pp. 62–63) McCone cabled the Station on October 6:

McCone directs that you withdraw recommendation to ambassador (concerning assassination plan) under McCone instructions, as we cannot be in position actively condoning such course of action and thereby engaging our responsibility therefore (Cable, CIA to Saigon, 10/6/63)

In response, the CIA Station in Saigon cabled Headquarters:

Action taken as directed. In addition, since DCM Trueheart was also present when original recommendation was made, specific withdrawal of recommendation at McCone's instruction was also conveyed to Trueheart. Ambassador Lodge commented that he shares McCone's opinion. (Cable, Saigon to CIA, 10/7/63)

Conein, the CIA official who dealt directly with the Generals,[2] testified that he was first told of McCone's response to the assassination alternative by Ambassador Lodge around October 20. (Conein, 6/20/75, p. 35) Conein testified (but did not so indicate in his detailed After-Action Report) that he then told General Don that the United States opposed assassination, and that the General responded, "Alright, you don't like it, we won't talk about it anymore." (Conein, 6/20/75, p. 36)

---

[1] Colby, who was then Chief, Far Eastern Division, drafted this cable for McCone. Colby testified:
"Q. So you were on notice as of that date that the Director personally opposed any inolvement by the CIA in an assassination?
"COLBY. I certainly was." (Colby, 6/20/75, p. 57)
[2] Conein described his role as follows: "My job was to convey the orders from my Ambassador and the instructions from my Ambassador to the people who were planning the coup, to monitor those individuals who were planning the coup, to get as much information so that our government would not be caught with their pants down." (Conein, 6/20/75, pp. 38–39)

The United States increased pressure on Diem to mend his ways. On October 17, General Richard Stillwell (MACV operations chief) informed Secretary Thuan that the United States was suspending aid to the Special Forces units responsible for the pagoda raids until they were transferred to the field and placed under Joint General Staff (JGS) command. (Pentagon Papers, p. 217) On October 27, Lodge traveled to Dalat with Diem, but did not receive any commitment from Diem to comply with American requests. (Pentagon Papers, p. 219)

On October 28, Conein met with General Don, who had received assurance from Lodge that Conein spoke for the United States. Don said that he would make the plans for the coup available to the Ambassador four hours before it took place, and suggested that Lodge not change his plans to go to the United States on October 31. (I.G. Report, C, p. 37; Pentagon Papers, p. 219)

On October 30, Lodge reported to Washington that he was powerless to stop the coup, and that the matter was entirely in Vietnamese hands. General Harkins disagreed and cabled his opposition to the coup to General Taylor. (Pentagon Papers, p. 220) A cable from Bundy to Lodge dated October 30 expressed White House concern and stated that "[w]e cannot accept conclusion that we have no power to delay or discourage a coup." (Cable, Bundy to Lodge, 10/30/63) A subsequent cable on that same day from Washington instructed Lodge to intercede with the Generals to call off the coup if he did not believe it would succeed. The instructions prescribed "strict non-involvement and somewhat less strict neutrality." (Pentagon Papers, p. 220)

Late in the morning of November 1, the first units involved in the coup began to deploy around Saigon. The Embassy was given only four minutes warning before the coup began. (Cable, MACV to Joint Chiefs of Staff, 11/1/63) An aide to Don told Conein to bring all available money to the Joint General Staff headquarters. Conein brought 3 million piasters (approximately $42,000) to the headquarters, which was given to Don to procure food for his troops and to pay death benefits to those killed in the coup. (Conein, 6/20/75, p. 72)[1]

Conein was at the Joint General Staff headquarters during most of the coup. (I.G. Report, C, pp. 41–42) At 1:40 p.m., the Generals proposed that Diem resign immediately, and guaranteed him and Nhu safe departure. (Conein After-Action Report, p. 15) The palace was surrounded shortly afterwards, and at 4:30 p.m. the Generals announced the coup on the radio and demanded the resignation of Diem and Nhu. Diem called Lodge and inquired about the United States' position. Lodge responded that the United States did not yet have a view, and expressed concern for Diem's safety. (Pentagon Papers, p. 221)

According to Conein's report, Minh told Nhu that if he and Diem did not resign within five minutes, the palace would be bombed. Minh then phoned Diem. Diem refused to talk with him and Minh ordered the bombing of the palace. Troops moved in on the palace, but Diem still refused to capitulate. Minh offered Diem a second chance to sur-

---

[1] Passing money to the coup leaders was considered sometime prior to the coup. On October 29, Lodge cabled that a request for funds should be anticipated. (Cables, Lodge to State, 10/29/63, and 10/30/63) Conein received the money on October 24, and kept it in a safe in his house.

render half an hour later, telling him that if he refused he would be "blasted off of the earth." Shortly before nightfall an air assault was launched on the Presidential Guard's barracks. (Conein After-Action Report, 11/1/63, pp. 17-18)

At 6:20 on the morning of November 2, Diem called General Don at the Joint General Staff headquarters and offered to surrender if he and Nhu were given safe conduct to an airport. Shortly afterwards, Diem offered to surrender unconditionally and ordered the Presidential Guard to cease firing. According to Conein, an escort for Diem appeared in front of the palace at 8:00 a.m., but Diem and Nhu were not present. (Conein After-Action Report, 11/1/63, p. 24)

Conein testified that he left the JGS headquarters amidst preparations by the Vietnamese generals to house Diem and Nhu there under proper security. After his return home he received a telephone call and was told to come to the Embassy. At the Embassy he was told that orders had come from the President of the United States to locate Diem. He further testified that he returned to JGS headquarters about 10:30 a.m. and asked General Big Minh where Diem was. After some discussion, Conein stated, Minh said that they were behind the General Staff Headquarters, but professed that they had died by their own hand. Minh offered to show the bodies to Conein but Conein declined because he feared that doing so might damage United States interests. (Conein, 6/20/75, pp. 55-57).

The details of Diem's and Nhu's deaths are not known.[1] There is no available evidence to give any indication of direct or indirect involvement of the United States.[2]

---

[1] Conein speculated that Diem and Nhu escaped through a tunnel from the palace and fled to a Catholic Church in Cholon. He opined that an informant must have identified them and called the General Staff headquarters. (Conein After-Action Report, 1/11/63, p. 23) A CIA source stated that Diem and Nhu had left the palace the previous evening with a Chinese businessman and arrived at the church at 8:00 on the morning of November 2. Ten minutes later they were picked up by soldiers and forced into an army vehicle. (Cable, Saigon to State, 11/2/63) Minh originally told Conein that Diem and Nhu had committed suicide, but Conein doubted that Catholics would have taken their own lives in a church. (Conein, 6/20/75, p. 56) The Inspector General's Report states that on November 16, 1963, a field-grade officer of unknown reliability gave the CIA two photographs of the bodies of Diem and Nhu in which it appeared their hands were tied behind their backs. (I.G. Report, C, pp. 43-44) The source reported that Diem and Nhu had been shot and stabbed while being conveyed to the Joint General Staff headquarters.

[2] It must be noted that on October 30, 1963, Ambassador Lodge notified Washington that there might be a request by key leaders for evacuation, and suggested Saigon as a point for evacuation. (Cable, Saigon to Washington, 10/30/63) Conein was charged with obtaining the airplane. Between 6:00 and 7:00 on the morning of November 2, Minh and Don asked Conein to procure an aircraft. Conein relayed the request to a Station Officer at the Embassy who replied that it would not be possible to get an aircraft for the next twenty-four hours, since it would have to be flown from Guam. Conein testified that a Station representative told him that Diem could be flown only to a country that offered him asylum and that the plane could not land in any other country. There were no aircraft immediately available that had sufficient range to reach a potential country of asylum. (Conein, 6/20/75, p. 54)

F. SCHNEIDER

1. SUMMARY

On September 4, 1970, Dr. Salvador Allende Gossens won a plurality in Chile's Presidential election.[1] Since no candidate had received a majority of the popular vote, the Chilean constitution required that a joint session of its Congress decide between the first and second place finishers. This constitutional requirement had, in the past, been proforma. The Congress had always selected the candidate who received the highest popular vote. The date set for the Congressional joint session was October 24, 1970.

On September 15, 1970, President Richard Nixon informed CIA Director Richard Helms that an Allende regime in Chile would not be acceptable to the United States. The CIA was instructed by President Nixon to play a direct role in organizing a military coup d'etat in Chile to prevent Allende's accession to the presidency. The Agency was to take this action without coordination with the Departments of State or Defense and without informing the U.S. Ambassador in Chile. While coup possibilities in general and other means of seeking to prevent Allende's accession to power were explored by the 40 Committee throughout this period, the 40 Committee was never informed of this direct CIA role. In practice, the Agency was to report, both for informational and approval purposes, to the President's Assistant for National Security Affairs, Henry Kissinger, or his deputy.

Between October 5 and October 20, 1970, the CIA made 21 contacts with key military and Carabinero (police) officials in Chile. Those Chileans who were inclined to stage a coup were given assurances of strong support at the highest levels of the U.S. Government, both before and after a coup.

One of the major obstacles faced by all the military conspirators in Chile was the strong opposition to a coup by the Commander-in-Chief of the Army, General Rene Schneider, who insisted the constitutional process be followed. As a result of his strong constitutional stand, the removal of General Schneider became a necessary ingredient in the coup plans of all the Chilean conspirators. Unable to have General Schneider retired or reassigned, the conspirators decided to kidnap him. An unsuccessful abduction attempt was made on October 19, 1970, by a group of Chilean military officers whom the CIA was actively supporting. A second kidnap attempt was made the following day,

---

[1] Dr. Allende, a long-time Senator and founder of the Socialist Party in Chile, was a candidate of the Popular Unity Coalition. The Coalition was made up of Communists, Socialists, Social Democrats, Radicals, and dissident Christian Democrats. Allende was a self-proclaimed Marxist and was making his fourth try for the presidency. His opponents were Rodomiro Tomic Romero, candidate of the ruling Christian Democratic Party, and Jorge Alessandri Rodriquez, candidate of the right-wing National Party. Dr. Allende won 36.3% of the popular vote; Alessandri was second with 35.3% of the vote. Dr. Allende's margin of victory was 39,000 votes out of a total of 3 million votes cast in the election. The incumbent President, Eduardo Frei Montalvo, a Christian Democrat, was ineligible for reelection. Chilean law prohibits Presidents from succeeding themselves.

again unsuccessfully. In the early morning hours of October 22, 1970, machine guns and ammunition were passed by the CIA to the group that had failed on October 19. That same day General Schneider was mortally wounded in an attempted kidnap on his way to work. The attempted kidnap and the shooting were apparently conducted by conspirators other than those to whom the CIA had provided weapons earlier in the day.

A Chilean military court found that high-ranking military officers, both active and retired, conspired to bring about a military coup and to kidnap General Schneider. Several of the officers whom the CIA had contacted and encouraged in their coup conspiracy were convicted of conspiring to kidnap General Schneider. Those convicted of carrying out the actual kidnap attempt and the killing of General Schneider were associates of retired General Roberto Viaux, who had initially been thought by the CIA to be the best hope. However, later the CIA discouraged General Viaux because the Agency felt other officers, such as General Camilo Valenzuela, were not sufficiently involved. General Viaux was convicted by the military court and received a twenty-year prison sentence for being the "intellectual author" of the Schneider kidnap attempt. General Valenzuela was sentenced by the military court to three years in exile for taking part in the conspiracy to prevent Allende's assumption of office. The military court found that the two Generals had been in contact throughout the coup plotting.

The principal facts leading up to the death of General Schneider (all of which are discussed in more detail below) are as follows:

1. By the end of September 1970, it appeared that the only feasible way for the CIA to implement the Presidential order to prevent Allende from coming to power was to foment a coup d'etat.

2. All of the known coup plots developed within the Chilean military entailed the removal of General Schneider by one means or another.

3. United States officials continued to encourage and support Chilean plans for a coup after it became known that the first step would be to kidnap General Schneider.

4. Two unsuccessful kidnap attempts were made, one on October 19, the other on October 20. Following these attempts, and with knowledge of their failure, the CIA passed three submachine guns and ammunition to Chilean officers who still planned to kidnap General Schneider.

5. In a third kidnap attempt on October 22, apparently conducted by Chileans other than those to whom weapons had been supplied, General Schneider was shot and subsequently died. The guns used in the abortive kidnapping of General Schneider were, in all probability, not those supplied by the CIA to the conspirators. The Chilean military court which investigated the Schneider killing determined that Schneider had been murdered by handguns, although one machine gun was at the scene of the killing.[1]

---

[1] The Committee has not been able to determine whether or not the machine gun at the scene of the Schneider killing was one of the three supplied by the CIA.

6. While there is no question that the CIA received a direct instruction from the President on September 15th to attempt to foment a coup, the Committee received sharply conflicting testimony about whether the White House was kept informed of, and authorized, the coup efforts in Chile after October 15. On one side of the conflict is the testimony of Henry Kissinger and General Alexander Haig; on the other, that of CIA officials. Kissinger testified that the White House stood down CIA efforts to promote a military coup d'etat in Chile on October 15, 1970. After that date, Kissinger testified—and Haig agreed—that the White House neither knew of, nor specifically approved, CIA coup activities in Chile. CIA officials, on the other hand, have testified that their activities in Chile after October 15 were known to and thus authorized by the White House.[1]

This conflict in testimony, which the Committee has been unable to resolve through its hearings or the documentary record, leaves unanswered the most serious question of whether the CIA was acting pursuant to higher authority (the CIA's view) or was pursuing coup activities in Chile without sufficient communication (the Kissinger/Haig view).

2. THE PRESIDENT'S INITIAL INSTRUCTION AND BACKGROUND

(a) *September 15 White House meeting*

On September 15, 1970, President Nixon met with his Assistant for National Security Affairs, Henry Kissinger, CIA Director Richard Helms, and Attorney General John Mitchell at the White House. The topic was Chile. Handwritten notes taken by Director Helms at that meeting reflect both its tenor and the President's instructions:

One in 10 chance perhaps, but save Chile!
worth spending
not concerned risks involved
no involvement of Embassy
$10,000,000 available, more if necessary
full-time job—best men we have
game plan
make the economy scream
48 hours for plan of action.

In his testimony before the Select Committee, Director Helms recalled coming away from the meeting on September 15 with:

* * * [the] impression * * * that the President came down very hard that he wanted something done, and he didn't much care how and that he was prepared to make money available.* * * This was a pretty all-inclusive order. * * * If I

---

[1] The basic issue is whether or not the CIA *informed* the White House of its activities. In context, informing was tantamount to being authorized. No one who testified believed that the CIA was required to seek step-by-step authorization for its activities; rather the burden was on the White House to object if a line of activity being pursued by the CIA seemed unwise. Both Kissinger and Haig agreed that if the CIA had proposed a persuasive plan to them, it almost certainly would have been approved. The CIA did not believe it needed specific White House authorization to transfer weapons to the Chileans; in fact, CIA Deputy Director (Plans) Thomas Karamessines testified that he did not formally approve the transfer, but rather that in the context of the project it was clear that the Agency had the authority to transfer weapons and that it was clear to Karamessines' subordinates that he would approve their decision to do so. He believed he probably was informed before the weapons actually were sent.

ever carried a marshall's baton in my knapsack out of the Oval Office, it was that day.[1] (Helms, 7/15/75, pp. 6, 10, 11)

However, none of the CIA officers believed that assassination was within the guidelines Helms had been given.

Senator HART of Colorado. . . . did the kind of carte blanche mandate you carried, the marshall's baton that you carried out in a knapsack to stop Allende from assuming office include physical elimination?

Mr. HELMS. Well, not in my mind, because when I became Director, I had already made up my mind that we weren't going to have any of that business when I was Director, and I had made that clear to my fellows, and I think they will tell you this.

The following day, September 16, Director Helms called a meeting at the CIA to discuss the Chilean situation. At this meeting, he related to his colleagues his understanding of the President's instructions:

2. The Director told the group that President Nixon had decided that an Allende regime in Chile was unacceptable to the United States. The President asked the Agency to prevent Allende from coming to power or to unseat him. The President authorized $10,000,000 for this purpose, if needed. Further, the Agency is to carry out this mission without coordination with the Departments of State or Defense. (Memorandum/Genesis of the Project, 9/16/70)

Henry Kissinger's recollection of the September 15 meeting with President Nixon is in accord with that of Richard Helms.[2] Although Dr. Kissinger did not recall the President's instructions to be as precise as those related by Director Helms, he did testify that:

* * * the primary thrust of the September 15th meeting was to urge Helms to do whatever he could to prevent Allende from being seated. (Kissinger, 8/12/75, p. 13)

*   *   *   *   *   *   *

It is clear that President Nixon wanted him [Helms] to encourage the Chilean military to cooperate or to take the initiative in preventing Allende from taking office. (Kissinger, 8/12/75, p. 12)

Operationally, the CIA set the President's instructions into motion on September 21. On that day two cables were sent from CIA Headquarters to Santiago informing the CIA Chief of Station (COS) of his new directive:

3. Purpose of exercise is to prevent Allende assumption of power. Parliamentary legerdemain has been discarded. Military solution is objective. (Cable 236, Hq. to Sta., 9/21/70)

*   *   *   *   *   *   *

---

[1] Director Helms also testified that the September 15th meeting with President Nixon may have been triggered by the presence of Augustin Edwards, the publisher of the Santiago daily *El Mercurio*, in Washington. That morning, at the request of Donald Kendall, President of Pepsi Cola, Henry Kissinger and John Mitchell had met for breakfast with Kendall and Edwards. (Mitchell calendar) The topic of conversation was the political situation in Chile and the plight of *El Mercurio* and other anti-Allende forces. According to Mr. Helms:

I recall that prior to this meeting [with the President] the editor of *El Mercurio* had come to Washington and I had been asked to go and talk to him at one of the hotels here, this having been arranged through Don Kendall, the head of the Pepsi Cola Company. * * * I have this impression that the President called this meeting where I have my handwritten notes because of Edwards' presence in Washington and what he heard from Kendall about what Edwards was saying about conditions in Chile and what was happening there. (Helms, 7/15/75, pp. 4–5)

[2] The documents, and the officials from whom the Committee has heard testimony, are in substantial agreement about what President Nixon authorized on September 15, namely CIA involvement in promoting a military coup d'etat in Chile. There is not, however, agreement about what was communicated between the CIA and the White House—and hence what was authorized by the latter—in the week between October 15 and the shooting of General Schneider on October 22. This matter will be discussed in Part V of this report.

B. (Track Two)—This is authority granted to CIA only, to work toward a military solution to problem. As part of authority we were explicitly told that 40 Committee, State, Ambassador and Embassy were not to be told of this Track Two nor involved in any matter. (Cable 240, Hq. to Sta., 9/21/70)

(b) *Background: Tracks I and II*

United States Government concern over an Allende regime in Chile did not begin with President Nixon's September 15 instruction to the CIA.[1] For more than a year, Chile had been on the 40 Committee's agenda. At an April 15, 1969, meeting of the 303 Committee (the predecessor of the 40 Committee) the question arose as to whether anything should be done with regard to the September 1970 Presidential election in Chile. At that time, Director Helms pointed out that "an election operation will not be effective unless an early enough start is made."[2] On March 25, 1970, the 40 Committee approved a joint Embassy/CIA proposal recommending that "spoiling" operations—propaganda and other activities—be undertaken by the CIA in an effort to prevent an election victory by Allende's Popular Unity (UP) Coalition. A total of $135,000 was authorized by the 40 Committee for this anti-Allende activity. On June 18, 1970, the U.S. Ambassador to Chile, Edward Korry, submitted a two-phase proposal to the Department of State and the CIA for review. The first phase involved an increase in support to the anti-Allende campaign. The second was a contingency plan to make "a $500,000 effort in Congress to persuade certain shifts in voting on 24 October 1970." On June 27, 1970, the 40 Committee increased funding for the anti-Allende "spoiling" operation to $390,000. A decision on Ambassador Korry's second proposal was deferred pending the results of the September 4 election.

The 40 Committee met twice between the time Allende received a plurality of the popular vote on September 4 and President Nixon issued his instruction to Director Helms on September 15.[3] At both these meetings the question of U.S. involvement in a military coup

---

[1] Covert U.S. Government involvement in large-scale political action programs in Chile began with the 1964 Presidential election. As in 1970, this was, in part, in response to the perceived threat of Salvador Allende. Over $3 million was spent by the CIA in the 1964 effort. (Colby, 7/14/75, p. 5)

[2] This and other references to 40 Committee discussions and actions regarding Chile are contained in a memorandum provided to the Committee by the CIA entitled "Policy Decisions Related to Our Covert Action Involvement in the September 1970 Chilean Presidential Election," dated October 9, 1970. On August 25, 1975, we subpoenaed all White House/National Security Council documents and records relating to the effort by the United States Government to prevent Salvador Allende from assuming office. On September 4, the Committee received 46 documents from the White House relating to Chile covering the period September 5 to October 14, 1970.

[3] Following the September 4 election, the CIA's Directorate of Intelligence circulated an intelligence community assessment of the impact of an Allende government on U.S. national interests. That assessment, dated September 7, 1970, stated:

Regarding threats to U.S. interests, we conclude that:
1. The U.S. has no vital national interests within Chile. There would, however, be tangible economic losses.
2. The world military balance of power would not be significantly altered by an Allende government.
3. An Allende victory would, however, create considerable political and psychological costs:
   a. Hemispheric cohesion would be threatened by the challenge that an Allende government would pose to the OAS, and by the reactions that it would create in other countries. We do not see, however, any likely threat to the peace of the region.
   b. An Allende victory would represent a definite psychological set-back to the U.S. and a definite psychological advance for the Marxist idea. (Intelligence Memorandum/ "Situation Following the Chilean Presidential Election," CIA's Directorate of Intelligence, (9/7/70)

against Allende was raised. Kissinger stressed the importance of these meetings when he testified before the Committee:

> I think the meeting of September 15th has to be seen in the context of two previous meetings of the 40 Committee on September 8th and September 14th in which the 40 Committee was asked to look at the pros and cons and the problems and prospects of a Chilean military coup to be organized with United States assistance. (Kissinger, 8/12/75, p. 5)

According to the summary of the 40 Committee meeting on September 8, the following was discussed:

> * * * all concerned realized that previous plans for a Phase II would have to be drastically redrawn. * * * The DCI made the point, however, that congressional action against Allende was not likely to succeed and that once Allende was in office the Chilean opposition to him would disintegrate and collapse rapidly. While not advocating a specific course of action, the Director further observed that a military golpe against Allende would have very little chance of success unless undertaken soon. Both the Chairman and the Attorney General supported this view. * * * At the close of the * * * meeting the Chairman directed the Embassy to prepare a "cold-blooded assessment" of:
> (1) the pros and cons and problems and prospects involved should a Chilean military coup be organized now with U.S. assistance, and
> (2) the pros and cons and problems and prospects involved in organizing an effective future Chilean opposition to Allende. (CIA Memorandum/Policy Decision Related to Our Covert Action Involvement in the September 1970 Chilean Presidential Election, 10/9/70)

Ambassador Korry responded to the 40 Committee's request for a "cold-blooded assessment" on September 12. He stated that "We [the Embassy] believe it now clear that Chilean military will not, repeat not, move to prevent Allende's accession, barring unlikely situation of national chaos and widespread violence." The Ambassador went on to say that "Our own military people [are] unanimous in rejecting possibility of meaningful military intervention in political situation." He concluded by stating: "What we are saying in this 'cold-blooded assessment' is that opportunities for further significant USG action with the Chilean military are nonexistent." (Memorandum/Ambassador's Response to Request for Analysis of Military Option in Present Chilean Situation, 9/12/70)

The CIA's response was in the same vein. Kissinger's assistant for Latin American affairs on the NSC staff summarized the CIA's "cold-blooded assessment" in a memo to his boss: "*Military action is impossible;* the military is incapable and unwilling to seize power. We have no capability to motivate or instigate a coup." (Memorandum for Dr. Kissinger/Chile—40 Committee Meeting, Monday—September 14, 1970)

On September 14, the 40 Committee met to discuss these reports and what action was to be taken:

> Particular attention was devoted to a CIA prepared review of political and military options in the Chilean electoral situation based on the Embassy and Station's "cold-blooded assessment." The Committee focused on the so-called "Rube Goldberg" gambit which would see Alessandri elected by the Congress on October 24th, resigning thereafter to leave Frei constitutionally free to run in a second election for the presidency.
>
> Ambassador Korry was asked to go directly to President Frei to see if he would be willing to commit himself to this line of action. A contingency of $250,000 was approved for "covert support of projects which Frei or his trusted team deem important." It was further agreed that a propaganda campaign be undertaken by the Agency to focus on the damage of an Allende takeover.[1]

---

[1] The $250,000 approved by the 40 Committee was never spent. The only proposal for using it which arose—bribing Chilean congressman to vote against Allende—was quickly perceived to be unworkable.

(CIA Memo/Policy Decision Related to Our Covert Action Involvement in the September 1970 Chilean Presidential Election, 10/9/70)

Following the September 14 Forty Committee meeting and President Nixon's September 15 instruction to the CIA, U.S. Government efforts to prevent Allende from assuming office proceeded on two tracks.[1] Track I comprised all covert activities approved by the 40 Committee, including the $250,000 contingency fund to bribe Chilean congressmen as well as propaganda and economic activities. These activities were designed to induce the opponents to Allende in Chile to prevent his assumption of power, either through political or military means. Track II activities in Chile were undertaken in response to President Nixon's September 15 order and were directed towards actively promoting and encouraging the Chilean military to move against Allende. In his testimony before the Committee, Kissinger stressed the links between Tracks I and II:

> * * * There was work by all of the agencies to try to prevent Allende from being seated, and there was work by all of the agencies on the so-called Track I to encourage the military to move against Allende * * * the difference between the September 15th meeting and what was being done in general within the government was that President Nixon was encouraging a more direct role for the CIA in actually organizing such a coup. (Kissinger, 8/12/75, p. 13)

Tracks I and II did, in fact, move together in the month after September 15. The authorization to Ambassador Korry, who was formally excluded from Track II, to encourage a military coup became broader and broader. In the 40 Committee meeting on September 14, he and other "appropriate members of the Embassy Mission" were authorized to intensify their contacts with Chilean military officers to assess their willingness to support the "Frei gambit"—a voluntary turn-over of power to the military by Frei, who would then have been eligible to run for President in a new election. (Memorandum/Policy Decisions Related to Our Covert Action Involvement in the September 1970 Chilean Presidential Election, 10/9/70)

In a situation report to Dr. Kissinger and Assistant Secretary Charles Meyer on September 21, Ambassador Korry indicated that in order to make the Frei gambit work, "if necessary, General Schneider would have to be neutralized, by displacement if necessary."[2]

---

[1] The terms Track I and Track II were known only to CIA and White House officials who were knowledgeable about the President's September 15 order to the CIA. The Committee sent letters to various senior officials inquiring if they were, in fact, not knowledgeable of the Track II activities. Those letters were sent to Secretary of State William Rogers, Secretary of Defense Melvin Laird, Deputy Secretary of Defense David Packard, Under Secretary of State for Political Affairs U. Alexis Johnson, Chairman of the Joint Chiefs of Staff Admiral Thomas Moorer, NSC Staff Member for Latin America Viron P. Vaky, Director of the State Department's Bureau of Intelligence and Research Ray S. Cline, and the Deputy Chief of Mission in Santiago Harry W. Shlaudeman. The Committee has received written responses from Messrs. Moorer, Johnson, Vaky, Shlaudeman and Cline. All except Cline have indicated that they had no knowledge of the Track II activity at the time; Cline indicated he heard of the activities in a general way, from his subordinate who handled 40 Committee work and from former associates at the CIA. In oral communications with Committee staff members, Secretaries Rogers and Laird have indicated they were unaware of Track II.

[2] In this same situation report, Ambassador Korry related a message that he had sent to President Frei through his Defense Minister indicating the economic pressures that would be brought to bear on Chile should Allende assume office:

> Frei should know that not a nut or bolt will be allowed to reach Chile under Allende. Once Allende comes to power we shall do all within our power to condemn Chile and the Chileans to utmost deprivation and poverty, a policy designed for a long time to come to accelerate the hard features of a Communist society in Chile. Hence, for Frei to believe that there will be much of an alternative to utter misery, such as seeing Chile muddle through, would be strictly illusory.

The use of economic instruments as levers on Frei and the Chilean military was a persistent subject of White House/CIA discussions and of instructions to the field. Helms' notes from the September 15 meeting with the President included the notation "make the economy scream." Economic leverage was the primary topic of a September 18 White House meeting involving Kissinger, Helms and Karamessines.

(Situation Report, Korry to Meyer and Kissinger, 9/21/70) In testifying, Kissinger felt the Korry report indicated "the degree to which Track I and Track II were merging, that is to say, that individuals on Track I were working on exactly the same problem as the CIA was working on Track II." (Kissinger, 8/12/75, p. 21)

Ambassador Korry's activities in Chile between September 4 and October 24 support Kissinger's view that the line separating Track I and Track II often became blurred. For example, the Ambassador was authorized to make his contacts in the Chilean military aware that if Allende were seated, the military could expect no further military assistance (MAP) from the United States. Later, in response to his own recommendation, Korry was authorized to inform the Chilean military that all MAP and military sales were being held in abeyance pending the outcome of the Congressional election on October 24. On October 7, Ambassador Korry received the following cable from Washington, apparently authorized by the 40 Committee:

> 2. * * * you are now authorized to inform discreetly the Chilean military through the channels available to you that if a successful effort is made to block Allende from taking office, we would reconsider the cuts we have thus far been forced to make in Chilean MAP and otherwise increase our presently programmed MAP for the Chilean Armed Forces. * * * If any steps the military should take should result in civil disorder, we would also be prepared promptly to deliver support and material that might be immediately required. (Cable 075517, Hq. to Sta., 10/7/70)

The essential difference between Tracks I and II, as evidenced by instructions to Ambassador Korry during this period, was not that Track II was coup-oriented and Track I was not. Both had this objective in mind. The difference between the two tracks was, simply, that the CIA's direct contacts with the Chilean military, and its active promotion and support for a coup *without* President Frei's involvement, were to be known only to a small group of individuals in the White House and the CIA. Kissinger testified that Track II matters were to be reported directly to the White House "for reasons of security." (Kissinger, 8/12/75, p. 14) Thomas Karamessines, the CIA's Deputy Director for Plans at the time and the principal CIA contact with the White House on Track II matters, testified on his understanding of why State, Defense, the 40 Committee and Ambassador Korry were excluded from Track II:

> That was not a decision that we made. But the best I can do is suggest that there was concern about two things. Number one, that there might be serious objections lodged, for example, by the State Department particularly if Track II were to be laid out at a Forty Committee meeting. And the only other thing I can contribute to that is that it was felt that the security of the activity would be better protected if knowledge of it were limited. (Karamessines, 8/6/75, p. 122)

(c) *CIA views of difficulty of project*

On one point the testimony of the CIA officials who were involved in Track II is unanimous: they all said they thought Track II was unlikely to succeed. That view ran from the working levels of the Agency to the top. They all said they felt they were being asked to do the impossible, that the risks and potential costs of the project were too great. At the same time, they felt they had been given an explicit Presidential order, and they tried to execute that order.

A few excerpts from the testimony follow:
Richard Helms, CIA Director—

* * * my heart sank over this meeting, because * * * the possibility of bringing off something like this seemed to me at that time to be just as remote as anything could be. In practical terms, the Army was constitutionalist. * * * And when you look here at the time frame in which the man was suddenly asking you to accomplish something, it seemed really almost inconceivable. * * *

What I came away from the meeting with the distinct impression that we were being asked to do almost the impossible and trying to indicate this was going to be pretty tough. * * * (Helms, 7/15/75, pp. 6-7)

Chief, Chile Task Force—

* * * it [was] my feeling that the odds [were] unacceptable, it [was] something that [was] not going to work, and we [were] going to be burned if we [got] into it * * * what [were] the chances of pulling off a coup successfully, or in any way stopping Allende from assuming the presidency? * * * we never even got to two chances out of 20. (Chief, Chile Task Force, 7/31/75, p. 16)

* * * I assure you that those people that I was in touch with at the Agency just about universally said, my God, why are we given this assignment? (Chief, Chile Task Force, 7/31/75, p. 53)

Deputy Chief, Western Hemisphere Division—

There was just no question that we had to make this effort, no matter what the odds were. And I think that most people felt that the odds were just pretty long. (Deputy Chief/WH Division, 7/15/75, p. 20)

Further, CIA officials believed their judgment of the project's difficulty was known to the White House. Helms commented on the September 15th meeting: "So realizing all of these things, I'm relatively certain that day that I pointed out this is going to be awfully tough." (Helms, 7/15/75, p. 16) Karamessines recalled pointing out to the President that "the Chilean military seemed to be disorganized and unwilling to do anything. And without their wanting to do something, there did not seem to be much hope." (Karamessines, 8/6/75, p. 10)

3. CIA'S IMPLEMENTATION OF TRACK II

(a) *Evolution of CIA strategy*

The President's instruction to the CIA on September 15 to prevent Allende's assumption of power was given in the context of a broad U.S. Government effort to achieve that end. The September 15 instruction to the CIA involved from the beginning the promotion of a military coup d'etat in Chile. Although there was talk of a coup in Chilean military circles, there was little indication that it would actually take place without active U.S. encouragement and support.

There was much talk among Chilean officers about the possibility of some kind of coup . . . but this was not the kind of talk that was being backed by, you know, serious organizational planning. (Karamessines, 8/6/75, p. 32)

(i) *The "Constitutional Coup" Approach*

Although efforts to achieve a political solution to the Allende victory continued simultaneous with Track II, the Agency premised its activities on the assumption that the political avenue was a dead end. On September 21, CIA Headquarters cabled its Station in Santiago:

Purpose of exercise is to prevent Allende assumption of power. Paramilitary legerdemain has been discarded. Military solution is objective. (Cable 236, Hq. to Sta., 9/21/70)

The initial strategy attempted to enlist President Frei in promoting a coup to perpetuate his presidency for six more years. The Agency decided to promise "help in any election which was an outgrowth of a successful military takeover." (Memo, Helms to Kissinger, 11/18/70) Under this plan Frei would invite the military to take over, dissolve the Congress, and proclaim a new election. Thomas Karamessines, the Deputy Director for Plans, testified:

> So this was in a sense not Track II, but in a sense another aspect of a quiet and hopefully non-violent military coup. * * * This was abandoned when the military were reluctant to push Frei publicly * * * and, number two, Frei was reluctant to leave on his own in the absence of pressure from the military. * * * There was left as the only chance of success a straight military coup. (Karamessines 8/6/75, p. 6)

At the same time, the Station in Santiago reported:

> Strong reasons for thinking neither Frei nor Schneider will act. For that reason any scenario in which either has to play an active role now appears utterly unrealistic. Overtures to lower echelon officers (e.g., Valenzuela) can of course be made. This involves promoting Army split. (Cable 424, Sta. to Hq., 9/23/70)

(ii) Military Solution

President Frei's failure even to attempt to dissuade his own party convention on October 3–4 from reaching a compromise with Allende ended all hope of using him to prevent an Allende presidency. (Memo, Helms to Kissinger, 11/18/70, p. 16) Thus, by the beginning of October, it was clear that a vehicle for a military solution would have to be found in the second echelon of Chilean officers, and that the top leadership of the Armed Services, particularly General Rene Schneider, constituted a stumbling block. (Cable 424, Sta. to Hq., 9/23/70; Cable 439, Sta. to Hq., 9/30/70) The Agency's task was to cause a coup in a highly unpromising situation and to overcome the formidable obstacles represented by Frei's inaction, Schneider's strong constitutionalism, and the absence of organization and enthusiasm among those officers who were interested in a coup.

A three-fold program was set into motion:

a. Collect intelligence on coup-minded officers;
b. Create a coup climate by propaganda,[1] disinformation, and terrorist activities intended to provoke the left to give a pretext for a coup: (Cable 611, Hq. to Sta., 10/7/70)
c. Inform those coup-minded officers that the U.S. Government would give them full support in a coup short of direct U.S. military intervention. (Cable 762, Hq. to Sta., 10/14/70)

---

[1] A cable sent from CIA Headquarters to Santiago on October 19 focused on creating an appropriate justification for a coup. The cable stated:
1. It still appears that Ref A coup has no pretext or justification that it can offer to make it acceptable in Chile or Latin America. It therefore would seem necessary to create one to bolster what will probably be their claim to a coup to save Chile from communism * * * You may wish include variety of themes in justification of coup to military for their use. These could include but are not limited to: (A) Firm intel. that Cubans planned to reorganize all intelligence services along Soviet/Cuban mold thus creating structure for police state. * * * (B) Economic situation collapsing. * * * (C) By quick recognition of Cuba and Communist countries Allende assumed U.S. would cut off material assistance to Armed Forces thus weakening them as constitutional barriers. Would then empty armories to Communist Peoples Militia with task to run campaign of terror based on alleged labor and economic sabotage. (Use some quotes from Allende on this.)
2. Station has written some excellent prop guidances. Using themes at hand and which best known to you we are now asking you to prepare intel report based on some well known facts and some fiction to justify coup, split opposition, and gain adherents for military group. With appropriate military contact can determine how to "discover" intel report which could even be planted during raids planned by Carabineros.
3. We urge you to get this idea and some concrete suggestions to plotters as soon as you can. Coup should have a justification to prosper. (Cable 882, Hq. to St., 10/19/70)

(b) The Chile task force

Because of the highly sensitive nature of the operation, a special task force was created in the CIA's Western Hemisphere Division to manage it. The task force was placed under the daily direction of the Deputy Director for Plans, Thomas Karamessines, and a group of the Agency's most experienced and skilled operators were detailed to the task force. One experienced CIA officer was summoned back to Washington from an overseas assignment to head the operation. With the exception of the Division Chief, William Broe, his deputy and the head of the Chile Branch, no other officers in the Division were aware of the task force's activities, not even those officers who normally had responsibility for Chile. The task force had a special communications channel to Santiago and Buenos Aires to compartment cable traffic about Track II. (Memo, Helms to Kissinger, 11/18/70, p. 30) Most of the significant operational decisions were made by the Chief of the Chile Task Force, Broe and Karamessines, who met on a daily basis.

It should be noted that all those involved with the task force described the pressure from the White House as intense. Indeed, Karamessines has said that Kissinger "left no doubt in my mind that he was under the heaviest of pressure to get this accomplished, and he in turn was placing us under the heaviest of pressures to get it accomplished." (Karamessines, 8/6/75, p. 7) The Deputy Chief of the Western Hemisphere Division testified that pressure was "as tough as I ever saw it in my time there, extreme." (Deputy Chief/WH Division, 7/18/75, p. 20) Broe testified that "I have never gone through a period as we did on the Chilean thing. I mean it was just constant, constant, * * * Just continual pressure. * * * It was coming from the White House." (Broe, 8/4/75, p. 55)

(c) Use of the U.S. military attache and interagency relations

The CIA Station in Santiago had inadequate contacts within the Chilean military to carry out its task. However, a U.S. military attache in Santiago knew the Chilean military very well due to his broad personal contacts among the Chilean officers. Following a proposal by the Chief of Station, the CIA decided to enlist the attache in collecting intelligence concerning the possibility of a coup and to use him as a channel to let the interested Chilean military know of U.S. support for a coup. Karamessines described this procedure for the Committee:

> We also needed contact with a wider segment of the military, the senior military which we had not maintained and did not have, but which we felt confident that our military representative in Chile had. * * * And we got the approval of the DIA to enlist the cooperation of the attache in our effort to procure intelligence. (Karamessines, 8/6/75, p. 6)

To obtain the attache's services, CIA officials prepared a suggested message for the Director of DIA to send to him in Santiago through CIA communications channels. Because the DIA Director, General Donald V. Bennett, was in Europe on official business, the Deputy Director of Central Intelligence, General Cushman, invited DIA Deputy Director Lt. General Jamie M. Philpott to his office on September 28, 1970.[1] During that meeting, General Cushman requested the assistance of the attache, and General Philpott signed a letter which authorized transmission of a message directing him:

> * * * to work closely with the CIA chief, or in his absence, his deputy, in contacting and advising the principal military figures who might play a decisive role in any move which might, eventually, deny the presidency to Allende.
>
> Do not, repeat not, advise the Ambassador or the Defense Attache of this message, or give them any indication of its portent. In the course of your routine activities, act in accordance with the Ambassador's instructions. Simultaneously, I wish—and now authorize you—to act in a concerted fashion with the CIA chief.
>
> This message is for your eyes only, and should not be discussed with any person other than those CIA officers who will be knowledgeable. CIA will identify them. (Cable 380, Hq. to Sta., 9/28/75)

For this and all subsequent messages intended for the attache, the secret CIA communications channel was used.

Both General Philpott and Thomas Karamessines testified that initially the attache would be used only to "obtain or procure" intelligence on Chilean military officers.[2] (Philpott, 8/5/75, p. 11; Karamessines, 8/6/75, p. 6) The September 28, 1970 message to the attache, however, did in fact trigger his deep involvement in the coup attempt. According to the attache's testimony, he received day-to-day instructions from the Chief of Station, and on occasion, the COS would show him messages, ostensibly from Generals Bennett and/or Philpott, directing him to take certain actions. The COS also transmitted messages from the attache to these Generals.

General Bennett testified that he never had knowledge of Track II and that he never received any communication relating thereto, nor did he ever authorize the transmission of any messages to the attache. General Philpott also testified that he had no recollection of anything connected with Track II after his initial meeting with General Cushman on September 28. (Philpott, 8/5/75, p. 16)

U.S. Army Colonel Robert C. Roth, who in September and October 1970 was the Chief of the Human Resources Division, Director of Collection, DIA, testified that he recalled working for Generals Bennett and Philpott on "a priority requirement to identify Chilean personalities who might be helpful in preventing the election of Allende as President of Chile." (Roth, 8/14/75, p. 6) Though Roth recalls no mention of Track II as such, the goal of this mission was identical to that described in the message of September 28 bearing Philpott's signature.

Beginning on October 15, Roth kept a chronology of his activities connected with Chile. This chronology reflects that there was a meeting on October 21 regarding the preparation of biographic material on Chilean generals which focused on their willingness to participate in a military coup. Generals Bennett, Philpott, and a CIA representative attended. The chronology also shows that on October 21, Roth delivered a message to Mr. Broe to be sent by CIA channels.[3] A

---

[1] General Bennett returned to the United States on the evening of October 10, 1970. General Philpott was Acting Director in Bennett's absence.
[2] In this connection it should be noted that when questioned about this letter, General Philpott testified that he recalled signing an authorization such as that contained in the first paragraph of Headquarters 380 but that he did not recall the authorizations and instructions in paragraphs two and three.
[3] Roth believes that General Philpott directed him to deliver this message and also pressed him on several occasions to seek a response from Broe to an earlier message to the attache. (Roth, 10/7/75, p. 53)

message was sent to the attache that same day, ostensibly from General Bennett, which authorized:

> FYI: Suspension temporarily imposed on MAP and FMS has been rescinded. This action does not repeat not imply change in our estimate of situation. On the contrary, it is intended to place us in a posture in which we can formally cut off assistance if Allende elected and situation develops as we anticipate. Request up date on situation. (Cable 446, Sta. to Hq., 10/21/70; Ref.: Cable 762, Hq. to Sta., (Cable 934, Hq. to Sta., 10/21/70)

Roth testified that this DIA project ended on October 23 when he followed Philpott's instructions to deliver biographic information on Chilean figures to Mr. Broe at CIA. Philpott also instructed him that "any further action on the subject would henceforth be the responsibility of the CIA and that DIA would perform normal support functions." (Roth, 8/14/75, p. 8) [1]

Both Bennett and Philpott testified that the activities described by Roth were routine DIA activities. However, Colonel Roth testified:

> I believe my impression at the time, or my recollection, is that I was informed that there was concern at the highest U.S. Governmental level over the possible election of Allende, that DIA then had a priority responsibility of coming up with the identities of key Chilean personalities that would be helpful, and so forth. I have nothing specific as to the nature of the instructions or the channels through which they came.
>
> Q. It was your sense at the time that you were working on a project that if it had not been initiated by, at least had the attention of or concern of, the highest level?
> Colonel ROTH. That was my impression at the time.
> Q. You understand from your work in the Defense Department that the highest level of government usually indicated the President of the United States?
> Colonel ROTH. I would assume that.

The CIA produced copies of several messages which identify Generals Bennett and Philpott as either the sender or recipient. Among these documents is a message relating to Track II which bears Philpott's purported signature. (Undated message, 10/14/70) General Philpott admitted that the signature appears to be his but doubted that it was and he could not recall signing it, or having seen it. (Philpott, 8/5/75, p. 22) CIA also produced messages of October 14 (Cable 762, Hq. to Sta., 10/14/70) and October 21 (Cable 934, Hq. to Sta., 10/21/70) conveying instructions from General Bennett to the attache. General Bennett testified he did not authorize these messages:

> It is beyond the responsibilities which I had in the military assistance area. It goes beyond the responsibility which I had in terms that I would have to get the authority or the approval of the Secretary through the Chairman for covert action of this magnitude. This message would not have been signed by me. (Bennett, 8/5/75, p. 21)

According to Karamessines, only the White House had the authority to issue the directives contained in those messages. (Karamessines, 8/6/75, p. 84)

The Department of Defense was unable to provide any documents bearing on the issue of the attache's Track II instructions or responses. A DOD file search under the direction of General Daniel O. Graham, Director of DIA, produced no copies of communication documents for the September–October 1970 period. (Graham, 8/5/75, p. 6) However,

---

[1] Roth's chronology also indicates that Philpott had asked that Broe be queried on two or three occasions regarding a report from the attache and that Philpott instructed that only he (Philpott) would communicate with Cushman if the need arose. (Roth, 8/14/75, p. 11) Roth also testified that Philpott advised him that communications with the attache would be by CIA channels. (Roth, 8/14/75, p. 41)

Roth testified that detailed memoranda for the record which he prepared on his activities are missing from the files. (Roth, 10/7/75. p. 58)

CIA officials maintain that they acted faithfully in transmitting messages to Generals Bennett and/or Philpott and in never sending a message without proper authorization. Mr. Karamessines was particularly forceful in this regard:

* * * I can recall no instance in my experience at the Central Intelligence Agency in which a message was received for an individual, an officer of the government anywhere, in whatever department, which was not faithfully, directly, promptly and fully and accurately delivered to that officer, or to his duly authorized representative. (Karamessines, 8/6/75, p. 79)

We may have played tricks overseas, but it stopped at the water's edge, and we didn't play tricks among ourselves or among our colleagues within the Agency or in other agencies. (Karamessines, 8/6/75, p. 79)

We could not remain in business for a day * * * if this had been the practice of the Agency. It would have been no time at all before we would have been found out, a single instance of the kind of thing you are suggesting might have taken place would have put us out of business. (Karamessines, 8/6/75, p. 80)

Dr. Kissinger denied he was ever informed of the attache's role or that he authorized any messages to be sent to the attache. (Kissinger, 8/12/75, p. 22)

The investigation to date has not resolved the conflict between the statements of the senior CIA, DIA and White House officials. There are four possibilities that could explain the conflict. First, Generals Bennett and Philpott were cognizant of Track II and communicated their general instructions to the attache. This possibility would be contrary to their sworn testimony. Second, General Bennett was not aware of Track II but General Philpott was and communicated general instructions to the attache. This possibility is supported by Roth's testimony but would be contrary to Philpott's sworn testimony and his duty to keep General Bennett informed. Third, the CIA acted on its own, and, after receiving initial authority from General Philpott, co-opted and ordered the attache without further informing any member of the Department of Defense or the White House. This possibility would be contrary to the sworn testimony of the Chief of the Chile Task Force, William Broe, Thomas Karamessines, and William Colby. Fourth, members of the White House staff authorized the CIA to convey orders to the attache on the basis of high or highest government authority. Further, that the White House staff directed that the attache's superiors in the Pentagon not be informed. This possibility would contradict the sworn testimony of Dr. Kissinger and General Alexander Haig.

(d) *Agents who posed as third country nationals*

In order to minimize the risks of making contact with dissident Chilean officers, the task force decided in late September to send four agents to Chile posing as third country nationals to supplement the attache's contacts with Chilean military officers. Headquarters felt this was necessary because "We don't want to miss a chance." (Cable 363, Hq. to Sta., 9/27/70) The agents were compartmented from each other and reported separately on their contacts to an operative in Santiago, who in turn reported to the Station. According to the testimony of the Chief of Station, they received their instructions from Washington and not from the Station.

(e) *Chief of Station*

Although most of the Station officers in Santiago did not know of Track II, the Chief and Deputy Chief of Station were knowledgeable and the Chief of Station initiated contacts on his own with Chilean officers. The COS has testified that he regarded Track II as unrealistic:

> I had left no doubt in the minds of my colleagues and superiors that I did not consider any kind of intervention in those constitutional processes desirable. * * * And one of the reasons certainly for my last recall [to Washington] was to be read the riot act—which was done in a very pleasant, but very intelligible manner. Specifically, I was told at that time that the Agency was not too interested in continuously being told by me that certain proposals which had been made could not be executed, or would be counterproductive. (Chief of Station (Felix), 8/1/75, p. 10)

The Chief of Station's objection to Track II did not go unnoticed. The following instruction to the COS was sent on October 7: "Report should not contain analysis and argumentation but simply report on action taken." (Cable 612, Hq. to Sta., 10/7/70) Very simply, Headquarters wanted the Station to take orders quietly as was the Agency itself.

Three examples of the Chief of Station's reporting bear out his claim to have dissented:

> Bear in mind that parameter of action is exceedingly narrow and available options are quite limited and relatively simple. (Cable 424, Sta. to Hq., 9/23/70)
>
> Feel necessary to caution against any false optimism. It is essential that we not become victims of our own propaganda. (Cable 441, Sta. to Hq., 10/1/70)
>
> Urge you do not convey impression that Station has sure-fire method of halting, let alone triggering coup attempts. (Cable 477, Sta. to Hq., 10/7/70, p. 2)

4. CIA EFFORTS TO PROMOTE A COUP

(a) *The Chilean Conspirators*

Anti-Allende coup plotting in Chile centered around several key individuals. One of these was retired General Roberto Viaux, the General who had led the "Tacnazo" insurrection a year before.[1] Following the "Tacnazo" revolt, and his dismissal from the Army, Viaux retained the support of many non-commissioned and junior officers as well as being the recognized leader of several right-wing civilian groups. (CIA Briefing Paper, "Special Mandate from the President on Chile," 7/15/75) Another individual around which plotting centered was General Camilo Valenzuela, Commander of the Santiago Garrison, who was in league with several other Chilean officers. (CIA Report on Chilean Task Force Activities, 11/18/70) These officers, with one possible exception, were in contact with Viaux as well.[2]

There was considerable communication among the various plotting elements. As Thomas Karamessines testified:

> * * * I might add here that it seemed that a good dozen or more Chilean senior officers were privy to what was going on * * * they were all talking to one another

---

[1] This revolt was engineered by Viaux ostensibly for the purposes of dramatizing the military's demand for higher pay, but was widely interpreted as an abortive coup.
[2] The record of meetings between Viaux and the active duty military officers is incomplete. The record does show, however, that several met with Viaux during the Track II period. One high ranking officer may have been a member of Viaux's inner circle of conspirators. Although a distinction can be made between the Viaux and Valenzuela groups, as CIA witnesses did throughout their testimony before the Committee, the principal distinction between the two was that the latter was led by active duty military officers. The two groups were in contact with each other. The record also indicates that they worked together in at least two of the three Schneider kidnap attempts.

exchanging views and trying to see how best to mount the kind of coup that they wanted to see take place. (Karamessines, 8/6/75, p. 10.)

(b) Contacts prior to October 15

The CIA's initial task in Chile was to assess the potential within the Chilean military to stage a coup. It recognized quickly that anti-Allende currents did exist in the military and the Carabineros (police), but were immobilized by "the tradition of military respect for the Constitution" and "the public and private stance of General Schneider, Commander-in-Chief of the Army, who advocated strict adherence to the Constitution." (CIA Report on Chilean Task Force Activities, 11/18/70), p. 17) The Agency's task, then, was to overcome "the apolitical, constitutional-oriented inertia of the Chilean military." (Ibid, p. 2)

Since the very top of the Chilean military, embodied by General Schneider and his second-in-command, General Prats, were hostile to the idea of a coup against Allende, discreet approaches were made to the second level of general officers. They were to be informed that the U.S. Government would support a coup both before and after it took place.[1] (Cable 611, Hq. to Sta., 10/7/70) This effort began in earnest on October 5 when the attache informed both an Army General ("Station's priority contact") and an Air Force General of the pro-coup U.S. policy. (Santiago 469, October 5; Santiago 473, October 6.)[2] Three days later the Chief of Station told a high ranking Carabinero official that "the U.S. Government favors a military solution and is willing to support it in any manner short of outright military intervention." (Task Force Log, 10/9/70) The official informed the COS that there was no chance of a coup by the Chilean Army high command. (Task Force Log, 10/10/70)

On October 7, the attache approached members of the War Academy in Santiago who in turn asked him to provide light weapons. This was the attache's first contact with the Army officer to whom he would ultimately pass three submachine guns on October 22.[3] At this meeting, the Army officer told the attache that he and his colleagues were:

* * * Trying to exert forces on Frei to eliminate Gen. Schneider to either replace him, send him out of the country. They had even studied plans to kidnap him. Schneider is the main barrier to all plans for the military to take over the government to prevent an Allende presidency. (Cable 483, Sta. to Hq., 10/8/70)

The next day, October 8, Headquarters cabled the Station in re-

---

[1] The military officers were told, for example, that should Allende be prevented from taking office, "The Chilean military will not be ostracized, but rather can continue to count on us for MAP support and maintenance of our close relationship." (Cable 075517, Hq. to Sta., 10/7/70)

[2] According to the CIA's wrap-up report on Track II, between October 5 and October 20, the CIA Station and the attache—for the most part the latter—made 21 contacts with key military and Carabinero officials. (CIA Report on Chilean Task Force Activities, 11/8/70)

[3] In his testimony, the attache indicated that the Army officer was affiliated with an Army general. (U.S. military attache, 8/4/75, p. 52) In a cable sent to Headquarters on October 18, in which the Army officer's request for three submachine guns was made, the Station indicated that the attache believed the officer, and his companion, a Navy officer were in league with a Navy admiral. (Cable 562, Sta. to Hq., 10/18/70) At another point in his testimony, the attache stated, "There was Valenzuela here and the Navy officer and the Army officer and the Air Force General over here." (The attache, 8/4/75, p. 107) The Committee has been unable to determine the exact affiliation of the Army officer. However, as previously stated, both the Army general and the Navy admiral were affiliated with General Valenzuela and the Navy admiral was in contact with General Viaux.

sponse to the attache-Army officer meeting. Headquarters took note of Schneider's resistance to coup plans and stated:

* * * This would make it more important than ever to remove him and to bring this new state of events . . . anything we or Station can do to effect removal of Schneider? We know this rhetorical question, but wish inspire thought on both ends on this matter. (Cable 628, Hq. to Sta., 10/8/70)

During the first week of intensive efforts chances of success looked bleak. The Chile Task Force Log commented:

* * * the highest levels of the armed forces unable to pull themselves together to block Allende. The Chilean military's tradition of non-intervention, Frei's reluctance to tarnish his historical image, General Schneider's firm constitutional stand, and most importantly, the lack of leadership within the government and military are working against a military takeover. (Task Force Log, 10/8/70)

The following day the Station made reference to the "rapid(ly) waning chances for success." (Cable 487, Sta. to Hq., 10/9/70) This pessimism was not dispelled by their simultaneous judgment: "Station has arrived at Viaux solution by process of elimination." (Cable 504, Sta. to Hq., 10/10/70) Three days later the Task Force agreed: "We continue to focus our attention on General Viaux who now appears to be the only military leader willing to block Allende." (Task Force Log, 10/13/70)

If Viaux was the CIA's only hope of staging a coup, things were bleak indeed. His own colleagues, including General Valenzuela, described him as "a General without an army." (Cable 495, Sta. to Hq., 10/9/70) Yet in the first two weeks of October he came to be regarded as the best hope for carrying out the CIA's Track II mandate.

Although the U.S. military attache was instructed not to involve himself with Viaux because of the high risk involved (Cable 461, Sta. to Hq., 10/5/70), he served initially as a contact to Viaux through a military attache of another country. This attache reported on October 5 that Viaux wanted several hundred paralyzing gas grenades to launch a coup on October 9. (Cable 476, Sta. to Hq., 10/6/70) Headquarters turned down the request, concluding that a "mini-coup at this juncture would be counterproductive" and Viaux should postpone his plans, "while encouraging him in a suitable manner to maintain his posture so that he may join larger movement later if it materializes." (Cable 585, Hq. to Sta., 10/6/70)

The primary purpose of the CIA agents who posed as third country nationals was to contact Viaux, and they very rapidly relieved the attache of his indirect role in that task. Viaux reiterated his demand for an air drop of weapons to one of these CIA agents, and again the response was the same: reject the demand for arms, but encourage him to keep planning. In essence the Agency was buying time with Viaux: "We wish to encourage Viaux to expand and refine his coup planning. Gain some influence over his actions." (Cable 689, Hq. to Sta., 10/10/70) To achieve this latter purpose, Headquarters authorized passing $20,000 in cash and a promise of $250,000 in life insurance to Viaux and his associates, as a demonstration of U.S. support. (Cable 729, Hq. to Sta., 10/13/70)

On October 13, Headquarters again indicated its concern over Schneider by asking: "What is to keep Schneider from making statement in early hours which will freeze those military leaders who might otherwise join Viaux?" (Cable 729, Hq. to Sta., 10/13/70.) The Station's response later that same day was "Viaux intends to kidnap Generals Schneider and Prats within the next 48 hours in order to precipitate a coup." (Cable 527, Sta. to Hq., 10/13/70) This Viaux kidnapping of Schneider was reported by the Station "as part of a coup that included Valenzuela." (Cable 529, Sta. to Hq., 10/13/70)

At about this time the Station began to receive encouragement from its other contacts. On October 14, ten days before the Chilean Congress was to vote, the Task Force Log concluded:

> Now we are beginning to see signs of increasing coup activity from other military quarters, specifically, an Army General [deleted] and Admiral [deleted], and the forces in Concepcion and Valdivis * * * (Task Force Log, 10/14/70)

(c) *October 15 decision*

To summarize, by October 15 General Viaux had advertised to his contact a desire to proceed with a coup, had indicated he would deal with the Schneider obstacle by kidnapping him, had met at least once with General Valenzuela and had once postponed his coup plans.[1]

On October 15 Thomas Karamessines met with Henry Kissinger and Alexander Haig at the White House to discuss the situation in Chile. According to the Agency's record of this meeting, Karamessines provided a rundown on Viaux, a meeting between two other Chilean military coup conspirators, and, in some detail, "the general situation in Chile from the coup-possibility viewpoint." (Memorandum of Conversation/Kissinger, Karamessines, and Haig, 10/15/70) A decision was made at the meeting "to de-fuse the Viaux coup plot, at least temporarily:"

> It was decided by those present that the Agency must get a message to Viaux warning him against any precipitate action. In essence the message should state: "We have reviewed your plans and based on your information and ours, we come to the conclusion that your plans for a coup at this time cannot succeed. Failing, they may reduce your capabilities in the future. Preserve your assets. We will stay in touch. The time will come when you with all your other friends can do something. You will continue to have our support." (Memorandum of Conversation, Kissinger, Karamessines, Haig, 10/15/70)

The meeting concluded, according to the Agency's record, "on Dr. Kissinger's note that the Agency should continue keeping the pressure on every Allende weak spot in sight—now, after the 24th of October, after 5 November, and into the future until such time as new marching orders are given. Mr. Karamessines stated that the Agency would comply."[2]

---

[1] The reason for Viaux postponing his coup plans was the subject of a cable from Santiago to Headquarters:

> We discount Viaux's statement that he had called off his coup attempt because of the CIA agent's impending visit. Other reporting indicated Viaux probably not able or intending move this weekend. (Cable 499, Sta. to Hq., 10/10/70)

There is also reason to believe that General Valenzuela was instrumental in persuading Viaux to postpone. According to the Chile Task Force Log:

> Station reported that on 12 October General Valenzuela met with General Viaux and attempted to persuade him not to attempt a coup. (Chile Task Force Log, 10/14/70)

[2] Secretary Kissinger's recollection of the October 15 meeting is not in accord with that of Mr. Karamessines or the cable (Headquarters 802) that was sent the following day to the Station in Santiago. This matter will be discussed in Part V of this report.

The following day CIA Headquarters cabled the results of the White House meeting to the Station in Santiago:

> 2. It is firm and continuing policy that Allende be overthrown by a coup.... We are to continue to generate maximum pressure toward this end utilizing every appropriate resource.
> 3. After the most careful consideration it was determined that a Viaux coup attempt carried out by him alone with the forces now at his disposal would fail. Thus it would be counterproductive to our Track Two objectives. It was decided that CIA get a message to Viaux warning him against precipitate action. (Cable 802, Hq. to Sta. 10/16/70)

The message was supplemented by orders to "continue to encourage him (Viaux) to amplify his planning; encourage him to join forces with other coup planners." (Cable 802, Hq. to Sta., 10/16/70) The message concluded: "There is great and continuing interest in the activities of Valenzuela *et al* and we wish them optimum good fortune." (Ibid)

(d) *Coup planning and attempts after October 15*

The decision to "de-fuse" General Viaux was passed to a Viaux associate on October 17. The associate responded that it did not matter because they had decided to proceed with the coup in any case. (Cable 533, Sta. to Hq., 10/17/70) At the final meeting of the CIA agent and the Viaux associate on October 18, the Agency was informed that the coup would proceed on October 22, "and that the abduction of General Schneider is the first link in chain of events to come." (Cable 568, Sta. to Hq., 10/19/70) An "emergency channel" of communication with Viaux was maintained. (Report on CIA Chilean Task Force Activities, 11/18/70, p. 21)

As previously stated, by mid-October things suddenly looked brighter for a coup being mounted by the high-level Chilean military contacts.[1] A CIA overview statement on Track II stated:

> Coup possibilities afforded by the active duty military group led by General Valenzuela and Admiral [deleted] had always seemed more promising than the capabilities of the Viaux group. These military officers had the ability and resources to act providing they decided to move and organized themselves accordingly. (CIA Briefing Paper, "Special Mandate from the President on Chile," 7/15/75, p. 5)

By mid-October the Chilean military officers appeared to be moving in this direction.

On the evening of October 17, the U.S. military attache met with the Chilean Army officer and the Navy officer. They requested 8 to 10 tear gas grenades, three 45-caliber machine guns and 500 rounds of ammunition. The Navy officer said he had three machine guns himself "but can be identified by serial numbers as having been issued to him. Therefore unable to use them." (Cable 562, Sta. to H., 10/18/70) The attache and the Chief of Station have testified that the officers wanted the machine guns for self-protection. The question, of course, is whether

---

[1] Two coup plotters, both Chilean generals, made one last attempt to persuade General Schneider to change his anti-coup position on October 15. The Station reported that the meeting turned out to be a "complete fiasco. Schneider refused to listen to their eloquent presentation of Communist action in Chile * * * and [remained] adamant in maintaining his non-involvement stance." (Cable 548, Sta. to Hq., 10/16/70)

the arms were intended for use, or were used, in the kidnapping of General Schneider. The fact that the weapons were provided the Army officer and the Navy officer and that Viaux associates were convicted of the Schneider killing suggests that the guns were not involved.

The machine guns and ammunition were sent from Washington by diplomatic pouch on the morning of October 19, although Headquarters was puzzled about their purpose: "Will continue make effort provide them but find our credulity stretched by Navy officer leading his troops with sterile guns. What is special purpose for these guns? We will try send them whether you can provide explanation or not." (Cable 854, Hq. to Sta., 10/18/70) The first installment was delivered to the Army officer and the Navy officer late in the evening of October 18 and consisted of the six tear gas grenades intended originally for Viaux.[1]

That same day, General Valenzuela informed the attache that he and three other high ranking military officers were prepared to sponsor a coup. (CIA Report on Chilean Task Force Activities, 11/18/70) Their plan was to begin with the kidnapping of General Schneider on the following evening, October 19, at a military dinner being given for Schneider,[2] after which Schneider would be flown to Argentina, Frei would resign and leave Chile, one of Valenzuela's colleagues would head the military junta, and dissolve Congress. With respect to the kidnapping of Schneider, the cable reported:

General Viaux knowledgeable of above operation but not directly involved. He has been sent to Viña to stay with prominent physician. Will be seen in public places during 19 and 20 October to demonstrate fact that above operation not his doing. Will be allowed to return to Santiago at end of week. Military will not admit involvement in Schneider's abduction which is to be blamed on leftists. (Cable 566, Sta. to Hq., 10/19/70)

The kidnapping of the evening of October 19 failed because General Schneider left in a private vehicle, rather than in his official car, and his police guard failed to be withdrawn. The Army officer assured the attache that another attempt would be made on October 20. (Cable 582, Sta. to Hq., 10/20/70) The attache was authorized to pay Valenzuela $50,000 "which was the price agreed upon between the plotters and the unidentified team of abductors," but the attache insisted that the kidnapping be completed before he paid the money. (Task Force

---

[1] As previously stated, after October 15 CIA efforts to promote a coup in Chile focussed on the active duty military officers—Valenzuela, et al.—rather than Viaux. An example of this shift in focus was the decision to provide the Army officer and the Navy officer the tear gas grenades originally intended for Viaux. A cable from Santiago explained the purpose of this action:

Station plans give six tear gas grenades to the attache for delivery to Armed Forces officers (deletion) instead of having CIA agents posing as third country nationals deliver them to Viaux group. Our reasoning is that the attache dealing with active duty officers. Also CIA agent leaving evening 18 October, and will not be replaced but the attache will stay here. Hence important that the attache credibility with Armed Forces officers be strengthened. (Cable 562, Sta. to Hq., 10/18/70.)

[2] The CIA agent who was in contact with Viaux at the time the Valenzuela plan was given to the attache apparently understood that Viaux was involved in the October 19 attempt. He stated:

Q. Were you told any of the details of how the (Viaux) kidnapping would be carried out?

Mr. SARNO. They indicated it was going to be at some sort of a banquet which the General (Schneider) would be attending. (Sarno, 7/29/75, p. 37)

Log, 10/20/70) At the same time General Valenzuela assured the attache that the military was now prepared to move. (Task Force Log, 10/20/70) The second abduction attempt on the 20th also failed and the Task Force concluded

> Since Valenzuela's group is apparently having considerable difficulty executing even the first step of its coup plan, the prospects for a coup succeeding or even occurring before 24 October now appears remote. (Task Force Log, 10/22/70)

(e) *The Shooting of General Schneider*

In the early morning hours of October 22 (2 a.m.), the attache delivered the three submachine guns with ammunition to the Army officer in an isolated section of Santiago.[1]

At about 7 am that day the group that intended to kidnap General Schneider met to discuss last-minute instructions. According to the findings of the Chilean Military Court which investigated the Schneider killing, neither the Army officer nor the Navy officer were there. Shortly after 8 am, General Schneider's car was intercepted on his way to work by the abductors and he was mortally wounded when he drew his handgun in self-defense. The Military Court determined that hand guns had been used to kill General Schneider, although it also found that one unloaded machine gun was at the scene of the killing.[2]

The first Station reports following the Schneider shooting said "Military Mission sources claim General Schneider machine gunned on way to work" (Cable 587, Sta. to Hq., 10/22/70) and "Assailants used grease guns. (Cable 589, Sta. to Hq., 10/22/70) The submachine guns had previously been described by the Station as "grease guns." Thus the initial reaction of the Station was that Schneider had been shot with the same kind of weapons delivered several hours earlier to the Army officer. Santiago then informed Headquarters "Station has instructed the attache to hand over $50,000 if Gen. Valenzuela requests" (Cable 592, Sta. to Hq., 10/22/70), thus indicating that the Station thought the kidnapping had been accomplished by Valenzuela's paid abductors. Later that day, the Station cabled Headquarters:

> Station unaware if assassination was premeditated or whether it constituted bungled abduction attempt. In any case, it important to bear in mind that move

---

[1] Although the attache's testimony and the cable traffic do not clearly establish the identity of the group to which the Army officer was affiliated (see page 240 of this report) two CIA statements on Track II tie the weapons and therefore the Army officer, to the Valenzuela group:

* * * The only assistance requested by Valenzuela to set the plan [of October 19] into motion through Schneider's abduction was several submachine guns, ammunition, a few tear gas grenades and gas masks (all of which were provided) plus $50,000 for expenses (which was to be passed upon demand). (CIA Report on Chilean Task Force Activities, 11/18/70, p. 22)

* * * Three sub-machine guns, together with six gas cannisters and masks, were passed to the Valenzuela group at 2 a.m. on 22 October. The reason why they still wanted the weapons was because there were two days remaining before the Congress decided the Presidential election and the Valenzuela group maintained some hope they could still carry out their plans. (CIA Briefing Paper, "Special Mandate from President on Chile," 7/15/75. p. 7)

[2] The Military Court determined that those who participated in the shooting of General Schneider on October 22 were part of the Viaux-led conspiracy. The Court also found that this same group had participated in the October 19 and 20 kidnap attempts.

In June 1972 General Viaux was convicted for complicity in the plot culminating in the death of General Schneider. He received a 20-year prison sentence for being "author of the crime of kidnapping which resulted in serious injury to the victim," and a five-year exile for conspiring to cause a military coup. General Valenzuela was also convicted on the latter charge. He received a sentence of three years in exile.

against Schneider was conceived by and executed at behest of senior Armed Forces officers. We know that General Valenzuela was involved. We also near certain that Admiral [deleted], Army officer and Navy officer witting and involved. We have reason for believing that General Viaux and numerous associates fully clued in, but cannot prove or disprove that execution or attempt against Schneider was entrusted to elements linked with Viaux. Important factor to bear in mind is that Armed Forces, and not retired officers or extreme rightists, set Schneider up for execution or abduction. * * * All we can say is that attempt against Schneider is affording Armed Forces one last opportunity to prevent Allende's election if they are willing to follow Valenzuela's scenario. (Cable 598, Sta. to Hq., 10/22/70)

(f) Post October 22 events

The shooting of General Schneider resulted immediately in a declaration of martial law, the appointment of General Prats to succeed Schneider as Commander in Chief, and the appointment of General Valenzuela as chief of Santiago province. These measures, and others taken, caused the Chile Task Force to make the following initial judgment:

With only 24 hours remaining before the Congressional runoff, a coup climate exists in Chile. * * * The attack on General Schneider has produced developments which closely follow Valenzuela's plan. * * * Consequently the plotters' positions have been enhanced. (Chile Task Force Log, 10/22/70)

On October 23, Director Helms reviewed and discussed Track II:

It was agreed * * * that a maximum effort has been achieved, and that now only the Chileans themselves can manage a successful coup. The Chileans have been guided to a point where a military solution is at least open to them. (Task Force Log, 10/24/70)

Although it was not immediately clear to CIA observers, the Station's prediction of October 9 that the shooting of Schneider (as a result of an abduction attempt) would "rally the Army firmly behind the flag of constitutionalism" was correct. (Cable 495, Sta. to Hq., 10/9/75) On October 24 Dr. Allende was confirmed by the Chilean Congress. General Schneider died the next day.

5. CIA/WHITE HOUSE COMMUNICATION DURING TRACK II

The testimony given to the Committee by Henry Kissinger and General Haig conflicts with that given by CIA officials.

Kissinger and Haig testified that on October 15, 1970, the White House stood down CIA efforts to promote a military coup d'etat in Chile. Both testified that after that date they were neither informed of, nor authorized, CIA Track II activities, including the kidnap plans of General Schneider and the passage of weapons to the military plotters.

By contrast, CIA officials testified that they operated before and after October 15 with the knowledge and approval of the White House.

The conflict pertains directly to the period after October 15, but it bears on the degree of communication between the White House and the CIA in the earlier period as well. For instance, Henry Kissinger testified that he was informed of no coup plan which began with the abduction of General Schneider. He was aware of General Viaux's plan—which he and Karamessines decided on October 15 to try to forestall—but did not know that it was to begin with Schneider's abduction.

CIA officials, especially Thomas Karamessines, stated that there was close consultation throughout Track II between the Agency and the White House. Karamessines testified that he met with Kissinger some six to ten times during the five weeks of Track II (Karamessines, 8/6/75, p. 66); and that he kept Kissinger generally informed of developments. (*Ibid.*, p. 56) The Committee has records of two meetings between Karamessines and Kissinger and of one telephone conversation between Karamessines and Kissinger's deputy, General Alexander Haig. Karamessines' daily calendar indicates that three other meetings with General Haig took place—but does not establish with certainty that the topic was Track II. The calendar also suggests that Karamessines and Kissinger met on three other occasions and so might have had the opportunity to discuss Track II.

Henry Kissinger's testimony before the Committee differs from Karamessines in two respects: he believed Track II was "turned off" on October 15,[1] and, after that date, he was informed neither of the coup plans of the Chilean conspirators nor of the passage of weapons to them. He said that Track II was:

> In the nature of a probe and not in the nature of a plan, * * * no plan for a coup was ever submitted to the White House. So my recollection of events, this was a request by President Nixon for Track II which led to two or three meetings which then on October 15th led to being turned off by the White House, after which Track II was dead as far as my office was concerned, and we never received another report on the subject. (Kissinger, 8/12/75, p. 15)
> In my mind Track II was finished on October 15th and I never received any further CIA information after October 15th on the basis of any records that I have been able to find. (Ibid., p. 59)

General Haig's testimony generally coincided with Kissinger's recollection:

> I left [the October 15th meeting] with the distinct impression that there was nothing that could be done in this covert area that offered promise or hope for success. I had the distinct impression that was Dr. Kissinger's conclusion, and that in effect these things—and I wasn't even really familiar with what these two groups were to do and how they were to do it, but they were to cease and desist. (Haig, 8/15/75, pp. 26–27)
> My recollection would be that we had no hope for a viable, covert plan of action. That is the impression I got. (Ibid., p. 29)

The following pages present the Committee's record of communication between the White House and the CIA from September 18 through December 21, 1970:

(a) *September*

September 18

Helms and Karamessines met with Kissinger at the White House. As Helms' notes of the September 15 meeting indicate, Kissinger wanted a plan within 48 hours. In the meeting on the 18th, according to CIA records, there was little discussion of a military coup. Rather

---

[1] Secretary Kissinger, in a written response to a Committee question, stated that he had not been able to find any "written instruction from the President to discontinue efforts to organize a coup. The President did, however, convey this decision to me orally in mid-October, 1970."
To date, the Committee has been unable to question former President Nixon on this point.

the conversation focused on "what economic leverage could be exercised in the Chilean situation." (Memorandum/Meeting with DDP, 9/18/70) The efficacy of economic pressure continued to be a subject of concern during the last days of September. Apparently that pressure was viewed as another inducement to Frei to opt for the "Frei gambit."

September 21

The 40 Committee met. The Committee has no confirmation that Chile was on the agenda at this meeting. Karamessines' calendar confirms that he attended; presumably Kissinger, the 40 Committee chairman, also attended, although the Committee has not been able to review his calendar. All that can be said about this meeting—and the meetings of the Senior Review Group, which Kissinger also chaired—is that the meetings afforded Karamessines and Kissinger an opportunity to meet privately and discuss Track II if they desired. In all these instances save the 40 Committee meeting on September 22, the Committee has no evidence to confirm that such a private Kissinger/Karamessines meeting actually took place. That the CIA prepared a memorandum of conversation for the private meeting on the 22nd but has been able to find none for other meetings may provide some support for the argument that no other such private meetings occurred.

September 22

Kissinger asked Karamessines to stay behind after a 40 Committee meeting called to discuss Track I. The two men also discussed Track II actions. According to the CIA record of the meeting, Kissinger told Karamessines that "our handling of the problem during the earlier meeting had been perfect and he added we were doing fine and keep it up." (Karamessines Memorandum for the Record/Chile, 9/22/70)

(b) *October*

October 5

A cable sent to Santiago, released by Karamessines, requested a report on how the Station planned to contact the three Chilean Generals, including Valenzuela, named in a cable of September 30. (Cable 449, Hq. to Sta., 9/30/70) The October 5 cable indicated that the report was needed for a discussion with Kissinger on October 6.[1] (Cable 556, Sta. to Hq., 10/5/70) Karamessines presumed such a meeting had taken place, although he had no specific memory of it. (Karamessines, 8/6/75, pp. 69-70) His calendar for October 6 indicates that he attended a 40 Committee meeting on Chile. (Karamessines calendar.) Kissinger chaired that meeting.

October 6

The Station reported that General Viaux was "ready to launch *golpe* evening 9 October, or morning 10 October." (Cable 472, Sta. to Hq., 10/6/70) In response, CIA Headquarters labeled the prospective coup one "with scant chance of success which will vitiate any further more serious action." The Station was directed to try to "stop

---

[1] In a written response to a Committee question, Kissinger stated that he was never informed that these contacts had been made.

ill-considered action at this time." (Cable 585, Hq. to Sta., 10/6/70)

Kissinger testified he had not been informed of the Viaux plan, supporting his recollection with the fact that the CIA memorandum of an October 10 conversation between Karamessines and Haig (see below) makes no mention of any previous plots. (Kissinger, 8/12/75, p. 24) Similarly, Kissinger did not remember having been informed that the CIA had called off a coup it regarded as premature. He stated:

> My perception at that period was that if they had a coup they would come * * * back to us before triggering it * * * at no time during the period did they, in fact, tell us * * * that they had a coup that might be ready to go. And, indeed, they generally told us the opposite. (Kissinger, 8/12/75, pp. 25–26)

As Karamessines' calendar indicated, there was a 40 Committee meeting on October 6. He attended this meeting, along with Richard Helms and William Broe of the CIA. According to the minutes of that meeting, CIA efforts to promote a military coup in Chile were not discussed. However, in an exchange with Charles Meyer, who was then the State Department's Assistant Secretary for Latin American Affairs, Dr. Kissinger stressed the desire of "higher authority" (President Nixon) to prevent Allende's assumption of office. According to the minutes:

> Mr. Meyer pointed to the need to determine a post-Allende position such as proposed in NSSM 97. It was agreed that an early NSC meeting was desirable on that subject. Mr. Kissinger said this presumed total acceptance of a fait accompli and higher authority had no intention of conceding before the 24th; on the contrary, he wanted no stone left unturned. (Memorandum for the Record/Minutes of the Meeting of the 40 Committee, 10/6/70, 10/7/70)

October 8

Karamessines met for lunch with General Haig. (Karamessines calendar.)

In his testimony, Haig recalled being aware that the CIA was in touch with two different groups of military plotters. He believed there must have been another meeting in which the CIA informed him of its on-going contacts.

> It seems to me, although the records don't reflect it, that there was a meeting in September, a very brief one, in which I must have been told that there was a specific program going underway. That probably would have been by Henry (Kissinger) and perhaps with Karamessines there. I am not sure. (Haig, 8/15/75, p. 12)

October 10

Karamessines discussed the Chilean situation by telephone with General Haig. He indicated that the Station had "made direct contact with a number of the senior military officers, especially those who had been reportedly very activist-minded and had received pessimistic reactions from all." (Memorandum/FUBELT, by William Broe, 10/10/70)

Haig recalled the telephone conversation with Karamessines on the 10th. His recollection accords with the CIA memorandum of conversation.

> I do know, and I know that from looking at the record this morning, that Karamessines made a telephone call to me in which he gave a progress report. I recall that, It was in effect a negative progress report, that they were just not coming up with it. (Haig, 8/15/75, p. 12)

Haig indicated to the Committee that he would have passed along the substance of that conversation to Kissinger, and that in general his role at the time was one of a conduit to Kissinger:

> I am quite confident that, given my own conception of my role at that time, that I would have conveyed that information to Henry, * * *. (Haig, 8/15/75, p. 13)
>
> Q. If Mr. Karamessines was unable to see Dr. Kissinger, and talked to you, what degree of latitude did you have concerning what you would pass on to Dr. Kissinger?
>
> General HAIG. At that time I would consider I had no degree of latitude, other than to convey to him what had been given to me. (Id., p. 15)

October 14

A cable to Santiago for the attache, ostensibly from General Bennett, authorized the attache to select two Chilean general officers and convey to them the following message: "High authority in Washington has authorized you to offer material support short of armed intervention to Chilean Armed Forces in any endeavors they may undertake to prevent the election of Allende on October 24." (Cable 762, Hq. to Sta., 10/14/70) Karamessines testified that in this case "high authority" would have been Kissinger or the President, for no one else could have given the attache such broad authorization. Karamessines presumed that the message had been drafted in, or at least cleared with, the White House. (Karamessines, 8/6/75, p. 91)

However, Kissinger did not recall having authorized the October 14th cable. He found the sequence of events puzzling; having been told on the 10th that little was happening, he would have expected in the meeting on the 15th (see below) to have discussed the results of the October 14th message. But the CIA record makes no mention of any such discussion. (Kissinger, 8/12/75, p. 53)

The 40 Committee met to discuss, among other topics, Chile. In addition to the 40 Committee principals (Kissinger, John Mitchell, David Packard, Alexis Johnson, Admiral Moorer), the meeting was attended by Karamessines, William Broe and General Robert Cushman of the CIA, Charles Meyer from State, and Ambassador Korry, who had returned to Washington from Santiago for a short period of consultation.

According to the minutes of that meeting, Kissinger asked Karamessines to give a rundown on the latest developments and present situation in Chile. Karamessines pointed out that "a coup climate does not presently exist." He noted that "the unpredictable General Viaux is the only individual seemingly ready to attempt a coup and * * * his chances of mounting a successful one were slight." Ambassador Korry agreed with Karamessines' assessment and stated that "as of now it seemed almost certain that Allende would be voted into office on October 24th." Kissinger then observed that "there presently appeared to be little the U.S. can do to influence the Chilean situation one way or another." Other participants at the meeting concurred. (Memorandum for the Record/Minutes of the Meeting of the 40 Committee, 10/14/70, 10/16/70)

October 15

Karamessines met with Kissinger and Haig at the White House to discuss Track II. According to the CIA memorandum of conversation,

Karamessines gave a run-down on Viaux, a meeting between two other Chilean military conspirators and "the general situation in Chile from the coup-possibility viewpoint." It was concluded that Viaux did not have more than one chance in twenty—perhaps less—to launch a successful coup. Kissinger ticked off the list of negative repercussions from an unsuccessful coup. The CIA record of the meeting continues:

> 5. It was decided by those present that the Agency must get a message to Viaux warning him against any precipitate action. In essence our message was to state: "We have reviewed your plans, and based on your information and ours, we come to the conclusion that your plans for a coup at this time cannot succeed. Failing, they may reduce your capabilities for the future. Preserve your assets. We will stay in touch. The time will come when you with all your other friends can do something. You will continue to have our support."
> 6. After the decision to de-fuse the Viaux coup plot, at least temporarily, Dr. Kissinger instructed Mr. Karamessines to preserve Agency assets in Chile, working clandestinely and securely to maintain the capability for Agency operations against Allende in the future.
> 8. The meeting concluded on Dr. Kissinger's note that the Agency should continue keeping the pressure on every Allende weak spot in sight—now, after the 24th of October, after 5 November, and into the future until such time as new marching orders are given. Mr. Karamessines stated that the Agency would comply. (Memorandum of Conversation/Dr. Kissinger, Mr. Karamessines, Gen. Haig at the White House, 10/15/70)

Kissinger, in his testimony before the Committee, regarded the CIA memorandum of conversation as substantially correct, although somewhat more detailed than he would have remembered. (Kissinger, 8/12/75, p. 52) He believed the Agency had been told to "stand down and preserve your assets."

Kissinger believed that the gist of the October 15th meeting as recorded in the CIA memorandum was incompatible with the order the CIA issued to its Station the next day, an order ostensibly based on the October 15th meeting. And, he noted, in writing its memorandum of the meeting of the 15th, the CIA had a "high incentive to preserve the maximum degree of authority." (Ibid., pp. 55–56) The October 16th order indicated that Track II had been reviewed at "high USG level" the previous day, and stated:

> 2. It is firm and continuing policy that Allende be overthrown by a coup. It would be much preferable to have this transpire prior to 24 October but efforts in this regard will continue vigorously beyond this date. * * *
> 4. There is great and continuing interest in the activities of Valenzuela et al. and we wish them optimum good fortune. (Cable 802, Hq. to Sta., 10/16/70)

Kissinger recalled the October 15th conversation as "turning off the coup plans rather than giving a new order to do them." (Kissinger, 8/12/75, p. 56) Haig agreed in his testimony.

> The conclusions of that meeting were that we had better not do anything rather than something that was not going to succeed. * * * My general feeling was, I left that meeting with the impression that there was nothing authorized." (Haig, 8/15/75, p. 13)

October 10–October 22 (approximate)

Karamessines and one or two others went with Kissinger to speak with the President, after a larger meeting. Karamessines believed this meeting took place between October 10 and 24. (Karamessines, 8/6/75, p. 89) According to Karamessines, the "President went out of his way to impress all of those there with his conviction that it was absolutely essential that the election of Mr. Allende to the presidency be thwarted."[1] As they were leaving the Oval Office, the President took Karamessines aside to reiterate the message. (Karamessines, 8/6/75, p. 8)

October 19

Station cabled Headquarters early in the morning, advising that the tear gas had been passed and outlining the Valenzuela coup plan, beginning with the kidnap of Schneider. In testimony before the Committee, Karamessines indicated he certainly would have reported the Valenzuela plan to Kissinger "very promptly, if for no other reason than that we didn't have all that much promising news to report to the White House. * * *" (Karamessines, 8/6/75, p. 72)

In the afternoon of the 19th, Karamessines met with General Haig at the White House. (Karamessines calendar.) By then, Karamessines would have had in hand the cable outlining the Valenzuela plan, since the cable had arrived that morning. However, General Haig had no recollection of the meeting with Karamessines on the 19th. Nor did he believe he had been informed of the Valenzuela plan. "This is all very new to me. I hadn't seen any of this, and I was not familiar with this particular plan * * * or $50,000, or any of the characters that are described in here." (Haig, 8/15/75, pp. 38–39)

Similarly, Kissinger testified that he had not been informed of the Valenzuela plan. He said he "was informed of nothing after October 15th. (Kissinger, 8/12/75, p. 65) He indicated that, according to his daily calendar, he had no conversation with either Karamessines or Helms between the 15th and the 19th. (*Ibid.*, p. 53) He indicated that he never knew that the CIA was in the process of passing guns and tear gas to Chilean military conspirators. He said "there was no further meeting on that subject. In anybody's record, mine or theirs [the CIA's], none of the information from the 16th on was familar to me." (*Ibid.*, p. 62)

Kissinger further testified he did not know that the United States was dealing with Chilean officers who plotted a coup which involved the abduction of General Schneider:

> Senator HART of Colorado. I am not sure that the record clearly shows your answer to the direct question of whether you knew or did not know that we were negotiating with military officers with regard to a plot that did involve the abduction of General Schneider.
> Secretary KISSINGER. I said I did not know. (Kissinger, 8/12/75, p. 86)

Nor did General Haig believe he had been informed of any abduction plans before the fact.

> Q. Were you aware during that period of time of the plans to kidnap General Schneider?
> General HAIG. I was aware after the fact. . . .
> Q. But you were never informed prior to his attempted abduction?
> General HAIG. I don't believe I was at all.

---

[1] If the meeting with the President occurred after October 15, that would lend credence to the testimony of CIA officials that they were not directed to end their coup efforts in the October 15th meeting. Unfortunately, the Committee has not had access to the daily calendars of President Nixon or Secretary Kissinger, which might pinpoint the date of the President's conversation with Karamessines.

October 20

A cable to the Station indicated that "while awaiting word on whatever events may have occurred 19 October, please let us know what you can on interim basis. * * * Headquarters must respond during morning 20 October to queries from high levels." (Cable 883, Hq. to Sta., 10/20/70) Karamessines testified that the references to "high levels" in the cable of the 20th meant White House officials, probably Kissinger. He felt quite certain that Kissinger would have been briefed in advance about Valenzuela's plan for the 19th and so would have been expected to ask what happened on the morning of the 20th. (Karamessines, 8/6/75, p. 73) In contrast, Kissinger interpreted that cable in precisely the opposite light. He felt it indicated that he had *not* been informed of the Valenzuela plan in advance. When news of the Schneider kidnap reached the White House, Kissinger believed he would have had "somebody pick up a telephone and say, 'What is this all about?'" (Kissinger, 8/12/75, p. 68)

October 22

Karamessines met with Haig at the White House. (Karamessines calendar) General Haig remembered that word of the shooting of Schneider came as " a great shock" to him, and he believed that Karamessines had told him about it in their meeting on the 22nd. He thought that Kissinger either was present at the meeting or that he, Haig, had gone immediately in to Kissinger's office to relate what Karamessines had told him. (Haig, 8/15/75, p. 36)

(c) *December*

December 2

A memorandum, dated December 2, 1970, from Helms to Kissinger stated that Helms had given a recapitulation on Track II to Attorney General Mitchell, who would deliver it personally to Kissinger. A handwritten note on the memorandum read: "sent to Kissinger via DCI [Helms]." (Memo, Helms to Kissinger, 12/12/70) The report, which was dated November 18, 1970, contained a full account of CIA activities during Track II, including the several plans to kidnap Schneider and the passage of weapons to the Chilean conspirators. (Report on CIA Chilean Task Force Activities, 15 September to 3 November 1970, 10/18/70)

In his testimony to the Committee, Kissinger did not recall receiving the report, although he doubted that he would have read such an "after action" report in any case. He testified that he could not find it in his files, in contrast to his finding a CIA report on Track I, dated November 19, 1970. Kissinger was puzzled by a number of aspects of the memorandum and report: why there were two reports, why the report of the 18th apparently was only called to his attention on the 2nd of December, and why it was to be delivered through Mitchell. (Kissinger, 8/12/75, pp. 71, 74)

(d) *Did Track II end?*

The Committee also received conflicting testimony about whether Track II ever ended, formally or in fact. As noted above, Kissinger indicated that Track II was supposed to have ended, as far as he was concerned, on October 15. It was formally terminated, according to Kissinger, by a new Presidential marching order issued prior to the October 24 vote of the Chilean Congress. The Committee does not have this new "marching order" in its possession. However, CIA officials from whom the Committee took testimony believed that there had been no such definitive end to Track II. It merely tapered off, to be replaced by a longer-term effort to effect a change of government in Chile. Karamessines' testimony was most explicit:

> Mr. KARAMESSINES. I am sure that the seeds that were laid in that effort in 1970 had their impact in 1973. I do not have any question about that in my mind either. (Karamessines, 8/6/75, p. 26)
>
> Q. Was Track II ever formally ended? Was there a specific order ending it?
>
> Mr. KARAMESSINES. As far as I was concerned, Track II was really never ended. What we were told to do in effect was, well, Allende is now President. So Track II, which sought to prevent him from becoming President, was technically out, it was done. But what we were told to do was to continue our efforts. Stay alert, and to do what we could to contribute to the eventual achievement of the objectives and purposes of Track II. That being the case, I don't think it is proper to say that Track II was ended. (Ibid., pp. 128-129)

When informed of Karamessines' testimony that Track II was never ended, Kissinger testified:

> The CHAIRMAN. Would you take issue with that, with the [Karamessines] testimony?
>
> Secretary KISSINGER. Totally. * * * It is clear that * * * after October 15th that there was no separate channel by the CIA to the White House and that all actions with respect to Chile were taken in the 40 Committee framework. There was no 40 Committee that authorized an approach to or contact with military people, no plots which I am familiar with, and all the covert operations in Chile after Allende's election by the Congress were directed towards maintaining the democratic opposition for the 1976 election. And that was the exclusive thrust, and if there was any further contact with military plotting, it was totally unauthorized and this is the first that I have heard of it. (Kissinger, 8/12/75, pp. 75-77)

IV. FINDINGS AND CONCLUSIONS

In evaluating the evidence and arriving at findings and conclusions, the Committee has been guided by the following standards. We believe these standards to be appropriate to the constitutional duty of a Congressional committee.

1. The Committee is not a court. Its primary role is not to determine individual guilt or innocence, but rather to draw upon the experiences of the past to better propose guidance for the future.
2. It is necessary to be cautious in reaching conclusions because of the amount of time that has passed since the events reviewed in this report, the inability of three Presidents and many other key figures to speak for themselves, the conflicting and ambiguous nature of much of the evidence, and the problems in assessing the weight to be given to particular documents and testimony.
3. The Committee has tried to be fair to the persons involved in the events under examination, while at the same time responding to a need to understand the facts in sufficient detail to lay a basis for informed recommendations.

With these standards in mind, the Committee has arrived at the following findings and conclusions.

A. FINDINGS CONCERNING THE PLOTS THEMSELVES

1. OFFICIALS OF THE UNITED STATES GOVERNMENT INITIATED PLOTS TO ASSASSINATE FIDEL CASTRO AND PATRICE LUMUMBA

The Committee finds that officials of the United States Government initiated and participated in plots to assassinate Patrice Lumumba and Fidel Castro.

The plot to kill Lumumba was conceived in the latter half of 1960 by officials of the United States Government, and quickly advanced to the point of sending poisons to the Congo to be used for the assassination.

The effort to assassinate Castro began in 1960 and continued until 1965. The plans to assassinate Castro using poison cigars, exploding seashells, and a contaminated diving suit did not advance beyond the laboratory phase. The plot involving underworld figures reached the stage of producing poison pills, establishing the contacts necessary to send them into Cuba, procuring potential assassins within Cuba, and apparently delivering the pills to the island itself. One 1960 episode involved a Cuban who initially had no intention of engaging in assassination, but who finally agreed, at the suggestion of the CIA, to attempt to assassinate Raul Castro if the opportunity arose. In the AM/LASH operation, which extended from 1963 through 1965, the CIA gave active support and encouragement to a Cuban whose intent to assassinate Castro was known, and provided him with the means of carrying out an assassination.

2. NO FOREIGN LEADERS WERE KILLED AS A RESULT OF ASSASSINATION PLOTS INITIATED BY OFFICIALS OF THE UNITED STATES

The poisons intended for use against Patrice Lumumba were never administered to him, and there is no evidence that the United States was in any way involved in Lumumba's death at the hands of his Congolese enemies. The efforts to assassinate Castro failed.

3. AMERICAN OFFICIALS ENCOURAGED OR WERE PRIVY TO COUP PLOTS WHICH RESULTED IN THE DEATHS OF TRUJILLO, DIEM, AND SCHNEIDER

American officials clearly desired the overthrow of Trujillo, offered both encouragement and guns to local dissidents who sought his overthrow and whose plans included assassination. American officials also supplied those dissidents with pistols and rifles.

American officials offered encouragement to the Vietnamese generals who plotted Diem's overthrow, and a CIA official in Vietnam gave the generals money after the coup had begun. However, Diem's assassination was neither desired nor suggested by officials of the United States.

The record reveals that United States officials offered encouragement to the Chilean dissidents who plotted the kidnapping of General Rene Schneider, but American officials did not desire or encourage Schneider's death. Certain high officials did know, however, that the dissidents planned to kidnap General Schneider.

As Director Colby testified before the Committee, the death of a foreign leader is a risk foreseeable in any coup attempt. In the cases we have considered, the risk of death was in fact known in varying degrees. It was widely known that the dissidents in the Dominican Republic intended to assassinate Trujillo. The contemplation of coup leaders at one time to assassinate Nhu, President Diem's brother, was communicated to the upper levels of the United States Government. While the CIA and perhaps the White House knew that the coup leaders in Chile planned to kidnap General Schneider, it was not anticipated that he would be killed, although the possibility of his death should have been recognized as a foreseeable risk of his kidnapping.

4. THE PLOTS OCCURRED IN A COLD WAR ATMOSPHERE PERCEIVED TO BE OF CRISIS PROPORTIONS

The Committee fully appreciates the importance of evaluating the assassination plots in the historical context within which they occurred. In the preface to this report, we described the perception, generally shared within the United States during the depths of the Cold War, that our country faced a monolithic enemy in Communism. That attitude helps explain the assassination plots which we have reviewed, although it does not justify them. Those involved nevertheless appeared to believe they were advancing the best interests of their country.

5. AMERICAN OFFICIALS HAD EXAGGERATED NOTIONS ABOUT THEIR ABILITY TO CONTROL THE ACTIONS OF COUP LEADERS

Running throughout the cases considered in this report was the expectation of American officials that they could control the actions of dissident groups which they were supporting in foreign countries.

Events demonstrated that the United States had no such power. This point is graphically demonstrated by cables exchanged shortly before the coup in Vietnam. Ambassador Lodge cabled Washington on October 30, 1963, that he was unable to halt a coup; a cable from William Bundy in response stated that "we cannot accept conclusion that we have no power to delay or discourage a coup." The coup took place three days later.

Shortly after the experience of the Bay of Pigs, CIA Headquarters requested operatives in the Dominican Republic to tell the dissidents to "turn off" the assassination attempt, because the United States was not prepared to "cope with the aftermath." The dissidents replied that the assassination was their affair and that it could not be turned off to suit the convenience of the United States Government.

6. CIA OFFICIALS MADE USE OF KNOWN UNDERWORLD FIGURES IN ASSASSINATION EFFORTS

Officials of the CIA made use of persons associated with the criminal underworld in attempting to achieve the assassination of Fidel Castro. These underworld figures were relied upon because it was believed that they had expertise and contacts that were not available to law-abiding citizens.

Foreign citizens with criminal backgrounds were also used by the CIA in two other cases that we have reviewed. In the development of the Executive Action capability, one foreign national with a criminal background was used to "spot" other members of the European underworld who might be used by the CIA for a variety of purposes, including assassination, if the need should arise. In the Lumumba case, two men with criminal backgrounds were used as field operatives by CIA officers in a volatile political situation in the Congo.

B. CONCLUSIONS CONCERNING THE PLOTS THEMSELVES

1. THE UNITED STATES SHOULD NOT ENGAGE IN ASSASSINATION

We condemn the use of assassination as a tool of foreign policy. Aside from pragmatic arguments against the use of assassination supplied to the Committee by witnesses with extensive experience in covert operations, we find that assassination violates moral precepts fundamental to our way of life.

In addition to moral considerations, there were several practical reasons advanced for not assassinating foreign leaders. These reasons are discussed in the section of this report recommending a statute making assassination a crime.

(a) Distinction between targeted assassinations instigated by the United States and support for dissidents seeking to overthrow local governments

Two of the five principal cases investigated by the Committee involved plots to kill foreign leaders (Lumumba and Castro) that were instigated by American officials. Three of the cases (Trujillo, Diem, and Schneider) involved killings in the course of coup attempts by local dissidents. These latter cases differed in the degree to which assassination was contemplated by the leaders of the coups and in the degree the coups were motivated by United States officials.

The Committee concludes that targeted assassinations instigated by the United States must be prohibited.

Coups involve varying degrees of risk of assassination. The possibility of assassination in coup attempts is one of the issues to be considered in determining the propriety of United States involvement in coups, particularly in those where the assassination of a foreign leader is a likely prospect.

This country was created by violent revolt against a regime believed to be tyrannous, and our founding fathers (the local dissidents of that era) received aid from foreign countries. Given that history, we should not today rule out support for dissident groups seeking to overthrow tyrants. But passing beyond that principle, there remain serious questions: for example, whether the national interest of the United States is genuinely involved; whether any such support should be overt rather than covert; what tactics should be used; and how such actions should be authorized and controlled by the coordinate branches of government. The Committee believes that its recommendations on the question of covert actions in support of coups must await the Committee's final report which will be issued after a full review of covert action in general.

(b) The setting in which the assassination plots occurred explains, but does not justify them

The Cold War setting in which the assassination plots took place does not change our view that assassination is unacceptable in our society. In addition to the moral and practical problems discussed elsewhere, we find three principal defects in any contention that the tenor of the period justified the assassination plots:

First, the assassination plots were not necessitated by imminent danger to the United States. Among the cases studied, Castro alone posed a physical threat to the United States, but then only during the period of the Cuban missile crisis. Attempts to assassinate Castro had begun long before that crisis, and assassination was not advanced by policymakers as a possible course of action during the crisis.

Second, we reject absolutely any notion that the United States should justify its actions by the standards of totalitarians. Our standards must be higher, and this difference is what the struggle is all about. Of course, we must defend our democracy. But in defending it, we must resist undermining the very virtues we are defending.

Third, such activities almost inevitably become known. The damage to American foreign policy, to the good name and reputation of the United States abroad, to the American people's faith and support of our government and its foreign policy is incalculable. This last point— the undermining of the American public's confidence in its government—is the most damaging consequence of all.

Two documents which have been supplied to the Committee graphically demonstrate attitudes which can lead to tactics that erode and could ultimately destroy the very ideals we must defend.

The first, document was written in 1954 by a special committee formed to advise the President on covert activities. The United States may, it said, have to adopt tactics "more ruthless than [those] employed by the enemy" in order to meet the threat from hostile nations. The report concluded that "long standing American concepts of American fair play must be reconsidered."[1]

Although those proposals did not involve assassinations, the attitudes underlying them were, as Director Colby testified, indicative of the setting within which the assassination plots were conceived. (Colby, 6/4/75, p. 117)

We do not think that traditional American notions of fair play need be abandoned when dealing with our adversaries. It may well be ourselves that we injure most if we adopt tactics "more ruthless than the enemy."

A second document which represents an attitude which we find improper was sent to the Congo in the fall of 1960 when the assassination of Patrice Lumumba was being considered. The chief of CIA's Africa Division recommended a particular agent—WI/ROGUE—because:

> He is indeed aware of the precepts of right and wrong, but if he is given an assignment which may be morally wrong in the eyes of the world, but necessary because his case officer ordered him to carry it out, then it is right, and he will dutifully undertake appropriate action for its execution without pangs of conscience. In a word, he can rationalize all actions.

The Committee finds this rationalization is not in keeping with the ideals of our nation.

2. THE UNITED STATES SHOULD NOT MAKE USE OF UNDERWORLD FIGURES FOR THEIR CRIMINAL TALENTS

We conclude that agencies of the United States must not use underworld figures for their criminal talents [2] in carrying out Agency operations. In addition to the corrosive effect upon our government,[3] the use of underworld figures involves the following dangers:

a. The use of underworld figures for "dirty business" gives them the power to blackmail the government and to avoid prosecution, for past or future crimes. For example, the figures involved in the Castro assassination operation used their involvement with the CIA to avoid

---

[1] The full text of the passage is as follows:

"* * * another important requirement is an aggressive covert psychological, political, and paramilitary organization far more effective, more unique, and, if necessary, more ruthless than that employed by the enemy. No one should be permitted to stand in the way of the prompt, efficient, and secure accomplishment of this mission.

"The second consideration, it is now clear that we are facing an implacable enemy whose avowed objective is world domination by whatever means at whatever cost. There are no rules in such a game. Hitherto acceptable norms of human conduct do not apply. If the U.S. is to survive, long standing American concepts of American fair play must be reconsidered."

[2] Pending our investigation of the use of informants by the FBI and other agencies, we reserve judgment on the use of known criminals as informants. We are concerned here only with the use of persons known to be actively engaged in criminal pursuits for their expertise in carrying out criminal acts.

[3] The corrosive effect of dealing with underworld figures is graphically demonstrated by the fact that Attorney General Robert Kennedy, who had devoted much of his professional life to fighting organized crime, did not issue an order against cooperating with such persons when he learned in May 1961 that the CIA had made use of Sam Giancana in a sensitive operation in Cuba.

In May, 1962, the Attorney General learned that the operation—which was described to him as terminated—had involved assassination. According to a CIA witness, the Attorney General was angered by the report and told those briefing him that he must be consulted before underworld figures were used again. He did not, however, direct that underworld figures must never again be used.

prosecution. The CIA also contemplated attempting to quash criminal charges brought in a foreign tribunal against QJ/WIN.

b. The use of persons experienced in criminal techniques and prone to criminal behavior increases the likelihood that criminal acts will occur. Sometimes agents in the field are necessarily given broad discretion. But the risk of improper activities is increased when persons of criminal background are used, particularly when they are selected precisely to take advantage of their criminal skills or contacts.

c. There is the danger that the United States Government will become an unwitting accomplice to criminal acts and that criminal figures will take advantage of their association with the government to advance their own projects and interests.

d. There is a fundamental impropriety in selecting persons because they are skilled at performing deeds which the laws of our society forbid.

The use of underworld figures by the United States Government for their criminal skills raises moral problems comparable to those recognized by Justice Brandeis in a different context five decades ago:

> Our government is the potent, the omnipresent teacher. For good or for ill, it teaches the whole people by its example. Crime is contagious. If the Government becomes a law-breaker, it breeds contempt for law; it invites every man to become a law unto himself. To declare that in the administration of the criminal law the end justifies the means—to declare that the Government may commit crimes in order to secure the conviction of the private criminal—would bring terrible retribution. Against that pernicious doctrine this Court should resolutely set its face. [*Olmstead* v. *U.S.*, 277 U.S. 439, 485 (1927)]

e. The spectacle of the Government consorting with criminal elements destroys respect for government and law and undermines the viability of democratic institutions.

C. Findings and Conclusions Relating to Authorization and Control

In the introduction to this report, we set forth in summary form our major conclusions concerning whether the assassination plots were authorized. The ensuing discussion elaborates and explains those conclusions.

The Committee analyzed the question of authorization for the assassination activities from two perspectives. First, the Committee examined whether officials in policymaking positions authorized or were aware of the assassination activities. Second, the Committee inquired whether the officials responsible for the operational details of the plots perceived that assassination had the approval of their superiors, or at least was the type of activity that their superiors would not disapprove.

No doubt, the CIA's general efforts against the regimes discussed in this report were authorized at the highest levels of the government. However, the record is unclear and serious doubt remains concerning whether assassination was authorized by the respective Presidents. Even if the plots were not expressly authorized, it does not follow that the Agency personnel believed they were acting improperly.

1. THE APPARENT LACK OF ACCOUNTABILITY IN THE COMMAND AND CONTROL SYSTEM WAS SUCH THAT THE ASSASSINATION PLOTS COULD HAVE BEEN UNDERTAKEN WITHOUT EXPRESS AUTHORIZATION

As emphasized throughout this report, we are unable to draw firm conclusions concerning who authorized the assassination plots. Even after our long investigation it is unclear whether the conflicting and inconclusive state of the evidence is due to the system of plausible denial or whether there were, in fact, serious shortcomings in the system of authorization which made it possible for assassination efforts to have been undertaken by agencies of the United States Government without express authority from officials above those agencies.[1]

Based on the record of our investigation, the Committee finds that the system of Executive command and control was so inherently ambiguous that it is difficult to be certain at what level assassination activity was known and authorized. This creates the disturbing prospect that assassination activity might have been undertaken by officials of the United States Government without its having been incontrovertibly clear that there was explicit authorization from the President of the United States. At the same time, this ambiguity and imprecision leaves open the possibility that there was a successful "plausible denial" and that a Presidential authorization was issued but is now obscured.

Whether or not assassination was authorized by a President of the United States, the President as the chief executive officer of the United States Government must take ultimate responsibility for major activities during his Administration. Just as these Presidents must be held accountable, however, their subordinates throughout the Government had a concomitant duty to fully disclose their plans and activities.

As part of their responsibility, these Presidents had a duty to determine the nature of major activities and to prevent undesired activities from taking place. This duty was particularly compelling when the Presidents had reason to believe that major undesired activities had previously occurred or were being advocated and might occur again. Whether or not the Presidents in fact knew about the assassination plots, and even if their subordinates failed in their duty of full disclosure, it still follows that the Presidents should have known about the plots. This sets a demanding standard, but one the Committee supports. The future of democracy rests upon such accountability.

2. FINDINGS RELATING TO THE LEVEL AT WHICH THE PLOTS WERE AUTHORIZED

(a) Diem

We find that neither the President nor any other official in the United States Government authorized the assassination of Diem and his brother Nhu. Both the DCI and top State Department officials

---

[1] As noted above, there are also certain inherent limitations in the extensive record compiled by the Committee. Many years have passed, several of the key figures are dead, and while we have been assured by the present Administration that all the relevant evidence has been produced, it is always possible that other more conclusive material exists, but has not been found.

did know, however, that the death of Nhu, at least at one point, had been contemplated by the coup leaders. But when the possibility that the coup leaders were considering assassination was brought to the attention of the DCI, he directed that the United States would have no part in such activity, and there is some evidence that this information was relayed to the coup leaders.

(b) *Schneider*

We find that neither the President nor any other official in the United States Government authorized the assassination of General Rene Schneider. The CIA, and perhaps the White House, did know that coup leaders contemplated a kidnapping, which, as it turned out resulted in Schneider's death.

(c) *Trujillo*

The Presidents and other senior officials in the Eisenhower and Kennedy Administrations sought the overthrow of Trujillo and approved or condoned actions to obtain that end.

The DCI and the Assistant Secretary of State for Inter-American Affairs knew that the Dominican dissidents viewed the removal of Trujillo as critical to any plans to overthrow his regime and that they intended to assassinate Trujillo if given the opportunity. It is uncertain precisely when officials at higher levels of government with responsibility for formulating policy learned that the dissidents equated assassination with overthrow. Clearly by early May 1961 senior American officials, including President Kennedy, knew that the dissidents intended to assassinate Trujillo. The White House and State Department, as well as the CIA, knew that the United States had provided the dissidents with rifles and pistols and that the dissidents had requested machine guns which they intended to use in connection with an assassination effort.

Thereafter, on May 16, 1961 President Kennedy approved National Security Council recommendations that the United States not initiate the overthrow of Trujillo until it was known what government would succeed the dictator. That recommendation was consistent with earlier attempts initiated by the CIA to discourage the planned assassination and thereby avoid potential problems from a power vacuum which might arise. After deciding to discourage the planned assassination, the DCI directed that the machine guns not be passed to the Dominican dissidents. That policy was reconfirmed by the State Department, the Special Group, and, in a cable of May 29, 1961, by President Kennedy himself.

The day before the assassination, President Kennedy cabled the State Department representative in the Dominican Republic that the United States "as [a] matter of general policy cannot condone assassination." However, the cable also stated that if the dissidents planning the imminent assassination of Trujillo succeeded, and thereby established a provisional government, the United States would recognize and support them.

The President's cable has been construed in several ways. One reading stresses the President's opposition to assassination "as a matter of general policy." Another stresses those portions of the cable which discuss pragmatic matters, including the risk that the United States' involvement might be exposed, and suggests that the last minute telegram was designed to avoid a charge that the United States shared responsibility for the assassination. A third construction would be that both of the prior readings are correct and that they are not mutually exclusive. However the cable is construed, its ambiguity illustrates the difficulty of seeking objectives which can only be accomplished by force—indeed, perhaps only by the assassination of a leader—and yet not wishing to take specific actions which seem abhorrent.

(d) *Lumumba*

The chain of events revealed by the documents and testimony is strong enough to permit a reasonable inference that the plot to assassinate Lumumba was authorized by President Eisenhower. Nevertheless, there is enough countervailing testimony by Eisenhower Administration officials and enough ambiguity and lack of clarity in the records of high-level policy meetings to preclude the Committee from making a finding that the President intended an assassination effort against Lumumba.

It is clear that the Director of Central Intelligence, Allen Dulles, authorized an assassination plot. There is, however, no evidence of United States involvement in bringing about the death of Lumumba at the hands of Congolese authorities.

Strong expressions of hostility toward Lumumba from the President and his National Security Assistant, followed immediately by CIA steps in furtherance of an assassination operation against Lumumba, are part of a sequence of events that, at the least, make it appear that Dulles believed assassination was a permissible means of complying with pressure from the President to remove Lumumba from the political scene.

Robert Johnson's testimony that he understood the President to have ordered Lumumba's assassination at an NSC meeting does, as he said, offer a "clue" about Presidential authorization. His testimony, however, should be read in light of the fact that NSC records during this period do not make clear whether or not the President ordered Lumumba's assassination and the fact that others attending those meetings testified that they did not recall hearing such a Presidential order.

Richard Bissell assumed that Presidential authorization for assassinating Lumumba had been communicated to him by Dulles, but Bissell had no specific recollection concerning when that communication occurred. The impression shared by the Congo Station Officer and the DDP's Special Assistant Joseph Scheider that the President authorized an assassination effort against Lumumba was derived solely from conversations Scheider had with Bissel and Bronson Tweedy. However, the impression thus held by Scheider and the Station Officer does not, in itself, establish Presidential authorization because neither Scheider nor the Station Officer had first-hand knowledge of Allen Dulles' statements about Presidential authorization, and because Scheider may have misconstrued Bissell's reference to "highest authority."

(e) *Castro*

There was insufficient evidence from which the Committee could conclude that Presidents Eisenhower, Kennedy, or Johnson, their close advisors, or the Special Group authorized the assassination of Castro.

The assassination plots against Castro were clearly authorized at least through the level of DDP. We also find that DCI Allen Dulles approved "thorough consideration" of the "elimination" of Castro. Further, it is also likely that Dulles knew about and authorized the actual plots that occurred during his tenure. Bissell and Edwards testified that they had briefed Dulles (and Cabell) on the plot involving underworld figures "circumlocutiously," but that they were certain that he had understood that the plot involved assassination. Their testimony is buttressed by the fact that Dulles knew about the plot to assassinate Lumumba which was being planned at the same time, and which also involved Bissell. We can find no evidence that McCone was aware of the plots which occurred during his tenure. His DDP, Richard Helms, testified that he never discussed the subject with McCone and was never expressly authorized by anyone to assassinate Castro.

The only suggestion of express Presidential authorization for the plots against Castro was Richard Bissell's opinion that Dulles would have informed Presidents Eisenhower and Kennedy by circumlocution only after the assassination had been planned and was underway. The assumptions underlying this opinion are too attenuated for the Committee to adopt it as a finding. First, this assumes that Dulles himself knew of the plot, a matter which is not entirely certain. Second, it assumes that Dulles went privately to the two Presidents—a course of action which Helms, who had far more covert action experience than Bissell, testified was precisely what the doctrine of plausible denial forbade CIA officials from doing. Third, it necessarily assumes that the Presidents would understand from a "circumlocutious" description that assassination was being discussed.

In view of the strained chain of assumptions and the contrary testimony of all the Presidential advisors, the men closest to both Eisenhower and Kennedy, the Committee makes no finding implicating Presidents who are not able to speak for themselves.

Helms and McCone testified that the Presidents under which they served never asked them to consider assassination.

There was no evidence whatsoever that President Johnson knew about or authorized any assassination activity during his Presidency.

3. CIA OFFICIALS INVOLVED IN THE ASSASSINATION OPERATIONS PERCEIVED ASSASSINATION TO HAVE BEEN A PERMISSIBLE COURSE OF ACTION

The CIA officials involved in the targeted assassination attempts testified that they had believed that their activities had been fully authorized.[1]

In the case of the Lumumba assassination operation, Richard Bissell testified that he had no direct recollection of authorization, but after having reviewed the cables and Special Group minutes, testified that authority must have flowed from Dulles through him to the subordinate levels in the Agency.

---

[1] The lower level operatives, such as the AM/LASH case officers, are not discussed in this section, since they had clear orders from their immediate superiors within the CIA.

In the case of the assassination effort against Castro, Bissell and Sheffield Edwards testified they believed the operation involving underworld figures had been authorized by Dulles when they briefed him shortly after the plot had been initiated. William Harvey testified he believed that the plots "were completely authorized at every appropriate level within and beyond the Agency," although he had "no personal knowledge whatever of the individuals' identities, times, exact words, or channels through which such authority may have passed." Harvey stated that he had been told by Richard Bissell that the effort against Castro had been authorized "from the highest level," and that Harvey had discussed the plots with Richard Helms, his immediate superior. Helms testified that although he had never discussed assassination with his superiors, he believed:

> * * * that in these actions we were taking against Cuba and against Fidel Castro's government in Cuba, that they were what we had been asked to do. * * * In other words we had been asked to get rid of Castro and * * * there were no limitations put on the means, and we felt we were acting well within the guidelines that we understood to be in play at this particular time.

The evidence points to a disturbing situation. Agency officials testified that they believed the effort to assassinate Castro to have been within the parameters of permissible action. But Administration officials responsible for formulating policy, including McCone, testified that they were not aware of the effort and did not authorize it. The explanation may lie in the fact that orders concerning overthrowing the Castro regime were stated in broad terms that were subject to differing interpretations by those responsible for carrying out those orders.

The various Presidents and their senior advisors strongly opposed the regimes of Castro and Trujillo, the accession to power of Allende, and the potential influence of Patrice Lumumba. Orders concerning action against those foreign leaders were given in vigorous language. For example, President Nixon's orders to prevent Allende from assuming power left Helms feeling that "if I ever carried a marshall's baton in my knapsack out of the Oval Office, it was that day." Similarly, General Lansdale described the Mongoose effort against Cuba as "a combat situation," and Attorney General Kennedy emphasized that "a solution to the Cuba problem today carries top priority." Helms testified that the pressure to "get rid of Castro and the Castro regime" was intense, and Bissell testified that he had been ordered to "get off your ass about Cuba."

It is possible that there was a failure of communication between policymakers and the agency personnel who were experienced in secret, and often violent, action. Although policymakers testified that assassination was not intended by such words as "get rid of Castro." Some of their subordinates in the Agency testified that they perceived that assassination was desired and that they should proceed without troubling their superiors.

The 1967 Inspector General's Report on assassinations appropriately observed:

> The point is that of frequent resort to synecdoche—the mention of a part when the whole is to be understood, or vice versa. Thus, we encounter repeated references to phrases such as "disposing of Castro," which may be read in the narrow, literal sense of assassinating him, when it is intended that it be read in the broader figurative sense of dislodging the Castro regime. Reversing the coin, we find people speaking vaguely of "doing something about Castro" when it is clear

that what they have specifically in mind is killing him. In a situation wherein those speaking may not have actually meant what they seemed to say or may not have said what they actually meant, they should not be surprised if their oral shorthand is interpreted differently than was intended.

Differing perceptions between superiors and their subordinates were graphically illustrated in the Castro context.[1] McCone, in a memorandum dated April 14, 1967, reflected as follows:

> Through the years the Cuban problem was discussed in terms such as "dispose of Castro," "remove Castro," "knock off Castro," etc., and this meant the overthrow of the Communist government in Cuba and the replacing of it with a democratic regime. Terms such as the above appear in many working papers, memoranda for the record, etc., and, as stated, all refer to a change in the Cuban government.[2]

Helms, who had considerable experience as a covert operator, gave precisely the opposite meaning to the same words, interpreting them as conveying authority for assassination.

Helms repeatedly testified that he felt that explicit authorization was unnecessary for the assassination of Castro in the early 1960's, but he said he did not construe the intense pressure from President Nixon in 1970 as providing authority to assassinate anyone. As Helms testified, the difference was not that the pressure to prevent Allende from assuming office was any less than the pressure to remove the Castro regime, but rather that "I had already made up my mind that we weren't going to have any of that business when I was Director."

Certain CIA contemporaries of Helms who were subjected to similar pressures in the Castro case rejected the thesis that implicit authority to assassinate Castro derived from the strong language of the policymakers. Bissell testified that he had believed that "formal and explicit approval" would be required for assassination, and Helms' assistant, George McManus, testified that "it never occurred to me" that the vigorous words of the Attorney General could be taken as authorizing assassination. The differing perceptions may have resulted from their different backgrounds and training. Neither Bissell (an academician whose Agency career for the six years before he became DDP had been in the field of technology) nor McManus (who had concentrated on intelligence and staff work) were experienced in covert operations.[3]

The perception of certain Agency officials that assassination was within the range of permissible activity was reinforced by the continuing approval of violent covert actions against Cuba that were sanc-

---

[1] Senator MATHIAS. Let me draw an example from history. When Thomas Becket was proving to be an annoyance, as Castro, the King said, "who will rid me of this troublesome priest?" He didn't say, "go out and murder him". He said, "who will rid me of this man," and let it go at that.
Mr. HELMS. That is a warming reference to the problem.
Senator MATHIAS. You feel that spans the generations and the centuries?
Mr. HELMS. I think it does, sir.
Senator MATHIAS. And that is typical of the kind of thing which might be said, which might be taken by the Director or by anybody else as presidential authorization to go forward?
Mr. HELMS. That is right. But in answer to that, I realize that one sort of grows up in tradition of the time and I think that any of us would have found it very difficult to discuss assassinations with a President of the U.S. I just think we all had the feeling that we were hired out to keep those things out of the oval office.
[2] It should be noted, however, that this memorandum was prepared several years after the assassination plots when a newspaper article alleged CIA involvement in attempts on Castro's life.
[3] Of course, this analysis cannot be carried too far. In the Lumumba case, for example, Johnson and Dillon, who were Administration officials with no covert operation experience, construed remarks as urging or permitting assassination, while other persons who were not in the Agency did not so interpret them.

tioned at the Presidential level, and by the failure of the successive administrations to make clear that assassination was not permissible. This point is one of the subjects considered in the next section.

4. THE FAILURE IN COMMUNICATION BETWEEN AGENCY OFFICIALS IN CHARGE OF THE ASSASSINATION OPERATIONS AND THEIR SUPERIORS IN THE AGENCY AND IN THE ADMINISTRATION WAS DUE TO: (A) THE FAILURE OF SUBORDINATES TO DISCLOSE THEIR PLANS AND OPERATIONS TO THEIR SUPERIORS; AND (B) THE FAILURE OF SUPERIORS IN THE CLIMATE OF VIOLENCE AND AGGRESSIVE COVERT ACTIONS SANCTIONED BY THE ADMINISTRATIONS TO RULE OUT ASSASSINATION AS A TOOL OF FOREIGN POLICY; TO MAKE CLEAR TO THEIR SUBORDINATES THAT ASSASSINATION WAS IMPERMISSIBLE; OR TO INQUIRE FURTHER AFTER RECEIVING INDICATIONS THAT IT WAS BEING CONSIDERED

While we cannot find that officials responsible for making policy decisions knew about or authorized the assassination attempts (with the possible exception of the Lumumba case), Agency operatives at least through the level of DDP nevertheless perceived assassination to have been permissible. This failure in communication was inexcusable in light of the gravity of assassination. The Committee finds that the failure of Agency officials to inform their superiors was reprehensible, and that the reasons that they offered for having neglected to inform their superiors are unacceptable. The Committee further finds that Administration officials failed to be sufficiently precise in their directions to the Agency, and that their attitude toward the possibility of assassination was ambiguous in the context of the violence of other activities that they did authorize.

(a) *Agency officials failed on several occasions to reveal the plots to their superiors, or to do so with sufficient detail and clarity*

Several of the cases considered in this report raise questions concerning whether officials of the CIA sufficiently informed their superiors in the Agency or officials outside the Agency about their activities.

(i) *Castro*

The failure of Agency officials to inform their superiors of the assassination efforts against Castro is particularly troubling.

On the basis of the testimony and documentary evidence before the Committee, it is not entirely certain that Dulles was ever made aware of the true nature of the underworld operation. The plot continued into McCone's term, apparently without McCone's or the Administration's knowledge or approval.

On some occasions when Richard Bissell had the opportunity to inform his superiors about the assassination effort against Castro, he either failed to inform them, failed to do so clearly, or misled them.

Bissell testified that he and Edwards told Dulles and Cabell about the assassination operation using underworld figures, but that they did so "circumlocutiously", and then only after contact had been made with the underworld and a price had been offered for Castro's death.

Perhaps Bissell should have checked back with Dulles at an earlier stage after having received approval to give "thorough consideration" to Castro's "elimination" from Dulles in December 1959.

Bissell further testified that he never raised the issue of assassination with non-CIA officials of either the Eisenhower or Kennedy Administration. His reason was that since he was under Dulles in the chain of command, he would normally have had no duty to discuss the matter with these Presidents or other Administration officials, and that he assumed that Dulles would have "circumlocutiously" spoken with Presidents Eisenhower and Kennedy about the operation. These reasons are insufficient. It was inexcusable to withhold such information from those responsible for formulating policy on the unverified assumption that they might have been "circumlocutiously" informed by Dulles.[1]

The failure either to inform those officials or to make certain that they had been informed by Dulles was particularly reprehensible in light of the fact that there were many occasions on which Bissell should have informed them, and his failure to do so was misleading. In the first weeks of the Kennedy Administration, Bissell met with Bundy and discussed the development of an assassination capability within CIA—Executive Action. But Bissell did not mention that an actual assassination attempt was underway. Bissell appeared before the Taylor-Kennedy Board of Inquiry which was formed to report to the President on the Bay of Pigs and the Cuban situation, but he testified that he did not inform the Board of the assassination operation.[2] As chief of the CIA directorate concerned with clandestine operations and the Bay of Pigs, Bissell frequently met with officials in the Eisenhower and Kennedy Administrations to discuss Cuban operations, and his advice was frequently sought. He did not tell them that the CIA had undertaken an effort to assassinate Castro, and did not ask if they favored proceeding with the effort. He was present at the meeting with Dulles and President Kennedy at which the new President was briefed on covert action in Cuba, but neither Dulles nor Bissell mentioned the assassination operation that was underway. Dulles himself may not have always been candid. On December 11, 1959, he approved the CIA's giving "thorough consideration to the elimination of Fidel Castro," but told the Special Group in a meeting the following month that "we do not have in mind the quick elimination of Castro, but rather actions designed to enable responsible opposition leaders to get a foothold."

The failures to make forthright disclosures to policy-makers continued during the time that Richard Helms was DDP. Helms' failure to inform McCone about the underworld operation (when it was reactivated under Harvey and poison pills were sent to Cuba) was a grave error in judgment, and Helms' excuses are unpersuasive. In May 1962 the Attorney General was told that the CIA's involve-

---
[1] Even assuming that Bissell correctly perceived that Dulles understood the nature of the operation, it was also inexcusable for Bissell not to have briefed Dulles in plain language. Further, even if one accepts Bissell's assumption that Dulles told the Presidents, they would have been told too late, because Bissell "guessed" they would have been told that the operation "had been planned and was being attempted."
[2] Dulles was also a member of the Board.

ment in an assassination plot had terminated with the Bay of Pigs. Not only did Edwards, who had briefed the Attorney General, know that the operation had not been terminated, but Helms did not inform the Attorney General that the operation was still active when he learned that the Attorney General had been misled. Helms did not inform McCone of the plot until August 1963, and did so then in a manner which indicated that the plot had been terminated before McCone became Director. Helms' denial that AM/LASH had been involved in an assassination effort in response to Secretary of State Rusk's inquiries was, as Helms conceded, not factual.

When Helms briefed President Johnson on the Castro plots, he apparently described the activities that had occurred during prior administrations but did not describe the AM/LASH operation which had continued until 1965. Helms also failed to inform the Warren Commission of the plots because the precise question was not asked.[1]

Helms told the Committee that he had never raised the assassination operation with McCone or other Kennedy Administration officials because of the sensitivity of the matter, because he had assumed that the project had been previously authorized, and because the aggressive character of the Kennedy Administration's program against the Castro regime led him to believe that assassination was permissible, even though he did not receive an express instruction to that effect. He added that he had never been convinced that the operation would succeed, and that he would have told McCone about it if he had ever believed that it would "go anyplace."

Helms' reasons for not having told his superiors about the assassination effort are unacceptable; indeed, many of them were reasons why he should have specifically raised the matter with higher authority. As Helms himself testified, assassination was of a high order of sensitivity. Administration policymakers, supported by intelligence estimates furnished by the Agency, had emphasized on several occasions that successors to Castro might be worse than Castro himself. In addition, the Special Group (Augmented) required that plans for covert actions against Cuba be submitted in detail for its approval. Although the Administration was exerting intense pressure on the CIA to do something about Castro and the Castro regime, it was a serious error to have undertaken so drastic an operation without making certain that there was full and unequivocal permission to proceed.

William Harvey, the officer in charge of the CIA's attempt using underworld figures to assassinate Castro, testified that he never discussed the plot with McCone or officials of the Kennedy Administration because he believed that it had been fully authorized by the previous Director, because he was uncertain whether it had a chance of succeeding, and because he believed that it was not his duty to inform higher authorities.

Nonetheless, the Committee believes there were occasions on which it was incumbent on Harvey to have disclosed the assassination operation. As head of Task Force W, the branch of the CIA responsible for covert operations in Cuba, Harvey reported directly to General Lansdale and the Special Group (Augmented). The Special Group

---

[1] John McCone was Director of the CIA and at least knew about the pre-Bay of Pigs plot during the Warren Commission's inquiry. McCone failed to disclose the plot to the Commission. Allen Dulles was on the Warren Commission. He did not inform the other members about the plots that had occurred during his term as DCI.

(Augmented) had made it known that covert operations in Cuba should be first approved by it, both by explicit instruction and by its practice that particular operations be submitted in "nauseating detail". Yet Harvey did not inform either General Lansdale or the Special Group (Augmented) of the assassination operation, either when he was explicitly requested to report to McCone, General Taylor, and the Special Group on his activities in Miami in April 1962, or when the subject of assassination was raised in the August 1962 meeting and McCone voiced his disapproval. Harvey testified that a matter as sensitive as assassination would never be raised in a gathering as large as the Special Group (Augmented).

The Committee finds the reasons advanced for not having informed those responsible for formulating policy about the assassination operation inadequate, misleading, and inconsistent. Some officials viewed assassination as too important and sensitive to discuss with superiors, while others considered it not sufficiently important. Harvey testified that it was premature to tell McCone about the underworld operation in April 1962, because it was not sufficiently advanced; but too late to tell him about it in August 1962, since by that time Harvey had decided to terminate it. On other occasions, officials thought disclosure was someone else's responsibility; Bissell said he thought it was up to Dulles, and Harvey believed it was up to Helms.

The Committee concludes that the failure to clearly inform policymakers of the assassination effort against Castro was grossly improper. The Committee believes that it should be incumbent on the DDP to report such a sensitive operation to his superior, the DCI, no matter how grave his doubts might be about the possible outcome of the operation. It follows that the DCI has the same duty to accurately inform his superiors.

(ii) Trujillo

In the Trujillo case there were several instances in which it appears that policymakers were not given sufficient information, or were not informed in a timely fashion.

At a meeting on December 29, 1960, Bissell presented a plan to the Special Group for supporting Dominican exile groups and local dissidents, and stated that the plan would not bring down the regime without "some decisive stroke against Trujillo himself." At a meeting on January 12, 1961, the Special Group authorized the passage of "limited supplies of small arms and other materials" to Dominican dissidents under certain conditions.

At this time, the fact that the dissidents had been contemplating the assassination of Trujillo had been known in the State Department at least through the level of the Assistant Secretary of State for Inter-American Affairs, and by senior officials of the CIA, including the DCI. Yet the internal State Department memorandum which was furnished to Undersecretary Livingston Merchant, and which was said to have been the basis for the Special Group's agreeing to the limited supply of small arms and other material (i.e., explosive devices), did not mention assassination. Instead, it spoke of "sabotage potential" and stated that there "would be no thought of toppling the [government] by any such minor measure [as the supplying of small arms and explosives]."

At a meeting of the Special Group on February 14, 1961, representatives of the CIA briefed the new members of the Group on outstanding

CIA projects. The Dominican Republic was one of the briefing topics. The minutes of that meeting indicate that Mr. Bundy requested a memorandum for "higher authority" on the subject of what plans could be made for a successor government to Trujillo. Bissell had no clear recollection as to the details of the February 14 briefing and was unable to recall whether or not the method of overthrow to be attempted by the dissidents was discussed. It is not known, therefore, whether the new members of the Special Group learned, at that time, of Bissell's assessment that overthrow of the regime required a decisive stroke against Trujillo himself. Robert McNamara recalled no mention at that meeting of any dissident plans to assassinate Trujillo.

On February 15 and 17, 1961, memoranda were prepared for the President by Secretary of State Rusk and by Richard Bissell respectively. Although both the Department of State and the CIA then had information concerning the dissidents' intent to assassinate Trujillo if possible, neither memorandum referred to such a contingency. Rusk disclaimed any knowledge of the dissidents intent to assassinate Trujillo until shortly before the event occurred, but Bissell admitted personal awareness of the assassination plans.

Bissell's February 17 memorandum indicated that dissident leaders had informed the CIA of "their plan of action which they felt could be implemented if they were provided with arms for 300 men, explosives, and remote control detonation devices." Various witnesses testified that supplying arms for 300 men would, standing alone, indicate a "non-targeted" use for the arms. One possible method of assassinating Trujillo which had long been discussed by the dissidents and which was the favored approach at the time of Bissell's memorandum envisioned assassination by means of a bomb detonated by remote control. But the memorandum made no reference to the use to which the explosive devices might be put. (There is no record of any query from recipients of the briefing paper as to the nature of the dissidents' "plan of action" or the uses for which the arms and explosives were intended.)

The passage of the carbines was approved by CIA Headquarters on March 31, 1961. Although the State Department's representative in the Dominican Republic concurred in the decision to pass the carbines, he was requested by the CIA not to communicate this information to State Department officials in Washington, and he complied with that request. Accordingly, neither the State Department nor the White House was aware of the passage for several weeks. Similarly, there was no contemporaneous disclosure outside the CIA, other than to the State Department representative in the Dominican Republic, that machine guns had been sent to the Dominican Republic via the diplomatic pouch.

A memorandum prepared by Adolph Berle, the State Department official from whom the CIA sought permission to pass the machine guns, states that "on cross-examination it developed that the real plan was to assassinate Trujillo and they wanted guns for that purpose." (Berle, Memorandum of Conversation, 5/3/61) Berle's memorandum states that he informed the CIA officials that "we did not wish to have anything to do with any assassination plots anywhere, any time." The CIA official reportedly said he felt the same way, even though on the previous day he had been one of the signers of a draft CIA cable which would have permitted passage of the machine guns to the dissidents for "* * * their additional protection on their proposed endeavor." (Draft HQs to Station Cable, 5/2/61)

Although the report of a new anti-Trujillo plot was discussed at a meeting of the Special Group on May 4, 1961, there is no indication that Berle, who was the Chairman of the Inter-Agency Task Force having responsibility for contingency planning for Cuba, the Dominican Republic, and Haiti, disclosed to higher authority the assassination information which he discovered by "cross-examination." The National Security Council met the next day and noted the President's view that the United States should not initiate the overthrow of Trujillo before it was known what government would succeed him. That National Security Council Record of Action was approved by the President on May 16, 1961. There is no record indicating whether Berle communicated to the President, or to members of the National Security Council, his knowledge as to the lethal intent of the dissidents who would be carrying out the overthrow of Trujillo.

(iii) Schneider

The issue here is not whether the objectives of the CIA were contrary to those of the Administration. It is clear that President Nixon desired to prevent Allende from assuming office, even if that required fomenting and supporting a coup in Chile. Nor did White House officials suggest that tactics employed (including as a first step kidnapping General Schneider) would have been unacceptable as a matter of principle. Rather, the issue posed is whether White House officials were consulted, and thus given an opportunity to weigh such matters as risk and likelihood of success, and to apply policy-making judgments to particular tactics. The record indicates that up to October 15 they were; after October 15 there is some doubt.

The documentary record with respect to the disputed post-October 15 period gives rise to conflicting inferences. On the one hand, Karamessines' calendar shows at least one White House contact in the critical period prior to the kidnapping of General Schneider on October 22. However, the absence of any substantive memoranda in CIA files—when contrasted with several such memoranda describing contacts with the White House between September 15 and October 15—may suggest a lack of significant communication on the part of the CIA as well as a lack of careful supervision on the part of the White House.

The standards applied within the CIA itself suggest a view that action which the Committee believes called for top-level policy discussion and decision was thought of as permissible, without any further consultation, on the basis of the initial instruction to prevent Allende from assuming power. Machine guns were sent to Chile and delivered to military figures there on the authority of middle level CIA officers without consultation even with the CIA officer in charge of the program. We find no suggestion of bad faith in the action of the middle level officers, but their failure to consult necessarily establishes that there was no advance permission from outside the CIA for the passage of machine guns. And it also suggests an unduly lax attitude within the CIA toward consultation with superiors. Further, this case demonstrates the problems inherent in giving an agency a "blank check" to engage in covert operations without specifying which actions are permissible and which are not, and without adequately supervising and monitoring these activities.

(b) *Administration officials failed to rule out assassination as a tool of foreign policy, to make clear to their subordinates that assassination was impermissible or to inquire further after receiving indications that assassination was being considered*

While we do not find that high Administration officials expressly approved of the assassination attempts, we have noted that certain agency officials nevertheless perceived assassination to have been authorized. Although those officials were remiss in not seeking express authorization for their activities, their superiors were also at fault for giving vague instructions and for not explicitly ruling out assassination. No written order prohibiting assassination was issued until 1972, and that order was an internal CIA directive issued by Director Helms.

(i) *Trujillo*

Immediately following the assassination of Trujillo, there were a number of high-level meetings about the Dominican Republic attended by the policymakers of the Kennedy Administration. All relevant facts concerning CIA and State Department support of the Dominican dissidents were fully known. No directive was issued by the President or the Special Group criticizing any aspect of United States involvement in the Dominican affair. Similarly, there is no record of any action having been taken prohibiting future support or encouragement of groups or individuals known to be planning the assassination of a foreign leader. The meetings and discussions following the Trujillo assassination represent another missed opportunity to establish an administration policy against assassination and may partially account for the CIA's assessment of the Dominican operation as a success a few years later. They may also have encouraged Agency personnel, involved in both the Trujillo and the Castro plots, in their belief that the Administration would not be unhappy if the Agency were able to make Castro disappear. No such claim, however, was made in testimony by any agency official.

(ii) *Schneider*

As explained above, there is no evidence that assassination was ever proposed as a method of carrying out the Presidential order to prevent Allende from assuming office. The Committee believes, however, that the granting of *carte blanche* authority to the CIA by the Executive in this case may have contributed to the tragic and unintended death of General Schneider. This was also partially due to assigning an impractical task to be accomplished within an unreasonably short time. Apart from the question of whether any intervention in Chile was justified under the circumstances of this case, the Committee believes that the Executive in any event should have defined the limits of permissible action.

(iii) *Lumumba*

We are unable to make a finding that President Eisenhower intentionally authorized an assassination effort against Lumumba due to the lack of absolute certainty in the evidence. However, it appears that the strong language used in discussions at the Special Group and NSC, as reflected in minutes of relevant meetings, led Dulles to believe that assassination was desired. The minutes contain language concerning the need to "dispose of" Lumumba, an "extremely strong feeling about the necessity for straightforward action," and a refusal to rule out any activity that might contribute to "getting rid of" Lumumba.

(iv) Castro

The efforts to assassinate Fidel Castro took place in an atmosphere of extreme pressure by Eisenhower and Kennedy Administration officials to discredit and overthrow the Castro regime. Shortly after Castro's ascendancy to power, Allen Dulles directed that "thorough consideration" be given to the "elimination" of Castro. Richard Helms recalled that:

> I remember vividly [that the pressure] was very intense. And therefore, when you go into the record, you find a lot of nutty schemes there and those nutty schemes were borne of the intensity of the pressure. And we were quite frustrated.

Bissell recalled that:

> During that entire period, the Administration was extremely sensitive about the defeat that had been inflicted, as they felt, on the U.S. at the Bay of Pigs, and were pursuing every possible means of getting rid of Castro.

Another CIA official stated that sometime in the Fall of 1961 Bissell was:

> * * * chewed out in the Cabinet Room in the White House by both the President and the Attorney General for, as he put it, sitting on his ass and not doing anything about getting rid of Castro and the Castro Regime.

General Lansdale informed the agencies cooperating in Operation MONGOOSE that "you're in a combat situation where we have been given full command." Secretary of Defense McNamara confirmed that "we were hysterical about Castro at the time of the Bay of Pigs and thereafter."

Many of the plans that were discussed and often approved contemplated violent action against Cuba. The operation which resulted in the Bay of Pigs was a major paramilitary onslaught that had the approval of the highest government officials, including the two Presidents. Thereafter, Attorney General Kennedy vehemently exhorted the Special Group (Augmented) that "a solution to the Cuban problem today carried top priority * * * no time, money, effort—or manpower is to be spared."[1] Subsequently, Operation MONGOOSE involved propaganda and sabotage operations aimed toward spurring a revolt of the Cuban people against Castro. Measures which were considered by the top policymakers included incapacitating sugar workers during harvest season by the use of chemicals; blowing up bridges and production plants; sabotaging merchandise in third countries— even those allied with the United States—prior to its delivery to Cuba; and arming insurgents on the island. Programs undertaken at the urging of the Administration included intensive efforts to recruit and arm dissidents within Cuba, and raids on plants, mines, and harbors. Consideration and approval of these measures may understandably have led the CIA to conclude that violent actions were an acceptable means of accomplishing important objectives.

---

[1] The Attorney General himself took a personal interest in the recruitment and development of assets within Cuba, on occasion recommending Cubans to the CIA as possible recruits and meeting in Washington and Florida with Cuban exiles active in the covert war against the Castro Government.

Discussions at the Special Group and NSC meetings might well have contributed to the perception of some CIA officials that assassination was a permissible tool in the effort to overthrow the Castro Regime. At a Special Group meeting in November 1960, Undersecretary Merchant inquired whether any planning had been undertaken for "direct, positive action" against Che Guevara, Raul Castro, and Fidel Castro. Cabell replied that such a capability did not exist, but he might well have left the meeting with the impression that assassination was not out of bounds. Lansdale's plan, which was submitted to the Special Group in January 1962, aimed at inducing "open revolt and overthrow of the Communist regime." Included in its final phase an "attack on the cadre of the regime, including key leaders." The proposal stated that "this should be a 'Special Target' operation * * *. Gangster elements might provide the best recruitment potential against police * * *." Although Lansdale's proposal was shelved, the type of aggressive action contemplated was not formally ruled out. Minutes from several Special Group meetings contain language such as "possible removal of Castro from the Cuban scene."

On several occasions, the subject of assassination was discussed in the presence of senior Administration officials. Those officials never consented to actual assassination efforts, but they failed to indicate that assassination was impermissible as a matter of principle.

In early 1961, McGeorge Bundy was informed of a CIA project described as the development of a capability to assassinate. Bundy raised no objection and, according to Bissell, may have been more affirmative.[1] Bissell stated that he did not construe Bundy's remarks as authorization for the underworld plot against Castro that was then underway. But the fact that he believed that the development of an assassination capability had, as he subsequently told Harvey, been approved by the White House, may well have contributed to the general perception that assassination was not prohibited.[2]

Documents received by the Committee indicate that in May 1961, Attorney General Kennedy and the Director of the FBI received information that the CIA was engaged in clandestine efforts against Castro which included the use of Sam Giancana and other underworld figures. The various documents referred to "dirty business," "clandestine efforts," and "plans" which were still "working" and might eventually "pay off." The Committee is unable to determine whether Hoover and the Attorney General ever inquired into the nature of the CIA operation, although there is no evidence that they did so inquire. The Committee believes that they should have inquired, and that their failure to do so was a dereliction of their duties.

Documents indicate that in May 1962, Attorney General Kennedy was told that the CIA had sought to assassinate Castro prior to the Bay of Pigs. According to the CIA officials who were present at the briefing, the Attorney General indicated his displeasure about the lack of consultation rather than about the impropriety of the attempt

---

[1] The Inspector General's Report states that Harvey's notes (which no longer exist) quoted Bissell as saying to Harvey: "The White House has twice urged me to create such as capability."

[2] Bundy, as the National Security Advisor to the President, had an obligation to tell the President of such a grave matter, even though it was only a discussion of a capability to assassinate. His failure to do so was a serious error.

itself. There is no evidence that the Attorney General told the CIA that it must not engage in assassination plots in the future.

At a meeting of the Special Group (Augmented) in August 1962, well after the assassination efforts were underway, Robert McNamara is said to have raised the question of whether the assassination of Cuban leaders should be explored, and General Lansdale issued an action memorandum assigning the CIA the task of preparing contingency plans for the assassination of Cuban leaders. While McCone testified that he had immediately made it clear that assassination was not to be discussed or condoned, Harvey's testimony and documents which he wrote after the event indicate that Harvey may have been confused over whether McCone had objected to the use of assassination, or whether he was only concerned that the subject not be put in writing. In any event, McCone went no further. He issued no general order banning consideration of assassination within the Agency.

One of the programs forwarded to General Lansdale by the Defense Department in the MONGOOSE program was entitled "Operation Bounty" and envisioned dropping leaflets in Cuba offering rewards for the assassination of Government leaders. Although the plan was vetoed by Lansdale, it indicates that persons in agencies other than the CIA perceived that assassination might be permissible.

While the ambivalence of Administration officials does not excuse the misleading conduct by Agency officials or justify their failure to seek explicit permission, this attitude displayed an insufficient concern about assassination which may have contributed to the perception that assassination was an acceptable tactic in accomplishing the Government's general objectives.

Moreover, with the exception of the tight guidelines issued by the Special Group (Augmented) concerning Operation MONGOOSE, precise limitations were never imposed on the CIA requiring prior permission for the details of other proposed covert operations against Cuba.

No general policy banning assassination was promulgated until Helms' intra-agency order in 1972. Considering the number of times the subject of assassination had arisen, Administration officials were remiss in not explicitly forbidding such activity.

The committee notes that many of the occasions on which CIA officials should have informed their superiors of the assassination efforts but failed to do so, or did so in a misleading manner, were also occasions on which Administration officials paradoxically may have reinforced the perception that assassination was permissible.

For example, when Bissell spoke with Bundy about an Executive Action capability, Bissell failed to indicate that an actual assassination operation was underway, but Bundy failed to rule out assassination as a tactic.

In May 1962, the Attorney General was misleadingly told about the effort to assassinate Castro prior to the Bay of Pigs, but not about the operation that was then going on. The Attorney General, however, did not state that assassination was improper.

When a senior administration official raised the question of whether assassination should be explored at a Special Group meeting, the assassination operation should have been revealed. A firm written order against engaging in assassination should also have been issued by McCone if, as he testified, he had exhibited strong aversion to assassination.

5. PRACTICES CURRENT AT THE TIME IN WHICH THE ASSASSINATION PLOTS OCCURRED WERE REVEALED BY THE RECORD TO CREATE THE RISK OF CONFUSION, RASHNESS AND IRRESPONSIBILITY IN THE VERY AREAS WHERE CLARITY AND SOBER JUDGMENT WERE MOST NECESSARY

Various witnesses described elements of the system within which the assassination plots were conceived. The Committee is disturbed by the custom that permitted the most sensitive matters to be presented to the highest levels of Government with the least clarity. We view the following points as particularly dangerous:

(1) The expansion of the doctrine of "plausible denial" beyond its intended purpose of hiding the involvement of the United States from other countries into an effort to shield higher officials from knowledge, and hence responsibility, for certain operations.

(2) The use of circumlocution or euphemism to describe serious matters—such as assassination—when precise meanings ought to be made clear.

(3) The theory that general approval of broad covert action programs is sufficient to justify specific actions such as assassination or the passage of weapons.

(4) The theory that authority granted, or assumed to be granted, by one DCI or one Administration could be presumed to continue without the necessity for reaffirming the authority with successor officials.

(5) The creation of covert capabilities without careful review and authorization by policymakers, and the further risk that such capabilities, once created, might be used without specific authorization.

(a) The danger inherent in overextending the doctrine of "plausible denial"

The original concept of "plausible denial" envisioned implementing covert actions in a manner calculated to conceal American involvement if the actions were exposed. The doctrine was at times a delusion and at times a snare. It was naive for policymakers to assume that sponsorship of actions as big as the Bay of Pigs invasion could be concealed. The Committee's investigation of assassination and the public disclosures which preceded the inquiry demonstrate that when the United States resorted to cloak-and-dagger tactics, its hand was ultimately exposed. We were particularly disturbed to find little evidence that the risks and consequences of disclosure were considered.

We find that the likelihood of reckless action is substantially increased when policymakers believe that their decisions will never be revealed. Whatever can be said in defense of the original purpose of plausible denial—a purpose which intends to conceal United States involvement from the outside world—the extension of the doctrine to the internal decision-making process of the Government is absurd. Any theory which, as a matter of doctrine, places elected officials on the periphery of the decision-making process is an invitation to error, an abdication of responsibility, and a perversion of democratic government. The doctrine is the antithesis of accountability.

(b) *The danger of using "Circumlocution" and "Euphemism"*

According to Richard Bissell, the extension of "plausible denial" to internal decision-making required the use of circumlocution and euphemism in speaking with Presidents and other senior officials.

Explaining this concept only heightens its absurdity. On the one hand, it assumes that senior officials should be shielded from the truth to enable them to deny knowledge if the truth comes out. On the other hand, the concept assumes that senior officials must be told enough, by way of double talk, to grasp the subject. As a consequence, the theory fails to accomplish its objective and only increases the risk of misunderstanding. Subordinate officials should describe their proposals in clear, precise, and brutally frank language; superiors are entitled to, and should demand, no less.

Euphemism may actually have been preferred—not because of "plausible denial"—but because the persons involved could not bring themselves to state in plain language what they intended to do. In some instances, moreover, subordinates may have assumed, rightly or wrongly, that the listening superiors did not want the issue squarely placed before them. "Assassinate," "murder" and "kill" are words many people do not want to speak or hear. They describe acts which should not even be proposed, let alone plotted. Failing to call dirty business by its rightful name may have increased the risk of dirty business being done.

(c) *The danger of generalized instructions*

Permitting specific acts to be taken on the basis of general approvals of broad strategies (e.g., keep Allende from assuming office, get rid of the Castro regime) blurs responsibility and accountability. Worse still, it increases the danger that subordinates may take steps which would have been disapproved if the policymakers had been informed. A further danger is that policymakers might intentionally use loose general instructions to evade responsibility for embarrassing activities.

In either event, we find that the gap between the general policy objectives and the specific actions undertaken to achieve them was far too wide.

It is important that policymakers review the manner in which their directives are implemented, particularly when the activities are sensitive, secret, and immune from public scrutiny.

(d) *The danger of "Floating Authorization"*

One justification advanced by Richard Helms and William Harvey for not informing John McCone about the use of underworld figures to attempt to assassinate Fidel Castro was their assertion that the project had already been approved by McCone's predecessor, Allen Dulles, and that further authorization was unnecessary, at least until the operation had reached a more advanced stage.

We find that the idea that authority might continue or "float" from one administration or director to the next and that there is no duty to reaffirm authority inhibits responsible decision-making. Circumstances may change or judgments differ. New officials should be given the opportunity to review significant programs.

(e) The problems connected with creating new covert capabilities

The development of a new capability raises numerous problems. Having a capability to engage in certain covert activity increases the probability that the activity will occur, since the capability represents a tool available for use. There is the further danger that authorization for the mere creation of a capability may be misunderstood as permitting its use without requiring further authorization.

Finally, an assassination capability should never have been created.

V. RECOMMENDATIONS

The Committee's long investigation of assassination has brought a number of important issues into sharp focus. Above all stands the question of whether assassination is an acceptable tool of American foreign policy. Recommendations on other issues must await the completion of our continuing investigation and the final report, but the Committee needs no more information to be convinced that a flat ban against assassination should be written into law.

We condemn assassination and reject it as an instrument of American policy. Surprisingly, however, there is presently no statute making it a crime to assassinate a foreign official outside the United States. Hence, for the reasons set forth below, the Committee recommends the prompt enactment of a statute making it a Federal crime to commit or attempt an assassination, or to conspire to do so.

A. GENERAL AGREEMENT THAT THE UNITED STATES MUST NOT ENGAGE IN ASSASSINATION

Our view that assassination has no place in America's arsenal is shared by the Administration.

President Ford, in the same statement in which he asked this Committee to deal with the assassination issue, stated:

> I am opposed to political assassination. This administration has not and will not use such means as instruments of national policy. (Presidential Press Conference, 6/9/75, *Weekly Compilation of Presidential Documents*, Vol. II, No. 24, p. 611.)

The witnesses who testified before the Committee uniformly condemned assassination. They denounced it as immoral, described it as impractical, and reminded us that an open society, more than any other, is particularly vulnerable to the risk that its own leaders may be assassinated. As President Kennedy reportedly said: "We can't get into that kind of thing, or we would all be targets." (Goodwin, 7/18/75, p. 4)

The current Director of Central Intelligence and his two predecessors testified emphatically that assassination should be banned. William Colby said:

> With respect to assassination, my position is clear, I just think it is wrong. And I have said so and made it very clear to my subordinates. (Colby, * * * 5/21/75, p. 89)

Richard Helms, who had been involved in an assassination plot before he became DCI, said he had concluded assassination should be ruled out for both moral and practical reasons:

> As a result of my experiences through the years, when I became Director I had made up my mind that this option * * * of killing foreign leaders, was something that I did not want to happen on my watch. My reasons for this were these:
> There are not only moral reasons but there are also some other rather practical reasons.

It is almost impossible in a democracy to keep anything like that secret * * *. Somebody would go to a Congressman, his Senator, he might go to a newspaper man, whatever the case may be, but it just is not a practical alternative, it seems to me, in our society.

Then there is another consideration * * * if you are going to try by this kind of means to remove a foreign leader, then who is going to take his place running that country, and are you essentially better off as a matter of practice when it is over than you were before? And I can give you I think a very solid example of this which happened in Vietnam when President Diem was eliminated from the scene. We then had a revolving door of prime ministers after that for quite some period of time, during which the Vietnamese Government at a time in its history when it should have been strong was nothing but a caretaker government * * *. In other words, that whole exercise turned out to the disadvantage of the United States.

* * * there is no sense in my sitting here with all the experience I have had and not sharing with the Committee my feelings this day. It isn't because I have lost my cool, or because I have lost my guts, it simply is because I don't think it is a viable option in the United States of America these days.

Chairman CHURCH. Doesn't it also follow, Mr. Helms—I agree with what you have said fully—but doesn't it also follow on the practical side, apart from the moral side, that since these secrets are bound to come out, when they do, they do very grave political damage to the United States in the world at large? I don't know to what extent the Russians involved themselves in political assassinations, but under their system they at least have a better prospect of keeping it concealed. Since we do like a free society and since these secrets are going to come out in due course, the revelation will then do serious injury to the good name and reputation of the United States.

Would you agree with that?

Mr. HELMS. Yes, I would.

Chairman CHURCH. And finally, if we were to reserve to ourselves the prerogative to assassinate foreign leaders, we may invite reciprocal action from foreign governments who assume that if it's our prerogative to do so, it is their prerogative as well, and that is another danger that we at least invite with this kind of action, wouldn't you agree?

Mr. HELMS: Yes, sir. (Helms, 6/13/75, pp. 76–78)

John McCone said he was opposed to assassinations because:

I didn't think it was proper from the standpoint of the U.S. Government and the Central Intelligence Agency. (McCone, 6/6/75. p. 15)

B. CIA DIRECTIVES BANNING ASSASSINATION

Helms in 1972 and Colby in 1973 issued internal CIA orders banning assassination. Helms' order said:

It has recently again been alleged in the press that CIA engages in assassination. As you are well aware, this is not the case, and Agency policy has long been clear on this issue. To underline it, however, I direct that no such activity or operation be undertaken, assisted or suggested by any of our personnel * * *. (Memo, Helms to Deputy Directors, 3/6/72)

In one of a series of orders arising out the CIA's own review of prior "questionable activity," Colby stated:

CIA will not engage in assassination nor induce, assist or suggest to others that assasination be employed. (Memo, Colby to Deputy Directors, 8/29/73)

C. THE NEED FOR A STATUTE

Commendable and welcome as they are, these CIA directives are not sufficient. Administrations change, CIA directors change, and someday in the future what was tried in the past may once again become a temptation. Assassination plots did happen. It would be irresponsible not to do all that can be done to prevent their happening again. A law is needed. Laws express our nation's values; they deter those who might be tempted to ignore those values and stiffen the will of those who want to resist the temptation.

The Committee recommends a statute [1] which would make it a criminal offense for persons subject to the jurisdiction of the United States (1) to conspire, within or outside the United States, to assassinate a foreign official; (2) to attempt to assassinate a foreign official, or (3) to assassinate a foreign official.

Present law makes it a crime to kill, or to conspire to kill, a foreign official or foreign official guest while such a person is in the United States. (18 U.S.C. 1116–1117). However, there is no law which makes it a crime to assassinate, to conspire to assassinate, or to attempt to assassinate a foreign official while such official is outside the United States. The Committee's proposed statute is designed to close this gap in the law.

Subsection (a) of the proposed statute would punish conspiracies within the United States; subsection (b) would punish conspiracies outside the United States. Subsection (b) is necessary to eliminate the loophole which would otherwise permit persons to simply leave the United States and conspire abroad. Subsections (c) and (d), respectively, would make it an offense to attempt to kill or to kill a foreign official outside the United States.

Subsections (a), (b), (c), and (d) would apply expressly to any "officer or employee of the United States" to make clear that the statute punishes conduct by United States Government personnel, as well as conduct by private citizens. In addition, subsection (a), which covers conspiracies within the United States, would apply to "any other person," regardless of citizenship. Non-citizens who conspired within the United States to assassinate a foreign official would clearly come within the jurisdiction of the law. Subsections (b), (c), and (d), which deal with conduct abroad, would apply to United States citizens, and to officers or employees of the United States, regardless of their citizenship. Criminal liability for acts committed abroad by persons who are not American citizens or who are not officers or employees of the United States is beyond the jurisdiction of the United States.

"Foreign official" is defined in subsection (e)(2) to make clear that an offense may be committed even though the "official" belongs to an insurgent force, an unrecognized government, or a political party. The Committee's investigation—as well as the reality of international politics—has shown that officials in such organizations are potential targets for assassination.[2] Killing, attempting to kill, or conspiring to kill would be punishable under the statute only if it were politically motivated. Political motivation would encompass acts against foreign officials because of their political views, actions, or statements.

The definition of "foreign official" in section (e)(2) also provides that such person must be an official of a foreign government or movement "with which the United States is not at war pursuant to a declaration of war or against which the United States Armed Forces

---

[1] The recommended statute is printed in Appendix A.
[2] For example, Lumumba was not an official of the Congolese government at the time of the plots against his life, and Trujillo, even though the dictator of the Dominican Republic, held no official governmental position in the latter period of his regime.

have not been introduced into hostilities or situations pursuant to the provisions of the War Powers Resolution." This definition makes it clear that, absent a declaration of war or the introduction of United States Armed Forces pursuant to the War Powers Resolution, the killing of foreign officials on account of their political views would be a criminal offense.

During the Committee's hearings, some witnesses, while strongly condemning assassination, asked whether assassination should absolutely be ruled out in a time of truly unusual national emergency. Adolf Hitler was cited as an example. Of course, the cases which the Committee investigated were not of that character. Indeed, in the Cuban missile crisis—the only situation of true national danger considered in this report—assassination was not even considered and, if used, might well have aggravated the crisis.

In a grave emergency, the President has a limited power to act, not in violation of the law, but in accord with his own responsibilities under the Constitution to defend the Nation. As the Supreme Court has stated, the Constitution "is not a suicide pact." (*Kennedy* v. *Mendoza-Martinez, 372* U.S. 144, 160 (1963))

During an unprecedented emergency, Abraham Lincoln claimed unprecedented power based on the need to preserve the nation:

* * * my oath to preserve the Constitution to the best of my ability, imposed upon me the duty of preserving, by every indispensable means, that government—that nation—of which that Constitution was the organic law. Was it possible to lose the nation, and yet preserve the Constitution? By general law, life and limb must be protected; yet often a limb must be amputated to save a life; but a life is never wisely given to save a limb. I felt that measures, otherwise unconstitutional, might become lawful, by becoming indispensable to the preservation of the Constitution, through the preservation of the nation * * *. (*The Complete Works of Abraham Lincoln,* Vol. X, pp. 65–66.) (Nicolay and Hay, Eds. 1894.)

Whatever the extent of the President's own constitutional powers, it is a fundamental principle of our constitutional system that those powers are checked and limited by Congress, including the impeachment power. As a necessary corollary, any action taken by a President pursuant to his limited inherent powers and in apparent conflict with the law must be disclosed to Congress. Only then can Congress judge whether the action truly represented, in Lincoln's phrase, an "indispensable necessity" to the life of the Nation.

As Lincoln explained in submitting his extraordinary actions to Congress for ratification:

In full view of his great responsibility he has, so far, done what he has deemed his duty. You will now, according to your own judgment, perform yours. (Abraham Lincoln, Message to Congress in Special Session, July 4, 1861.)

EPILOGUE

The Committee does not believe that the acts which it has examined represent the real American character. They do not reflect the ideals which have given the people of this country and of the world hope for a better, fuller, fairer life. We regard the assassination plots as aberrations.

The United States must not adopt the tactics of the enemy. Means are as important as ends. Crisis makes it tempting to ignore the wise restraints that make men free. But each time we do so, each time the means we use are wrong, our inner strength, the strength which makes us free, is lessened.

Despite our distaste for what we have seen, we have great faith in this country. The story is sad, but this country has the strength to hear the story and to learn from it. We must remain a people who confront our mistakes and resolve not to repeat them. If we do not, we will decline; but, if we do, our future will be worthy of the best of our past.

STATEMENT OF JOINDER

I hereby join in the foregoing report.

[signature]

Frank Church, *Chairman.*

[signature]

John Tower, *Vice Chairman.*

*Philip A. Hart, Michigan.

[signature]

Walter F. Mondale, Minnesota.

[signature]

Walter D. Huddleston, Kentucky.

---

*See Separate Views of Senator Philip Hart, p. 297.

ROBERT MORGAN, North Carolina.

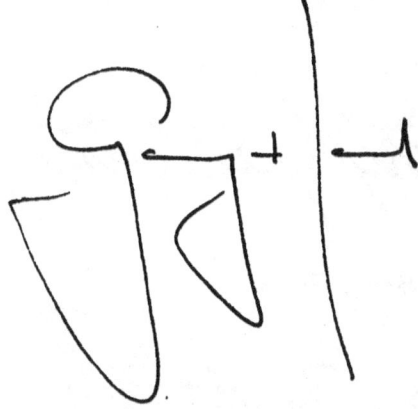

GARY HART, Colorado.

Howard Baker,
Tennessee.

Barry Goldwater,
Arizona.

Charles McC. Mathias, Jr.,
Maryland.

Richard S. Schweiker,
Pennsylvania.

Appendix A

[S. ——, 94th Cong., 1st sess.]

A BILL To make unlawful the entering into a conspiracy to assassinate a foreign official outside the United States, the assassination of a foreign official outside the United States, or the attempted assassination of a foreign official outside the United States, and for other purposes

Be it enacted by the Senate and House of Representatives of the United States of America in Congress assembled, That title 18, United States Code, is amended by adding immediately after Section 1117 the following new section:

"§ 1118. Conspiracy to assassinate foreign official outside the United States; attempted assassination of foreign official outside the United States; assassination of foreign official outside United States.

"(a) If any officer or employee of the United States or any other person while within the United States or the special maritime and territorial jurisdiction of the United States, conspires with any other such officer, employee or person to kill any foreign official because of such official's political views, actions or statements, while such official is outside the United States and such jurisdiction, and one or more such officers or employees or persons does any overt act within the United States or such jurisdiction to effect the object of the conspiracy, each shall be punished by imprisonment for any term of years or for life.

"(b) Whoever being an officer or employee of the United States, or a citizen of the United States, while outside the United States and the special maritime and territorial jurisdiction of the United States, conspires with any other such officer or employee or with any other person or persons to kill any foreign official, because of such official's political views, actions or statements, while such official is outside the United States and such jurisdiction, and one or more such officers, employees, citizens or other persons does any overt act to effect the object of the conspiracy, shall be punished by imprisonment for any term of years or life.

"(c) Whoever being an officer or employee of the United States, or a citizen of the United States, while outside the United States and the special maritime and territorial jurisdiction of the United States, attempts to kill any foreign official, because of such official's political views, actions or statements, while such official is outside the United States and such jurisdiction, shall be punished by imprisonment for any term of years or life.

"(d) Whoever being an officer or employee of the United States, or a citizen of the United States, while outside the United States and the special maritime and territorial jurisdiction of the United States, kills any foreign official, because of such official's political views, actions or statements, while such official is outside the United States and such jurisdiction, shall be punished as provided under sections 1111 and 1112 of this title, except that any such officer or employee or citizen who is found guilty of murder in the first degree shall be sentenced to imprisonment for life.

"(e) As used in this section, the term—

"(1) 'officer or employee of the United States' means any officer or employee, whether elected or appointed, in the executive, legislative, or judicial branch of the Government of the United States (including the District of Columbia) and its territories and possessions, and includes any officer or member of the armed forces;

"(2) 'foreign official' means a Chief of State or the political equivalent, President, Vice President, Prime Minister, Premier, Foreign Minister, Ambassador, or other officer, employee, or agent; (a) of a foreign government with which the United States is not at war pursuant to a declaration of war or against which United States Armed Forces have not been introduced into hostilities or situations pursuant to the provisions of the War Powers Resolution; or (b) of a foreign political group, party, military force, movement or other association with which the United States is not at war pursuant to a declaration of war or against which United States Armed Forces have not been introduced into hostilities or situations pursuant to the provisions of the War Powers Resolution; or (c) of an international organization;

"(3) 'foreign government' means the government of a foreign country, irrespective of recognition by the United States;

"(4) 'international organization' means a public international organization designated as such pursuant to section 1 of the International Organizations Immunity Act (22 U.S.C. 288);

"(5) 'citizen of the United States' means, in addition to a United States citizen, any national of the United States, and any person who has been and is classified as an alien admitted to the United States as a permanent resident under the laws of the United States."

SEC. 2. The analysis of chapter 51 of title 18, United States Code, is amended by adding at the end thereof the following:

"1118. Conspiracy to assassinate foreign official outside United States; attempted assassination of foreign official outside United States; assassination of foreign official outside United States."

Appendix B

Chronology of Major Events

The following capsule summary sets forth in chronological sequence major events covered in this Report. The purpose of the chronology is to remind the reader that the assassination plots and related events, which are organized in the Report around attempts against various leaders, often occurred during the same time frame, and can only be fully understood by considering the entire picture.

This chronology necessarily abbreviates and characterizes events, and does not indicate when certain things should have happened but did not. It is not a substitute for the full discussion of the events which appears in the body of the Report at the pages indicated in brackets. The Committee's interpretation of what occurred is fully set forth in the Findings and Conclusion of this Report.

1959

December 11—Dulles approves "thorough consideration be given to the elimination of Fidel Castro." (p. 92)

1960

January 13—Special Group meeting considers Castro's overthrow. (p. 92)

Spring 1960—Meetings on covert action against Cuba at levels of CIA, Special Group, and NSC. (p. 93)

Sometime in Spring 1960—Ambassador Farland establishes links with Dominican Republic dissidents. (p. 193)

April 1960—President Eisenhower approves contingency plan for Dominican Republic—if situation deteriorates, U.S. to take action to remove Trujillo when successor regime lined up. (p. 192)

Late Spring-Early Summer—Bissell discusses assassination capabilities with Scheider. (pp. 20–21)

June 30—Congolese independence declared. Lumumba is Premier. Kasavubu is President.

July 1—CIA memo recommending delivery of sniper rifles to Dominican dissidents approved. (p. 194)

July 11—Tshombe declares Katanga independent.

July 13—UN Security Council calls for Belgian troop withdrawal from Congo and sends UN peacekeeping force.

July 14—Kasavubu and Lumumba suggest Soviet aid may be requested.

July 27—Lumumba visits Washington and receives aid pledge from Secretary Herter.

Event involving CIA request that a Cuban arrange an "accident" involving Raul Castro. (pp. 72, 93)

August 1960—U.S. interrupts diplomatic relations with Dominican Republic.

August 1960—Bissell and Edwards have discussion concerning use of underworld figures to aid in assassination of Castro. (p. 74)

August 18–26—NSC and Special Group discusses action against Lumumba and Dulles cables Congo station that Lumumba's "removal must be an urgent and prime objective . . ." (p. 52)

Early September—Scheider is ordered by Bissell to make preparations for assassination of an African leader. (p. 21)

Late September—Bissell and Edwards brief Dulles and Cabell about operation against Castro. (p. 194)

Late September—Initial meeting between Rosselli, Maheu, and CIA support chief. A subsequent meeting takes place in Florida. (p. 76)

September 5—Kasavubu dismisses Lumumba; power struggle ensues.

September 14—Mobutu, Chief of Staff of Congolese Army, takes over government by coup.

September 15—Lumumba seeks protective custody of UN guard.

September 16–20—CIA cables indicate Lumumba is seen as a continued threat

(291)

while in custody—as capable of mounting a counterattack or appealing to the public. (p. 18)

September 17-19—Tweedy and Tweedy's Deputy tell Scheider to go to Congo to deliver poisons to Hedgman and instruct him to assassinate Lumumba if possible. (p. 21)

September 19—Tweedy cables Hedgman that Scheider will come to Congo on sensitive mission. (p. 22)

September 21—NSC meeting in which it is noted that Lumumba, although deposed, remains a threat. (p. 62)

September 26—Scheider goes to Congo. (p. 24)

October 3—CIA memo sets forth plans to support Dominican dissidents.

October 5—Scheider leaves Congo. (p. 24)

October 18—Memo from Hoover to intelligence agencies detailing Giancana's statements about an imminent Castro assassination but not mentioning CIA. (p. 79)

October 31—Bissell asks Mulroney to go to Congo. (p. 37)

Las Vegas wiretap discovered. (p. 77)

November 3—Special Group discusses covert action against Castro regime. (p. 98)

November 3—Mulroney arrives in Congo. (p. 40)

Sometime after November 8—Dulles and Bissell jointly brief President-elect Kennedy on details of planned invasion of Cuba. (p. 196)

December 1—Mobutu's troops capture Lumumba.

December 3—Lumumba imprisoned at Thysville.

December 29—Special Group approves plan of covert assistance to internal and external Dominican dissidents. (p. 196)

1961

January 12—Special Group meeting approved "limited supply of small arms and other material" to Dominican dissidents. (p. 196)

January 17—Lumumba transferred by Congolese government to Elizabethville where he is killed at hands of Katanga authorities.

January 22—President Kennedy succeeds President Eisenhower.

Sometime between January 22 and April 15 (sequence unknown)—Bissell and Bundy have discussion concerning an "executive action" capability. (p. 181)

President raises with Smathers subject of assassination, indicating his disapproval. (p. 123)

Rosselli passes pills to a Cuban in Miami. (p. 80)

January 25-26—Harvey discusses Executive action with CIA subordinates. (p. 183)

February 10 and February 15—Meeting in New York City between Dominican dissidents and CIA officials. (p. 198)

February 13—Lumumba's death announced by Katanga Interior Minister Munungo.

February 14—Special Group meeting at which new members are briefed by Dulles and Bissell on "specific actions taken by the predecessor group during the past year. (p. 202)

February 15—Rusk memo to President on Dominican Republic. (p. 203)

February 17—Bissell memo to Bundy speaks of Dominican dissident "plan of action". (p. 204)

March 13—Requests for arms and explosives made by Dominican dissidents to CIA and passed on to Washington. (p. 198)

March 15—Request by Station to Headquarters for three pistols for Dominican dissidents. (p. 199)

March 20—Station raises with Headquarters the Dominican dissident request for machine guns. (p. 201)

March 24—Cable advises pistols are being pouched for the Dominican dissidents. (p. 200)

March 31—Headquarters approves passing of carbines to Dominican Republic. (p. 100)

April 7—Carbines passed to "action group" and eventually to one of the assassins. (p. 200)

April 10—Bissell approves shipping machine guns to Dominican Republic by pouch. (p. 202)

April 15-17—Bay of Pigs invasion fails.

April 17—CIA order not to pass machine guns to Dominican dissidents without Headquarters approval. (p. 205)

April 18—Maheu tells FBI of CIA involvement in Las Vegas wiretap. (p. 126)
April 19–20—The Cuban involved in the underworld assassination plot and the Bay of Pigs invasion attends meeting at which the President, other Cubans, and high Administration officials not witting of the plot are present. (p. 124)
April 20—Headquarters advises Station not to pass machine guns to Dominican dissidents. (p. 206)
April 22–June 19—Taylor/Kennedy Board of Inquiry into Bay of Pigs invasion. (pp. 121, 135)
April 25—Cable advises Headquarters of imminent assassination attempt against Trujillo and possible use of U.S.-supplied weapons. (p. 206)
April 26—Headquarters orders Dominican Republic Station that there is no authority to pass additional arms and tells Station to advise dissidents that U.S. not prepared to cope with aftermath of assassination. (p. 206)
May 3—Berle determines Dominican dissidents seek machine guns to assassinate Trujillo and speaks against involvement in such an effort. (p. 207)
May 4—Special Group meeting at which DCI reports new anti-Trujillo plot. (p. 208)
May 5—NSC notes President's view that the U.S. should not initiate the overthrow of Trujillo until it knows what government will succeed him. (p. 209)
May 16—President approves Record of Actions of May 5, 1961, NSC meeting. (p. 209)
May 16—State Department is told that assassination attempt against Trujillo is imminent. (p. 208)
May 18—Special Group stands by decision not to pass machine guns being sought by Dominican dissidents. (p. 126)
May 22—Hoover memo to Attorney General Kennedy noting CIA had used Giancana in "clandestine efforts" against Castro. (p. 126)
May 29—President advises State Department official in Dominican Republic that U.S. "must not run risk of U.S. association with political assassination, since U.S. as a matter of general policy cannot condone assassination". This principle is "overriding" and "must prevail in doubtful situation." (p. 213)
May 30—Trujillo ambushed and assassinated near San Cristobal, Dominician Republic.
June 1 and period shortly thereafter—State Department and CIA review of actions taken in dealing with dissidents in Dominican Republic. (p. 214)
October 5—National Security Action Memorandum 100 directs assessment of potential courses of action if Castro were removed from the Cuban scene. CIA makes intelligence estimate. (p. 136)
November 9—President tells Tad Szulc that he is under pressure from advisors to order Castro's assassination, but does not name advisors. (p. 138)
November 15—Bissell asks Harvey to assume control of underworld operation on stand-by basis. (p. 83)
November 16—President Kennedy gives speech mentioning opposition to assassination. (p. 139)
November 29—John McCone succeeds Allen Dulles as Director, CIA.
November 1961—Operation MONGOOSE created. (p. 139)

1962

January 18—Lansdale assigns 32 planning tasks against Castro regime. (p. 142)
January 19—MONGOOSE meeting at which Attorney General says solution to Cuban problem today carries top priority. (p. 141)
January 29—CIA objects to prosecution of Maheu for Las Vegas wiretap. (p. 129)
February 19—Richard Helms succeeds Richard Bissell as Deputy Director, Plans, CIA.
Early April—Harvey establishes contact with Rosselli. (p. 83)
Late April—Harvey passes poison pills to Rosselli in Miami. (p. 84)
May 7—Houston and Edwards brief Attorney General on pre-Bay of Pigs underworld assassination plot. Thereafter decision made not to prosecute. (p. 131)
August 8—Special Group (Augmented) adopts a stepped-up plan designed to inspire internal revolt in Cuba. (p. 147)
August 10—The subject of assassination is raised at a meeting of the Special Group (Augmented). (p. 161)
September 7—Rosselli tells Harvey the pills are still in Cuba. (p. 84)
October 4—Attorney General advises Special Group (Augmented) that President wants more priority given to operations against Castro regime. (p. 147)
October 22–28—Cuban Missile Crisis.
November—Operation MONGOOSE ends.

1963

Early 1963—CIA Technical Services Division explores exploding seashell and contaminated diving suit schemes. (p. 85)
April 1963—Special Group discusses the contingency of Castro's death. (p. 170)
May 8—South Vietnamese troops in Hue fire on Buddhists, triggering nation-wide Buddist protest. (p. 217)
May 18—U.S. Ambassador Nolting meets with Diem to outline steps to redress Buddist grievances. (p. 217)
June 19—Special Group authorizes sabotage program against Cuba. (p. 173)
July 4—Vietnamese General Minh, Don, Kim, and Khiem agree on necessity of coup. (p. 218)
August 16—McCone is given memorandum detailing pre-Bay of Pigs assassination plot against Castro. (p. 107)
August 24—DEPTEL 243 is sent to Ambassador Lodge in Saigon telling him to press for dramatic actions to redress Buddhist grievances, including removal of Nhu and his wife. (p. 218)
August 26—CIA officers advise Vietnamese Generals Khiem and Khanh of DEPTEL 243. (p. 219)
August 29—A White House message authorizes Saigon to confirm that U.S. will support a coup if it appears it will succeed. (p. 219)
August 31—Attempted generals' coup in South Vietnam fails. (p. 220)
Fall 1963—Atwood explores possible accommodation with Castro. (p. 173)
October 2—McNamara and Taylor return from fact-finding mission in Vietnam and report that, although the war is progressing favorably, there is political turmoil. (p. 220)
October 3—General Minh outlines to Saigon Station a course of action which includes assassinating Diem's brothers, Nhu and Can. (p. 220)
October 5-6—CIA Headquarters directs Saigon that Minh's course of action not acceptable. (p. 221)
November 2—Diem is assassinated following a coup. (p. 223)
November 22—President Kennedy assassinated.
Vice President Johnson becomes President.
AM/LASH given poison pen device for assassinating Castro. (pp. 89, 175)

1964

March–May—Caches of arms delivered to AM/LASH in Cuba. (pp. 89, 175)
April 7—Special Group discontinues CIA-controlled sabotage raids against Cuba. (p. 177)

1965

Early 1965—AM/LASH put in contact with leader of anti-Castro group and receives weapon with silencer from him. (p. 89)

1966

1966—Helms reports to Rusk that CIA not involved with AM/LASH in Castro assassination plot. (p. 178)

1967

May 1967—Helms briefs President on 1967 Inspector General's Report. (p. 179)

1968

January 20—President Johnson leaves office, President Nixon inaugurated.

1970

September 4—Dr. Allende wins a plurality in Chile's Presidential election. (p. 225)
September 8 and 14—40 Committee discusses Chilean situation. Question of U.S. involvement in a military coup against Allende raised. (p. 229)
September 15—President Nixon instructs CIA Director Helms to prevent Allende's accession to office. The CIA is to play a direct role in organizing a military coup d'etat. This involvement comes to be known as Track II. (p. 227)
September 28—U.S. Military Attache in Santiago instructed to assist CIA in promoting coup. (p. 235)

October 5—CIA makes first contact with Chilean military conspirators. (p. 240)

October 13—CIA Station informs Headquarters that retired General Viaux intends to kidnap General Schneider to precipitate a coup. Viaux's plan is reported to Headquarters as part of a coup plot that includes General Valenzuela. (p. 242)

October 15—Karamessines meets with Kissinger and Haig at the White House. A decision is made to defuse the Viaux coup plot, at least temporarily. (pp. 242, 250)

October 16—Headquarters informs CIA Station of Viaux decision and instructs it to continue to generate maximum pressure to overthrow Allende by coup. (p. 243)

October 17—CIA informs Viaux associate of decision. Agent told that Viaux would proceed with coup in any case and that the abduction of Schneider is first link in chain of events. (p. 243)

U.S. Military Attache meets with Chilean Army officer and Navy officer. They request tear gas, grenades, and three sterile submachine guns, with ammunition. (p. 243)

October 18—General Valenzuela informs U.S. Military Attache that he and senior military officers prepared to sponsor a coup. (p. 244)

October 18—Tear gas grenades delivered to Chilean Army officer and Navy Captain. (p. 244)

October 19—Weapons sent from CIA Headquarters by diplomatic pouch to Santiago. (p. 244)

First Schneider abduction attempt fails. (p. 244)

October 20—Second Schneider abduction attempt fails. (p. 244)

October 22—Three submachine guns delivered to Chilean Army officer by U.S. Military Attache. (p. 245)

General Schneider is shot in kidnap attempt. (p. 245)

October 24—Dr. Allende confirmed by Chilean Congress. (p. 246)

October 25—General Schneider dies. (p. 246)

1972

Helms issues directive against assassination.

1973

Colby issues directive against assassination.

SEPARATE VIEWS OF SENATOR PHILIP A. HART

Because of illness, I was unable to attend meetings of the committee for the several months immediately preceding the issuance of this report. Inasmuch as I did not participate in hearings on assassination during this period, nor in much of the committee's deliberations on the findings and the drafting of the report, it would be inappropriate and perhaps misleading for me to sign the report as one of its authors.

However, while expressing no view on the report and its findings, I feel that I did participate in enough committee hearings on the subject to conclude that the United States should never engage in political assassination in peacetime. Therefore, I support the committee's recommendation for a statute making such activity a crime.

In addition, I endorse the Committee's decision to make the facts of this chapter in our history known to the American people.

PHILIP A. HART.

ADDITIONAL VIEWS OF SENATOR ROBERT MORGAN

Our Nation needs a strong, secure, and effective intelligence community. Our memory of Pearl Harbor and testimony taken in hearings with regard to that catastrophe as well as testimony taken during these hearings clearly establish the need for a central intelligence agency to coordinate the intelligence gathered by our various agencies of Government. If the United States had had a coordinating intelligence agency in 1941, the disaster at Pearl Harbor would, in my opinion, have been averted. That we have now, and continue to have, such an agency is essential if we are to avert any future threats to our national security. Our national security is, after all else, of paramount importance.

We must recognize, however, that our national security can be subverted by overzealous governmental action as well as antagonistic domestic or foreign agents. Our Nation cannot remain intact if we ourselves subvert our own ideals; consequently, it is as important for our government to abide by them. In the words of U.S. Supreme Court Justice Louis Brandeis:

> Decency, security, and liberty alike demand that governmental officials shall be subjected to the same rules of conduct as the citizen. In a government of laws, existence of the government will be imperiled if it fails to observe the law scrupulously. Our government is the potent, the omnipresent teacher. For good or for ill, it teaches the whole people by its example. If the government becomes a lawbreaker, it breeds contempt for the law; it invites every man to become a law unto himself; it invites anarchy. To declare in the administration of [a democracy such as ours] the end justifies the means * * * would bring terrible retribution. Against that pernicious doctrine, [we] resolutely set [our] face.

It is argued, and in many cases justifiably so, that in dealing with our national security, and especially with hostile or adversary forces abroad, extraordinary means are necessary. So long as the Soviets maintain KGB agents around the world, we must maintain an effective intelligence gathering capability. However, this report deals with a particular activity of the government, which in the absence of armed conflict, would, if true, shock the conscience and morals of most Americans. That this investigation was necessary was unfortunate, but it was made so by the broadly circulated and printed reports of alleged assassination plots, some of which were given credence by public statements by various officials. It was my belief in the beginning, and still is, that it would be far better to ascertain the truth as far as possible, and clear the air, to the end that our intelligence agencies could get back to their assigned tasks.

I have weighed in my own mind for many days and nights how much of the information contained in this report should be made available to the American public and thus to the world, including our potential adversaries. That the public has a right to know is incontrovertible, but whether that right extends to information which could damage our image and national security is not so easily determined. Is it satisfactory for the members of the Congress, the duly elected representatives of the people, to hold such information in trust for the people? In some cases of national security the answer can and must be "yes", and in the future, such information must be held by competent and aggressive oversight committees.

In the present situation too much water has gone over the dam for such secrecy and to refuse to make as full and complete a disclosure as is consistent with the safety and protection of our present intelligence personnel would only add to the intrigue, and the issue could not be put to rest. So though I have in some instances voted with some of my colleagues to retain much information in executive session, I have concurred with the issuance of this report after being assured that the release of it would not violate any law with regard to classified matter and after the respective agencies have had another chance to recommend exclusion of extremely sensitive matters.

Throughout the hearings one issue has remained paramount in my mind. If the alleged acts happened, were they the result of overanxious, over-zealous intelligence agents who were acting like "a rogue elephant on the rampage", or, were they basically the acts of responsible, well-disciplined intelligence agents acting in response to orders of "higher authority"? To me the conclusion is important. If the first is true, then the agencies must be revamped or possibly dismantled and new agencies created to replace them. If the second is true, then clearer lines of authority must be established and stringent oversight by the duly elected representatives of the people must take place.

During the course of these hearings, I have been impressed by the belief held by the principals that those illegal and immoral acts engaged in by our intelligence agencies were sanctioned by higher authority and even by the "highest authority." I am convinced by the large amount of circumstantial evidence that this is true. Although illegal and immoral activities carried out by our intelligence agencies cannot be justified by any argument, it is, I think, important to note that these actions were carried out in the belief that they were sanctioned by higher authority, even though this Committee has been unable to establish whether or not presidential authority was given. Some of the acts conducted by these agencies could have been, and probably were, beyond the scope of the projects authorized. In addition, the agencies may have conducted other activities which, in spite of this investigation, are still unknown to this Committee. Thus, they cannot be absolved of all the blame.

Since our intelligence agencies act on both a compartmentalized and need-to-know basis, it is difficult to establish in retrospect who was informed and what authority was given. It is also difficult to establish what was told to those who were informed since circumlocution was also a standard practice within the chain of authority. The practice was, after all, adopted to insure official deniability as well as to acquire consent. And the effectiveness of these techniques of "need-to-know" and "circumlocution" is attested by the fact that this Committee not only has been unable to establish whose consent was given but has also been unable to establish who was not involved. We have been able to establish neither responsibility nor innocence. In this situation, the presumption of innocence cannot be applied without question, since the mere willingness to participate in circumlocutious briefings implies a willingness to deny responsibility at crucial times. Consequently, I also believe that responsibility for the illegal actions of our intelligence agencies must be shared; it should not be carried entirely by our intelligence community.

In drafting legislation to circumscribe the activities of intelligence gathering agencies, I would stress the need to guarantee their ability to function effectively in our complex and dangerous world. The effectiveness of our intelligence agencies must not be limited solely by sound and practical applications of law drafted with clear objectives in mind. We must know what we want our intelligence agencies to do and what we do not want them to do. Then we can confidently allow them to function in the knowledge that they will not only defend the law but abide by it. Only in that way can we be certain that our society will be preserved as an embodiment of our openly democratic ideals. Although we must have intelligence, we also must preserve our open society, for to destroy the latter for the sake of the former would be a complete perversion of our goals.

While we may realize that investigations of this nature into sensitive governmental actions in effect strengthen our country, we would be foolhardy to think for a moment that our enemies, and perhaps even friends, will openly acknowledge this significant accomplishment. We can assume, for instance, that our opponents will go to great lengths to publicize and distribute propaganda based on this report inimical to the best interests of the United States. That this, in fact, will be done only serves to reinforce my belief that we need, and must have, as strong an intelligence capability as possible. And while this Committee is charged with the responsibility of investigating and reporting on the misdeeds of the Central Intelligence Agency, we cannot reveal the details of the many meaningful accomplishments of the Agency which without a doubt have been beneficial to our country. That we have such an agency now, that we maintain our intelligence potential in these times of continuing international tension is essential to our society and continued existence as a nation.

The release of this report, based on the public's right to know, does not compromise our right to be secure. The report details only the actions of Agency employees in the cases under investigation and does not unnecessarily reveal confidential intelligence sources and methods. One can, however, successfully predict the impact the report will have in the news media. A review of previous revelations concerning assassinations which have appeared in the press have gone a long way towards sensationalizing this country's involvement in assassination plots. This report confirms some prior public allegations while it disproves others. While some may shudder upon learning that the events related in the report actually took place, we can all take great pride in the ability of this country to look frankly at problems within our system of government, and accordingly, in our ability to govern ourselves. History will undoubtedly record our ability to openly reveal and discuss improper, unpopular governmental actions as one of the basic elements in the continued existence of our free society and the general ability we, as a nation, have achieved to subject ourselves and our government to the rule of law.

ROBERT MORGAN.

ADDITIONAL VIEWS OF SENATOR HOWARD H. BAKER, JR.

Altogether, I think the Committee's report represents a remarkably good treatment of the large volume of testimony and documentation which was received by us and a fair reconciliation of the conflicts that developed.

While it is clear from the record that assassination planning and efforts did in fact occur during the late 1950's to the mid-1960's, it is not equally clear from the record that they were fully authorized by the respective Presidents serving during that time. I entirely agree with and subscribe to the Committee's central finding that:

> the system of Executive command and control was so inherently ambiguous that it is difficult to be certain at what level assassination activity was known and authorized. This creates the disturbing prospect that assassination activity might have been undertaken by officials of the United States Government without it having been uncontrovertibly clear that there was explicit authorization from the President of the United States. At the same time, this ambiguity and imprecision leaves open the possibility that there was a successful "plausible denial" and that a Presidential authorization was issued but is now obscured. (Committee Report, Findings and Conclusions p. 261)

Or put another way, in the Inspector General's report on this subject in 1967:

> This reconstruction of agency involvement in plans to assassinate Fidel Castro is at best an imperfect history. Because of the extreme sensitivity of the operation being discussed or attempted, as a matter of principle no official records were kept of planning, of approvals, or implementation. The few written records that do exist are either largely tangential to the main events or put on paper from memory years afterwards . . . For the most part . . . we have had to rely on information given to us orally by people whose memories are fogged by time. (I. G. Report, p. 1)

However, it is my personal view that on balance the likelihood that Presidents knew of the assassination plots is greater than the likelihood that they did not. This impression stems from the record of course, but as well from observing and hearing the witnesses testify and by applying the usual courtroom tests for determining the worth and value of the witnesses' testimony: the demeanor of the witnesses while testifying; the completeness or the incompleteness of their statements; whether the testimony has the ring of truth; prior consistent or inconsistent statements; inconsistencies in the course of their testimony before the Committee; the probability or improbability of their testimony; their means of knowledge; their interest in the subject. All of these things are best judged by observing the testimony of the witnesses.

It is because of this, that I had hoped for public hearings on this subject, carefully sanitized to avoid the disclosure of properly classified information and the identification of "sources and methods". It seems to me that without a record clearly supporting a conclusion of Presidential responsibility, or the absence of it, that a public examination of the witnesses was more important than would otherwise be the case. The Committee determined not to hold public hearings and I abide by that decision.

Accompanying these views is an Appendix of record evidence and documentation which relate to these conclusions and impressions. While the Appendix in large part deals with the Castro situation, I believe it is fairly representative of the problems we have encountered.

HOWARD H. BAKER.

APPENDIX

FOR ADDITIONAL VIEWS OF SENATOR HOWARD H. BAKER, JR.

	Page
I. The Testimony and Evidence Regarding Authority From Those Involved in the Operational Activities of the Plots	307
II. The Testimony and Evidence Regarding Authority From Those CIA Officials Knowledgeable of the Plots	308
Pre-Bay of Pigs	308
Post-Bay of Pigs	310
III. The Testimony and Evidence Regarding How Authority Would Have Been Obtained—The Troubling Doctrine of Plausible Denial	313
IV. The Concept of Assassination Was Discussed at the Highest Levels of Government and Not Affirmatively Disavowed	318
A. Executive Action	318
B. The August 10 Meeting	319
1. The Testimony: Who Raised the Suggestion of the Assassination of Castro?	320
(a) Testimony of McCone	320
(b) Harvey's Testimony	321
(c) Goodwin's Testimony	321
(d) Lansdale's Testimony	322
(e) Testimony of Rusk, Bundy, and Gilpatric	322
(f) Testimony of Robert McNamara	323
(g) Testimony of Parrott	323
(h) Testimony of Walter Elder	323
C. Conversations With President Kennedy About the Use of Assassination	324
1. President Kennedy's Meeting With Tad Szulc on November 9, 1961	324
2. Conversation Between President Kennedy and Senator George Smathers	325
D. President Eisenhower's Discussion at the August 18, 1960, National Security Council Meeting	326
V. Did the Investigation of Giancana and Rosselli Reveal Their Involvement in the Assassination Plots to the FBI, Department of Justice, Attorney General, or the President?	327
A. The FBI Memoranda	328
1. The October 18, 1960, Memorandum	328
2. The May 22, 1961, Memorandum	329
B. President Kennedy's Meeting With the Cuban Exile Leader	330
C. The Events of 1962	333
VI. The MONGOOSE Program—The Environment in Which the Assassination Plots Arose	333
VII. Whose Idea Was the Use of the Underworld in an Assassination Plot Against Castro?	338

I. The testimony and evidence regarding authority from those involved in the operational activities of the plots

Our investigation was unable to uncover any documentary evidence bearing directly on the issue of authority for the assassination plots. Testimony, however, was taken from all of those involved at the operational level of the assassination plots. To a man, they were convinced the assassination operations were specifically approved by the United States Government.

The CIA Case Officer selected for the plot activities, testified about his feelings toward the authorization of the plots, as follows:

> I was in World War II. And I was told that there was an enemy, and I was told that I was supposed to do it in the interest of national defense support. And I felt that this was coming from a higher up and in their wisdom and judgment this was the way to go. I was just doing as I was directed. (O.C., 5/30/75, p. 41)

Robert Maheu, the man contacted by the case officer initially in an attempt to recruit underworld assistance, testified that he felt the assassination plots were not only authorized but were an adjunct to the Bay of Pigs invasion:

> I was taking my instructions from [the Case Officer] and Col. Edwards. I had no way of knowing where they were receiving their instructions * * * I personally never discussed this matter with any higher authority than [the Case Officer] and Col. Edwards during those days. (Maheu, 7/30/75, p. 5)
>
> * * * * * * *
>
> * * * The government felt it was important to dispose of Mr. Castro as part of the overall invasion plan * * * (Maheu, 7/29/75, p. 13; 7/30/75, pp. 7–9)

Maheu throughout his testimony reiterated his contention that he would never have accepted the Case Officer's request for assistance with the assassination plans had he not been convinced they were government sponsored:[1]

John Roselli was also firm in his testimony that he regarded the assassination plots, as, in effect, part of the United States "war" against Castro. He testified as follows:

> Q. What did Mr. Maheu discuss with you in the first meeting * * *?
> A. * * * he was told that some high government official had given him word to recruit me, if I would be willing to help the government.
>
> * * * * * * *
>
> Q. When you were asked to help arrange for the assassination of Mr. Castro, what was your understanding of who in the United States government wanted you to do this?
> A. Well, anybody in the United States government. My point was if I am recruited in the army and I was in the Second World War, it is like being recruited in the army and if it comes through from higher authority I don't

---

[1] Maheu had been involved in a wide variety of ventures for the CIA. He was also, at the time of the plots, cultivating Howard Hughes as a client (and indeed told Hughes of the project during its active stage). The Committee's Report discusses the full breadth of Maheu's motivation in accepting this assignment. (Committee Report, pp. 74–75).

ask any questions how high it was as long as there were government people. I was satisfied that I was doing a duty for my country.

*   *   *   *   *   *   *

Q. Now, you were asked to help join in an effort to kill somebody. Why did you agree to do that?
A. It was a government project. (Roselli, 6/24/75, pp. 7, 57-58, 59)

Our evidence established that throughout his lengthy involvement in the plots Roselli paid for almost all of his expenses.[1] Moreover, at the time of the Cuban Missile Crisis both Harvey and Roselli agreed that Roselli was active in providing pure "intelligence" on what was occurring in Cuba. Nevertheless, the evidence adduced by the Committee strongly suggests that the underworld was also quite interested in getting rid of Castro because of his actions barring their control of the Havana gambling enterprises. And, Roselli did attempt to use his CIA involvement to his advantage in later years in an attempt to deter prosecution of him for other unrelated matters. (*See* Committee Report, p. 85)[2]

Whatever the totality of the motivation of all those involved in the operational end of the plots, the uncontroverted evidence is that they all truly believed the U.S. Government was behind the project.

II. The Testimony and Evidence Regarding Authority From Those CIA Officials Knowledgeable of the Plots

The Committee's Report discusses the evidence relating to whether the assassination plots were authorized by higher authority outside the CIA. That is, of course, the ultimate issue of our inquiry. To properly address that issue, I feel it is important to note that each of the supervisory officials of the Agency testified that they fully believed that the plots were authorized by the "highest authority."[3] During the Pre-Bay of Pigs phase Bissell and Edwards were the CIA officials admittedly knowledgeable of the plots. Both felt that the plots were fully authorized. During the Post-Bay of Pigs phase Bissell turned the project over to William Harvey and his immediate superior Richard Helms. Both confirmed Bissell's earlier testimony that the plots were authorized both within and without the CIA.

PRE-BAY OF PIGS

Bissell testified that the plots were authorized by "highest authority" which he felt meant knowledge and approval by the President. He testified that it would not have been "consonant with the operations of the CIA" to conduct such highly sensitive activities without the President's permission or knowledge. (Bissell, 6/9/75, pp. 37-38) Bissell elaborated:

---

[1] This was corroborated by the testimony of the Case officer, Maheu, and Harvey.
[2] At least Harvey (and perhaps others) recognized that the use of the underworld could lead to demands in later years. When he was first apprised of the details of the Roselli project he observed that:

"* * * it was a very, or it appeared to be, and in my opinion was, at that time, a very real possibility of this government being blackmailed either by Cubans for political purposes or by figures in organized crime for their own self-protection or aggrandizement, which, as it turned out, did not happen, but at that time was a very pregnant possibility." (Harvey, 6/25/75, pp. 67-68)

[3] Our investigation established that "highest authority" was a euphemism, used both at the CIA and cabinet level, for the President of the United States.

Q. * * * (I)n the ordinary course of the operations of the CIA as you know it under their traditions, their rules and regulations, their policies as you knew them, what is your opinion—(w)as the President, President-elect briefed or was he not in the light of all these circumstances?

Bissell: I believe at some stage the President and the President-elect both were advised that such an operation had been planned and was being attempted.

Q. By whom?

Bissell: I would guess through some channel by Allen Dulles.

* * * * * * *

Senator Morgan: Mr. Bissell, it's a serious matter to attribute knowledge of this sort to the President of the United States, especially one who cannot speak for himself. Is it fair to assume that out of an abundance of caution you are simply telling us that you have no knowledge unless you are absolutely certain? * * * I gather that you think * * * it (assassination plot information) came out but because of the seriousness of the accusation you are just being extremely cautious * * * Is that a fair assumption to make?

Bissell: That is very close to a fair assumption, sir. It's just that I have no direct knowledge, firsthand knowledge of his (the President) being advised but my belief is that he knew of it (assassination plans). (Bissell, 6/9/75, pp. 55–56)

Bissell emphasized that because of the Agency's structure, in which he was only DDP and not DCI, Allen Dulles would be the "only person" who could have informed the President of the assassination plots. (Bissell, 6/9/75, p. 60). And, he summed up why he felt certain that such authorization was obtained from the President by Dulles:

I had no direct evidence that (the President) was advised. I do agree with you that given the practices of the Agency, its relation to the Presidency and to the White House and given also everything I know of Mr. Dulles' character and integrity, I would expect he had perhaps obliquely advised both of the Presidents of this auxiliary operation, the assassination attempt. (Bissell, 6/9/75, p. 47) [1]

Bissell testified that it was not at all unusual that he, Bissell, did not personally discuss authorization for the project with either the President or one of his aides in the White House.[2] He stated that he believed that, since his position was that of DDP reporting directly to the DCI, the DCI, and not Bissell, "in a matter of this sensitivity * * * would handle higher-level clearances." (Bissell, 6/9/75, p. 26)

On matters of this sort I left the question of advising senior officers of the government and obtaining clearances in Allen Dulles' hands. (Bissell, 6/9/75, p. 29)

Bissell concluded his testimony by describing the tight control which was applied to such a project:

Assuming for the moment that I am correct (that the President approved the plots), since the effort would have been to minimize the possibility of embarrassment to the President, it is, I think, understandable that neither I nor anyone else in the Agency would have discussed this operation on our own initiative with, for instance, members of the White House staff. The effort would have been to hold to the absolute minimum the number of people who knew that the President had been consulted, had been notified and had given, perhaps only tacitly, his authorization. (Bissell, 6/11/75, p. 6)

---

[1] How Bissell felt the President would have been advised, through the method of plausible denial, is treated in Part III of these views. *infra*.

[2] Bissell did discuss assassination capability with a senior White House official and the record is patently clear that at a minimum he received no discouragement and at a maximum was "ordered" to develop an assassination capability. As I discuss in Part IV of these views, these conversations may have contributed to his strong subjective notion that assassination was authorized.

The only other supervisory official who testified about authorization during this Pre-Bay of Pigs period was Col. Sheffield Edwards.[1]

Col. Edwards was quite ill at the time of his appearance before the Committee (and has since died) and was unable to undergo a lengthy inquiry. He was, however, certain in his belief that the assassination plans were approved by the top echelon of the CIA. He testified before the Committee as follows:

* * * (T)his possible project was approved by Allen W. Dulles, Director of CIA, and by General Cabell, the Deputy Director. They are both dead.

The Chairman: How do you know, Colonel, that the project had been approved by these two gentlemen?

Edwards: I personally briefed Allen Dulles * * * and Cabell. (**Edwards**, 5/30/75, pp. 5–6)

Edwards was also interviewed by the Rockefeller Commission (Edwards interview, 4/9/75, p. 5):

Q. Now, who inside the Agency besides Bissell did you have any contact with on the top echelon?

A. Very important. The plan was approved by Allen W. Dulles and General Cabell.

As Director of Security of the CIA, Edwards appeared to have little direct contact with the White House and therefore was unable to enlighten the Committee on the issue of authorization to the plots outside the CIA.[2] His testimony, however, corroborates the feelings of the others involved in the plots that at no time did they view their actions as beyond the bounds of appropriate authority.

Post-Bay of Pigs

The assassination project or activities continued into a second or post-Bay of Pigs phase. As the Committee's Report discusses, William Harvey was selected by Bissell to take over the project. Harvey testified that he had no doubt, throughout his involvement in the assassination plots, that the project was authorized by the "highest authority,"[3] which to him meant the President of the United States. He testified that:

I can conceive of it [assassination] being perfectly within the province of an intelligence service, * * * on proper orders from the highest * * * authority (and)

* * * * * * *

the approval [for assassination] * * * must come from the Chief Executive, the President. (Harvey, 6/25/75, pp. 22, 24, 31–32)

Harvey emphasized at the outset of his testimony that he as a subordinate officer of the CIA did not have direct knowledge concerning the source of such authority. He described the authorization process as necessarily being conducted on a higher level:

[T]he fact that I say that authority for an assassination must * * * come from the President does not mean that I as an officer in CIA am entitled to know or to inquire exactly as to the where, why, what, when and in what words this authority may have been transmitted. (Harvey, 6/25/75, p. 32)

---

[1] *See* discussion regarding knowledge or lack thereof of J. C. King, then Chief of the CIA's Western Hemisphere Division. *infra*, Part *VII*.

[2] He did participate in the May 7, 1962, briefing of Attorney General Kennedy, which I treat in Part V, *infra,* and which is described in depth in the Committee's Report, pp. 131–134.

[3] See ft. 3, pg. 308, *supra.*

Harvey continually asserted and re-asserted throughout his testimony, at several appearances before the Committee, that

> I was completely convinced during this entire period, that this operation had the full authority of every pertinent echelon of CIA and had full authority of the White House, either from the President or from someone authorized and known to be authorized to speak for the President. But I won't answer, so this does not get out of context, that I have no personal knowledge whatever of the individual's identities, times, exact words or channels through which such authority may have been passed. (Harvey, 6/25/75, p. 31)

Harvey was then questioned about (1) whether he had any doubts that the plots were authorized and (2) why he did not personally confirm the authorization by specifically asking high government officials about it. Harvey answered that, "[I]t was my conviction at the time * * * that [the plots] were completely authorized at every appropriate level within and beyond the Agency." (Harvey, 6/25/75, p. 69) He explained that he felt he was always operating under appropriate orders from the top and that it simply was not his place (or purpose, particularly within the framework of plausible denial) in the bureaucracy to go "topside to question the orders of his superiors." (Harvey, 7/11/75, p. 73) In response to a question by Senator Goldwater, he described his feelings this way:

> I did not feel that it was up to me, after being requested, instructed, ordered, whichever you want to put it, to assume (control of this operation), and after being told, if you will, by a responsible officer at a senior level who was my immediate superior, that this did have the necessary and requisite approval that you referred to, Senator Goldwater, that it was up to me to go to the Director and say, now what about this? (Harvey, 6/25/75, p. 84)

At his final appearance before the Committee, Harvey explained:

> * * * if I had not been firmly convinced that this had full authority right straight down the chain of command, * * * I (would) have said to Bissell, all right, if I'm going to undertake this, which at best is a damned dicey operation or undertaking, I want to know who authorized it and under what circumstances. But I had every right to believe organizationally, humanly, whatever way you want to put it, that nothing that was being told to me by Bissell had not in fact come to him from the Director of Central Intelligence, or with the knowledge of the Director of Central Intelligence. (Harvey 7/11/75, pp. 73-74)

Harvey specifically rejected the idea that he would have entertained the thought of embarking on an assassination project on his own:

> I think what you are saying is had I not had reason to believe and been firmly convinced that this was an authorized, direct and fully approved and ordered, both operational and policy decision, would I, William Harvey, have gone out on my own and planned anybody's assassination, and the answer to that is a flat no. (Harvey, 7/11/75, p. 72)

Harvey best summarized his involvement in the plots as follows:

> At no time during this entire period we are talking about did I ever personally believe or have any feeling that I was either free-wheeling or end-running or engaging in any activity that was not in response to a considered, decided U.S. policy, properly approved, admittedly; perhaps through channels and at levels I personally had no involvement in, or firsthand acquaintance with, and did not consider it at that point my province to, if you will, cross examine either the Deputy Director or the Director concerning it. (Harvey, 6/25/75, p. 83)

The only other supervisory official of the CIA who admittedly was knowledgeable of the plots during the Post-Bay of Pigs phase was Richard Helms, presently U.S. Ambassador to Iran. Helms was at that time DDP (taking over from Bissell in February, 1962) and John

McCone was DCI (taking over from Dulles in November, 1961.[1] Helms had not been involved in the planning for the abortive Bay of Pigs invasion and had no knowledge of the Pre-Bay of Pigs assassination plots (Helms, 6/13/75, pp. 17–18). Harvey testified that he had "briefed" Helms some time in early 1961 regarding Bissell's directive to Harvey to begin working on an assassination capability." (Harvey, 6/25/75, pp. 42–44)[2] Thereafter, Helms said he was not "brought into Cuban operations" until after McCone had become Director in "late 1961 or early 1962." (Helms, 6/13/75, p. 18)

Our evidence established, however, that Helms was not brought into the picture affirmatively until April, 1962, when Harvey discussed with him the contacting of Roselli. Helms explained that:

> Harvey * * * says he came to me and said he wanted to recruit this man * * * (Roselli) which I didn't like at the time * * * But I decided to go along with it, since (Roselli) had been used in a previous operation, which hadn't worked. He was, therefore, in that sense, around our neck as a possible embarrassment. if he (Roselli) did have some connections and we didn't have very many in those days into Cuba someplace, maybe he would turn out to be a useful fellow. (Helms, 7/17/75, p. 8)

Helms testified that he was never convinced that this operation would be successful but since it had already been approved, he felt that "we haven't got very much, why don't we try". Helms, 7/17/75, pp. 23–24)

Helms, as our Report demonstrates, was much less involved in the plots than either Bissell or Harvey and perhaps because of this testified that:

> * * * [t]here is something about the whole chain of episode in connection with this Roselli business that I am simply not able to bring back in a coherent fashion. And there was something about the ineffectuality of all this, or the lack of conviction that anything ever happened, that I believe in the end made this thing simply collapse, disappear. And I don't recall what I was briefed on at the time. You saw the IG Report [which] says that I was kept currently informed. Maybe I was and maybe I wasn't, and today I don't remember it. * * * But I do not recall ever having been convinced that any attempt was really made on Castro's life. (Helms, 7/12/75, p. 38)

Nevertheless, Helms did recall being advised of the plots by Harvey and indicating his approval. He testified that he felt the assassination attempts, while he was skeptical as to how far they actually progressed, were authorized by the White House. Helms, however, like Harvey and Bissell, did not have any personal knowledge as to how or through whom such authorization passed.[3]

---

[1] McCone denied any knowledge of or authorization for the assassination plots which went on during his tenure as DCI. McCone testified that he learned of the plots for the first time in August 1963 when Helms briefed him. This discussion and the failure of McCone to issue any directive thereafter affirmatively banning such actions (which continued into 1964 and 1965) is discussed in the Committee's Report, pp. 99–108.

[2] Harvey testified he told Helms exactly what Bissell told him, i.e., that the White House had twice urged Bissell to set up an Executive Action capability. (Harvey, 6/25/75, pp. 42–44)

[3] Helms, in effect, stepped into the middle of a project run originally by Bissell and passed on in November, 1961, to Harvey. Dulles remained as DCI until November, 1961— well long enough to have briefed the incoming Kennedy Administration on whether to continue the assassination actions. Helms did not know whether Dulles obtained such authorization or for that matter whether McCone did so. As developed hereinafter, everything which was transpiring around him led him to believe such authorization was obtained. See Helms, 6/25/75, pp. 67–69, 34, 90, 101–103. Part VI *infra*, of these views provides a look at just what kind of environment surrounded Helms and the CIA in 1962. Helms, however, never asked anyone in higher positions if the plots were in fact authorized even when he had the opportunity to do so—exhibiting, at a minimum, very bad judgment.

Helms testified that while no one in the Administration gave him a direct order to assassinate Castro, neither did he expect one.[1] It was, however, made abundantly clear to him by the Kennedy Administration that the CIA's mission was to "get rid of Castro";

> The desire (of the Administration) was "can't you fellows [CIA] find some way to get rid of Castro and the Castro regime?" (Helms, 7/17/75, p. 17)

Helms testified that he had no doubts but that the assassination attempts were within the authorized U.S. policy toward Castro:

> I believe it was the policy at the time to get rid of Castro and if killing him was one of the things that was to be done in this connection, that was within what was expected. (Helms, 6/13/75, p. 137)

Thus, Helms told the Committee that the plot activities were both presented to him in 1962 as an ongoing project previously authorized and that such actions appeared to be clearly within the ambit of authority which he felt existed at the time. The latter concept, stressed by Helms in his testimony, was that assassination plots were consistent with the environment of the time. Helms' view that assassination was within the approved policy during the atmosphere of the time is corroborated by the authors of the CIA's 1967 Inspector General's Report who took pains to point out:

> We cannot overemphasize the extent to which responsible Agency officers felt themselves subject to the Kennedy Administration's severe pressure to do something about Castro and his regime. The fruitless and, in retrospect, often unrealistic plotting should be viewed in that light. (IG Report, p. 4)

Helms testified that during this 1961–1962 period

> The highest authorities of government were anxious that the Castro government fall and that in some fashion Castro go away (Helms, 6/13/75, p. 62)

*   *   *   *   *   *   *

> and if he (Castro) had disappeared from the scene they would not have been unhappy. (Helms, 6/13/75, pp. 72–73)

Helms summed up his testimony, in effect, by stating in colloquy with Senator Mathias that, though no direct order was given to him, "some spark had been transmitted that (assassination) was within the permissible limits." (Helms, 6/25/75, p. 72) Helms' and Harvey's total understanding of the authorization of assassination plotting together with the ingrained system of deniability present in intelligence operations, I feel, explains, but does not excuse their actions in not directly confronting a superior or a While House official and saying: "By the way, are these assassination plots really authorized." I think it blinks reality to suggest that such a thing would have occurred. True, the system must be changed, but these assassination activities must be viewed in light of the modus operandi which existed at the time.

III. *The Testimony and Evidence Regarding How Authority Would Have Been Obtained—the Troubling Doctrine of Plausible Denial*

The Committee received considerable evidence on the manner or modus operandi which would have been employed to advise the President of matters of great sensitivity, such as the assassination plots. The

---

[1] How Bissell, Harvey, and Helms felt the plots would have been authorized is treated in part III of these views.

Committee Report defines and discusses the mode or method of operating which has come to be known as plausible denial. (Committee Report, pp. 11–12) Members of the Committee have given its application to the assassination plots differing degrees of weight. In these views I assign it substantial weight because of the frequency with which it wove its way through the evidence concerning the critical issue of authorization.

Simply stated, plausible denial is the system which dictates that any acts that are perpetrated shall be done in such a way so as to ensure that the U.S. Government cannot be blamed. In its most common meaning in the intelligence community, plausible denial dictates the use of "cut-outs," or, various levels of knowledge with the lowest level not being told that the work that is being done is on behalf of the U.S. Government. The system is designed to insulate the President from the responsibility for projects which may go awry.

We know that efforts were made to employ this system in the Castro plots through the use of Maheu to initiate the contact with Rosselli and Giancana, the CIA Case Officer assuming the false identity of an employee of Maheu, and the use of the "cover story" of the U.S. business interests in explaining the plots to the Cubans. The agent (in this case the Cubans) may assume or guess that the person he was doing the work for was a government representative, but, an admission of government involvement was avoided.

Additionally, we found the system used in the records of the Special Group which avoid direct attribution to the President and refer to the President as "higher authority," or "his associate." This was true in almost all the cases we examined.[1] Moreover, the testimony revealed that the prevailing practice on all sensitive matters was to brief the President without obtaining his express approval. Maxwell Taylor testified that the President would simply listen to what the person briefing him had to say without responding affirmatively so that "the record (did not) say that the President personally approved (the project). (Taylor, 7/9/75, p. 25)

Thus, whenever we attempted to climb the authority ladder to determine the highest level of knowledge and approval of assassination plots we encountered the use of plausible denial. Indeed, Bissell testified that he and Edwards used the system to "circumlocutiously" advise Dulles of the assassination plans because "the Director (Dulles) preferred the use of * * * (that) sort of (circumlocutious) language * * *." (Bissell, 6/9/75, p. 25) Bissell testified that it would be through the use of plausible denial that he felt approval for the assassination plots would have been obtained from the President by Dulles.

Bissell testified that Dulles would have advised the President of the assassination plots by obliquely describing the operation but continuing "until the President got the word." (Bissell, 6/11/75, pp. 12–14) He described how Dulles could have preserved deniability yet obtained approval from the President:

> I have expressed the opinion and am making it clear, it is not based on hard evidence that probably the President knew something of this * * * I very much

---

[1] See "Guidelines for Operation MONGOOSE" (Draft), March 5, 1962; Memorandum for the Record, Special Group Augmented, "Discussion of Operation MONGOOSE with the President" of March 16, 1962 and accompanying footnote of March 22, 1962; Memorandum for the Record, Special Group Meeting, August 25, 1960.

doubt if he at any time was told any of the details. My guess is that indeed whoever informed him, that is Dulles directly or Dulles through a staff member, would have had the same desire that you referred to to shield the President and to shield him in the sense of intimating or making clear that something of the sort was going forward, but giving the President as little information about it as possible, and the purpose of it would have been to give the President an opportunity, if he so elected, to cancel it, to order it cancelled, or to allow it to continue but without, in effect, extracting from him an explicit endorsement of the detailed specific plan.

Senator MATHIAS. What you're saying is this is a highly subjective kind of operation in which an intimation can be given in which the President can clearly be told what is happening, but be told in, I think the words you used, a *circumlocutious* way, that he might not even blink unless he wanted to. Is that right?

Mr. BISSELL. That is correct, sir. (Bissell, 6/9/75, pp. 60-61)

Bissell made it clear that his perception of what happened at levels of authority above him spanned more than one administration. Indeed, he continually spoke of President Eisenhower and Kennedy together:

> In the case of an operation of high sensitivity of the sort that we are discussing, there was a further objective that would have been pursued at various levels, and that was specifically with respect to the President to protect the President. And therefore the way in which I believe that Allen Dulles would have attempted to do that was to have indicated to the two successive Presidents the general objective of the operation that was contemplated, to make it sufficiently clear so that the President—either President Eisenhower or President Kennedy—could have ordered the termination of the operation, but to give the President just as little information about it as possible beyond an understanding of its general purpose. Such an approach to the President would have had as its purpose to leave him in the position to deny knowledge of the operation if it should surface.
>
> My belief—a belief based, as I have said, only to my knowledge of command relationship, of Allen Dulles as an individual, and of his mode of operations—is that authorization was obtained by him in the manner that I have indicated. I used the word on Monday "circumlocutious," and it was to this approach that I referred. (Bissell, 6/11/75, pp. 5-6)

William Harvey and Richard Helms also felt that they doubted that there would ever be a direct written or even oral order communicated to the DCI on a matter such as the assassination plots. Helms elaborated on why he felt the plots were authorized even though he was unable to point to a direct written or oral order to carry them out:

> [Assassination plots would not be] authorized in any formal way * * * These schemes * * * would have taken place in the context of doing what you could to get rid of Castro, and the difficulty with this kind of thing, as you gentlemen are all painfully aware, is that nobody wants to embarrass a President of the United States discussing the assassination of foreign leaders in his presence. This is something that has got to be dealt with in some other fashion. Even though you use euphemisms you've still got a problem * * *
>
> Now, when President Eisenhower took responsibility for the U-2 flights that was on his own * * * [h]e wasn't obliged to do that * * * he had his mechanism to blame it on, if he wanted to. (Helms, 6/13/75, p. 29)

Helms added that apprising the President of such a matter was no easy or simple task:

> Senator MATHIAS. When Mr. Bissell was here I think I asked him whether the job of communicating with superior authority was one of protecting superior authority, and specifically the President, protecting him from knowledge and at the same time informing him, which is a difficult and delicate job, and he agreed that that was really the difficulty.
>
> And you this morning have said that in advising a President or very high authority of any particular delicate subject, that you resorted to euphemism.
>
> Mr. HELMS. Yes, sir. (Helms, 6/13/75, pp. 65-66)

*   *   *   *   *   *   *

Senator MATHIAS. Did Presidents indulge in euphemisms as well as Directors?

Mr. HELMS. I don't know. I found in my experience that Presidents used the entire range of the English language from euphemisms on the one extreme to very explicit talk on the other.

Senator MATHIAS. Let me draw an example from history. When Thomas A. Beckett was proving to be an annoyance, as Castro, the King said who will rid me of this man. He didn't say to somebody go out and murder him. He said who will rid me of this man, and let it go at that * * *

Mr. HELMS. That is a warming reference to the problem.

Senator MATHIAS. You feel that spans the generations and the centuries?

Mr. HELMS. I think it does, sir.

Senator MATHIAS. And that is typical of the kind of thing which might be said, which might be taken by the Director or by anybody else as Presidential authorization to go forward?

Mr. HELMS. That is right. But in answer to that, I realize that one sort of grows up in tradition of the time and I think that any of us would have found it very difficult to discuss assassinations with a President of the United States. I just think we all had the feeling that we were hired out to keep those things out of the Oval Office.

Senator MATHIAS. And yet at the same time you felt that some spark had been transmitted, that that was within the permissible limits?

Mr. HELMS. Yes; and if he had disappeared from the scene they would not have been unhappy. (Helms, 6/13/75, pp. 71-73)

The Executive Assistant to Harvey, described what he thought the approval process might be in the following exchange with Senator Schweiker:

Senator SCHWEIKER. We keep coming back to this confusing status where we see the assassination plans and plots falling out very prolifically, and we see that higher authority as in your case has authorized them, but somewhere along there we lost track. And I guess my question is, would a logical explanation of this very confusing situation be that some of the powers that be just decided not to discuss them in the formal sessions, and just verbally passed on instructions through the chain of command, but not in the formal committee special group apparatus?

Might that be a logical explanation of why we are continually confused by the kind of testimony that you have given, and let me say that others have given, too?

EXECUTIVE ASSISTANT: I wouldn't expect any President to sign a piece of paper directing an assassination for any reason. I don't think that is done in any government.

Senator SCHWEIKER. So that kind of an explanation would make sense from your experience in government?

EXECUTIVE ASSISTANT: Yes, sir.

Senator SCHWEIKER. And explain the discrepancy that we keep running into in terms of different situations analogous to yourself?

EXECUTIVE ASSISTANT: Sure. I don't think you are going to find a piece of paper for everything that this Agency or any other Agency has done. There are lots of things that get done by word of mouth.

The CHAIRMAN: But does this leave us in a situation where the direct connection between the President or the Special Group Augmented, the high policy making authority, with respect to knowledge of and direction to assassination of Mr. Castro must be based upon assumption or speculation?

EXECUTIVE ASSISTANT: I think it is based upon the integrity of the people who passed on the orders. And it is all oral. (Executive Assistant to Harvey, 6/18/75, pp. 54-55)

Harvey, reporting directly to first Bissell and then Helms, also exhibited in his testimony an ingrained reluctance to even discuss assassination in front of his superiors unless specifically asked about it. He was sure that the way the system of deniability operated

* * * no one would want to charge the President personally with the complete, dirty-handed details of [the assassination plans]. (Harvey, 6/25/75, p. 82)

Moreover, when he was first advised by Bissell that the White House was urging the CIA to set up an assassination capability,[1] Harvey was asked during his testimony why he had not inquired of Bissell as to who in the White House had communicated with him. Harvey answered that:

> I did not ask him, and he did not volunteer and I would have considered it somewhat improper to ask and grossly improper if he had volunteered on his part. (Harvey, 6/25/75, p. 87)

Again, when queried by the Committee as to why he never raised the subject of assassination at any of the Special Group Meetings he attended, Harvey responded that he:

> * * * felt that if the White House (tasked) this (operation to the CIA) and wanted the Special Group to know about it, it was up to the White House to brief the Special Group and not up to me to brief them, and I would have considered that I would have been very far out of line and would have been subject to severe censure. (Harvey, 7/11/75, p. 77)

It seems to me that Harvey's failure to specifically raise the subject of assassination in meetings with high level Government officials is attributable to more to his attempt to effectuate the system of plausible denial than to any sinister motive to conceal the plots from his superiors. Helms very frankly, and in my view honestly, confirmed Harvey's understanding of deniability and the "protection" of one's higher authority as follows:

> Mr. HELMS. I don't know whether it was in training experience tradition or exactly what one points to, but I think to go up to a Cabinet officer and say, am I right in assuming that you want me to assassinate Castro or to try to assassinate Castro, is a question it wouldn't have occurred to me to ask. (Helms, 7/17/75, p. 51)

Whether that protection extended to a duty to lie to protect higher authority is a matter we were not able to resolve. Bissell, while emphasizing that he had been truthful in his testimony before the Committee, said:

> "* * * There are occasions when I would go a long way to protect the President of the United States from certain kinds of embarrassment." (Bissell, 6/11/75, pp. 62–63)

* * * * * * *

> "(Senator Goldwater) Q. * * * Would you tell a falsehood to protect a President of the United States?
> A. Well, under certain circumstances, I would indeed, Senator. I would tell a falsehood, for instance, to the Press or in public announcements * * * and that is perhaps a little different thing, but I would certainly be at ease to do so if the revelation of an operation would be directly embarrassing to the President." (Bissell, 7/22/75, pp. 50–51)

The testimony set out above provides us with the best look at what most likely occurred in terms of *how* authorization was obtained by the CIA for the assassination plots. Whether such conversations did in fact occur is something we will never be able to prove conclusively. What remains are impressions of what probably occurred. This testimony in large part forms the basis of my impressions.

---

[1] Assassination capability of "Execution Action," as it came to be known is described in Part IV of these views, *infra*.

IV. The concept of assassination was discussed at the highest levels of Government and not affirmatively disavowed

The Committee's investigation revealed that the "concept" of assassination was actually discussed on several occasions at the highest levels of Government. While I find it disturbing that something as drastic as assassination was apparently calmly talked about within our Government, it is even more troublesome that assassination was never clearly and unequivocally disavowed in a manner which left no doubt, at any level of government, that such a course of action would not be tolerated under any circumstances. Some of the discussions of assassination were plainly that. Other times the "capability" for assassination or language which may have been interpreted by some as a euphemism for assassination were the topics of debate within the Executive Branch. The fine distinction between approval of a "capability" for assassination and approval of planning and plotting for actual assassination may be a distinction without difference. If not, it is clearly a dangerous and foolish distinction to make. So too was the ever so common use of loose language and euphemisms. As the Committee's Report notes, the frequent usage of terms such as "get rid of," "eliminate," "removal of Cuban leaders," "disappear simultaneously," "straightforward action," "direct positive action" together with continual discussion of contingency plans to take effect upon the demise of Castro within an intelligence community operating under an ingrained system of deniability combined to create a mosaic of confusion and misunderstanding.

A. Executive Action

Executive Action is treated in the Committee's Report, pp. 181–190. The impact of Executive Action, at least upon me, is one of more substantial weight than that accorded in the Report. In my view, the gravity and seriousness of Executive Action is twofold. First, in some ways I find an untargeted capability to perform assassinations even more sinister than the overt planning against a specific antagonistic target. While the plotting against Castro can never be justified, at least the argument can be made that we were battling what was at that time perceived to be a hostile communist force 90 miles from our shores. A standby assassination ability that is capable of being employed anywhere for any reason addresses no particular threat, perceived or real. It is highly a dangerous "capability" to maintain.

Second, the approval, whether actual or apparent, of the maintenance of an assassination capability surely contributed to the CIA's view that the assassination plots were fully authorized. It strains my imagination to argue that assassination capability (Executive Action) on the one hand and assassination "plotting" on the other hand fit neatly into separate little compartments. For example, while Bundy was either affirmatively ordering the CIA to set up an assassination capability or at least implicity approving it, did the CIA officers knowledgeable of such White House approval find it consistent with and supportive of their feeling that the assassination plots were authorized? Were Bissell, Helms and Harvey, aware that the White

House had approved or urged assassination "capability," far off base in their beliefs that the Castro plotting also bore the White House imprimatur? To me, these questions provide obvious answers.

Third, Bissell testified that when he and Bundy were discussing Executive Action he "might have" spoken of "Castro as a possible victim" (Bissell, 6/11/75, p. 50) and:

> I might very well have spoken of others [besides Castro], I might well have spoken of Lumumba. I might possibly have spoken of Trujillo. They were some of the cases where this kind of thing was considered.
>
> * * * * * * *
>
> I might well have used the three names that I just gave, because they were the sorts of individuals [Castro, Lumumba, Trujillo] at that moment in history against whom such a capability might possibly have been employed. (Bissell, 6/11/75, pp. 50–51)

Thus, we have yet another example of the CIA's planning in Trujillo, Lumumba and Castro blended together, along with Executive Action, in a common web of perceived authority.

The fact that Executive Action and actual plots were at times blended together is best illustrated by Harvey's testimony of his discussion with Bissell about the creation of an Executive Action capability. He recalled that Bissell advised him at that time of a then going operation involving "the names of Maheu and possibly Roselli and Giancana," "which was a part of the Agency's effort to develop * * * a capability for Executive Action." (Harvey, 7/11/75, pp. 55, 61) Harvey said that he was told that "in connection with * * * our charge to create such a capability [Executive Action], [t]here is one operation already going." (Harvey, 7/11/75, p. 53)

These are some of the questions and concerns which I have about the "Executive Action" testimony and evidence the Committee has received. What I consider to be the most important parts of our documentary evidence and testimony concerning Executive Action are set out comprehensively in the Committee's Report, pp. 181–190.

B. THE AUGUST 10 MEETING

The Special Group Augmented met on August 10, 1962. Sixteen persons, all high Government officials, attended the meeting. I treat this meeting separately because I accord it more importance than does the Committee's report. It is one of the few times where the Committee has established, upon convincing evidence, that assassination was raised and overtly discussed as a possible course of action. While, as the Committee Report concludes, the August 10 meeting was not directly related to the Castro attempts, I feel it is instructive for several reasons. First, it is about the only concrete example of what occurred when we know the subject of assassination was raised publicly and the discussion was written up. Second, it contributed to the hostile atmosphere in which these various assassination plots grew. Third, it demonstrates that despite the clear record that assassination was discussed, not everyone present can "recall" the discussion and no one will admit that he raised assassination as a possible course of action. Fourth, the written record of the meeting (the minutes) contains no reference to it.[1] In short, the August 10 meeting serves as a microcosm for the whole system of deniability.

The Committee Report, pp. 161–169, describes this meeting in detail. I will not recount the facts again, but will focus instead on the testimony regarding who suggested it.

1.—THE TESTIMONY—WHO RAISED THE SUGGESTION OF THE ASSASSINATION OF CASTRO?

(a) TESTIMONY OF MCCONE

McCone testified that the question of a "liquidation" or removal of Castro and other Cuban leaders arose at the August 10 meeting in the context of "exploring the alternatives that were available" for the next phase of MONGOOSE. (McCone, 6/6/75, p. 33) He noted that:

* * * during those days it was almost common for one person or another to say, we ought to dispose of Castro ... But at no time did anyone come to me, or come to other authorities to my knowledge, with a plan for the actual undertaking of an assassination. (McCone, 6/6/75, p. 3.)

McCone testified that he did not recall who made this suggestion, but that he and Mr. Murrow took "strong exception" to assassination he said:

Q. "* * * I take it then, that according to your best recollection the subject of liquidating Castro and possibly other top Cuban leaders did come up at this meeting, and you did take strong exception to it?"
A. "Yes. I was not alone in that. Mr. Murrow took exception. I remember that very clearly." (McCone, 6/6/75, p. 33)

Despite remembering very clearly his response, McCone testified he couldn't "recall" who it was that made the suggestion. (*Ibid.*)

McCone then testified that although he had no independent recollection of who raised the subject of assassination, he was able to reconstruct from the documentary record that was Secretary of Defense Robert McNamara who made the suggestion. McCone relied upon his own memorandum, which was written in 1967, and the August 13 Harvey Memorandum. McCone's memorandum was prepared April 14, 1967, after McCone left the CIA. He dictated the memorandum as his recollection of the August 10, 1962 meeting. The memorandum was prompted by a telephone call from the newspaper columnist Jack Anderson, who at that time was preparing a column on Castro assassination attempts. After talking with Anderson on the telephone, at Robert Kennedy's request, McCone dictated the April 14, 1967 memorandum, which stated that at one of several MONGOOSE meetings on August 8, 9 or 10, 1962. "I recall a suggestion being made to liquidate top people in the Castro regime, including Castro." (McCone, Ex. 4, p. 1) While

---

[1] I find it disturbing, but not surprising, that our exhaustive inquiry did not satisfactorily establish either why the minutes show no reference to assassination nor who suggested assassination. No one was candid enough to say, yes, I raised it but not in a serious vein or in a moment of frustration. Rather, we are left either to question the credibility of the witnesses or conclude that assassination was so commonplace or insignificant that it did not make an impression on anyone. In any case, it is not a pleasant picture.

this 1967 memorandum does not state that McNamara raised the concept of assassination, it does state that:

> Immediately after the meeting, I called on Secretary McNamara personally and re-emphasized my position, in which he heartily agreed. I did this because Operation MONGOOSE—an interdepartmental affair—was under the operational control of (the Defense Department) * * * (*Id.*)

McCone continued in his testimony that "At no time did the suggestion receive serious consideration by the Special Group (Augmented) nor by any individual responsible for policy." (McCone, Ex. 4). He emphasized that after he spoke with Harvey about the Lansdale memorandum he:

> [i]nsisted that that Memorandum be withdrawn because no decision was made on this subject, and since no decision was made, then Lansdale was quite out of order in tasking the Central Intelligence Agency to consider the matter. (McCone, 6/6, pp. 38–39)

McCone concluded his testimony about the August 10 meeting and its aftermath by saying that "The subject was just dropped" after his objection. (McCone, 6/6/75, p. 37)[1]

(b) Harvey's Testimony

Harvey testified that Robert McNamara raised the subject of assassination by stating at the August 10 meeting "shouldn't we consider the elimination or assassination of Fidel?" (Harvey, 7/11/75, pp. 29–30) When asked whether he was certain or merely guessing that it was McNamara and not someone else who made the suggestion, Harvey responded:

> No, I am not guessing . . . [t]o the best of my recollection, it was surfaced by Robert McNamara. (Harvey, 7/11/75, p. 86)

Harvey also testified that his independent recollection of McNamara raising the subject was in accord with his memorandum of August 14 (written shortly after the meeting) which also referred to McNamara bringing up the assassination suggestion.

(c) Testimony of Goodwin

The testimony of Goodwin was, like Lansdale's appearance before the Committee, not a model of clarity. Goodwin was interviewed by the staff on May 27, 1975. (Goodwin Exhibit 2, 7/18/75) At that time he told the staff that McNamara had suggested assassinating Castro or "getting rid of Castro" at the August 10 meeting. Indeed, he told the staff that "etched on his memory" was the following exchange:

> McNamara got up to leave during a discussion of how to get rid of Castro and said, "The only way to get rid of Castro was to kill him."

Goodwin then said that McNamara followed this comment up by saying, "I really mean it." At that point, Goodwin told the Committee

---

[1] This conclusion was not in accord with Harvey's recollection that after the August 10 meeting Lansdale tried to raise the subject of assassination with him on several occasions. *See* I.G. Report, p. 115; Harvey 7/11/75, pp. 3–5.

staff that Bissell said, "Oh, you mean Executive Action." Goodwin said he didn't think the comments were followed up on by McNamara (although Lansdale and Harvey were both at the meeting) and that "it was pretty foolish for McNamara to talk about that kind of a subject in front of 15 other people." (Goodwin interview, 5/25/75, p. 1)

When Goodwin appeared before the Committee, about six weeks later, his testimony was significantly different. He testified with respect to who raised the suggestion of assassination at the August 10 meeting that: "I am unable to say with any certainty who it was." (Goodwin, 7/18/75, p. 8)

Goodwin was later questioned about statements he was quoted as having made to authors Taylor Branch and George Crile, III.[1] He was quoted in the article as having said that at one of the Cuban task force meetings, McNamara said that "Castro's assassination was the only productive way of dealing with Cuba" and that he, Goodwin, was "surprised and appalled" at such statements. In his testimony, Goodwin said he was misquoted and that he did not tell the authors "it was definitely McNamara." (Goodwin, 7/18/75, p. 33). Goodwin concluded by testifying that, some 15 years after the August 10 meeting, he could not testify about who raised the assassination suggestion with "substantial certainty" (*Id.* at p. 35).

(d) LANSDALE'S TESTIMONY

Lansdale testified that he simply had a poor recollection of the August 10 meeting. He was not sure what occurred at the meeting, other than that assassination was raised and that "one or two people sitting in there (at the meeting) said it was something that shouldn't be considered," (Lansdale, 7/8/75, p. 123) and that "others * * * might have" joined McNamara in proposing or urging it. (Lansdale, 7/8/75, p. 127) Moreover, Lansdale could not explain why he ordered the CIA to draw up an assassination plan if the consensus of the Special Group was negative.[2] He said he didn't "remember the reason why" he sent out such a memorandum. (Lansdale, 7/8/75, pp. 122–23, 20–21) Lansdale summarized his recollection as follows:

> I believe that the subject of assassination was brought up at a meeting * * * by Robert McNamara * * * and (McNamara) was usually very brief and terse in his remarks, and it might have been something like, well, look into that * * * (Lansdale, 7/8/75, pp. 116, 126).

Lansdale could not offer any explanation for why the minutes of the meeting were silent on the matter except that it was decided not to make it "a matter of official record." (Lansdale exhibit 16, p. 1)

(e) TESTIMONY OF RUSK, BUNDY, AND GILPATRIC

Rusk, Bundy, and Gilpatric all testified that they had "no recollection" of assassination being discussed at the August 10 meeting. (Rusk, 7/10/75, p. 63; Bundy, 7/11/75, pp. 27, 89; Gilpatric, 7/8/75, p. 48) [3]

---
[1] They co-authored the article entitled "The Kennedy Vendetta," which appeared in Harper's Magazine, July, 1975.
[2] Lansdale, like Goodwin, denied the accuracy of two news stories quoting him as saying he was ordered to develop such a plan. *See* Committee Report, pp. 167–169.
[3] Indeed, Gilpatric testified that "I didn't think I was present for that meeting." (Gilpatric, 7/17/75, p. 48)

(f) TESTIMONY OF MCNAMARA

McNamara testified concerning the August 10 meeting that he did not even recall that particular meeting. (McNamara, 7/11/75, p. 11) He said that he had "no recollection of raising [the assassination suggestion] at any time." (McNamara, 7/11/75, p. 12) McNamara, throughout his testimony, stated that he doubted that he proposed such a tactic. He said at one point:

> I have talked with Messrs. Taylor, Bundy, Gilpatric and Rusk [and they also] have no recollection of me raising it. It is entirely out of character with what I believe I thought at the time and I do not read into those words (Harvey's memorandum) a statement that I did propose it. (McNamara, 7/11/75, p. 18)

(g) TESTIMONY OF PARROTT

Parrott, the author of the August 10 Minutes, testified that he did not recall a discussion of assassination at that meeting, but the fact that the minutes do not reflect such a discussion is not an indication that the matter did not come up. Parrott pointed out that his minutes "were not intended to be a verbatim transcript of everything that was said." (Parrott, 7/10/75, p. 34) Parrott further stated that the purpose of his minutes was "to interpret what the decisions were and to record those and to use them as a useful action document." (Parrott, 7/10/75, p. 35) Parrott testified:

> "We had 15 or 16 people (at the August 10, 1962, meeting) * * * all of them well informed, all of them highly articulate.
> This meeting, as I recall, went on for several hours * * * Now I'm sure that particularly in a group like this that there were a great many proposals made that were just shot down immediately. (Parrott, 7/10/75, pp. 34–35)

Parrott further testified that he did not record proposals "that were quickly rejected at the August 10 meeting. (Parrott, 7/10/75, p. 35) He stated that, although he had no recollection of a discussion of Castro's assassination at the August 10 meeting, he would infer from the related documents (the Lansdale and Harvey memoranda of August 13 and 14) that the subject was raised but "it never got off the ground * * * [a]nd therefore, I did not record it." (Parrott, 7/10/75, p. 35) Parrott said it was not his practice to intentionally not record such discussions in the minutes.

(h) TESTIMONY OF ELDER

Walter Elder testified that although he was not present at the August 10 meeting, he was present when McCone returned to the Agency and "called McNamara on the phone and * * * took exception to the discussion of assassination as improper." (Elder, 8/13/75, pp. 22–23) Elder described the conversation (which he heard in McCone's office on a speaker phone) as follows:

> A. * * * (McCone) said, "Bob, the subject you just brought up, I think it is highly improper. I do not think it should be discussed. It is not an action that should ever be condoned. It is not proper for us to discuss, and I intend to have it expunged from the record."
> Q. Did McNamara say he did not bring it up?
> A. No, he did not.
> Q. Is that the total conversation as you remember it?
> A. This was back in 1962. That was the gist of it.

C. Conversations With President Kennedy About the Use of Assassination

The only evidence the Committee heard of the discussion of assassinations with a President were two conversations with President Kennedy.[1] Both occurred during the active phase of the Castro plots, during the year 1961. Neither conversation aided us in our effort to determine whether President Kennedy or any other President specifically or implicitly authorized the CIA's assassination plots and plans. They established that President Kennedy said he was being urged to authorize Castro's assassination. Yet, none of the Presidential advisors were aware of any such urgings and testified that they thought they would have been if the President had been so urged.

1. President Kennedy's Meeting With Tad Szulc on November 9, 1961

In early November 1961, Szulc was asked by Richard Goodwin, then Special Assistant to President Kennedy, to meet with Attorney General Robert Kennedy on November 8, 1961, to discuss the situation in Cuba. The meeting was an "off-the-record" one which Szulc attended as a friend of Goodwin's and not as a reporter. (Szulc, 6/10/75, p. 24) During the meeting with Robert Kennedy, the discussion centered on "the situation in Cuba following the [Bay of Pigs] invasion [and] the pros and cons of some different possible actions by the U.S. Government in that context." (Szulc, 6/10/75, p. 25) The word assassination did not come up during this meeting. (Szulc, 6/10/75, p. 31)

At the close of the meeting, Robert Kennedy asked Szulc to meet with President Kennedy. (Szulc, 6/10/75, p. 25) On November 9, 1961, Szulc, accompanied by Goodwin, met with President Kennedy for over an hour in the Oval Office. (Szulc, 6/10/75, p. 25) Szulc recalled that the President discussed "a number of his views on Cuba in the wake of the Bay of Pigs, asked me a number of questions concerning my conversations with Premier Castro, and * * * what the United States could [or] might do in * * * either a hostile way or in establishing some kind of dialogue * * *" (Szulc, 6/10/75, pp. 25–26)

Szulc testified that after this general discussion, the President then asked, *"what would you think if I ordered Castro to be assassinated?"* (Szulc, 6/10/75, p. 26; Szulc Notes of Conversation with President Kennedy, November 9, 1961 (Emphasis Added.) Szulc testified that he replied that an assassination would not necessarily cause a change in the Cuban system, and that it was Szulc's personal view that the United States should not be party to murders and political assassinations. (Szulc, 6/10/75, p. 26) Szulc testified that thereupon the President said, "I agree with you completely." Szulc stated further:

> He [President Kennedy] then went on for a few minutes to make the point how strongly he and his brother felt that the U.S. for moral reasons should never be in a situation of having recourse to assassination in foreign policy. (Szulc, 6/10/75, p. 27)

---

[1] The testimony regarding the August 18, 1960 meeting of the National Security Council at which President Eisenhower said something which one Robert Johnson thought was as an assassination suggestion is discussed *infra;* see also Committee Report, pp. 55–60.

Szulc's notes of the meeting with the President state:

> JFK then said he was testing me, that he felt the same way—he added "I'm glad you feel the same way—because indeed U.S. morally must not be part [sic] to assassinations."

Szulc's notes of the conversation further state:

> JFK said he raised question because he was under terrific pressure from advisers (think he said intelligence people, but not positive) to okay a Castro murder, said [sic] he was resisting pressures. (Szulc Note of Conversation with President Kennedy, November 9, 1961)

Szulc stated, relying on his memory, that it is "possible" and he "believed" that President Kennedy used such words as "someone in the intelligence business," as the source of the pressure for a Castro assassination. (Szulc, 6/10/75, p. 29) The President did not identify the person or persons. (Szulc, 6/10/75, p. 27)

Goodwin also testified before the Committee about the Szulc/Kennedy conversation. He said that, after asking Szulc for his reaction to a suggestion that Castro be assassinated, President Kennedy said only, "we can't get into that kind of thing, or we would all be targets." (Goodwin, 7/18/75, pp. 4, 11)

This conversation, if accurately related to the Committee, and if the President was accurate in his remarks to Szulc, is particularly troublesome to me. It raises a number of questions on the issue of authority. The central question, of course, is who, in November 1961, was putting pressure on the President to authorize Castro's assassination? On November 29, 1961, John McCone replaced Allen Dulles as DCI;[1] thus. on November 9, Dulles was still DCI. Bissell was then still DDP. Helms and Harvey were both within the DDP. Yet, everyone has uniformly denied ever even mentioning assassination to President Kennedy, let alone "pressuring" him to approve it.[2] Moreover, the CIA itself, in a paper drafted and submitted to the President only one month earlier, had concluded that Castro's death would not be "fatal to the regime" and recommended against any such action. *See* Committee Report, pp. 136–137.

Thus, this piece of evidence, like many others, does not fit neatly into the puzzle. Whether Allen Dulles ever spoke to President Kennedy about approval is a matter which cannot be conclusively resolved.

2. CONVERSATION BETWEEN PRESIDENT KENNEDY AND SENATOR GEORGE SMATHERS

George Smathers, former United States Senator representing the State of Florida, testified that in a conversation he had with President Kennedy as they walked together on the White House lawn:

> * * * [President Kennedy] asked me what reaction I thought there would be throughout South America were Fidel Castro to be assassinated * * * I told the President that even as much as I disliked Fidel Castro that I did not think it would be a good idea for there to be even considered an assassination of Fidel Castro, and the President of the United States completely agreed with me, that it would be a very unwise thing to do, the reason obviously being that no matter

---
[1] McCone's appointment was announced on September 27, 1961, but he spent some time "getting up to speed" on Agency operations, through briefings with Dulles, and took office on November 29. (*See* Elder, 8/13/75, pp. 8–9, 12–14)
[2] McCone, Helms, Bissell, Harvey, and all members of the Special Group and Special Group Augmented have testified that at no time did they ever discuss assassination with President Kennedy. Allen Dulles is deceased.

who did it and no matter how it was done and no matter what, that the United States would receive full credit for it, and it would work to his great disadvantage with all of the other countries in Central and South America * * * I disapproved of it, and he completely disapproved of the idea. (Smathers, 7/23/75, pp. 6, 7)

Smathers testified that he had the "impression" that the President raised the subject of assassination with him because someone "had apparently discussed this and other possibilities with respect to Cuba" with the President. (Smathers, 7/23/75, pp. 16, 25) Smathers had no direct knowledge of any such discussion, nor did he know who might have been involved. (Smathers, 7/23/75, pp. 16, 25) Moreover, the President did not indicate directly that assassination had been proposed to him. (Smathers, 7/23/75, p. 18)

According to Smathers, the President "asked me what reaction I thought there would be through South America were Fidel Castro to be assassinated." (Smathers, 7/23/75, p. 6) Smathers responded that he thought it would work to "great disadvantage" with the nations of Central and South America because they would blame the U.S. for any assassination of Castro.

Thereafter, Smathers said he tried to raise the subject of Cuba with President Kennedy and the President told him in no uncertain terms that he should not raise the subject with him again. Smathers particularly recalled one incident, which occurred after the above-quoted conversation, which stuck in his memory. He recalled that one evening he was at the President's home and during conversation:

I just happened to mention, * * * something about Cuba, and the President took his fork and cracked the plate * * * and says, for Gods sakes, quit talking about Cuba * * * (Smathers, 7/23/75, p. 22)

Senator Smathers concluded his testimony by indicating that in general he felt he was "taking the tougher stance" on Cuba than was President Kennedy (Smathers, 7/23/75, p. 24) but that he disapproved even thinking of assassinating Castro and that in his opinion President Kennedy was definitely "not interested in the assassination of Fidel Castro." (Smathers, 7/23/75, p. 16)

This second time that President Kennedy talked about assassination he again expressed the opinion that assassination should not be used by the United States. The subject was one, however, which appeared to be on his mind and, again, we are unable to establish who, if anyone, raised assassination with the President.

D. President Eisenhower's Discussion at the August 18, 1960 National Security Council Meeting

A discussion of United States policy towards the Congo occurred at the National Security Council on August 18, 1960. Robert H. Johnson, an NSC staff member from July 1951 to January 1962, attended that meeting as he had others and took the minutes. He testified that:

I attended one such NSC meeting in the summer of 1960. I should note parenthetically that I have refreshed my memory as to the probable time of the meeting by checking the historical record of international developments. At that meeting, there was a discussion of developments of what was then the Congo, now Zaire. I do not remember the context of the discussion. It is my guess that it was precipitated by the intelligence briefing by the Director of Central Intelligence on world developments with which every NSC meeting at that time began.

At some time during that discussion President Eisenhower said something—I can no longer remember his words—that came across to me as an order for the assassination of Lumumba who was then at the center of political conflict and controversy in the Congo. There was no discussion; the meeting simply moved on. I remember my sense of that moment quite clearly because the President's statement came as a great shock to me. I cannot, however, reconstruct the moment more specifically. (Johnson, 6/18/75, p. 6)

Senator Mathias then asked:

But what comes across is that you do have a memory, if not of exact words, but of your own reaction to a Presidential order which you consider to be an order for an assassination.
Mr. JOHNSON. That is correct.
Senator MATHIAS. And that although precise words have escaped you in the passage of 15 years, that sense of shock remains?
Mr. JOHNSON. Right, Yes, Sir. (Johnson, 6/18/75, p. 8)

Johnson, however, qualified his remarks as follows:

* * * I must confess that in thinking about the incident more recently I have had some doubts. As is well known, it was quite uncharacteristic of President Eisenhower to make or announce policy decisions in NSC meetings. Certainly it was strange if he departed from that normal pattern on a subject so sensitive as this. Moreover, it was not long after this, I believe, that Lumumba was dismissed as premier by Kasavubu in an action that was a quasi-coup. I have come to wonder whether what I really had [heard] was only an order for some such political action. All I can tell you with any certainty at the present moment is my sense of that moment in the Cabinet Room of the White House. (Robert H. Johnson, 6/18/75, pp. 5–7)

The minutes do not, however, reflect the exchange to which Johnson alluded.[1] Nor, does any other participant of the same meeting remember any such statement. Douglas Dillon, who was also present, suggests that the sentiment of the time was to get rid of Lumumba and that perhaps that is what was said. *See* Committee Report, pp. 57–60.

A fine line appears to exist between getting rid of someone and taking steps toward their assassination. Again, we find conversations which mean different things to different people. This is one more example of why I fully agree with the Committee's central finding that we cannot conclusively establish whether the assassination plots were authorized, yet come away with the impression that the CIA's actions were not far afield from what the policymakers desired.

V. *Did the Investigation of Giancana and Roselli Reveal Their Involvement in the Assassination Plots to the FBI, Department of Justice, Attorney General or the President?*

On October 31, 1960, at the very early stages of the Castro plotting in Florida, the wiretap installed through Maheu at the request of Giancana was discovered in another person's Las Vegas apartment. *See* Committee's Report, pp. 77–79. The FBI commenced an investigation which soon led to both Maheu and Giancana. During the course of the investigation information regarding the CIA's involvement with underworld figures was disclosed to the FBI, Justice Department

---

[1] Johnson, following the meeting, "checked with a superior as to whether I should include the President's statement in my de-briefing of the Planning Board and as to how I should handle it in my memorandum of the discussion. I suspect—but no longer have an exact recollection—that I omitted it from the de-briefing. It was not unusual to occasionally omit some particularly sensitive subject from the de-briefing." (Johnson, 6/18/75, p. 7; 9/13/75, pp. 11–13)

officials, and Attorney General Kennedy. In addition, our investigation revealed that during the Florida assassination plotting the FBI actually had Roselli and Giancana under surveillance and had a bug in their various abodes.[1] This section will describe what evidence the Committee gathered concerning what information was transmitted to the Executive Branch during the period of the Las Vegas wiretap investigation and what action was taken because of it.

A. THE FBI MEMORANDA

1. THE OCTOBER 18, 1960 MEMORANDUM

The first relevant memorandum discovered by the Committee's investigation was a memorandum sent by Director Hoover to Allen W. Dulles, DCI, marked "Attention: Deputy Director, Plans."[2] The memorandum reported that an FBI "source" had obtained the following information:

> According to the source, during recent conversation with several friends, Giancana stated that Fidel Castro was to be done away with very shortly. When doubt was expressed regarding this statement Giancana reportedly assured those present that Castro's assassination would occur in November. Moreover, he allegedly indicated that he had already met with the assassin-to-be on three occasions, the last meeting taking place on a boat docked at the Fontainbleau Hotel, Miami Beach, Florida. Reportedly, Giancana claimed that everything has been perfected for the killing of Castro and that the "assassin" had arranged with a girl, not further described, to drop a "pill" in some drink or food of Castro's.

Bissell, however, was the CIA's DDP (to whose attention the memo was directed) at the time and testified that he did not recall seeing the memorandum. (Bissell, 7/22/75, p. 40) He said that under CIA procedures a copy would also have been given to the DCI Dulles. (Bissell, 7/22/75, p. 40)

The FBI copy of the Hoover/Dulles memorandum contained the following additional information:

> By separate airtel [night cable] we have instructed the field to be most alert for any additional information concerning alleged plots against Castro and to submit recommendations for close surveillance of Giancana in the event he makes trip to the Miami area or other trips which may be for the purpose of contacting people implicated in this plot.

I find the October 18, 1960, memorandum particularly significant since it reveals intimate knowledge of the Castro plots including the method to be used (poison pills) and the place of most meetings. (Fontainbleau Hotel). I have a hard time believing this memorandum was dismissed as idle chatter, particularly as the FBI's investigation proceeded forward and yet additional information was obtained. Our investigation, however, has not determined exactly who was advised, orally or otherwise, of this October 18 memorandum or what was done about it.

---

[1] See FBI documents; Meheu 7/29/75, pp. 66–67, 9/23/75, pp. 13–16; Roselli 9/22/75, pp. 13, 19, 20–21, 47, 55.

[2] Copies of this memorandum were sent to Assistant Chief of Staff for Intelligence, Department of the Army, Attention: Chief, Security Division; Office of Special Investigations. Air Force, Attention: Chief, Counterintelligence Division; Director of Naval Intelligence; Assistant Attorney General J. Walter Yeagley; Office of Security, Department of State.

Courtney Evans was then the FBI's liaison with Attorney General Kennedy and the President. He had worked closely with the then Senator John Kennedy and Robert Kennedy on the McClellan Committee, which had investigated the relationship between organized labor and organized crime. After becoming Attorney General, Robert Kennedy singled out Giancana as one of the underworld leaders to be given the most intense investigation. Evans was questioned by the Committee about the October 18 memorandum. He testified that he did not recall ever having seen it, that he had never heard from any source of an assassination plot involving the Central Intelligence Agency and members of the underworld during his tenure with the Bureau, and that he never discussed assassination with the Attorney General. (Evans, 8/27/75, pp. 55–57) He testified that while he did not recall the memorandum, if it had been sent to him, it would have been sent by Thomas McAndrews, who was Chief of the Organized Crime Section of the Special Investigative Division of the Bureau.

McAndrews, who was responsible for distributing information to the entire intelligence community from the FBI, could not recall ever having given the October 18 memorandum to his superior, Evans. When asked if he believed the information contained in that memorandum had ever been brought to the attention of Attorney General Kennedy, McAndrews testified:

I think he was briefed specifically on it, either in writing or orally * * * I think it was done. But I can't say for sure. (McAndrews, 9/17/75, p. 27)

Ralph Hill, who was the Special Agent in charge of the investigation of Giancana, stated that he recalled the information in the October 18 memorandum, but that he did not recall the memorandum itself. He stated that because of the Attorney General's interest in organized crime figures, it was the practice for field reports concerning Giancana to be given to Courtney Evans, who would then forward them to the Attorney General.

As the FBI investigation of the Las Vegas wiretap proceeded forward, Sheffield Edwards, the CIA's Director of Security, was in continual contact with the Bureau about the case. Edwards was unable to be questioned about either the October 18 memorandum or his contacts with the FBI due to his infirm condition. Bissell, however, testified that he knew during the spring of 1961 that Edwards was seeking to persuade the Justice Department not to prosecute the parties involved in the tap, including Maheu, Roselli and Giancana. While he believed that Edwards had told the Bureau the truth, he did not expect that Edwards would have revealed that the CIA operation involved assassination. (Bissell, 6/9/75, pp. 63–65)

2. THE MAY 22, 1961 MEMORANDUM

The information which Edwards was providing the FBI in response to inquiry about the Las Vegas tap was eventually forwarded by Director Hoover directly to Attorney General Kennedy by memorandum of May 22, 1961. The memorandum, while not directly mentioning the word "assassination," reported that the CIA had relied on Giancana because of his contacts with gambling figures who might have sources for use "in connection with CIA's clandestine efforts against the Castro government." The memorandum continued that "none of Giancana's efforts have materialized to date and that several of the plans still are working and may eventually 'pay off'." It described the activities as "dirty business" and said the CIA could not afford having knowledge of the actions of Maheu and Giancana in pursuit of any mission for the CIA. The May 22 memorandum stated:

> Colonel Edwards advised that in connection with CIA's operation against Castro he personally contacted Robert Maheu during the Fall of 1960 for the purpose of using Maheu as a "cut-out" in contacts with Sam Giancana, a known hoodlum in the Chicago area. Colonel Edwards said that since the underworld controlled gambling activities in Cuba under the Batista government, it was assumed that this element would still continue to have sources and contacts in Cuba which perhaps could be utilized successfully in connection with CIA's clandestine efforts against the Castro government. As a result, Maheu's services were solicited as a "cut-out" because of his possible entree into underworld circles. Maheu obtained Sam Giancana's assistance in this regard and according to Edwards, Giancana gave every indication of cooperating through Maheu in attempting to accomplish several clandestine efforts in Cuba. Edwards added that none of Giancana's efforts have materialized to date and that several of the plans still are working and may eventually "pay off."
>
> Colonel Edwards related that he had no direct contact with Giancana; that Giancana's activities were completely "back stopped" by Maheu and that Maheu would frequently report Giancana's action and information to Edwards. No details or methods used by Maheu or Giancana in accomplishing their missions were ever reported to Edwards. Colonel Edwards said that since this is "dirty business" he could not afford to have knowledge of the actions of Maheu and Giancana in pursuit of any mission for CIA. Colonel Edwards added that he has neither given Maheu any instruction to use technical installations of any type nor has the subject of technical installations ever come up between Edwards and Maheu in connection with Giancana's activity.

* * * * * * *

> Mr. Bissell, in his recent briefings of General Taylor and the Attorney General and in connection with their inquiries into CIA relating to the Cuban situation told the Attorney General that some of the associated planning included the use of Giancana and the underworld against Castro.

The memorandum thus provided a graphic though elusive description of the assassination plots in terms which I think would lead one receiving the memorandum to ask: What dirty business? What exactly are the "clandestine efforts" of the CIA against Castro? What "plans" are still working and may eventually "pay off?" Perhaps, though, the system of plausible denial dictated that such questions would not be asked. In any event, our investigation did not reveal whether such questions were asked and if so what answers were given.[1]

B. PRESIDENT KENNEDY'S MEETING WITH THE CUBAN EXILE LEADER

Before reviewing what our investigation revealed as to what happened to the May 22 memorandum, I feel it important to review the time period in which it was written. First, the portion of the memorandum which reads "none of Giancana's efforts have materialized to date" seems to refer to the recent passage of poison pills in April 1961 to the Cuban exile leader who was active in the plots around this

---

[1] All officials still living who the record established saw the memoranda testified they never learned that the memorandum was describing assassination efforts.

period of time.[1] Second, the memorandum was received by Attorney General Kennedy in aftermath of the Bay of Pigs and at the height of the Taylor/Kennedy Bay of Pigs inquiry which met from April through June of 1961. (*See* Committee's Report at pp. 121–23) Moreover, Allen Dulles was one of the members of the Taylor/Kennedy Board and obviously available to answer inquiries about the May 22 memorandum. Third, our investigation determined President Kennedy met in person with the Cuban exile leader on April 19–20, 1961, apparently to discuss the failure of the Bay of Pigs.[2] Thereafter, on May 18, 1961, the Taylor/Kennedy Board of Inquiry interviewed the Cuban exile leader, and other members of Cuban groups. The record reveals that the subject matter of this interview was the Bay of Pigs operation and that Attorney General Kennedy was present.

Those still living who participated in the Taylor/Kennedy inquiry have testified they never heard of the assassination plots from any of the witnesses. The May 22 memorandum, however, references Bissell's briefing Attorney General Kennedy about the fact that the CIA's "asssociated planning included the use of Giancana against Castro." Bissell's testimony about what he told Kennedy at that time is treated at length in the Committee's Report, pp. 121–23. Suffice it to say he again had a very bad memory as to what, if anything, he told Attorney General Kennedy about the plots.[3]

The May 22 memorandum was accompanied by a short cover memorandum stating that Edwards had acknowledged the "attempted" use of Maheu and "hoodlum elements" by the CIA in "anti-Castro activities," but that the "purpose for placing the wiretap * * * [had] not been determined * * *." (FBI memo to Attorney General, 5/22/61)

The May 22 memorandum to Attorney General Kennedy was stamped "received," and contained a notation in the margin, in Kennedy's hand, as follows: "Courtney I hope this will be followed up vigorously." "Courtney" was Courtney Evans. Evans, as indicated earlier, testified that he neither knew anything about any assassination plots nor discussed the subject with Attorney General Kennedy. However, Evans did write a memorandum to Allen Belmont, Assistant Director of the FBI, dated June 6, 1961, which stated:

> We checked with CIA and ascertained that CIA has used Maheu as an intermediary in contacting Sam Giancana, the notorious Chicago hoodum. This was in connection with anti-Castro activities. CIA, however, did not give any instructions to Maheu to use any technical installations. In connection with this information received from CIA concerning their attempted utilization of the hood-

---

[1] According to FBI memoranda dated December 21, 1960, and January 18, 1961, the Cuban exile leader was associated with anti-Castro activities financed by United States rackateers, including Santos Trafficante, who hoped to secure illegal monopolies in the event of Castro's overthrow. Cuban exile leader was also used by Roselli in the second passage of pills to Cuba in April 1962.
[2] While there is no record of this meeting, other members of Cuban groups and Secretary of Defense McNamara and General Lemnitzer were present. McNamara has testified that he never heard the assassination plots discussed with the President or anyone else. (McNamara, 7/11/75, p. 73)
[3] Bissell at one point answered:
Q. * * * you're saying that in briefing the Attorney General you are telling him you are using the underworld against Castro, and you intended to mean, Mr. Attorney General, we are trying to kill him.
A. I thought it signaled just exactly that to the Attorney General, I'm sure. (Bissell, 7/22/75, p. 54)
But, he later equivocated about what he said, the net result being that we just cannot be sure what he may have said to Attorney General Kennedy.

lum element. CIA requested this information be handled on a "need-to-know" basis.

We are conducting a full investigation in this wiretap case requested by the Department and the field has been instructed to press this investigation vigorously. Accordingly, the Attorney General will be orally assured that we are following up vigorously and the results of our investigation will be furnished to the Department promptly.

At the time Director Hoover sent the May 22, 1961 memorandum to the Justice Department, indicating that there was a CIA/Giancana link, the Bureau and Justice files contained the October 18, 1960 memorandum revealing that Giancana had earlier talked about an assassination attempt. This memorandum of October 18, 1960 did not reveal any Giancana/CIA connections. It did, however, mention assassination. Anyone reading the memorandum of October 18, 1960 and knowing that the CIA was associated with Giancana in a project "against Castro" should have realized the connection. There is no evidence, however, that the Attorney General ever saw the October 18 memorandum. Nor is there any evidence that anyone put the two memorandums together or, for that matter, asked enough questions of the right people to determine that the project or activities or plans "against Castro" were in fact assassination plots.

Given the information transmitted in the memorandum of 1960 and 1961 that developed from the FBI investigation of the Las Vegas tap together with bugs in the listening devices in various buildings of the underworld figures and the physical surveillance in Florida adds up to one of three possibilities; (1) the plots became known to those who wanted to know and were allowed to continue; (2) no one learned of them because they "didn't want to know;" or (3) the information was never sufficiently put together enough to reveal the plots. The evidence, however, will not permit me to even guess which of the three possibilities actually occurred. We will never know for certain whether in May of 1961, almost a year before the second passage of poison pills in April 1962, anyone realized that there were ongoing assassination plans and yet did nothing about them.

C. THE EVENTS OF 1962

Both the Castro plots and the Giancana wiretap investigation did not exhibit much activity between the May 22, 1961 memorandum and the advent of 1962. The events surrounding the May 7, 1962 briefing are dealt with at length in the Committee's Report. I mention them briefly here so that they may be viewed together with the events preceding them in 1960 and 1961. In this manner I believe a fuller picture of the problems of who knew what when is presented.

The ambiguity reflected in the Committee's Report over what occurred in the May 7 briefing is heightened by the May 14, 1962, memorandum which purports to describe the May 7 briefing. The May 14 memorandum was prepared at the Attorney General's request by Edwards, with Houston's assistance.

The May 14 memorandum described the assassination plots as a "sensitive operation against Fidel Castro," and said that "(a)fter the failure of the invasion of Cuba word was sent through Maheu to Roselli to call off the operation," and that "neither this Agency (CIA) nor (Edwards) knew of" the proposed Las Vegas wiretap. Thus, the memorandum did not fully or accurately describe the assassination operation and actually falsely stated other facts, e.g., that the plots were concluded in May of 1961 when they were continuing and that the CIA was not involved in authorizing the Giancana tap when it apparently did. Moreover, the Attorney General had already seen the May 22, 1961 memorandum (discussed *supra*) which said that in late May of 1961 "[plans were] still working" and might "eventually pay off." And, the Attorney General was presumably also aware that the CIA had been involved in the proposed tap (from reading the May 22, 1961 memorandum). Therefore, the May 14, 1962, memorandum contained several statements which seem to be known inaccuracies.

The answer to all these ambiguities may be that the May 14 memorandum was intended to be false to serve as a "cover" for the real facts. Alternatively, the memorandum may just have resulted from the apparent confusion between Houston and Edwards and a general reluctance to detail in writing something like an assassination operation.

It is clear, however, that at the May 7 briefing the "operation" against Castro was described as an assassination attempt because of the meeting between Attorney General Kennedy and Hoover two days later. Hoover's May 10 memorandum describing the May 9 meeting, noted that Kennedy described the operation as involving the CIA's hiring "Robert A. Maheu, a private detective in Washington, D.C., to approach Giancana with a proposition of paying $150,000 to hire some gunmen to go into Cuba to kill Castro."

Whatever occurred at the May 7 meeting and whatever the reasons for the May 14 memorandum, the major concern which arises for me is that no affirmative action was taken. Despite the fact that the Attorney General, the Director of the FBI, the General Counsel and the Director of Security of the CIA, all discussed assassination plots against Castro, no written order was levied upon all CIA employees banning any such actions.[1]

Indeed, John McCone, the Director of the CIA in May of 1962, testified that he was not even told of the plots until August of 1963, and then only because of a newspaper article (Committee Report, pp. 99–108) [2]. And, all the advisors to President Kennedy testified that they also never heard anything about it. For example, Herbert J. Miller, Jr. testified that he had never heard about assassination efforts and that if the Attorney General had, "he would have told me." (Miller, 8/11/75, pp. 17–22) Of course, we know that the Attorney General did know, at least as of May 7, 1962. Whether he informed President Kennedy we do not know. The confusion over who did or did not know, and if so when, again demonstrates the glaring need for better command and control within both the intelligence community and the Executive Branch.

VI. The MONGOOSE Program—The Environment in Which the Assassination Plots Arose

The Committee Report discusses in some detail the occurrences during the so-called "MONGOOSE Program" against Cuba by the Ken-

---

[1] In another aspect of the Committee's investigation the command and control structure also failed to provide a specific written order which, according to one CIA employee, would have ensured the destruction of certain toxins. (Gordon, 9/16/75, pp. 166–67)

[2] This is so even though our record indicates that McCone and Attorney General Kennedy were personal friends and, in the words of McCone's former Executive Assistant Walt Elder "quite close." (Elder 8/13/75, pp. 52) (*See also* Helms, 6/13/75, p. 69)

nedy Administration from November 1961 through October 1962, and, for the most part, I find little to differ with in the presentation. I thought that, because of the length of the Committee's Report, it would be useful to succinctly set out some examples of how and why the pressure on the CIA and other agencies was so great during this period. Even a brief look at these events demonstrates what the environment was. This is not to excuse what occurred but to describe the quite unique atmosphere which existed during these various assassination plots. While MONGOOSE was a program directed only against Cuba, it in some ways set the tone for actions taken in other countries. These examples, along with other evidence of that period, will, I hope, shed some additional light on why assassination plots may not have struck those involved at the CIA level as immediately *verboten*.

Richard Helms has testified that during the time he was DDP the prevailing mood in the Administration regarding Castro was, in essence, "anything goes." He stated that (1) the injunction laid down by the Administration was to "get rid of" the Castro regime, and (2) no limitations were placed on the means.

Helms testified that in October or November of 1961:

* * * the Agency was instructed—to get going on plans to get rid of Castro by some device which obviously would have to be covert because nobody had any stomach anymore for any invasions or any military fiascos of that kind. (Helms, 6/13/75, pp. 16–17)

He characterized the atmosphere of the 1961–62 MONGOOSE period as

pretty intense, and I remember vividly it was very intense * * * [N]utty schemes were born of the intensity of the pressure. And we were quite frustrated. (Helms, 6/13/75, p. 26)

And by the time of the missile crisis the pressure was described as "no doubt about it, it was white heat." (*Id.* p. 27)

Helms was not the only witness who testified that the pressure to remove Castro by any means was real. The Executive Assistant to Harvey in the DDP testified that in the early fall of 1961 Bissell told him that he was called to the White House where he was:

chewed out in the Cabinet Room of the White House by both the President and the Attorney General for, as he puts it, sitting on his ass and not doing anything about getting rid of Castro and the Castro regime. (Executive Assistant, 6/18/75, pp. 8, 37–38)

The Executive Assistant added that he understood that the CIA had been ordered during the MONGOOSE period to remove the Castro regime and that "no holds were barred * * * we had no limitation." (Executive Assistant, 6/18/75, p. 37)

Former Secretary of Defense Robert S. McNamara noted that

we were hysterical about Castro at the time of the Bay of Pigs and thereafter. And there was pressure from JFK and RFK to do something about Castro. (McNamara, 7/11/75, p. 93)

The Inspector General's Report described the pressurized environs in which the assassination plots were spawned as follows:

We cannot overemphasize the extent to which responsible Agency officers felt themselves subject to the Kennedy Administration's severe pressure to do something about Castro and his regime. The fruitless and, in retrospect, often unrealistic plotting should be viewed in that light. (IG Report, p. 4)

The events, meetings and proposals concerning the "Cuba problem" which occurred after the defeat at the Bay of Pigs largely explain why those involved felt engulfed by the "pressure" to get rid of Castro. After the Taylor/Kennedy Report (Committee Report, pp. 135-36) was completed in June 1961, President Kennedy set up a completely new covert structure for dealing with the Cuban situation. In November 1961 a new program was mounted against Cuba which came to be known as "Operation MONGOOSE." And, before it was concluded in October 1962 a wide variety of actions were debated, considered and employed against Cuba. While not all proposals were approved their mere consideration contributed to the climate at the time.

President Kennedy's November 30, 1961, memorandum formally established the MONGOOSE program and named Edward G. Lansdale as its Chief of Operations. On December 1, 1961, the Attorney General informed the Special Group that "higher authority" had decided that higher priority should be given to Cuba.

The parameters of what was or was not considered authorized under the MONGOOSE program was graphically demonstrated in Roswell Gilpatric's testimony:

Q. Going back, then, to the general MONGOOSE Special Group (Augmented) atmosphere here, could you give the Committee your best recollection of your perception at that time of the limits of the authority of the Special Group with respect to what could and could not be done about Castro?

Mr. GILPATRIC. Well, the only limit that I felt the Special Group was under, was Senator Goldwater said, we had no power. We were an advisory group, we were staffing the President of the United States and the Attorney General, but within our charter, so to speak, the one thing that was off limits was military invasion. That, as I understood it, was something that the group was not to go into. The Joint Chiefs had contingency plans for the invasion of Cuba. They always have had, probably, they've probably got new ones today, but that kind of overt military action was out of bounds as I understood it as far as the Special Group was concerned.

We were talking about covert, clandestine operations to be conducted through the CIA using, perhaps, paramilitary measures, but not the armed forces of the United States in a support role.

Q. Would the killing of Castro by a paramilitary group have been within bounds?

Mr. GILPATRIC. I know of no restriction that would have barred it. (Gilpatric, 7/17/75, pp. 44-45)

Early in the MONGOOSE Program, on December 7, 1961, Gen. Lansdale sent a memorandum concerning the Cuba Project to Maxwell Taylor, U. A. Johnson, Roswell Gilpatric, and John McCone, then DCI. Lansdale noted that the President's November 30 memorandum would be implemented and that MONGOOSE would accomplish an overthrow of Castro by means of a popular movement of Cubans from within Cuba. He recommended exploiting the potential of the underworld in Cuban cities to harass and bleed the Communist control apparatus. The Lansdale memorandum read in part:

This effort may, on a very sensitive basis, enlist the assistance of American links to the Cuban underworld. (Memorandum, December 7, 1961)

The Lansdale program assigned some 32 planning tasks for the agencies participating in MONGOOSE (including the CIA). These tasks ranged from intelligence collection to the use of military force. The next day an additional 33rd task was added to a plan to utilize biological and chemical warfare against the Cuban sugar crop workers.

Although the proposal was eventually rejected as unfeasible, the consideration of such a drastic tactic was no doubt borne out of the frustration and concern of the times.

On January 19, 1962, the Attorney General once again addressed the Special Group and emphasized that the President felt that immediate action against Cuba was necessary. The Attorney General emphasized that the solution of the Cuban problem was:

> The top priority in the U.S. government—all else is secondary—no time, money, effort, or manpower is to be spared * * * Yesterday * * * the President had indicated (to the Attorney General) that the final chapter had not been written—its got to be done and will be done. (McManus Memorandum, January 19, 1962)

After the Attorney General addressed the group on that occasion, Lansdale sent a memorandum to the members of the "Caribbean Survey Group" (another euphemism for the Cuba Project) dated the next day which stated:

> As he (the Attorney General) so adequately tasked us, there will be no acceptable alibi. If the capability must be developed, then we must acquire it on a priority basis. It seems clear that the matter of funds and authority offers absolutely no defense for losing time or for doing less than the very best possible effort in your tasks.
>
> *   *   *   *   *   *   *
>
> It is our job to put the American genius to work on this project, quickly and effectively. This demands a change from business-as-usual and a hard facing of the fact *that we are in a combat situation*—where we have been given full command. (Memorandum, January 20, 1962, p. 1) (Emphasis supplied.)

On January 24, 1962, the CIA submitted its plan for developing the assets needed for the Cuba Project. The plan included the use of Cuban "crime syndicate" members as intermediaries who would make appeals inside of Cuba, but it noted that controlling indigenous nationals was difficult.

General Lansdale's Program Review for the Cuba Project of February 20, 1962, included his "Basic Action Plan." Phase IV of that plan had as one of its components:

> Attack on the cadre of the regime, including key leaders * * * This should be a "Special Target" operation. CIA defector operations are vital here. Gangster elements might provide the best recruitment potential for actions against police G-2 officials. Bloc technicians should be added to the list of targets. CW (Chemical Warfare) agents should be fully considered.

Lansdale testified that the "actions" and "attack" referred to in this component meant killing. (Lansdale, 7/8/75, p. 106) And, he also testified that he had suggested to various agency representatives involved in the MONGOOSE program that they contact "criminal elements" for possible use in the program against Cuba. (Lansdale, 7/8/75, p. 107)

On January 30, 1962, a Defense Department proposal was sent to Lansdale entitled "Operation Bounty." The proposal involved a:

> system of financial rewards, commensurate with position and stature, for killing or delivering alive known Communists. (Lansdale ex #1, Memorandum of January 30, 1962, p. 1)

Under Operation Bounty leaflets were to be dropped into Cuba listing rewards for the death of various individuals. The rewards ranged from $5,000 for an "informer" to $100,000 for "government officials."

A reward of "2¢" was listed for Castro himself. (*Id.*, p. 3)[1] While the Bounty proposal never got off the ground operationally, yet it is another indicia of the climate of the time.

As the MONGOOSE program advanced, the Special Group recognized that the Cuban program, considering what was being proposed, created a potentially volatile situation. The March 5, 1962 SGA Minutes acknowledged that:

> Agents infiltrated into Cuba would be trained in paramilitary as well as intelligence skills and * * * once the agents are within the country, they cannot be effectively controlled from the U.S.

Nevertheless, under the program, agent teams were dispatched into Cuba. A Lansdale memorandum of March 13, 1962, to the Special Group Augmented advised that:

> (1) Two teams of agents dispatched April 1 through 15, 1962; (2) Two teams of agents dispatched April 16 through 30, 1962; (3) Two teams dispatched to Cuba May 1 through 15, 1962; (4) Four teams of agents dispatched to Cuba May 16 through 31; (5) Ten to fifteen teams of agents dispatched to Cuba June 1 through 31, 1962.

In addition to the agent infiltrations, the MONGOOSE program also continued to include stepped up sabotage proposals. The unsuccessful attempt to blow up the Matahambre mine was approved on August 30, 1962, and an August 31, 1962 memorandum from Lansdale to the SGA selected sabotage targets as "the Matahambre Mine and various refineries, nickel plants * * *" The same memorandum suggested:

> encouraging destruction of crops by fire, chemicals, and weeds, hampering of harvest by work slowdown, destruction of bags, cartons, and other shipping containers.

While the MONGOOSE program ended around the time of the Cuban missile crisis in October 1962, sabotage continued. For example, the Special Group minutes of June 19, 1963, show that the following proposed sabotage program was approved:

> A meeting was held this morning with higher authority, on the above subject. Present were Mr. McNamara and General McKee; Mr. Harriman; Mr. McCone and Mr. Fitzgerald; and Mr. Bundy.
>
> * * * * * * *
>
> Mr. Fitzgerald then gave the outlines of the proposed program. It will be directed at four major segments of the Cuban economy: (a) electric power; (b) petroleum refineries and storage facilities; (c) railroad and highway transportation; and (d) production and manufacturing. (He pointed out that many targets in the last category could be put out of operation by successful sabotage of power facilities.) The first operation is planned for mid-July. Raids will be conducted from outside Cuba, using Cuban agents under CIA control. Missions will be staged from a U.S. key.
>
> * * * * * * *
>
> A question was asked as to whether the Cubans would retaliate in kind. The answer was that they would certainly have this capability but that they have not retaliated to date, in spite of a number of publicized exile raids.

I set out the above events as examples of the atmosphere and environment which I can easily see might lead one to conclude that an assassination effort, presumably approved by higher authority, fit within the realm of approved action against Castro and Cuba.

---

[1] The reward for Castro was supposed to "denigrate * * * Castro in the eyes of the Cuban population." (Lansdale, 7/8/75, p. 26) The logic of the effort, however, escapes me.

VII. Whose Idea Was the Use of the Underworld in an Assassination Plot Against Castro

A final matter I would like to treat briefly is a question which the Committee Report does not specifically address, *i.e.*, the origin of the Castro plots. I describe the testimony here not because it matters much where within the CIA the proposal originated, but because it sheds additional light on why it is so difficult to pin down responsibility for assassination.

The Inspector General's investigation did not focus on any one particular individual as the originator of the plots, noting that the "first seriously-pursued CIA plan to assassinate Castro had its inception in August 1960." Concerning the plots' origin, the Inspector General's Report stated:

> Richard Bissell, Deputy Director for Plans, asked Sheffield Edwards, Director of Security, if Edwards could establish contact with the U.S. gambling syndicate that was active in Cuba. The objective clearly was the assassination of Castro although Edwards claims that there was a studied avoidance of the term in his conversation with Bissell. Bissell recalls that the idea originated with J. C. King, then Chief of WH Division, although King now recalls having only limited knowledge of such a plan and at a much later date—mid 1962. (I.G. Report, p. 14)

However, when King was interviewed by the Committee, he denied that the Castro underworld plots originated with him. He said that he remembered nothing about the plots but could not dispute Bissell and Edwards. (King Interview, p. 1.)

Moreover, Bissell and Edwards each had differing recollections concerning who proposed the idea of utilizing the underworld in an assassination effort against Castro. Each testified that the other came to him with the idea. Edwards testified that:

> Q. Now, did you in the fall of 1960 receive some instructions from Mr. Bissell in connection with Mr. Castro?
> A. Yes.
> Q. And did he tell you to find somebody who could accomplish the assassination of Mr. Castro?
> A. No, he told me if I had access, to see if I had access to any source that I feel might accomplish that end, yes.
>
> * * * * *
>
> Q. And this refreshes your recollection that you were approached in August 1960 by Mr. Bissell.
> A. I was approached by Mr. Bissell. Now, I'm not sure that it shows here that it was approved, this possible project was approved by Allen W. Dulles, Director of CIA, and by General Cabell, the Deputy Director. They are both dead.
>
> * * * * *
>
> I mean, I told him that Mr. Bissell, the Deputy for Plans, had asked me if I had any sources and Bissell was there as I recall. I'm pretty sure he was there. And it was a brief conversation, it was a sensitive conversation. (Edwards, 5/30/75, pp. 3, 5, 7)

On the other hand, Bissell described the origin as follows:

> My own recollection was that Shef Edwards himself brought up the possibility of using this channel. * * * I am sure that I did encourage Shef Edwards to see what could be done through this channel.
>
> * * * I think he [Edwards] either said in as many words or strongly inferred that the plan would be put into effect unless at that time or subsequently he was told by Mr. Dulles that it should not be.
>
> * * * * *

You have hit on an important point which is that this operation, the planning for this operation and the support of this operation was conducted in a manner completely different from that of any other operation I ever knew of in the Agency was conducted. The main difference was that an operation directed against a foreign government was handled through the Director of Security's chain of command by his people and with his contacts, and as you are aware, he did not report to me, he was not in my chain of command. This was done, as I made clear, with my foreknowledge, but operationally, this matter was in his hands.

* * * * * * *

I received reports quite infrequently from Shef Edwards. I felt a high confidence in his competence to pursue this matter and none in my own. * * * I knew a plan had been drawn up and I knew that Edwards had been authorized to pursue it, and I knew in a general way what the plan involved. (Bissell, 6/9/75, pp. 22, 23, 32, 72)

* * * * * * *

I think the question it undoubtedly did raise in my mind at the time was whether the specific operation *that had been initiated by Mr. Edwards* with my knowledge and encouragement, whether the operation was threatened with being blown. (Bissell, 7/22/75, p. 59, emphasis added)

The testimony set out above demonstrates that none of the witnesses were rushing forward to take credit for initiating the Castro schemes. And, plots to use the underworld to attempt to assassinate Castro are events which should stick in one's memory. Nevertheless, this aspect of our investigation, as in many other areas of our inquiry on assassination, has not provided concise, clear evidence nor easy answers.

ADDITIONAL VIEWS OF SENATOR BARRY GOLDWATER

My signature appended to the Majority Report of this Committee indicates I am greatly appreciative of the dedicated work done by the Senate members of the Committee and the complete staff.

I am in disagreement with the general idea of an interim report. In fact, as I will indicate, I was opposed to getting into the subject of assassinations at all. Although my signature appears on the Majority Report, I have additional views concerning this whole subject which I am compelled to make part of this report.

A majority of the Select Committee voted in favor of an interim assassination report, because they believed it was necessary to lay the matter at rest so that the Committee could get on with other work. While I respect the decision of the Committee, I disagree for the following reasons:

(1) An interim report is tentative in nature. If the Select Committee is unable to pass on the subject matter of assassinations with finality, I submit it should wait until it can do so. Further, it is questionable that there is any public need requiring an interim report.

(2) A lengthy report with numerous names and replete with quotes can pose security and diplomatic problems in the absence of time to carefully scrutinize the document. Americans and our friends abroad may suffer embarrassment or notoriety.

(3) The interim report deals with such subjects as "plausible deniability", "command and control", and covert operation methods. The Select Committee is placing itself in the position of generalizing on these subjects based on four case studies presented to the full Committee. Although the document does contain disclaimers as to final conclusions on these matters, nevertheless conclusions in those areas are implied.

(4) It is possible that the Select Committee may uncover new material bearing on assassinations as it proceeds into other areas of investigation leading to the further possibility that its findings might have to be altered in the final report.

In view of the foregoing, I believe the reader of the interim report might want to ask himself these questions:
Does it serve any national interest?
Does it enhance the legislative process?
Does it raise more questions than it answers?

I, for one, oppose the interim assassination report because I feel the Committee should have all the evidence at hand before publishing a report. Problems raised by the conduct of covert operations have an important bearing on the work of the Select Committee. Important also are the lines of authority established by various administrations. However, the Committee has received scant information on covert operations and command and control as of this writing.

What have been the results of the assassination investigation?

The full Committee has considered four case studies involving Rafael Trujillo, President of the Dominican Republic; Ngo Dinh Diem, President of South Vietnam; and General Rene Schneider, Chief of Staff of the Chilean Armed Forces; and attempts on the life of Fidel Castro during the early 1960's. In the first three cases, evidence presented to the full Committee failed to establish any direct U.S. involvement in the deaths.

One case not examined in detail by the full Committee, requires comment. The Committee has received evidence that "higher authority" than the CIA ordered the removal by whatever means necessary of the late African leader Patrice Lumumba. On January 17, 1961, Lumumba was killed in Katanga, and a subsequent United Nations report found no U.S. involvement. The findings of the United Nations are supported by evidence received by the Select Committee. This case tends to reinforce findings given further on concerning the CIA's responsiveness to Presidential orders and directives.

The attempts upon the life of Fidel Castro fall into a different category. During the early 1960's the United States was in a state of near war with Cuba. Fidel Castro and Che Guevara were promoting and abetting the export of revolution to other countries of the Western Hemisphere. Russian ballistic missiles were installed on Cuban soil altering the balance of power between the United States and the Soviet Union and creating a serious threat to America's survival.

The ill-conducted Bay of Pigs invasion was mounted because Fidel Castro was clearly thought to be a threat to the United States and friendly nations in Latin America. Castro's removal seemed necessary, if not vital, in those days and was supported by nearly all responsible officials in Washington. Congress generally supported President Kennedy in his Cuban policy.

The Select Committee has received circumstantial evidence that Attorney General Robert Kennedy was aware of the attempts on Fidel Castro's life before, during, and after they occurred. There can be no doubt of the unusual circumstances where the President has his brother as Attorney General, and there can be no doubt of the close relationship existing between these two.

When the Select Committee decided to conduct an investigation into assassinations, I warned the Committee that Presidential involvement or authority was a certainty. Moreover, I was very concerned that harm would come to the office of the Presidency giving comfort to our Nation's detractors and enemies.

Nothing has happened in the intervening weeks to change my views. Unfortunately, the word assassination has been thrown around to the extent that the office of the Presidency and the CIA appear to the untutored as Murder, Inc.

The mere fact that key officials are called with respect to so-called assassination hearings tend to reinforce this image. For example, the Select Committee has been taking testimony on the Allende election in Chile in 1970 and the circumstances surrounding the death of General Rene Schneider. In the early hours of October 22, General Schneider was shot while some Chileans were trying to abduct him. Their purpose was to remove General Schneider from the office of

Commander-in-Chief so that a military coup to oust Allende could proceed.

The conspirators planned to remove General Schneider to Argentina for safekeeping. The last thing in the world they wanted was his death, because they knew this would be severely criticized in Chile. Unfortunately, General Schneider pulled his pistol in an attempt to resist his abductors. In the ensuing melee, General Schneider was shot and ultimately died.

Two things have been confirmed by the record: First, the Schneider death can in no way be characterized as an assassination. Second, there was no direct American involvement in his abduction or death.

Nevertheless, the words "assassination", "Chile", and "Allende" have become linked with those who testify regardless of the actual facts of the case. While this is true of any Congressional investigation, in this instance it becomes more burdensome to the witnesses because murder is involved.

With the understanding that new information may be received in the coming months by the Select Committee, I offer these conclusions:

I. Since World War II, Presidents have directly or indirectly approved of all actions taken by the CIA which have been the subject of the Select Committee investigation. If any Presidents were unaware of CIA activities, it was a result of their failure to insist on detailed briefings or reports. The intelligence community is, and must be, responsive to Presidential requests and orders.

II. Since World War II, no President or his agents ordered an assassination that was *actually* committed. Moreover, there is no evidence that any agency of the U.S. Government committed an assassination. There is no doubt that it was the policy of the U.S. Government, for example, to seek the ouster of Presidents Ngo Dinh Diem and Rafael Trujillo, but their removal and death cannot be *directly* attributed to the U.S. Government.

III. The CIA at all times was acting within the law, or had every reason to believe it was acting legally, in taking action on the behalf of Presidents Eisenhower, Kennedy, Johnson, and Nixon.

IV. If there have been failures, abuses, mistakes, or bad judgment they are the result of individual actions and are deviations from the normal high standards established by the U.S. intelligence services.

V. The United States has been served by men and women in our intelligence services who have exhibited great courage, loyalty and dedication.

The Select Committee may be faced with a dilemma that cannot be resolved: tyrannicide. The appalling atrocities committed by Hitler and Stalin raise a question which may be unanswerable but which needs to be carefully examined because the human carnage they created cries out for it. Stated another way, should a President of the United States have the right to aid the destruction of either a Josef Stalin or Adolf Hitler in peacetime? Assassination during wartime does not seem to be at issue. Here we have a fundamental question which may have confronted Presidents in the past, and which could confront a future President.

Since the Select Committee came into being in late January, it has been my belief that the investigation should be held in executive session with one final and complete report to the Senate and ultimately to the American people. The difficulty of distinguishing between those matters that are part of the public record from those that must remain classified are difficult to keep in mind. Accordingly, Members of the Select Committee and its staff are now faced with an increased possibility of inadvertent disclosure of information that could be damaging to America's foreign policy.

Finally, Congressional investigations into the intelligence services are failing to turn up any categories of abuses not already known. More open hearings in the abuse area can lead us into lines of inquiry that may well do serious harm to the Nation's intelligence services. Congress now possesses sufficient information in the abuse area to start the legislative wheels turning. We may have passed the point where public investigation into the intelligence services has produced irretrievable harm. I hope not. It is not too late to put on the brakes.

BARRY GOLDWATER.

SUPPLEMENTAL VIEWS OF SENATOR CHARLES McC. MATHIAS, JR.

As much as I regret the necessity for this report, I concur in the findings reported.

Painful political problems are seldom solved by silence. As crude as the story unfolded here may seem, it can be the source of important lessons for the future.

The facts are necessary in order to frame, with authority, a new, comprehensive statutory charter for the intelligence agencies of the United States. The proposal of that charter is the most useful work that the Select Committee can accomplish and the basic justification for its existence. The main tasks of the Select Committee remain to be done in the next three months.

It will be asked why it is necessary to publish the report outside the Select Committee, or at most beyond the Capitol. One of the tenets of American political philosophy holds that "Knowledge will forever govern ignorance and a people who mean to be their own Governors must arm themselves with the power which knowledge gives." The duty which James Madison defines in these words is of the essence of democracy and it can be positive and stimulating. This report portrays a darker side, but life does present us with responsibilities that must be discharged if stench is to be prevented from causing rot and disease.

Much of what is reported herein is inconclusive. There should be no illusions that even the work done so far by the Select Committee on this aberrant chapter in United States policy has produced anything more than an oblique insight into the destructive effect of excessive secrecy upon the practices of governments. It is a glimpse of the exercise of great power without many of the checks and balances that serve to guard our liberties and protect our values.

Nearly 30 years have passed since Congress created the Central Intelligence Agency in 1947. In that time the thousands of men and women who have worked in our intelligence services have rendered a vital contribution to the American people.

In the aftermath of Watergate and its lessons about the abuse of power, it is clear that Congress faces a most serious task—to determine the proper role of our intelligence agencies within our constitutional system of government.

The assassination plots discussed in the report are profoundly disturbing, not because they are unique, but because they represent steps backward. History has often witnessed the practice of assassination as an instrument to transfer or to terminate political power. History also shows that men and governments have come to recognize the compelling force of ethical principles. The torturer who was once an adjunct of the courts themselves is today an international outlaw. By recognizing the sacredness of human life, mankind has sought to shed such barbarisms, barbarisms that have usually led to further violence and often to the destruction of the leaders and nations who resorted to them.

When practiced against a domestic leader, assassination is common murder. When practiced against a foreign leader, assassination is an act of war without that sorry sanction that war gives to the taking of human life. There can be no place in a world striving toward civilization for either practicing or condoning assassination.

Principles are impersonal. If they are right for the weak, they are right for the strong. Moral strength is more enduring than mere power. It is these concepts that should guide nations and history teaches that a contrary course brings tragedy not only to the victim but to the assassin as well. Nothing found in these pages will contradict the lessons mankind has read and ought to have learned.

Our purpose in studying the evidence of assassination plots was not to damage our intelligence services or to injure the reputations of past Administrations. Rather, we sought to stop the erosion of society's values caused by excessive secrecy and unchecked Executive power by making the factual record as accurate and clear as possible.

We talk candidly with our fellow Americans, but we speak also to our friends around the world. They should be advised of our efforts at self-correction and our adherence to our traditional values and beliefs.

CHARLES McC. MATHIAS, Jr.

Abbreviations of citations

Example	Source
Bundy, 7/1/75, p. 34	Bundy testimony to the Senate Select Committee, July 1, 1975, p. 34.
Goodpaster, 7/17/75, II, pp. 13–14	Goodpaster testimony to the Senate Select Committee, July 17, 1975, afternoon session, pp. 13–14.
Helms, Rockefeller Commission, 3/5/75, p. 61.	Helms testimony to the Commission on CIA Activities Within the United States, Mar. 5, 1975, p. 61.
Memo, Bissell to Smith, 10/1/54	Memorandum from Bissell to Smith Oct. 1, 1954.
Cable, Bissell to Smith, 10/1/54	Cable from Bissell to Smith, Oct. 1, 1954.
Cable HQ to Sta., 10/5/70	Cable from Headquarters to Station, Oct. 5, 1970.
Cable, Smith, Jones to Hedgman, 10/5/57.	Cable from Smith and Jones to Hedgman, Oct. 5, 1957.
Cable, Smith to Jones, Hedgman, 10/5/57.	Cable from Smith to Jones and Hedgman, Oct. 5, 1957.
Memo to Smith, 6/5/60	Unsigned memorandum to Smith, June 5, 1960.
Memo from Hedgman, 6/5/60	Unaddressed memorandum from Hedgman, June 5, 1960.
NSDM 97, 8/18/70	National Security Decision Memorandum No. 97, Aug. 18, 1970.
Smith affidavit, 6/5/63, p. 1	Smith affidavit given to the Senate Select Committee, June 5, 1963, p. 1.
Special Group Minutes, 10/6/61	Minutes of a meeting of the Special Group, Oct. 6, 1961.
SGA Minutes, 10/6/61	Minutes of a meeting of the Special Group (Augmented), Oct. 6, 1961.
I. G. Report, p. 98	Apr. 4, 1967, Report on Plots to Assassinate Castro prepared by the Inspector General of CIA for the Director, p. 98.
I. G. Report, B, p. 22	Undated [c. March–May 1967] Report on the Assassination of Trujillo prepared by the CIA. I. G. for the Director, p. 22.
I. G. Report, C, p. 22	May 31, 1967, Report on the Assassination of Diem prepared by the CIA. I.G. for the Director, p. 22.
Pentagon Papers, p. 422	Senator Gravel Edition, *"The Pentagon Papers,"* the Defense Department History of U.S. Decisionmaking on Vietnam, Beacon Press, Boston, p. 422.
Mecklin, p. 158	Mecklin, John, *"Mission in Torment,"* an Intimate Account of the U.S. Role in Vietnam, Doubleday & Co., 1965, p. 158.

This report is the result of an impressive effort by the entire Committee staff. The Committee wishes to express its appreciation to the members of the support, research, and professional staffs, and, in particular, to the following professional staff members who made a substantial contribution to this report:

Frederick D. Baron	Edward F. Greissing
David W. Bushong	Karl F. Inderfurth
M. Elizabeth Culbreth	Robert K. Kelley
Rhett B. Dawson	Lawrence Kieves
Thomas C. Dawson	Charles B. Kirbow
Joseph F. Dennin	Michael J. Madigan
Dorothy C. Dillon	Andrew W. Postal
Daniel E. Dwyer, Jr.	Gordon C. Rhea
Joseph E. diGenova	Gregory F. Treverton
	Burton V. Wides

www.ingramcontent.com/pod-product-compliance
Lightning Source LLC
Chambersburg PA
CBHW032016230426
43671CB00005B/100